Criminal Investigation

Criminal Investigation

SEVENTH EDITION

JAMES N. GILBERT

University of Nebraska at Kearney

PEARSON

Prentice
Hall

Upper Saddle River, New Jersey 07458

Library of Congress Cataloging-in-Publication Data

Gilbert, James N.
    Criminal investigation / James N. Gilbert.—7th ed.
        p. cm.
    Includes bibliographical references and index.
    ISBN 0-13-196207-8
    1. Criminal investigation.   2. Criminal investigation—United States.   I. Title.
HV8073.G53 2006
363.25—dc22   2006042808

Editor-in-Chief: Vernon R. Anthony
Executive Editor: Frank Mortimer, Jr.
Associate Editor: Sarah Holle
Marketing Manager: Adam Kloza
Editorial Assistant: Jillian Allison
Production Management: GGS Book Services
Production Editor: Trish Finley
Director of Manufacturing and Production: Bruce Johnson

Managing Editor: Mary Carnis
Production Liaison: Barbara Marttine Cappuccio
Manufacturing Manager: Ilene Sanford
Manufacturing Buyer: Cathleen Petersen
Senior Design Coordinator: Mary Siener
Cover Designer: Robert Aleman
Cover Image: H. Winkler/A.B./zefa/Corbis
Printer/Binder: R. R. Donnelley & Sons Company

Pearson Prentice Hall™ is a trademark of Pearson Education, Inc.
Pearson® is a registered trademark of Pearson plc
Prentice Hall® is a registered trademark of Pearson Education, Inc.

Pearson Education LTD
Pearson Education Singapore, Pte. Ltd
Pearson Education, Canada, Ltd
Pearson Education–Japan
Pearson Education Australia PTY, Limited
Pearson Education North Asia Ltd
Pearson Educación de Mexico, S.A. de C.V.
Pearson Education Malaysia, Pte. Ltd

*For Libby and Jenne
and my parents*

Contents

Preface

Criminal Investigation, Seventh Edition, is designed to develop an analytical understanding of the investigative process. In doing so, this new edition focuses on merging theoretical and proven practical aspects of crime detection and solution. The text can be used by students with no prior investigative knowledge or as a thorough reference source by law enforcement practitioners. Criminal justice instructors will find that the detailed discussion allows ample latitude for their personal approaches and experiences.

ORIENTATION AND ORGANIZATION

As in previous editions, the importance of basic investigative foundations is stressed throughout. Additionally, the book explains the essential interrelationship of forensic science and the investigative process. The workings of the modern crime laboratory are presented in such a fashion that the reader will comprehend criminalistic potential of evidence. The chapters are designed to acquaint the student with the subject in a naturally expanding fashion—from the colorful historical origins of criminal investigation to the future possibilities. Each commonly encountered major crime is legally defined and discussed in terms of current status, offender characteristics, and investigative techniques. Each chapter includes key terms, objectives, exercises, and relevant Web sites to guide the criminal justice student and facilitate comprehension of pertinent concepts.

FEATURES NEW TO THIS EDITION

Although many popular and time-proven features of past editions have been retained, the seventh edition contains considerable new material directly relevant to the investigative challenge of the twenty-first century. Each chapter has been extensively revised and updated with the latest research data from government and academic sources. Investigative profiles featuring first-person accounts by working investigative practitioners appear throughout the text. End-of-chapter relevant Web site sources are also new to this edition, as are numerous updated photos and charts. Unique material detailing the problematic "CSI effect," the expanding federal DNA database *CODIS*, cyberstalking, low copy DNA, methamphetamine labs, identity theft, and the future possibilities of investigative biometrics and complete coverage on hate crimes will be found in this edition, as will expanded information regarding the latest drug trends and futuristic directions of criminal investigation.

The seventh edition remains faithful to the overall design and readability of the previous editions while incorporating significant amounts of new material necessary to prepare students for the investigative challenge that awaits them.

ACKNOWLEDGMENTS

It is impossible to compile the necessary materials for a textbook of this nature without the assistance of many people. Merely thanking them in print does not convey adequately my appreciation for their invaluable assistance. However, I gratefully thank the following individuals for taking time from busy schedules to provide me with information and materials: Chief O. H. Sylvester, Berkeley, Calif., Police Department; Chief William Dye, Captain John Jones, Lieutenant Thomas Whipple, and Officer Larry Coffey, Champaign, Ill., Police Department; Sergeant Gary Brinkley, University of Illinois Police Department; Andrew Brooks Jr., Chicago Police Department; Michael Heath, former Coroner, Champaign County, Ill.; Homer Boynton Jr. and Paul Zolbe, Federal Bureau of Investigation; John Wiley, U.S. Secret Service; James Barrett, First National Bank of Maryland; Jack Larsen, Audio Intelligence Devices; Barrie McArthur, Diversified Technology, Inc.; Courtney Owens, Identi-Kit Company; Herbert MacDonell, Laboratory of Forensic Science; Martin Reiser, Los Angeles Police Department; Donald Parkinson, Macomb County, Ill., State's Attorney Office; R. Keppel, Metropolitan Police, New Scotland Yard; Detective Lieutenant David Townsend, Michigan State Police; Chief George Maher, Nassau County, N.Y., Police Department; John Hopkins, National Automobile Theft Bureau; Detective Alfred Young, New York City Police Department; William Escudier, Ni-Tec, Inc.; Superintendent Adam Reiss, Ohio State Police; William Gaines and Michael Marlow, Parkland College, Champaign, Ill.; W. C. Linn, Pinkerton's Inc.; Paul Roche, Prefecture of Police, Paris, France; Captain Wesley Allen, Lieutenant Henry Kelley, Criminalist Joseph Orantes, and Detective Gary Yoshonis, San Diego Police Department; Richard Arther, Scientific Lie Detection, Inc.; Captain J. S. Leitch, Seattle Police Department; Donald Penven, Sirchie Fingerprint Laboratories; George Moss, Varda Silent Alarm Company; Director Daniel Dowd and Assistant Director Kenneth Sundberg, Crime Laboratory Bureau— Wisconsin Department of Justice; Director William McDonald, Central Connecticut State University Department of Public Safety; Thomas Deakin, Editor, FBI Law Enforcement Bulletin; Robert Dorion, Forensic Odontologist; James Wallace, Mississippi Bureau of Narcotics; Glenn Whiteacre, Ocala Police Department; Detective James L. Trainum, Washington, D.C., Metropolitan Police Department; Professor Alec Jeffreys, University of Leicester, England; Commissioner James T. Moore, Florida Department of Law Enforcement; Horace Heafner, National Center for Missing and Exploited Children; Deborah L. Kallgren, Cellmark Diagnostics; Mark Potok, Southern Poverty Law Center; David M. White, State College Police Department; Dr. Henry Lee, Director, Connecticut State Police Forensic Laboratory; Captain Melissa Ownby, Beaumont, Texas, Police Department; Georgia Nelson, Options in Psychology; and Professor David Stock, New Mexico Military Institute.

The following people were especially helpful with this edition: Nate and Jennifer Hunter, Hunter Computer Consulting and Investigative Services; Gary Plank, Behavioral Profiler, Nebraska State Patrol; Susan Gilbert and Marion Brady, North Las Vegas Police Department; April Tardy and Michael Havstad, Los Angeles County Sheriff's Department; Noel Griffin, Florida Department of Law Enforcement; Paul Marquardt, Bureau of Alcohol, Tobacco, Firearms and Explosives; Dr. Henry Lee, Forensic Research Training Center; Shari Goodyear, Indiana County Pennsylvania District

Attorney's Office; Russ Schanlaub, Northwestern Indiana Bi-State Drug Task Force; Dr. Paul McCauley, Indiana University of Pennsylvania; Jennifer Johnson, Georgia Bureau of Investigation; Dr. John Daugman, University of Cambridge; Gary Smith, Northfield, Minn., Police Department; Dagny Putman, Centers for Disease Control; and Lisa Horn, ESRI (selected screen shots used in text courtesy of ESRI. Copyright ESRI. All rights reserved. ArcMap/ArcInfo Graphical User Interface is the intellectual property of ESRI and is used herein with permission). Finally, special thanks to Jim Whetstone, Parkland College, for providing my initial opportunity to teach and learn.

I thank the following reviewers for their thoughtful recommendations on this edition: Reginald Nealy, West Chester University, West Chester, PA; Neal Baldwin, California State-Fullerton, Fullerton, CA; and Lee Ayers-Schlosser, Southern Oregon University, Ashland, OR.

Criminal Investigation

Historical Origins of Criminal Investigation

KEY TERMS

Allan Pinkerton
Alphonse Bertillon
anthropometry
Bill of Rights
Bow Street Runners
CID
criminalistics
detective
Eugène Vidocq
Fourteenth Amendment

Industrial Revolution
Jonathan Wild
Metropolitan Police Act
modus operandi
parliamentary reward system
polygraph
portrait parlé
thief-taking
Thomas Byrnes
Will West case

LEARNING OBJECTIVES

1. to understand the historical evolution of the criminal investigative process;
2. to appreciate the relationship of European and American origins of criminal investigation and the criminal justice system;
3. to comprehend the concept of thief-catching;
4. to be able to account for similarities and differences of early American criminal investigators and their European counterparts;
5. to be familiar with American investigators who were instrumental to the development of present-day criminal investigation;
6. to comprehend the development of forensic science;
7. to be able to list prominent European and American criminalists; and
8. to understand the importance of legal influences on the development of criminal investigation.

THE EVOLUTION OF THE DETECTIVE

The vast history of criminal investigation can be appreciated only in the light of our distant past. Acts deemed unacceptable to a group have always been remedied by some means. In early groups, known as *tribes* or *clans*, methods existed for detecting and resolving undesirable acts. The methods used, although primitive beyond comparison to today's, were based on assigning responsibility to a given individual or family. If a member of a particular family violated the moral code of a tribe, the other family members were held responsible for detection, apprehension, and even execution of the offending member. In these ancient times, it was not unusual for entire communities to be held responsible for criminal acts of individual members. The community was then obliged to detect from within which member had committed the act.

As civilization developed, social and cultural traditions were codified into formal laws. An early example is the Laws of Hammurabi, developed in Babylon about 2100 B.C.[1] Such codification necessitated means of detecting those who refused to obey the law. The majority of individuals involved in ancient criminal detection were members of the military. The civilizations of Egypt, Rome, and Greece assigned criminal detection responsibilities almost exclusively to military units.

European Origins

During the Middle Ages, criminal detection shifted from a government responsibility to its ancient predecessor—group responsibility. A system of mutual protection, known as the Frank-Pledge system, again placed control of fellow human beings on the shoulders of each individual. Communities were subdivided into smaller groups consisting of ten families. The members of each subgroup, known as a *tithing*, were responsible for detecting and controlling any negative behavior on the part of a group member.[2] It would not be until 1066, when the Duke of Normandy conquered England, that criminal detection and public protection would again shift back to the government. From the reign of the Duke of Normandy to the early 1700s, what we now know as criminal investigation was largely unknown. What existed in its place were efforts aimed mainly at crime *prevention*. Once a crime was discovered, no matter how serious, further investigation was not pursued effectively.

Law enforcement through the seventeenth century was a conglomeration of government- and merchant-financed patrols. These early patrols, known as *watches*, were literally composed of the dregs of society. Ill-paid and frequently lacking even the barest elements of honest character, those manning the patrols were almost totally ineffective. Not only did the watches fail to deter criminal activity, but in some cases they aided it by their participation. An early English magistrate, Patrick Colquhoun, stated that "those very men who are paid for protecting the public are not only instruments of oppression in many instances, by extorting money most unwarrantably, but are frequently accessories in aiding and abetting or concealing the commission of crimes which it is their duty to detect and suppress."[3] In the late seventeenth century, a victim of criminal wrongdoing could purchase the investigative services of a minor court official; however, it was a rare situation when any satisfactory outcome was realized.

With the advent of the eighteenth century, major population shifts began to occur in Europe. England and France (specifically, the cities of London and Paris) experienced an unprecedented rise in criminal activity. The **Industrial Revolution** was at hand and would be in effect until well into the nineteenth century. Rapid social and cultural changes marked the beginning and growth of modern industrialism. With the shifting masses of people from rural areas to metropolitan cities came the inevitable negative consequences. Suddenly, or so it seemed to Londoners, a person could not venture into the streets without the fear of being victimized. Early historical accounts of the period are filled with descriptions of rising crime, with no public or government solutions to the problem.

Criminal elements in London became so powerful that parts of the city were surrendered to them. In his *History of Crime in England*, published in 1876, L. O. Pike stated that "in practice there were criminal quarters where the officers of justice were set at defiance, and where no man's life was safe unless he had the privilege of being an inhabitant."

The European governments struggled to keep social order by resorting to severe and often brutal methods of punishment. Literally hundreds of crimes became capital offenses. The stealing of a deer, counterfeiting bank notes—even the most petty of thefts—became capital offenses. In some criminal cases "immediate death" was not quickly forthcoming. Edward Burnworth, an English highwayman, had 424 pounds placed on his chest for over an hour before he finally confessed and was executed.[4]

The government of England, in an attempt to stop the floodtide of crime, placed into effect a system for refunding expenses of prosecutors and witnesses, known as the **parliamentary reward system**. This concept attached financial rewards to various felony crimes. Upon the conviction of a felony suspect, the reward (normally 40 English pounds) was paid to those officials who were responsible for the apprehension and prosecution of the offender. In addition, those involved in the detection and arrest were rewarded the guilty party's horse, furniture, arms, money, and even personal clothing. This system proved to be a dismal failure. Police officials were accused of arresting only felony criminals, in expectation of the parliamentary reward. The system was finally abolished in 1818.

Thief-Taking. As a direct result of London's crime problems came the rather disappointing origin of modern criminal investigation. A concept known in Europe as thief-catching, or **thief-taking**, became widely accepted in the early 1700s. A master criminal, one **Jonathan Wild** (Figure 1.1),

FIGURE 1.1 Early print of Jonathan Wild, English thief-catcher. *(Source: New York Public Library.)*

became London's most effective criminal investigator in the 1720s. Wild's actions made popular the logic of employing one who was a thief to catch a thief. It was utterly inconceivable to early law enforcement officials that anyone but a criminal could successfully detect crime.

Jonathan Wild was a young buckle maker in rural England when he moved to London. Before long he became well known to London's criminal element as a brothel operator. Wild conceived the novel idea of charging a fee for locating and returning stolen property to its rightful owners. His private business prospered quickly and soon expanded into apprehending criminals wanted by the government. When Wild became displeased with a member of his organization (he employed numerous criminals as assistants), he would arrest his former associate and surrender the subject to local magistrates for a reward. Such methods made Wild unpopular with the criminal element and the officials. Accordingly, he was the subject of many threats and physical attacks. On one occasion, while Wild was testifying against a former friend in court, the suspect leaped at Wild in an unsuccessful attempt to cut his throat.

Jonathan Wild's business operations were questionable, to say the least. His normal method of operation, upon learning of a theft, was to persuade the thieves to give him the stolen goods in return for a portion of the money paid by the victim for the return of the property. He, like other thief-catchers to follow, was found guilty of stealing the very items returned to grateful owners. In addition, he was charged with helping a friend escape from infamous Newgate prison. Wild's career came to an abrupt end when he was executed on May 24, 1725. Despite his success at criminal detection (he was responsible for the arrest and execution of more than 120 felons), the London public disliked Wild. As he was being taken to his execution site, hundreds of people jeered, showering him with stones and dirt.[5] After his death, however, Wild became something of a folk hero. His body was disinterred, and the skull and skeleton were exhibited publicly as late as 1860.

Another notorious thief-catcher and former convict was **Eugène Vidocq** (Figure 1.2). Vidocq based his operations in Paris and was active some 80 years after the death of Jonathan Wild. He was equally as successful and unscrupulous as his predecessor, but Vidocq's investigative operations had one major advantage. He and those criminals under his direction operated with the complete sanction of the police. At the end of a lengthy

FIGURE 1.2   Eugène Vidocq, criminal turned Paris investigator. *(Source: New York Public Library.)*

criminal career in 1809, Vidocq offered his services as an informer to the Paris police authorities. Several years later he was arrested for counterfeiting and again offered to inform in return for a light prison term. The prefecture (chief of police) agreed, assigning Vidocq to inform on fellow prison inmates. For a short time, Vidocq performed this function well. In return for his services, he was permitted to escape from a wagon while being transferred from one prison to another. For many years, while posing as an active criminal, Vidocq supplied the Paris police with information. As a result of his capability to detect crime, Eugène Vidocq surfaced as a secret informer in 1817 and, under police authorization, formed the first Paris police detective bureau. It initially consisted of four detectives, increasing in intervals to 28. Vidocq and his fellow thief-catchers proved remarkably successful. Between January and December 1817, with only 12 members, the squad effected 772 arrests. Those arrested included 15 murderers, 108 burglars, 5 armed robbers, and more than 250 thieves of various descriptions.[6] Because of his unprecedented success in criminal investigation, police officials grew envious of Vidocq's ability. In response to police charges that his men were picking pockets, Vidocq ordered that his detectives wear gloves at all times, stating that a pocket can be picked only by a bare hand. Vidocq's name soon became famous throughout Europe. Changing disguises as often as ten times a day, he continued to infiltrate criminal groups. Purposely clean shaven, he would suddenly assume a full beard, changing to a moustache as he felt necessary.

After ten years of active detective work, Vidocq resigned his post—much to the relief of the Paris police. He now had sufficient capital to begin his own private investigative business. Instantly successful, Vidocq was besieged by thousands of crime victims seeking the return of stolen property. In addition to pursuing criminals and recovering stolen goods, Vidocq formed what he termed a "trade protection society." For a fee, any shopkeeper or business establishment could obtain particulars concerning the financial solvency of new customers. At one time, over 8,000 shopkeepers subscribed to this service, which was the forerunner of our present-day credit check.

The Paris police officials continued to view Vidocq's operations with envy and suspicion. As a result, Vidocq was arrested more than 200 times for such charges as "abuse of confidence." He was never convicted, but the legal expense of these repeated arrests and the widely circulated rumors of dishonesty brought about Vidocq's impoverishment. For many years prior to his death in 1857, he was reduced to appearing before audiences dressed as a convict. Frequently changing costumes, he would lecture on his past adventures as a thief-catcher. His memoirs, published in Paris in 1829, did much to popularize the methods of criminal investigation in use at that time. Despite his tarnished criminal past, Vidocq is credited with founding la Sûreté, France's national detective organization.

The methods of the thief-catchers were indeed crude when contrasted with modern means. But one must consider the context in which thief-taking thrived. Victims of criminal offenses had little recourse but to employ the likes of Wild and Vidocq. At the time there existed no public agency or police institution that utilized dependable methods of criminal investigation. The prevailing law enforcement method of operation was based on the prevention of crime by police presence. When this failed, and a crime was discovered, the official investigative effort began—and ended—with the report or discovery of the criminal act. Police authorities in the eighteenth century were very reluctant to work in any plainclothes investigative capacity. The use of criminal informants, undercover operations, surveillances, and similar methods was considered beneath the dignity of the police officer. Thus, these tactics for many years were relegated to the thief-catcher.

The English Detective.   As the populations of European cities continued to swell, criminal activity increased. Criminal competition became so acute that large numbers of thieves would leave their major area of operation. Traveling to and from small villages, they would rob and steal until public outcry forced them back to the larger cities. Not only did the level of street crime become intolerable, but the counterfeiting of coins grew to unprecedented proportions. In 1696, the government of England withdrew all detectable counterfeit coinage from circulation. This amounted to £1,200,000, or roughly $2,100,000. The government was then forced to impose a tax on windows, collecting a tax fee from each individual who owned a home or business with one or more windows.[7]

With increased crime, the public demand for government-supported criminal detection grew. In 1748, Henry Fielding, the English author of the novel *Tom Jones*, was appointed magistrate for the areas of Westminster and Middlesex. He operated out of a court in London located on Bow Street. Shortly after his taking office, the London population saw a group of police officers attached to the Bow Street Court and not in uniform, performing criminal investigative functions. This was a novel occurrence indeed, for never before had the English people experienced police officers who were not readily identifiable. In failing health, Henry Fielding relinquished control of the Bow Street Court to his brother, Sir John Fielding, in 1753. Under the younger Fielding's personal guidance, these early investigators, known as the **Bow Street Runners**, became quite effective (see Figure 1.3). Many of the practices of this small group are still in effect, such as developing paid informants, printing wanted notices, using criminal raids, and bearing firearms and handcuffs.

Although John Fielding was blind, he would often visit crime scenes, take information, and set his investigators on the track of a suspect. Presiding over criminal cases in court, Fielding would sit quietly with bandages over his eyes. Detecting a falsehood in a witness's statement, he would dramatically descend from the bench, waving a switch and demanding the truth.

The population of London in the early 1800s was more than one million, with a crime rate considered one of the worst in history. In the short

FIGURE 1.3 Contemporary print of one of the Bow Street Runners, England's first plainclothes investigators. *(Source: London Metropolitan Police, New Scotland Yard.)*

span of seven years, from 1821 to 1828, there was a felony arrest increase of 41 percent compared to a 15 percent increase in population. This resulted in a ratio of one criminal to every 822 London citizens.[8] The Bow Street Runners were soon overwhelmed by the demands of an increasingly alarmed public. Fielding personally attributed the increase in crime to "a new kind of drunkenness . . . by that poison called Gin." He estimated that more than 100,000 London citizens used the "poison" as their principal sustenance. Armed robberies became so frequent on England's highways that passengers robbed between sunrise and sunset could sue the county for the amount of their loss.

To remedy the public outcry, a prominent London resident, Patrick Colquhoun, proposed the unique idea of a sizable uniformed force to police the city. His proposal was considered too radical and was dismissed. Yet, in 1829, Sir Robert Peel (Figure 1.4) reiterated the idea in the House of Commons. The eventual passage of his recommendations, known as the **Metropolitan Police Act**, was to have a tremendous impact on the history of criminal justice in general and on the development of criminal investigation specifically.

Peel's new force was housed in a building that formerly had been occupied by Scottish royalty. Thus, from the beginning, all police officers and the public at large referred to the London Metropolitan Police as Scotland Yard; the officers were nicknamed *bobbies*, after Sir Robert. Peel possessed a tremendous intellect for police organization. His concepts and actions serve, even now, as a model for police administrators. By the 1840s, others were administering the Metropolitan Police, but the concept of using both uniformed and plainclothes officers in a full-time capacity was firmly established. The general public as well as many government officials, however, viewed the police out of uniform with continual misgiving. One London politician viewed detectives as "police spies armed with extraordinary authority to harass and dog the steps of peaceable citizens, to enter their houses and exercise the right of search on any small pretence or trumped up story."[9]

FIGURE 1.4 Sir Robert Peel, founder and chief organizer of the London Metropolitan Police. *(Source: London Metropolitan Police, New Scotland Yard.)*

Much of the credit for the eventual popularity of Scotland Yard can be attributed to the famous English novelist Charles Dickens. Dickens edited a popular magazine in London in which appeared many articles describing the noble investigative efforts of "the Yard." He befriended many of the investigators and accompanied them on several cases. It was through Dickens's writings and other literary efforts that London's public became gradually more acceptant of the officer in plain clothes. In his novel *Bleak House*, published in 1853, Dickens introduced the term **detective**, the first recorded appearance in print of the word specifically designating an investigative law enforcement officer.

The Yard's detectives began to refer to different criminal types by colorful names, such as the following listed by the English journalist Henry Mayhew in his *London Labour and the London Poor*, published in 1861:

- Mobsmen—those who plunder by manual dexterity, also known as light-fingered gentry.
- Tail buzzers—those who dive into coat pockets for snuff boxes and pocket-books.
- Wires [this term is still in use today]—those who pick pockets.
- Snoozers—those who sleep at railway hotels, and decamp with some passenger's luggage in the morning.
- Star glazers—those who cut the panes out of shop windows.
- Dead lukers—those who steal coats and umbrellas from passages at dusk, or on Sunday afternoons.

In 1877, the investigators of Scotland Yard were organized into a new section known as the Criminal Investigation Department. Its new head was Howard Vincent, a London lawyer without field police experience, who had observed operations of the Paris police. The Criminal Investigation Department, or **CID** as it became known, now contained several hundred detectives. Although many unsolved sensational crimes would pressure the CID into near extinction, an accepted method of criminal investigation had been established.

U.S. Origins

The growth of criminal investigation in the United States parallels European development in a broad sense, with some notable differences regarding particulars. The early populations of major European cities were far greater than those of developing metropolitan areas in this country. For this reason, the need for numerous detectives did not materialize in the United States until approximately 1840.

The European custom of volunteer night watches had been used in major American cities since 1636. In 1656 came the first New York City patrol, dubbed the *rattle watch*.[10] It consisted of a mere six men sounding rattles, yelling such phrases as "By the grace of God two o'clock in peace!" It was not until the early 1830s that daytime paid police patrols were instituted. In the less populated areas of the country, there was no police presence until the late 1880s.

In the northern and eastern areas of the United States, law enforcement was organized along English and French lines. An assortment of sheriffs, marshals, and constables worked in the various New England states. The South had many more armed patrols, but these early patrols were mainly instituted to prevent the escape of slaves rather than for any legitimate law enforcement function. The concept of thief-catching was put to little use in the United States. But there was individual action of a vigilante nature, the offer of rewards, and recovery of stolen goods for a fee.

As criminal occurrences became more numerous during the nineteenth century, public pressure on elected officials to take positive action brought results. Many of America's early public detectives, such as Francis Tukey and Allan Pinkerton, were appointed to their positions by influential mayors. America's political system differed dramatically from the governmental structures of Europe. The government of England, for example, was highly centralized, as was the English police force. In the United States the opposite was frequently true, with mayors in the major cities holding considerable political power. When crime rose to an unacceptable level, the American public complained not to Washington but to their local mayors. Until the nineteenth century, American mayors often personally administered many forms of punishment. In the late 1700s, the mayor of New York City publicly "whipped a woman at the whipping post . . . and afforded much amusement to the spectators by her resistance," reported a local paper.[11] In Boston, Mayor Josiah Quincy Jr. ran a virtual war on crime, culminating in the appointment of Francis Tukey as Boston's new marshal in 1846. Tukey, using many of the investigative methods pioneered by Quincy, such as the surprise police raid, soon hired three officers to serve as Boston's first detectives. Following Boston's lead, Chicago Mayor Levi D. Boone, alarmed over the lack of police effort in the recovery of stolen property, appointed 30-year-old Allan Pinkerton as that city's first detective in 1849.[12]

The rise of the official plainclothes detective in the United States was a rapid one, particularly when contrasted with its counterpart in England. The American public wanted results in the apprehension of criminals and recovery of stolen property. When the use of detectives proved successful in achieving those results, the practice was immediately accepted, with none of the English history of suspicion and hostility toward nonuniformed officers.

The detective bureau organized by the mayor of Philadelphia in 1859 was a typical example of an early U.S. investigative unit. According to a historian of the period, the operation consisted of

> one or two men being on duty at the Central office continually, watching the railroad stations and steamboat landings. Chief of Detectives Wood instructed his men to report to him immediately the presence in the city of any known criminals. When he would send for them and offer the alternative of leaving the city within 25 hours or being locked up, they were not slow in choosing the first.[13]

Although their methods were obviously primitive by today's standards, the Philadelphia investigators were very effective. During its first year, the eight-man unit arrested 481 suspects and recovered more than $25,686 in stolen property.[14]

Frequently, it was more difficult to persuade early U.S. police officers into uniforms than out of them into plain clothes. It was thought that the police uniform too closely resembled regular army uniforms. At this early point in the country's history, the majority of army regulars was recruited from the lowest social classes. It was not until the close of the Civil War in 1865 that the blue uniform became a symbol of honor.[15]

By the 1890s nearly all heavily populated U.S. cities had full-time detectives operating from police headquarters. Crime continued to rise to shocking levels, with major cities like New York reporting more than 80,000 criminal offenses in 1868. To make matters worse, the American criminal population was boosted by the tidal wave of immigrants. Seeking jobs where none existed and living in such slum districts as the notorious Five Points area in lower Manhattan, some of the country's newest citizens turned to crime in desperation.

The detectives' forces grew considerably after the Civil War with the return of veterans into the ranks. The end of the war also added to the national crime problem. Thousands of battle veterans had developed demanding narcotics habits as a result of the continuous morphine treatments they received while recovering from battle wounds. In need of funds to support their addictions, many turned to criminal activities. The number of veterans addicted to morphine, a derivative of opium, was so great that the condition was soon popularly known as the "soldier disease."

Inspector **Thomas Byrnes** (Figure 1.5), chief of detectives in New York City, was one of the most famous investigators of the nineteenth century. An unusually keen-minded individual with 32 years of police experience, he trained his detectives in recognizing individual criminal technique. This method was later to be known as **modus operandi**, or *method of operation*, and is considered an essential tool of investigation to this day. Thomas Byrnes wrote *Professional Criminals of America*, in which he described the working traits of hundreds of active criminals. This book, published in 1886, became a classic work on the operational methodology of the U.S. criminal. Byrnes resigned under pressure from the new president of the Board of Police Commissioners, Theodore Roosevelt, and worked as an insurance investigator for many years thereafter.

While the eastern, central, and southern states developed departments of criminal investigation, the West coped with crime in a different fashion. Here were large expanses of land with relatively small populations, so that regular patrol forces were a rare sight. Instead, the appointed U.S. marshal or locally elected sheriff with an occasional deputy bore the entire burden of patrol, criminal apprehension, and investigation. Such broad responsibilities necessitated some unique methods of law enforcement, particularly when the population swelled during government westward expansion programs. Occasionally, ranchers would band together for apprehension purposes after the discovery of criminal activity. This technique of "raising the hue and cry" was a throwback to the ancient Anglo-Saxon practice of calling one's neighbors to join in the pursuit by sounding an animal horn. In areas somewhat

FIGURE 1.5 Inspector Thomas Byrnes, American founder of criminal modus operandi. *(Source: New York Public Library.)*

more densely populated, various "vigilance committees" composed of local citizens organized pursuit posses to apprehend suspected criminal violators. The same committee would then judge the suspect's guilt or innocence and finally execute sentence. This type of unofficial law enforcement was quite common in the California mining areas during the gold rush of 1848.

The advent of a state-authorized form of policing began in Texas with the formation of the legendary Texas Rangers organization in 1835. Many of the western states developed departments that devoted a majority of their time to field criminal investigation. An excerpt from the official report of Captain T. H. Rynning of the Arizona Rangers described the following typical field duties in 1903:

> We have recovered and restored to their rightful owners, a great many strayed and stolen cattle, horses, sheep and goats, as well as quantities of other stolen property. . . . We have captured and turned over many fugitives from justice from other states and from Mexico; also many U.S. offenders, principally smugglers, Chinese unlawfully in the United States, persons selling whiskey to Indians, and others have been captured and turned over to U.S. authorities. . . . The conditions throughout the Territory are most gratifying. Law and order prevail. There has not been a train robbery, nor lynching in the Territory during the past two years; the old gang of rustlers, smugglers, and wandering outlaws have all been broken up. . . . But two men have been killed resisting arrest during this period, which I consider a remarkable record considering the great number of arrests made on serious charges.

Rynning ended his report by listing the arrest figures compiled by only one captain, one lieutenant, and twenty rangers as

> 297 felony arrests, 762 misdemeanor charges. . . . 16 arrests for petit larceny, 37 concealed weapons, 25 assaults, 9 selling whiskey to Indians, 39 violations of stock and butcher license laws, 5 violations of game laws, 23 for keeping and frequenting opium resorts, 7 running bunco games and gambling games without license, 266 for disturbing the peace and drunk and disorderly, 339 other misdemeanors and vagrants.[16]

Such were the daily activities of the criminal investigator of the West.

The investigative development of the U.S. West was similar to the Canadian development in many respects. The North West Mounted Police came into existence on August 30, 1873. Like their U.S. counterparts, these officers had to demonstrate great versatility in the performance of their duties, which included battling whiskey-smuggling operations and investigating cattle and horse thefts. The expertise of the "Mounties" in their early criminal detection efforts can be illustrated by an 1899 murder investigation. As a result of a thorough investigation of the murder-robbery of three men, more than 400 evidence exhibits were presented to secure a conviction of the suspect.[17]

Allan Pinkerton—America's Foremost Private Detective.   No discussion concerning the history of criminal investigation in the United States could be complete without mention of **Allan Pinkerton** (Figure 1.6). This individual truly deserves the title of "America's Founder of Criminal Investigation." Born August 25, 1819, in Glasgow, Scotland, he fled to the United States fearing political arrest in his native country. By profession he was a self-employed barrel and cask maker, but Pinkerton's instinctive detective abilities soon emerged. While scouting for wood supplies to be used in his business, he detected and later apprehended a local gang of counterfeiters.

FIGURE 1.6 Allan Pinkerton, America's most famous private investigator. *(Source: Pinkerton's Inc.)*

Soon after his counterfeiting adventure, local citizens besieged him for assistance in recovering stolen property and other investigative matters. His reputation quickly grew to the extent that he finally abandoned his barrel business to devote full-time energies to crime detection.

Working for a brief time as deputy sheriff in Cook County, Illinois, Pinkerton became the first detective of the Chicago Police Department in 1849. The following year he worked in the same city as a special U.S. mail agent, detecting mail thieves. Absorbing the fundamentals of detective work at city, county, and federal levels, Allan Pinkerton opened his private detective agency in the early 1850s. In partnership with Chicago attorney Edward Rucker, the immediately successful business was formally known as the North-Western Police Agency.[18]

A tremendous need for the Pinkerton Agency existed in the United States of the 1850s. Other private investigators were in operation at the time, many of them also being former police officers. However, for the most part they lacked those characteristics that would account for Pinkerton's success. Widespread incompetence and corruption were all too commonplace in the contemporary public and private police departments. Jurisdictional restrictions also imposed severe handicaps, often resulting in the escape of criminal suspects across county or state lines.

During this early era of U.S. development, considerable areas of land were being populated as access to them was afforded by the growing railroad system. Yet, in many instances, little or no law enforcement was in effect in the so-called boomtowns. Pinkerton and the many private investigators he hired were not burdened by the jurisdictional restrictions imposed on public officers.

Pinkerton's fame as an inventive and effective investigator had already been established prior to the U.S. Civil War. Among numerous methods pioneered by the Pinkerton Agency were "shadowing" (the art of suspect surveillance) and assuming a "role" (working in an undercover capacity). The agency was also the first to hire a female detective, Kate Warne, in 1856. Pinkerton was an incorruptible individual who established a code of ethics and adhered to it to the letter. He adamantly prohibited his employees from working for one political party against another. Gratuities or rewards were also denied them—a rarity indeed for the times in which the agency operated.

With the outbreak of the Civil War in 1861, Pinkerton immediately offered his services to the federal government. Assigned the task of protecting President Abraham Lincoln, he is credited with detecting and preventing at least one assassination plot. During the war years, his duties included the elaborate operation of an espionage unit and the gathering of military intelligence. Pinkerton, not content to merely administer others, personally made several undercover missions under the alias of Major E. J. Allen. Despite a series of near fatal discoveries, he posed as a Confederate supporter; on one occasion, he was given a personal tour of enemy lines by a top-ranking command officer!

Following the war, Pinkerton's business activities seemingly had no limits. Working in all parts of the United States from branch offices, he administered investigations that ranged from the pursuit of train robbers to the infiltration of secret terrorist labor organizations.

Allan Pinkerton took an active and personal role in his agency until shortly before his death on July 1, 1884. He is credited with establishing the practice of handwriting examination in U.S. courts and promoting a plan to centralize criminal identification records (the forerunner of the Federal Bureau of Investigation Records Division in Washington, D.C.). He also advanced the cause of international police cooperation by sharing information with Scotland Yard and the French Sûreté, thus providing a foundation for the modern international Interpol organization. The Pinkerton Detective Agency provided an honest, efficient model that hundreds of public detectives strived to emulate. Much of the success of today's investigator can be attributed to the dynamic, farsighted Pinkerton.

Criminal Investigation on the Federal Level.   Federal criminal investigation in the United States dates to September 24, 1789, when Congress created the office of the attorney general. Up to the close of the Civil War in 1865, most federal investigations were contracted out to private detectives (Figure 1.7). From 1865 to 1870, the need for specialized agencies within the government led to the creation of the U.S. Secret Service, the Internal Revenue Service, the Custom Service, and finally to the Department of Justice.

The Federal Bureau of Investigation is without question the best known of the federal investigative agencies. The attorney general established the Bureau of Investigation of the Department of Justice in 1909; however, the FBI of today was not organized until 1924 under the directorship of J. Edgar Hoover. From its inception, the bureau has significantly contributed to the overall development of criminal investigation. The creation of a nationwide identification file in Washington, D.C., operated by the FBI, was a major step in consolidating identification records of thousands of individual police departments. Prior to 1924, the identification files were housed in two separate facilities. Since 1896, the International Association of Chiefs of Police had recognized the need for a central repository of criminal identification records. This organization established an identification bureau in Chicago to contain the records and photographs of active criminals. In addition, Leavenworth Federal Penitentiary had for many years been a national collection point for criminal records and fingerprint cards. With the establishment of the records division of the FBI, all existing records were located in one central file for the first time.

Another major contribution of the FBI began with the authorization by Congress to collect and publish uniform crime statistics. From the first bulletin, issued in 1930, to the present, the *Uniform Crime Reports Bulletin*

FIGURE 1.7   A typical turn-of-the-century criminal investigator reviewing case reports. *(Source: Pinkerton's Inc.)*

has been an indispensable measuring gauge for the level of crime in America. The FBI laboratory has set a national standard for criminalistics examination. Created in 1932 with but a single microscope, the laboratory is the largest facility of its kind, processing a wide variety of criminal evidence daily.

Possibly the greatest benefit to the development of criminal investigation has been the image of the FBI. The bureau recognized early the importance of public support. By creating a reputation for investigative competence and individual honesty, the bureau was instrumental in elevating the status of all U.S. criminal investigators.

DEVELOPMENT OF CRIMINALISTICS

Before the 1900s, criminal investigation relied almost exclusively upon the interaction of people. Detectives used their skills as interviewers and persuaders to obtain information regarding innocence or guilt. This form of information gathering, including the frequent use of the informant, was nearly always the sole means of field criminal detection. Today the emphasis is very different. Current methods involve, to a large extent, what is known as **criminalistics**, or the more generic term *forensic science*. The term *criminalistics* originated in an 1893 German text, *Handbook for Understanding a System for Criminalistics*, authored by Hans Gross. An Austrian magistrate and criminology professor, Gross described the importance of a scientifically trained investigator who could also function as a liaison between specialized scientists and police officials.[19] In its simplest form, criminalistics is the application of many fields of natural science to the detection of crime. Chemistry, physics, biology, and mathematics are frequently considered the backbone of forensic science.

Although many crime laboratories existed throughout Europe in the early 1900s, the oldest forensic laboratory in the United States was established in 1923 by the Los Angeles Police Department. Other large police agencies soon developed forensic units, often following sensational criminal events. For example, the Chicago police, assisted by business and civic leaders, established a scientific crime detection laboratory at Northwestern University following the infamous 1929 St. Valentine's Day murders. Additional widespread interest and development of criminalistics followed the 1935 kidnapping trial of Bruno Hauptmann. Convicted of murdering the infant son of Charles Lindbergh, a national hero who completed the first solo nonstop flight across the Atlantic, the determination of Hauptmann's guilt was heavily based on forensic evidence. The establishment of the FBI laboratory in the early 1930s, however, had the greatest impact on the rapid growth of forensic laboratories in this country. There are currently more than 350 public crime laboratories operating in the United States.[20]

In the relatively short span of less than 90 years, criminalistics has become an indispensable cornerstone of criminal investigation. Many thousands of criminal convictions each year can be traced directly to the efforts of the criminalist. To appreciate why and how this development occurred, we again examine nineteenth-century Europe.

Alphonse Bertillon

The detective had become an undisputed part of police organization by the late 1890s. Yet there appeared to be no significant drop in the level of crime. Many critics of the police pointed out that there actually seemed to be a corresponding *rise* in crime resulting from the direct presence of the detective. But this phenomenon was due to the increased efficiency of the European police. As more detectives operated in the field, more arrests were made; statistical rates alone would indicate a growth in crime. As detective work became popularized by the literary media, Europe's scientific community sensed that criminal investigation was a field in which their talents had an untold future.

Although there is no one individual who can be termed the founder of criminalistics, Frenchman **Alphonse Bertillon** (Figure 1.8) is unquestionably the founder of criminal identification, in addition to being instrumental

FIGURE 1.8   The founder of criminal identification by body measurement, Alphonse Bertillon. *(Source: New York Public Library.)*

in the development of forensic science. Born in Paris on April 24, 1853, Bertillon was the second son of a prominent physician-statistician who had founded a society and school of anthropology.[21] Under family pressure to be a physician, Bertillon's poor academic achievements soon forced him from college into the French army.

Shortly after Bertillon's military discharge in 1879, his father secured for him a minor clerk position with the Paris police. His main duty was to copy onto cards the physical descriptions of arrested and wanted suspects. Bertillon soon sensed the inadequacy of the existing methods of criminal identification. He noted that the mere recording of basic factors, such as name, height, weight, and hair color, did not ensure identification of the criminal recidivists (crime repeaters), who could always change names or physical appearance. This was a problem that, for centuries, the French police had been unable to resolve. Primitive methods, such as branding and tattooing, had been used well into the nineteenth century. Although French police routinely photographed arrested criminals, a practice started in 1840, it was quite difficult to identify a suspect by the crude, poorly defined images. The problem of identifying past offenders was so acute that a financial reward was offered to any French police officer who could identify a recently arrested suspect.

Sharing his father's interest in anthropology was indeed fortunate, for it enabled Bertillon to devise a radical new method of criminal identification that was as amazingly logical as it was simple. He reasoned that a foolproof method of identification should be based on physical characteristics that are unchanging and not susceptible to alteration. Anthropology had demonstrated that the human skeleton after the early growing years became fixed and individual. Thus, Bertillon constructed his method of identification, called **anthropometry**, on the uniqueness of the human frame. By this method, the human body was measured in 11 key places (see Figure 1.9). The 11 measurements were then recorded with the color of the eyes, hair, and skin. Bertillon calculated that by using his recording system, the chances against two different suspects having the same measurements would be 4,194,304 to 1.[22] Accordingly, a method of criminal identification based on scientific principles was born.

Although his method was far superior to any other method of identification in use, Bertillon had considerable difficulty in persuading police officials of its merit. Both the Paris chief of police and the chief of detectives resented what they considered to be the intrusion of "mere scientific theory" into practical police work. The system of anthropometry was finally adopted in 1882, but it was not formally recognized until 1888.

Alphonse Bertillon was promoted to chief of the Department of Judicial Identity in 1888. This department was the identification bureau of the French police and aided the field detectives in evidence investigation. Bertillon concentrated much of his research time into the development of police photography. He is credited with the development of the modern police "*mug shot*," or the standardized method of photographing arrested suspects. He persuaded the Paris police to adopt the method of photographing suspects both full face and side profile with each subject sitting the same distance from the camera (see Figure 1.10). Yet another of his photographic innovations was the *metric photograph*. This type of photograph was enclosed within a metric scale along the photograph's border. The scale could be used to measure the distance in the photograph if the subject was on a flat surface and at a right angle to the camera. Although the metric photograph could not be relied upon for an exact measurement, it nevertheless gave a fairly accurate representation of the scene.

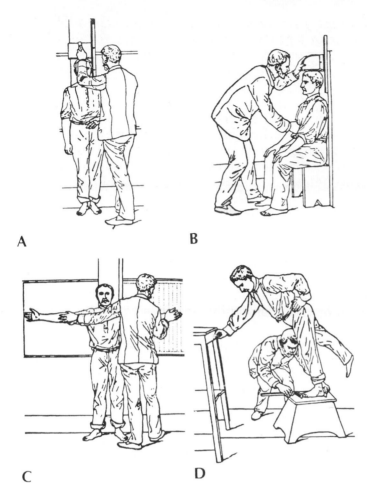

A   B

C   D

FIGURE 1.9   Four of the 11 measurements essential to the criminal identification method of anthropometry. *A*. Measuring the height; *B*. the trunk; *C*. the reach; *D*. the left foot. *(Source: Federal Bureau of Investigation.)*

Bertillon's now famous **portrait parlé** was an outgrowth of his anthropometrical system. The portrait parlé, or speaking picture, aided the police in identifying individuals by providing detailed descriptions of the human head and features. It was developed to be used in lieu of an actual photograph or as a method of obtaining an accurate description of the suspect from an observant victim. The basis of the method was to emphasize the uniqueness of each part of the head and face.

Bertillon was instrumental in other forms of criminalistics, including the science of fingerprinting. Although he did not originate the fingerprinting technique, Bertillon appreciated its possibilities. In 1902, he was the first identification expert in Europe to solve a murder case solely by means of fingerprint evidence.

To his death in 1914, Bertillon never accepted the method of fingerprinting as being superior to anthropometry. Anthropometry was widely adopted by police departments in Europe and the United States for more than 20 years. However, as the infant science of fingerprinting became better known, anthropometry quickly disappeared as a standard method of criminal identification. The now famous **Will West case** was probably most instrumental in hastening the demise of anthropometry. In 1903, a man by the name of Will West was committed to the U.S. Penitentiary at Leavenworth, Kansas.

FIGURE 1.10 One side of a typical Bertillon card showing the various measurements and the standard photograph, circa 1910. *(Source: Federal Bureau of Investigation.)*

Shortly after his arrival, he was measured using the Bertillon system and photographed. West denied having been in the penitentiary before, but the measuring clerk, using his Bertillon measurements, checked his records. The clerk found a previous file with nearly identical measurements and a photograph of a man who appeared to be the prisoner sitting before him. Will West continued to deny that the record was his and stubbornly maintained that he had never before been measured. The record clerk turned the file over and was shocked to read that the card belonged to inmate William West, who was already a prisoner in Leavenworth, having been committed to a life sentence on September 9, 1901, for murder.[23] (See Figure 1.11.)

The West incident drew attention to the chief weakness of Bertillon's system: its dependence on highly accurate methods of measurement. The 11 measurements were only as accurate as the ability of the individual physically measuring the suspect. If the measurer was careless, the figures written on the card would be inaccurate. If the suspect was then rearrested and accurately measured, the second set of figures would significantly differ from the first. Accordingly, the entire purpose of the system would fail, for a file search would not indicate the original arrest and measuring. Juan Vucetich, a founder of fingerprint classification, was particularly frustrated by identification difficulties associated with the Bertillon method. According to Vucetich, his research on fingerprints was in reaction to this frustration.

Bertillon's system of anthropometry was short lived, yet it served as the foundation of all future methods of identification classification. The current

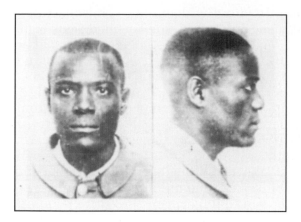

WILLIAM WEST
177.5/188.0/91.3/19.8/15.9/14.8/6.5/27.5/12.2/9.6/50.3
(Bertillon measurements)

WILL WEST
178.5/187.0/91.2/19.7/15.8/14.8/6.6/28.2/12.3/9.7/50.2
(Bertillon measurements)

FIGURE 1.11 The remarkable facial and physical similarities of Will and William West emphasized the need for a more reliable identification method to replace anthropometry. *(Source: Federal Bureau of Investigation.)*

method, in which fingerprints are classified and systematically filed, can be linked to Bertillon's methods. The true value of anthropometry is in the influence it had on police identification and record keeping. For the first time, police authorities became convinced of the value of science in its application to police problems.

Contributors to Criminalistics

Criminalistics was primarily a European phenomenon during its formative years. An early police authority, Raymond Fosdick, noted in his influential book *American Police Systems* that European agencies instituted the majority of criminal identification discoveries long before their U.S. counterparts.[24] Yet few authorities would disagree that the United States now ranks second to none in its legal forensic capabilities.

A complete listing of all the men and women who have contributed scientific expertise in the development of criminal investigation would fill several books. However, the following selected individuals are presented as early and contemporary criminalistic authorities:

- **Juan Vucetich (1858–1926).** Vucetich was an early pioneer in the development and classification of fingerprints. In 1898, in Argentina, he introduced a system of fingerprint classification credited by many to be the first complete system. It found widespread use, especially in Latin countries, and is still used in the original or modified form in many South American police departments. Vucetich had no formal education. He emigrated to Argentina in 1884 from the Dalmatian island of Lessina and joined the police department in Buenos Aires. In 1889, he was appointed chief of the Anthropometric Bureau, instituting the Bertillon method of identification. By 1891, he had devised a system of fingerprint classification based on ten fingers. Shortly thereafter, he became the first individual in South America to secure a criminal conviction based upon fingerprints as the sole clue.

Juan Vucetich was a firm believer in the identification value of fingerprints, not only in criminal investigation but in noncriminal cases as well. On July 20, 1919, his proposal to fingerprint the entire population of Argentina became law, with Vucetich appointed director of the project. The Argentine population did not share his enthusiasm for the project, and various protests, riots, and attacks on his office forced a quick repeal of the law. Vucetich died in 1926, a well-known forensic scientist and founder of the field of fingerprint classification.

- **Francis Galton (1822–1911).** Known as the first individual to publish a definitive study of *dactylography* (fingerprint identification), Galton compiled much scientific data to prove that fingerprints are both unchanging and unique for each individual. He demonstrated mathematically that there are approximately 64,000,000,000 chances to one of two fingerprints being identical. A cousin of Charles Darwin, Galton was a physician who never practiced. His scientific interests were broad, his major fields of study being statistical research and anthropology.

  In addition to his work in fingerprinting, Galton researched the virtually unknown field of composite photography during the latter part of his life. He superimposed photographs of hundreds of human faces, attempting to demonstrate anthropological characteristics common to all criminal types. Galton was knighted by the English government for his many scientific achievements.

- **Edward Richard Henry (1850–1931).** Still another important pioneer in the science of fingerprinting, Henry developed his interest in criminal identification while serving as inspector-general of the Bengal police in India. Finding anthropometry unsatisfactory, he studied under Francis Galton, basing much of his later work on Galton's principles. After studying Vucetich's system of fingerprint classification, Henry devised a classification scheme based on patterns and shapes. It was considered to be a simple yet comprehensive method, which he described in his book *Classification and Uses of Finger-Prints*, published in 1901. Henry's work is credited as the major factor in the persuasion of Scotland Yard to adopt fingerprinting as a means of criminal identification. Following his scientific studies, Henry became commissioner of the London Metropolitan Police in 1903.

  The Henry system of fingerprint classification is currently used by nearly all English-speaking countries. However, it was found to be inadequate for fingerprint collections of more than 100,000 sets. Accordingly, the original Henry system has been combined with an extended FBI system.

- **Arthur Conan Doyle (1859–1930).** Born in Edinburgh, Scotland, Doyle is well known for creating the fictional detective Sherlock Holmes of Baker Street, London, and his friend Dr. Watson. Doyle was a medical doctor who abandoned his practice to become a full-time writer.

He developed his famous character into a scientifically trained investigator, thereby popularizing criminal investigation based on forensic principles.

Sherlock Holmes was introduced in Doyle's first novel, *A Study in Scarlet*, published in 1887. The novels were amazingly accurate predictors of future criminalistic discoveries. For example, in the Holmes adventure *A Case of Identity*, the fictional detective traced a document to a specific typewriter.[25] This work was published in 1893, before forensic scientists had investigated such a possibility. Many leading criminalists, including Bertillon, were avid readers of the Sherlock Holmes series.

Doyle was a prolific writer. Fifty-six short stories and four novels feature the imperturbable Sherlock Holmes practicing the scientific method of criminal investigation.

- **Karl Landsteiner (1868–1943).** An Austrian medical doctor, researcher, and pathologist, Landsteiner discovered in 1901 the agglutination of human blood. This discovery demonstrated that blood possesses certain characteristics, which allowed the designations A, B, AB, and O. Landsteiner's work pioneered a specialty of forensic serology, the scientific study of bodily fluids, particularly blood. Dr. Landsteiner's discovery enabled other criminalists, such as Leone Lattes, to assist criminal investigators by developing methods used to blood-type dried bloodstains. Awarded a 1930 Nobel prize for his blood grouping research, Landsteiner relocated to the United States in 1922.

- **Calvin H. Goddard (1891–1955).** A U.S. Army physician, hospital administrator, and historian, Dr. Goddard developed the now standard system of tracing bullets and associated evidence to weapons from which they were fired. Dismayed by the amount of conjecture and lack of expertise associated with the examination and comparison of firearms, Goddard founded the New York–based Bureau of Forensic Ballistics in 1926. Aided by fellow criminalists Charles Waite, Philip Gravelle, and John Fisher, the bureau perfected the bullet-comparison microscope and assembled the first complete collection of handguns, powders, and bullets for comparison purposes. Recalled to the Army during World War II, Goddard developed the military police criminal investigation laboratory of the Far East Command in Tokyo. A popular expert witness, he testified at the Sacco-Vanzetti trial and served as an investigative consultant for the infamous St. Valentine's Day Massacre.

- **Hans Gross (1847–1915).** A professor of law at the University of Graz, Austria, Gross's career touched many areas of the criminal justice system. He had at various times been a public prosecutor, judge, investigator, and criminalist. He was one of the first to stress the scene of a crime as an indispensable starting point for gathering evidence.

  Gross was an expert in many areas of criminalistics, including blood-stain removal and glass breakage. He is possibly best known for his field handbook of criminal investigation, first published in Munich in 1893. This work became a standard guide for field investigators; it repeatedly emphasized using evidence rather than relying solely on informants as a means of crime solution.

- **Robert Heindl (1883–1958).** Heindl was a German criminalist and chief of many bureaus of criminal investigation. It was on his initiative that fingerprint classification was introduced in Germany around 1900. The reliability of witnesses' observations and statements intrigued Heindl. In a series of scientifically controlled experiments, he found that witnesses generally overestimated suspect height by five inches and age by eight years. He also found that men have more accurate form perception than women. After considerable historical study, Dr. Heindl concluded that the Egyptians used a method of identification quite similar to Bertillon's portraite parlé. He further documented a continuous effort to develop a method of criminal identification since earliest civilized human society.

Heindl was a forensic scientist who continually aided the field detective. When he became aware of a field problem to which scientific methodology could be applied, he responded quickly with research and, frequently, a solution. His book containing a classification of all known tire patterns was used with success in one of the earliest cases involving such evidence.

- **Edmond Locard (1877–1966).** One of the foremost criminalists in the world, Locard founded the internationally known Institute of Criminalistics in Lyons, France. His research particularly concerned the analysis of minute evidence. An early researcher of the science of *poroscopy*, the identification of sweat pores, he proved that pores vary in number, size, and position in each individual.

  In addition to writing many police science books, Dr. Locard was author of an encyclopedia of criminalistics (*Traité de Criminalistique*), as well as numerous articles published in scientific journals. He was responsible for training many criminalists who later gained fame. Locard's principle, "Every contact leaves a trace," is well worth remembering by all criminal investigators.

- **Rudolph Reiss (1876–1929).** Both as a university professor of police science and as a director of several crime laboratories, Reiss aided the field of forensic science. An early student of Bertillon, he specialized in forensic photography, being one of the first to teach a university course in this subject. Reiss published his classic *Judicial Photography* in 1903.

  Reiss taught at the University of Lausanne, Switzerland, for many years and directed a crime laboratory in Yugoslavia until his retirement. He is well known for his work on ink discharge, forged fingerprints, and developing methods for preserving footprints.

- **Harry Soderman (1902–1956).** Born in Sweden, Soderman received a doctor of science degree from the University of Lyon in 1928 as a student under Edmond Locard. For many years he was a private criminalist in Stockholm, becoming the head of the Institute of Police Science at the University of Stockholm in 1931. An authority on crime laboratories, he assisted the New York Police Department in establishing their laboratory in 1934.

  Collaborating with New York City Police Inspector John O'Connell, Soderman wrote *Modern Criminal Investigation* in 1935. It became a classic text, presenting forensic science materials in a practical way to thousands of detectives. He also authored many manuals on police science and instructed police on subjects from firearms examination to collecting dust from the clothing of suspects. Soderman was one of the founding members of the international Interpol organization.

- **August Vollmer (1876–1955).** Born in America, Vollmer (Figure 1.12) was known principally for his concepts of police organization and administration. He had a tremendous influence on the development of criminalistics in the United States. In 1905, he was elected town marshal of Berkeley, California, where he instituted concepts of police administration and science that significantly increased law enforcement professionalism.

FIGURE 1.12　August Vollmer, expert police administrator and early promoter of criminalistics. *(Source: Berkeley Police Department.)*

Vollmer organized and headed the Institute for Criminology and Criminalistics at the University of California at Berkeley. This institute was the first of its kind in the United States and paved the way for many criminalistic laboratories throughout the country.

Vollmer encouraged his Berkeley officers to experiment in all areas of criminology and forensic science. Under his supervision, officer John A. Larson developed the first practical **polygraph** (lie detector) in 1921 (see Figure 1.13). Larson later became a physician and expert in the application of the law to medicine. In addition to forensic science exploration, Chief Vollmer was the first police administrator to institute formalized in-service detective training.[26]

Retiring in 1932, Vollmer assumed a professorship of criminology at the University of California; considering his lack of even a high school education, this was a remarkable achievement. He also served as a police and criminalistic consultant to numerous law enforcement agencies.

FIGURE 1.13　The first practical polygraph, developed by John Larson under the supervision of Chief August Vollmer in 1921. *(Source: Berkeley Police Department.)*

- **Paul L. Kirk (1902–1970).** Dr. Kirk is perhaps the best-known U.S. criminalist. Holding a doctorate in biochemistry, he joined the faculty of the University of California in 1925, becoming head of the Department of Criminalistics in 1954. He founded crime laboratories in Chicago and St. Louis, among other U.S. cities. His classic textbook *Crime Investigation: Physical Evidence and the Police Laboratory* is a widely used sourcebook.

  In 1952, Kirk invented a new density-measuring device for soil samples found at outdoor crime scenes. In the same year, he accumulated an extensive crime scene investigation kit that was highly portable, yet extensively equipped. Kirk constantly emphasized that the field officer was the key to successful crime investigation. In his view, it was vital for field officers to know precisely what types of evidence to collect and why.

  The death of Dr. Kirk was a great loss to the field of forensic science. Through his well-publicized testimonies as an expert witness in several sensational criminal trials, such as the Sam Sheppard murder case, he familiarized the general public with some of the uses of criminalistics.

- **Alec Jeffreys (1950–).** In 1984, a British biologist, Professor Jeffreys (Figure 1.14), discovered the concept of DNA profiling, commonly called "genetic fingerprinting," at the University of Leicester in England. DNA (deoxyribonucleic acid) is a genetic compound found in every cell of the human body. Dr. Jeffreys's discovery has enabled criminalists to individualize DNA traces commonly encountered in evidence such as blood, semen, and hair roots, among other bodily compounds. Despite its name, this method of individualizing human trace evidence has nothing to do with traditional fingerprinting.

FIGURE 1.14 Dr. Alec Jeffreys, biologist and genetics expert, discovered the concept of DNA genetic fingerprinting. *(Source: Dr. Alec Jeffreys, University of Leicester.)*

INVESTIGATIVE PROFILE

Dr. Henry C. Lee, Ph.D.
Forensic Scientist
Director, Forensic Research Training Center, Meriden, Connecticut
Former Chief Criminalist for the State of Connecticut, and Commissioner, Connecticut
Department of Public Safety

I've been involved with criminal investigations and forensic science for the past 45 years, and every day has been a fascinating challenge. I was born in China and grew up in Taiwan, where I joined the Taipei Police Department, rising to the rank of captain. But as I was always interested in the application of science to crime detection, I decided in 1965 to immigrate to the United States to pursue higher education in forensic science and chemistry. I obtained my bachelor's degree in forensic science from John Jay College in New York City and by 1975 earned my masters and Ph.D. in biochemistry from New York University. After completing my doctorate, I became a faculty member at the University of New Haven and created the Forensic Sciences program.

I've been very fortunate to have participated in so many changes and developments in the world of forensic science. As a crime lab director, I've observed many tremendous advancements in instrumentation and testing techniques; particularly in the areas of human identification and crime scene interpretation. DNA testing, blood splatter analysis, recent findings in hair and fiber examinations, new methods of obtaining latent fingerprints, and many other advances have significantly expanded the field. The importance and prestige of forensic science is a far cry from what was encountered in the early part of my career. Because of the increased effectiveness of criminalistics and heightened public expectations, all police officers must be trained to appreciate the capabilities of forensic science. And I'm pleased to note that at last the public and people working in the justice system are content to just let science speak for itself. Early in my career, you couldn't testify for the defense, only for the prosecution. I've testified over 1,000 times in court and assisted in 7,000 major cases. While I worked with prosecutors in the majority of these investigations, I also regularly assisted defense attorneys. Evidence must be thought of as being totally neutral and objective. Today's forensic scientist must let evidence speak for itself; it is not our concern why something was done. We focus on how something was done and what evidence this action produced. Then we apply pure science to the evidence, identifying a suspect or gaining insight into what occurred or how a crime was committed.

My career has had so many positive aspects. It's always been exciting, always challenging, and constantly different. I particularly enjoy the way logic must always be utilized within my work. Crime laboratory experts quickly learn that they must mix scientific knowledge with logic and one's investigative instincts. From this reasoning process often comes the answers that solve crimes. These three elements were used in the infamous "wood chipper" case in which a husband murdered his wife, dismembered her body, and ran the body parts through a wood chipper. We used science to identify the victim through hundreds of tiny bits of bone and teeth and logic and instinct to trace the rental of the wood chipper to the killer. Like any other justice career, there are negatives as well. It's not a job; it is a profession, and you often bring the cases home with you. So you ponder the cases when you go to bed, when you eat, when you drive. And there's a lot of tragedy, for the victim's family thinks you should have an instant answer, that science can solve anything, and quickly. But it often takes a long time for the answers, and sometimes there will be no answer for them at all.

Students who are thinking about a career in forensic science need to be aware that the field has two separate career paths. There are those who are evidence technicians, and they perform a different function than forensic scientists working in a crime laboratory. Technicians are part of a team that processes crime scenes. Forensic scientists, or criminalists as they are also known, typically have advanced graduate degrees and are conducting experiments in a local, state, or federal crime lab. Forensic scientists must have a solid foundation in the natural sciences and a high tolerance for repetitive work. After all, they annually conduct hundreds or even thousands of experiments of a specialized nature, like drug screenings or DNA comparisons.

Forensic science has literally opened the world to me, and I've consulted in England, Bosnia, South America, and the Middle East, among other locations around the world. I've been involved in many of the most sensational cases in recent American criminal history, including the O.J. Simpson case, the Kennedy assassination, and the Jon Benet Ramsey murder investigation. When I'm not consulting, I enjoy writing about my specialty. I'm the author of a number of books dealing with scientific investigation, and I edit five scientific publications. To achieve prominence in your chosen profession, you have to realize that every profession is unique. And every profession needs a few who are the best, who can develop and improve that profession. Why not pick an area within your limits, then set the goal of no limit for that profession? Within that area you choose, choose to strive for the best.

DNA profiling was first used by British criminal investigators in 1987. At that time, a double homicide was solved when the perpetrator's DNA matched semen DNA located at the murder scene. The discovery of this technique has opened a new and vastly important area of criminal identification. Hundreds of otherwise unsolvable homicide and rape investigations have been resolved through DNA analysis and suspect comparison. In addition to solving violent crimes, Dr. Jeffreys's profiling technique is now regularly used in many noncriminal cases, such as paternity suits.[27]

LEGAL INFLUENCES ON THE DEVELOPMENT OF CRIMINAL INVESTIGATION

Criminal investigation in the United States is strictly governed by the application of law. All investigators must be cognizant of the prescribed legal guidelines applicable to every step of the detection process. The historical development of criminal law into its present state was neither rapid nor without considerable resistance. Criminal law and the procedures for dealing with criminal evidence are the end results of centuries of questioning and defining the need for applying criminal justice.

Many ancient civilizations contributed to what we now recognize as U.S. criminal law and procedure. Various criminal codes of the United States were particularly influenced by early cultures of foreign origin. An examination of Louisiana's criminal law reveals obvious French origin; more subtle Spanish influences can be noted in criminal codes of the West. However, the major foundation of our criminal procedure is indisputably based on English common law.

The signing of the Magna Carta, the founding document of the English constitution, in 1215, was the true beginning of the eventual application of law to U.S. police procedure. Early criminal codes in the United States basically defined crime and applied punishments for each violation. The U.S. colonies before the Revolution had no codes by which methods of criminal detection could be judged. Accordingly, the early constables used any and all means they deemed necessary to obtain evidence. The use of coercion and force to obtain confessions was unfortunately all too common. Restrictions on methods of arrest were nearly nonexistent, and the frequent searching and seizing of evidence was accomplished by any means available.

Following the successful outcome of the American Revolution, the founding fathers drew together the Constitution in 1789. It is significant that the Constitution and the **Bill of Rights**, adopted in 1791, had little influence on individual state criminal procedure. The Bill of Rights (the first ten amendments of the Constitution) was directed toward federal law enforcement agencies.

In 1868, the **Fourteenth Amendment** was added to the U.S. Constitution. This addition was responsible, in large measure, for the current state of professional criminal procedure and investigation. The Fourteenth Amendment requires that "no state shall deprive any person of life, liberty or property without due process of law, nor deny . . . the equal protection of the laws." Through a long series of decisions rendered by the U.S. Supreme Court, the Fourteenth Amendment was gradually applied to the individual states. The effect of this action was to bring about sweeping changes in criminal procedure.

By the late 1960s, certain provisions of the Bill of Rights (the Fourth, Fifth, and Sixth Amendments in particular) had been applied to all states through the Fourteenth Amendment. This had a profound effect on thousands of criminal investigators throughout the country. Restrictions that had for many years applied to federal investigations, such as methods of search and seizure (Fourth Amendment), methods of obtaining information and confessions (Fifth Amendment), and the assistance of counsel requirements (Sixth Amendment), now applied to local criminal investigations.

Although all ten amendments of the Bill of Rights are important to law enforcement operations, the Fourth, Fifth, and Sixth Amendments have historically had the greatest direct impact on criminal investigation. The Fourth Amendment to the Constitution provides that

> the right of the people to be secure in their persons, houses, papers, and effects, against unreasonable searches and seizures, shall not be violated, and no Warrants shall issue, but upon probable cause, supported by Oath or affirmation, and particularly describing the place to be searched, and the persons or things to be seized.

The Fourth Amendment was inspired by English outrages pertaining to searches, seizures, and arrests prior to the American Revolution. It was written into the Constitution to assure citizens that government officials would respect rights regarding the seizure of persons and things and the associated right to privacy.[28] The framers of the Constitution purposely wrote the amendments to be somewhat vague, knowing that future generations would interpret the amendments through court actions. Thus, the Constitution forbade unreasonable searches and seizures but did not define what types of police action are to be judged unreasonable.

American courts have historically guided law enforcement officers in interpreting the Fourth and other amendments. For example, it was unclear to investigators whether evidence obtained in violation of the Fourth Amendment could still be admitted in state courts. Through the landmark U.S. Supreme Court decision of *Mapp v. Ohio* (1961), the Court held that the exclusionary rule, which had already been in effect for federal cases since 1914, also applied to state criminal proceedings. The admission of evidence obtained as a result of unreasonable searches and seizures is prohibited in a legal proceeding by the exclusionary rule.[29]

In a democracy such as the United States, the right to privacy is of extreme importance for all citizens. Although this right was not expressed explicitly in the Constitution, it is implied as a principle in several amendments, including the Fourth. A legal right to privacy was recognized by the U.S. Supreme Court in 1965 and has been formalized through many state and federal rulings of importance to investigators.[30] Matters of privacy can affect a large variety of criminal cases, such as an investigator's decision to use an electronic information-gathering device or to examine a suspect's phone bill or bank account. Because the right to privacy is not an absolute, courts have generally ruled that this right can be forfeited when law enforcement officers show sufficient probable cause to believe that an individual is involved in criminal activity. As outlined in the Fourth Amendment, probable cause must be demonstrated by the police to independent judicial officials, who then authorize investigators to intrude on a person's right to privacy, generally by issuing a warrant.

The Fifth Amendment addresses many areas of importance; however, the following section has particular significance for the criminal investigator:

> . . . nor shall [any person] be compelled in any criminal case to be a witness against himself, nor be deprived of life, liberty, or property, without due process of law.

In addition, the Sixth Amendment passage, ". . . and to have the Assistance of Counsel for his defence," is often combined with Fifth Amendment rulings.

The right not to be compelled to testify or to incriminate oneself is historically very old. Ancient Hebrew law, common law, and the early canon law of the church all stated this principle. Accordingly, the writers of the Constitution specifically detailed this right, no doubt foreseeing its importance as the country expanded and crime increased. Since then, the Fifth and Sixth Amendments have been interpreted heavily in the investigative areas of suspect interviewing and the notification of the right to an attorney.

The U.S. Supreme Court cases of *Escobedo* (1964) and *Miranda* (1966) provide examples of Fifth and Sixth Amendment rulings that have an impact on investigators daily. These decisions instructed officers to advise criminal suspects of their rights to silence and counsel as a protection against self-incrimination prior to trial. Such judicial interpretations are historically recent, as tradition dictated such rights to apply only at the time of trial.

The now famous criminal cases of *Mapp, Escobedo, Miranda*, and others have achieved desirable results. Rather than providing legal obstacles by "handcuffing the police," the reverse has occurred. With constitutional guidelines in effect, criminal investigators were obliged to concentrate on physical evidence as an essential element of their investigations. This has directly affected the growth and importance of criminalistics. The deemphasizing of the confession as a single indicator of absolute guilt has also compelled the detective to focus on other areas of criminal investigation.

Thus, the law has ensured criminal investigations that are as just as is humanly possible. The modern detective is legally and morally bound to conduct *all* investigations with due process of law, ensuring every person the equal protection of the law.

▲ SUMMARY

Modern criminal investigation has evolved from ancient origins that included clan or family obligation to resolve crime. Responsibility then passed to military units and, during the Middle Ages, shifted from a governmental duty to a system of mutual protection within the village. When an expanding population eventually shifted the obligation of crime investigation back to government officials, watches and patrols were formed to deter crime. The failure of such methods demanded a reactive effort to apprehend criminal suspects and recover stolen property. The offering of rewards and the public employment of criminals to apprehend other lawbreakers were widespread practices. The efforts of early thief-catchers Jonathan Wild and Eugène Vidocq met with mixed results, as officials and public pressures demanded an end to this method of investigation.

As crime rates and urban populations continued to increase, the responsibility for policing and crime investigation passed firmly into the hands of government. England pioneered the system by establishing the Bow Street Runners, an early unit of plainclothes investigators. With the passage of the Metropolitan Police Act, Sir Robert Peel advanced the investigative effort by permanently establishing an effective police force for the city of London.

The evolution of criminal investigation in the United States occurred somewhat later than its development in Europe. The need for intense investigative effort did not arise in the United States until the middle of the nineteenth century. The development of investigative methods in America was aided significantly by the innovative efforts of Allan Pinkerton. Originally a government law enforcement officer, Pinkerton established an efficient, honest, and extensive private detective agency that served as a model for many public detective units. Through the creation of the Federal Bureau of Investigation, the positive image of the American investigator was solidly presented to the American people.

After the turn of the century, the traditional use of a confession or an informant as the sole means of proving guilt was devalued. Physical evidence connecting a suspect to a crime became very important, thus creating the need for forensic science, or criminalistics. The application of science to crime investigation was pioneered by many Europeans, of whom Alphonse Bertillon was one of the most important and farsighted. Among his many achievements, Bertillon created a method of criminal identification based on skeleton measurement, known as anthropometry. His method was widely used until replaced by the superiority of fingerprinting.

Many other individuals contributed to the development of criminalistics with unique discoveries or scientific theories. Dactylography (fingerprint identification) was fully developed into a system of classification by the early 1900s, at a time when other pioneering work was being completed in the areas of blood research and crime scene processing.

Criminal investigations are only as good as their adherence to the law. The Constitution and Bill of Rights serve as historical foundations and evolving contemporary guides for modern investigators. Although originally applied to federal criminal cases, the procedures and protections articulated in the Constitution were made applicable to state investigative actions through the Fourteenth Amendment. The Fourth, Fifth, and Sixth Amendments of the Bill of Rights are of particular significance to law enforcement officers, as the law of criminal procedure is interpreted mainly through these amendments. The Fourth Amendment deals with the issues of arrest, search, and seizure and the associated issue of the right to privacy. The Fifth and Sixth Amendments concern themselves with investigative practices associated with the right against self-incrimination and the right to counsel. As legal rulings continue to develop from state and federal judicial interpretations, investigators will continue to be guided in their responsibilities and obligations.

■ EXERCISES

1. Prepare a research paper on the level of criminality in early London.
2. Prepare a research paper on the life and accomplishments of Allan Pinkerton.

3. Research and demonstrate to the class how a criminal suspect was measured through anthropometry.

4. Research the forensic science capability of your community. Determine where and how local police agencies process their physical evidence.

5. Prepare a research paper detailing major criminal cases heard by your state's supreme court. Detail how the appeals relate to issues within the Fourth, Fifth, or Sixth Amendments.

RELEVANT WEB SITES

http://www.met.police.uk/history/

Official site of the London Metropolitan Police. Details the historical development of the organization and includes a historical timeline. Contains extensive information on notorious past and present English criminal investigations, including the "Jack the Ripper" case.

http://www.troopers.state.ny.us/.Forensic_science/

Operated by the New York State Police, this site details the developmental growth of a large state forensic laboratory. Illustrates the various functions and examinations commonly encountered in a modern state laboratory.

http://www.fbi.gov/

Official site of the Federal Bureau of Investigation with extensive information on FBI history and many associated areas of investigative interest.

http://www.forensic-evidence.com

Contains extensive links pertaining to criminal investigation, evidence, and forensic science. Includes essays on Alphonse Bertillon, fingerprints, handwriting, and constitutional issues related to criminalistics.

Introduction of Basic Concepts

KEY TERMS

assignment by caseload
assignment by priority
assignment by specialization
critical thinking
deductive reasoning
inductive reasoning
intuition
investigative ethics

legal knowledge
observational skill
organizational ability
persistence
police investigator
private investigator
public investigator

LEARNING OBJECTIVES

1. to appreciate the importance of criminal investigation to the criminal justice system as a whole;
2. to know what constitutes a successful criminal investigation;
3. to be able to list and define the desirable traits of the investigator;
4. to be able to explain and contrast deductive and inductive reasoning;
5. to appreciate the importance of investigative ethics and the common causes of misconduct;
6. to be familiar with the organization and staffing of investigation divisions in various agencies on the local, state, and federal levels; and
7. to understand how various cases are assigned to investigators through generalized, specialized, and priority designations.

CRIME AND THE INVESTIGATOR

- Researchers surveying homicides in the United States have discovered that murder is the leading cause of death for women in the workplace and for black men 25 to 34 years of age.
- In a once-tranquil state park system, 3,525 crimes were reported during a recent year—including 4 murders, 6 rapes, 20 assaults with a deadly weapon, 22 indecent exposures, 9 arsons, and 6 robberies.
- The chance of becoming a victim of violent crime is greater than that of being injured in an auto accident, burned by fire, or divorced.
- A mother and five children died in a burning apartment in Newark, New Jersey, because they had nailed their apartment door shut for fear of becoming crime victims.
- One U.S. household in four annually has at least one member who will be a victim of theft, burglary, rape, or robbery.
- One in five teenagers has been the victim of a violent crime, and they are twice as likely as any other group to be shot, stabbed, sexually assaulted, beaten, or otherwise attacked.

Crime is a major concern in the United States. The possibility of becoming a victim of crime, particularly of a violent assault, is the number one fear of millions of Americans. This concern is well founded, as 5.3 million people over the age of 12 annually will be victimized by violent crimes.[1] That nearly 14 million serious crimes are reported yearly to the police indicates only part of the situation. An annual study by the Bureau of Justice Statistics surveys American households to determine the extent of serious crime not being reported to law enforcement authorities. Initiated in 1973, the National Crime Survey measures the number of crimes unreported to the police as opposed to reported crime, which is documented annually by the FBI's *Uniform Crime Reports Bulletin*. The results of the National Crime Survey are disturbing to the entire criminal justice system, indicating that people and households in the United States face 49 million crime attempts a year when unreported and reported crime occurrences are combined.[2]

The efficient criminal investigator is in a position to make a significant contribution toward reducing the crime level in the United States. It is true that the investigator is but one part of the law enforcement institution, but he or she is indisputably a vital part. To great numbers of the public the investigator represents the successful return of stolen property or the satisfaction that justice is being done by the identification and arrest of an assailant. When these and other investigative functions do not occur, many negative outcomes occur. Victims of crimes may not report violations to the police feeling that "nothing can be done." It is significant that approximately 50 percent of the people interviewed in an unreported crime study failed to notify the police because they believed "the police would not want to be bothered" or "nothing would come of it."

If the criminal justice system is to be considered a success, each of the three components—law enforcement, courts, and corrections—must operate in a competent, just manner. The investigation function will directly affect the workings of both the judiciary and the correctional system. Inasmuch as more than 2,800 deeds are classified as federal crimes and an even greater number as state and local offenses, investigators have ample statutory support to charge law violators. However, an illegally conducted or poorly prepared investigation will be rejected in court. The dismissal of a criminal case is all too often blamed on the judiciary alone. The indiscriminating media or public may look no further to discover the *cause* of a dismissal. Public opinion of the effectiveness of the judiciary suffers, with court officials resenting inept criminal investigations.

All segments of the population have been affected by the disturbing national crime problem. Since 1930, when national statistics were first collected, crime rates have steadily increased. Even though rates have recently experienced modest declines, since 1961, the rate of serious crime has more than doubled and, in one recent year, rose an alarming 17 percent. In New York City alone, more than 710,000 felony offenses are reported annually to the police. Although many crime categories are currently leveling or demonstrating slight declines, our national crime rate continues to be intolerably high and the leading national problem for most Americans.[3] The concept that crime is confined solely to the inner cities is rapidly being proven false; the greatest increases of criminal offenses are occurring in the "peaceful" suburbs and rural areas. American criminality has given the police and the public cause for concern. And the national average of only 20 percent of all reported crime resulting in arrest is far from encouraging.

Today's criminal investigator faces a formidable challenge. There can never be enough education, training, and retraining to prepare the officer for the task at hand. The success or failure of the officer's efforts will mirror the success or failure of our system of justice.

CRIMINAL INVESTIGATION—THE PARTIAL SOLUTION

Criminal investigation is a logical, objective, legal inquiry involving a possible criminal activity. The results of the inquiry, if successful, will answer the following questions:

1. Did a criminal violation as described by a code or statute occur?
2. Where and at what time and date did the crime occur?
3. Who were the individuals involved in the planning, execution, and after-effects of the violation?
4. Is a witness to the criminal activity present?
5. Is there evidence of the criminal offense?
6. In what manner or by what method was the crime perpetrated?
7. Is there an indication of guilt or innocence to aid judicial officials in determining a just solution to the case?

It must be realized that to answer these questions completely is no simple task. Very frequently, incomplete criminal cases in which some of the questions remain open are presented to prosecuting officials. This is not always the fault of the individual investigator; many other components have a direct bearing on the completeness of the investigation. For example, the attitude of the victim, the physical condition of the scene of the crime, the presence or absence of witnesses—all play a part in the inquiry. Yet it is the investigator who is ultimately accountable. The duties of today's investigator are numerous and frequently difficult. To meet the responsibility of investigating crime, an individual should possess certain traits that are of enormous benefit on the job.

Desirable Traits of the Investigator

Of the many personality traits indispensable to the investigator, surely *superior reasoning ability* ranks near the top. The ability to analyze logically a multitude of facts and determine how they interrelate is basic to the investigative purpose. Although this ability is essential at all levels of law enforcement, the investigator is confronted with continual mental challenges on a daily basis. Unlike noninvestigative coworkers, a full-time investigator does not usually initiate a case; that is, the majority of cases with which an investigator is concerned are assigned or developed by others, rather than originating from "on the scene" intervention. However, because most preliminary investigations are handled by patrol officers who regularly engage in investigative matters in addition to their patrol duties, the traits desirable in an investigator are required in all within the department.

Superior reasoning ability is closely related to the concept of **critical thinking**. Originally developed by psychologists and educators, this method of reasoning challenges one to adopt an attitude of fair-mindedness, intellectual caution, and an openness to question common or assumed beliefs.[4] Critical thinkers will find supportable reasons to accept or reject an assumption and are never hesitant to seek an explanation of the "why" of an event. Finally, active critical thinking avoids the emotional approach so easily evoked during criminal inquiries. Investigators, like everyone else, have emotions, but to reason clearly they must think as rationally as possible, basing their reasoning on facts.

Developing critical and analytical thinking is the means for understanding and using information that emerges during the investigative process. Properly used, critical thinking leads to sound conclusions based on independent ideas. The following elements form the foundation of the critical thinking process:

1. Differentiating between fact and opinion
2. Determining cause-and-effect relationships
3. Determining the accuracy and completeness of information presented
4. Recognizing logical fallacies and faulty reasoning
5. Developing inferential skills through deductive or inductive reasoning[5]

A fact is a statement or observation that can be verified by other verifiable points of information, whereas an opinion is merely one's impression or personal belief. During the course of an investigation, a considerable amount of information must be processed. Factual data will generally guide the course and direction of the case, whereas opinions serve only a secondary, less valuable function. Cause-and-effect thinking often serves a directional purpose during the investigative process, as one or more facts generate further related factual insights. Critical thinking also focuses on a determination of how accurate and complete one's gathered facts are. By examining these factors, the investigator can be guided to gather additional information or move into another area of inquiry.

Critical thinkers must be able to recognize faulty logic, as inaccurate logic only serves to divert an investigation. Faulty reasoning often centers on generalization, stereotyping, oversimplifying, or incorrect assumptions. Critical thinking reminds the officer to avoid such problems by focusing on facts. Conclusions based on insufficient data or on simplistically labeling items or people without concern for individualist traits only serve to distort the inquiry.

Methods of reasoning that assist critical thinking and that are peculiar to the investigative process are basically of two types: **deductive** and **inductive**. Because either method can be misleading when used in a narrow frame of reference, many investigators employ a combination of the two or emphasize one over the other, depending on the nature of the investigation. The deductive method of reasoning forms a general conclusion prior to having a complete explanation based on facts. With the deductive conclusion in mind, the investigator considers the emerging evidence, contrasting it with the conclusion to determine its validity. Let us assume that an investigator is examining a crime scene involving a subject found dead by a gunshot would to the head. A handgun is located near the hand of the deceased, and the officer is informed that the subject had had a painful terminal illness. The officer concludes that the gunshot wound was self-inflicted—an example of deductive reasoning. If the officer had not formed a conclusion as to the cause of death but waited for the results of further investigation and evidence gathering and then formed a conclusion based on all known facts, inductive reasoning would have been at work.

Although the use of inductive reasoning may prevent a narrowing of perceptions and speculation, its exclusive use may also postpone or eliminate the direction and momentum necessary to gather evidence or to make an arrest. Because successful arrest and/or property recovery is highly dependent on action during the early stages of an investigation, the passage of too much time will often work against the success of a case. Yet totally focused deductive thinking may block inquiry into other significant areas, a serious error if the original conclusion was faulty. It is but human nature to support a conviction once it is formed, thus making further evaluation of information less than objective. Accordingly, an investigator may base the selection of deductive or inductive reasoning on the nature of a particular criminal inquiry. Complex inquiries, such as complicated white-collar crimes or major drug cases, are well suited for the inductive method, whereas those cases in which the passage of time works against the probability of success, robbery or burglary, for example, are often better served by deductive reasoning.

The investigator is occasionally perceived as an individual completely devoid of imagination and curiosity. The origins of this stereotype date back to early literature portraying the "bumbling" inspector whose dullness is accentuated as he is repeatedly outwitted by a brilliant private investigator or other second party. This image has been perpetuated by the media, despite its lack of authenticity. The present-day investigator must have both *imagination* and *curiosity*—and the ability to use them advantageously. To simply assemble the facts of a case may not be enough to "get the whole picture." Imagination—forming mental images of what is not present or creating new ideas by combining previous experiences—is indispensable in the many investigations that are not complete. An investigator who has difficulty accounting for factors that are not immediately apparent is working at a disadvantage. Curiosity is a desire to learn by being inquisitive. Can there be a trait that is more necessary to law enforcement at all levels? The continual examining and questioning of all facets of an investigation challenges the officer to be objective.

Intuition is frequently cited as a necessary quality of the investigator. This trait is defined as immediate apprehension or cognition—quick and ready insight without the conscious use of reasoning. It has often been pointed out that many police officers have a "sixth sense," resulting in hunches that those outside the profession rarely perceive. In fact, intuition is often the result of a combination of experience and training. Applying one's past experiences to a situation is generally a subconscious thought process. This, of course, applies to knowledge acquired during education and training.

The ability to observe is a normal condition for most people. Yet **observational skill** must be highly developed in the investigator. The act of observing is a noting and recording of facts. Under most circumstances, the investigator will use the senses of seeing and hearing, the former being the more significant. The power of observation can be developed so that it is far above the normal level. For example, the criminal investigator must be able to note visual details while observing a subject for only a brief time. The accuracy of descriptions of facial features, clothing, automobiles, and so forth is often of crucial importance in a criminal case. Obtaining accurate search warrants, providing descriptions of wanted suspects and vehicles, and reliable testimony in court all depend upon the power of observation.

Few people have so-called photographic memories, but the ability to retain visual images can be heightened through progressive memory training. The military has for many years demonstrated this learning ability in programs designed to train pilots and gun crews to recognize aircraft during brief viewings. Silhouettes of aircraft, ships, and other military objects are projected onto a screen at timed intervals. After viewing the silhouettes for progressively shorter periods of time, pilots develop a capacity to recognize the object in fractions of a second. The same kind of conditioning can be applied to the criminal investigator either formally or by self-training.

The nature of investigative work frequently demands a high degree of **organizational ability**. Like the successful business executive, the police investigator is continually processing various types of information. Written information, verbal information, current case assignments, and follow-ups of past investigations all require an ability to organize. The investigating officer is receiving and processing formal reports from a multitude of sources. This demands an orderly method of information retention that will result in the availability of records and facts when needed.

Of the many qualities that characterize the skillful investigator, a substantial **legal knowledge** may be the most significant. The age of the detective who ignored legal restrictions or rarely applied them is fortunately long past. Today's investigator must possess a solid grounding in criminal law and, to a lesser degree, in civil law. It is not uncommon, particularly in large municipalities, for the prosecuting attorney to rely heavily on the investigator's judgment for legal evaluation of a case. This is normally due to the large number of criminal cases assigned to the prosecutor, leaving little time for pretrial discussion. Thus, the assistance of an officer who is able to determine an illegal or questionable aspect of a case is very important to the prosecution. Although civil investigations (cases involving private wrongs) do not generally involve the investigator of a police agency, many citizens will report civil violations for police action. The officer must then be able to distinguish between a criminal violation and a civil violation in order to determine appropriate action.

A wide variety of situations and people are encountered in criminal investigation. An officer may meet a corporation president in the morning, then take a statement from an illiterate narcotics addict in the afternoon. Such great diversity requires an ability to interact with all types of individuals in an equally convincing manner. To achieve this, *cultural understanding* and a *wide range of interests* are desirable. The investigator should continually strive to be well rounded. This applies to reading areas and to interests in general. Proficiency in many areas of investigative work, such as report writing, interviewing, developing informants, and performing undercover operations, is closely related to personality flexibility.

An awareness and understanding of cultures different from the investigator's own can be of great advantage. Such insight can assist appreciably in information gathering, interviewing, informant recruiting, and many other tasks commonly encountered during criminal investigation. Because specific behaviors and traits are unique to various cultural groups, development of an awareness of cultural diversity can provide the investigator with new insights. For example, the Hispanic population, the fastest-growing minority group in the United States, has many unique cultural mannerisms, which may include a preference to deal with male officers, a tendency to avoid eye contact with authority figures, or a habit of standing closer during conversations than Anglo-Americans.[6] In gaining cross-cultural insight through departmental training, college classes, or self-education, investigators will expand their general knowledge and effectiveness.

The investigator must be persistent to a degree beyond that of the average citizen. **Persistence** can be defined as continuing in the face of opposition or refusing to give up when faced with an adverse situation. The overall task of the investigator is no easy one—particularly when confronted with a difficult case. To persist until all available facts of an investigation are known and until satisfied that further effort will be unproductive is the working definition of persistence for the investigator.

In an effort to assist law enforcement agencies in selecting superior investigators and evaluating their performance, the Department of Justice researched numerous departments throughout the United States. Their findings indicate that above-average past job performance leading to frequent suspect conviction, college study, and strong verbal ability are good indicators for investigative success. The selection process for investigative positions should also be focused on job relatedness, applicant fairness, and valid requirements that can be legally defended.[7]

Investigative Ethics

Much more than a desirable personality trait, ethical conduct is absolutely essential for investigative professionalism. **Investigative Ethics** can be defined as the practical normative study of the rightness or wrongness of human conduct. Although all areas of criminal justice involve decisions that relate to ethical conduct, the police investigator often faces frequent and immediate ethical pressures. The professionalization of criminal investigation has rapidly intensified in the past ten years, particularly in the areas of technology and field techniques, yet there has been comparatively little research and discussion concerning investigative ethics. As sociologists have demonstrated, a culture's values and conduct are often the final areas of change in a transforming society, preceded by changes in technology and economics.[8] All law enforcement personnel assigned to line functions (duties that bring officers into continuous contact with the public) make frequent judgments or discretionary decisions. Whereas officers performing patrol duties generally decide ethical questions pertaining to prearrest and arrest, investigators focus on the ethical situations resulting from an arrest.

The development of American criminal investigation has included far too many examples of unethical and illegal field practices. Despite a renewed nationwide interest in police misconduct sparked by the videotaped beating of Rodney King in 1991, examples of unethical police behavior have been sporadic rather than a continuous problem.[9] Yet although the vast majority of criminal investigators do not engage in unprofessional or illegal tactics, some are indeed corrupt. As the public fascination with police procedure has been a constant since the early 1800s, modern media presentations of unethical conduct are frequent, illustrating police corruption or misconduct to a national audience. Unfortunately, the problem of unethical investigative conduct is real, one that must be addressed by present and future investigators.

The causes of unethical behavior are many, including pressure to make additional arrests, greed, peer influence, or an "end justifies the means" attitude. Specific examples of unethical investigative behaviors resulting from these causes include entrapment, misconduct during suspect interviews, courtroom deception, and evidence fabrication. The criminal investigator is under considerable pressure to produce results, and in most police agencies, results are still heavily measured by arrest rates. An unethical investigator may increase arrest rates by using the illegal tactic of entrapment, behavior that encourages an innocent person to commit a crime he or she would not otherwise commit. Interviewing procedures may be altered, evidence may be "planted," or outright courtroom deception may occur. All of these behaviors can be originally motivated by greed or improper peer influence, but many unethical acts are actually committed because an investigator believes a criminal suspect will otherwise escape justice. Regardless of the specific motive, the number of federal, state, and local law enforcement personnel being imprisoned for illegal conduct committed during the course of their duties has recently increased. Although the number of police officials behind bars represents only a small fraction of all sworn police, recent increases demonstrate the need for continued ethical discussion and education among present and potential law enforcement personnel.

Professional investigative behavior resists the common temptations inherent in many criminal cases. For example, an investigator may strongly believe a suspect guilty and, in the absence of judicial proof, may attempt to fabricate evidence to gain a conviction. Another may justify any action that assists the arrest of a particularly reprehensible subject, such as a child molester or a narcotics dealer. In addition, constant exposure to victims of crime and a corresponding lack of arrests can cause a great deal of cumulative stress. Finally, the attitude of corrupted peers may encourage an investigator to alter the facts to achieve an illegal conviction or to commit other negative acts, such as outright theft. Theft of property or money is often connected to narcotics or gambling investigations. These cases provide the easiest access to ready cash, and corrupt individuals who steal from subjects of their investigations may rationalize their behavior by convincing themselves that such crimes are victimless.

The development of an ethical work attitude is fundamental to all efforts undertaken by an investigator. Such an attitude may have naturally been instilled through previous moral training by the family or other social institutions, or it may be developed. The investigator confronted with a temptation of unethical conduct should speculate as to the true consequences of an illegal or immoral action. Although the consequences may be gratifying in the short run, they are almost always highly destructive in a personal or professional sense. To visualize just how damaging unethical investigative behavior can be, an officer needs only to imagine an American system of justice wherein all criminal justice personnel act unethically.

The American Society for Public Administration has developed a series of questions to assist public officials in evaluating their ethical beliefs. The questions can help to create a sound foundation for professional conduct and can assist investigators in developing insight and resistance against field stress:

1. Do I confront difficult ethical decisions directly and attempt to think through the alternatives and principles involved?
2. Am I inclined to make decisions on the grounds of convenience, expediency, pressure, or impulse?
3. If someone asked me to explain my professional ethics, what would I say?
4. Have my values and ethics changed since I began working? If so, why and how? What are the primary influences that have changed my thinking?
5. Where do my professional loyalties ultimately lie? With the Constitution, the law, my organization, superiors, or the general public? Do I feel torn by these loyalties? How do I deal with the conflicts?[10]

Proper ethical attitude, which implies performance of one's investigative duties in a legal and moral fashion, must be continually maintained. Just as patrol officers condition themselves for various felony calls by mentally rehearsing how they will handle such assignments, investigators must prepare themselves for the pressures that are unique to their assignments.

Despite the many stresses associated with the enforcement and investigative functions, the professional investigator will adopt a just and uncompromising attitude. The truly ethical investigator maintains a constant level of professionalism and allows no deviation from that standard. Rather than succumbing to unethical logic and engaging in unprofessional means to justify a seemingly desirable end, the investigator should realize that no conviction is worth sacrificing one's personal and professional integrity.

Current State of the Art

Criminal investigators may be classified according to three basic types: the **police investigator**, the **public investigator**, and the **private investigator**.

The Police Investigator.   A law enforcement officer working toward the resolution of a criminal matter through investigative action, this type of investigator outnumbers the other two types. All police departments and sheriff's offices have some types of investigative capacity. However, not every police agency has plainclothes investigators assigned to a detective division. Of the more than 15,000 local and county law enforcement agencies in the United States employing nearly 800,000 sworn officers, a large number are not of significant size to justify a full-time detective. A reliable method of determining the ratio of investigators to the size of the department or population of the community has not been resolved. Some police departments determine the size of their detective divisions to be approximately 10 percent of the total sworn personnel.[11] In general, however, when the patrol division is unable to operate with maximum effectiveness due to increased investigative duties, a need for separate investigative responsibility is present.

In medium-sized and large law enforcement agencies, sizable detective divisions, or bureaus of investigation, are found. The division may be commanded by a captain, lieutenant, or sergeant, depending on the size of the unit. Smaller police departments may utilize patrol officers on an "as needed" basis or have command officers, such as the chief, perform investigative functions.

Within the detective division, cases may be assigned to specialized investigators according to the nature of the case, or a caseload basis of assignment may prevail. **Assignment by specialization** (e.g., assigning a rape investigation to an investigator working all sex-related offenses) is normally desirable. This method utilizes an investigator's specialized training and experience in a particular crime and enhances success by grouping crimes with common elements together. Criminal suspects tend to specialize in their operations, often committing the same type of crime repeatedly. An officer who has specialized in investigating a certain crime becomes adept at recognizing individual criminal mannerisms or unique methods of operation. An example of a highly specialized detective bureau is that of New York City (Figure 2.1), where certain investigators work full time on cases concerning thefts of fine art objects.

An undesirable outcome of specialization may occur when certain officers are assigned an unmanageable number of cases. If one investigator is responsible for all narcotics cases and another investigator is responsible for

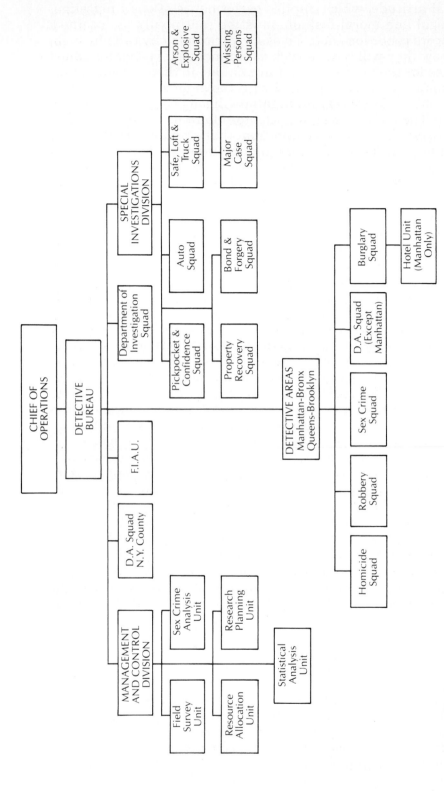

FIGURE 2.1 Organizational guide—New York Detective Bureau. *(Source: New York City Police Department.)*

all armed-robbery investigations, the narcotics detective may have five times the workload of the robbery investigator. For this reason, an accurate study must be undertaken to determine the number of investigators to be assigned to a particular crime category. The number will depend on the frequency of the given crime.

Assignment by caseload involves no consideration of the nature of a crime. This method assumes all officers to be generalists, equally competent to investigate any type of crime. Assignments are made on a rotation basis (i.e., each succeeding case is given to the next investigator until the cases are equally distributed). Generally, to assign cases without regard to their difficulty and complexity or to discount the training and experience of the investigator is a poor administrative practice. An example of a typical generalized detective bureau is the ten-officer operation of the Hattiesburg, Mississippi, police department (Figure 2.2).

In communities where serious crime is frequent, investigative divisions normally use **assignment by priority** to each investigation. Ideally each case should receive an equal amount of investigative effort and be acted on as soon as it is reported. However, the large volume of cases assigned to the detective division, the limited number of investigators, and the relative seriousness of each offense make a priority ranking necessary. Crimes or attempted crimes against persons, such as homicide, rape, deviant sexual conduct, robbery, and assaults with injury, are given the highest priority. When the criminal act is directed against property, such as burglary, larceny, and auto theft, a second priority is assigned. All other investigations, such as fraud and embezzlement, are given the least urgent ranking. Of course, rankings in the third priority, when the amount of loss is large (say, an embezzlement of thousands of dollars), can be more serious than minor thefts in the second priority (see Figure 2.3).

Assignment by priority does not mean that some cases are never investigated. It is a method that recognizes that some crimes endanger the safety of the community to a greater degree than other types of offenses. Because humans are obviously more significant than items of property, solutions of those criminal offenses against people demand a greater urgency. In small or medium-sized police departments, where investigators tend to be generalists, priority assignments are necessary. In large law enforcement agencies, the detective divisions are sufficient to preclude priority assignments.

In addition to municipal and county police investigators, considerable numbers of detectives work at the state and federal levels. They have

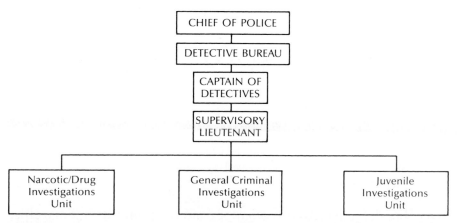

FIGURE 2.2 Organizational guide—Hattiesburg Detective Bureau. *(Source: Hattiesburg, Mississippi, Police Department.)*

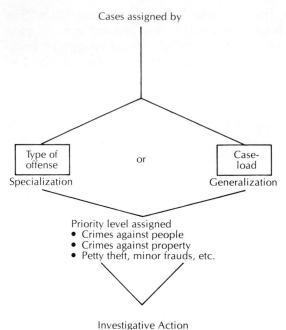

Cases assigned by

Type of offense | or | Case-load

Specialization   Generalization

Priority level assigned
• Crimes against people
• Crimes against property
• Petty theft, minor frauds, etc.

Investigative Action

FIGURE 2.3   Case assignment criteria.

statewide jurisdiction and perform a variety of duties. Investigative responsibilities normally include assisting local police departments on request, narcotics and dangerous drug cases, organized crime investigations, and intercounty criminal violations. Such agencies as the Florida Department of Law Enforcement and the Kansas Bureau of Investigation typify the organization and function of many state agencies (see Figure 2.4).

In addition to the specialized state investigative units, state police agencies, which typically provide enforcement on public highways, also have plainclothes investigators. The size of the investigative unit will vary according to the enforcement emphasis of the individual agency. State agencies that are basically traffic oriented, such as the California Highway Patrol, have a relatively small investigative staff.

Of the more than 88,000 federal law enforcement personnel, 40,000 are plain clothed criminal investigators found mainly in the Treasury Department, Department of Justice, and Department of Defense. Treasury investigators work in specific agencies, such as the U.S. Secret Service or Internal Revenue Service, and perform a wide variety of tasks. The Department of Justice houses the Federal Bureau of Investigation and Drug Enforcement Administration, among other agencies. The Department of Defense includes the criminal investigative departments of the Army, Navy, Air Force, and Marine Corps.

The Public Investigator.   Public investigators perform duties that are frequently similar methodologically to those of police investigators. They are employed by many public agencies, such as the local and county public defender's office, coroner's office, and the U.S. Office of Personnel Management. Public investigators are normally empowered by state or federal statute to perform a specific information-gathering task. Occasionally, a public investigation may overlap into the criminal area, bringing a public investigator into close contact with a police detective. An investigator from the public defender's office interviewing a police detective regarding the statements of a defendant is an example.

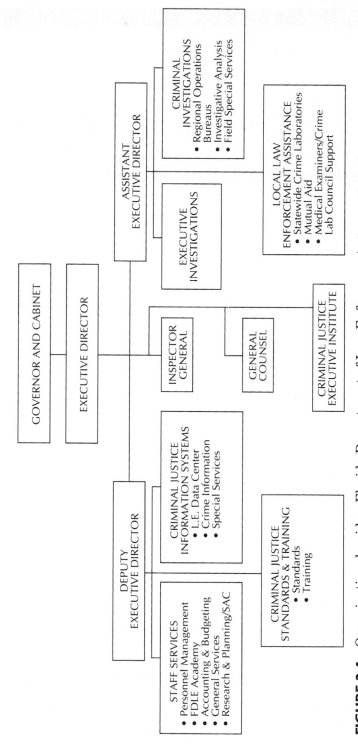

FIGURE 2.4 Organizational guide—Florida Department of Law Enforcement. (*Source: Florida Department of Law Enforcement.*)

INVESTIGATIVE PROFILE

Shari L. Goodyear
County Detective
District Attorney's Office
Indiana, Pennsylvania

I'm a criminal investigator within a Western Pennsylvania district attorney's office. While I've held this position since 2002, my original interest in public service work dates back to 1983. I've always been attracted to jobs where I could help people and contribute to my community. This may be due to my family history, as I have relatives who are working in the medical field or in law enforcement on some level. My uncle was a county commissioner and eventually became a district judge. I was really quite inspired by him, and he taught me in my early years how important it was to be honest and observant and really listen to people. So I first began public service as an emergency medical technician (EMT) and volunteer firefighter. I had to take considerable training for both positions, and these jobs put me in constant touch with law enforcement personnel. We would work together at accident and fire scenes, and I admired their duties and professionalism. Then I worked in the private security field as a loss prevention specialist at a large retail chain store. This was the position that actually launched me into police work. This job had similarities to public law enforcement, as it dealt with employee theft and shoplifting problems. This motivated me to attend our regional police academy, and I graduated in 1998 with my certification. I was then hired as a part-time police officer in Cambria County and began working with the county's drug task force.

My most memorable drug case was an OCDETF (organized crime and drug enforcement task force) investigation that focused on drug trafficking over a five-county area. I became part of a drug task force operation that was composed of many law enforcement agencies, including the Pennsylvania state attorney general's bureau of narcotics. This assignment involved a considerable amount of undercover work stretching over two years. It resulted in the arrest of 23 targeted drug dealers who had sold cocaine, heroin, and pills throughout the region. As a result of my drug work, I came into close contact with the county district attorney's office and was offered a job with them. The Indiana County district attorney office has three investigators, five assistant district attorneys, and the district attorney, who is an elected official. My work as an investigator is really diverse, which is something that I truly enjoy about the position. On any given day I might be involved in preparing and serving subpoenas, interviewing and identifying witnesses for court, processing juvenile criminal complaints, or working various narcotics cases. We regularly coordinate with police agencies throughout the county, as our office is responsible for determining if a subject they've arrested should be prosecuted. The DA's office determines if there really was sufficient probable cause for an arrest and, if so, prepares the case for trial. So my duties are actually far more diverse and unpredictable than many standard detective assignments.

Lately we have been preparing a large number of juvenile cases, and I'd estimate at least 60 percent of my work is in this area. All the juvenile petitions filled with the probation office come into our office, and I prepare the case files for court. Juvenile criminal cases are very important and take a lot of work, as these offenders have unique rights and the greatest possibility of being rehabilitated. I'm also busy doing two other rather unique duties: a check restitution program and a tobacco compliance operation. I'm the coordinator of a new program that seeks to recover restitution for bad checks that have been passed in businesses throughout the county. We identify and locate the suspects and offer them a chance to provide restitution, which avoids a far stiffer sentence than normal. I also direct the tobacco compliance check program. The funding is structured in the form of a grant from the Pennsylvania Department of Health and is provided to the Armstrong-Indiana Drug and Alcohol Commission. The commission mandates we follow the Centers for Disease Control model program for tobacco prevention and control initiatives. The funds finance compliance checks and deterrence programs aimed at preventing juvenile smoking. I'm also the assistant TAC officer for a countywide information collection agency. I assist the chief county detective in ensuring that all agencies accessing and operating the system are following proper operating rules. Although my county detective position would be enough for most people, I also work as a part-time uniformed patrol officer with the West Hills Regional Police Department in Johnson, Pennsylvania. I find patrol work keeps me sharp, and I'm continually developing informant sources that help my investigative work. I guess it's obvious that I just live and breathe law enforcement.

What I enjoy most about my detective position is trying to stay one step ahead of the perpetrators. It is a constant mental challenge and learning process. Also, there is no routine to this line of work—nothing is ever mundane. The downside is the long hours, as you are always on call as well. And of course all this can be difficult on the family, but still I wouldn't trade it for anything else. It is an honor to be a female detective since law enforcement in the past had been predominantly male. But there are still some remaining challenges. I find some of our elderly citizens still tend to think police work is a male-dominated career. I do not expect any different treatment from my fellow officers based on my gender. All incoming assignments and investigations are delegated to each officer regardless of gender. While on duty, I do not tolerate any derogatory comments from any potential perpetrator. There are some investigative situations where a woman is an asset beyond what a man can accomplish. I've worked a number of rape cases in which victims would give statements only to a female officer. I think sometimes women have a superior listening ability and can show empathy at a scene more naturally than some male investigators. I'm a trained negotiator and had a case in which a woman was threatening suicide by slashing at her wrists as we arrived on scene. When a male officer approached and spoke to her, she quickly raised the knife to her throat. When I addressed her, she would lower the knife. It turned out she was angry with a male friend and would calm down around another woman.

If a student wants to secure a job like mine, she or he needs to approach police departments and get involved in ride-along programs. See if police work is really what you think it is rather than just what you see on television. Same thing goes for sitting in on real court trials at your local courthouse. A good police officer must be able to take the investigate work he or she has performed and be able to testify well in court. Also, I really recommend doing work as an EMT or volunteer work in your area like I did with the fire department. My job still involves a significant amount of undercover work. I know a lot of criminal justice students are interested in this type of work, but undercover is not for everyone. You have to be prepared to do a lot of research on the suspects you have targeted for drug buys, and you do considerable surveillance. An undercover officer must also be a quick thinker and be able to improvise and adapt to any situation that confronts you. But most of all, you have to be quick on your toes and not afraid to ask questions of your superior officers; you just never know what will come up.

The Private Investigator. The fundamental difference between the private detective and other types is the investigative objective. Whereas police and public investigators are primarily concerned with the interests of society, the private detective serves organizational and individual interests.[12] Frequently portrayed in the media but most often inaccurately, private detectives are utilized in three major areas: to gather information in private noncriminal matters, to assist attorneys in gathering legal information of a criminal and noncriminal nature, and to aid private industries. Many private investigators are former police detectives or federal agents. In a similar fashion to the public investigation, the private investigation may overlap into a criminal area. However, the private investigator has no authority by statute to investigate a legally prescribed crime and should in all cases involving criminal violations inform the appropriate law enforcement agency.

While the number of private investigators does not equal police detectives, these numbers are substantial, with 8,700 licensed private investigators in California alone. However, the number of private detectives may be significantly diminishing. Many private investigators have noted a serious decline in the request for their services due to unrestricted public access to the Internet. As many potential clients conduct their own investigations on the Internet (gathering data or locating lost friends or relatives), the need to hire an information expert has declined.

The requirements necessary to be a private detective vary greatly from state to state. To receive a license in California, one is required to complete 6,000 hours of supervised training over a three-year period, while other states do not require private investigators to be licensed.[13]

▲ SUMMARY

As crime continues to be a major problem to society, the criminal justice system struggles to maintain its effectiveness. Investigation, although but a partial solution to the elimination of crime, is a highly important function. The other major elements of our system of justice, courts and corrections are largely dependent upon successful investigations. Through proper apprehensions, the investigator provides the rest of the system with clientele and, frequently, effects the return of stolen property.

The investigation of crime is a legal inquiry based on logic and objectivity. If investigation is properly accomplished, a specific crime will be defined, and answers to the traditional questions of who, what, where, when, how, and possibly why will become evident. Although no two investigators have exactly the same personality traits, some attributes are highly desirable in all. These include superior reasoning, imagination and curiosity, intuition, observational skill, organizational ability, sufficient legal knowledge, wide range of interests, understanding of cultural diversity, and the ability to persevere until successful.

Improper or illegal conduct is a potential problem for all members of the criminal justice system. Unethical behaviors have far-reaching and often disastrous consequences for individuals and entire law enforcement agencies. Common areas of unethical behavior within the investigative process include entrapment, interviewing violations, courtroom deception, and misconduct during vice investigations, particularly in the area of narcotics. Although there are numerous causative factors for unethical misconduct, a misguided "the end justifies any means" attitude is often the underlying motivation.

There are three basic types of investigators: the law enforcement investigator, the public investigator, and the private investigator. The police investigator may be a uniformed or plainclothes officer, involved in the inquiry phases of a criminal event. Police investigators generally work their cases through assignment by supervisory personnel, with investigations allotted by a system of specialization or caseload. Assignment by specialization uses an investigator's expertise in a particular area of criminality. Accordingly, cases are assigned to specialized officers according to the nature of the offenses. The caseload method assumes all investigators to be equally competent in dealing with any type of case, with no effort to match a particular type of investigation to the skills of an individual.

Law enforcement investigators are found within all levels of government, local, state, and federal, the majority of criminal investigations being performed on the local level. Another type of government-affiliated investigator, the public investigator, deals with noncriminal matters frequently involving background inquiries or general information gathering. Private investigators are profit-oriented individuals not associated with govern-ment agencies. Their clients often include private citizens, lawyers, insur-ance companies, and other private interests.

EXERCISES

1. Study the national crime rate and contrast it with the reported and cleared crime rate in your community.
2. Interview a local police investigator to determine his or her opinion as to the most important personality traits of an investigator.
3. Study a local department's investigation division to ascertain the method of case assignment and organization.
4. Interview a public investigator assigned to a local prosecutor's or public defender's office. Compare and contrast the job responsibilities and duties with those of the police investigator.
5. Research a recent well-publicized example of unethical police behavior. Determine the specific methods of misconduct and speculate as to the possible causes of the incident. How could the misconduct have been prevented?

RELEVANT WEB SITES

http://www.criticalthinking.org/aboutCT/definingCT.shtm

Site devoted to the reasoning process of critical thinking. Defines the concept and provides links to resources and associated areas of professional development.

The Investigative Method

KEY TERMS

affidavit
burden of proof
circumstantial evidence
concluding investigation
corpus delicti rule
direct evidence
evidence
exclusionary rule
exculpatory evidence
hypothesis
inculpatory evidence
in-depth investigation

means
motive
opportunity factor
physical evidence
probable cause
preliminary investigation
res gestae declarations
rule of discovery
search warrant
solvability factors
tests of suitability

LEARNING OBJECTIVES

1. to understand how the scientific method applies to criminal investigation;
2. to be able to explain the necessity of legal guidelines and restrictions of the investigative function;
3. to comprehend the significance and application of evidence to the criminal proceeding;
4. to be able to list and define the three major phases of a criminal investigation;
5. to be familiar with the ways in which a criminal case can be brought to the attention of a law enforcement agency; and
6. to appreciate the relationship of time to the probability of successful case solution.

STARTING POINTS OF THE CRIMINAL INVESTIGATION

The criminal investigation process covers an extensive scope of duties, methods, and objectives. If unprepared, the novice investigator may well be bewildered by what seems to be a mass of unrelated information. "Where do I begin?" This statement is all too often voiced by a frustrated officer lacking a method of organization. The scientific community has developed an orderly method of arriving at a conclusion based upon logic and progressive reasoning. This procedure, known as the *scientific method*, is applicable to the investigation of crime. The scientific method provides the investigator with a framework in which to structure an inquiry. Basically, this method of inquiry is divided into five separate stages as follows (Figure 3.1):

---

1. State the problem.
2. Form the hypothesis.
3. Observe and experiment.
4. Interpret the data.
5. Draw conclusions.

State the Problem

- Identify suspect
- Locate suspect
- Effect arrest
- Recover property

Form the Hypothesis

- Motive
- Knowledge
- Means

Observe and Experiment

- Evaluate results of hypothesis
- Reject hypothesis, if necessary
- Experiment with another hypothesis

Interpret the Data

- Interpret results of final observations and experimentation

Draw Conclusions

- Has the stated problem been answered?
- Does evidence support hypothesis?
- Has each stage of investigative method been conducted in a totally legal fashion?
- Does data interpretation support a recommendation for prosecution?

FIGURE 3.1   The investigative method.

To *state the problem* of a criminal investigation would appear to be an obvious and automatic task. A detective is assigned a case involving an armed robbery of a grocery store in which money is taken from a concealed safe. The problem would be to identify, locate, and arrest the perpetrator of the crime and attempt to recover all stolen property. Yet upon careful consideration, it will become clear that the identification, location, arrest, and recovery steps do not completely cover the actual problem.

To properly view the officer's function in the criminal justice system, he or she must realize that an officer's actions have a major bearing on the success or failure of justice. If we define justice as rendering to each his or her due, then a convicted criminal violator must receive justice from the judicial and correctional systems. This cannot be achieved unless the investigation is legally conducted. Consequently, a complete statement of the problem is to *identify, locate, arrest, obtain evidence, and recover stolen property in a thorough legal manner designed to ensure the greatest probability of justice.*

To form a **hypothesis** is to construct an explanation for an occurrence. Why was a grocery store the subject for an armed robbery? Why did the suspect select this particular grocery store? How did the suspect know the location of the safe? Traditionally, an inquiry into motive, knowledge, opportunity, and means of a particular crime will produce one or more explanations.

Motive is defined as that which causes a person to act in a certain manner. The motive for a particular criminal activity often will be self-explanatory. Monetary gain is the most common of all the various causative factors. If a person's home is broken into and a stereo system stolen, the motive is not complex. The suspect has gained monetarily by selling the stereo or has benefited materially by keeping the property. In some investigations, however, motive is of prime importance to explain the criminal occurrence. In cases involving arson, bombings, and murder, when the offender is not known, the success of the inquiry may depend upon motive. During the course of a murder investigation, the officer must consider the benefit factor of the case. In arriving at a possible hypothesis, it must be taken into account who would benefit by the death of the victim. Similar reasoning should be applied to the typical arson case or any investigation in which the benefit factor is other than obviously material.

In some criminal offenses, special knowledge is needed to commit the crime. Nearly anyone can walk into an unlocked home and steal property, but to gain entry into a massive locked safe or to counterfeit $20 bills requires knowledge not readily accessible to the majority of people. Precisely because of the small pool of subjects, the knowledge factor must be considered.

The **opportunity factor** determines if a given suspect could have been physically present during the commission of the criminal activity. Although this factor is essential to verify, it can be overlooked because of its lack of complexity. The investigator must be able to prove or question alibis that inevitably arise in many criminal cases. A suspect's whereabouts and known movements must be carefully checked to either rule out a suspect or conclude that he remains under suspicion because of lack of proof regarding his presence at another locality during the crime.

The least useful of the factors used to formulate a hypothesis involves the **means** and opportunity necessary to perpetrate the crime. This is because the majority of crimes can be committed with means available to nearly everyone. Shoplifting merchandise requires no more than a hand; to randomly hold up a gas station requires only a firearm. On the other hand, to detonate an explosive composed of nitroglycerin not only requires knowledge but also a means of obtaining the necessary chemicals.

When the investigator can propose an explanation for the occurrence of a crime, the search for suspects becomes an inquiry based on logical possibilities that serve as guidelines. The officer must use caution, however, in attempting to support a hypothesis, for the hypothesis may be wrong.

The third phase of the scientific method requires *observation* and *experimentation* as applied to the proposed explanation. This process serves as a check for a hypothesis that is incorrect. The investigator evaluates information obtained from applying the theory to various sources. The conclusion reached is that a former employee was involved in the grocery store robbery. A listing of all former and present employees of the store is obtained. Interviews are conducted, former employees are located, and possibly the polygraph is used. By these methods, the investigator is testing the theory for the probability of its being correct.

After the hypothesis of a former employee being involved is subjected to observation and experimentation, *interpretation of data* is conducted. The investigator must be as objective as possible in this interpretation. Does the information obtained thus far support the former-employee theory? Does it tend to diminish the theory? The data may be reviewed by another investigator to provide a second opinion. The officer may conclude, at this point, that the hypothesis is not valid and that additional experimentation based on alternate theories is indicated.

The final step of the scientific or investigative method is to *draw a conclusion*. A conclusion is a judgment, or a summing up of the hypothesis relating to the original problem. If the investigator's interpretation of the information supports the former-employee theory, this theory may be accepted as valid and pursued to an identification and arrest.

It should be stressed that the scientific method can be readily applied to criminal investigations, but the investigation of crime is not, and can never be, scientific in an absolute sense. In the natural sciences, when a given set of factors that have been proven to produce a specific result is applied, an identical result will be obtained. Two chemical compounds will always produce a certain type of acid, two plus three will always equal five, and the sun will always rise in the east. Yet if a grocery store is held up and money taken from a hidden safe, it cannot be assumed automatically that a former employee was involved. Crime involves an element for which scientific precision is lacking—the human element. Human beings can never be counted upon to react in a specific manner all of the time. Within the same police department, two officers may reach opposite conclusions based on the same circumstances. If the scientific method is applied in evaluating various hypotheses involving a crime, however, the investigator will be better able to arrive at a conclusion that is based on logic.

Legal Guidelines and Restrictions

If the criminal justice system is to be truly just, all of its various components must adhere to formal rules of conduct, known as law. Law enforcement officers are in a real sense the "arm of the law"; it is by their actions that the law becomes an actual positive force.

The criminal investigator is obligated to have as much knowledge of legal matters as of police techniques. If the overall reputation of a police agency is that of being just, efficient, and professional, it is probable that investigating officers in that agency are carefully observing legal guidelines and restrictions.

All criminal investigators are guided by various legal decisions that have greatly affected the manner in which an investigation is conducted. Hundreds of past and present court decisions have been influential in governing the conduct of each investigator. Although the historical development of our law and rules of evidence can be traced back through the centuries, legal decisions rendered during the past 60 years have been of utmost significance.

It is not uncommon to hear some individuals protest what they feel are "obstacles to effective police work" or court decisions that have "handcuffed the police." However, the police have actually benefited from the legal restrictions that affect their work. Many methods used during a typical criminal investigation, such as techniques of interviewing, the employment of informers, and the procurement of information by other means, are now pursued in a more competent manner as a direct result of legal guidelines. Increased professionalism and greater public support of the police can be largely attributed to the current legal guidelines adhered to by modern investigators. One has only to examine the crude methods used by detectives before the turn of the century to realize the necessity of judicial review.

Although all law enforcement officers must be aware of what actions constitute various criminal acts, the law of evidence and procedure is of prime importance to the investigator. Criminal investigators are normally assigned cases developed by the patrol division. They review basic reports written by patrol officers and learn what actions have been taken. In addition, they discover what evidence has been obtained and the manner in which it was obtained. The investigator must have the capability to analyze acquired evidence to determine whether it will be legally admissible in a criminal trial. This is necessary for three basic reasons: (a) to evaluate the importance of evidence obtained by others, (b) to obtain evidence properly during the continuing investigation, and (c) to assist the prosecuting attorney.

Evidence is anything properly admissible in a court that will aid the function of a criminal proceeding in establishing guilt or innocence. The many different types of evidence are of varying importance. Within the overall development of criminal law, the admissibility of evidence has been determined by an evolving process. Much like certain types of human behavior deemed to be criminal, actions that produce legally admissible evidence are quite changeable over time. Prior to the application of the exclusionary rule to local investigations, evidence obtained without a search warrant or even a confession beaten out of a suspect could be admitted in a trial. Now seized evidence generally requires a warrant unless obtained incident to an arrest, and information obtained from interrogation of a suspect must be demonstrated to be voluntary. As the rules of evidence continue to evolve, judges will decide the proper admissibility of evidence obtained by investigators. Such determinations are often based on the most recent state or federal Supreme Court decisions.

Evidence serves two very important and different functions. **Inculpatory evidence** is incriminating, for it tends to establish guilt. **Exculpatory evidence** exonerates, or clears a person of blame or legal guilt. Because the majority of criminal investigations focus on locating inculpatory evidence, it is easy to lose sight of the dual function of all investigations. The ultimate objective is the discovery of truth; all other outcomes are secondary to this function. Many investigations produce both types of evidence, or the same item of evidence may be used to achieve both objectives. For example, a latent fingerprint may clear several suspects who were believed to be guilty while establishing the clear guilt of another. It is important to note that state and federal courts require the prosecutor's office to give all exculpatory evidence in its possession to defense counsel. Thus, in the interests of fairness and justice, all evidence that suggests, indicates, or tends to prove innocence falls within this category.[1]

Types of Evidence

In general, evidence that is inanimate, or nonhuman, is valued more highly than evidence involving human beings. This is due to the fallibility of the human condition (e.g., loss of memory, prejudice, or purposeful altering of truth).

Direct evidence is relatively important in a criminal trial and will normally prove a fact without support. Such evidence has been obtained from the physiological senses of the individual, giving direct personal knowledge of what is being testified to. *Indirect evidence*, also known as **circumstantial evidence**, does not directly prove a fact at issue but may establish a strong inference as to the truth of that fact. Circumstantial evidence is generally added to other types of evidence and may or may not be used during the trial, depending on the inference drawn. A third category is **physical evidence** or *real evidence*. Real evidence can be any kind of object associated with the investigation, but it must be a physical, tangible item, unlike other forms of evidence that may result from sensory observations or inferences. A fourth variety of evidence often encountered in criminal investigations is *documentary evidence*. Although this form of evidence is similar to real evidence in that the item must be of a physical nature, documentary evidence need not be the actual item but an acceptable representation of it. Documentary evidence represents, portrays, or otherwise documents that a particular item of evidence exists or legally demonstrates the item's appearance at a particular time. Commonly encountered types of documentary evidence include forensic laboratory reports, photographic or video pictures, judicial transcripts, and various investigative reports.[2]

An investigator must be able to determine the category of the evidence pertaining to the case at hand. When a witness describes how he saw a suspect reach into a jewelry showcase, grasp a ring, and place the ring in his pocket, the witness's testimony is direct evidence. If various witnesses testify that the suspect spoke to them of having stolen a ring from a jewelry showcase, their testimony is considered to be indirect evidence. When a search of the suspect's residence locates a diamond ring similar in description to the stolen ring, that is physical evidence. An accurate computer image and description of the stolen ring provided by the jewelry store would constitute documentary evidence. By realizing the relative importance of the four types of evidence, the officer can judge the strength of the case. The probability of successful prosecution can then be determined and further investigative actions planned.

Evidence in any form may be admissible during a trial; if an objection is offered, the judge may determine that it fails to meet the rules of evidence. The rule of evidence admissibility provides three standards, or **tests of suitability**, to determine if an item of evidence will be allowed to have a bearing on the case. *Evidence must be competent, relevant, and material to be held admissible.*

Competent evidence is responsible evidence, sufficient to prove a fact has a bearing on the case. Competent evidence can pertain to physical items, documents, and people. When an evidence item is shown to possess qualities that render it trustworthy or reliable—such as the proper fashion in which it was obtained, the way it was maintained or preserved, or its present correct form or condition—the evidence is competent. Naturally, if an investigator obtains evidence in an untrustworthy fashion or fails to preserve it in a proper manner, the court will likely declare the item untrustworthy and thus incompetent to be received as evidence during a trial. *Relevant evidence* is pertinent and relates directly to the matter under consideration. As long as a given item of evidence tends to prove or disprove any circumstance related to the criminal investigation, it is relevant to that proposition. In most criminal cases, the question of relevance pertains to three elements: time, the event, and people. For evidence to be relevant, it must pertain to the specific day and period of time at issue, the criminal act itself, or those who are involved in the offense. In a similar but less specific fashion, that which is judged to be *material evidence* has a logical connection with the issue under investigation and has a bearing on the determination of truth. From a practical standpoint, materiality is not frequently raised as an evidence objection, for the concept is legally quite similar to questions of relevancy.

Certain general types of evidence have been held to be inadmissible during a criminal trial. For example, if evidence is obtained by an investigator in an unlawful manner, it cannot be admitted. This principle, known as the **exclusionary rule**, applies to violation of constitutional rights. Evidence obtained from unlawful interrogations, illegal searches, or by entrapment or denying a suspect right to counsel also cannot be admitted. Although some recent Supreme Court decisions provide some exceptions to the exclusionary rule, the overall application of the principle continues. As with many legal doctrines, there can be exceptions to the exclusionary rule. Although not commonly encountered, the inevitable discovery exception to the exclusionary rule can occur. This exception allows evidence to be admitted during a trial even though it was seized in violation of the Constitution. Under the exception, courts generally will not suppress illegally seized evidence if the prosecution can establish that the evidence inevitably would have been discovered lawfully. For example, although an auto may be searched illegally and incriminating evidence prohibited from trial, a body in the trunk would inevitably be discovered when the car was inventoried after the seizure. While the dead body could be allowed as evidence even though the search was ruled to be illegal, other evidence that would not inevitably be discovered due to size or location would still be inadmissable.

Evidence that is judged to be hearsay will not be admitted, in general. The rule dealing with this type of evidence governs testimony of a secondary nature, given by a witness who is relating the statements of another person. There are exceptions to the hearsay rule of which the investigator should be aware. If a suspect makes an admission that establishes an element of a criminal act, the investigator to whom the admission was made will be allowed to testify. If the suspect offers a confession by which all the elements of a crime are established, the investigator who obtained the confession may testify in regard to it. There are many additional exceptions to the rule, which include references to official records, the defendant having adequate opportunity to cross-examine the accuser at trial, the defendant waiving the right of trial confrontation, the defendant having adequate opportunity to cross-examine the accuser at prior judicial proceedings, or *res gestae* **declarations**.

Res gestae declarations are words or statements made during the commission of an offense. The words may be spoken by anyone (e.g., witness, victim, or suspect) and are admissible even if heard by an individual who did not witness the crime. Statements of this type are admissible in criminal courts because judges feel that what is said during a crime is normally spontaneous rather than preconceived. Furthermore, because of the heightened excitement, such statements tend to be truthful.

During the course of a typical criminal trial, the defense attorney may exercise the **rule of discovery**. This procedure allows the defendant, through the actions of an attorney, to examine documents, reports, and other types of information in the possession of the police and prosecution. A criminal investigator must continually keep in mind the possibility that the rule of discovery will be exercised. Information of a confidential nature or information that would embarrass the investigator should always be kept out of documents subject to defense review. This procedure aids both the defense and prosecution in a criminal case: Frequently, by reviewing incriminating information compiled by the state, a defendant may elect to forgo a trial and plead guilty.

Evidence in criminal cases frequently results from the exercise of probable cause by police officers. **Probable cause** is a legal justification for police action that is purposely lacking in a precise definition. When law enforcement officers are aware of facts and circumstances that would be suspicious to a person of reasonable and prudent caution, action may be taken to obtain evidence. If officers do *not* have justifiable probable cause and obtain evidence, this evidence will generally be inadmissible.

Criminal investigators also acquire considerable amounts of evidence through the execution of a **search warrant**. A search warrant is a written court order directing the police to search premises for stolen property or illegal substances of some kind. It requires police to confiscate and produce the property before the court. Warrants can be issued only when probable cause is sufficient to convince a judge of the warrant's worth. This type of qualifying probable cause is often based on the investigator's personal observation of suspected criminal activity, reliable informant information, information obtained following a subject's arrest, and the timeliness of the information. Some states require that all search warrants be served during daylight hours unless the warrant specifically authorizes a nighttime search based on public interest. Investigators must justify this request within an **affid-avit**, an attachment to the warrant wherein the police detail their probable cause for the warrant to be issued.

Arrests based upon proper probable cause but without a warrant often yield incriminating evidence. Patrol officers and detectives often make warrantless arrests and search suspects shortly after the arrest. The ability to conduct and seize evidence in this fashion is known as *search incident to arrest* and produces far greater amounts of evidence than through search warrants. As a general principle, the Fourth Amendment of the Bill of Rights gives citizens a reasonable expectation of privacy from government intrusion. Accordingly, a warrant is generally required to conduct a search. However, the Supreme Court has recognized various exceptions to this principle that allow police searches and seizures of property without a warrant. These include consent searches, emergency searches, certain types of motor vehicle searches, inventory searches, and searches incident to arrest. A warrantless search may be conducted during a lawful custodial arrest. The scope of the search includes the immediate person of the arrestee, personal items in his possession, the area into which he or she could reach to retrieve a weapon at the time of the arrest, any means of escape or destructible evidence, as well as a search of immediately adjoining areas for people posing a threat. This authority to search and seize is based upon the dual concerns of officer safety and preservation of evidence for trial.

It is the prosecution that must bear the burden of proof in a criminal case. The **burden of proof** involves a continuous demonstration of guilt, or a proving of each element of a crime, against the accused. In order to successfully establish proof, a thorough understanding of the ***corpus delicti rule*** is necessary. The term *corpus delicti* is a Latin term meaning "body of the crime"—the fact necessary to prove that a crime was committed. All the essential elements of an offense constitute the *corpus delicti*; the criminal investigator must have a thorough knowledge of each of these elements or specified parts. For example, California defines the crime of first-degree burglary as having five necessary elements, or facts in issue, which together form the *corpus delicti* for the offense: entry of an occupied building at night with the intent to commit a theft or other crime. Like pieces of a puzzle that are necessary to visualize an entire image, each element must be proven independently (see Figure 3.2). Thus, evidence to prove one element is not relevant, or adequate, to prove another element, whereas all the evidence is material to the case. Not only must it be established that a crime was committed, but the investigation will seek to prove that the defendant committed the specific elements of the offense.

Investigators should take the initiative to provide themselves with adequate background on the subject of criminal evidence. It is strongly recommended that all investigators receive additional education beyond the basic instruction given during initial training at the police academy. College-level courses in evidence and procedure or in-service training seminars by prosecutors are well suited for this purpose.

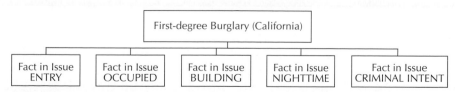

FIGURE 3.2 *Corpus delicti* for first-degree burglary.

PHASES OF THE CRIMINAL INVESTIGATION

The investigation of criminal offenses by the police can be divided into three general phases (Figure 3.3):

1. the preliminary investigation,
2. the in-depth investigation, and
3. the concluding investigation.

The Preliminary Investigation

The **preliminary investigation** involves the first exposure of the criminal offense to the investigative effort. It cannot be emphasized too strongly that this step is vital to the success of the investigation. The preliminary investigation serves as the foundation for the case; therefore, it must be a proper foundation or the entire investigation is in jeopardy.

A criminal offense may be brought to the attention of a law enforcement agency in various ways (Figure 3.4). The majority of crimes processed by investigators are *reported by either victims or witnesses*. A family returns home from a vacation to find a burglary, or a shop owner unlocks the store to discover the safe has been broken into. A large proportion of crimes are reported by witnesses who may have observed an offense or by individuals who have had their suspicions aroused by some unusual occurrence.

A second way in which the investigative process is begun is by *self-initiation* on the part of the investigator (i.e., criminal investigators seek out criminal offenses without citizen input). Officers working in a vice unit frequently initiate their cases. Information locating a probable criminal offense may come from informants, as is common in narcotics cases, or from the investigator's own experience. An investigator who is solicited for an act of prostitution by purposely walking a certain street is self-initiating a criminal

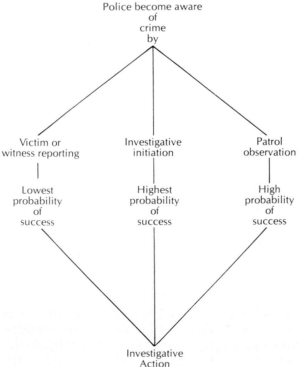

FIGURE 3.3 Crime awareness process.

Preliminary Investigation

- Offense determined
- Suspect arrested, if possible
- Crime scene protected
- Victims and witnesses identified
- Basic statements taken
- Crime scene processed

In-Depth Investigation

- Preliminary investigation data reexamined
- Crime scene revisited

- Crime scene processed further
- Existing and new victims and witnesses located and interviewed
- Documents processed
- Facts and evidence gathered
- Application of criminalistics arranged

Concluding Investigation

- Case suspended
- Case successfully concluded and prepared for prosecution

FIGURE 3.4   Investigation phases.

case. Investigators may "stake out" a business that has a high probability of being held up by an armed-robbery suspect as an additional method of self-initiation.

A third origin of investigations of criminal cases is *patrol observation.* For example, when patrol officers observe a dark business office that normally has a light above the safe, a burglary may be discovered. An officer who observes a subject exchanging small containers for money may pursue the matter, suspecting that narcotics may be sold.

Each of the three ways in which the police become involved in a preliminary investigation has a corresponding rate of success (see Figure 3.4). Criminal cases that are self-initiated by investigators generally have the greatest probability of being successfully prosecuted. This is because the investigator has the opportunity to establish the *corpus delicti* by personal observation or by being the actual victim. Because the investigator is trained to know the specific elements of an offense and because of the professionalism with which the investigator testifies in court, the majority of self-initiated cases result in convictions.

Cases observed by patrol officers also have a high proportion of successful convictions. However, if the officer discovers a crime scene but has not observed the actual commission of the offense, the likelihood that the investigation will be successful decreases substantially. Preliminary investigations initiated by citizen reporting generally have the lowest rate of success. This may be due to many factors involving both the police and the reporting citizen. As we will discuss in detail in Chapter 5, the protection of a crime scene from contamination is of great importance. The typical citizen-reported crime involves one or more people who are physically in the crime scene before, during, and after the offense or people who are physically in the scene while notifying the police. Thus, the probability of the scene being altered or of physical evidence being destroyed increases.

It has been statistically documented that certain categories of crimes have greater solution rates than others, based on category alone. Criminal homicide traditionally has a high clearance rate by arrest (approximately 65 percent), whereas larceny investigations generally have a low rate of clearance (approximately 20 percent).[3] This is due to many factors, including varying degrees of investigative effort determined by the relative seriousness of the offense (see Table 3.1).

Regardless of the method by which the police become aware of the offense, the preliminary investigation begins at that moment of awareness. From the arrival of the first police officer to the last day of the trial, the criminal investigation process is in effect. The quality of the preliminary

TABLE 3.1 Clearance Rates by Arrest of Major Felony Crimes

Crimes of Violence

Criminal homicide	63 percent
Aggravated assault	60 percent
Rape	44 percent
Robbery	26 percent

Crimes Against Property

Burglary	13 percent
Larceny-theft	18 percent
Motor vehicle theft	13 percent
Arson	17 percent

Source: Federal Bureau of Investigation, Uniform Crime Report.

inquiry is vital to the effectiveness of the in-depth and concluding investigations. In many sizable police agencies, it is the patrol division that performs this first investigative operation.

The National Advisory Commission on Criminal Justice Standards and Goals (comprising a panel of experts who have published studies on police investigation and other related matters) recommends that every police agency employing 75 or more people should assign full-time criminal investigators.[4] Since there are thousands of police agencies with fewer than 75 people, not only the preliminary investigation but all follow-up investigations will be handled by patrol officers. Yet, even in the largest police departments, such as New York City with 4,000 detectives, the responsibility for the preliminary inquiry is delegated to the patrol officer. The reasons for this are based upon logic and years of experimentation to establish which method has the greatest probability of success. The patrol division operates on a 24-hour basis, every day of the year; the investigative division generally does not. The patrol division, mobile at all times, has the quickest response time; the investigator must travel to the scene from his or her office or other distant point. Therefore, unless the case is self-initiated by the investigator, it is the patrol officer who will process the preliminary investigation.

The preliminary investigation most often begins at the scene of the offense and proceeds outward. As one would expect, the response time of the assigned patrol officer is of crucial significance; an arrival time that is unduly slow can have many negative consequences. Upon arrival, the officer should quickly survey the scene to determine if first aid is needed and to form initial judgments for future actions. A basic question that must be answered soon after the officer's arrival will determine the course of the inquiry. Has an offense been committed that the police are empowered to investigate? Since many calls for police service involve matters that are civil rather than criminal, it is important to waste no time in answering this question.

When the officer is satisfied that a criminal offense has occurred, further actions are taken, depending on the specific nature of the crime. If the crime is robbery, a detailed description must be transmitted as soon as possible. If the offense is burglary and the suspect was not seen, protection of the crime scene becomes the first immediate duty. When the officer arrives at a scene involving personal injury, the injured must be taken care of first, even if the officer believes that an arrest could be made by pursuing the suspect.

Generally, regardless of the crime involved, protection of the crime scene is one of the first procedures. The preliminary inquiry focuses on the crime scene as the major area of importance. As the spokes of a wheel radiate from the center, various investigative leads are drawn from the crime scene. Many large police agencies utilize patrol officers in a crime scene protection capacity, this being their sole responsibility in the preliminary investigation. In this way, patrol officers protect the scene and transfer full investigative responsibility to the first arriving detective.

The outcome of the preliminary investigation is governed by the passage of time. As a general principle, the probability of a successful case decreases with the passage of time, starting from when the suspect commits the offense. When officers arrest a suspect at the scene or in close proximity to the scene, the probability of a successful conviction is at its highest. The longer the interval without an arrest, the lower the probability of success. Many factors play a part in this phenomenon. The longer a suspect remains at large, the greater the likelihood of

1. physical escape from the scene,
2. inaccurate witness or victim identification,
3. destruction or disposal of evidence taken from the scene by the suspect,
4. victims or witnesses being unwilling to testify in court,
5. police suspension of the case,
6. construction of credible alibis by suspects, and
7. possible contamination or loss of physical evidence.

In addition to protecting the crime scene, preliminary responsibilities may include the collection, marking, preservation, and transportation of evidence. If the officer incorrectly processes evidence in any of the aforementioned steps, the entire investigation may be jeopardized.

Besides the crime scene, another major focus of the investigation is people. Victims, witnesses—anyone who can add information to the initial inquiry—are of value to the preliminary investigation. If victims and witnesses are present at the scene, the victim is given priority for the officer's attention. A basic interview is conducted with the victim, keeping in mind that the victim will be interviewed again during the in-depth investigation. The purpose of the preliminary interview is not to record all details of the offense but to obtain the basic facts upon which the in-depth inquiry will be based.

Witnesses must be located and identified with haste during the preliminary investigation. With the arrival of the officer, there is a tendency for some witnesses to leave the scene or to alter their observations by discussing the event with others. This is an additional justification for a brief victim interview and a reason why all victims should be asked to identify others who may have been present during the commission of the offense.

Although the preliminary investigation is frequently a patrol function and the in-depth inquiry an investigative function, occasionally friction develops between the two divisions. The problem is almost always due to a lack of communication. Patrol officers justifiably feel resentful when they complete a proper preliminary inquiry and are never informed of the outcome of the case. It is the responsibility of the investigative division to see that this type of information gets back to the patrol officer.

To determine whether a specific case should proceed past the preliminary investigation stage, many police agencies use **solvability factors**. Developed in the early 1970s by the Rochester (New York) Police Department, solvability factors have become a widely used tool in determining the probability of a successful criminal investigation. This method recognizes that some cases will be inherently difficult to solve because they lack suitable information to allow apprehension. Its aim is to conclude quickly those cases with little probability of success and to focus investigative resources on cases demonstrating workable leads. Using such logic, police agencies have reported impressive increases in arrest and conviction rates.

Following extensive research, the Rochester Police Department determined that 12 common areas of information were strongly linked with successful criminal investigations:

1. Was there a witness to the crime?
2. Can the suspect be named?
3. Can the suspect be located?
4. Can the suspect be described?
5. Can the suspect be identified?
6. Can a suspect vehicle be identified?
7. Is stolen property traceable?
8. Is a clear suspect method of operation present?
9. Is there significant physical evidence present?
10. Is there a positive report concerning the physical evidence by a trained technician?
11. Is it reasonable to conclude that the case can be solved by normal investigative effort?
12. Was there clear limited opportunity for anyone but the suspect to have committed the crime?

During the preliminary investigation, officers focus their efforts toward the solvability factors, actively pursuing information relative to the 12 questions. The preliminary reports are then carefully examined by investigators to assess the potential solvability of the case or its suspension from active investigative efforts.[5] Accordingly, one or more affirmative answers to the solvability factors indicate a case with substantial potential for success, whereas cases lacking one or more affirmative answers are generally designated as inactive investigations.

In theory, all criminal cases should receive equal investigative effort, yet reality dictates otherwise. Excessive caseloads, limited resources, and the natural connection of strong investigative leads to successful arrests determine why some cases are investigated past the preliminary stage.

The In-Depth Investigation

The second investigative stage of a criminal offense is the follow-up, or the *continuing inquiry*. The **in-depth investigation** phase follows up initial leads stemming from the preliminary investigation. Traditionally this stage of the inquiry has been the sole responsibility of the detective because the continuing investigation is frequently defined as occurring when the patrol division yields responsibility to the detective division.[6]

There is no precise moment at which the preliminary investigation is transformed into the in-depth investigation. In some police agencies, a time factor may be used, such as a departmental order specifying eight hours as the maximum preliminary inquiry period. In some law enforcement agencies, the in-depth inquiry begins with the arrival of a plainclothes detective on the scene. Regardless of how the in-depth inquiry is designated, the investigative methods employed are standard.

The in-depth investigation usually involves a longer time span than the preliminary inquiry. While preliminary duties can be accomplished in hours, the continuing duties frequently involve days, weeks, or even many months. The investigator is well suited to perform this phase of the case, particularly if the assigned offense relates to his or her specialty. Although patrol officers are assigned specific geographic areas of responsibility and are expected to remain within those areas, investigators may pursue leads throughout the city without neglecting their primary mission. In addition, the investigating officer, through experience and training, has a greater knowledge of investigative resources than the patrol officer. In the performance of their duties, investigators develop informants both in and out of the criminal world. They also have a greater knowledge of what information may be yielded from official records from within the department and from government or private agencies.

The in-depth inquiry begins with a general reexamination of all facts, leads, and other types of information secured during the preliminary investigation. The detective must determine if the preliminary inquiry was complete and attempt to answer the following:

1. Was the crime scene processed in a proper manner?
2. If a suspect was arrested, was the arrest legally competent?
3. Of the physical evidence secured, which should be examined by the crime laboratory, and what specific examinations should be requested?
4. Are the identifying data concerning victims and witnesses correct?
5. Has the preliminary officer been contacted in regard to leads or areas of inquiry not found in the formal preliminary report?

Once the investigator is satisfied that the preliminary investigation has been conducted in a satisfactory manner, gathering of information independent of the initial stage begins. The specific duties involved will, of course, depend on the type of offense being investigated; however, the following tasks are normally associated with all serious in-depth inquiries:

1. A return to the crime scene for
   (a) familiarization of localities, objects, and so forth (particularly necessary for an investigator who has not yet viewed the scene);
   (b) additional thorough search for physical evidence;
   (c) location of victims or witnesses not identified who are in the immediate crime scene vicinity; and
   (d) verification of suspect, victim, or witness statements that are associated with the physical structure of the scene. (For example, is it possible, when standing in Room A, to witness an incident in Room B?)
2. The processing and coordination of reports, records, and documents having some bearing on the inquiry. This would involve
   (a) checking local, state, and federal agencies for arrest records of a suspect, if identified;
   (b) examining the *modus operandi* file (a file describing individual methods of operation by specific suspects); and
   (c) examining field interview records for similar descriptions of a suspect, auto, and so forth. (Field interview records are cards filled out by patrol officers listing names, physical factors, and clothing descriptions of subjects suspicious to the officer.)
3. The application of criminalistics to the case by initiating or completing the following:
   (a) packaging and transporting physical evidence to a crime laboratory;
   (b) accounting for the return of crime laboratory reports for each examination requested; and
   (c) arranging for expert criminalistic processing of the crime scene, if necessary.

4. The gathering of investigative leads by obtaining information from the following:
   (a) informants of a criminal background, paid or otherwise;
   (b) merchants or other noncriminal informants who may aid in the recovery of stolen property;
   (c) a thorough neighborhood search for witnesses or those who may provide any type of pertinent information; and
   (d) an appeal to the public for information by utilization of the media or other sources.

The investigator may obtain information in other ways, the specific offense often indicating a course of inquiry. For example, an unsuccessful business that has been completely destroyed by fire suggests the possibility of arson for insurance motives. Or the murder of the leader of a violent street gang may point toward an inquiry involving rival gangs. It should be emphasized that the detective must be flexible in the investigative approach. No two investigations will be the same.

The Concluding Investigation

This final stage, the **concluding investigation**, is the direct outgrowth of the previous two stages. If the preliminary and in-depth investigations have been unsuccessful in identifying, locating, and arresting a suspect, certain administrative decisions concerning the continuation of the case must be made. An active inquiry cannot continue indefinitely. Although in theory it would be ideal if an investigator could pursue a case until it was solved by arrest, in reality this is not feasible. The volume of crime, limitations of investigative personnel, and lack of investigative leads all require a method for case suspension. The standard method used in most police agencies is to suspend the active investigation of a case when all areas of inquiry have been dealt with thoroughly but without success. If the offender remains unidentified despite the best efforts of the investigator, the case will be withdrawn from active investigation until new leads are developed. On the other hand, if the preliminary and in-depth investigations have been successful, a suspect will have been arrested and the criminal offense reconstructed. In this situation, the concluding investigation is primarily concerned with preparing a solid case to maximize the probability of a conviction.

During the concluding inquiry, the investigating officer works closely with the prosecuting attorney. Theoretically, the preparation of a criminal case for court is the sole responsibility of the prosecutor, but in many jurisdictions, the large caseload assigned to each prosecutor limits the actual time given to each case. It is the investigator, then, who must assist the prosecutor if the case preparation is to be a sound one. Most officers are not trained attorneys, yet much of what is done during this stage has a direct bearing on the rules of law. A criminal case should be prepared for trial in the following manner:

1. Review the suspect's arrest to ascertain its legality.
2. Review all suspect statements and admissions as to their legality.
3. Review the manner in which all relevant evidence has been secured.
4. Reexamine legal requirements of victim and witness statements and identifications of the suspect.
5. Review and compile all notes, reports, and documents that may be used during the trial.
6. Review all information secured by the use of informants and make decisions about the possibility of their use in court.

7. Review the prosecution's strategy and the nature of the detective's testimony to be used during the trial.

8. Arrange for all necessary expert-witness testimony.

It should be obvious from the preceding discussion that an investigator's legal knowledge must be considerable. An understanding of what constitutes legal arrests, searches and seizures, and admissible evidence is fundamental to a successful career as a criminal investigator.

Clearance and Conviction Rates

The efficiency of our criminal justice system is determined by varying standards. To a great extent, police effectiveness is still judged by rates of arrest, of either an entire agency or of an individual investigator. Although it may not always be fair or even logical to judge police effectiveness by this standard alone, it continues to be the criterion used by much of the public.

As a national average, police are successful in clearing by arrest approximately 20 percent of all serious felonies reported to their agencies. Police departments judge solution rate by counting clearances, that is, the number of cases in which a known criminal offense has resulted in the arrest, citation, or judicial summoning of an individual in connection with the offense.[7] The success of a particular investigation is not, however, a uniform factor among all crimes. Some investigations have a naturally higher probability of success than others (see Figure 3.4). For example, criminal homicide investigations generally involve perpetrators who know their victims and who make little or no real effort to avoid apprehension. In addition, the extreme seriousness of the crime dictates maximum investigative effort, with an exhaustive search for forensic evidence. On the other hand, there is traditionally a much lower rate of arrest in cases of burglary. Many factors contribute to this unfortunate fact, including heavy caseloads and the large amount of stolen property that is unidentifiable when recovered. The main reason for the low rate of clearance is, however, the lack of a suspect identification, as this type of criminal purposely avoids contact with victims or witnesses (see Table 3.1).

Of those cases successfully concluded by an arrest, an unfortunately large number are not carried onward into the judicial process (see Figure 3.5). National studies indicate that approximately 40 percent of all felony arrests brought by police for prosecution are rejected in some manner. Some investigations are either dropped outright by a prosecutor prior to court examination

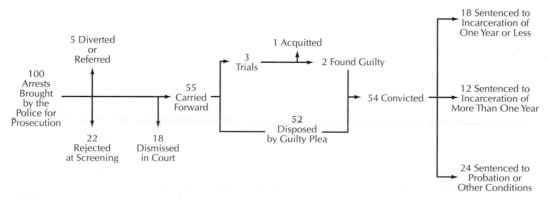

FIGURE 3.5 Typical outcome of 100 felony crime investigations resulting in arrest and brought for prosecution. *(Source: U.S. Department of Justice, Bureau of Justice Statistics.)*

or dismissed by a judge in one of the various judicial screenings. Prosecutors tend to reject cases because of problems of insufficient evidence, whereas judges tend to dismiss cases because of legal violations relating to due process.[8] However, those cases that are carried forward to the trial stage are typically strong, as evidenced by only 2 percent not resulting in conviction.

Such data can be very helpful to the investigator, demonstrating that in many cases, evidence linking a suspect to an offense is not located, collected, or processed effectively. Although it is true that certain types of investigations are inherently difficult in this regard, there is considerable room for improvement. On the positive side, research indicates that the screening process is quite effective in predicting which cases will result in conviction.

▲ SUMMARY

All complex tasks must have a plan that constructs a method of reasoning, or framework, to complete the task. Because the task of crime investigation can be highly complex, an orderly method of logic derived from the scientific method is a starting point for the investigator. Although this framework will not automatically resolve crime inquiries, it provides progressive structure to an investigation, giving the officer great latitude to employ his or her own resources. A five-step process, the method initially states the problem, forms a hypothesis, observes and experiments, interprets data, and, finally, draws conclusions.

As in the twentieth century, the twenty-first century will require an increased adherence by investigators to the laws of evidence and procedure. An effective criminal investigator is equally skilled in field techniques and legal knowledge. Although most investigators are not lawyers, their legal knowledge must be extensive for several important reasons. Investigators generally have the responsibility of reviewing preliminary reports for legal correctness, and they assist prosecutors in evaluating cases for court presentation.

Evidence can be anything that has importance to the state's case or to the defendant's. Evidence may be obtained from the direct observations of an individual or may be in a tangible or physical form. Regardless of its source, evidence to be admitted into trial must be competent, relevant, and material to the issue being litigated.

The investigative process can be divided into specific phases according to task or, in large agencies, according to assigned personnel. Division by task breaks the investigation into three distinct phases: preliminary, in-depth, and concluding investigation. The preliminary investigation forms the foundation for all future actions and generally focuses on the crime scene. As information and evidence are gathered in this phase, the use of solvability factors can be helpful. This method seeks to conclude those cases with little probability of success and encourages focusing of investigative resources on those cases with leads demonstrating high probability of apprehension. The in-depth investigation expands from the crime scene and, using preliminary information as a base, widens into new areas of inquiry. Specifically, the in-depth investigation has four general areas of inquiry: a return to the crime scene for additional information, the processing and coordinating of documents, the application of criminalistics to recovered evidence, and the gathering of new investigative leads.

The concluding investigation seeks to resolve the case through prosecution or suspension. Successful cases will be prepared for prosecution through close coordination between the investigator and the state's attorney. During this stage, evidence is reviewed for future court admissibility, and involved citizens are examined and briefed as to the possibility of their becoming witnesses. Because only a few cases can be actively investigated for extended periods of time without results, many must be suspended lacking an apprehension. Generally, when all investigative leads have been exhausted without results, the case will be put in the suspended-status category.

Clearing cases through arrest is a major concern for the criminal investigator because his or her effectiveness is often measured by this standard. Nationally, police are successful in making arrests in 20 percent of all reported serious felonies. That some investigations are more likely to result in apprehension than others is due to various factors. Cases in which the perpetrator is known or that involve physical harm to the victim receive intense investigative effort. Cases involving property generally have the lowest arrest rates. A lack of suspect identification and the absence of physical evidence to connect a perpetrator to the stolen property often account for such low apprehension rates.

Of all serious cases that do result in arrest, 40 percent are rejected either by the prosecutor or by the judge prior to trial. The majority of rejections are typically due to problems of insufficient evidence. Obtaining evidence is often a complicated process, yet the high rate of case dismissal indicates a need for further education and training in this vital area.

▪ EXERCISES

1. Observe a local criminal trial for the manner in which evidence is presented and ruled upon.
2. Interview a commanding officer of a local department's investigation bureau. Determine how cases are brought to the bureau's attention through the various reporting methods.
3. Find out how local departments define and conduct their preliminary, in-depth, and concluding investigations. Determine how the agencies assign officers to these phases (by department order, tradition, commander's judgment, and so forth).

● RELEVANT WEB SITES

http://phyun5.ucr.edu/"wudka/Physics7/Notes_www?node5.html

Defines the principles of the scientific method, which can then be applied to the investigative function. Explains the difference between a fact, a theory, and a hypothesis.

http://www.trialbehavior.com/news/csi.htm

Details the importance of criminal evidence to the trial process. Gives considerable coverage to the impact that forensic science has on the admissibility of evidence during criminal trials. Explains the "CSI effect" upon the rules of evidence.

Note-Taking and Reports

KEY TERMS

closing report
field note-taking
outline note-taking
police report
preliminary report

progress report
prosecution report
suspended case
verbatim notes

LEARNING OBJECTIVES

1. to understand how note-taking aids the criminal investigator;
2. to be able to list and define the various styles of note-taking;
3. to see how field notes relate to the formal report;
4. to understand the purposes of the police report;
5. to be able to list the elements of a well-written report; and
6. to be familiar with the various types of investigative reports and the circumstances in which they are used.

INTRODUCTION

Reports generated by the police agency serve as a factual base for the entire criminal justice system. Even prior to the actual arrest of a suspect, notes and reports are being compiled. After the arrest, reports literally follow the suspect through the judicial process and often assist correctional personnel. Note-taking and report writing are intrinsic to an officer's job. Notes are compiled during all phases of an investigation and serve as source material for the report. The report is a formal presentation of facts that serves as the official police record.

NOTE-TAKING

It would be difficult indeed for an officer to write an investigative report at the crime scene. Because the report becomes the official police record stating the details of the offense, care must be taken to ensure completeness and accuracy. Consequently, an investigator who is processing a crime scene, interviewing victims and witnesses, and dealing with a myriad of other tasks cannot write a proper report at the same time. Yet information must be recorded for use at a time when the formal report will be compiled. The method by which this is accomplished is known as *field note-taking* (Figure 4.1). All police officers utilize **field notes**, regardless of their specific assignment. Field notes are written impressions and facts gathered during an initial inquiry. They may be observations, statements, or general impressions gathered during an investigation. Field notes aid the investigator in the following ways:

1. They serve as the factual foundation for the report.
2. They serve as memory aids.
3. They enhance the credibility of the officer and the report.

All crime scenes, regardless of the specific offense, must be described in some way. Property scenes typically involve the listing of stolen items. Offenses that are person to person normally involve the taking of detailed

FIGURE 4.1 Officers must take accurate field notes, for the notes will serve as the factual base for formal reports. *(Source: Bob Daemmrich / Pictor / ImageState / International Stock Photography Ltd.)*

statements from victims and witnesses. Such information is first set down in fieldnote form, to be used at a later date in the formal report. Field notes are generally recorded in a small loose-leaf notebook. Bound notebooks may pose court-related problems, for the officer cannot remove specific pages for reference while testifying. Careful note-taking will provide specific information in regard to the following areas of investigative importance:

1. location and time of offense;
2. names and identifying data of victims, witnesses, or suspects;
3. verbatim statements;
4. property and injury listings;
5. investigative data and method of operation; and
6. crime scene recording.

Note-taking is a procedure that is relatively new to police work. Officers in nineteenth-century American police agencies rarely took field notes or even carried the necessary paper or writing instruments. Police record keeping at this time was in its infancy, with formal reports a rarity. Investigators relied upon memory to recall facts during a judicial proceeding, producing testimony that often fell short of being accurate. As crime increased and the quality of policing advanced, it became common practice to record information during the initial investigation. Present-day crime frequency demands that accurate note-taking be accomplished to aid the officer's memory. Most often an officer will wait until the end of a work shift to write the formal report. If the officer has no field notes to rely upon to document the report, errors will undoubtedly occur. Furthermore, the use of notes increases the credibility of the investigator and the credibility of the written report. Juries are aware of the limitations of the human memory; thus, documenting the accuracy of the report by producing field notes compiled at the scene creates a favorable impression. When an investigator's overall credibility can be demonstrated, it is helpful to the prosecution.

Field notes will be taken at all scenes, but the officer must use discretion in determining at what point during the initial questioning the writing process begins. Certain individuals are intimidated by an investigator who immediately produces a notebook and begins writing. Many statements are initially inaccurate or confused—in need of several retellings before the facts should be recorded. An investigator must make specific judgments regarding the information that will be noted. Generally speaking, factual information that is material to the offense being investigated should be written down. If a witness offers an opinion or personal judgment, this information may be noted, but such data should always be labeled as opinion. Keeping in mind that field notes are often viewed by the jury, the officer must make certain that opinionated data are carefully identified as such.

The precise manner in which notes are set down will vary with the personal preference of the investigator and the type of information being recorded. Some investigators use **outline note-taking**. This method is normally arranged either by subject or time. For example, all data pertaining to stolen property would be listed under the heading "A. Stolen Property." Or a listing of occurrences by way of a sequential time frame is used. Each heading would represent a specific time period, with all pertinent events listed beneath it. An alternate style, which lends itself well to taking statements, is the use of **verbatim notes**. Verbatim notes are the precise words of the individual giving the statement. The verbatim style can be of great courtroom value. If the investigator testifies that recorded statements were taken word for word, defense arguments that the information was distorted during the recording are avoided. When the verbatim method is used, however, the officer must take care to indicate that the statement is precise. Words and sentences that are verbatim should be so indicated by the use of quotation marks.[1] Field notes used to record the crime scene should be kept separate from statement recordings. Crime scene notes are used to identify scene photographs and record significant evidence data.

Field notes should always be as accurate and brief as possible. Yet accuracy should never be sacrificed for the sake of brevity or vice versa. If, in order to be accurate, a statement requires lengthy notes, then the officer should take considerable notes. Brevity is attained through experience and practice. With increased opportunities to practice note-taking, an officer will find that considerable verbiage can be accurately condensed into a brief series of notes. Obviously, such condensation applies only to cases of a nonverbatim nature. Just as the college student selects pertinent lecture material to record rather than attempting to write down the instructor's every word, so the investigator screens verbal information at the crime scene. Notes should be legible and orderly in appearance and organization. Notes taken in haste, or without organization, are often difficult to interpret when writing the formal report. Two separate cases should not be reported on one note page; confusion about the origin of the information may result. The officer's handwriting should be legible to avoid errors and to permit other investigators to read the information without difficulty.

An investigator should follow a similar pattern of note-taking regardless of the specific case. Such initial information as name, address, and phone number should be secured at the beginning of the process. There may, however, be certain exceptions in which identifying information is best obtained in the later stages of the questioning. Some people are hesitant to provide information to the police—they may even refuse to relate any information—if the officer initially requests personal data. If such hesitancy is sensed, it is normally preferable to gain the individual's confidence first by obtaining information that is not personal. The personal information can then quite often be secured at the close of the note-taking, when the person's initial apprehension has diminished.

Criminal courts allow the defense to review materials used by the officer during testimony. For this reason alone, certain types of words, terms, and negative statements should never appear in the notes. The proper name of any informant or individual who does not want to be publicly identified should not be written in the notes. Such names should not be recorded even if the intent is to remove the name or destroy the page later: If the officer should forget that this information is in the notes, an embarrassing situation could occur during testimony. Peculiar habits or mannerisms of a victim or witness should not be noted. Again, such information may be utilized to discredit the professionalism of the officer or to offend a friendly witness. Vulgar terms, slang, and words peculiar to certain geographic localities have no place in police field notes. If the investigator is taking a verbatim statement, however, *all* words, regardless of their effect, should be recorded exactly as they are stated. When the officer has concluded the note-taking process, proper names and numbers should be read back to avoid errors.

Notes are equally important to the proper functioning of a police agency and to the success of the investigator. Since the written report evolves from the field notes, the quality of the notes will affect the final report. Correct police reports constitute an essential element in achieving due process during the judicial proceeding. Thus, the precision of the data in such reports serves the interest of all parties during a trial. Police supervisors will partially evaluate an officer's overall performance by the accuracy and completeness of reports.[2] If the original field notes are not up to standard, the reports will reflect the shortcomings. Field notes are the starting point for a chain of written information that will be retained indefinitely. The recovery of stolen property and the identification of suspects often depend on the accuracy of the information obtained during the note-taking process.

REPORTS

Police reports are the natural culmination of field notes and are often prescribed by law or agency policy. Reports are the formalizing or gathering together of information into a permanent written record. A considerable amount of an officer's time—about 15 to 20 percent—is invested in completing reports. Although police reports serve many important purposes, they primarily preserve information. Information gathered during the daily workings of a police agency varies from the inconsequential to the highly significant. Investigative reports document information that has been deemed significant by the police officer. Or the very nature of the data may call for a report. Certain types of information received by a police agency are automatically recorded in a formal-report form. For example, an anonymous telephone bomb threat to the agency will be the subject of a report without the necessity for individual judgment. But the majority of police reports are the result of officer discretion. When a crime scene is processed, the officer alone determines the type of report necessary, based upon a judgment of the existence of a criminal offense. Further investigation again involves the officer's judgment regarding the necessity of follow-up reports. Finally, the investigator decides whether to resolve the investigation through a termination report.

Written reports are essential to the administrative operation of the police agency. They are, in a sense, the fuel that propels the agency to operate properly. Reports link the various divisions so that effective coordinated work can be accomplished. Modern police work requires a considerable number of individuals working together toward a single goal. The communications division may receive and report the complaint, the patrol division responds, the detective and criminalistics divisions investigate, and the jail division finally processes the perpetrator. During the entire course of the investigation, reports are generated and acted upon. Furthermore, reports that have been prepared for past cases are frequently of value in aiding current inquiries. And, as mentioned previously, they are indicators of the efficiency of the investigator. In addition, investigative reports have the potential of being viewed by a wide variety of individuals (see Figure 4.2). They are carefully reviewed by various supervisors and routinely used to evaluate the investigator's work performance. Other than in the smallest agencies, reports will likely be read by any number of fellow investigators

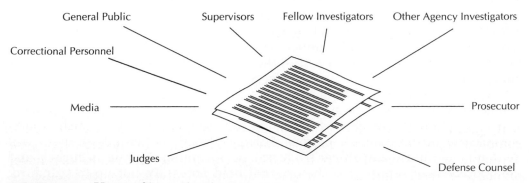

FIGURE 4.2   Users of investigative reports.

working together or by additional newly assigned officers. Because many criminal investigations involve many cities or are multicounty or even interstate investigations, the original reports may be reviewed by officials from a multitude of other law enforcement agencies. As the case works its way through the judicial process, various reports can, and likely will, be thoroughly read by prosecutors, defense attorneys, and judges. It is not uncommon for reports to be reviewed even by appellate judges. Correctional workers, such as probation officers, typically refer to police reports in preparing their presentence investigations for the court. Finally, the reports may be given careful scrutiny by the media and various citizens.

Although sensitive portions of a report can be withheld, most agencies must release law enforcement reports as public documents to qualifying segments of the media or the public. By statute or case law in most states and by tradition in every state, various police reports are available to citizens. For example, a Texas state appellate court decision held that most parts of a police offense report must be made available to the public and the press.[3]

A thorough police report should answer six traditional questions: who, what, when, where, why, and how. Certain investigations yield answers to all of the questions; other cases resolve only some of the inquiries. Generally, the questions can be answered with factual information, with the occasional exceptions of "why" and "how" a particular offense was committed.

General Guidelines

The majority of police reports must contain precise data. Although certain intelligence reports may include some subjective material, the typical offense report must be totally objective. Opinions of the investigator or conclusions that are not based upon fact do not belong in the report. There is always the possibility that a report may be read aloud in court or viewed by the defense before the trial. A report stating opinions that have been shown to be incorrect at the time of the reading damages the officer's credibility.

Information contained in the report should be based on fact. Facts are events that have actually happened or occurrences that a logical person would judge to be true without further proof. The majority of the facts stated in a report will have been experienced by the officer directly. Events and objects that have been seen and statements that have been heard by the investigator form the factual basis for the police report. Some factual material that has not been personally experienced by the officer may also be included. This is information acquired from credible sources such as the files of the police agency.

The written police report should be well organized. One of the most common mistakes of an inexperienced investigator is the failure to organize before and during the report writing. Prior to the actual writing of the report, an officer should outline the content in the order of occurrence. This is particularly necessary if the step has not been taken in the field notes. With the growing use of tape-recorded reports, proper organization is even more essential because although written reports can illustrate at a glance what has been said, the taped report must be played back to accomplish this. Thus, some officers inadvertently omit data or repeat information rather than play the entire tape back for accuracy.

Just as field notes should be accurate and brief, so should the report. But, again, one factor should not be sacrificed for the sake of the other. A complete report states in a concise manner all the pertinent facts that were available at the time of the writing. The report should not read like a novel or contain irrelevant descriptions. The length of the report should be manageable; in an overdrawn narrative important points can be overlooked.

As with field notes, vulgarisms and slang terms should never be used, unless they are quoted verbatim for some investigative purpose. If such terms or phrases are used, they must be identified by enclosing them in quotation marks or by setting them apart in a specified area. The final test of a proper report is the clarity of its overall meaning. This is particularly significant with investigative reports, for they are often more speculative than offense reports taken at the crime scene. The investigator must be careful to convey the message in a manner that is understandable to all. If care is taken throughout the report to choose precisely those words and phrases that best express the investigator's thought, the meaning of each sentence will be clear, allowing no room for misinterpretation or speculation as to what was really meant.

A professionally written law enforcement report can be thought of as containing five essential elements, often referred to as the five Cs. These five elements are necessary to ensure a correct investigative report:

1. Completeness
2. Conciseness
3. Clearness
4. Correctness
5. Courteousness or fairness

A complete report must cover all details concerned with the incident or occurrence and include all facts as they are known to the officer at the time the report is written. A complete report is a document that would give a clear picture of what really occurred to a total stranger. A necessary part of completeness is the use of full and thorough sentences without the use of special jargon. Also, a complete report anticipates questions about information that may be lacking. The report should address what specific information is lacking or incomplete and what specific efforts were made to obtain the missing data. Why the officer failed to obtain the information and what efforts are recommended to obtain it should be mentioned. A concise report is not simply brief; it gets to the point by making every sentence count. Such pertinency is accomplished by avoiding editorializing and repetition.

Clarity must constantly be strived for in law enforcement reports, as a clear report allows the reader to comprehend the incident as the writer observed it. The report writer should use words that directly describe the event rather than the writer's response to the situation. Clarity can also be achieved by avoiding words that can be interpreted in different ways by different groups of people. Police report correctness pertains to writing that lacks personal judgments or conclusions reached without the support of evidence or facts. Correctness leads to accuracy, which is the overall objective of the report-writing process. Correctness or accuracy is best achieved by limiting the data in the report to sensory observations, most commonly sight, hearing, and touch. As the report reflects the integrity of the writer, every effort to maintain accuracy should be made. Finally, the police reporting process must be courteous or fair at all times. Fair reports lack personal antagonism or subjective opinions that alter the essential objectivity of the document. Because the investigative process objective is to gather the facts and report them, any attempt to judge or otherwise use theories to replace facts must be avoided.[4]

Types of Investigative Reports

All police agencies have specific reporting procedures that the investigator must follow. When an officer is assigned to a case involving any felony violation or certain misdemeanor offenses, the formal reporting process is initiated.

It begins with the preliminary investigation report, followed by progress reports and perhaps a prosecution report.

Preliminary Reports. Although information is gathered as soon as a complaint is received, the reporting process formally begins when the officer completes the **preliminary report**. Of all reports of any type written in police agencies, the preliminary is the most commonly prepared, as nearly half of all reports are preliminary documents. This type of report is often referred to as the case report; it is the first detailed listing of the facts of the case (see Figure 4.3). Preliminary reports are often filled out by assigned patrol personnel and serve as the factual foundation for later investigative work. Preliminary reports record the following information:

1. the offense;
2. current date and time;
3. date and time of offense, if known;
4. identification data pertaining to the victim or other reporting party;
5. location of the offense;
6. method of operation;
7. identification data pertaining to the suspect; and
8. identification of the officer.

Preliminary investigation reports also provide space for miscellaneous details that are important to the case. Information such as a listing of stolen property or a description of the weather during the offense may be listed in this section. The officer will attach to the report or write on the back of the preliminary report a concise narration of the results of the preliminary investigation. This narration will state precisely how and when the officer

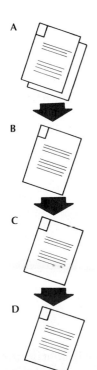

A
- Preliminary reports prepared by investigating officer and duplicated.
- One copy kept by investigation division.

B
- Original reviewed and signed by supervising officer, then forwarded to record division.

C
- Upon receipt of original, index cards prepared by record division to be filed in central index by
  (a) name of victim, suspect, reporting party;
  (b) type of crime;
  (c) location of crime; and
  (d) description or number of stolen property.

D
- Original filed in numerical order within central report file.

FIGURE 4.3 Report flow handling of offense report—preliminary stage.

was assigned to the offense and the condition of the scene, victim, witness, or suspect. A discussion or listing of the various investigative procedures that have been accomplished will follow, with only factual data included.

Progress Reports.   Progress reports, as the name implies, are designed to provide the investigator with a reporting method to describe the progress of the investigation. Such reports are normally due at specified intervals. Many agencies use the 15-day interval, in which the first progress report must be submitted 15 days after the preliminary report and every 15 days thereafter. Progress reports are designed to ensure constant follow-up to the initial crime occurrence. This type of report is common to all detective bureaus, for whenever additional investigative data are developed, they should be documented immediately.[5] Thus, progress reports can and should be submitted to the case file at any time before the 15-day due date (see Figure 4.4).

Theoretically, the progress report should be strictly factual in content. However, many police agencies use progress reports to state various conclusions arrived at by the investigative officer. Judgments pertaining to the reliability of a witness, the importance of specific evidence, or the truthfulness of a statement are often found in progress reports. Many agencies, however, do not include such material in progress reports, as it may have a negative effect in the courtroom.

The majority of police agencies resolve an investigation through the progress report. When a particular investigation is to be ended, a statement is entered on the final progress report explaining the reasons for the termination. Cases are normally terminated when no new leads are available or when the perpetrator has been arrested. The decision to terminate the case normally originates with the investigator. A supervisor either concurs or rejects the investigator's recommendation. When investigations are not solved by an arrest but terminated for lack of leads, they are termed "suspended." **Suspended cases**, for all practical purposes, receive no

A
- Progress reports prepared by investigating officer and duplicated.
- One copy kept by investigation division.

B
- Original reviewed and signed by supervising officer, then forwarded to record division.

C
- Upon receipt of original, progress report filed numerically with preliminary report by record division.
- Index cards prepared and filed, if additional information is developed.

D
- Report flow terminated by supervisory approval for
  (a) lack of investigative leads; or
  (b) arrest of perpetrator.

FIGURE 4.4   Report flow handling of progress report—in-depth investigation.

further police effort. However, the case is not actually considered closed; it is kept in an "open" status, awaiting further developments.

A closed status is assigned to investigations that are terminated by the arrest or, in some cases, the identification of the perpetrator. It is important to note that closed status does not depend on a suspect's *conviction*. It is the *arrest* that concludes the police investigation.

Closing and Prosecution Reports.   Some police agencies have a formal reporting procedure for the closing of an investigation. The same rationale used in closing a case through the progress report applies, with the information listed on a separate closing form. Certain agencies routinely prepare **prosecution reports**, which are designed to aid the prosecutor in preparing the state's case. Although such reports are still a rarity, they serve a very important function. Prosecution reports are compiled to filter out essential information of judicial significance from the general mass of data. Information concerning the identity of victims and witnesses and all data pertaining to victim or witness credibility are included in this report. Additional information regarding the evidence located at the scene, laboratory test results, and the transmission of such evidence are also included. Additionally, this type of report frequently includes crime scene photographs, crime scene sketches, and other recording aids. There is no specific list of what should be included in a prosecution report; any information judged to be of value in the preparation and prosecution of the case may be of importance.

The prosecution report should be used with greater frequency. It serves as an investigative link between the police agency and prosecution, and it is appreciated by prosecutors to a greater extent than is commonly imagined. Many prosecutors feel that investigators abandon an investigation after an arrest has been made. A California superior court judge once commented that "it is a general police attitude that their job is over when they have caught somebody." Although this type of attitude may not be so general, the fact that it exists at all is unfortunate. An excellent example of a police agency that aids the prosecution is the Los Angeles County Sheriff's Departments, homicide division. This division prepares and forwards to the prosecutor a well-organized, indexed, bound notebook containing the original report of investigating deputies, statements by all witnesses, lists of evidence, photographs of the crime scene and victims or suspects, and a discussion of all possible defense theories. It is termed the "murder book" and has been cited as a major contributory factor toward the higher-than-average homicide conviction rate of this agency.[6]

Compiling data from various sources into a professional police report is not an easy task. To the beginning criminal investigator, report writing is often viewed as one of the most arduous duties of the position. Most difficulties can be linked to a single problem area: a lack of organization prior to and during the report-writing process. Preliminary, progress, and **closing reports** are all dependent on a clear and orderly arrangement of data. Yet information cannot be obtained without clear communication between the report writer and the information source. Many factors serve to complicate the communication process, including initial distractions. Distractions hinder both the giver and the recorder of data. The investigator should make every effort to obtain reporting facts in an environment free of distractions. A second problem area relates to the speed with which the brain processes spoken information. Information is absorbed and processed through hearing nearly three times faster than most people speak. Because of this lag time, it is easy for officers to lose their concentration and become distracted while a reporting party is still speaking.[7]

All three types of investigative reports must reflect the tightest possible organization and clarity. Readers absorb information relatively quickly and are basically seeking data that answer the age-old question, "What happened?" Facts must be stated as briefly as possible to hold the reader's interest while still containing all pertinent data. Each report should state clearly in the opening sentences what the significant points are to avoid reader confusion or misinterpretation. Simplicity is often difficult to achieve, however, in cases involving multiple suspects, a host of different offenses, or a complex method of operation. Depending on the nature of the investigation, preliminary reports are often the most difficult initially, with progress and closing reports becoming less complicated. This is often the situation in dramatic cases of violence involving one or more unknown perpetrators. As information develops through the investigative process, reports are typically easier to organize and compose as the clarity of the crime becomes apparent. Other cases may be the opposite, with scant preliminary information and increasing amounts of information added throughout the progress reports. Regardless of the types of cases, each report must reflect the writer's attempt to simplify incoming information into organized, factual statements that allow the data to tell a coherent story.

▲ SUMMARY

The reporting process serves as the foundation for successful investigation and provides the entire criminal justice system with necessary information. Sound reports cannot be written without complete and accurate notes. Field notes are taken by all officers and serve as the basis for the more formalized report. In addition, field notes are often used in court proceedings to assist officers in recalling events and detailed information precisely. Law enforcement personnel use various styles when taking notes at crime scenes and while recording information from victims and witnesses. Two of the more common methods are using an outline format and taking down the words of an individual verbatim.

Police reports become a permanent record of the investigated event and then will be reviewed by many individuals within and outside the law enforcement agency. In addition to recording and formalizing the justice process, professionally written reports are essential for successful career advancement. All information contained in law enforcement reports must be based on facts. Opinions or other conclusions not based on factual material have no place in most police reports. A limited variety of documents, such as intelligence summaries, may contain subjective material.

Investigative reports are generally of three main varieties: preliminary, progress, and closing. The preliminary report is essential to the completion of all other related documents because it serves as the source document. Accordingly, great care must be taken to ensure its accuracy. Most preliminary reports are completed shortly after the initial investigation of an offense. The progress report, or follow-up report, is the second type of investigative report; it documents the investigative efforts being made to clear the case. The final stage of reporting, the closing report, or concluding report, is used by agencies seeking a formal document to terminate a case. During this stage, prosecution reports may also be completed. Such documents contain information of immediate interest to the state prosecutor and emphasize judicially significant facts.

Note-taking and report writing will always be of great importance to the criminal investigator. That report quality affects the course of the investigator's career is indisputable. The majority of top police administrators are excellent report writers. If an officer performs well in the field but cannot give that performance proper expression through the written report, the officer is handicapped in terms of career. Although each police agency trains the officer in the specifics of report writing, criminal justice students should develop proper English usage and good writing habits as early as possible in their academic studies.

EXERCISES

1. Using role-playing techniques, interview a student "crime victim." Record the victim's statements using a selected note-taking method. Use the notes to prepare a preliminary investigation report.
2. Examine report forms from various police agencies in your county. Compare and contrast the rules of the agencies regarding the use of these forms.

RELEVANT WEB SITES

http://www.writingcomission.org/pr/writing_for_employ.html

Created by the National Commission on Writing, this site provides information on how important proper reporting writing is for professional development.

http://www.infoplease.com/homwork/writingskills1.html

An extensive collection of essays illustrating proper methods of note-taking and report writing for college students and professionals.

The Crime Scene Focus

KEY TERMS

chain of custody
coordinated photo series
crime scene
crime scene equipment kits
crime scene sketch
CSI effect
digital photography
equivocal death scenes
grid search method
measurement marker
personation

photographic distortion
physical evidence
projection
rectangular coordinate method
response time
sector search method
spiral search method
staging
strip search method
theory of transfer
triangulation

LEARNING OBJECTIVES

1. to see why the crime scene has become a major element of the criminal investigation process;
2. to appreciate the importance of proper crime scene protection;
3. to understand the methods used in proper crime scene photography;
4. to be able to draw an accurate crime scene sketch;
5. to be able to compare and contrast crime scene photography and the crime scene sketch;
6. to be familiar with the methods of searching a crime scene;
7. to understand the collection and marking phases of the crime scene focus; and
8. to appreciate the significance of proper crime scene equipment.

INTRODUCTION

Literally thousands of criminal investigations are processed each year, but there has yet to be found the so-called typical crime scene. Despite frequent similarities, no two scenes contain identical elements. Consider two finger-prints of a general grouping. Both appear similar, yet when closely examined, numerous differences are evident. Crime scenes, too, may appear very much the same yet each crime locality presents a unique mental and professional challenge to the investigator.

A **crime scene** is a location at which a suspected criminal offense has occurred. Processing the crime scene is normally one of the most important phases of the investigation. It is here that the investigator focuses in the search for physical evidence. All crime scenes, to a variable degree, contain physical evidence. This may be visible to the naked eye or minute to the point of being microscopic. Physical evidence comprises all objects and material found in connection with an investigation that are instrumental in discovering the facts.

Criminal investigators of the past did not fully realize the potential of the crime scene. Police officials during the nineteenth and early twentieth centuries relied primarily on informational sources, such as the informant, for solutions to crimes in which the suspect was not known. When a suspect was located, the confession (or lack of it) was of primary importance to the trial.

Fortunately, law enforcement officers now realize the true significance of the crime scene in the judicial process. This is due, in part, to numerous court decisions that have decreased the importance of the confession. The traditional confession, though still of considerable consequence, must now be supported by physical evidence, eyewitness testimony, or some other corroborative factor. Thus, the importance of the crime scene continues to grow. It is a reasonable assumption that court proceedings will continue to place more emphasis on physical evidence and less on written and verbal statements of the suspect.

The importance of careful observation at the scene of a crime cannot be overemphasized. The crime scene frequently provides the key to the solution of a case. Yet crime scene processing can be deceptive to those untrained in its intricacies. The very evidence that may be essential for a successful case will not always be recognized as such. Often, a seemingly insignificant item will assume tremendous importance during a criminal trial. It follows that all evidence should be processed with equal competency and thoroughness. If protection of the crime scene is ignored or halfheartedly attempted, the value of any evidence collected will be severely limited. The searching and recording phases are also essential; they locate and officially record all significant evidence. Of equal importance is the manner in which evidence is collected. Improper methods may result in the rejection of an item of evidence during the trial. Finally, the crime scene focus is completed with the proper transportation of the evidence.

GENERAL PRINCIPLES

The investigator must be prepared to apply crime scene skills virtually anywhere; crime is pervasive—it knows no boundaries. It is a common misconception that most crimes conveniently occur indoors, in spacious, well-lighted rooms. Unfortunately, they do not. Criminal offenses occur in nearly every locality imaginable: indoors, outdoors, in automobiles—literally in any place, at any time.

The true challenge of the crime scene is in the area of detection. Again, evidence that could solve the crime will frequently be present at the scene. Successfully locating this evidence is essential, for such tracing clues can often aid in locating the perpetrator of the offense. Or the evidence may help investigators determine the type of criminal offense that has taken place. Further, the evidence may identify the victim, if the victim's identity is not known. The officer should not totally limit the search for physical evidence to the crime scene locality. Physical evidence can also be found on the person of the victim or suspect or within their immediate environment.

The investigator attempts to reconstruct what took place at the crime scene. *Reconstruction of the scene* is accomplished by carefully noting where evidence is located in relationship to its known former position. The officer must also be attentive to objects that seem foreign to the crime scene environment. Bloodstains, articles of clothing lying about, and scattered items in an otherwise orderly room would be examples of foreign objects. Because every item of physical evidence is potentially important to the case, the officer must be extremely thorough. An important rule that applies to all investigations is that *each and every item of evidence found at the scene should be considered essential until proven otherwise.*

There are basically two types of crime scenes. The *indoor scene* is by far the more common, with the *outdoor scene* occurring at the approximate rate of 30 percent. The indoor scene is normally located within a residence or commercial building. The outdoor scene may be a very large area, such as a park or wooded area, or a smaller area such as a residential backyard.

Surely the most difficult outdoor crime scene to date would be the World Trade Center mass murder scene of September 11, 2001 (see Figure 5.1). The terrorist attack upon the two massive buildings claimed the lives of 2,823 victims, and it took a full year to thoroughly process 1.2 million tons of debris. In addition to searching the destroyed buildings for evidence and human remains, investigators processed 1,400 vehicles parked within the scene at the time of the attack.

It is not uncommon for a single investigation to involve both types of crime scenes. For example, a victim may be taken forcibly from a home to an outdoor area where another crime occurs. The investigative method used in studying both the indoor and outdoor scenes is similar. However, there may be problems associated with one crime scene that are not found at another (see Figure 5.2). Poor weather, lack of sufficient lighting, curious people, and

FIGURE 5.1   The terror attack upon the World Trade Center proved to be the largest criminal homicide investigation in the history of the United States. *(Source: Joel Meyerowitz, Getty Images / Time Life Pictures.)*

FIGURE 5.2 The outdoor crime scene presents a unique challenge to the investigator because of its size and potential for contamination. *(Source: AP Wide World Photos.)*

other difficult conditions are common. A skillful investigator is equally competent to process both the indoor and the outdoor scene.

In most jurisdictions, the uniformed police officer will generally be the first authority to arrive at the scene. When a crime is reported to a police agency, a patrol officer is notified by radio to proceed quickly to the scene. Rapid **response time** is frequently instrumental to the success or failure of an entire investigation, for the longer a crime scene remains unprotected, the greater chance for *crime scene contamination*. Contamination of the scene takes place when evidence is altered, removed, or destroyed in any manner.

Crime scene protection is extremely important in regard to subsequent success in admitting evidence in judicial proceedings. Only items demonstrated to be authentic to the scene and free from contamination will be allowed to be entered as evidence during a trial. It must be kept in mind that anytime anyone enters a scene, he or she brings something to the scene and when leaving takes something away. This is the **theory of transfer**. Transfer of objects or materials is helpful in regard to the movements of criminal suspects but is a natural enemy of the investigator in an unprotected crime scene.

It is the primary duty of the first officer to arrive to protect the entire scene. The true size of the scene may be deceiving in that the suspect had to enter and exit from it. For many individuals, the attraction of a crime scene is nearly irresistible; frequently, they will do their utmost to enter it. Thus, one of the major problems of protecting the scene is keeping the curious public and fellow police officers away. It is not uncommon for officers to find people already present when they arrive. The duty of the officer then becomes twofold: unauthorized individuals must be kept from entering, and those found within the scene must be evicted. The officer should stand at the outer perimeter of the scene, allowing only authorized personnel to enter. A polite but firm authority must be exerted to stop all who do not belong in the crime scene area immediately—even other officers not assigned to the scene. The officer yields protection responsibility only to a superior officer, the arriving investigator. Most police agencies specify by department regulations to whom and under what circumstances responsibility should be yielded.

The problem of crime scene contamination by fellow law enforcement officers cannot be overly stressed, as most crime scene technicians continually rank this problem as their greatest concern. This form of contamination is of course unintentional but can be prevented by strict scene control. The curiosity of other officers and their urge to help those assigned to the scene often cause alteration and outright destruction of evidence. Frequently, the most valuable types of evidence, such as trace evidence, are the most vulnerable to contamination. Trace evidence is quite fragile and must undergo sensitive laboratory analysis to yield its fullest results. Evidence such as blood, fingerprints, hairs or fibers, and footwear evidence are very susceptible to destruction by too many officers at a crime scene. Officers must understand by training and by agency policy that the false media image of crime scenes filled with uniformed officers and detectives is a destructive myth. For a scene to be effectively processed, only the minimum number of assigned personnel can be allowed within the scene; a crime scene is no place for a crowd.[1]

Recording Procedures

Photography.   Photography is the first means by which the crime scene is processed and, in many ways, the most important. Proper photographs provide a permanent record of how the scene appeared after the offense was discovered. Additionally, the photographs support the investigator's testimony during a trial. It is vital that crime scene photographs be taken before any items are moved or altered. If physical evidence is moved before being photographed, the pictures may not stand up as evidence. This is due to the legal objection that the photographs do not represent the scene in its true state.

Crime scene photographs are generally taken in a **coordinated photo series**. Very general pictures are taken first, with more specific ones following. For example, the first photographs of a gas station armed robbery are long-range pictures of the entire building. These are followed by views of the room in which the robbery actually took place. The final photos are close-up views of single items of physical evidence located in the room.

It is important to be aware of the problem of **photographic distortion**. The photograph must not misrepresent the scene, person, or object that it purports to depict. If the photographer selects a proper point of view with natural perspective, the probability of a distortion-free photograph increases (see Figure 5.3). Obviously the type of camera selected by the investigator also has a bearing on the quality of the photographs. Generally speaking, the more expensive 35mm cameras tend to produce a better-quality photo than less expensive cameras that develop prints shortly after exposure.[2]

The use of **digital photography** is rapidly gaining widespread usage among investigators. This method of photography allows the rapid transmission of crime scene photos from computer to computer. Rather than using traditional film, digital cameras capture an image electronically. The digitized data is stored either on the camera's internal floppy disk, on a removable media card, or within Ram memory. The electronic images are then transmitted from one computer to another and printed. Digital pictures are generally far more clear and detailed than other types of photographs. Since there is virtually no delay for photo processing, the images can be instantly transmitted to police supervisors, fellow off-site investigators, prosecutors, or judges at the very earliest stages of an investigation.

In photographing small items found at the crime scene, a **measurement marker** should be used. A ruler or an easily recognized small object, such as a coin, can be placed next to the evidence and photographed so that the true size of the evidence item becomes apparent. Photographs containing evidence markers may be objected to in court, however. Normally the objection is based

FIGURE 5.3 *A.* An example of photographic distortion, this photograph was taken at eye level: (1) victim, (2) skid mark caused by the rifle stock, (3) rifle, (4) cartridge. *B.* The same scene photographed from a 20-foot scaffold. Note that the height and direct angle of lens to subject reduces the distortion. *(Source: Gary Smith, Northfield, MN, Police Department.)*

on the theory that the photograph does not truly represent the original scene as the photographer found it. The investigator should first photograph the evidence "as is," minus any type of foreign object. Markers can then be added for additional pictures. That is, two sets of crime scene photographs should be taken whenever there is the need for an evidence marker. The extra expenditure of film is fully justified by the importance of successfully entering the photographs as evidence during a criminal trial.

Each photograph taken at the crime scene must be fully identified. Very few things can be more embarrassing to the investigator than being unable to identify photographs during courtroom testimony. *Identification data* include the following:

1. Data to identify the subject of the photograph. Often, crime scene photographs contain many extraneous items of little significance to the investigation.
2. Data to identify the location of the photograph. The state, city, street address, and detailed location of the room within the building are items frequently listed.
3. Data to identify the photographer (e.g., name, police agency, badge, or identification number).
4. The case number, if known at the time of marking. The case number may be automatically assigned when the call is dispatched or assigned at a later date.
5. The time the photograph was taken, accurate to the minute.

6. The date the photograph was taken. The investigator must take care in marking this item, for crimes occur with some frequency during the early morning hours, when dates have recently changed.
7. The series number, if applicable.
8. Data to describe weather conditions, photographic equipment, shutter speeds, film type, and developing and printing techniques. Many defense attorneys ask highly technical questions with the intent of discrediting the officer's competence. The astute investigator will be prepared.

The preceding data are recorded in the investigator's field notes or directly onto the photographs if the prints have been developed at the scene. It is preferable that the individual who took the photographs also mark them; however, this is not an absolute evidentiary requirement in most courts.

Cameras used for photographing crime scenes vary considerably. Some law enforcement agencies use relatively inexpensive models that will develop the photograph at the scene. Others exclusively use cameras of a more complex nature; these take film that must be developed in a darkroom. The selection of a proper crime scene camera is according to the personal preference of the investigator and/or department policy. Police agencies having rather large budget allowances for this purpose can offer their officers a choice of camera systems. Smaller departments normally select one type of camera for all investigative purposes.

It is important to ensure that portable light sources are available at all crime scenes. The lighting present at the scene may be inadequate—the scene may even be completely dark. Proper lighting is an essential element for professional quality photographs. Nothing can be more frustrating to the investigator than to have to delay the photo series because of lack of light.

Many law enforcement agencies now use videotaping in addition to traditional still photographs. Videotapes often can provide a more complete and realistic idea of how the scene appeared. Crime scenes in which damage is extensive, such as explosion and fire scenes, are well suited to the videotape technique. Yet the use of the still camera continues to be the most practical method of recording a crime scene.

All significant crime scenes should be thoroughly photographed with quality color film. It is not uncommon for hundreds of still photos to be taken at major felony crime scenes. Occasionally, some color photographs may be difficult to admit into evidence. Defense attorneys and some judges may voice objections that color photographs, particularly of such violent crimes as homicide, rape, and assault, may incite feelings of prejudice against a defendant. When such objections are valid, black-and-white photos may be printed from the original color proof sheets. Generally, indoor crime scenes produce four to five photos of rooms devoid of obvious evidence, as well as numerous photos of crime scene rooms and all noteworthy evidence within. The photos must be taken before any evidence is marked or touched, as the photos should record the scene exactly as encountered. Finally, investigators or crime scene technicians should take care not to include extraneous persons in their photographs, as the presence of human subjects compromises the integrity of the scene and may taint the photo as evidence.[3]

The Crime Scene Sketch. After the scene has been photographed and searched, a **crime scene sketch** (Figure 5.4) is made. The crime scene sketch is a measured drawing of a scene showing the location of all important items, particularly physical evidence. The sketch is generally drawn by the investigator; however, the investigator may assign the duty to another officer. The sketch is highly significant in that it can be even more revealing than a photograph. Unnecessary detail can be eliminated in a sketch, whereas

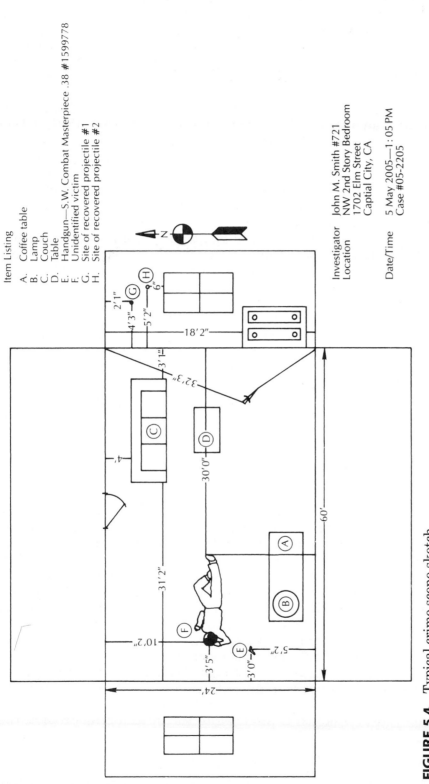

Item Listing

A. Coffee table
B. Lamp
C. Couch
D. Table
E. Handgun—S.W. Combat Masterpiece .38 #1599778
F. Unidentified victim
G. Site of recovered projectile #1
H. Site of recovered projectile #2

Investigator   John M. Smith #721
Location   NW 2nd Story Bedroom
               1702 Elm Street
               Capital City, CA

Date/Time   5 May 2005—1:05 PM
               Case #05-2205

FIGURE 5.4   Typical crime scene sketch.

everything in the range of the camera is recorded. Furthermore, a sketch will not distort the true location of objects, as many photographs tend to do.

All objects that are included in the sketch must be accurately measured. The investigator who is doing the drawing generally takes the measurements as well. Careful measurements are critical, for during a trial the position of a certain item of physical evidence may indicate guilt or innocence. Objects should be measured with a device that will indicate both feet and inches. A steel measuring tape, capable of reaching at least 25 feet, should be used.

Crime scene sketches are usually drawn using three basic methods of locating objects: the rectangular coordinate method, the straight-line method, and triangulation. In the **rectangular coordinate method**, two right angles are drawn from the item being measured to the nearest permanent object. The *straight-line method* is generally used to show the location of items against a wall, such as a piece of furniture. **Triangulation** is commonly used to determine distances outdoors, although it can easily be used indoors. Two fixed points, such as the corners of a room or a telephone pole and the corner of a building, are selected as points of reference. Measurements are then taken from the evidence object to each point, forming a triangle. Thus, the point of intersection of the two lines will be the exact location of the evidence item.

The investigator often encounters important evidence that is located either on the walls or the ceiling of the scene. A three-dimensional view of the scene can be accomplished by means of **projection**, also called an *"exploded" sketch*. In this type of sketch, the walls and ceiling are pictured as if on the same plane as the floor. This is like drawing a box, the edges of which have been cut and the sides folded outward, exposing the sides and top.

The officer should decide what will be included in the sketch before actually beginning to draw. Although it is important to include all relevant items, a common error is to be overly detailed. Only physical evidence items and large furniture items necessary for proper measurements should be included in the sketch. An officer need not be an accomplished artist to draw a proper crime scene sketch. The usefulness of the sketch depends on accurate measurements, not on how realistically the objects are drawn.

All measurements recorded in the crime scene sketch should be made from permanent objects. If movable objects are used, the value of the sketch is greatly decreased. For example, if a jury returned to a crime scene to verify the investigator's sketch and found that the objects used to position evidence had been moved, the reliability of the sketch would be open to question. Indoors, walls or corners serve well to locate items. Outdoors, such objects as trees, buildings, and telephone poles may be used.

Because the crime scene sketch often assumes great importance during a criminal trial, the investigator must verify all measurements. One acceptable method is to have a second officer remeasure the locations of all significant evidence. The investigator's on-the-scene rough sketch is usually in pencil, but the final sketch should always be rendered using a nonperishable medium, such as permanent ink.

Before the finished sketch is attached to the official crime report, the following data should be included:

1. the name of the investigator making the sketch, with identifying badge number;
2. a detailed location of the scene, including city, state, street address, and location of room within the building;
3. the date and time the sketch was made—time given for completion of the rough sketch, not the finished sketch;

4. the evidence listing, showing the location of important physical evidence by letter or number;
5. the case number of the investigation;
6. a directional arrow, or compass heading; and
7. the scale, or the words "not drawn to scale."

In regard to the last item, crime scene sketches may be drawn to scale or not to scale, depending on the judgment of the investigator. A scaled sketch accurately represents the measurements taken at the scene in relative proportion. When scales are used, it is important to select one that is suitable to the type of scene being recorded. Most sketches are drawn on normal 8-by-10 graph paper, using the following scales:

1. One-half inch equals one foot for a small-room sketch.
2. One-fourth inch equals one foot for a large-room sketch.
3. One-half inch equals ten feet for scenes located in large buildings.
4. One-fourth inch equals twenty feet for large outdoor scenes.

Some officers elect not to use a scaled crime scene sketch. Although scaled drawings give an accurately proportioned view of the scene, they are time consuming to prepare. Consequently, sketches that are not to scale are often used. Accurate measurements must be secured regardless of the lack of scale.

Computerized Sketches and Models.   The recent use of computers to assist investigators in diagraming a scene accurately has greatly enhanced the accuracy and ease of crime scene sketching. Many police agencies have adapted computer-aided design (CAD) programs to the crime scene process. Using this method, an officer can diagram a crime scene directly on the computer, illustrating the type and location of evidence from the program's inventory of commonly encountered items. Once the basic measurements of the scene are entered into the computer, the investigator can use the program to measure distances accurately from one evidence item to another. Other helpful features not possible in traditionally drawn sketches enable users to view the scene in complete perspective in addition to being able to pan around the scene or zoom to a close-up.[4]

The use of crime scene models is often necessary in complex or serious felony crime scenes. The manner in which evidence is presented during a trial can have a dramatic impact on the outcome of a trial. Although photos, videotapes, and crime scene renderings are important in documenting a scene, visual scale models have also proven to be extremely helpful. Although often costly, scale models effectively hold the attention of juries and assist the prosecution in several ways. Being three-dimensional, the model presents a dramatic and clear representation of the entire scene, allowing jurors to relate visually to incidents and evidence explained during the trial. Additionally, the model can be relocated to the deliberation room for use as an aid by the jury members.[5]

Accurate crime scene recording has also been enhanced through the use of laser technology. By employing laser light to measure a scene, the time needed to process the scene is greatly reduced while precise, detailed three-dimensional virtual models are created. Such systems are capable of producing 25,000 measurements per second as the laser beam sweeps the scene. When the beam strikes an object, it reflects back, recording both the location and the range of each encountered object. The investigator can then selectively collect a mass of geometrical data, including the coordinates of any location or the distance between any two points. The data create a virtual scene that can be retrieved at any time, producing distortion-free images that allow viewing from any direction or view perspective.[6]

Searching the Crime Scene

When confronted with strong evidence of client guilt, defense attorneys frequently attack the investigator's case at its weakest point. Unfortunately, as well illustrated by the O.J. Simpson murder trial, the attack often centers on the various phases of crime scene processing. If any element of crime scene investigation can be brought into question, such as the thoroughness of how the evidence was gathered or whether contamination was possible, an otherwise open-and-shut case can be ruined (see Figure 5.5). Investigators in the Multnomah County Sheriff's Office in Portland, Oregon, are properly concerned about scene contamination to the point of keeping a "contamination list" at every serious crime scene. The list is completed by the first officer at the scene and records the time of entry and departure as well as the reason for entering by all people at the scene, including family members, fire/rescue personnel, and other police officers. Additionally, officers are trained to allow access to indoor scenes through only one door, stationing an individual by the door to enforce compliance. Often unrealistically influenced by media portrayals, the general public has come to expect a near meticulous crime scene investigation. Investigators must be aware of the changing social expectations in this regard and take every precaution to ensure that guilty suspects do not escape justice as a result of crime scene work that was less than thorough.

The primary motivation for searching the crime scene is to locate evidence. The evidence may be obvious or not immediately apparent. Any article or material a suspect leaves at a crime scene or takes from the scene or

FIGURE 5.5   Dr. Henry Lee, former director of the Connecticut State Police Forensic Laboratory, processes a felony crime scene. Note that he wears fiber-free overalls and gloves to avoid crime scene contamination. *(Source: Connecticut State Police Forensic Laboratory.)*

that may be otherwise connected with the crime is considered to be evidence. Control and teamwork are at the heart of any successful crime scene search. The entire operation must be under the control of one individual. It may be an investigator or a uniformed officer of high rank. The officer in charge directs all searching activity—assigning various duties to other officers and making sure that there is no confusion. In some situations, the officer in charge may participate in the actual search; however, when a major crime has occurred, the assigning and directing responsibilities of the officer in charge preclude physical participation in the search by that officer.

The physical nature of the crime scene will generally suggest to the officer in charge what type of search will be effected. If the scene is indoors, the search will be limited by the size of the building or room. The outdoor scene will require a search method designed for large, unrestricted areas. Before the actual search of a crime scene begins, all concerned must be restrained in their tendency to rush into the search area. Investigators, too, are governed by human emotion and may become overly eager to process a scene. In their haste, such delicate evidence as bloodstains and foot impressions may be literally trampled into oblivion. The experienced officer always pauses and surveys the scene visually before physically moving in so as not to inadvertently damage any of the evidence.

One of the most common indoor methods of search is termed the **strip search method** (Figure 5.6A). The searcher starts at one end of the scene and walks directly across until the opposite end is reached. The searcher then turns and walks back toward the original end, searching not the same ground previously covered but to the right or left of the original path. The strip method can be completed using any number of searchers. Of course, the greater the number of searchers used in any method, the greater the probability for complete coverage. Another method used for both indoor and outdoor scenes is known as the **spiral search method** (Figure 5.6B). The spiral search usually begins from the outer perimeter of the scene, moving inward in a constricting circular fashion. This system is particularly suited for use by one individual in a small indoor scene.

Outdoor scenes or very spacious rooms require search methods designed especially to cover large areas. The **sector search method**

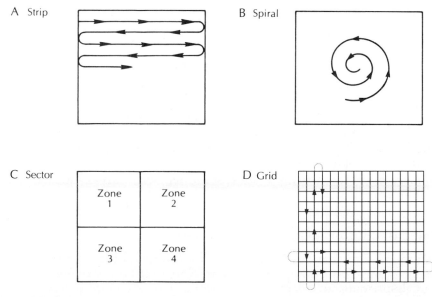

FIGURE 5.6 Search methods.

(Figure 5.6C) is frequently employed for this purpose. This method divides the scene into equal sectors, or zones. One searcher is normally assigned to each sector with responsibility for all that occurs there. The **grid search method** (Figure 5.6D) is very useful for large crime scenes or scenes that must be searched for small items of evidence in an extremely thorough fashion. The entire search area is crisscrossed by one or more investigators so that all areas are actually crossed several times. This search method was used to search effectively the site of an airplane crash. A PSA flight mysteriously crashed in California, killing all on board. Thousands of evidence fragments were scattered throughout a large rural outdoor scene. After recovering the flight recorder, investigators speculated that an armed passenger had possibly shot the crew, causing the disaster. A complete grid search was undertaken of the complex debris-covered scene, locating the suspect's weapon and suicide note.

An investigator is often cognizant of the probable type of crime that has occurred before the search begins. However, "jumping to conclusions" regarding the nature of a criminal offense should be avoided. By forming a preconceived notion, the officer may be unconsciously limiting the search effectiveness. For example, if the victim has a gunshot wound, the investigator may assume that only gun-related evidence may be present at the scene. This assumption may "blind" the searcher in locating other important physical evidence of a nonfirearm nature. It is very important to be aware that many crime scenes are deceiving as to what type of offense has actually occurred.

During the crime scene search, the investigator is likely to find **physical evidence**. Although the crime scene has been photographed before being searched, it still may be necessary to photograph newly found items. Such items should never be handled immediately. Before physical evidence is disturbed or altered, it should be recorded in regard to the following information:

1. time and date the evidence was found;
2. the location at which it was found;
3. the name of the investigator who located the evidence;
4. a description of the item;
5. identifying marks, if any, to further distinguish or individualize the item; and
6. the names of officers who witnessed the find, to add credibility to the investigator's statements during the trial.

The preceding information is recorded in the field notebook as soon as possible after the discovery. It bears repeating that all entries in the notebook should be made carefully, for if the notebook is introduced as evidence in court, it may be examined by the attorney representing the defendant.

All police officers recognize the importance of frequently encountered physical evidence, such as firearms and shell casings. Smaller items, such as chips of wood, hairs, paint flakes, and glass fragments, may also be very important, but they often escape detection. Both large and minute items of physical evidence must be thoroughly searched for at the scene. The investigator has no way of determining which evidence will have the greater significance at a later date. The ultimate purpose of recovering physical evidence is to aid in the solution of the offense by

1. establishing tracing, or identifying the suspect;
2. establishing the suspect's *modus operandi* (MO) or indicating similar MOs;
3. proving or disproving an alibi;
4. connecting or eliminating suspects;

5. identifying stolen property, contraband, and other illegal property;

6. identifying victims, if their identities are unknown;

7. providing investigative leads; and

8. proving a statutory element of the offense.

When evidence is found at the scene, the investigator must be able to account for it. Accounting responsibilities begin when the item is first located and do not end until the evidence reaches the courtroom. Being able to account for the location and possession of evidence is known as *maintaining the* **chain of custody**. This accountability procedure is very important, for if a break in the chain occurs, the item will not be admitted as evidence in court. When a handgun is found at the scene of a criminal offense, the investigator carefully records where and how it was found and transports the item to police headquarters. The handgun is then transferred to an evidence room for safekeeping. When the gun is placed in the evidence room, a formal written receipt is made of this transfer. Any time the evidence is moved or transferred, receipts are obtained. By following strict accountability procedures, the chain of custody remains intact.

Evidence Collection

The collection of physical evidence is basically a two-step procedure. The investigator first searches for and collects all large, obvious items. Following this initial collection, the smaller items of physical evidence are collected. By dividing the collection process, a more thorough search is effected (see Figure 5.7). The modern crime scene can be a two-edged sword in that evidence must be thoroughly located, recorded, and processed yet handled as little as possible to avoid contamination.

The methods used by the investigator in collecting physical evidence vary according to the item encountered. All objects of solid form must be handled with great care. This is due to the possibility of obliterating fingerprints that may be on the object. Depending on the officer's discretion, evidence will either

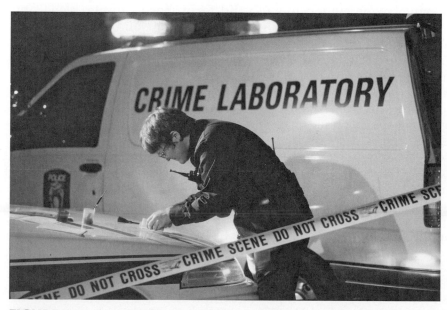

FIGURE 5.7 An investigator records, examines, and packages evidence at an outdoor crime scene. *(Source: Ron Chapple / Ron Chapple Photography.)*

be processed for latent fingerprints at the scene or transported for this purpose to a crime laboratory. All officers at the crime scene involved in evidence collection should take care not to alter the scene by leaving their own fingerprints. This rather obvious but occasionally overlooked problem is easily remedied. Each officer should wear gloves that are clean and of lightweight material, such as white cotton. If, for some reason, gloves are not available at the scene, a clean, flexible material may be wrapped around the investigator's hands to function as gloves.

During the phase of the search involving small types of physical evidence, the officer must constantly keep in mind that even the most minute object may be significant. Fibers, hairs, liquids, bodily fluids, and latent fingerprints are regularly encountered at crime scenes. When minute items are located, they should be picked up with considerable care. Metal tweezers or forceps are often used to pick up minute solid items with minimum disturbance. Care must be taken not to scratch or damage the item or otherwise alter its original condition.

Marking Evidence

After an item of evidence is located and recorded in field notes, it must be properly marked. It is a legal requirement that all solid evidence be inscribed for future identification. The marking of evidence occurs during the searching phase as each item of evidence is located and collected. The type of mark placed on the object depends on the following factors:

1. the size of the object,
2. the physical nature of the object (e.g., solid or liquid),
3. the value of the object, and
4. the number of like objects.

If the evidence object is of sufficient size, the markings should include the case number, date, time, and initials of the marker. However, not all evidence is large enough to bear numerous markings. Evidence too small to be marked directly must be placed in a container and the exterior surface of the container marked.

Not all crime scene evidence is of solid form. For example, blood and other bodily fluids and some types of narcotics are nonsolid evidence items frequently present at a crime scene. Obviously, the fluid or semifluid type of evidence cannot be marked directly. If this is attempted, contamination will occur. Such evidence must be carefully packaged in airtight containers (e.g., cellophane bags or glass vials). All pertinent information is then marked directly on the container, using an indelible marking instrument.

During the course of an investigation, the officer may encounter evidence that is of great value monetarily. For example, rare art objects, valuable firearms, and other expensive items may be recovered during theft investigations. In marking such items as evidence, consideration should be shown as to where the markings are placed. It is generally possible to find a place for marking that is not too obvious. For example, an expensive firearm may be properly marked on an area covered by the wooden stock.

It is common for certain types of items to be numerous. Some investigations can yield several thousand pieces of evidence, such as large drug quantities recovered during a narcotics raid. If the officer does not wish to mark all the items recovered or if the marking is physically impossible, they may be packaged collectively in a single container. All of the items must be accurately counted, however, and the total number marked on the outside surface of the container.

Packaging Evidence

Some of the evidence recovered at the crime scene may consist of highly breakable items that must be securely packaged. Frequently, the packaging must be completed at the crime scene, although in some situations, the physical evidence can be packaged at police headquarters. Evidence is packaged mainly to be sent to a forensic laboratory for analysis. If the evidence is to arrive at the laboratory in proper condition, the following rules should always be observed:

1. Evidence to be analyzed should be packaged in separate containers.
2. Clean packaging materials should be used.
3. A strong sealing material should be used to enclose the package.
4. Cloth items should not be folded unnecessarily.
5. If evidence is found at the scene within a container, it should be left in the original container to be transported.
6. A letter of transmittal stating what type of analysis is needed must be included.
7. The evidence should always be sent registered mail, with a receipt secured.

Evidence Staging and Personation

A final general principle relates to the detection of deceptive crime scenes and observing other scenes that personalize the criminal suspect. Although most scenes are not purposely altered to mislead the investigator, a significant number are. All crime scenes tell a story to the perceptive criminal investigator, but **staging** attempts to redirect the investigation away from logical truth. Staged crime scenes are generally accomplished to protect the victim or immediate family or to steer the inquiry away from the most logical suspect. Staged scenes are commonly encountered in false burglaries or robberies, often to try to explain missing money or valuables that have been used for illegal or vice-related purposes. Other similar misleading attempts may be related to death investigations involving suicides or accidental deaths that are sexually connected. Such cases are frequently altered to appear as criminal homicides because of embarrassment linked to the true cause of death. Staged crime scenes should become apparent through various inconsistencies present at the scene. Additionally, the scene may not correspond to the explanation given by the suspect. A scene in which tables and chairs have been turned over for no apparent reason or a window has been pried open from inside may be a staged burglary. Although the investigator must use care not to upset legitimate crime victims by an unreasonably suspicious attitude, he or she must be alert for inconsistencies and contradictions that become apparent during the processing of the crime scene. Staged scenes should not be confused with **equivocal scenes**. Equivocal scenes are open to interpretation because of natural conditions or circumstances rather than purposeful efforts to deceive. An investigator may enter a death scene and find a deceased victim with a knife in her chest. While no staging was accomplished, the death may intially be explained by two or more interpretations. It may have resulted from accidental, suicidal, or homicidal means, but until further investigation reveals the true cause, it will remain equivocal.[7]

If a criminal suspect imparts unique personality traits by actions or evidence at a crime scene, a process of **personation** has occurred. Violent crime scenes in particular have a high probability of containing indicators of individual personality. Criminal homicide, sexual assault, robbery, and other crimes reflect personality through behavior resulting from extreme emotion and

INVESTIGATIVE PROFILE

Marion Brady
Crime Scene Investigator
North Las Vegas Police Department
North Las Vegas, Nevada

Like many people in the Las Vegas area, I'm originally from somewhere else. My family moved here from New Jersey when I was a teenager, and I eventually attended the University of Nevada at Reno planning to go into corporate law. But since my interest in becoming an attorney wasn't all that intense, I took a career placement exam that predicted I'd do very well as either a military officer or a police officer. With this in mind, I was soon taking criminal justice classes, which I loved, and after a ride along with the Reno police, I knew law enforcement was a match. I changed my major from political science to criminal justice and obtained an internship with the Washoe County Sheriff's Department, leading to a position as a reserve deputy sheriff. When I graduated, I joined this agency full time and spent five interesting years as a deputy sheriff. I then secured a lateral position as a police officer with my present employer, the North Las Vegas Police Department. Many people don't realize that the greater Las Vegas area actually has four separate urban police agencies, with our agency employing over 300 sworn officers.

I then spent five years as a patrol officer in North Las Vegas before promoting to crime scene investigator (CSI) in 1997. Even from the beginning of my career when I was a patrol deputy, I'd been just fascinated with crime scenes. I spent as much time assisting the CSI people as I could and always asked tons of questions. So when the opportunity presented itself, I happily transferred into the Investigative Bureau and underwent the 400-hour training program for new CSI personnel. Now, over eight years later, I've had over 4,000 hours of crime scene training, and I'm one of the department trainers regarding crime scene investigation. Our agency has eight CSIs, five of whom are civilians and three sworn police officers like myself. I've worked approximately 200 homicides and attempted murders, 1,000 burglaries, and nearly 90 sexual assaults and made at least 25,000 fingerprint comparisons. Not long ago I was fortunate enough to attend the National Forensic Academy in Tennessee, which is a ten-week intensive course of study concentrating on forensics and crime scene processing. The training included everything from class lectures to processing actual bodies in various stages of outdoor decomposition. One of the training exercises simulated a plane crash caused by a weapon of mass destruction. An aircraft cabin was actually exploded with human forms made of ballistic gelatin so we could realistically process scattered body parts.

I look forward to my work each and every day. It is the challenge of the crime scene that fascinates me, as I enjoy discovering what can be learned from evidence, which of course cannot speak but must be found and interpreted. I also enjoy testifying in court regarding my actions at crime scenes and particularly like breaking down confusing scientific jargon into everyday words and concepts the average juror can comprehend. The demands of the job are of course many. Sometimes I'm overwhelmed at complex scenes, as there may not be enough people to help. This can be particularly true when there are multiple crime scenes happening at once in different parts of the community. Once I was working a fatal traffic accident during a blazing hot August day and then had to rush over to a double homicide on the opposite side of town. It was over 115 degrees, and between the two scenes I spent the entire day out in the sun. I ended up in the hospital with heat stroke and passed multiple crystallized kidney stones due to the intense dehydration.

The television CSI image is amusing, but it has generated a lot of positive interest in forensics and crime scene processing. Of course we can't solve complex cases in an hour like on television, and most CSI people don't interrogate suspects and run around arresting them. These duties are generally performed by the detectives. But my cases are endlessly interesting, with never a dull moment, and so professionally challenging. People do the strangest things, resulting in some really strange crime scenes. For example, there was this case in which a guy contracted AIDS and gave it to his girlfriend. When she found out he had infected her, she shot him to death. After leaving his body in the bedroom for three days, she enlisted the aid of her daughter to dispose of the body. They wrapped him in trash bags and jammed his body headfirst into a large plastic bucket-like container. They then dug through a concrete patio slab and buried the bucket in a four-foot hole. Many months passed, and the daughter, who had moved to California, confessed her crime to a minister who had her contact the police. When I processed this scene, it was a real challenge, as it was not only a criminal homicide scene but also something like an archaeological dig. Great care had to be taken as we processed each layer of dirt, clothing, and the badly decomposed body.

Criminal justice students who want to go into CSI work need to prepare themselves by taking forensic science courses or various courses in the natural sciences. Previously being a police officer is not necessary in many police departments like it used to be, but it certainly helps. But they'll never regret getting into this specialty. For we speak for the victims by processing these crime scenes. I've been able to prove child abuse by locating a bloody hair on a wall where a baby's head has been slammed, and I've identified fugitive murderers through fingerprint comparison who had been arrested for minor crimes under a false name. It is a very satisfying job, and I have no intention of ever doing anything else.

deviant psychology inherent in planning and committing such crimes. Officers should be alert to any unusual behaviors by suspects beyond that necessary to commit the criminal offense, as such actions are true indicators of personation. By removing only certain items from a scene or positioning the murder victim in a unique fashion, the suspect symbolically imparts unique identifying meaning to the scene. When serial, or recurring, offenders engage in repetitive, ritualistic acts at numerous scenes, their conduct can be termed signature actions.[8]

CRIME SCENE EQUIPMENT

The equipment needed for proper crime scene processing is of the utmost importance. The investigator who arrives at a scene without the essential tools for collection, marking, and packaging of evidence will undoubtedly be in a considerable predicament. **Crime scene equipment kits** (Figure 5.8) should be prepared and available to all officers. These kits should be stored in a readily accessible area and contain standard equipment used for processing the majority of scenes.

All crime scene equipment kits contain the tools necessary for processing latent fingerprints. Because large numbers of small items are generally encountered at crime scenes, a wide variety of containers must be on hand. Paper envelopes are commonly used to hold solid items of physical evidence,

FIGURE 5.8 A fully equipped crime scene kit. (*Source: Sirchie Fingerprint Laboratories.*)

whereas glass vials are essential for liquids. There must never be any question as to the absolute cleanliness of the containers. If it can be proved that a container was contaminated with a foreign material before the evidence was placed within, the item may not be admissible during the trial. It is unwise to use containers constructed from metal because of the contamination possibilities. Any container the investigator decides to use must be able to be sealed in an airtight manner.

The tools the investigator chooses to bring to each crime scene are often a matter of personal preference. Some investigators have at their disposal every crime scene tool imaginable. Officers who are members of small departments with limited budgets must be highly selective in purchasing crime scene equipment. The following crime scene tools are absolutely necessary for even the most basic indoor or outdoor scenes:

1. camera and adequate film supply;
2. lighting equipment;
3. assorted tape measures and rulers;
4. latent fingerprint equipment (see Chapter 17);
5. gloves;
6. forceps or metal tweezers;
7. a small pair of scissors;
8. a small saw;
9. an assortment of filter paper or sterile swabs used to collect liquid evidence;
10. marking instruments;
11. evidence containers of varying types;
12. evidence tape with which to seal evidence containers;
13. casting materials for the preparation and taking of molds and casts; also, rubber containers for the mix;
14. a magnifying device (subject to ridicule in fiction but nonetheless highly functional in reality); and
15. personal protection items to be used within crime scenes where the possibility of infectious disease is suspected (e.g., disposable boots, gowns, masks, and protective eyewear).

The preceding list covers items that are generally necessary. Certain types of offenses, however, require such specialized equipment as metal detectors, narcotic test kits, vacuum sweepers, and other devices. With increased crime scene processing experience, the investigator will be able to predict what equipment is needed for a particular crime and the frequency of its use. Many police agencies have converted vans into specialized crime scene response vehicles. A fully equipped crime scene van allows technicians and investigators immediate access to a large variety of equipment necessary to process most major felonies.

Specialized Crime Scene Personnel

Although all police officers are trained to process crime scenes to some degree, many serious, unusual, or complex scenes will require the skill of specialized personnel. Crime scenes are generally processed by three types of individuals: law enforcement officers (patrol officers or detectives), crime scene investigators (CSIs), and criminality. Since most crime scenes are neither unusually serious crimes like homicide or rape nor beyond the skill level of most experienced investigators, CSI technicians and criminality are typically not present. However, specialists are summoned when the investigator or supervisors deem a scene to justify their expertise. It is far more common for CSI staff to process such scenes than lab-bound criminality. Contrary to fictional television shows, criminality rarely leave their crime laboratories. Possessing advanced graduate degrees, criminality are hired to conduct various laboratory procedures on evidence sent or brought to them. While they do occasionally testify in court as to the results of their laboratory work, they usually delegate crime scene procession to others.

Although some detectives are cross trained to be crime scene investigators, most CSI personnel are full-time crime scene specialists. They are highly trained to protect, record, search, and recover physical evidence. While they have a detailed knowledge of evidence-testing methods used by criminality, they do not conduct laboratory forensic procedures after transporting evidence to the criminalist. Because of various fictional media presentations, CSI work has been glamorized far beyond the realism of their important work. Movie and television presentations typically compact CSI staff and criminality into one person and falsely show forensic personnel interrogating and arresting suspects. Such tasks are nearly always performed by patrol or detective personnel. Additionally, the popularity and glamor of such shows have created a negative situation commonly referred to as the **CSI effect**. This pertains to unrealistic jury expectations that can cause difficulty in successful trial prosecutions. Since CSI television plots revolve around forensic evidence being recovered and quickly solving all cases, real juries may fail to realize that most prosecutions are actually based on nonforensic circumstantial evidence. Falsely believing that the lack of DNA, fired bullets, hairs and fibers, or other forms of trace evidence automatically equates to reasonable doubt, jurors may illogically fail to convict because of the effect of televised fiction.

▲ SUMMARY

The crime scene has tremendous potential in solving or aiding criminal investigations. Waiting at every scene are evidentiary clues that invite discovery. If each officer uses the proper crime scene methodology that has been developed by a century of trial and error, consistent and successful evidence discovery will result. To summarize precisely why it is vital to focus on the crime scene during a criminal investigation, the words of the presiding judge in *Harris v. United States* are particularly applicable:

> Wherever he steps, whatever he touches, whatever he leaves, even unconsciously, will serve as silent evidence against him. Not only his fingerprints or his footprints, but his hair, the fibers from his clothing, the glass he breaks, the toolmark he leaves, the paint he scratches, the blood or semen that he deposits or collects—all these and more bear mute witness against him. This is evidence that does not forget. It is not confused by the excitement of the moment. It is not absent because human witnesses are. It is factual evidence. Physical evidence cannot be wrong; it cannot perjure itself; it cannot be wholly absent. Only its interpretation can err. Only human failure to find it, study and understand it, can diminish its value.[9]

The scene of a crime traditionally provides the investigator with numerous opportunities for case solution. Historically, crime scenes were not nearly as significant as they now are to the investigative process. Judicial review, technology, and police professionalism have combined to increase the importance of physical evidence, resulting in a corresponding decrease in the value of the confession. In past decades, the confession alone was often enough to secure a conviction. Contemporary court rulings generally insist on additional supporting evidence for a determination of guilt.

Crime scene investigation is a sequential process, involving carefully thought-out actions that follow one another in a logical order. Although the first concern upon arrival at the scene is to treat the injured and arrest suspects, protection of the area is an immediate responsibility. As evidence of great importance may be located within the scene, protection will prevent any alteration or contamination that could devalue the evidence item. In addition to allowing the location, recording, and collecting of evidence, crime scenes aid the investigator in reconstructing the criminal event. Accordingly, the position and movements of those involved can often be determined by a thorough investigation of the scene.

The true dimensions of a crime scene can be deceptive; most are actually much larger than they appear. Although most crime scenes are indoor locations, outdoor scenes pose a particular challenge because of the associated potential for contamination and loss of control. Once the crime scene dimensions have been determined and protection achieved, a sequential processing begins. The first phase involves a limited search and complete recording through photography and sketching. Although crime scene photos are essential to illustrate the locality in a realistic fashion, sketches of the scene show precise measurements—important information that cannot be achieved through photography alone. A complete search of the area is necessary to locate evidence. A professional search requires considerable organization and control of personnel as well as a method of searching that ensures thorough coverage of the scene.

As evidence is located within the crime scene, care must be taken to maintain the judicial integrity of each item. Through a process informally known as the chain of evidence or custody, investigators must be able in later judicial proceedings to account for the location and possession of evidence from the time of discovery onward. As evidence is located, it must be properly marked, packaged, and transported to an evidence collection room. Great care must be maintained throughout this process to avoid damaging the evidence. Some law enforcement agencies employ criminalists or specially trained crime scene technicians to process crime scenes, but the majority of agencies continue to utilize officers assigned to patrol and investigative responsibilities.

EXERCISES

1. Practice photographic methods that are applicable to indoor and outdoor crime scenes.
2. Select a room in your home and draw it as an indoor crime scene sketch.
3. Practice marking and packaging solid evidence objects.
4. Assemble a basic crime scene processing kit or visit a local police agency and examine its crime scene equipment.
5. Interview a local criminal investigator concerning common crime scene problems that are encountered.
6. Participate in a group project in which half of the group members construct a mock crime scene and the others process the scene in accordance with the principles learned.

RELEVANT WEB SITES

http://www.forensicdata.com/homicidecrime.htm

Illustrates how computer images are created through the use of known trajectory points to re-create and demonstrate suspect and victim movements at crime scenes and accident sites. Computer re-creations demonstrate sequence of events, distance and angles of shots fired, and relative locations of individuals at scenes.

http://www.crime-scene-investigator.net/index.html

Extensive collection of crime scene essays by law enforcement professionals pertaining to evidence collection guidelines and the recording and preservation of physical evidence.

http://www.drhenrylee.com/home.shtml

Official home page of leading forensic scientist Dr. Henry Lee, with links discussing crime scene processing at his many famous cases. Includes a forensic lab tour.

Interviewing

KEY TERMS

coercion
cognitive interview
denial
duress
emotionally affected victim
Escobedo decision
Gault decision
hypnosis
interview
interrogation
legal stipulation
Miranda decision

Miranda warning
narcoanalysis
obsessive-compulsive
paranoid
polygraph
psychopath
psychotic
victim compensation
videotaping
voice polygraph
witness protection units

LEARNING OBJECTIVES

1. to appreciate the importance of verbal skills to the successful criminal investigation;
2. to be able to list the factors that contribute to the difficulty of the information-gathering process;
3. to be familiar with phases and procedures associated with the victim interview;
4. to be familiar with phases and procedures associated with the witness interview;
5. to be able to list the factors that influence the reliability of victim and witness interviews;
6. to be able to contrast the suspect interview and the victim/witness interview;
7. to be aware of the legal requirements of the suspect interview;
8. to understand the application of various questioning techniques to specific personality types;
9. to be aware of aspects of the juvenile interview; and
10. to appreciate criminalistic contributions to the interview process.

INTRODUCTION

Although many skills and talents are required of the criminal investigator, the ability to obtain information verbally ranks paramount. Verbal communication with victims, witnesses, suspects, and others is certainly one of the most vital aspects of the investigator's work and one that demands constant involvement; thus, it has become a generally accepted principle that good interviewing ability is the mark of a successful investigator. Police questioning of individuals has been divided, by tradition, into two formal categories: interviewing and interrogation. The **interview** has been associated with the questioning of those not suspected as law violators.[1] **Interrogation**, on the other hand, has been used in connection with the questioning of suspected law violators. In this chapter, the two definitions are merged under one broad subject heading—*interviewing*. The term *interrogation* has come to acquire a negative connotation that is misleading but persistent. In the minds of far too many, the term conjures up the image of a "third-degree" approach—a darkened room in which a confession is forced from an unfortunate individual by brutal and coercive means. For this reason, it is recommended that investigators refer to all police questionings as interviews. This is particularly suggested on reports, which are frequently cited, and for courtroom testimony. Defense attorneys, upon hearing an investigator refer to questioning as an interrogation, may seize upon this usage to influence the jury to the defendant's advantage.

An interview may be defined as a communication involving two or more people for the purpose of obtaining information. The information-gathering process will vary in difficulty in direct proportion to the following factors:

1. cooperative attitude of the subject,
2. perceptive ability of the subject,
3. skill of the investigator,
4. emotional state of the subject, and
5. legal knowledge of the investigator.

The degree to which a subject is cooperative is of the greatest importance in the interview situation. Individuals have different reasons for hesitating to cooperate. These vary from a fear of being apprehended for direct participation in the crime to "not wanting to get involved." Many individuals can view the same criminal offense and differ widely in relating what they perceived. The human condition is that our interpretation of events is colored by such factors as our personal interests and emotional makeup. Finally, the skill and training of the officer, coupled with sound legal knowledge, are essential to the successful interview.

VICTIM INTERVIEWS

Of the various types of interviews, those involving victims are the most common. The victim interview may be relatively simple or a prolonged and difficult experience demanding maximum skill from the officer. The emotional state of the victim will determine the degree of difficulty. The majority of victim interviews involve people who have been victimized by some form of theft and who have not been in contact with the perpetrator. A smaller number will involve individuals emotionally affected by direct contact with the criminal. Regardless of the emotional state of the victim or the nature of the offense, the victim interview is conducted in a three-step process. The first step of the interview involves thorough preparation by the investigator. Because the police interview always has a purpose, to gather information or determine guilt, careful research before any conversation is desirable. Although it is not always possible, the officer should determine the following before actually interviewing the victim: (a) the nature of the crime, (b) the identity and background of the victim, and (c) the emotional state of the victim.

Since many criminal investigations are initially handled by patrol personnel, the investigator's interview with the victim may take place hours or even days after the crime was committed. The preliminary report prepared by the patrol officer provides the investigator with much-needed information. The type of crime, details of the offense, and basic victim information are included in this initial report. Also of importance are the patrol officer's judgments that are not included in the written report. In attempting to establish the background and emotional/mental state of the victim, sources other than the formal report must be consulted. Once the victim's name, address, and other standard identifying information are obtained, a file search should be completed. Police agency records should be checked for past complaints and all other information linked to the particular victim in question. It should not be implied that the investigation is more concerned with the background of the victim than with the identity of the offender; however, no investigation is complete unless all areas that might yield pertinent information, including the victim's past, have been researched. For example, if a file check reveals numerous similar crime reports involving the victim in which his or her statements have been determined as unfounded because of a suspected mental illness, this information would be useful to the investigator for the current interview.

The second step of the victim interview is the actual face-to-face questioning. The questioning process will vary in minor details but will generally involve many "retellings." It is a rare interview in which the victim gives his or her account in one complete version. The questioning techniques used by the investigator generally are determined by the emotional condition of the victim.

The final step of the victim interview is the conclusion, or the closing attitude left with the subject. The manner in which the interview is closed is highly important and will be detailed in the discussion dealing with witness interviews.

The Emotionally Affected Victim

Ideally, criminal investigators should interview all victims, regardless of the type of crime or extent of contact with the perpetrator. Actually, however, the volume of reported crime allows investigators the time to interview only a small portion of the total number of victims. Victims who have seen the offender but who have not experienced direct contact will be questioned in the same manner as witnesses. Criminal offenses of a felony nature, in which the victim has been in contact with the offender, always involve the questioning process. But these victims need special consideration by the investigator. Direct-contact situations involve verbal or physical actions directed against the victim. The victim's emotional reaction to such direct contact may complicate the interview process.

Unless one has been a victim of a serious crime, it is difficult to appreciate the emotional and psychological problems that may result. An individual returning home to discover a burglary normally experiences a period of anger, fear, and anxiety. Such feelings will generally diminish, and in a relatively short period of time, the victim will regain normal emotional composure. But the victim who has direct contact with an offender, such as the rape or robbery victim, frequently undergoes emotional reactions that are long term and often severe. The officer must understand why these reactions occur and appreciate the emotional dilemma in which victims find themselves. Contact with a criminal during the commission of a crime affects individuals differently. Yet psychologists have demonstrated that most people react in a standard manner following their victimization during a criminal offense. The human condition initially denies a shocking or painful experience.[2] "I can't believe this has happened" or "this just can't be" are expressions the investigator may hear as victims attempt to deny an emotionally shocking experience. It is important that the investigator refrain from forcing the victim to confront the reality of certain situations. Demanding that a victim acknowledge that the assault or rape actually occurred may cause that victim serious psychological problems. The preferable course of action is to demonstrate an understanding of the pain and humiliation suffered by the victim. The officer may decide to postpone the interview to allow the passage of time to dull the victim's **denial** efforts.

Another common reaction to criminal contact is extreme frustration. This frustration may take the form of anger toward themselves and/or toward others. This is particularly common with victims of sex crimes because of the social stigma associated with rape, indecent exposure, and similar offenses. These people may feel that their actions somehow contributed to their being singled out as victims. This inward blaming could make the interview difficult, as the victim may attempt to alter answers to relieve guilt. If this type of emotional reaction is noted, the investigator should assure the victim that his or her actions did not contribute to the crime. Other victims may express their frustration by condemning the police. The investigator should not take offense; the accusations are part of a natural reaction. The criminal is not present, the victim does not want to take the blame, so the police authorities become a convenient scapegoat. In this situation, the officer should demonstrate understanding by acknowledging the emotional stress of the victim. The victim who accuses the police of allowing crime—specifically, his or her victimization—desperately needs an outlet for frustration and blame, however misdirected it may be.

Victims of particularly violent crimes in which their lives may have been threatened have experienced such fear that they may hesitate to blame the criminal. This psychological reaction is common to victims of kidnapping; fear of death blocks the victim's acknowledgment of the kidnapper as a threat to minimize the frightening reality of the situation. Fortunately, it is only a matter of time until the victim psychologically realizes that he or she is safe and can focus on the criminal in proper perspective. When most people are physically threatened or feel a sense of personal danger, their value as accurate observers diminishes. Experienced police officers have often noted that descriptions of suspects with weapons are poor at best. This is because individuals confronted with a threatening object such as a gun or knife tend to focus on the weapon as the source of danger. Therefore, the investigator should not totally rely on physical descriptions of suspects from victims who have been threatened in this manner.

The emotional state of the victim during the interview may be misleading. Two victims experiencing contact with a suspect in an identical manner may react quite differently. One victim may be completely hysterical, whereas the other appears to be completely calm, often showing no emotion at all. Outward appearances are often deceiving, for it may be that the calm victim has experienced more emotional disturbance than the hysterical victim. For this reason, it is unwise to jump to conclusions based on outward victim appearance. In many situations, a victim who was totally calm during repeated questioning sessions becomes emotionally undone upon encountering the suspect during a trial. Criminal investigators fulfill a very important role interviewing the emotionally affected victim—they serve to provide immediate direct therapy to the victim. Their intervention in the victim's emotional crisis with helping techniques provides needed support at a crucial time. Although investigators are not specifically trained to be psychological counselors, the victim interview demands their best guidance efforts. A U.S. Department of Justice study of 3,000 individuals in the Milwaukee area revealed that the most commonly experienced problems of crime victims are mental or emotional suffering and property loss.[3]

Possibly the most difficult of all emotionally affected interviews are those that concern subjects who are suffering extreme grief. Many types of criminal investigations involve victims or others who are directly involved in the grieving process. Relatives of homicide victims, witnesses or friends of suicide subjects, rape victims, and many others typically experience the seven common stages associated with extreme psychological loss. Initially, the subject will experience the previously discussed emotions of shock, denial, and anger. However, those suffering from extreme grief frequently exhibit four additional stages as they react to the criminal event. Following the anger so common to many victims, a subject may exhibit signs of extreme depression or progress into a stage of detachment from others. These are serious psychological difficulties for many victims because in extreme cases they may lead to suicide. Accordingly, proper intervention is essential, requiring prompt referral to trained mental health professionals. As the individual works through the grieving process, the final two stages of dialogue and acceptance should become evident. The ability and willingness to talk about the disturbing event can be focused on the investigator or others and is a healthy signal that the person is accepting his unfortunate victimization.

To be a crime victim in the United States is expensive. The cost of emotional suffering cannot be measured in terms of dollars and cents; however, according to a recent study by the National Institute of Justice, personal crime accounts for $105 billion annually in medical costs, lost earnings, and public program costs related to victim assistance. Violent crime alone costs individuals and the general public billions in mental health care, as 20 percent of all psychological health care in the United States is attributable to treating victims of crime.[4] This high dollar loss associated with crime has prompted some states to institute **victim compensation** legislation, which is designed to assist victims financially—normally those victimized by serious personal crime.

WITNESS INTERVIEWS

The witness has proven to be both a blessing and a problem to the criminal justice system. Witnesses are absolutely essential to our investigative process, for they often provide descriptions that result in an arrest. They are crucial to our judicial system, as well, for they provide testimony that is frequently instrumental in securing a conviction. Yet, historically, the eyewitness has been a most unreliable source of evidence. Every police officer can recall situations in which individuals were "absolutely positive" in identifying a suspect, only to be proven wrong at a later date. For example, one Los Angeles investigation of a bank robbery suspect resulted in a conviction based mainly on eyewitness identification by no less than seven witnesses. Following the conviction, it was proven that the suspect could not possibly have committed the crime, demonstrating the inaccuracy of each of the seven witnesses. The witness occupies a dubious position in our justice system—considered essential yet viewed with mistrust.

A witness is defined as one who sees or knows by personal presence and perception. Our legal system, in a further effort to qualify the reliability of witness testimony, has assigned three general requirements:

1. that the witness was conscious during the event,
2. that the witness was physically present during the event, and
3. that the witness was psychologically and mentally attentive.

These requirements—consciousness, presence, and attentiveness—are reviewed at several stages during the justice process. Initially, it is the task of the investigator to interview the witness in an effort to ascertain that these qualifications are met. It is important that this be accomplished early in the investigation, for it may prove damaging to the prosecution if the defense reveals the lack of one or more reliability requirements later on. To determine if a witness is reliable, the officer should have a basic knowledge of factors that influence the accuracy of perception (see Figure 6.1). The varying degrees of accuracy with which people, objects, and events are perceived depend on the following:

1. physiological abilities,
2. external factors,
3. emotional involvement, and
4. personal screening.

People, objects, and events are perceived through the five senses, sight and hearing being the most important in judging witness reliability. The visual accuracy of eyewitness testimony is very important and is frequently scrutinized during a trial. Therefore, the officer must determine, at the outset, the visual ability of the witness. Does the witness have normal eyesight? If not, was the witness wearing corrective lenses at the time the event in question took place? Hearing, or the aural sense, is often of equal importance to testimony reliability. The exact words used by an offender can serve to determine the method of operation and facilitate identification during a lineup. The importance of determining the degree to which the witness can see or hear accurately cannot be overemphasized. The officer should make a determination by direct questions to the witness and confirm answers with relatives, friends, and doctors.

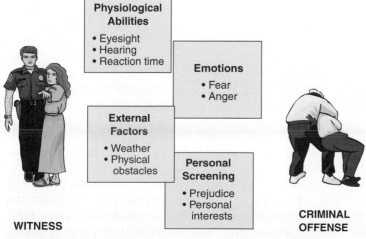

FIGURE 6.1 Factors influencing witness observation.

Of all the various factors that can influence the reliability of witness testimony, external conditions may be the most critically examined in the courtroom. External factors are conditions not intrinsic to the individual but that affect his or her ability to acquire and relate information. The weather conditions during the event, the distance of the witness from the event, and the obstacles between the witness and the event are all considered external conditions. Every statement the officer believes will have an important bearing on the case should be considered with regard to external obstacles. Even when the witness is certain that no external factor interfered, a return to the scene for confirmation is in order. It is not uncommon for juries to visit a crime scene in an attempt to determine an angle of sight or obstructions that could invalidate the credibility of the witness. During witness questioning, detailed time and light conditions should be noted. The time of day, the extent of artificial light, and weather conditions all have a bearing on the accuracy of perception.

Just as the victim is emotionally affected by a crime, so too is the witness. The emotional state of the witness is another factor influencing reliability of perceived events. The inaccuracy of people functioning under emotional stress is well documented. When individuals are in fearful situations, their powers of observation diminish significantly. In a calm, normal state, free of external or internal stress, observation tends to be the most accurate. Witnesses normally have little or no expectation that they are about to observe an emotionally shocking event; they are generally caught off guard. An inexperienced investigator may be incredulous that a witness who has observed an armed robber for five minutes at a distance of ten feet is unable to testify even to the race of the robber. Yet this situation is not uncommon. It is a natural reaction for most people to fixate on a threatening object, such as a gun, and totally ignore the physical features of the person holding the firearm.

Other emotions besides fear can alter witness testimony. Extreme anger, disgust, and prejudice can likewise affect perceptive ability. When individuals are angry to the point of rage, they may screen out all spoken words while focusing on the object of their anger. Furthermore, prejudiced individuals may distort facts to suit preconceived biases. This situation is often encountered in investigations involving racially prejudiced witnesses or victims. All of us practice personal screening to some degree in our everyday lives. A shoe clerk will tend to observe the type and quality of shoes a person is wearing. A firearms collector will focus on the type and condition of a gun more intently than the average person. Personal interests and experiences may hinder the questioning process, or they may work to its benefit. By focusing on a particular item, a witness may ignore other factors of importance. On the other hand, a professional soldier with lengthy combat experience may perceive a violent crime quite accurately—his training, experience, and stress conditioning boost the accuracy of his perception far above that of the typical witness.

Witness interviews are conducted in a three-step process, as are victim and suspect questionings. Each major step of the preparation, questioning, and closing has additional subtasks associated with it that must be completed. The preparation phase of witness interviewing involves considerable foresight on the part of the investigator in attempting to anticipate situations that may complicate the task and taking steps to avoid them. For example, witnesses should always be separated before the actual questioning. Individuals have a tendency to be influenced by others to a surprising degree. If one witness who has accurately observed a crime converses with five witnesses with inaccurate observations, the single witness is very likely to alter testimony to conform to the prevailing view. Research detailing human information retention levels confirms the importance of victim and/or witness separation. While people retain only 30 percent of what they see, they will retain 60 percent of what they discuss with others (see Table 6.1). Since what is discussed may be false, it is critical to separate witnesses before accurate observations become altered by misleading information.[5] In preparing for witness questioning, the time and place of the interview should be selected to accommodate the witness. Since most people feel more comfortable in familiar surroundings, the home of the witness is generally preferred over the formal surroundings of the police agency.

During the interview questioning stage, the investigator will initially ask the witness to tell what happened. It is advisable to let the witness relate the complete experience without interruption. The witness has been waiting in anticipation to reveal the story—often for several hours, sometimes for days. Because many people feel apprehensive when confronted by a law enforcement officer, they are often tense during the initial stage of the interview. This tension is often relieved by letting them tell the story fully, without interruption.

Most witnesses are not intimidated by note-taking on the investigator's part. In fact, the witness normally expects this note-taking—it concurs with the media image of the investigator. During the initial telling of the event, the officer should make basic notes. After the initial telling, the notes serve as a guide for the detailed statement. To obtain the final, detailed statement, any number of retellings by the witness may be necessary. During the questioning, the investigator should constantly bear in mind the requirements for a reliable witness. Questions should be asked to be sure these requirements are satisfied or to demonstrate that the witness is unreliable.

The investigator frequently must use discretion during witness questioning—for example, in selecting the questioning technique that would be most successful. Some witnesses are in need of constant questioning for each statement they make. They may feel unsure of themselves, giving vague answers so the investigator will probe for more. Other witnesses resent this method and consider it an indication that they are not trusted. Investigators should be aware that the manner of questioning can substantially influence the statement of a witness. For example, if the officer asks, "Did you observe in which hand the suspect held the gun?" the witness may form a mental image of a suspect with a gun, even if no gun was actually observed during the event. The answer to the question may assume a firearm was present. If, instead, the officer asks, "Did you notice anything in the hands of the suspect?" the problem is circumvented.

Cognitive Interviewing

The **cognitive interview** technique, initially developed in the early 1980s, is gaining rapid acceptance throughout the criminal justice system. This questioning process is based on the principles of cognitive psychology—the

TABLE 6.1 Information Retention Levels

Method of Retention	Amount Retained
What is read	10 percent
What is heard	30 percent
What is seen	30 percent
What is seen and heard	40 percent
What is discussed with others	60 percent

Source: K. Spencer, Center for Excellence in Teaching, Johns Hopkins University, Baltimore, MD.

scientific study of memory that emphasizes research in memory retention, perception, and communication.[6] The cognitive method utilizes interviewing techniques that aid witnesses and victims in retrieving and elaborating on information recalled from memory. Designed to enhance recall but not to detect deception, this method is used with cooperating subjects rather than with criminal perpetrators.[7] When using this technique, the investigator continually uses mnemonics, questions designed to improve or focus memory recall.

The cognitive method relies on a four-step process in which the investigator guides the subject back to the criminal event. The initial phase of the questioning generally reconstructs the circumstances of the incident. The investigator may instruct the subject to focus on details of the physical environment of the scene. The subject may be asked to think about what a room looked like or to recall specifics within it, such as the location of furniture. In addition, subjects may think about the weather, lighting, or any nearby people, vehicles, or other objects present at the time of the event. Finally, subjects should recall how they were feeling and think about their reactions during the time of the crime.[8] This phase of the technique attempts to assist in a subject's recall by increasing the overlap of elements in stored memory and those retrieved with the help of cues. The second phase in the technique of cognitive interviewing is designed to encourage the subject to report all information freely during the interview. Specifically, the interviewee should do most of the talking. The investigator explains that some individuals hold back information because they are not sure that it is important to the case. It must be strongly emphasized that no information should be withheld, even details that may not be thought of as important.

The final two questioning methods of the cognitive technique are based on the assumption that memory has several access routes. If information is not accessible with one type of memory retrieval cue, it may very well be accessible with a different cue. The third phase instructs the subject to recall the events in a different order rather than the traditional order of beginning to end. Asking the subject to recall incidents in reverse order can provide the right memory cues. Recall may also be enhanced by starting with whatever impressed the subject most during the event, then examining other incidents by moving both forward and backward in time. In the fourth and final stage, the subject is encouraged to change perspectives. This can be accomplished by having the subject recall the incident from different perspectives that may have been possible at the scene or by adopting the perspectives of others who were present.

Cognitive interviews are improved by limiting interruptions. The interview site should be selected with care, as it must be free of distractions. Questions should be phrased with simple terms, avoiding official jargon. It is also important to instruct subjects to speak slowly (this assists memory recall) and for the investigator to aid this process by also speaking slowly. Although investigators should follow up any significant comments made by a subject, unnecessary interruptions must be avoided as the witness relates recalled details.

Following the four general phases of the method, the cognitive technique is completed with a series of questions. The questions are designed to elicit items of information commonly encountered in criminal cases but easily forgotten by many subjects:

1. Physical appearance: Did the suspect remind the subject of anyone? If so, can the subject state who and why?
2. Names: If the subject thinks a name was spoken but cannot remember, try going through the alphabet to determine the first letter of the name.

What was the first letter of the name the subject heard? Can the subject think of the number of syllables in the name?

3. Numbers: In some cases, a number is seen or heard but cannot be specifically remembered. Was it a high or low number? How many digits might there have been, and were there letters in the sequence?
4. Speech: Did the suspect's voice remind the witness of someone else's voice? If so, why? Was there anything unusual about the voice?
5. Conversation: If specific conversations cannot be recalled, the subject should be instructed to think about his reactions to what was said and the reactions of others present. Were any unusual words or phrases used?

Following the cognitive interview, it is common for subjects to recall important information hours or even days later. Information may come to conscious memory as a result of the stimulating effect of the questioning. Thus, investigators should always close the interview by explaining this possibility and the importance of contacting the investigator quickly with any additional information.

Some criminal investigators have used various elements of the cognitive interview for many years. However, a number of research studies strongly suggest that when all the techniques are used together, the probability of memory recall is greatly enhanced. For example, a study a few years ago tested the cognitive method among robbery detectives of the Miami (Florida) Police Department. The study demonstrated that criminal investigators who conducted interviews with crime victims and eyewitnesses were able to elicit nearly 50 percent more information by using the cognitive technique than with traditional interviewing methods.[9]

The questioning process should continue until the investigator is satisfied that all information of value has been gathered. At that point, the interview will be closed. The closing phase should be accomplished with one major objective in mind—to leave the witness with a positive impression of the police. If the witness proves to be reliable, he or she will be reexamined many times, including important courtroom questioning. The witness must be given the assurance, by the professionalism of the investigator, that participation in the criminal justice system is not a negative experience.

The professionalism of the investigator assumes a sensitivity to the witness's fear of suspect reprisal. Criminal investigators should assure witnesses that any threats against them or acts of intimidation will be investigated and resolved by police action. The investigator should be sympathetic, stressing that it is only natural to be concerned about suspect reprisal but also assuring the witness such acts rarely take place.

Prosecutors must also be sensitive to such witness apprehension, assuring witnesses that not-in-custody suspects, waiting at the courthouse for their cases to be called, will not be allowed to enter the area in which witnesses are waiting to testify. To further ensure the safety and confidence of witnesses, **witness protection units** have been created. Such units, staffed by investigators from the police agency and prosecutor's office, provide security to witnesses who have been threatened or who are extremely fearful of reprisal. The units maintain high visibility to deter reprisals and vigorously investigate and prepare for prosecution all actual threats. In some urban communities, witness intimidation is becoming a particularly serious and growing problem. In 2005, Baltimore police estimated that 35 to 50 percent of nonfatal shooting cases could not proceed to prosecution because of reluctant witnesses, and nearly 90 percent of all homicide cases involved some manner of witness intimidation. Community fear of witness retaliation was heightened by the circulation of a two-hour DVD produced by a drug gang titled "Stop Snitching," which threatened death to witnesses. Investigators responded with a police DVD, "Keep Talking," which detailed the effectiveness of the department's witness protection unit.[10] When threats of state or federal witnesses reach the potential of murder, some elect to enter the U.S. Marshals Service Witness Protection Program. Currently, more than 7,500 witnesses and 9,600 family members have been relocated and given new identities since 1970.

As many criminal investigators have suspected for some time, communications between police officials, prosecutors, and witnesses are often not ideal. One research study has proposed giving each witness a printed card at the crime scene, detailing responsibilities and duties, with the address of the prosecutor's office printed on the card.[11] The attitude of the prosecutor during the witness interview is very important to the eventual outcome of the case. Although prosecutors interview hundreds of witnesses, each interview must be tactful and considerate.

SUSPECT INTERVIEWS

Interviewing a suspected criminal offender tests the questioning skill of the investigator in a variety of ways. This type of interview differs from all others in that the individual being questioned is suspected in the commission of a crime. The suspect may be under formal arrest or free to leave at any time. The suspect may, indeed, be guilty or innocent of any wrongdoing. The suspect may refuse to be interviewed or permit the interview to proclaim innocence or attempt to deceive the investigator.

Thorough preparation is always necessary before conducting the interview. Since the majority of suspect interviews take place at a location other than the crime scene, the investigator normally has ample time to prepare. The degree of preparation is dictated by the type of crime: its seriousness, the number of victims involved, and amount of information available pertaining to the suspect. Initially, all arrest and offense reports associated with the crime should be reviewed. Additional arrest information on the suspect should be secured from the investigator's agency and the other involved departments. Witness reports should then be examined, and arresting officers should be interviewed for insight into the suspect's personality. Thorough preparation may also include a visit to the crime scene.

The time and place of the interview must be carefully considered. The majority of suspect interviews are conducted in the police agency; in this case, the formal setting of the police facility works to the investigator's advantage. It serves to remind the suspect of the seriousness of the situation and tends to thwart the notion that the investigator can be deceived. The suspect interview should take place within a short time following the arrest. Some investigators feel that interviewing a suspect directly after physical apprehension is counterproductive because of the suspect's state of mental and physical stress. It is feared that anger and frustration resulting from a loss of freedom may disrupt the interview. However, most investigators support the widely held belief that the earlier a suspect is interviewed, the more spontaneous and truthful the answers will be in that the suspect thereby has less time in which to fabricate deceptive answers and explanations.

It has been assumed that an interview room should be as sparse in appearance as possible. This assumption is based on the theory that a room devoid of all but the barest essentials will create a tense environment, with a greater probability for a confession. Indeed, a sparse setting may be successful with some suspects; others may find it too intimidating and refuse to be interviewed. The experienced repeat offender will be oblivious to any type of surroundings.

Legal Requirements of the Suspect Interview

Before actual questioning begins, the investigator should state his or her name, agency, and position within the agency. Following this introduction, the suspect must be made aware of certain constitutional guarantees. The now famous ***Miranda* decision** of 1966 and the ***Escobedo* decision** of 1964 are Supreme Court rulings that have tremendous significance to the suspect interview. The *Escobedo* case involved a murder investigation that focused on Danny Escobedo as the suspect. Following his arrest by Chicago investigators, the suspect was interviewed by detectives on two separate occasions. In the course of the second interview, the suspect admitted guilt and gave a full confession. Although he was found guilty and sentenced to life imprisonment, Escobedo's conviction was overturned by the Supreme Court because of procedures resulting from the interview. During the interview, Escobedo asked to converse with his attorney, who was present in the police agency. This request was denied by the investigators.[12] In ruling on the case, the Supreme Court held that the suspect's Sixth Amendment right had been violated when he was denied the assistance of counsel. Following the *Escobedo* decision, there was considerable confusion among investigators and lower criminal courts as to what warnings were to be given to persons in custody before questioning. The resulting *Miranda* decision served to clarify the Supreme Court's view on the procedures to be followed in a criminal interview.

A kidnapping and rape investigation in Phoenix, Arizona, resulted in the arrest of Ernesto Miranda as the suspect. Following a lineup identification by the victim, the suspect was interviewed for two hours—a relatively short period of time for a major case of this nature. During this time period, Miranda confessed orally, then gave investigators a written confession regarding the offense.[13] The suspect was subsequently convicted, with the Arizona Supreme Court upholding the lower-court decision. The U.S. Supreme Court reversed this decision, stating that the suspect's right to counsel and his protection against self-incrimination had been violated. As a result of this landmark decision, the so-called **Miranda warning** has become mandatory. Suspects taken into custody or deprived of their freedom of action, who are to be questioned by law enforcement officers, must be warned in substantially the following terms:

1. You have the right to remain silent.
2. Anything that you say can be used against you.
3. You have the right to talk with a lawyer and have the attorney present during questioning.
4. If you cannot afford an attorney, one will be appointed to represent you before any questioning at your request.

The suspect must then be asked if he or she understands the rights as they have been stated. The burden of proving the suspect's understanding rests with the police and prosecution. Therefore, it is always preferable to have the suspect sign a statement indicating complete understanding. Investigators must stop the questioning at any time the suspect invokes the right to remain silent.

There has been considerable debate over whether the Miranda warnings must be given immediately after any arrest or only in cases in which questioning is initiated by the police. It is the opinion of many prosecution officials and numerous courts that the warnings should apply only when questioning is to be initiated by a law enforcement officer. Thus, the immediate warnings following an arrest are not necessary unless the arresting officer attempts to question the suspect. If immediate warnings are given by arresting patrol officers who have no intention to question, the suspect may invoke his right to remain silent as a result of the tension created by his immediate arrest. This often creates a legal dilemma when detectives attempt to question the suspect at a later time.

A more recent U.S. Supreme Court decision, *Minnick v. Mississippi* (1990), clarified the issue of whether police can reinitiate questioning of a suspect who has requested and conferred with an attorney but does not have counsel present for later interviews. The court held that police cannot restart questioning of a suspect without counsel, even though an attorney had previously conferred with the suspect.[14]

A virtual storm of controversy has surrounded the *Miranda* decision's effect on the suspect interview. When the decision was announced in 1966, police officials were nearly unanimous in their belief that no sane suspect would ever again consent to an interview. Yet, in the more than three decades of interviewing that have passed since the decision, many police officials have come to believe that their initial fears were groundless. Various studies have indicated that no appreciable increase in crime or increase in suspect refusal has resulted from the decision.

It is commonly assumed that the main purpose of the suspect interview is to obtain a confession or elicit an admission of guilt. Actually, these are secondary objectives. Primarily, the interview is used to gather information. The emphasis on information gathering has resulted from the gradual loss of credibility associated with the confession. During the first half of the twentieth century, there was substantial incriminating value attached to either the oral or the written confession. Criminal courts, with few exceptions, viewed the confession as a total indicator of guilt. Consequently, many suspects were convicted on the basis of the confession alone, with supportive evidence totally lacking. Interviews were almost always conducted with confession as the goal. The second half of the century saw a gradual shift in emphasis. Judges, defense attorneys, and juries began to value the confession less and less; consequently, the importance of supportive evidence increased. This is not to say that the confession is currently without value in securing a conviction. It can still be very instrumental. However, few criminal prosecutions will be successful without additional evidence. Thus, it is important to realize that interviewing does not stop once the suspect states "I did it." The interview should be directed to how, why, and where the crime was committed.

Ethical Interviewing

What is ethical or acceptable during a criminal interview basically centers on two factors: legal precedent and voluntariness. The ethics of suspect interviewing have been established over many decades by various court cases challenging police questioning behavior. Numerous decisions by state appellate courts and the U.S. Supreme Court have determined various acceptable and unacceptable interviewing techniques, which are summarized in Table 6.2. It is important to note that although such techniques apply in most states, investigators must determine specific state law in their local jurisdictions. For example, Florida courts have ruled that law enforcement authorities cannot pretend to possess forensic evidence they do not have, whereas in California and most other states, this practice is permissible.[15] The legal precedent for utilizing acceptable forms of interview deception is grounded in a series of Supreme Court decisions. The opinion of the Court is clearly detailed in *Fraizer v. Cupp* (1969), in which it stated that "strategic deception of the suspect by police, where it is not sufficient to overbear the suspect's will but merely prompts him to act from a consciousness of guilt, does not make a statement involuntary."[16]

TABLE 6.2   Suspect Interview Tactics

Acceptable	Unacceptable
In an effort to obtain a confession or admission of guilt, the following interview tactics are legally acceptable in most states; in some states, restrictions apply. After police have fully informed suspects of their rights, they may:	The following tactics are legally unacceptable and should never be used during a suspect interview:
• Explain the real evidence against the suspect • Appeal to suspect's religion, sense of guilt, family embarrassment, etc. • Bring in other investigators to interview suspect • Leave suspect alone for short periods of time • Alter witness statements for suspect's comprehension • Lead suspect to believe in nonexistent evidence	• Physically come in contact with suspect • Threaten suspect • Promise better treatment in court • Deprive suspect of clothing • Deny suspect food, water, bathroom, or sleep • Question without Miranda rights • Try to continue questioning or badger suspect who has invoked right to remain silent • Question suspect waiting to consult with attorney

The voluntariness of a confession is determined by the suspect's vulnerability as well as the specific interview tactics employed by the police. Interviewing tactics will be judged as unethical and illegal if they overreach, intimidate, or coerce, defeating the free and independent exercise of the suspect's will. Most courts, however, view police trickery that simply exaggerates the strength of evidence against the suspect as not interfering with the defendant's free and deliberate choice to confess. Such logic never applies to the Miranda warning, and investigators must not attempt to trick a suspect into waiving his or her constitutional right to remain silent. Although most state and federal courts tolerate a high degree of game playing or creative use of deception during the interview, judicial authorities will not permit such tactics to overcome the suspect's will. Thus, investigators must carefully tailor their interviewing strategies to each individual defendant and should seek advice from the agency's legal adviser prior to questioning.[17]

The Questioning Process

Following the legal warning and introduction, the actual questioning process begins. The challenge of the suspect interview has been demonstrated by repeated research studies in which traditional methods of detecting deception succeed only 50 percent of the time even for experienced investigators.[18] The area in which the questioning is to take place should be isolated from normally busy areas of the police agency. The room should be situated so that the investigator and suspect will not be interrupted by others. The officer may elect to record the interview electronically or to have a stenographer present. It is still a source of constant amazement to new police officers that any suspect elects to talk with the police. Should not the Miranda warning convince a suspect of even subnormal intelligence to remain silent? It is indeed fortunate for the criminal justice system that human nature, particularly the nature of the criminal, can be counted on. Basically, the reason that so many suspects waive their right to silence, allow the interview, and eventually admit their guilt is the suspect's own ego. Guilty suspects habitually act in this manner in the belief that they can outwit the police through deception. Even a large portion of older, experienced criminals waive their rights and choose to talk with the police.

To understand the behavior of the criminal, psychological makeup must be considered. The behavioral approach is rapidly becoming more important in many areas of criminal investigation, such as crime scene analysis and profiling, and its effectiveness in interviewing has been proven beyond doubt. Law enforcement contact with the mentally ill or emotionally disturbed criminal suspect is becoming more common. Although no one is certain what percentage of the nation's population can be classified as mentally ill, the American Psychiatric Association recognizes more than 220 possible mental disturbances. The deinstitutionalization of mental hospital patients, cuts in public assistance and counseling, and rising economic fears have elevated the mentally ill population to the fastest-growing segment in local jails nationwide. Approximately 10 percent of all contacts between the police and public involve a mentally or emotionally ill individual.[19] Although patrol officers tend to encounter such subjects during domestic complaints, theft calls, and a variety of disturbance incidents, investigators are mainly concerned with successful interviewing techniques tailored to a particular personality disturbance.

The investigator may have some indication of the suspect's personality from examination of the records. Also, because behavior indicates personality, the nature of the crime and the suspect's particular method of operation convey personality type. In the majority of suspect interviews, however, personality characteristics are revealed during the initial minutes. The interviewing officer's attitude should be friendly yet professional. Being overly friendly—calling suspects by their first names, nicknames, or slang expressions, for example—will only cause resentment. After the Miranda warning is given, the investigator normally has to take the verbal initiative. The opening statement must be selected with care. If the statement implies that the "police know all," some suspects may demand to be informed of the evidence linking them to the offense. Additionally, if the statement is too aggressive, such as "We know you did it," a suspect may be frightened into silence. The opening statement should refer to an area not directly connected to criminal activity. For most suspects, apprehension is at a peak at the start of the interview; the hours before have been spent planning denials and deceptions. Therefore, an investigator who initially asks nonthreatening questions, such as "How have you been treated so far?" or "What kind of work do you do?" forces suspects to drop their guard mentally. This initial conversation quickly sets the tone for the entire interview, hopefully establishing a rapport between investigator and suspect that enables the officer to focus on the criminal offense.

The investigator is at a critical point when the questioning shifts from general conversation to the specific offense. Regardless of the calming effect of the initial conversation, the suspect now realizes that the responses to the questions may determine either a release or continued confinement. At this stage the investigator should attempt to classify the suspect in terms of the following behavioral categories:

1. normal personality;
2. psychopathic personality;
3. paranoid personality;
4. obsessive-compulsive personality; or
5. psychotic personality.

Depending on which personality type best describes the suspect, a specific questioning technique should be chosen. Collective law enforcement experience and the science of psychology dictate that certain forms of questioning are well suited for specific behavioral personalities. By tailoring specific questions to a recognized type, the investigator is far more likely to succeed during the interview.

There are, of course, large numbers of criminal suspects who are emotionally and **psychologically normal**. In fact, this type of suspect is the most commonly encountered. They may be first offenders or repeat offenders who, for various reasons, have selected criminality as a way of life. Primarily because of their normal thinking patterns, they experience some degree of guilt as a result of their criminal activities. By focusing the questioning on these guilt feelings, the investigator can often obtain a full confession. Guilt is a heavy emotional burden for any normal person. The number of suspects who voluntarily surrender themselves for arrest in unsolved cases underscores this point each year. A normal individual is quite fearful and tense before and during the interview. Regardless of social or economic level, this suspect will react to basic anxieties in a manner advantageous to the investigator. Most people, including normal offenders, have either a fear of or respect for authority or some degree of both. Psychologically, this may result from the conditioning received as a child in a submissive role relative to the parents. The criminal investigator is an obvious representation of authority to the suspect. If the suspect has been conditioned through life to answer truthfully when questioned by an authority figure, the officer's task is simplified considerably. Of course, not all suspects cooperate so readily during the questioning process. A particular fear, which is more intense in the suspect's mind than any other factor, can block the natural desire to relieve guilt. Fear of reprisal by other suspects, fear of social disgrace, fear of going to prison—all contribute to a reluctance to admit guilt. The officer must determine the nature of the suspects fear and attempt to work through it.

Normal subjects typically exhibit considerable physiological symptoms that suggest fear and tension. The suspect's body language can yield important clues in determining whether the suspect is telling the truth. A suspect who sits with arms tightly crossed in a rigid fashion and who avoids the eyes of the officer is obviously nervous. Restlessness, laborious breathing, and difficulty with word pronunciation are additional indicators of fear. When signs of nervousness are apparent, the investigator can choose either to play up the fear, exploiting it to gain an advantage, or attempt to relieve it. A normal suspect's fear tends to intensify when an officer makes such statements as "You seem to be really nervous."

In addition to using fear as a motivator toward confession, many psychologically normal suspects will respond if investigators provide an acceptable or "dignified" way to admit their criminal involvement. Like most people, criminals often employ psychological defense mechanisms to justify their behavior. Three such defense mechanisms are particularly common, collectively known as the RPMs of criminal interviewing: rationalization, projection, and minimization. When suspects rationalize, they attempt to offer reasonable explanations for their illegal actions that will not lead to a negative judgment. Projection attempts to displace the blame onto something or someone other than the suspect, while minimization reduces the importance or gravity of the wrongdoing. Since many suspects are close to providing a confession due to guilt or fear, the proper suggestion of one or more of the RPMs often provides a convincing reason to confess. When the investigator downplays the seriousness of the crime, blames it on other forces, or suggests that a perfectly understandable rationale exists for what the suspect did, a confession or admission of guilt often follows.

The natural guilt and fear levels of normal suspects decrease with crime repetition. The habitual criminal frequently commits offenses with partners or associates, however, and this fact can be used to the officer's benefit. The officer should be aware that the suspect may be upset that he or she alone was apprehended and can capitalize on the desire to share the misfortune.

Of the various abnormal personality types that are common to criminality, the psychopathic personality is the most common.[20] The **psychopath**, often termed the *sociopath* or *antisocial offender*, has, for whatever reason, experienced abnormal emotional and psychological development. Often emotionally immature, psychopathic individuals are typically highly compulsive and lacking in social responsibility. Because they rarely learn from past negative experiences, prior police encounters may have no bearing on their present antisocial actions. Of particular interest to the investigator is the psychopath's inability to feel guilt as a result of wrongdoing. Finally, it is characteristic of this type of suspect to consider him- or herself to be extremely clever—able to lie or manipulate situations. Although above average in intelligence, most psychopathic offenders waive their right to silence. When this type of suspect hears the Miranda warnings, the very personality traits that brought about the arrest serve to reject the admonishments.

Obtaining a confession or admission of guilt from the psychopathic suspect is not an easy task. Being highly manipulative by nature, they immediately sense when the police are attempting to trick or "con" with fabrications or references to evidence that does not exist. This offender will respond to an interview environment that stresses only what he or she can get out of the encounter. Several interviews may be necessary, as the suspect needs frequent demonstrations of attention and stimulation. Antisocial offenders are also often narcissistic; that is, they have an exaggerated admiration of themselves. Questions that appeal to their immature self-image through flattery are frequently effective. Accordingly, the investigator can phrase questions as "I can see you're intelligent" or "I need help in understanding; can you help me understand?" Such questions are often eagerly answered by individuals who believe in their superiority to others. The investigator must be ready to demonstrate a solid, convincing case in which a confession or admission of guilt appeals to the suspect's best interest. As psychopaths generally believe they are superior to the police, they readily engage in conversation, although their answers often need to be guided back to the matter at hand.

Psychopaths often commit crimes that reflect their personalities. Offenses that are dependent on verbal persuasion or manipulation, such as various forms of fraud, are frequently committed by this type of criminal. Additionally, more serious violent felonies that appeal to an impulsive, present-oriented personality seeking immediate gratification, such as rape, are often linked to the psychopath.

Although psychopathic criminal personalities are the most common, the suspect with **paranoia** is encountered in many investigations. This individual often has fixed delusions, typically of a suspicious nature. Tending to be resentful and bitter, paranoid suspects feel they are being singled out and mistreated by their enemies. They blame everything and everyone but themselves. Interviewing a paranoid suspect often tests an investigator's tolerance and professionalism. The paranoiac, depending on the severity of the mental illness, often frustrates questioning techniques employed by even the most experienced investigators. Paranoid suspects conveniently find a multitude of excuses for their behavior. They suspect that the world is against them or that people have it in for them. In an attempt to gain support for these suspicions—to lend credence to them—they may reveal desired information. At the root of the paranoiac's mental problem is a fearful belief of inferiority. A nonthreatening interview environment is highly desirable for a successful interview. The suspect should sense that the investigator is honest and open and only seeks to understand what is troubling the suspect. Great pains must be taken to ensure that paranoid individuals do not focus their suspicions and persecutory delusions on the interviewer. If the interview is being recorded or filmed, the suspect should be informed. Regardless of how foolish the suspect's fears and suspicions are to the investigator, a sense of understanding, reassurance, and concern must be directed toward the suspect. Criminal offenses associated with the paranoid personality can be troublesome or extremely serious. Because of their unreasonable fears and suspicions, suspects may threaten others or continually complain to local or federal authorities about various conspiracies. When the disorder becomes more serious, paranoiacs may explode into violence, harming family members, neighbors, or coworkers.

Interviews focusing on **obsessive-compulsive** offenders also call for specific questioning techniques. This suspect exhibits a tendency to fixate, or irrationally focus on a thought, idea, or other person. Such mental patterns may then move to a compulsive level in which some type of act is performed in an effort to relieve the anxieties of the obsession. When interviewing obsessive-compulsive suspects, investigators soon note the high degree of anxiety and guilt within the subject. Additionally, such individuals have a constant need to be in control and present a personality that is rigid and perfection oriented. As obsessive-compulsive offenders are so filled with anxiety, the interview often needs more of an initial warm-up phase prior to pertinent questioning. After the suspect's anxiety has been reduced, indirect questions pertaining to the crime should begin. Remembering that obsessive-compulsive offenders may go into great detail in areas not pertinent to the questions, the interviewer must continually keep the answers on the subject. Building rapport is particularly important with this type of suspect, and because of the obsessive-compulsive's timid exterior and ample guilt, the order of questions is significant. Beginning questions should be benign, whereas later questions should be increasingly specific regarding the crime. Criminal offenses associated with this offender may be considered nuisance oriented or can escalate into serious interpersonal behaviors. Common crimes often include obscene phone calls, sending unwanted letters, or minor theft. More serious offenses committed by the obsessive-compulsive offender may involve stalking, arson, or sexually compulsive acts such as exhibitionism or rape.[21]

Occasionally, the officer encounters a suspect who is grossly disturbed. Individuals who are **psychotic** often commit bizarre crimes of a violent nature or offenses that lack any typical motive. Attempts to question this type of individual are normally futile because the suspect is generally totally out of touch with reality. Severe cases of schizophrenia and other mental illnesses characterized by a loss of reality are equally difficult for the interviewing officer. When interviews are attempted, the investigator should not encourage or expand the subject's fantasy or delusions but attempt to filter the facts through what is being stated. Grossly disturbed individuals can be easily identified by their incoherent ramblings, bizarre behavior, and withdrawn attitudes. Unlike the previously discussed behavioral types, psychotic offenders are generally not legally accountable for their offenses and are best treated by specialists, such as psychiatrists. Grossly disturbed offenders who have lost touch with reality commit a wide and often eccentric variety of crimes. Offenses may range from disturbance calls in which citizens are frightened by the incomprehensible statements or actions of the psychotic to disorganized criminal homicides, that is, homicides that lack planning or a common motive.

General Suspect Questioning Techniques

Certain basic questioning techniques are applicable regardless of the type of individual being interviewed. Questions that encourage a yes-or-no response should never be used for the obvious reason that they do not elicit as much information as possible. Instead, the open-ended question, such as "And then what happened?" or "What did you do then?" should frequently be employed. Criminal suspects often deliberately attempt to shift the questioning so as to subvert the purpose of the interview. The officer must remain in charge by directing the flow of conversation back to the original question. An even-tempered, confident, businesslike demeanor should be maintained by the officer throughout the questioning. A show of temper or distracting emotions of any nature can enable a suspect to take control. While common in detective fiction, the rapid-fire questioning of a suspect by multiple police is generally ineffective. Like most people, criminal suspects tend to be more talkative about stressful topics when in the company of one (or occasionally two) investigators. When two officers are present during the interview, one will actively participate, while the second should quietly take notes.[22]

Other important points include the order of things stated, false supportive phrases, and the use of silence. Generally, things said first are the most important, so the investigator should pay close attention to the suspect's choice or order of words. False supportive phrases such as "actually," "definitely," or "to tell the truth" communicate the suspect's lack of confidence in what he or she is stating. Finally, silence on both the suspect's and officer's part can be effectively used as a tool during the interview. Many individuals are uncomfortable with silence, as they expect the police to continually talk and ask rapid questions. Accordingly, the officer may elect not to respond to a question or statement, allowing the suspect to become uneasy and fill the silence with further statements. Conversely, the officer may eliminate or control the use of silence by the suspect by using neutral responses such as "You haven't finished your statement" or "Go on." Most suspect questioning techniques apply the old interviewing adage of "It's not just what they say, but how they say it."[23]

The use of **coercion** has no place in the police interview. Forcing an admission of guilt from a suspect obviously negates the possibility of a voluntary statement. Statements that are not voluntarily given adversely affect the admissibility of the information as evidence. The use of **duress** must likewise be avoided. Whereas coercion implies the use of physical force, duress implies a mental compulsion that can negate the voluntariness of a statement. The very nature of the police interview may force the officer to walk a fine line in the avoidance of duress. If the investigator creates an atmosphere of such fear that the suspect's ability to reason is restrained, then duress can be cited to render a statement inadmissible. Additionally, there should be no prominent display of firearms or any similar type of equipment in view of the suspect during the interview.

No police officer has the authority to grant immunity from prosecution or a reduction of sentence to any suspect. Contrary to what media presentation seems to suggest, investigators do not indicate or imply in any way that, by confessing, the suspect will be aided by police authorities. Officers may state, however, that a suspect's cooperation will be brought to the attention of prosecution officials. In the event that a suspect indicates a readiness to reveal information on the condition that immunity or a reduction of sentence is guaranteed, the interview should cease until the prosecutor can be contacted.

Juvenile Subject Interviews

Because of the significant increase in juvenile crime participation, the criminal investigator should be prepared to interview the younger offender with some frequency. Of the 15 million annual total arrests, suspects under the age of 18 account for approximately 19 percent of those arrested. During a recent year, juvenile arrests accounted for 17 percent of those arrested for violent crimes and 35 percent of all property crimes.[24] In many crime categories, such as burglary, motor vehicle theft, arson, and vandalism, the juvenile has a particularly high likelihood of arrest.

In a similar fashion to the *Miranda* decision, the Supreme Court completely restructured the juvenile suspect interview through the **Gault decision**. Fifteen-year-old Gerald Gault was arrested on June 8, 1964, as a result of his alleged participation in making obscene phone calls. Following his detention in a juvenile home for three days, during which his parents had no notice of his arrest or detention, the suspect was released to appear at a hearing several days later. During the hearing, Gault was not given warnings as to right to counsel, the right to remain silent, or self-incrimination. Furthermore, the complainant was not required to be present. At the conclusion of the hearing, the subject was sentenced to a state industrial school for "the period of his minority"—the six years before he would reach 21.[25]

The Supreme Court considered the Gault case during its 1967 session, ruling that juvenile subjects are entitled to the same equal protection under the law as adult suspects. As a direct result of this decision, it is mandatory that the juvenile interview offer the same constitutional protections set forth in the *Miranda* decision. If the age or emotional condition of the juvenile does not allow for an understanding of these rights, the parents or legal guardian must understand and act on the warnings.

Even before the legal protections now afforded juvenile subjects were in place, the interaction of juveniles with police was treated with special care. Because of concerns with rehabilitation and the suggestibility of minors, a special sensitivity has traditionally surrounded this type of interview. Some agencies require the presence of a parent during the interview or encourage the investigator to summon a parent in cases that involve certain felony offenses. Large police departments often require the presence of an officer from the juvenile unit to assist the investigator. Other agencies require that all juvenile interviews be conducted by juvenile unit officers exclusively.

Recording the Suspect Interview

It is to the investigator's advantage to have a record of the interview, particularly if an admission of guilt or total confession is elicited from the suspect. A record of the interview may be taken by a stenographer, tape-recorded, or even filmed by videotape. The investigator must use discretion in selecting the means of documentation and the time at which the interview will be recorded. The presence of a stenographer may inhibit the responses of the suspect, as may the obvious presence of a tape recorder. A record of the interview is useful in that it presents to the court and jury an accurate review of what transpired. Additionally, such a record may discourage the suspect's denial that a confession was made and vindicate officers should there be claims of coercion or duress.

When the investigator has obtained a confession from the suspect, the confession should be put in writing. The suspect may be allowed to write out the statement, or the stenographer, under the investigator's direction, may prepare the statement for the suspect's signature. In either case, the confession should be worded in the suspect's terminology and manner of speaking. If the confession is not being filmed and the officer is alone with the suspect, additional witnesses should be present to observe the voluntariness of the procedure. If a statement is prepared for the suspect, he or she should sign it and state in writing that the admission or confession was given with a full understanding of constitutional rights and that it was given voluntarily.

Close analysis of statements written by subjects or even victims or witnesses can often aid the investigator in determining possible deception. Researchers have noted questionable truthfulness by focusing on three sections of written statements: the introduction, the criminal incident, and the conclusion. One study of 60 written criminal case statements revealed the following:

1. In truthful statements, the section that describes the criminal incident is generally the longest part of the overall statement, while deceptive statements have longer introductions (where the writer describes details leading up to the crime) than other sections.
2. Truthful statements often include a greater number of unique sensory details than deceptive statements, particularly in the criminal incident section. Sensory details relate to information linked to the five sensory perceptions of sight, sound, smell, taste, and touch.
3. In the closing or concluding sections of most truthful statements, subjects generally describe their emotions, while deceptive writers tend not to. This is particularly noted in interpersonal offenses, such as homicide, rape, or aggravated assault, among others.[26]

Videotaping

Videotaping is a visual and aural method of recording suspect confessions or admissions or statements given by important witnesses. When video cameras reached consumer markets in the United States in the late 1970s, they were primarily used to document family recreational activities and provide surveillance in retail stores and banks. Audiovisual technology began to find a place in law enforcement in the mid-1980s. Initially used as a training tool or to record crime scenes, civil disorders, and lineups, videotaping is now a standard tool during many criminal interviews. Surveys reveal that at least 60 percent of all police agencies currently use videotape to document interrogations or confessions in various types of cases.[27] Although the technique can be used to record victim or witness statements, it is primarily employed with the suspect interview. The superiority of videotaping is based on its positive impact on a judge or jury. Because the tape shows suspect voluntariness, the jury need not rely on the often contradictory testimony of witnesses. In addition, taped confessions accelerate pretrial hearings by indicating the voluntariness of a confession to a judge ruling on motions concerning coercion. Major police departments, such as those in New York City and St. Louis, have videotaped many thousands of confessions to date. Both departments report a guilty-plea rate of more than 85 percent in cases recorded by videotaping.[28] By 2005, many law enforcement agencies on all levels were recording suspect interviews as a matter of general policy. In some jurisdictions, like Washington, D.C., and the state of Minnesota, legal codes mandate that all suspect interviews are to be taped whenever possible. Other states have tailored videotaping laws to be crime specific. The Illinois legislature enacted a statute providing that unrecorded custodial suspect interviews in homicide investigations are presumed inadmissible unless a statutory exception applies.[29] Accordingly, it is expected that relatively soon nearly all custodial suspect interviews will be entirely recorded as a matter of policy or law.

Videotaping by private citizens has become quite popular in a large segment of the population; well over 14 million Americans currently own video cameras. The use of privately filmed videotapes is not uncommon in the course of various criminal investigations or judicial proceedings. The famous

Zapruder film of President Kennedy's 1963 motorcade assassination was one of the first private films of criminal violence, and the 1991 videotape of the beating of Rodney King by police sparked national interest in the private use of this information-gathering method.

A police taping session should be recorded by a video technician who may be a specially trained investigator. Although most videotaping sessions are overt, or known to the subject of the recording, the investigator may elect to use a hidden, or covert, tape. Some state or local laws prohibit the use of hidden taping sessions, even though federal law does not. A "reasonable expectation of privacy," a federal constitutional doctrine, does not exist during a station house interview. Most states are "one party consent" jurisdictions in which only one party in a conversation need give permission to record the conversation. In states that require both parties to consent to the recording of a conversation, suspects must be informed that their interview will be videotaped and permission then secured prior to the taping. The investigator conducting the session should first state the location, persons present, date, and time, even if the tape contains a frame-by-frame time bar. The advisement of rights should follow, even if such warnings have been given prior to the recording. As for all suspect interviews, the location of the taping must be selected with care; an officelike environment is superior (Figure 6.2). Objections to videotaping typically center on the ethical issue of privacy, prejudicial effects on juries, and the possible altering of tapes. Civil and criminal courts are currently determining the evolving law concerning video filming by private citizens of other citizens. However, tapes filmed by law enforcement officers must submit to the same rules of procedure applied to all evidence, with particular emphasis on whether the tape would unduly prejudice jury members through its graphic content. Although tapes can be edited to mislead the viewer, laboratory analysis can determine whether a video was shot with a particular camera or its images altered through various electronic means.

See Figure 6.3 for a tabular summary of the interview process as it pertains to victims, witnesses, and suspects.

FIGURE 6.2 Investigators question and record a suspect's statement. The routine taping of felony suspect interviews is becoming increasingly more common as a means of establishing confession validity for judicial proceedings. *(Source: Getty Images, Inc.–Liaison.)*

Preparation	Questioning	Closing
Victims and Witnesses • Research subject if possible • Anticipate problems • Separate witnesses/victims • Select calming environment	• Make introduction • Let subject relate observations without interruptions • Take notes • Guide the retelling • Evaluate subject's statement in terms of reliable witness requirements	• Leave subject with positive impression • Inform subject as to possibility of repeat interviews and court-room testimony
Suspects • Thoroughly research suspect's social and criminal history • Review all associated reports and documents • Confer with arresting officers • Select advantageous time and place	• Make introduction • Thoroughly explain constitutional guarantees • Evaluate suspect as to psychological makeup • Select questioning technique suitable to suspect's personality • Use questions that encourage full explanations • Remain in charge of questioning • Record interview • Consider use of scientific techniques (polygraph, etc.)	• Transfer suspect's oral confession or statement of facts to written form with witness present • Try to leave suspect with positive impression, considering the possibility of future interviews

FIGURE 6.3 The interview process.

CRIMINALISTIC APPLICATIONS

Scientific knowledge and technology have been instrumental in the development of methods to aid the investigator in securing information from a subject. Data obtained by these methods vary, however, in objective accuracy and in courtroom admissibility.

Polygraph

Police officials and scientists have devoted considerable effort to develop a device capable of determining deception. Scientific efforts to measure an individual's blood pressure as an indication of question evasion trace back to the mid-1800s. The present-day **polygraph** or "lie detector" (Figure 6.4) has found wide use in police departments throughout the country; however, it is an instrument still surrounded by mystery and needless confusion.

Basically stated, the polygraph measures physiological changes of the body that are triggered by emotional responses to specific verbal questions. Physical reactions are noted and measured in graphlike fashion, specifically, respiration, blood pressure, and galvanic skin reflex. A rubber tubelike apparatus attached to the front of the subject's chest measures changes in breathing. Pulse rate and blood pressure are recorded by means of a flexible cuff, of the type used by physicians, attached to the upper portion of either arm. The galvanic skin reflex is measured by passing a harmless electrical current through the tips of the subject's fingers. Experts in the field have noted an increase in electrical current during a deception—a reaction that is still not fully understood.

The polygraph is a very useful tool to the criminal investigator for a number of reasons. First of all, the device can have a remarkable "power of suggestion" for some suspects, even if it is not actually used. Literally

FIGURE 6.4 This subject has been prepared for a polygraph examination.
(*Source: Hunter Investigative Service.*)

hundreds of detailed confessions are obtained each year by the mere presence of the machine. Many suspects stubbornly deny guilt during the interview yet give a confession just prior to the polygraph examination. This is due to the belief that "the machine can't be beat." Those suspects who elect to take the test often confess their guilt during the examination or immediately thereafter. Finally, careful analysis of the test findings may give the officer leads to pursue in subsequent interviews.

Although many factors can influence polygraph accuracy, the following are four particular areas of concern:[30]

1. the examiner;
2. the examinee;
3. the thoroughness of the investigation; and
4. environmental conditions.

Polygraph examinations are practically useless unless they are conducted by a highly trained professional examiner. A credible examiner should have completed training at a reputable polygraph school accredited by the American Polygraph Association. In addition, the examiner should receive continuing refresher training. For example, the FBI requires all agent examiners to undergo refresher training at intervals not to exceed two years. A final factor that contributes to examiner competency is the frequency of polygraph examinations. There is no specific number that demonstrates professionalism, but many federal agencies require their examiners to conduct a minimum of 50 examinations per year.[31]

The second major factor that affects the accuracy of the examination concerns the subject to be tested. Physical and emotional conditions have the most immediate influence on testing accuracy. Lack of food or rest or the presence of unusual stress can often invalidate the polygraph examination. Because an intensive or prolonged traditional questioning session is often quite stressful, it is generally not wise to administer the polygraph test following such an interview. Suspects who are unable to distinguish between reality and fantasy (psychotics) and those who are incapable of showing genuine emotion in reaction to deception (extreme psychopaths) are often poor subjects for the examination.

A thorough gathering of investigative facts is essential prior to the polygraph examination. Because a successful examination is dependent on what information the investigator supplies to the examiner, the investigator provides all details of the case, including prior suspect statements, crime scene data, forensic reports, and other case facts. Thorough conferences with the investigator will yield a series of questions to be asked of the suspect. Following the actual test, the operator and the investigator go over the reaction of the suspect to each pertinent question. If the suspect has not confessed during the examination, the investigator decides in what manner the information obtained is to be used in future interviews.

The final factor, concerning environmental conditions, is equally important to the accuracy of the polygraph examination. The place of the examination must be free from distraction, and once the test has begun the examiner and subject should not be interrupted. The presence of additional people during the examination tends to distract the suspect and invalidate the findings. In addition, the polygraph examiner should not be hurried either to begin or to complete the examination.

Currently, polygraph results are not generally accepted as evidence in criminal proceedings. However, if the prosecuting and defense attorneys agree to raise no objection to their admissibility (known as **legal stipulation**), the results can be allowed in most states. Suspects must willingly agree to take the examination. Fortunately, many guilty suspects of the psychopathic personality type quite willingly take the test in the belief that they can further deceive the officer. Additionally, suspects who are innocent of alleged offenses may elect to be examined to document their innocence.

The reason polygraph data are not readily admitted as legal evidence is that their accuracy is affected by circumstances external to the instrument, such as the skill of the operator, the mental and physical condition of the suspect, and the number of past interviews on the matter being explored.

In the recent past, polygraph examinations were widely used within private industry for screening job applicants and preventing employee theft. Nearly two million such examinations were routinely given each year by various corporations or contracted private security investigators. However, the continuing controversy over the voluntary nature of the test caused 22 states to enact a variety of restrictions during the 1970s and 1980s. The issue was finally resolved in the passage of the national Employee Polygraph Protection Act of 1988. The federal law now bans all random polygraph examinations and most uses of the device for preemployment purposes. Accordingly, an employer cannot ask or tell job applicants to take a polygraph as part of the job-interviewing process. Moreover, an employee under investigation may not be fired for refusing to take a polygraph examination or be fired solely because of the test results if an examination is taken.

The law does permit exceptions to the general ban in that polygraph examinations may still be compulsory in companies that manufacture or dispense drugs, in some types of security firms, and in businesses doing sensitive work under contract to the federal government. Other private industries can still request employees to take an examination as part of an internal criminal investigation, but the firm must justify a reasonable suspicion that the employee was involved in the alleged offense. The suspected employee must be notified in writing 48 hours in advance and may have a lawyer present during the testing. In addition to select private employment exemptions, judicial rulings allow law enforcement agencies on all levels to use the polygraph to screen applicants. Fully 62 percent of all police agencies currently use the polygraph for screening new employees, a significant rise from only 16 percent in 1962 (Figure 6.5).

So-called **voice polygraphs**, or devices that analyze the degree of "stress" in a suspect's speech, are currently used by many law enforcement agencies. Voice-stress evaluators monitor the vocal quality of an individual, producing a graphlike reading that indicates possible deception. A major advantage of this type of device is that it is attachment free. Stress-related modulation in the voice is the sole factor monitored, allowing the suspect to be free of traditional polygraph body attachments. Also, voice stress analysis can be performed on previously recorded voices, or during real-time telephone conversations. Vocal-stress devices have been shown to produce confessions in a manner similar to that of the body polygraph. However, the widespread use of voice stress analysis may never become a reality since many forensic experts have questioned the capability of these devices.

Hypnosis

The use of **hypnosis** as an information-gathering aid is occasionally employed within the criminal justice system. Various criminal investigators from agencies throughout the United States currently use this technique in selected interviews of victims, witnesses, and, to a lesser degree, suspects. Furthermore, certain police agencies may use hypnosis as an in-service

Early 1900s	Psychologists speculate that deception can be detected by noting changes in blood pressure and pulse. First relatively crude machines are developed.
1920s	John Larson perfects polygraph and introduces practice of asking a combination of relevant and irrelevant questions during examination.
1930s	Polygraph designed by Leonard Keeler at Northwestern University provides first results to be submitted as evidence before a jury.
1940s	Attorney John Reid develops the control question, a standard against which examiners can measure a subject's response.
1950s	Concerns from judicial officials emerge questioning the reliability of the polygraph, results not allowed in most criminal proceedings. The Catholic Church condemns the practice as "an intrusion into man's interior domain."
1960s	Use of the polygraph expands into the workplace and is frequently used as condition of hiring and the investigation of on-the-job theft allegations.
1970s	Polygraph continues to be heavily used in private sector with 2 million exams given annually. Protests intensify over job privacy issues and inaccuracy of the tests.
1980s **1990s**	U.S. Congress passes Act in 1988 banning most uses of the polygraph in the private employment sector. The use of the device to screen most criminal justice applicants is exempted from ban. Device is used mainly as investigative tool on voluntary suspects, victims, and witnesses to verify allegations and claims of innocence.
2000s	Computer software developed to aid in accuracy of polygraph results. Brain wave and blood flow patterns are researched for future deception value.

FIGURE 6.5   Progression of the Polygraph. *(Source: American Polygraph Association, Omaha World Herald.)*

training aid. Officers have found self-hypnosis beneficial in recalling suspect descriptions, stolen license and auto descriptions, and similar information. Hypnosis was used as early as 5,000 years ago, yet even today it is difficult to define precisely. Basically, hypnosis places an individual in a state between wakefulness and light sleep. It allows for complete relaxation and intense concentration, hence promoting a heightened suggestibility. The so-called hypnotic trance is not actually possible, for the subject is never really asleep. The hypnotic state has been likened to intense daydreaming or to the total absorption that may be experienced when reading a book of great interest. For a subject to enter a hypnotic state, there must be a total focusing of attention. This is usually achieved by means of a light, voice and eyes, or some other type of attention-fixing device. Motor activities must cease and the subject be silent while the method of induction is repeatedly used until the hypnotic state is achieved.

The use of hypnosis in a criminal investigation must always be voluntary. Although the method has been used in the suspect interview, it is of greater value in victim and witness questioning. In these interviews, hypnosis has been used successfully to overcome two frequent problem areas. First, a victim often experiences difficulty in relating descriptions of an emotionally shocking crime. Because the experience has been highly traumatic, conscious memory may be repressed as a form of self-protection. Since the victim did experience the offense, the information is in the mind, but it cannot be retrieved using normal questioning techniques. Hypnosis may serve as the key to unlock the subconscious memory, allowing the victim to relate important information fully.

The second problem area involves the inability of witnesses to remember details of investigative significance. Witnesses frequently cannot relate even the most basic descriptive factors, such as the color of an auto, race of an offender, or type of clothing. Fortunately, hypnosis has proved to be an effective memory stimulant in hundreds of cases. While in the hypnotic state, the victim or witness is free of stress and anxiety so that a mental image of the event can be reconstructed. It has been estimated by law enforcement hypnosis experts that in 60 percent of all felony investigations, information can be obtained beyond that secured through traditional means when hypnosis is applied.[32]

The use of investigative hypnosis is not without its critics. The California Attorneys for Criminal Justice, an association of more than 1,500 defense lawyers, argued that the effectiveness of hypnosis has been overrated. As a result of the group's petition to prohibit the use of investigative hypnosis, the California Supreme Court banned the testimony of witnesses who have been hypnotized.[33] Many other states have followed California's example by restricting hypnotic-induced testimony. Objections are based on the premise that what a subject thinks is being recalled from memory may be totally false and that the memory may be inaccurate. Some defense attorneys also think that the hypnotic session may implant memories so that the hypnotized subject accepts them as his or her own. Although hypnosis may not reach the evidence standards required for admission in many courts, its use remains valuable for uncovering leads when no other sources are available.

Case Study of Investigative Hypnosis.　　A case occurred in the city of Los Angeles in which a victim was shot to death. A witness was located who had been in the victim's apartment for about 20 minutes while the suspect was present. However, the witness could not recall significant details of the event other than that shots were fired and that her friend's body was subsequently found outside the apartment door. The police department's staff psychologist was asked to conduct a hypnotic session. It is significant to note that investigators and a police artist were present throughout the session and actively participated in the dialogue with the witness. Before hypnotic induction began, the witness was told that the mind was like a videotape machine in which everything was recorded and stored. The witness was then instructed to relax and cooperate by fixing her eyes on a thumbtack that had been taped to a metal blind directly in front of her. Following the visual fixation, various induction techniques were used to achieve the hypnotic state, at which point the TV method of questioning was employed. After the witness had described her television viewing habits in detail, it was suggested to her that she was presently watching television in a similar manner. It was further suggested that she was going to view a special television movie that she could slow down or stop. She could also close in on scenes to allow her to see clear details. It was stressed to the witness that no matter what she viewed, she would remain relaxed and detached. Using the TV technique, the witness mentally reconstructed the events of the night her friend was murdered. She related that she and the victim were socializing when a suspect entered the apartment. At this moment, it was suggested to the witness that the film would stop, showing her a close-up of the suspect's features. The witness had ingested alcohol and drugs on the night of the murder; however, a detailed facial description was obtained despite the altered state of her perceptive ability. After describing the suspect, the witness related that her friend walked to the kitchen, placed a gun in his back pocket, and went outside with the suspect. The witness then heard a number of shots, turned the lights out, and called the police. At this point in the questioning, with the witness's approval, the investigators and police artist asked questions. As a result, a composite picture of the suspect was drawn that subsequently proved to be very accurate.

Following the questioning session, it was suggested to the witness that she would remember the things she had seen only if she chose to and that when she awoke she would feel relaxed and rested. It is significant that while the witness was still in the hypnotic state, it was suggested that if she should recall other details in the days to follow, she would feel free to call the investigators with this information. The witness was then brought out of the hypnotic state. She reported that she felt very relaxed.[34]

This murder investigation was subsequently solved through the use of information revealed during the session and other information developed later on. The investigators reported that the hypnosis interview was of considerable help in identifying the suspect and in gaining corroborating evidence.

Narcoanalysis

Narcoanalysis, or the use of so-called truth serums, is generally not considered an acceptable interviewing technique. Drug compounds, such as sodium pentothal or phenobarbital solution, are injected into the subject's bloodstream to produce a sleeplike state—a narcosis—wherein the subject is relieved of inhibitions. Information may then be revealed that is unobtainable via conscious questioning. Although often used by psychiatrists and other mental health practitioners, narcoanalysis is rarely used by the criminal investigator. It has proved to be scientifically unreliable and physically dangerous as well. The information revealed during a narcosis may be inaccurate or totally spurious because of the effect of the drug. As with all drugs of a barbiturate composition, the danger of respiratory failure and impaired brain function is present. Accordingly, any truth serum test must always be administered by a physician.

Narcoanalysis can only be used with those who voluntarily choose to subject themselves to the technique. Occasionally, suspects may request narcoanalysis to "prove" their innocence or as a memory aid to strengthen an alibi. When hypnosis has proved ineffective, narcoanalysis has been used as an alternate technique with both victims and witnesses. The results of the examination are generally not admissible in a criminal case, unless prosecution and defense stipulate otherwise.

▲ SUMMARY

The ability to obtain verbal information from crime victims, witnesses, and suspects is absolutely crucial to the investigative process. Although suspect interviews receive considerable media attention, victim and witness questionings are far more numerous. The successful victim or witness interview depends on many factors in regard to the attitude of both investigator and subject. Investigators should prepare thoroughly prior to the interview, as all pertinent documents should be reviewed and necessary file checks conducted. Victim or witness interviews can be generally guided by the degree of emotionality present within the subject. Those subjects who have been emotionally affected by their victimization must be interviewed with great sensitivity, for the psychological impact of the crime may still be evident, influencing their statements and recollections. Many factors can alter a subject's perception of a criminal event, including physiological abilities, emotions, external factors, and personal feelings. Each of these factors can distort perception and recall of an event. The cognitive interviewing technique has proven to be very effective in screening such factors and is an excellent supplement to traditional questioning methods.

Suspect interviews vary greatly from the questioning of victims and witnesses. There are many legal concerns associated with this form of questioning, beginning with the mandatory advisement of rights. Criminal suspects often regard the police interview as a hostile encounter, which makes this type of questioning more difficult than all others. To enhance the probability of obtaining an admission of guilt or a full confession, the investigator should attempt to match the questioning to the personality of the subject. Most suspect interviews involve individuals who are psychologically normal. These suspects generally perceive their actions to have been wrong and experience the normal emotions of guilt and anxiety. Other suspects lack these normal reactions to criminality, necessitating interviewing techniques more suited to their abnormal personalities. The psychopathic personality, quite common among suspects with psychological abnormalities, requires questioning suited to those who lack the capacity to experience guilt or remorse.

Many methods outside the traditional questioning process are selectively used to enhance the interview. Use of the polygraph, generally to detect deception, is not uncommon, although the test results are typically not admissible in criminal trials. The polygraph is valuable in producing investigative leads but must be used with caution, as many factors can invalidate its findings. Investigative hypnosis has also been used with some frequency. Although this form of questioning can be admitted as evidence in court, great care must be taken to avoid challenges based on the improper use of subject suggestibility.

EXERCISES

1. Have a selected group of students create a visually shocking event. Have student "witnesses" individually write their descriptions of the event. Compare the impressions for accuracy.

2. Using role playing techniques, create a mock interview posing as investigator and suspect.

3. Write a research paper detailing the personality traits of the psychopath, paranoiac, and psychotic personalities.

4. Prepare a research paper concerning the legal debate surrounding investigative hypnosis. Detail the case law in your state.

5. Involve students in role playing and videotape victim, witness, and suspect interviews. Simulate the ways in which emotionally affected victims might challenge the investigator and the attitudes typically encountered in criminal suspects. Present and review the tapes for class discussion.

RELEVANT WEB SITES

http://www.tourolaw.edu/patch/Miranda/

Details the full text of the U.S. Supreme Court decision justifying its opinion that created the now famous Miranda warning.

http://coloradorobbery.org/Articles/criminal_interrogation.htm

Site of Colorado Association of Robbery Investigators. Includes an extensive essay on how and why criminal suspects confess to the police.

http://www.psyweb.com/Mdisord/jsp/mental.jsp

Extensive mental health site that includes definitions of common mental illnesses. Of particular value to criminal investigators is the section pertaining to personality disorders.

Traditional Sources of Information

KEY TERMS

consensual crimes
doctrine of informer privilege
documentary information
electronic surveillance
entrapment
Freedom of Information Act
informants with ulterior motives
National Crime Information
   Center

National Criminal Justice
   Reference Service
paid informants
Privacy Act
reward programs
voluntary informant

LEARNING OBJECTIVES

1. to appreciate the importance of informational sources to the investigative process;
2. to be able to list and define human information sources;
3. to be aware of legal considerations regarding the informant;
4. to be able to list and define documented information sources;
5. to be aware of privacy considerations that influence information gathering;
6. to have thorough knowledge of federal legislation that has recently influenced information gathering and record keeping;
7. to understand the issues pertaining to electronic information gathering; and
8. to be familiar with recently developed scientific aids that have expanded criminal justice information gathering.

INTRODUCTION

Information is absolutely essential to the investigative process. Sources of information have always been the structural framework upon which the investigation is built. In media presentations, the investigator's information-gathering efforts are generally ignored. The hours (often weeks) of examining documents, interviewing informants, and searching files simply do not provide sufficient excitement for movies or television. However, all effective investigators have mastered information-gathering techniques. They know where and how to obtain information. In some cases, the information gathered dictates whether to follow an investigative lead or to scrap it, thereby determining the direction of the inquiry. Information is frequently necessary to identify an offender or to provide background on a probable suspect. Finally, information gathered from a multitude of sources is essential for the prosecution of the suspect.

HUMAN SOURCES OF INFORMATION

Although not always the most reliable sources of information, people are the most frequent sources. Human beings vary considerably in their motivation, accuracy, and willingness to reveal their knowledge to the authorities. Each individual who reports a crime to the police or answers an investigator's inquiry is providing information. Although some people give information only if paid to do so, the majority of people volunteer information through a sense of civic duty. The general reliability of human informational sources is questionable. In the previous chapter we saw how various factors affect a person's accuracy of perception. Physiological abilities, emotional state, physical conditions, maturity, and a host of other factors play a part in information processing so that no two people experience an object or event in precisely the same way.

VOLUNTARY INFORMANTS

It is unfortunate that the term *informant* has acquired such a negative connotation. As children, we learn to disapprove of "tattletales," or those who inform on others. In fact, an entire terminology has evolved, used by citizens and police alike, to describe the informant. "Snitch," "fink," "rat," "stoolie," and many other descriptors are all too common. Yet, few citizens consider themselves "stoolies" when they phone the police to report a loud party or a suspicious individual loitering in the street. The source of information can be a citizen with an impeccable background or an individual with a long criminal history. In either case, information has been obtained through an informant. The stigma attached to the term only serves to complicate the information-gathering process. Many individuals who wish to provide information to the police hesitate to do so for fear of being somehow connected with the criminal element. Anyone, regardless of a criminal or law-abiding background, who provides information to the police without ulterior motive or payment is a **voluntary informant**.

Voluntary informants run the entire social and economic spectrum. This type of informational source may be a garbage collector who observes a strange car parked in front of a home or a physician who treats an individual with a gunshot wound. The only common denominator is the voluntariness of the information. Civic responsibility, fear, or general suspicion often motivate voluntary informants to contact a police agency without being solicited, but much valuable information would never reach the police if the investigator failed to take the initiative. For a variety of reasons, some people will gladly relate information to police officers, but only if the officer initiates the contact. Thus, it is necessary for the investigator to pursue voluntary informants actively during the course of an investigation.

The nature of the crime, its location, and the probable identity of the perpetrator all serve to guide the investigator in contacting the voluntary informant. Obviously, if an offense occurs in front of a bar, the investigator will seek information within. A burglary offense calls for the questioning of known burglars or those who associate with such individuals. If the officer has an indication of the identity of the suspect, associates, relatives, and others are contacted for information. People in certain occupations have traditionally been found to have a high probability of yielding valuable information. Bartenders, pawnshop operators, taxi drivers, massage parlor personnel, and street vendors in general are some of them. Generally, those associated with businesses in used goods or entertainment or who operate "in the street" in some manner are sources worth cultivating.

Investigators obtain voluntary information from informants in three general ways: by *personal cultivation*, by *departmental reference*, and by *unsolicited contact*. All officers should attempt to cultivate voluntary informants. Often, contacts made during a past investigation prove to be useful to the present case. If, for example, an officer conducted a past interview with a nightclub owner in a professional manner, the owner might be predisposed to provide information at a later date when solicited by the officer. A friendly, nonbelligerent, concerned attitude invites respect and confidence. An officer known for a positive attitude and reliability will find that reputation helpful in establishing rapport. Police officers often overlook a major source of voluntary information—the very suspects they arrest. An arrest does not have to be antagonistic. Of course, there will be some suspects who hate the police on general principle, but a surprisingly large number do not view an arrest as a personal affront. If treated fairly and in a professional manner, these suspects often voluntarily provide investigative information. The offer of a cigarette or an extra phone call to a suspect's relative can go far toward establishing a friendly rapport.

Many police agencies have established files listing voluntary informants cultivated in prior investigations. The file may be cross-referenced by name, type of information obtained, and occupation. Such information may prove to be very useful or of no value at all, depending on the informant. Although some informants will voluntarily provide information to any investigator, many will talk only to officers with whom a personal rapport has been established. Again, the stigma of being labeled an informant may prohibit the recontacting of some individuals.

Unsolicited contacts are voluntary informants who self-initiate the police contact. Identified subjects who report criminal activity without being solicited or subjects who give anonymous tips over the phone or by letter fall into this category. Anonymity may be essential for some voluntary informants. Many people wish to provide the police with information, yet the apprehension of being publicly identified stifles contact. Other individuals, for seemingly irrational reasons, fear face-to-face contact with an officer. They will provide information only on a totally anonymous basis. Some informants fear reprisal and simply do not trust the police to safeguard their identity. For these reasons, subjects who phone the police with information should not be pressured to reveal their identity. When asked, "May we have your name?" and the subject states, "I would rather not say," no further demand should be made.

Numerous police agencies have wisely instituted programs that recognize the necessity of guaranteed anonymity. One such program, known as the Robotphone, was developed in Northern Ireland by the Royal Ulster Constabulary. When an informant dials the well-publicized Robotphone number, a recording device takes the information. This program has been highly successful in aiding officers in criminal investigations and in identifying terrorist suspects.[1] An important element of the program is the absence of a live police interviewer at one end of the telephone. Apparently, many voluntary informants will provide information to a machine much more readily than to a human being, either in person or over the phone. This method has been adopted by many American police agencies with equal success. TIP (Turn in a Pusher) and Secret Witness are two that have shown dramatic results.

In addition to newspaper programs or anonymous Web sites, television series currently dramatize unsolved case histories spotlighting wanted fugitives. A significant number of nationally prominent criminal investigations have been cleared as a result of televised reenactments, as the programs reach more than 60 million households. To date, as a result of the most popular of such programs, *America's Most Wanted*, 48 missing children have been recovered and more than 870 fugitives arrested, including eight who appeared on the FBI's Ten Most Wanted list.[2] For many years, the Drug Enforcement Administration (DEA) has operated a toll-free number designed to gather narcotics information. Any individual calling the number is assured absolute anonymity. There are programs offering monetary rewards in addition to guaranteed anonymity, but many highly successful ones have no monetary provisions.

Informants with Ulterior Motives

Some individuals provide the police with information for self-serving reasons. Such **informants with ulterior motives** do not demand or receive money for their information; however, serving as an informant benefits them in some fashion. Civic duty may be stated as the reason they are informing, but their true motivation may be something quite different. Revenge has always been a strong motivating factor for this type of informant. A person may seek to inflict harm on another for a real or imagined injury. Criminals who feel they have been cheated in the division of stolen property often anonymously inform on their former partners. Wives may inform on husbands whom they suspect to have been unfaithful or vice versa. Occasionally, a victim who has been swindled in a bunco scheme through greed motivations may anonymously inform for revenge.

Some arrested suspects provide information in the belief that their cooperation will result in their release or a reduced sentence. As previously mentioned, officers must never indicate that they have the authority to reduce a suspect's sentence; only the prosecuting attorney, in cooperation with the court, has this authority. Officers can indicate that a suspect's cooperation will be brought to the attention of the prosecutor, but they can go no further in attempting to elicit information.

Informing to eliminate fellow criminal competitors has traditionally benefited the investigator. Many criminals operate along typically businesslike lines of profit and loss. When one suspect is economically threatened by the competition of others, the result may be a timely phone call alerting the investigator to the competitor's illegal activity. With the increase in illegal drug sales, investigators have noted a sharp increase in this type of informant. Other common ulterior motives are guilt and the desire to receive attention. Regardless of the true motivation involved and despite the often distasteful people with whom the officer must converse, all informants must be given equal credence and consideration.

Paid Informants

Any individual who receives monetary compensation for information is a **paid informant**. Paid informants vary in background and criminal association, but all provide information for money. In the majority of cases, the paid informant is either actively involved in crime or has close contacts with those who are. Because of public sensitivity concerning the use of informants, many police agencies reveal few details concerning the practice. Yet the paid informant and the police have been strange working companions for many years. From the earliest organized police forces to the present day, the paid informant has been in constant demand. The failings of human nature—greed, in this case—suggest that this source of information will always be with us. Police agencies on the local, state, and federal levels spend millions of dollars annually for the informant's services. Recently, the Internal Revenue Service paid $6.6 million to 708 individuals who provided confidential information relating to income tax cheating.[3] The FBI, Treasury Department, and a host of other federal investigative agencies have sizable portions of their annual budgets earmarked for this purpose. State investigative agencies also routinely pay informants, with the majority of the money spent in cases relating to narcotics and organized crime.

Critics of the use of paid informants point to the huge amounts of money involved and to the immorality of police paying unscrupulous individuals (frequently criminals) for information. Yet the paid informant is a necessary, even essential, element of criminal investigation. It is perhaps unfortunate that these individuals have become so important, but the very nature of criminality demands their use. Crime is secretive and perpetrated by people who take great pains to avoid identification. Consequently, the task of criminal identification is a difficult one, demanding the use of all legal aids available to the officer, including the paid informant.

Certain investigations involving **consensual crimes**, in which complaints are rarely filed, often demand the use of paid informants. Narcotics crimes and prostitution fall into this category. Information gathered from paid informants often results in the recovery and return of substantial amounts of stolen property. For example, during one year, informants paid by the FBI accounted for 14,233 arrests and the recovery of more than $51 million in money and merchandise.[4] The DEA is another agency that is highly dependent on paid information. At any given time, the DEA maintains 4,000 informants who receive various payments totaling from $2 million to $4 million a year.[5] Although such expenditures may seem extravagant, the results they produce are significant. As former FBI director William Webster has written, "The informant is the single most important tool in law enforcement."[6]

Although the typical paid informant is a criminal type, many individuals with noncriminal backgrounds provide valuable information in exchange for money. The practice dates back nearly two centuries in this country. The offering of rewards for a suspect's identity or whereabouts was commonplace in the United States from the late 1700s to the turn of the century. In many areas of the country, cash payments were nearly the sole method of criminal apprehension because of the absence of any effective criminal investigation. A revival of interest in the cash reward appears to be gaining in popularity. Chiefly motivated by the increase in serious crime during the mid-1960s, numerous private and public agencies began to offer cash for information used in crime solution. In some cities, banks post photographs of robbery suspects on billboards and in buses. The Maryland Association for Bank Security has developed a highly successful Bank Robbery Reward Plan. Reward posters (Figure 7.1) are posted in all of the members' bank branches and related Web sites stating that cash rewards will be paid for information leading to convictions for bank robbery. Many newspapers and radio and television stations have also instituted programs designed to reach individuals with information for sale.

In many American communities, "Crime Stoppers" or similarly titled programs have become commonplace and highly effective in producing apprehensions. Through such programs, typically promoted in newspapers and sometimes in radio and television spots, cash rewards are paid for information leading to arrests and convictions in unsolved crimes. Reporting methods are devised that guarantee anonymity to the informant. Many such local programs are funded by private sources, such as a business community or a chamber of commerce. Police investigators typically provide the facts of an unsolved investigation for public announcement and assist in the evaluation of incoming tips.

The *Detroit News* advertised to its readers that rewards of $1,000 to $5,000 would be paid for information leading to convictions in specific crimes. In six years of operation, this program helped solve 31 murders and many more felony offenses. Readers of the *Sacramento Bee*, in response to a similar program, solved 93 crimes and provided information leading to 48 major arrests during an 18-month period.[7] A trend that uses a newspaper format identifies wanted criminal suspects by name. Ads are purchased in local shopping-oriented papers by police or county prosecution officials, listing suspects' names and birth dates. One such program in Barron County, Wisconsin, listed 346 individuals wanted by the authorities. The advertisement quickly resulted in 12 arrests through informant information and in the voluntary surrender of 72 suspects after they became aware of the newspaper advertisement.

FIGURE 7.1 Citizen tips through various media sources have led to the capture of thousands of dangerous felons during the past decade. Here, an FBI official, White House reporter, and the host of a television series dedicated to apprehending fugitives celebrate the fiftieth anniversary of the FBI's Ten Most Wanted program. (*Source: Dennis Cook / AP Wide World Photos.*)

Reward programs are obviously of great benefit to the police; however, such programs must be closely supervised. A mutual cooperation and understanding must be established between the police and program agency. Investigators must stress to the citizens who operate such programs that criminal investigation is strictly a police responsibility. Accordingly, all information obtained through the program must be turned over to the police for proper investigation. Independent agencies other than the police should then determine the amount of reward to be paid to the informant.

The legality of an anonymous tip to the police has been upheld many times by various state supreme courts. The U.S. Supreme Court, as recently as 1990, determined that an anonymous tip, corroborated by independent investigative work, can provide reasonable grounds for suspicion and investigatory detention of a suspect. In *Alabama v. White*, the Court ruled that an anonymous informant who had access to information concerning a suspect's movements would also be likely to have access to reliable information about the suspect's illegal activities.[8]

Managing the Paid Informant

Informants who receive money for the information they supply must be managed very carefully. The paid informant is typically a career criminal or someone marginally involved in criminal activities. Obviously, this type of individual is untrustworthy—likely to take advantage of any mistake in management by the officer. One of the most important rules of informant management is that the investigator must always control the informant and never the informant the investigator. It is the investigator who must decide the details of the informant's activities, such as the manner in which evidence is gathered, meeting locations, and the amount of money paid for specific information.

Not only does the investigator manage the paid informant's activities in the field closely—all contacts involving money must be scrupulously managed. All funds paid to informants must be documented to protect the investigator and the police agency. Receipts should be obtained from the informant following payment, showing the amount paid, date, and signature of the recipient. Documentation of payment protects the officer from allegations that no payment was made or that a portion of the payment was withheld. Informants often hesitate to sign such receipts for fear of their identity being revealed. The investigator must give assurance that the receipt is for purposes of record keeping only and will remain confidential. Before any informant is paid, the investigator has an obligation to confirm the accuracy of the information. It is desirable that information be cross-checked using different sources, if at all possible. Similar information from other informants or confirmation by field surveillance will periodically serve to establish an informant's general reliability. If such checks are not made, informants may begin to supply information that is inaccurate or totally fictitious.

This type of informant is usually involved in a criminal organization, supplying information that will lead to a long investigation. All paid informants, regardless of the nature of their information, should be thoroughly identified by the police agency. This includes photographs, physical description, name, address, and fingerprints. Such information serves to identify and locate the informant for other officers and enables the background check to be made. Information gathered on the informant should be filed in a secure area. Although most state and federal investigative agencies allow open access to such files for all investigators, local agencies tend to restrict availability to the detective division. In addition, many local agencies require investigators wishing to review the files to obtain permission from the chief law enforcement executive or command-level supervisors.[9]

A successful working relationship between investigator and informant is based on trust. The informant must have considerable trust and confidence in the ability of the officer. The informant's position is sometimes a very dangerous one; injury or even loss of life could result from an error in judgment. Consequently, the investigator must take great care to protect the informant's identity from everyone, with the exception of those who have a legitimate need to know. The investigator should never use the informant's true name in conversation or in investigative reports. Code names or number designations should be substituted. Obviously, when a meeting is required, the informant should never come to the police agency. Meetings should be held in out-of-the-way places, with a different locality selected for each meeting.

Police agencies that routinely use paid informants would do well to adhere to guidelines developed by the attorney general of the United States. Although the following guidelines were specifically developed for the FBI and DEA, they are applicable in theory to all police agencies:

1. When dealing with paid informants, a documented record of payment will be kept.
2. Supervisors will conduct frequent reviews of the activities of each informant.
3. The police agency will notify other authorities when an informant commits a crime in the jurisdiction of those authorities.
4. A background investigation will be completed for all informants.
5. Officers will be prohibited from making deals with informants who are seeking leniency in exchange for information.
6. Prosecution officials will review investigations using paid informants for legal adherence.
7. Officers will obtain the approval of a supervisor before using a paid informant
   (a) who is under 18 years of age,
   (b) who is currently on parole or probation,
   (c) who is undergoing treatment for drug addiction or who was addicted to drugs in the past, or
   (d) who has been convicted of two or more felony offenses.[10]

Informant Legal Considerations

A frequent area of difficulty arising from the use of informants in criminal investigations concerns the protection of their identities during the trial. The majority of informants, particularly the paid variety, do not wish to testify in public. Fortunately, our judicial system has historically recognized the need for informant confidentiality. State and federal courts have developed a doctrine known as the **doctrine of informer privilege**, which recognizes that an informant's identity should not be disclosed during the trial for two basic reasons, as follows: (a) disclosure may result in retaliation and harm to the informant, and (b) confidentiality ensures a continued flow of information to the police. However, courts are also rightly concerned with providing a fair trial to the defendant. In response to these seemingly conflicting concerns, courts have developed certain "balancing" procedures to determine whether the informant should be required to testify in a particular criminal trial. Can a defendant be tried fairly without the opportunity to confront the informant? Is the informant's presence for cross-examination necessary and material to the suspect's defense? The court must weigh these factors carefully, examining the nature of the informant's involvement in the offense being considered. If the information provided by the informant merely initiated the investigation and the police subsequently established the elements of the crime through their own efforts, the informant's identity is rarely necessary. However, when the informant was physically present to witness the offense or participated in some element of the offense, an appearance in court may well be required. If the informant witnesses events between the officer and suspect, the officer's testimony will normally negate the necessity of having the informant testify. Occasionally, judges may interview informants privately to determine if their testimony would differ from the officer's and thus be important to the suspect's defense.

Certain types of investigations may involve an informant who has directly participated in an illegal transaction, for example, the purchase of narcotics. As a general principle, if an informant participates directly in the offense, either by handling evidence or otherwise engaging in the transaction, that informant becomes a material witness; that is, the informant's testimony may be important in the determination of guilt or innocence. Thus, the informant's testimony will be required by the defense, necessitating a court appearance.

A second commonly contested legal issue involving informants is **entrapment**. A common defense in cases involving informants or undercover police officers, entrapment can be asserted to challenge the legality of various investigative techniques. Often used as a criminal defense by drug defendants and other suspects charged in a variety of vice crimes, a claim of entrapment asserts that police have induced an individual to commit a crime. When defendants make such claims, the burden of proof falls on investigators to prove the defendant was, in fact, predisposed to commit the criminal offense. Inducement generally requires more than merely establishing that an officer approaches and requests a defendant to engage in criminal conduct. Government conduct is required that creates a substantial risk that an undisposed person or otherwise law-abiding citizen would commit the offense.

To ensure that undercover investigations do not give rise to successful claims of entrapment by suspects, officers should be aware of three essential points. First, investigators should be prepared to articulate to the court a legitimate law enforcement purpose for beginning the undercover operation. Second, officers should avoid using persistent or coercive techniques and instead merely create an opportunity or provide the facilities for the suspect to commit the offense. Finally, investigators must document the factors demonstrating why a defendant was disposed to commit the criminal act prior to police contact. Such factors often include a prior arrest record, the suspect's familiarity with drug terminology, and eagerness to engage in criminal activity.

Many of the search warrants issued each year in the United States are based on information supplied by informants. Although the law varies from state to state, a search warrant will be issued if the informant is reliable and knowledgeable and has timely information.

Informant reliability is determined mainly from past associations between the informant and the authorities. If the informant has aided the police by identifying criminal suspects or locating wanted suspects or has generally supplied information that has proved to be accurate, reliability can be established. Accurate knowledge is necessary for the establishment of probable cause. The warrant can be issued only when the probable cause is sufficient to convince the judge of the warrant's worth. The investigator must determine if the informant's knowledge is firsthand and based on actual perception.

It is probable that the use of informants will continue to cause controversy and disagreement. Many defense attorneys feel that it is blatantly unconstitutional for informants to acquire information to be used in investigations. The objection centers on the lack of protection against self-incrimination when suspects are questioned by paid informants. Under the *Miranda* decision, police are required to warn a suspect of rights to silence and counsel, but an informant is free to question an unwary suspect without any such warnings.

A final legal informant consideration involves the use of *cellmate informants*. Cellmate informants are undercover police officers or fellow prisoners who obtain incriminating information from suspects confined in a correctional institution. Criminal investigators have found this technique to be an effective tool with certain types of suspects who are likely to boast while in jail or prison. The U.S. Supreme Court in *Illinois v. Perkins* (1990) held that the use of cellmate informants does not violate the *Miranda* rule. Undercover officers or actual cellmates need not give the warning before inquiring about a crime, as a prison cell lacks the psychologically compelling atmosphere that *Miranda* was designed to protect against. When an imprisoned suspect has previously invoked his right to silence during an earlier phase of the investigation, however, the legal use of cellmate informants is questionable in many circumstances.[11]

DOCUMENTARY SOURCES OF INFORMATION

Few people outside the law enforcement profession realize the investigative importance of documentary sources of information. **Documentary information** is any type of information of a printed nature or data otherwise recorded and stored for retrieval. Such information may be obtained from within the police agency, from other criminal justice agencies, and from sources not connected with law enforcement. The media image of the criminal investigator rarely includes the paperwork aspect of the job. The investigator deals with people and crime scenes on a continual basis, but much time is spent tracking down and evaluating "paper information." It is a rare felony investigation in which an officer does not spend many hours processing reports, files, and records in an effort to document the case. Such duties require patience, knowledge, and a systematic thoroughness for proper results.

Internal Agency Sources

The first step in becoming skilled in gathering and evaluating documentary information is to be aware of the typical municipal police agency as a source. Since police departments vary considerably in size and budget, no two agencies will be identical in their information-gathering capabilities. However, all medium-sized and large departments have the same general reporting and recording systems. The majority of police agencies have some type of *master file* containing the following information:

1. names and addresses of individuals who have been arrested or questioned in some manner or who have reported an offense, witnessed an offense, or who have otherwise made contact with the police agency;
2. references to crime reports by the name of the reporting party, victim, or suspect or by the assigned officer;

3. reports of all traffic accidents and other traffic contacts; and

4. name listing of all suspects having warrants for their arrest.

In addition to the master file, police agencies typically have records located in the division in which the greatest use will be made of them. The detective division often has a *modus operandi* (MO) file, cross-indexed by type of crime, name of criminal, and method of criminal operation. Investigators frequently refer to photographic files of previously arrested subjects. This type of file or book is arranged by the type of crime committed and is used to aid victims or witnesses in identifications. Printed bulletins and notifications of recent crimes are also found in the detective division. Depending on the size of the agency, files of informants and of criminal intelligence may also be available to the investigator.

The patrol division is capable of helping the investigative efforts of the entire department; it operates around the clock and has tremendous information-gathering potential. Patrol divisions that routinely use the field interview gather much important information that is ultimately recorded and filed for future reference.

The jail division routinely records the names of suspects who are currently confined, along with the offense and background information from the booking form. The booking form may be very useful in that it lists the address, date of birth, physical description, place of employment, occupation, possessions at time of arrest, and other important data on the suspect. The jail department also houses fingerprint cards and photos taken at the time of arrest.

The identification division of a police agency often is a source of files of a forensic nature. Records of latent fingerprints, crime scene photos, tool marks and impressions, paint samples, and ballistics materials are normally stored in this area. The property room contains stolen or recovered items that are held until trial. Records of such property indicate the basic physical description of the item, serial numbers, recovering officer, and other pertinent information.

Criminal Justice Agency Sources

Cooperation is the backbone of effective criminal investigation. The long-standing tradition of sharing documentary information among the various enforcement agencies has benefited the entire criminal justice system. Criminal investigators should be aware that, in addition to their own agencies, a multitude of other agencies at the local, state, and federal levels may serve as information sources. Each level provides unique and often essential services to aid the investigative process.

Local agency sources are normally municipal police departments, county sheriff's offices, and county probation and parole bureaus. Neighboring municipal police departments provide similar information, yet the specifics of the information are unique to each source. Because of the increased mobility of the criminal, similar crimes in several adjacent communities are occurring with greater frequency. Close communication and cooperation among local agencies may result in the recognition of such a pattern. Cooperation with a sheriff's department can also result in the acquisition of valuable intelligence information. Since the sheriff's department has an enforcement responsibility to the entire county, the documentary information found there is of a broader scope than that of a typical municipal police agency. The sheriff is also responsible for the operation of the county jail, including the collection and storage of all booking information resulting from jail procedures.

Probation, parole, and prison records have considerable information of possible value to the investigator. All convicted offenders who are placed on probation or released on parole have been investigated by these departments. The detailed background investigations on these offenders may provide insights not available elsewhere. The extent of such data can be appreciated when one considers there are currently over four million people on probation and 700,000 on parole. These figures do not include the millions of Americans who have previously been under probation and parole supervision. Prison records can provide data regarding inmate associates, gang affiliations, and DNA profiles. The coroner's or medical examiner's office is responsible for the investigation of suspicious or violent deaths. To arrive at a determination of the cause of death, this office conducts a postmortem examination of the deceased. Such a procedure involves the compilation of considerable information regarding the victim, witnesses to the death, and all other pertinent areas of inquiry.

State governments provide investigative assistance through various specialized departments. They also consolidate information from local enforcement agencies. The attorney general of each state is considered its chief law enforcement officer. The major function of the Office of the Attorney General is to review existing state statutes, supervise local prosecutors, and investigate specific criminal or civil violations. State attorney generals frequently aid local agencies by conducting training seminars or by issuing statewide bulletins of enforcement interest. *Alert*, a monthly news bulletin published by the Office of the Attorney General of Maine, interprets the latest laws and court actions affecting police officers' job execution. Many states have sizable investigative agencies, such as the California Department of Justice and the Florida Department of Law Enforcement, that provide investigative assistance to requesting local agencies or instigate investigations into multicounty crimes. State investigative bureaus can assist the local investigator by providing informants, undercover agents, and intelligence information. In addition to state investigative agencies, the majority of states have bureaus of identification.

Identification bureaus provide a central location for crime reports, DNA profiles, fingerprint cards, MO files, laboratory equipment, and personnel for all enforcement agencies within the state. The trend in recent years has been to combine the state identification bureau with the state investigation department, merging the two into a single agency. Occasionally, the state police or highway patrol of a given state also functions as an identification bureau. There are approximately 55 million criminal history records in state criminal identification repositories throughout the United States.

Within the government structure of each state, the motor vehicle bureau contains much documentary information of possible investigative value. This department is often administered by the secretary of state. Since our society is highly mobile, the automobile has become increasingly more important as a tracing clue in various crimes. Contained within the department are records of all motorized vehicles within the state and licensing information on all drivers. The licensing information can be very useful, containing a detailed physical description, date of birth, address, signature, handwriting sample, and photograph.

Federal criminal justice agencies exercise wide territorial authority and are varied in the specific enforcement assistance they can provide to local officers. The Department of Justice agencies include the FBI, the DEA, the Bureau of Prisons, and the Law Enforcement Assistance Administration. The FBI has a long history of providing valuable information to local law enforcement agencies. Having the most massive data collection of any justice agency, the FBI has compiled records on nearly 80 million individuals and organizations since its founding in 1908, with 800,000 new names added to its files each year. Information has been gathered from routine background inquiries, national security checks, and standard criminal investigations.[12] In addition to investigating the 206 federal offenses over which it has jurisdiction, the FBI serves any requesting police agency via the following:

1. **The National Crime Information Center (NCIC).** On January 27, 1967, the NCIC computerized electronic data exchange became operational. Developed to complement computerized systems already in operation by local and state enforcement agencies, this system records enormous amounts of criminal information in a central computer bank in Washington. The system is designed to link thousands of police agencies by remote computer terminals to the control center. Agencies using the service can instantaneously determine if a suspect is wanted in another jurisdiction or if recovered property is stolen. Participating agencies also have the capability of entering information into the system concerning locally wanted people, automobiles, and other types of property. The NCIC system contains more than 20 million records on wanted and missing persons, stolen property, and other matters. It has proved to be an extremely useful system. Nearly 60,000 authorized users conduct a million transactions daily. Among its many uses, the NCIC system has proven to be extremely helpful in apprehending wanted fugitives, as more than 300,000 entries are contained in the Wanted Persons File. Technological advances planned for the near future will allow users to receive and transmit suspect fingerprints and photographs. A wanted suspect's fingerprints will be computer transmitted, searched, and matched from the Wanted Persons File within 20 seconds.[13]

2. **The Criminalistics Laboratory Information System (CLIS).** This computerized information system collects and disseminates forensic science data for law enforcement agencies throughout the United States. The data are collected, identified, and stored for online retrieval through NCIC terminals. Information on the latest analysis methods, crime scene collection procedures, and the like is instantly available for any officer.

3. **The FBI Laboratory.** The largest forensic laboratory in the world, its facilities are available without cost to any U.S. enforcement agency. More than 900,000 forensic examinations are conducted yearly in all areas of criminalistics. In addition to forensic testing, the laboratory operates the National Fraudulent Check File, the Anonymous Letter File, the Bank Robbery Note File, the National Stolen Coin File, and the National Stolen Art File. The check file is a national repository for fraudulent checks that has proven very helpful in tracking fraudulent check passers moving rapidly from one community to another. When a fraudulent check is submitted, handwriting and other factors are compared against previously submitted checks. Additional descriptive data on the suspect MO, photographs, and identification records of check passers are furnished to requesting enforcement agencies. The bank note file connects robberies to individual perpetrators through analysis of holdup notes. During a recent year, 1,129 such notes were searched in the computerized files, resulting in 144 associations with other robbery notes. The art file contains more than 4,000 detailed descriptions of stolen fine art and helps establish the method of operation.[14]

4. **The FBI Identification Division.** Formed in 1924, this division receives fingerprint cards of arrested suspects and others from 7,200 contributing agencies. The sets of fingerprints submitted daily number 25,000. The identification division informs police agencies of a suspect's prior record

and possible wanted status. Deceased subjects are also identified. The fingerprint collection of this division is in excess of 175 million cards.

5. **The Combined DNA Index System (CODIS).** Because of the DNA Identification Act of 1994, the FBI was authorized to establish a national DNA database for law enforcement purposes. The CODIS system enables public laboratories on the local, state, federal, and international levels to exchange and compare DNA profiles via computer. The system allows investigators to compare identified DNA profiles against genetic evidence secured from past unsolved crimes or recently arrested suspects and assists in establishing the identity of suspects and victims. The central FBI CODIS computer index currently contains over 2.3 million DNA profiles from all 50 states and 18 foreign countries. To date, at least 5,000 unsolved crimes have been cleared by the system, and many thousands of felons have been correctly identified who otherwise might have remained unknown.

The Federal Bureau of Prisons administers federal correctional institutions throughout the United States. Information concerning a suspect's conduct while in prison, personal acquaintances, medical and psychological data, and photographs are available to the officer from this source. The DEA was established in 1973 to control narcotics and dangerous drug abuse. The agency is additionally responsible for supervising licensing and inspection of those individuals who are legally allowed to handle and prescribe narcotics. The DEA provides numerous training seminars in narcotics investigation to local police agencies and maintains a laboratory for narcotics analysis. Local police agencies may use the record resources of the DEA, such as the known-addicts file. All suspects who have been arrested or otherwise identified as narcotics users are fully identified in this file. The DEA also routinely provides undercover agents to assist departments that lack the expertise, personnel, or budget for undercover operations.

The U.S. Department of the Treasury comprises the Internal Revenue Service (IRS) and the Bureau of Alcohol, Tobacco, Firearms and Explosives (ATF). Organized in 2003, the U.S. Department of Homeland Security houses the Secret Service and newly combined Bureau of Immigration and Customs Enforcement (ICE). Homeland Security was primarily formed to keep America secure from terrorist attack, and is particularly focused on safeguarding the country's borders, airports, seaports, and waterways. Further responsibilities of this federal department include developing the latest security technologies, responding to natural disasters or terroristic assaults, and analyzing intelligence reports leading to publicized threat-level alerts. The Bureau of Customs prevents smuggling and regulates the transfer of people and property into and out of the country. This agency additionally maintains files on suspects who have engaged in smuggling activities, including the method of operation used by such suspects. The IRS oversees and enforces the internal revenue statutes. The Intelligence Division of the IRS maintains information on tax evaders, including many organized crime and narcotics suspects. The Secret Service has considerable information on counterfeiting suspects and those suspected of threatening persons protected by this agency. The Secret Service also maintains a forensic section to analyze forged or counterfeited currency and securities.

The ATF operates as a separate bureau of the Treasury Department. Information on suspects who have been investigated or convicted of crimes in these areas is available in this bureau. A national office laboratory in Washington, D.C., offers a wide variety of services to enforcement officers. These include firearm and toolmark examination, chemical and instrumental analysis, and questioned document examination. Local investigators who encounter cases involving explosive devices almost always consult with ATF investigators; the latter are experts on the handling and field practices that are called for in such cases.

The U.S. Department of Defense includes the Army, Navy, Marines, and Air Force, in addition to civilian intelligence-gathering agencies. Each branch of the armed forces has specific internal enforcement agencies. Records are maintained on individuals who have been members of the armed forces and civilian individuals who have been the subject of criminal or intelligence investigations.

Other law enforcement agencies of the federal government can assist the investigator in various ways. For example, the U.S. Postal Service can provide a change of address and record information that appears on the outside surface of an envelope. Or the Federal Aviation Administration (FAA) can provide detailed information regarding aircraft and data concerning suspects who are licensed pilots. With the rapid increase in narcotics cases involving aircraft, the FAA has been consulted with considerable frequency. Immigration and Customs Enforcement can provide fingerprints, photos, and other data on suspects who are aliens or naturalized Americans. Because of the sizable number of federal agencies and their specialized areas of inquiry, it is advisable for every local police agency to obtain a directory of the federal government. Directories listing the name, address, and function of each federal agency are available online or from the Government Printing Office in Washington, D.C.

A relatively new but very helpful agency is the **National Criminal Justice Reference Service** (NCJRS). This federal department has become the largest criminal justice information network in the world. The NCJRS was created to furnish research findings to criminal justice professionals and operates five clearinghouses that provide free information to criminal investigators and other justice practitioners.

Outside Sources

Sources not connected with law enforcement vary substantially in quality and accessibility. Many publishing companies issue annual directories of individuals with common interests or backgrounds. Various *Who's Who*–type publications or Web sites can supply the investigator with biographical data on certain prominent individuals. There are a number of financial listings of varying usefulness. Dunn and Bradstreet has financial data on businesses. Standard and Poor's *Register of Corporations, Directors and Executives* and Moody's *Bank and Finance Manual* also list business and corporation information. The annual *Physician's Desk Reference* lists more than 2,500 drug and narcotic products. Although this publication is intended for physicians, the compound analysis of the various drugs and the physical side-effect information that is given can help an officer who is working narcotics. The book also contains a visual products section in which the color, size, and product markings of many dangerous drugs are illustrated. Other directories are available that list subscribing professional people, such as physicians, engineers, and educators. Names, addresses and phone numbers are given and sometimes background data.

Private industry has given rise to numerous credit reporting agencies for investigating the financial background of potential customers. Hundreds of major businesses make use of such agencies. Many retailers deal with local credit bureaus that compile and exchange information on the local level only. The national computer-based services and local credit bureaus have similar types of documentary information. Such information is limited because it is normally obtained from an individual during application for credit. Full name, address, previous places of residence, past and current employment, and various indicators of financial worth are normally listed. Similar information is documented in central depositories that are operated by banks and finance companies; however, because of the greater risk involved, this information is generally more extensive and detailed. Employee records, phone company information, medical files, and student records may additionally assist the officer.

The availability of private information sources is as great or as limited as the resourcefulness of the investigator. In today's computer-driven society, it is a rare individual indeed who has not deposited documentary information somewhere. If the investigator has procured some general information concerning a suspect, such as a name or place of employment, few private sources of information will remain untouched.

PHYSICAL SOURCES OF INFORMATION

The Crime Scene

The scene of the criminal offense is the source of most of the physical information pertinent to the investigation. All evidence secured from the crime scene is reviewed as to its information potential. It may be determined that additional examinations by others are required. Crime scene evidence often has significant value in providing the officer with suspect-tracing information. Latent fingerprints, clothing, and bodily fluids are only a few of the hundreds of tracing clues that may result from a thorough search of the scene.

It is important for the investigator to realize that the informational value of physical evidence may best be judged by specialists with the necessary expertise. Although an officer may be very experienced and have considerable knowledge of forensic science, evidence should be submitted to the police laboratory for all value judgments. Criminalistics is a relatively young and rapidly expanding science. Consequently, evidence that was valueless in past investigations may be very useful to the present case as a result of new forensic discoveries.

PRIVACY CONSIDERATIONS

Public concern with the right to privacy can be attributed in part to the tremendous growth of computerization. Never before in U.S. history has government and industry had so great a capability to gather and use information. In a modern-day sense, privacy is often a legal right; however, the legal right of an individual to remain publicly anonymous is far from absolute. U.S. courts are often faced with a true dilemma when confronted with privacy considerations. On the one hand, there is the need of government and industry to store and disseminate information; on the other, there is the right of individual protection against the storage and dissemination of incorrect or damaging data.

Philosophical Objections to Information Gathering

Many Americans feel threatened by the information-gathering capacity of private and public sectors of the population. A feeling that individuality has been sacrificed to "the right to know" is commonly expressed by some opponents of data collection systems. Other opponents argue that the personal development of an individual can be seriously damaged by computer files.

They fear that individuals may become overly concerned with how they are presented in a file and attempt to structure their lives to conform with the computer's expectations. Philosophical objections range from situational opposition to the rejection of all information gathering in any format. Additionally, many citizens feel that secretive data systems hamper effective government. The objections to information gathering are not groundless, for large computerized systems do make mistakes. Individuals can suffer financially or otherwise from false information routinely released by an impersonal data center.

The historical and philosophical development of our country has been rooted in the right to individuality and privacy. Thus, the investigator may be in a difficult position. Criminal investigation in a large, mobile society is inherently difficult, demanding the development and use of modern information systems. Yet, despite the difficulties and the need to overcome them, right of individual privacy must be observed.

Private Information Gathering

Information is collected, stored, and released by thousands of private agencies. Business concerns, data-processing bureaus, and many other non-government sources annually gather a tremendous amount of information on thousands of individuals. It is estimated that more than 100 million people are the subject of detailed computerized files in one or more private-industry computers.[15] The development of computer processing has been of great benefit to commercial business. Private industry has the capacity to check financial stability, past credit ratings, and other financial risk factors with computer assistance. Masses of paper that at one time were difficult to store and utilize can be stored in data banks at greatly reduced size. A matchbox can hold computer record information that, in print, would fill a cathedral (see Figure 7.2).

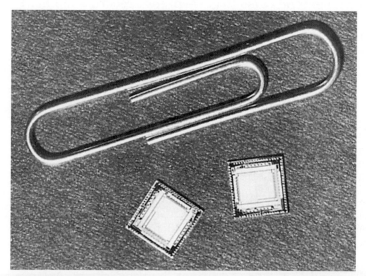

FIGURE 7.2 The first computer, completed in 1946, used 18,000 vacuum tubes and required 1,800 square feet of floor space. Today's computers are rarely larger than a portable television. They use tiny silicon chips, such as those pictured above with a paper clip to indicate relative size. Each of the chips shown is capable of storing the contents of a large public library.
(Source: International Business Machines Corporation.)

Credit bureaus have traditionally been an aid to the investigator; the information they record frequently helps to identify or trace a suspect. Credit investigators gather much useful information on people who apply for credit, loans, or life or automobile insurance and on those who apply for certain types of employment. For example, the Medical Information Bureau of Boston collects and stores medical history forms from 90 percent of all life insurance companies. Any person applying for life insurance with a subscriber company has a completed medical history form stored in the bureau's computer banks if one or more of 250 specified medical or psychiatric illnesses is cited.[16] The bureau's files currently number more than 11 million. Many other data-reporting agencies operate in a similar manner, storing information received during the application procedure for credit, loans, or other services.

The capacity to store and evaluate information automatically has produced correspondence privacy difficulties. Widespread reports of misuse of information by private industry led to the passage of the Fair Credit Reporting Act of 1970. The act gave an individual the authority to obtain, on demand, a report of what was in his or her credit file and to challenge any information found to be untrue. This had the impact of making it more difficult for the officer to gain access to private information files. Criminal investigators who, in the past, obtained such information through personal contact now find private sources reluctant to release information. In many situations, a court order is necessary to obtain the requested information, as is the case with telephone records.

Criminal Justice Information Gathering

Law enforcement agencies on the local, state, and federal level have developed effective record-keeping data systems. Most police departments have totally computerized record divisions. It has been estimated that the federal government operates more than 8,000 record systems containing information that would total 92 billion pages.[17] Public suspicion and mistrust of private industry data gathering extends also to government record keeping. To counteract fears that false information was being filed against individuals or that U.S. citizens had no access to tax-supported record systems, Congress passed the **Freedom of Information Act** (FOIA) in 1966. This act recognized the "people's right to know" by setting up a formal request procedure for public access to government records. Prior to the FOIA, an individual had to prove a direct interest in the information requested. The 1966 act did away with that stipulation—if an individual took legal action to demand information, the burden of proving a legitimate reason for denial rested with the government. Because of various complaints (mainly from the news media) that the act was cumbersome, new legislation was proposed to amend it. On December 31, 1974, the **Privacy Act** was enacted by Congress. The Privacy Act has had a major impact on all federal agencies and particularly federal law enforcement agencies.

Essentially, the Privacy Act and FOIA opened federal records to the individuals to whom they pertain. The individual has the right to review and amend incorrect information and to subject the report to judicial review if the agency refuses to amend the data. Additionally, the Privacy Act prescribed information collection procedures designed to improve the accuracy of the data. The Privacy Act does contain specific exemptions, prohibiting the review and release of information that falls into the following categories:

1. information classified as necessary for the national security;
2. information relating to the internal personnel rules and practices of an agency;

3. privileged trade-secret information; and

4. information concerning personnel, medical files, or investigative records that, if disclosed, might jeopardize the right to fair trial, invade personal privacy, or expose confidential sources.

Each federal agency must determine the investigative effects of data disclosure. It is fortunate for law enforcement that such exemptions are stipulated in the act. Otherwise criminal suspects undergoing a current investigation could keep abreast of each investigative development and learn the identity of all sources, obviously undermining the investigative effort.

Although the Privacy Act was directed toward all federal agencies, it has greatly influenced record keeping on the state and local levels. Many state legislatures have enacted state laws based on the Privacy Act. The majority of the states specify that information may be reviewed only by law enforcement personnel. For example, the Illinois statute states, "No file or record . . . shall be made public, except as may be necessary in the identification of persons suspected or accused of crime . . . and no information . . . shall be given or furnished by said Department to any such person."[18]

Accordingly, the Crime Control Act gives the subject of a specific criminal-history record file the right to inspect and challenge inaccuracies. It is important to note that investigative records and criminal intelligence files are not classified as criminal-history record information; thus, a subject may not review and correct such files. To prevent access to these files, all information pertaining to the five points previously listed must be maintained in separate files.

It is probable that additional legislation will be proposed governing the accessibility of police information. Although some individuals welcome continued efforts to "open up government," the necessity of restricted access to police records must be appreciated. This concern is particularly true given the investigating demand of the war on terror. Without the assumption of confidentiality, informational sources will be more difficult to locate. Many investigators report a current trend toward reluctance to be interviewed on the part of subjects. Such informants fear their identities will be disclosed under the FOIA. Other problems relate to the time and money necessary to implement accessibility. Since the FOIA amendments in 1974, many federal agencies have been overwhelmed by requests for information. The FBI alone has a backlog of more than 5,000 such requests that cannot be acted upon because of staff limitations. Since the Privacy Act, federal requests have averaged more than 12,500 a month, with resulting monthly processing costs of $8.2 million.[19] Since so many requests for FBI files are repeated for similar notorious cases, the agency decided in 1998 to place a large number of commonly requested files online so they would be available through open Internet access. Many famous investigations are now readily available via computer, totaling an extraordinary 1.3 million pages of information.

Electronic Surveillance

The use of electronic devices to gather information continues to be highly controversial. Government officials and some segments of the general public are sharply split on the issue. Many Americans are generally confused. Listening surreptitiously to private conversations of others has been practiced for many centuries. Historical accounts are filled with descriptions of individuals (both public and private) attempting to gather information by eavesdropping.

In the United States, *wiretapping* was not practiced with any degree of frequency until the outbreak of the Civil War. From 1861 to 1865, surreptitious "tapping" of telegraphic lines became a standard military practice.

Confederate cavalry leaders became particularly adept, with General John Morgan employing the services of a tapping expert to accompany his troops and gather information.[20] The interception of telephone calls did not come until the turn of the century, when telephone usage became commonplace.

Electronic surveillance, or *eavesdropping*, normally refers to the listening in on spoken interactions via devices that gather and amplify sound. Unlike wiretapping, this technique does not depend on a physical entry into a circuit. Wiretapping and electronic surveillance techniques were greatly improved during World War II and are currently in a highly sophisticated state of electronic development. Prior to 1968, electronic information gathering was practiced by public and private individuals but not on a consistent basis. Although many states prohibited the practice, the statutes were unclear about what specifically constituted the practice. In June 1968, Congress passed the Omnibus Crime Control and Safe Streets Act, which legalized electronic surveillance by law enforcement officers. The act was the first federal legislation in history to allow federal, state, and local officers to intercept wire and oral communications—with certain specified safeguards. Congress was prompted to pass the act to control organized crime and certain other serious criminal offenses.

The Omnibus Crime Control Act specified that electronic surveillance of a judicially unauthorized nature was illegal. It additionally specified punishments for violations and banned the manufacture, distribution, possession, and advertising of devices used to eavesdrop. The act also set forth procedures by which to apply for authorization to practice electronic surveillance and specified certain criminal cases in which the practice would be permitted. Certainly, the prohibition of private eavesdropping is one of the act's strong points. Private eavesdropping was common prior to 1968, with private investigators and other unauthorized individuals frequently engaging such means in investigations involving divorce and other domestic situations.

The thrust of the Omnibus Crime Control Act was to provide law enforcement with a modern, effective tool with which to combat organized crime and other serious offenses. Since the passage of the act, it has been documented that many law enforcement agencies have made use of electronic surveillance. Figures published by the federal government for 2004 are typical of recent usage patterns. They indicate that 1,710 wiretap requests were approved by federal and state judges. Each wiretap averaged nearly 2,000 conversations. The majority of court-authorized electronic surveillances are requested by state and local law enforcement agencies. In a recent year, nearly 60 percent of all requests were made by local rather than federal authorities. Of the total warrants issued, 73 percent were sought in drug investigations, with most of the other warrants being used for gambling and organized crime cases. As cell phones, pagers, e-mail, and fax machines have become more common, a growing number of court-authorized wiretaps have been used in cases that involve this expanding wireless electronic technology. Nearly nine of every ten wiretaps targeted portable devices, such as cell phones and pagers.

Although the majority of the states have statutes sanctioning court-ordered electronic surveillance, it is far from a common police practice. Annual reports submitted to Congress indicate that only a minority of the states having the power to use electronic surveillance actually use such means. Overall, the use of electronic surveillance has been greatly exaggerated in media accounts and other popular outlets. In reality, only slightly more than 8,000 criminal wiretaps have been authorized by courts in the past ten years. Yet the effectiveness of this selective method of investigation is well illustrated by the 22,000 convictions that resulted from the 8,000 surveillances.[21] In 2004 alone, wiretaps resulted in 4,506 arrests, which concluded in 634 convictions.

Wiretapping and electronic surveillance should not be confused with recording conversations in which the officer is one of the parties. The federal statute applies to the surveillance of those conversations that do not include the officer as a participant. In undercover fieldwork, recording devices concealed on the officer's body are frequently used. Since the undercover officer, or informant, is one of the parties to the conversation, court authorization is not normally necessary. Some states have enacted statutes demanding that such recordings be authorized by a local state's attorney or district prosecutor. For example, Illinois requires that an investigator secure the consent of a state's attorney to record conversations, even in cases in which the investigator is one of the parties. To date, 40 states and the federal government allow the taping of conversations if one party agrees to the recording.

▲ SUMMARY

In addition to obtaining information through interviewing, investigators must be skilled at gathering data from other sources. Information can be obtained from human, documentary, and physical sources. Human sources include citizens providing information as a result of civic duty, suspicion, or other natural motivations. Some provide information purely for monetary gain; others have ulterior motives. All human-oriented information must be evaluated objectively, and efforts must be made to corroborate the data through supporting sources. The paid informant often needs strict supervision and control, for such individuals typically have been or currently are involved in criminal activities.

The use of documentary sources of information necessitates a complete understanding of the location and type of data within the investigator's agency. A multitude of other criminal justice organizations also have informational sources of frequent benefit to the investigative process. Many federal data-gathering services are available to the investigator, including vast criminal history files and the National Crime Information Center. Sources of data not connected with law enforcement vary from privately published directories to information gathered by the credit and banking industries. Most physical evidence, however, is obtained from actual crime scenes. This form of evidence is often evaluated by experts trained in the science of criminalistics.

As technology devises newer and better methods to obtain investigative information, a corresponding concern with privacy arises. Privacy concerns are often difficult to resolve in a completely satisfactory fashion, for the rights of individuals must be balanced with the need of government to serve and protect effectively.

■ EXERCISES

1. Complete a research paper on the use of police informants from a historical and present-day perspective.
2. Interview a local police official as to departmental policy regarding the use of paid informants.
3. Research the degree and type of court-authorized electronic surveillance conducted by police in your city, county, or state.

RELEVANT WEB SITES

http://www.icje.org/id114.htm

Extensive essay details entrapment problems in handling informants. Links to essays on informant liability issues.

http://www.fas.org/irp/agency/doj/fbi/is/ncic.htm

Site of National Crime Information Center operated by the FBI. Details the various categories of individuals covered by the system. Links to sites dealing with the Privacy Act.

Computer-Aided Investigations and Computer Crime

KEY TERMS

artificial intelligence
computer crime
cyberstalking
distance learning

electronic mail
Internet
microcomputer
World Wide Web

LEARNING OBJECTIVES

1. to understand the importance of computer information systems;
2. to be able to explain how computer technology aids the investigative function;
3. to define the internal agency uses of the computer;
4. to define the external investigative uses of the computer;
5. to comprehend the nature and resources of the Internet;
6. to understand how Web sites on the World Wide Web can assist criminal investigation;
7. to be able to discuss the investigative procedures and legal considerations applicable to computer crime; and
8. to be able to list the characteristics and methods of operation unique to computer crime suspects.

INTRODUCTION

Criminal investigation and other law enforcement information-gathering techniques generate considerable amounts of potentially important data. The public image of police work suggests a role other than that of information processing, but in fact, police departments are highly information-intensive organizations. Unless the information is managed properly to ensure its availability to the officer, however, it cannot be used to its full potential. Much of the process of crime investigation is in actuality the continuous management of information. Even the most routine case can generate a massive amount of data, and complex felony investigations often amass staggering volumes of paper. Fortunately, in the course of a decade, modern technology has made the task of information management and retrieval much more efficient.

Computer science has increased the information-gathering and management capacity of law enforcement dramatically. Because of their speed in performing data processing and analyzing complex information, computers have become an integral part of law enforcement. As studies demonstrate that nearly 67 percent of the average police officer's time is spent doing some form of information processing, defined as "paperwork," the computer is becoming a standard tool in law enforcement and society in general.[1] The storage and processing of information by computers are rapidly replacing traditional paper methods in many areas of society. One-third of all the mail sent between businesses is now carried by electronic means, and 30 percent of all corporate information now exists only in electronic form.[2] Finally, 22 million Americans have access to the Internet at their workplace, and 71 million U.S. households (nearly three-quarters of the nation's total households) contain personal computers. Of these households, 61.2 million have direct Internet access. College students in particular are far more adept with the computer and using the Internet than the general population. Close to 90 percent of all college students have visited the Internet, 85 percent own their own computer, and at least 72 percent check e-mail messages daily.

Accordingly, with each passing year, the United States is moving from a paper society to a culture of electronic impulses. Nearly every facet of life, from personal banking to libraries to medical and business records, is electronically recorded and transmitted without a paper trail. The rewards of the computer revolution include greater efficiency, convenience, and masses of information at one's fingertips. Law enforcement computers currently perform a multitude of tasks that were more difficult and time consuming when accomplished by nonelectronic means. In addition to the sharing of information by many agencies throughout a region, state, nation, or the world, computers perform numerous internal functions of great investigative significance.

Law enforcement use of the computer is as significant as was the adoption of the police radio or even the motorized patrol. Computer technology began in earnest in 1946 with a military computer 18 feet high and 80 feet long.[3] This massive and relatively crude technology has developed into the modern microcomputer capable of performing more than one million instructions per second. Police agencies began to develop computer capabilities during the late 1960s with the National Law Enforcement Tele-communications System (NLETS). NLETS attempted to link law enforcement computers in most states to increase information sharing. In 1967, the National Crime Information Center (NCIC) became operational. NCIC became the first true crime database in the United States, providing extensive crime information to all states from a single federal source.

Most investigators use a **microcomputer**, a small, highly effective computer system consisting of a typewriter-like keyboard and monitor or video screen. The microcomputer's affordability, size, and versatility have produced an ideal system for the investigative process. With the development of the computer chip in 1973, the possibility of small, affordable computers aiding law enforcement became a reality. The personal computer, a desktop or portable microcomputer intended for individual use, was introduced by the IBM Corporation in 1981. As the computer industry perfected its technology, small and large police agencies alike began to purchase microcomputers to use in criminal investigations. Because computer size and cost continued to decrease, the personal computer is now available in portable laptop models, with handheld models already in limited use. More than 70 million personal computers have been sold in the United States alone. Studies demonstrate that the majority of those in the criminal justice system are currently computer literate, and nearly all investigative professionals have become computer literate.[4] This chapter's discussion focuses on the investigative use of the computer and details its criminal use and abuse.

INVESTIGATIVE USES OF THE COMPUTER

Internal Uses

The current widespread usage of computers has significantly aided the internal operations of individual agencies. The management of criminal investigations by various supervisors has long been a difficult task because of the volume of data generated by each case. Accordingly, a major challenge of the investigative process is coordinating incoming information into an understandable central pool of data. Because various officers write numerous reports during the three main phases of an investigation, several management challenges can arise. In medium to large agencies, most preliminary and some follow-up reports are written by patrol division officers, with all remaining reports completed by investigators. A resulting problem has been the lack of communication between the patrol and detective divisions after the investigative responsibility has been transferred. With the use of computers, incoming report information is much more readily communicated within an agency. Officers need only inquire through personal computers to determine the status of a given case with which they have previously been involved, and supervisors can issue updates to individuals or entire units through computer-generated summaries. A fully computerized law enforcement agency has the advantage of rapid and direct communication from officer to officer, supervisor to officer, or division to division. Such directness encourages the sharing of information, which eliminates much of the former resentment caused by lack of communication within an agency.

Modern computer information processing has also significantly assisted the investigative supervisor. Much of the success of criminal investigation depends directly on effective first-line supervision. Although investigative supervisors have a wide range of duties, a primary responsibility is certification of the completion and accuracy of preliminary investigative reports written by patrol officers or investigators. Because of rapid completion of reports by computer and the related ease of review and correction by word processing, supervisors can now better control data accuracy. In addition, supervisors are able to monitor the progress of investigators by instantly obtaining a computer summary of a specific officer's case file and related efforts.

Through the use of computers, an agency's investigative reports can form the foundation for improved crime analysis. When large amounts of data are to be analyzed, the need for automation is increased. By submitting standardized crime report forms, a computer can analyze the data using such factors as time of day or type of victim or premises to help officers predict future offenses within their jurisdiction. In one instance, the Dallas (Texas) Police Department used its computer system, the Real-Time Deployment Protect (RTD), to analyze tasks previously done by hand. The RTD system has efficiently deployed the department's tactical and detective divisions in combating high-crime trends. Reported crimes in each of the 11 patrol beats in the city are evaluated by type of crime, method of operation, type of victim, and other criteria. The computer then compares the current day's reported crimes with the average number of daily crimes for a specified previous period. Using these data, the system then provides daily information reports for dissemination to the department's officers. Most larger police agencies, such as the New York City Police Department, have internal computer systems that specialize in particular crime analysis.

Traditionally, police internal computer systems have been confined to the functions of storage and retrieval of data, with enhanced speed of operation. However, a new generation of computers and knowledgeable investigators has developed a programming technique of considerable potential. Termed **artificial intelligence**, or expert system concept, this computer program has the ability to manipulate data and infer conclusions from guidelines that are based on information supplied by investigators. The system uses technology and police expertise to aid case solution by collecting, storing, and analyzing data that can match information taken from crime scenes with potential perpetrators. Such systems depend on sources of information stored in the computer, known as databases, and the ability of the computer to match such information with particular investigations or suspects. For example, an officer responds to a burglary crime scene and writes his or her report on a personal computer. The report information is entered into another computer containing a program that checks the thoroughness of the preliminary investigation through a series of tutorial questions. Depending on the officer's answers, the computer may instruct that certain steps be completed to ensure a complete investigation. Such systems also have the capability of matching unique methods of operation with specific criminal suspects. Finally, the system has the ability to produce solvability scores based on the reporting information entered through the tutorial questions. The probability scoring indicates to the investigator and supervisor the extent to which an agency's resources should be committed to a specific case.[5]

Other *internal computer uses* focus on training, accident and crime scene reconstructions, tracking complex financial investigations, and agency communication. Computers can be used to improve training by providing individualized test and answer examinations or more complex "what if" scenarios that utilize movielike sight and sound stories through the use of a CD-ROM unit. For example, an investigator can be trained to skillfully process a criminal homicide crime scene by viewing an interactive CD that projects a re-created crime on the computer monitor. The story can be programmed to stop and quiz the officer at various points during the investigation while simultaneously instructing as to proper procedures and tactics. The reconstruction of various crime scenes is greatly enhanced by the use of the computer. Programs allow officers to give the computer various types of crime scene information, often taken from crime scene sketches and notes, and then realistically recreate a three-dimensional scene. Such reconstructed scenes can then be altered on the computer to be viewed from various angles or directions, assisting the officer in the analysis of evidence by location and position.

Internal computer systems are also well suited to certain types of complex criminal investigations. Fraud cases that involve extensive financial transactions, such as check cases, embezzlements, and bunco operations, can be analyzed rapidly and thoroughly by computer. Additionally, elaborate narcotics investigations involving numerous suspects and victims can be tracked effectively in this manner.

The computer is capable of increasing effective and timely communication throughout a law enforcement agency. A key component is the use of **electronic mail**, commonly termed e-mail. Electronic messaging allows every member of the agency who has access to a computer to communicate electronically with one or more fellow officers. Instead of past methods that depended on individuals receiving and reading paper memos or hoping officers would observe and read a posted bulletin board notice, e-mail messages are instantly sent to computers.[6] The messages may be sent to one detective or sent by the push of a single key to hundreds or thousands of computer screens. Other benefits of e-mail include the sender's being able to track who has read the message, thus ensuring accountability for the contents of the directive, plus paperless storage, printing, and future retrieval of the information by all who receive it. The widespread use of electronic messaging increases the speed with which field officers receive important messages, notices, and directives. Criminal investigators can also use this technology to inform officers of what happened to a case they may have handled in its preliminary stage or to alert fellow investigators or patrol officers of emerging crime trends. Other applications of computer technology in the agency include but are not limited to case management, tracking dispositions of investigations, narcotics and evidence control, firearms registration, and processing warrant information.

Through computer usage investigators are able to load information directly into databases without the redundant step of manual entry by clerks. Supervision has improved, morale has increased, and greater efficiency has been achieved. The ultimate benefit may well be higher clearance rates. Finally, considerable financial and personnel resources spent on manual reporting can now be diverted to other essential areas. The benefits of internal use of the computer are summarized in Figure 8.1.

Investigative Reports
• Preliminary
• Follow-up
• Closing

1. Entered in computer by investigator
2. Data transferred to permanent storage by disk or directly into main unit
3. Data entered into main computer for storage, analysis, and retrieval
4. Information can be retrieved for:
   • Solvability scoring
   • Suspect identification
   • Supervision and management
   • Property identification
   • Crime trend analysis
   • Method of operation determination
   • Agency sharing

FIGURE 8.1   Use of the computer in the management of information.

External Uses

In addition to improving internal police operations significantly, the information technology revolution has extensive external applications. Interagency data sharing is rapidly bringing together the previously fragmented system of law enforcement documentation. Through the use of computers, agencies can have instant electronic access to information from regional departments, state agencies, and federal investigative departments. Basic information such as the nation's 50 million criminal history records can now be displayed immediately on linked computers. Such basic information may prove helpful in many investigations, and interagency sharing of crime-specific information is also greatly enhanced. The state of Washington's Homicide Investigation and Tracking System (HITS) well illustrates the effectiveness of this concept. HITS relies on state agencies to submit information voluntarily concerning murders, attempted murders, missing persons for whom foul play is suspected, unidentified possible murder victims, and predatory sex offenses. The computer program then collates and analyzes the important characteristics of the reported crimes. Information is provided detailing cases with similar characteristics, and known suspects are identified and located by community residence. Finally, the HITS program provides investigators with names of experts who can assist with homicides or sex crimes and furnishes technical advice regarding crime scene and evidence processing.[7]

Many other states have regional or statewide programs similar to Washington's HITS computer technology. Most regional programs are patterned after the federal Violent Criminal Apprehension Program (VICAP), administered by the FBI. The VICAP program gathers and analyzes violent crime data provided by all the states, maintaining a unified investigative tracking tool for the nation's police. In Connecticut, 14 police agencies have pooled their information resources to form that state's first regional police computerized information system. Known as the Case Incident Regional Reporting System (CIRRS), it allows departments to share criminal case record information through a computer terminal located in each department.

Internet Resources

Not only have computers significantly improved both internal agency operations and external interagency information sharing, but the national and international resources of the Internet have vast potential to aid the investigative function. The **Internet** is an informational superhighway composed of an interconnected worldwide network of computer data pools. The Internet electronically links millions of computer users with more than 32,000 networks in 135 countries.[8] Thousands of police agencies are currently using the Internet as both a bridge to their constituents and a means to communicate with other law officers around the world. This technology has tremendous implications for criminal investigators. The Internet enables users to access a vast and varied array of information that is physically located in distant places. Yet the most useful feature may be its interactive quality whereby users are able to engage in electronic discussions with one another, either one-on-one or in groups. Using this tool, officers can communicate across the United States and throughout the world, sharing or seeking information on various crimes and investigative strategies.[9] Although investigators have always networked by telephone or letter, the Internet provides an instant method of posting or answering questions on electronic message boards. During a recent case, Hawaiian investigators posted information concerning a missing material witness on a restricted

Internet messaging site. An officer in Michigan read the information, located the subject, and notified Hawaiian authorities seconds after the discovery. In another case, Las Vegas detectives successfully tracked a fugitive rape suspect from their jurisdiction to Scotland using Internet e-mail.

A growing number of police agencies are providing information through the use of Web sites. *Web sites* are graphics-based documents located on the **World Wide Web**, an electronic locality that contains text, graphics, sound, and interactive potential. Web sites are Internet areas in which one or more home pages can be found. A *home page* refers to a personalized collection of information pertaining to a specific agency, business, or individual. A Web site may contain one or many home pages and is updated or altered by the agency or individual controlling the site. Besides a computer, Web sites are located through the use of a *modem*, a device that uses telephone lines to dial up the various large computer systems that comprise the Internet.[10] Web sites can be located through many searching methods, including commercial online services, entering the Web site address, or simply searching for the name of the police agency. After locating an agency's Web site, citizens or fellow officers can obtain a wide variety of data including the history of the department, current crime statistics, names and descriptions of wanted fugitives, and crime prevention tips. In the near future, many law enforcement agencies will also use their sites to allow citizens to file simple crime reports and confidentially leave tips for reporting illegal activities or locating wanted suspects (Figure 8.2).

The FBI and many other state and local law enforcement agencies are already using their Web sites to post wanted fugitive notices. The bureau's famous Ten Most Wanted list, complete with photos, is now available on the Internet and in the summer of 1996 led to the first electronic capture of a major fugitive. A 14-year-old American boy living in Guatemala located the FBI's Web site and was shocked to find a local family friend's photo and description. Using an alias, convicted bank robber Leslie Rogge had fled the

FIGURE 8.2 Many law enforcement agencies such as the Beaumont (Texas) Police Department have designed Internet Web sites for interagency and citizen information review. *(Source: Captain Melissa Ownby, Beaumont Police Department.)*

United States and settled in South America. The teenager notified authorities, and Rogge was arrested and returned to Florida to serve a 25-year prison sentence (Figure 8.3).[11] The FBI continues to use its Web site to gather tips in other investigations, such as the Oklahoma City bombing of the federal building and the UNABOMBER investigation.

Other advantages of external police usage of the Internet include distance learning, global outreach, and increased technological understanding. **Distance learning** refers to long-distance training and education in which participants can interact with the instructor via satellite transmission. It is now possible for such training to be accomplished through linked computer systems. A Secret Service instructor could instruct hundreds of investigators across the United States or the world in the newest anticounterfeiting techniques. With computerized long-distance learning, the instruction could be transmitted directly to the various agencies without the training agent leaving the federal academy in Georgia.

In addition to having the capacity to interact with fellow investigators within the United States, the Internet allows unlimited opportunities for worldwide communication. Through the Internet, police are able to reach fellow officers in any country in the world. As criminals become more internationally mobile, particularly in the areas of drug trafficking, high-level thefts, and fraud, the ability to communicate instantly through electronic means is essential. Finally, external usage of the computer has the potential to increase an agency's technological skill in many areas related to the investigation of crime. The now common use of computer-automated fingerprint identification as detailed in Chapter 17 is an early example of the ability of computer technology to improve criminal identification greatly. Technologically enhanced computer programs are being developed in many areas of the investigative function. A recent program can identify wanted suspects or imposters who have disguised themselves by electronically

FIGURE 8.3   Fourteen-year-old Sebastian Strzalkowski brought about the first computer-assisted arrest of an FBI Ten Most Wanted fugitive when he recognized an escaped bank robber as his neighbor while viewing the bureau's Internet Web site. (*Source: Associated Press.*)

TABLE 8.1 Investigative Benefits of the Computer

Internal Uses	External Uses
Paperless report writing	Interagency Internet communication with local, state, federal, and foreign justice agencies regarding
Rapid report review by supervisors	• wanted fugitives
Case status communication between patrol and detective units	• distinctive suspect method of operation
	• stolen property
Crime analysis projection	• missing persons
Artificial intelligence	Communication of fingerprints, DNA, and other forensic identification data
Training and scene reconstruction	Posting of community information through agency home page and Web site
Personnel notices through e-mail	

comparing their facial characteristics with previous photos. In a similar fashion to matching fingerprints, the computer matches physiological characteristics by "seeing through" superficial attempts at facial disguise.[12]

As agencies share computer program technical advances, investigative improvements in suspect identification, surveillance equipment, crime scene processing, and forensic methods will be communicated among investigators more rapidly than former methods that relied on paper notifications or training seminars. As technology advances, access and use of the Internet will become a standard means of communication for most Americans. Methods currently exist for low-cost Internet access through a standard television set, which will open electronic communication to even greater portions of the justice system and general public. The investigative benefits of internal and external use of the computer are summarized in Table 8.1.

Computer Crime

Prior to the 1980s, computer crime was a relatively rare occurrence. Few criminal investigators encountered frauds involving computers; therefore, special training in this crime category was nearly nonexistent. Now, however, computers are rapidly replacing written communications in many commercial and personal settings, with a resulting increase in computer-related crime. **Computer crime** is any criminal offense in which the computer is either the tool or the object of a crime. Although the FBI's *Uniform Crime Report* does not collect accurate data on computer-oriented crime, it is estimated that high-tech computer criminals steal $3 billion to $5 billion annually.[13] Cases of computer crime can occur in many environments, with the greatest number reported in commercial settings (see Table 8.2). A recent

TABLE 8.2 Computer Crime Victims

Type of Organization	Percentage of Victimization
Commercial organizations	36
Governmental agencies	17
Telecommunications companies	17
Banks	12
Individuals	12
Universities	4

Source: National Center for Computer Crime Data.

study by the state of Florida determined that 24 percent of all businesses having computer systems at their facilities had experienced computer-related crime within the last 12 months.[14] The true extent of computer crime is currently unknown, as perhaps fewer than 15 percent of the cases are reported to law enforcement agencies.

The computer is an electronic machine that performs rapid, complex calculations and makes decisions based on programmed instructions. These operations are typically achieved through the transformation of received data into numerous electrical impulses. Computers are an economic necessity for industry and government. All computers are subject to misuse or crime. Computers were not initially designed with technical security in mind, which afforded knowledgeable suspects relatively easy access in most cases. Furthermore, information can often be added or removed from data banks without leaving physical traces; hence, there is no traditional crime scene. Yet the greatest difficulty in combatting the computer crime lies in the so-called computer mystique. Many people, including some in law enforcement, are still mystified by computer technology. Even with a general operating knowledge, a detailed understanding of programming is needed to fully comprehend most cases of computer crime.

Suspect Method of Operation

The recent growth of the computer industry has vastly increased the possibility of computer crime. Several factors unique to the twenty-first century have increased the opportunity for abuse. The sheer number of people now trained to use computers has grown dramatically. Most students now have a working knowledge of the computer, as do an equally large number of employees. Additionally, many millions of terminals are in private hands.

Computer misuse occurs during one of the essential operations that most computers perform. The initial operation of the computer involves receiving information in the form of usable data. Information can take many forms—bills, intelligence data, orders for products, and so forth—yet all information must be transformed into an electronic language that the device can work with. Consequently, the information is transformed into electrical impulses that can be "read" by the machine's optical devices. When the data are entered into the computer program by means of various devices, the *input* phase of the computer process has been completed.

Following data input, the computer acts on the data through a series of instructions known as the *program*. These instructions are devised by a *programmer* and written by a *coder* into a specific language that is understood by the computer. Computers must be presented with precise solutions to problems they are to solve to achieve a desired result. A device physically separate from yet electronically connected to the computer, known as the *central processing unit (CPU)*, directs and regulates the program within the computer. When the electrical signals are transformed into readable data (printouts, updated master tapes), the *output* phase of the computer process is completed. Output information is generally transcribed through a *printer*, a device that converts the data into readable, typewritten form. Programmed information can be stored indefinitely within the computer or translated from electrical signals back into readable information at the discretion of the operator. The physical electronic devices that operate the computer are known as *hardware*. The various operating instructions that are programmed into the computer are referred to as *software*.[15]

At any point, from the initial informational input stage through the ending data output stage, operation of the computer is open to misuse. Information may be altered or obliterated as it is being transformed into electronic impulses, or programs may be added, deleted, or altered in some way. Additionally, the data output may be altered, or the offender may simply gain access to the information for intelligence purposes.

There are six basic motivations for using computers in criminal situations: *monetary gain, property resale, intelligence gathering, destruction of the system, criminal record keeping*, and *predatory stalking*.

Monetary Gain.   Computer crime involving a motive of monetary gain is widespread both in private industry and throughout government. The offender acquires money or documents that can be converted into cash by sabotaging the proper operations of the computer. Monetary gain motivations are common in the area of high corporate finance, in which an estimated $400 billion is transferred through the industry each day by computer control. Banking institutions, stock brokerage firms, payroll departments, and government agencies all may be defrauded through computer misuse. Suspects may gain monetarily from the computer either directly or as a second party. If the offender is the authorized operator or programmer for the computer system, altering the operation is a relatively simple matter. If the offender is not authorized to operate the computer but has the technical knowledge to alter operations, the individual must initially gain access to the device.

Monetary gain can be accomplished in a variety of ways, depending on the computer system and the offender's familiarity with it. Possibly one of the most common techniques is to divert incoming funds. This method commonly occurs in the banking industry, when funds are transferred from legitimate accounts to fictitious accounts. The offender programs any number of fraudulent accounts to receive funds that are systematically diverted from legitimate accounts. Generally, only small amounts are diverted, so that the crime will not be immediately noticed by the account holders or internal audit systems. Some offenders, however, divert large amounts of money, confident that the anonymity of the computer will hide their identities. Some computer criminals, who have control over computers that issue checks, program the device to issue a completely fraudulent check to themselves or to an accomplice. A case involving an employee of the U.S. Department of Transportation is typical of this method of operation. The employee issued to himself more than $850,000 within a two-month period by manipulating computers to transfer tax funds to his name. Before his arrest by government investigators, he had purchased eight luxury cars, an expensive home, a tavern, numerous television and stereo systems, and several diamonds.

Another form of monetary gain through computer crime involves adding fictitious costs to items purchased for a particular company. This fraud is typically perpetrated by higher-level employees of the company who periodically collect the overcosts, leaving the computer's data banks with normal bills and unexplained losses. A common form of indirect monetary gain is accomplished when computers are used for unauthorized purposes. Employees use the computers for noncompany work when supervisors are not present to avoid paying for computer time. When a company computer is used in this manner, the resulting "downtime" (periods of inoperation causing loss of profits) constitutes a form of computer crime. Employees working in private businesses or completing advanced degrees requiring research often abuse their employer's computers through this technique.

Additional crimes for monetary gain have involved software theft and cellular phone account fraud. Because computers are enjoying widespread growth and popular usage, copyrighted commercial software is frequently illegally duplicated. This simple process may not appear to be a serious crime problem, but the illegal copying of a single $400 software package is the economic equivalent of eight strong-arm robberies, as strong-arm robbery averages a $50 loss per incident.[16] Another growing crime area aided by computer technology is the theft and usage of cellular phone numbers. Suspects obtain cellular billing identification codes by using computer-connected scanning devices, which capture an individual's account number when the victim's phone is in use. Once the suspect obtains the computerized billing code, it is a fairly simple technological matter to program the phone codes for illegal and often extensive unauthorized usage.

While managers of government and business computer systems are generally well aware of their vulnerability to unauthorized intrusion, most private citizens give little thought to the possibility of intrusion into their home personal computers. When one considers the considerable amount of financial information now generally stored within personal computers, illegal entry by "hackers" is becoming far more common than it was just a decade ago. The problem has become so widespread that the federal government released a software program and list of standards in 2002 designed to assist citizens in securing their home computers against illegal entry. The standards and software are designed to locate security flaws and make suggestions on how to thwart unauthorized electronic entry into private computer files.

Because most home computers are now as powerful as business computers and because hundreds of thousands of Americans conduct shopping and banking transactions through their computers, the vulnerability level has also risen accordingly. Home computers that are connected directly to the Internet through high-speed cable lines that remain open all the time are even more vulnerable. Most home computer owners are also slow to secure their computers with the latest antivirus and firewall software designed to plug security holes. Additionally, because many home computer owners think only business and government computers are routinely subject to attack, they tend to lack prudent suspicion regarding Internet threats and are too willing to click on e-mails that might be infected with malicious programs designed to secure financial information to aid in illegal monetary gain.

Property Resale.   The property that is resold is acquired through unauthorized computer diversion. This type of computer crime can be accomplished internally by an employee or externally by a nonemployee. The defrauded companies are those that stock valuable property and make normal deliveries of such property. Offenders acquire the proper ordering information and sabotage the computer's ordering system by directing the computer to order and deliver the valuable property to themselves or accomplices. The delivery address will be one that cannot be traced. Even if the computer reveals that the bogus order was placed, the identity of the individual who initiated the order cannot be obtained in most cases.

Intelligence Gathering.   In this form of computer theft, information that is stored in the computer is obtained in an unauthorized manner. Such information may be desired by a business competitor, an individual, or a foreign government. The diverted information may result in a profit (as is the case in private industry), or the data can be used for nonprofit purposes. There have been many cases of computer theft in which business secrets have been acquired by a dishonest employee and sold to another business that is a direct competitor. Confidential formulas used in soft drinks, cosmetics, baked goods, and other products have been diverted in this manner. Sensitive information concerning criminal operations or secret government activities is also subject to theft.

Computer criminals may acquire intelligence relatively easily if they are employed by the agency possessing the information they desire. Depending on their position and responsibilities within the agency, they may have the code necessary to enter the computer and gather the data. Computers storing confidential information may have security systems that include entry codes or use data encryption; however, many computers have no such systems. *Entry codes* are signals (word, number, or card codes) that activate the computer to reveal confidential information. Without the use of the code, the device will not respond to questions pertaining to the sensitive data. The most sophisticated entry code systems are currently using finger-print images, voiceprints, and even lip prints. The term *data encryption* pertains to the conversion of sensitive data into a secret code when it is entered into the computer. The data can be decoded into understandable form only if the computer operator knows the proper procedure to break the code.

Intelligence may be stolen from computers by persons who are not employed by the agency possessing the desired data. Offenders may surreptitiously enter the computer's data banks, either by direct physical operation of the computer or by use of the telephone. The physical-operation technique involves burglarizing the premises; it is not a common technique, since most computer rooms operate on a 24-hour basis. Many computers are programmed to operate in conjunction with telephone wires. Information can be altered, added, and sometimes obliterated by "phoning the computer" with the proper number.

Destruction.   Destruction of certain elements of the computer system or of the entire system may be the goal of some offenders. Disgruntled employees and individuals who object to the processing of certain information are typical. The computer may also be sabotaged by offenders employed by business competitors. The physical destruction of the system is often accomplished through fire, or essential data or programs may be erased.

Criminal Record Keeping.   Computers are frequently used by suspects to store records of their illegal activities or otherwise support criminal enterprises. It is becoming increasingly likely that investigators will encounter computers and associated software during the execution of search warrants. Various crimes demand a system of record keeping owing to numerous cash transfers among large numbers of subjects. Narcotics, gambling, loan-sharking, money laundering, and other criminal activities are often recorded on home personal computers. Computers and all related software are specified on search warrants and seized during raids and searches by criminal investigators.

Predatory Stalking.   A rapidly increasing number of computer crimes are of the stalking variety, in which so-called *cyberstalkers* harass or intimidate victims via the Internet or e-mail. Many such offenders are predatory sex criminals targeting victims for solicitation of rape or other sex crimes, while others target victims for harassment purposes only. The head of the sex crimes unit in the Manhattan District Attorney's Office reports that about 20 percent of the unit's cases involve **cyberstalking**. When computers are used to stalk, harass, or illegally solicit protected groups, suspects are engaging in predatory stalking. In addition to transmitting child pornography illegally through the Internet, some sex offenders routinely use the computer to solicit minors for sexual activities. By gaining the trust of juveniles through Internet "conversations" or by posing as a younger individual, suspects attempt to lure victims to a site for sexual purposes. This type of criminal offender also commonly engages in transmitting child pornography by computer. In 1995, federal agents executed 125 search warrants of homes and businesses leading to the arrests of a dozen suspects for computer-related pornography violations. Although now common, this two-year investigation was the first time in law enforcement history that federal authorities probed the misuse of a nationwide computer network in which information and graphic material were exchanged between computers. As it is a violation of federal law to create, possess, or disseminate child pornography, the case illustrates how child sex offenders have abused the Internet to further their crimes.

In a California case, a male stalker assumed a female acquaintance's identity and posted ads in her name over the Internet soliciting sexual contact. The victim, who did not even own a computer, was suddenly besieged by strangers leaving lewd messages on her phone, with several showing up at her doorstep. After a joint investigation by federal and state officials, the suspect was arrested and charged under a California law that criminalizes stalking and harassment on the Internet, in addition to computer fraud and solicitation for rape violations. Other predatory computer-oriented criminal activity involves stalking or harassment of a nonsexual nature. Some suspects use computers to intimidate former acquaintances in the same intrusive fashion that harassing phone calls can be used. Additionally, it is not uncommon for some individuals to use e-mail to harass, threaten, or torment others. While such crimes can be classified as stalking and prosecuted on the local level or charged as a federal interstate transmission of a threat, specific computer stalking statutes are far more effective. California was one of the first states to amend its general stalking statute to specifically cover cyberstalking. Currently all states now have laws that explicitly cover stalking on the Internet or through other electronic communications means.

Cyberstalking is rapidly emerging as the predominant computer crime across the nation. An examination of cases reported to the New York City Police Department's Computer Investigation Unit revealed the extent of this offense. This group investigates any crime involving a computer or connected technology. Of all cases reported to the unit over a four-and-a-half-year period, 201, or 43 percent, were harassment by computer. Subsequent arrests revealed offenders to be overwhelmingly male (at 80 percent), 74 percent being white, with an average age of 24. Approximately 26 percent of the offenders were juveniles. Victims were female in 52 percent of the cases, 85 percent being white, with an average age of 35. E-mails were by far the most common method of computer harassment at nearly 80 percent, followed by instant messages and chat room stalking. Message boards and Web sites were the least likely method of operation to be utilized by suspects.[17]

Another expanding crime, that of identity theft, is often thought of as a computer crime. Although a computer is commonly used in some varieties of this offense, other forms of identity theft are committed without computer assistance. For a detailed discussion of identity theft, see Chapter 13.

Suspect Characteristics

With the exception of the predatory offender, many computer criminals generally follow the profile common to the white-collar offender. Such individuals tend to be of more than average intelligence, particularly when contrasted with other criminal types. Many of them view their actions not as theft or fraud but as the mere "borrowing" of money or information. They tend to be otherwise highly honest and would never steal directly from a person. The attitude of "the little guy against the system" is prevalent among the offenders.

Suspects are generally young, white, well educated, highly motivated, and first-time offenders. Whereas the bank embezzler is often 40 to 60 years of age, the computer thief is generally under 35. Since, in most cases, direct access to and operational familiarity with the data system is required, the thief is often a computer operator or programmer. Rarely will such an individual be a professional criminal with a history of police involvement. For this reason, when an apprehension takes place, the offender will generally confess and reveal the exact method of operation. Other types of criminal suspects are neither particularly skilled with the computer nor employed as computer operators or programmers, however. Such suspects are often career criminals who have recently learned the fundamentals of personal computing to further their criminal record keeping.

Computer crime has attracted organized crime elements in several reported cases throughout the United States. Typically, the organized crime member does not commit the actual computer theft but employs or coerces a programmer. In some cases, programmers or computer room supervisors become involved with organized crime as a result of gambling loans. Employees who fail to pay back debts are persuaded to commit computer crime as a method of repayment to organized crime. Predatory computer suspects generally possess the traits and characteristics specific to sex criminals and other types who are obsessively focused.

Computer criminals often are quite confident that they will not be apprehended. Many other types of criminals share this trait, but it appears with somewhat greater frequency in this crime category. To some degree the confidence is justified since the arrest rate for computer crime is unfortunately very low. The sophisticated technology of the computer, poor supervisory and auditing methods, and a lack of police familiarity with the computer all contribute to a disproportionate rate of arrests to committed offenses.

Investigative and Preventive Methods

Basic to all computer investigations by the police is a knowledge of electronic data processing. Criminal investigators can gain a working knowledge of computer operations through special seminars conducted by police training agencies and many private industries. Considerable computer forensics training is provided by the National White Collar Crime Center, a nonprofit organization funded by Congress that conducts numerous no-cost seminars across the nation. Additional free investigative training is sponsored by the Bureau of Justice Assistance, an arm of the U.S. Department of Justice.[18] In the majority of cases, the police will be contacted after a computer crime has been committed, or computer evidence will be seized during the execution of a search warrant. Generally, the company discovers a loss through audit procedures, or internal security personnel suspect the offense. The investigator is expected to confirm the theft and satisfy the legal requirements necessary to establish fraud or theft. Since some criminal investigators may not be highly trained in data processing, company employees who are familiar with the operation of the computer should initially brief the officer. In some cases, if the loss is substantial or the method of operation is complex, private computer theft experts should be consulted.

When the method of operation is understood and a suspect is not initially identified, the basic methods of investigation are used. From the beginning of the computer investigation, officers must perceive the similarity of electronic evidence to standard, more familiar evidence like fingerprints or DNA. All such evidence including electronically generated evidence is typically latent in nature. The evidence cannot be initially "seen" but must be made visible by special means. This unique form of evidence is neither physical nor human but exists as electronic impulses.[19] The officer determines which individuals had access to the computer, which ones had possible motives, and which had the required knowledge and operational skill to accomplish the crime. If indications are that the offender is not an employee, the investigative task is obviously confounded.

When a group of probable suspects is identified, background investigations should be accomplished on each one. Since the guilty party is generally a first-time offender, the results of the background check may not be significant. The interview phase of the computer crime inquiry is typically the most important phase of the investigation. The investigator should take advantage of the suspect's criminal naïveté by using appropriate interviewing techniques. The polygraph is ideally suited for this type of investigation. In cases involving large losses, the bank records and spending patterns of a suspect may coincide with money losses recorded by the computer. Offenders often work with accomplices in computer crime cases. Accordingly, an identified suspect should be questioned closely as to this possibility or placed under surveillance prior to the arrest in an effort to identify accomplices.

Since most cases of computer crime involve unknown perpetrators, employees with access to the typical data processing system must be identified. Most automated data processing systems involve the following groups of employees:

1. **Coders:** Individuals who transfer the computer program into a language that is understood by the computer. This task is often accomplished through keypunch operations, in which data are transferred onto specially prepared cards.
2. **Computer Operators:** Individuals who physically control the operation of the computer and associated devices. Operators perform such functions as loading a tape transport, placing cards in the input hopper, removing the printout, and ensuring the continuous operation of the system.
3. **Programmers:** Individuals who design, write, debug, and document algorithms (special problem-solving programs based on mathematics) that direct the computer to perform the desired task.
4. **Systems Analysts:** Individuals who define the problem to be solved and develop a clear, well-defined solution. Analysts also ensure the proper installation and operation of the computer program.
5. **System Users:** Individuals who use the output of the computer system (paymasters, personnel managers, executives, department heads, etc.).
6. **Data Processing Managers:** Supervisory personnel who oversee the various personnel connected with the data processing operation.

The basic investigative task in the unknown-suspect computer crime is to determine which of the aforementioned groups and, specifically, which individuals within those groups had the motive, opportunity, and knowledge to misuse the computer. Since many types of computer crime are impossible without collusion between two of the groups, the inquiry should not focus entirely on a single one. Also, it should not be overlooked that maintenance employees have general access to a computer system, although their technical knowledge is normally insufficient to accomplish the offense.

Although the crime scene in this offense lacks many of the traditional tracing clues, several standard criminalistic techniques may be applied. Latent fingerprints may be developed on input or output materials to possibly identify the unauthorized user. In attempting to trace input source documents to a particular suspect's typewriter or output printer, many of the same factors used in standard typewriter comparison tests can be considered. Further, when paper printouts are torn from the output printer, the torn sheet can often be matched back to the paper in the printer. Ribbon shreds or unique marks left by the mechanical operation of the printer may further connect a specific printer with an unauthorized printout recovered from a suspect.

As it is likely that computers and associated materials will be seized as evidence in a wide variety of criminal investigations, the following procedures should be followed to ensure the admissibility of computer-related evidence:

- Only investigators specially trained in retrieving computer information should come in contact with the evidence.
- If investigators expect to encounter computer evidence during the execution of a search warrant, specific information describing the computer and associated materials must be stated in the warrant.
- Before seized computer programs are run, complete copies should be made.
- Evidence must be sealed to prevent unauthorized access, then marked and stored properly to ensure a legal chain of custody.
- Photos should be taken of the computer crime scene, including photos showing the back of the computer (recording how the various wires are connected).
- If non–law enforcement personnel are to be contacted for assistance, only true experts should be consulted, such as university professors of computer science. Retail computer sales personnel are typically not qualified legally to process seized computers or testify as trial experts.[20]

Crimes of the cyberstalking variety demand that investigators understand how electronic evidence can be obtained from computer providers, as such offenses often involve secretive, false, or coded computer identities. In a similar fashion to the issuing of a standard search warrant, judges issue warrants that require Internet providers to surrender information pertaining to computer users who have allegedly committed a crime using the provider as a conduit to the Internet. Most electronic evidence takes two forms: e-mails or anonymous postings to Web sites. Since computer users leave an indelible electronic trail of their activities despite a false or coded identity, investigators can follow such leads directly back to the suspect who originally wrote them, provided they are armed with search warrants.

The majority of evidence seized from computers will result from the execution of a search warrant. The Fourth Amendment guarantee of a reasonable expectation of privacy applies to computer files stored within home computers. Law enforcement officers are typically prohibited from entering and searching computer-related items unless they possess a search warrant authorizing both entry into the residence and a search of the computer and related items. In regard to workplace computer searches, courts may permit warrantless searches if employees have been put on notice by their employers that no expectation of privacy exists regarding office computers. However, since in some workplace environments this notice may not exist or supervisors may not have the authority to grant permission to search, investigators should obtain a warrant whenever possible. The affidavit establishing probable cause for the issuance of a computer search warrant should detail what is being sought, how it is linked to criminality, and why it is believed to be at the scene. Additionally, the computer to be searched should be fully described, along with other items commonly encountered, such as Zip drives, CDs, scanners, printers, and associated cameras.

Fortunately for the investigator, high-tech cases that focus upon finding leads within computer files and hard drives are often more successful than the public expects. Detectives are increasingly relying upon "digital footprints" that the user believes to be erased, hidden, or destroyed but are in most cases retrievable. Investigations in which criminal perpetrators or missing persons use a computer prior to their crimes or disappearance are subject to the now routine search of their computer's contents as detectives seek criminal evidence or answers to where a missing individual may be located. Using a type of "out of sight, out of mind" mentality, most computer users believe that by erasing data they have destroyed the information. Yet to those skilled in data retrieval, deleted e-mails or other erased documents such as visited Web sites are often recovered through the use of various types of utility software. In one recent case, a runaway teenage girl narrowly missed being the victim of an assault. Recovered e-mails revealed that she had left to meet a subject she had been corresponding with via an online chat room. She had no idea that the subject planned to harm her when they met. Fortunately, her e-mails indicated the out-of-state location of the meeting, where police intercepted the girl and arrested the suspect.

Other investigative methods may involve either the task force approach or proactive electronic undercover tactics. There are now hundreds of multiagency cyber crimes task forces operating around the United States. The cyber task force is a cooperative effort that often involves a dozen or more agencies on the federal, state, and local levels banding together to fight computer crime. Specific offenses typically include Internet fraud, child pornography, computer hacking, the spread of viruses, identity theft, and the unauthorized access to computer networks. This concept pools the collective talent of a number of investigators in addition to a shared operating budget. For example, a cyber crime task force recently organized in eastern Nebraska included among its members the FBI, U.S. Secret Service, U.S. Postal Inspection Service, Internal Revenue Service, Nebraska State Patrol, Omaha and Lincoln police agencies, and five other municipal or county police agencies. Each agency contributed equipment, investigative expertise, and operating expenses to investigate cyber crime within their region. Proactive electronic undercover tactics involve police monitoring of computer Web sites and chat rooms in an effort to detect and prevent child sexual abuse or other types of computer crime. Often posing as juveniles, police officers may engage, via e-mail, suspects who are attempting to lure minors into a meeting for sexual assault purposes. When the adult subject electronically propositions or attempts to entice for sexual conduct a person he believes to be a juvenile, a crime is committed, and an arrest follows.

Legal Considerations

On the federal level, the United States Code contains more than 40 sections within Title 18 that can be used to prosecute computer-related criminal offenses. However, the statutes were initially constructed to combat offenses other than computer crime. Consequently, successful prosecution was difficult until the enactment of the Federal Computer Systems Protection Act in 1977. The act was the first bill to specifically address the problem of computer misuse.

Computer crime on the state level can be prosecuted through statutes dealing with general fraud and theft. However, since most fraud and theft statutes require that the property be obtained by deception or taken to permanently deprive, certain types of computer misuse may not fit these definitions. State laws pertaining to misappropriation of trade secrets, obtaining services under false pretenses, or credit card fraud may also be applied to computer crime. The credit card fraud statute may be particularly applicable if the offender has used a fictitious account number to gain access to the computer system. Suspects who use the telephone to "tap into" computers may additionally be guilty of fraud perpetrated by the telephone. Finally, in cases of computer crime in which business competitors receive data from dishonest employees, the business may be prosecuted for receiving stolen property. Although computer criminals may be prosecuted through theft and fraud laws, every state now has a specific computer crime law. The first state computer crime statute was enacted in Florida in 1978, with Arizona's statute following two months later. Although states have a separate criminal code section for computer crime, many have placed it in other categories. Arizona has placed its computer crime provision under its organized crime and fraud section, whereas North Dakota's code is found within its racketeer and corrupt organization codes. California, like many other states, has elected to place its computer crime code in the crimes against property section. The majority of state computer crime codes prohibit entering a computer system without authorization, stealing information from one, or causing a system to go out of service.[21]

Computer crime cannot be controlled effectively by common crime prevention techniques. Routine patrol and most other traditional methods of deterring criminal behavior will not reach into the computer room of a large corporation. Consequently, prevention efforts must be focused within the facility. Deterrence can be achieved if employees are aware of the existence of a knowledgeable internal security unit. The private security unit may choose to institute a periodic polygraph examination as a means of deterrence or a system of computer checks and audits. As with all security practices, all relevant legal rights of search and seizure must be followed by security personnel in regard to the employee's right to privacy.

Unique legal considerations will apply to investigative tactics in which police use proactive undercover methods, posing as potential victims or assuming other identities. This type of tactic is often challenged through a defense of entrapment. When investigators pose, via the computer, as juveniles or potential fraud victims or seek to acquire illegal items like narcotics or stolen property, arrested parties often claim the officers illegally entrapped them into committing the crime. The court will carefully review the actions of police by examining the nature and content of the e-mail exchange between the police and the arrested suspect. If it appears that the police induced a subject to commit a criminal act when the subject was neither predisposed nor originally contemplating the crime, the case will be dismissed. Accordingly, investigators must be careful not to suggest online criminality when there is no evidence in prior e-mails that a subject is predisposed to commit a crime.

Supervisory control should be instituted to provide for a full account of identities of persons who use the computer, including the time of operation. The room that houses the computer and rooms in which remote terminals are located should be limited to authorized employees only.

▲ SUMMARY

The application of computer technology has revolutionized the investigative information-gathering process. Because of their speed in performing data processing and analyzing data, computers have increased the ability of investigators to process reports rapidly and to communicate data.

Additionally, the storage capacity of computers is rapidly replacing traditional paper methods within most law enforcement agencies.

Investigators are now continuously using the microcomputer during the normal course of their duties. Use of the computer assists police in both internal and external matters. Internal uses include easier report review by supervisory officers and sharing of information through e-mail throughout the agency. Another internal function involves the analysis of crime data in order to connect a series of crimes to a single suspect or to predict future criminality by locality and type. The external use of the computer through the Internet enables a single agency to communicate with numerous other departments. Interagency sharing of information is both rapid and far more complete than past noncomputerized methods of official communication. Regional, statewide, and international computer transmissions are currently being utilized to locate fugitives, stolen property, and missing persons. Finally, computers are providing justice information of interest to the general public and to answer computer inquiries from citizens.

Although computerization has benefited the investigative process immeasurably, various crimes relating to computers have become correspondingly more common. Computer misuse is generally motivated by monetary gain, property resale, or outright destruction of valuable records. Suspects involved in this type of offense are often well educated and have work experience within the computer industry. Although computer criminals may be prosecuted through state theft and fraud laws, specific computer criminal statutes now exist in most states.

■ EXERCISES

1. Survey a local police or sheriff's agency in your area and determine to what degree computers are being used for investigative purposes.
2. Interview a college official to determine what security measures are used to prevent unauthorized computer entry of student records.
3. Prepare a research paper on the historical development of the modern personal computer.
4. Search the Internet for Web sites and home pages pertaining to law enforcement or topics relating to criminal investigation. Report to your class on how the sites were located and their Internet addresses.

● RELEVANT WEB SITES

http://www.usdoj.gov/criminal/cybercrime/compcrime.html

Extensive site dealing with computer crime operated by the U.S. Department of Justice. Details various computer crime cases and federal statutes that apply to computer crime cases and provides guidance to investigators dealing with computer scenes and associated evidence.

http://www.emergency.com/fbi-nccs.htm

Explains the structure and function of the FBI's National Computer Crime Squad. Details the variety of computer crime cases the unit is authorized to investigate or assist other agencies with.

Burglary

KEY TERMS

burglary
circular fracture lines
cone fracture
fence
informant file
management by objective
neighborhood check
punch attack

radial fracture lines
rip attack
soil density gradient test
spectrophotometer
sting operation
toolmark
vulnerability analysis

LEARNING OBJECTIVES

1. to know the legal meaning of the term *burglary*;
2. to be aware of the current state of burglary in regard to frequency, time, and place of occurrence;
3. to be able to list offender characteristics associated with burglary;
4. to be able to define the three major categories of burglary;
5. to be familiar with suspect methods of operation relative to the various types of burglary;
6. to be able to define the various types of safe burglaries;
7. to understand the three major investigative areas of the burglary inquiry;
8. to be aware of recent burglary research findings and their importance to the investigator;
9. to be able to define the four major strategies for the reduction of burglary; and
10. to be familiar with those areas of forensic science that directly apply to the burglary investigation.

INTRODUCTION

Laws pertaining to the offense of burglary have evolved after the adage, "A man's home is his castle." English judges during the fifteenth century sought to differentiate the mere stealing of an object from stealing that was perpetrated in one's residence. Thus, the early common law defined burglary as the breaking and entering of the dwelling of another, in the nighttime, with intent to commit a felony therein. Conviction of common-law burglary required the proof of each of the elements of the definition. If any element was lacking, the crime of burglary had not occurred.

The development of current statutory burglary laws has been achieved by redefining or eliminating many of the common-law elements. Under most state statutes, for example, there is no requirement that an actual break occur because forcible entry is no longer considered an element of burglary. Also, the meaning of the term *dwelling* has been broadened to include a wide variety of structures ranging from a telephone booth to an automobile. Each individual state penal code describes specific structures into which the suspect must enter to commit the offense of burglary. A suspect may enter through an unlocked door or enter without authority into a dwelling having no door at all. However, many states do distinguish among various burglaries, depending on the presence or absence of physical breaking. For example, Florida specifies that a burglary involving breaking and entering is punishable by imprisonment to 20 years. By contrast, burglary in that state involving entering *without* breaking is punishable by imprisonment to ten years. Other states specify degrees of burglary depending on the nature of the suspect's actions. In the state of New York, punishments are stricter for burglaries committed during the night by armed suspects and for burglaries involving the assault of an individual than for daytime burglaries by unarmed suspects or burglaries not involving assault.

The modern definition of **burglary**, which has evolved from the early common-law offense definitions, does vary slightly from state to state. In general, however, burglary involves an individual who

(a) without authority
(b) knowingly enters
(c) a building or structure
(d) with the intent to commit a felony or theft.

It is significant to realize that burglary does not always involve the successful taking of property. A suspect can be charged with the offense without actually having taken any property whatsoever. The essential element that must be proved is the *intent* to commit a felony or theft. There have been many cases in which, after having been apprehended in a dwelling without authority, the suspect claims that the dwelling was entered by mistake. If the officer can demonstrate that the suspect intended to commit the crime by exhibiting tools normally carried by burglars found on the suspect's person or by linking a forced entry to the suspect, then the intent will have been established.

CURRENT STATE OF BURGLARY

The *Uniform Crime Report* established that slightly over two million burglaries were reported during a recent year.[1] Although this reported rate of burglary is extremely serious, the true number of burglaries annually is actually near five million. National Crime Surveys conducted by the Department of Justice indicate that only 50 percent of all burglary victims actually report the offense to the police.[2] Sixty-two percent of all burglaries involved forcible entry, 31 percent were without force, and the remainder were unsuccessful forcible-entry attempts. For many years, burglary was one of the most rapidly increasing felony crimes in the nation. In recent years, the reported rate has actually dropped; the 2004 rate of occurrence was 21 percent below the 1994 level.

Some criminologists speculate that three main factors may be significantly responsible for the decline of burglary: (a) drug addicts have switched from burglary to the more probable cash-producing crime of robbery, (b) there has been an increase in home-security devices as well as traditional prevention methods, and (c) a greater number of career burglars have been apprehended and imprisoned for long sentences.

Burglary currently constitutes 18 percent of all major felony crime in the United States, with 21 percent of all property crime falling into this category. These facts are not encouraging, despite the recent overall drop, to either police or the general public. A reported burglary is committed in the United States every 15 seconds, which ranks the crime second only to that of larceny. Although only some larcenies are felonies, the crime of burglary is always a felony. Burglary, then, becomes the most common U.S. felony offense. Consider that during a typical 50-minute college lecture, more than 200 burglaries are committed.

Law enforcement investigators clear by arrest approximately 13 percent of all reported burglary offenses. Burglary has been a serious problem to the investigator from the earliest days of thief-taking. For the average citizen, burglary is the most common serious crime in which he or she is liable to become a victim. One person in a hundred will be a burglary victim, with the true number being no doubt higher because of the significant number of unreported burglaries. Furthermore, the true number of victims is much greater, for entire families are affected by a single burglary.

Many people experience the workings of the criminal justice system for the first time as victims of a burglary—and, as such, they are in a position to evaluate the effectiveness of their police. That only 13 percent of all reported burglaries are cleared by arrest is a fact that few victims are prepared to face. Because of many factors, including the television image of the investigator, the U.S. public often fails to understand the rationale for the low clearance rate. Actually, far fewer than 13 percent of the victims will have their stolen property returned, for an arrest does not always mean property recovery. With the average burglary loss per victim at approximately $1,600, it is obvious that the officer's image in terms of effectiveness is bound to suffer. However, despite the problem of low clearance, many victims may base their evaluation of police performance on factors other than solely whether their burglary case was solved. A recent University of Texas research survey demonstrated that burglary victims evaluate police efficiency regarding burglary by how they were treated during the course of the investigation. Accordingly, a person whose burglary was never solved will not automatically believe the police to be poorly managed or that the investigator is inefficient.[3]

The typical burglary occurs in a residence in the daytime during the summer months. Residences continue to be the most frequent target of burglaries, accounting for 66 percent. This is due primarily to two factors: ease of entry and lack of detection. It is generally much easier to gain entry into the typical home as compared to a business establishment. Burglars are aware that the majority of victims are not home during normal working hours and that it is uncommon for people to note carefully who is in their neighborhood. Burglary rates rise to their peak during the summer months. This is due to a variety of factors, including vacations, open windows and doors for ventilation, and greater numbers of people walking through the neighborhood. Yet seasonal rates for burglary are not remarkably high during the summer, for although rates are lower in other months, the pattern of victimization is relatively close to that in peak summer months.[4] Therefore, burglary cannot be considered a fixed cyclical crime of highly significant seasonality.

OFFENDER CHARACTERISTICS

Profiling offender characteristics for a particular general offense category is not possible with a high degree of precision. However, certain general conclusions and specific regional findings have been determined by recent research. The FBI *Uniform Crime Report* indicates that the typical burglary suspect is a white male, under the age of 25, living in a metropolitan area.

A substantial majority of these annually arrested for burglary are relatively young. Currently, 17 percent of arrested burglary suspects from all types of geographic areas are under the age of 18. The highest degree of juvenile involvement is found in small cities under 10,000 in population, where juveniles account for 25 percent of all burglary arrests. Other factors may contribute to the large number of youthful suspects, including considerable free time and lack of supervision while parents work. Sociological developments, such as an increasing lack of family structure and a day-to-day lifestyle that is characteristic of many lower-class homes, may contribute to prevalence of the youthful burglar. The stereotype of the youthful suspect from a lower-class background can be misleading, however. It is interesting to note that burglaries in comparatively affluent suburban areas have risen to a point at which they closely approximate rates in the poorer inner cities. One may only speculate as to the comparatively small number of older offenders arrested for burglary. It may be that burglary is a "beginning" offense from which the older criminal has "graduated," becoming more involved in other criminal activities yielding greater profit. Possibly, as offenders age and are apprehended for various crimes, their prison sentences become longer, making them unavailable for criminal activities for increasingly greater periods. Finally, as some studies suggest, it may be that fewer older burglars are arrested because of their sophisticated methods of operation.

Burglary suspects are more prone to violence than previously assumed by criminal justice researchers. Burglary, traditionally regarded as a nonviolent crime, actually carries a significant risk of violence if a member of the burglarized household is at home. Research indicates that burglary suspects commit three-fifths of all rapes and robberies that occur in the home and one-third of all household assaults. Further, victims are at home during a burglary in 13 percent of all cases, resulting in 30 percent of these victims being violently attacked by the suspect.[5]

Contrary to the popular stereotype of a stranger suspect, a substantial percentage of household burglaries are committed by suspects related to or known by the victim. Spouses, ex-spouses, relatives, and acquaintances have been found to commit 37 percent of all burglaries in which offender characteristics are known, whereas 48 percent of cases are classified as involving actual stranger suspects. Additional suspect characteristics document the high level of drug abuse among burglary perpetrators. In surveys among imprisoned burglars, 50 percent report having been under the influence of drugs or drunk during the commission of their crimes. Specifically, 42 percent admitted being under the influence of a narcotic or dangerous drug other than alcohol at the time of the offense. The rate of drug abuse during the commission of a felony is highest for burglars among all types of convicted criminals, with the single exception of those imprisoned for drug offenses.[6]

Contrary to the popular media image, the typical burglar is not a skilled professional criminal. The majority of burglaries are committed by forcible entry, most often by blunt force of an unskilled nature. The significant number of juvenile offenders also contributes to the general level of amateurism found among most burglary suspects. If an extensive number of prior arrests indicates a lack of criminal professionalism, most burglary suspects clearly qualify. Burglars tend to have unusually high rates of prior arrest and conviction, both factors demonstrating a lack of criminal sophistication. A Rand research study of burglary and robbery suspects in 14 large urban jurisdictions concluded that 23 percent were on probation or parole when arrested, 75 percent had prior arrests, and more than 50 percent had prior convictions and/or incarcerations.[7]

BURGLARY TYPES

Residential

Two of every three burglaries reported to the police are burglaries of residences. *Residential burglaries* involve places of habitation for one or more people—an apartment, mobile home, or other type of dwelling. That residences are consistently selected by strangers as targets is due to a combination of factors.

The typical home is far from being secure in any sense of the word. Houses are rarely designed with physical security in mind. During construction, inadequate locking devices are usually installed because of cost consideration. When the home is occupied, few owners take the trouble to secure their dwellings or even give the possibility of burglary a serious thought. The same is true for apartments. Apartments are particularly prone to burglary because of the transient nature of the occupants.

Burglars are aware of the ease by which entry can be gained into the average residence. The youthful offender quickly acquires the low-level knowledge necessary to break into the majority of homes and apartments. A Seattle, Washington, study indicated that in 40 percent of residential burglaries, entrance was gained through open doors or windows.[8] Shrubs, trees, fences, or other such landscaping features that obscure visibility of the residence contribute significantly to successful suspect entry.

Business

A *business burglary* can involve any type of retail business operation or service. The target may be a large department store or a small, family-operated grocery store. Business burglaries typically occur during the hours of darkness and involve individuals with higher levels of skill. Generally speaking, burglars who select retail businesses as targets are older and more experienced than the residential offender. The business burglar's skill is necessitated by the greater physical resistance encountered during forceful entry. The majority of businesses have at least adequate door and window locks or bars to resist simple forceful entry. Frequently, the business burglar must make use of specialized tools to force often difficult entry. In addition to physical entry prevention devices, many businesses are equipped with alarm systems. These range in sophistication from the simple bell alarm to silent telephone alarms that notify the police electronically. Such electronic alarms are becoming more commonplace throughout the country. For example, in Cedar Rapids, Iowa, nearly one of ten businesses has a burglary telephone alarm operating during nonbusiness hours.[9] The business burglar, in addition to being skillful at entering, is often skilled in opening locked safes. Since many retail businesses lock operating cash in safes, the business burglar naturally expects to encounter the secured safe.

General Dwelling

General-dwelling burglaries do not occur as often as either of the other two types. Private offices, medical offices, government buildings, schools, and churches are examples of general dwellings. Many suspects select this type of dwelling for specific reasons involving the type of property they expect to find. Medical offices and veterinary practices are frequently burglarized in the expectation of finding narcotics and dangerous drugs. Schools are frequently selected for the large amount of business equipment and computers found there. Burglars who select medical offices and other types of treatment-oriented dwellings often have been inside the office during working hours as a patient.

METHODS OF OPERATION

To investigate various types of burglary successfully the officer must be familiar with the behavior of the burglar. *Method of operation* (MO), or in formal Latin, *modus operandi*, pertains to the notion that human behavior tends to repeat itself. All of us repeat behaviors daily that are closely similar to past behaviors. The pattern in which we dress, the route traveled to school or work, how we wash our hands, and a thousand other behaviors are remarkably similar to past actions. Not only are present behaviors similar to past actions, but our future actions will also conform to this principle. Human methods of operation are additionally reinforced if a given action is repeatedly successful in achieving its goal. For instance, a student using an outline method of note-taking and a certain type of pen obtains complete notes. It is highly likely that the student will continue to use such methods to take notes in the future. In a similar fashion, the burglar may continually use a certain type of screwdriver to pry open glass patio doors. Its past use has been successful in obtaining entry, which reinforces present and future use of the tool in a similar manner.

In addition to the variable of successful past usage, situational stress plays an important role in forming a method of operation. Under stressful conditions people often revert to familiar past actions. Thus, a criminal committing a crime under the stress of imminent arrest and danger of injury or discovery will naturally revert to past methods of behavior. Such repeated individualized methods of criminal technique become very important in suspect identification and in linking present offenses to past crimes.

Methods of operation in burglaries, as in most other types of serious felonies, are normally quite standardized. Methods of entry, search, and exit that have proven successful in the commission of past crimes will continue to be used by the suspect. By carefully studying methods of operation, the investigator may be able to connect many burglaries to a single individual. Such information can narrow a wide number of suspects and can establish a predictive pattern, thus allowing stakeouts to produce an apprehension.

Residential Methods

Entry. All completed burglaries involve a point of entry, a method of search, and a point of exit. The *point of entry* refers to the location selected by the burglar to enter the dwelling. The residential burglar frequently selects a point of entry with regard to the following factors:

1. public visibility,
2. degree of resistance, and
3. time necessary to gain entry.

Residential burglars generally cruise a selected neighborhood, observing homes for "signals" indicating a probable target. They are looking for residences that appear to be unoccupied, signaled by the absence of cars, lights, or other factors. After selecting the residence, the burglar looks for an entry point that is obscured from public view by some physical feature, such as shrubbery or a fence. After the burglar confirms that no one is home, often by knocking on the door or looking through a window, the primary entry point is selected and entry attempted. Initially burglars try all doors and windows since their experience has demonstrated that many homes are normally unlocked. If such efforts fail, a forced entry will be attempted.

The site of the residential forced entry is carefully chosen by the protection it affords from public view. In the majority of cases, a rear door, sliding patio door, or window will be selected. Burglars are generally fast workers, constantly alert for indications that their presence has been discovered by an observant neighbor. The time necessary to gain entry is a major factor in determining whether the burglary will be carried out to completion. Few burglars stay at the scene long enough to force a securely locked door; teenage offenders in particular do not even attempt entry once a secure lock is encountered.

Methods of forced entry in residential dwellings are varied but rarely sophisticated. In contrast to the ingenious housebreaker of movies and television, the typical residential burglar employs only two basic methods of forced entry: celluloid insertion and physical force. *Celluloid insertion* involves the placement of a flexible plasticlike object, such as a photo negative, credit card, or plastic ruler, between the door and the frame. The celluloid is then brought down until it strikes the latch, releasing the spring that locked the door. This method is successful only with spring-latch locks; it is not effective with the deadbolt variety. However, the majority of homes and apartments continue to be equipped with spring-latch locks and other less expensive locking mechanisms.

When the burglar encounters a securely locked door that defies celluloid entry, he may revert to *physical force*. Such crude methods as forcing a fist, elbow, or foot through a window or sliding glass door may be used. The burglar who is more prepared may be equipped with specific tools (see Figure 9.1). A crowbar, screwdriver, or other such metal tool may be sharpened on one end to pry open a window. Occasionally, the investigator may encounter a series of forced entries involving the use of a pipe wrench. The pipe wrench is attached to the doorknob and twisted, forcing open the locking device by leverage.

Officers often encounter home or apartment burglaries in which there are no signs of forced entry, yet it is determined that the residence was locked before the burglary. A skilled suspect, often an older, mechanically inclined individual, may have used various picks or other devices to gain entry. *Lock picks* and *tension wrenches* are very effective devices in the hands of skilled burglars. When they are inserted into the key opening and carefully manipulated, few locks will fail to open. The majority of locks are designed and constructed to resist blunt force; consequently, they are

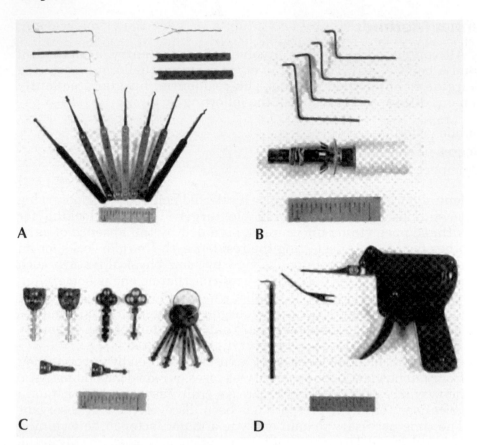

FIGURE 9.1 Common burglary tools. *A.* An assortment of lock picks and tension wrenches used to bypass common residential, business, and vehicle locks; *B.* Lever-type tension wrenches and a tubular lock pick. Wrenches shaped in this manner are typically used on letterboxes and padlocks. The tubular lock pick is designed for locks with circular pin arrangements, such as those on vending machines and coin boxes; *C.* Warded pass keys. These are filed to leave only the tip so that they key will fit many different locks of a general type. The commercially available set with the ring can open more than 200 types of padlocks; *D.* A pick gun. When used in conjunction with the tension wrench, locks can be bypassed without the manual manipulation of a pick. A simple pull of the trigger provides the necessary picking action.
(Source: Andrew Brooks Jr., Chicago Police Department.)

vulnerable to picking. A more recent device, known as the *pick gun*, enables a burglar to pick a lock mechanically. The device provides the manipulative action by simply pulling a trigger. Such sophisticated methods of entry as picking and the use of the pick gun are relatively rare; the great majority of residential burglars repeatedly use force and celluloid insertion.

Search. The burglar's method of operation once inside the dwelling is not as consistent as the method of entry. How the burglar searches for property is commonly known as the *prowl*. Hard goods that can be easily converted into cash are commonly sought. Stereo systems, radios, small television sets, guns, jewelry, and, of course, cash are favored items. Many burglars always start searching in one specific room of the dwelling, say, the bedroom. This searching behavior is often due to past success in finding valuable property in one room in particular. Some burglars always select the bathroom for initial searching, hoping to find drugs, either for personal use or for resale.

The more experienced burglar attempts to leave the crime scene as undisturbed as possible. This is particularly true when force is not required to enter the residence. By leaving no immediate sign of forced entry and prowl, the theft may not be perceived by the victim for some time. However, the typical prowl is a hurried one in which there is no regard for secrecy. The contents of drawers are overturned, frequently in a central location, and items are broken and damaged, leaving the home with the appearance of a disaster area. Juvenile suspects often vandalize the interior of the dwelling as well as commit the theft.

It is important for the investigator to attempt to reconstruct the search method used by the suspect. Although not an easy task, reconstruction of prowl may identify a particular offender. This is often the case when a police agency operates an MO file of past burglaries, indicating specific methods of entry, prowl, and exit, by suspect.

Exit.   The *point of exit* by which the suspect leaves the dwelling is the least significant factor in the method of operation. Rarely is the exit different from the entry point, and under normal conditions, force is not necessary. Yet, in some cases, burglars may choose to exit from a point different from the entry site. Burglaries involving the removal of large, heavy objects, such as console television sets, may force an exit through a door, although entrance was gained through a side window. It is very important to investigate both entry and exit, for the probability of discovering physical evidence is increased if both sites are located.

Business and General-Dwelling Methods

Entry.   As previously mentioned, the burglar who selects a business establishment as the target for the crime is often more highly skilled than the residential burglar. Commercial buildings generally have superior locking devices and alarms. Accessible glass entry points are kept to a minimum. For these reasons, the business burglar is often equipped with tools necessary to effect entry.

This type of burglar does not typically select a business on a random basis. Some degree of advance planning is involved, if only on the most basic of levels. Windows and skylights are preferred areas of entry. Businesses that do not have obvious alarm systems are naturally preferred over those that do. In those structures employing some type of alarm system, a surprisingly high percentage of alarms fail to function.

When an entry point is selected, force is applied in a variety of ways. Panes of glass may be cut, doors pried or picked, and bars occasionally burned or cut away. In increasing numbers, sophisticated burglary alarm systems are being rendered useless. Some professional burglars use elaborate "bypass" methods to gain entry undetected. While not common, burglars with considerable electronic know-how are growing in number.

Search.   After entry has been gained into the commercial dwelling, the prowl is normally shorter in duration and more specific than the residential prowl. Since many business burglaries are the result of preplanning, the location of valuable property is generally known. Localities with open public access, such as pharmacies and restaurants, are almost always observed by the burglar before an actual burglary during business hours.

The use of safes in retail businesses is common practice; thus, forcibly opened safes are primary evidence leads in numerous burglary investigations. However, with the growing tendency of retail businesses to rely upon credit cards and checks, less cash is being kept on hand. As a result, many professional burglars plan the safe burglary to coincide with a timely delivery of money. There are many methods used to gain entry into a locked safe. Once a method has been selected, the success of the entry attempt often depends upon three factors:

1. the size of the safe,
2. the skill of the burglar, and
3. the degree of preplanning involved.

Some safes are designed primarily to protect contents from fire; these are portable and are easily broken into. Others are massive in size and thickness and are constructed with burglary prevention in mind. A small, lightweight safe may be "packed out" (transported) to a remote area by a burglar, who can then force it open without regard for time or noise factors.

Nearly all forcible safe entry methods involve attacking the safe at its weak points or attacking the locking mechanism itself (see Figure 9.2). A method commonly known as a **rip attack**, or *peel job*, involves peeling the metal sheets from a weakened corner location. A crowbar or other metal object is then inserted into a drilled hole and leverage applied. Many safes are forced by a **punch attack**, the preferred method of the experienced safe burglar. It is a comparatively clean and quiet method, requiring somewhat more skill than the rip attack. The safe dial is forced off by a blow from a sledgehammer or like object, leaving the spindle and essential locking mechanism open to attack. A safe may also be attacked by a burning torch or explosive charge. Burning typically requires heavy and cumbersome equipment, such as an oxygen and acetylene tank. The use of explosives is very rare, although it is frequently portrayed in the media. Most safes have fire prevention insulating materials built into them, so it is common to encounter such materials in the form of fine powder throughout the scene. Because it is probable that the suspect's shoes and clothing will contain traces of the material, samples of the insulation should be collected for later forensic comparison.

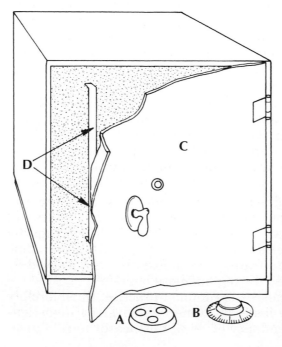

FIGURE 9.2 Safe attack methods. Entry is gained by initially punching the dial ring (*A*) and dial (*B*) from the safe door front plate (*C*) to weaken and expose the locking mechanism (*D*). The safe door may then be "ripped" or "peeled" back, further exposing the locking bar.

When the investigator encounters a safe that has been opened without any apparent sign of force, three conclusions are possible: Either a master burglar has manipulated the dial by the faint sounds of the tumblers, or the door was not properly locked, or the door was opened by someone who knew or had access to the combination. The majority of modern safes are of sufficient quality to have internal mechanisms that operate in virtual silence; these cannot be opened even with the use of a medical stethoscope. Consequently, the probable conclusion in this circumstance is that the safe door was not properly locked or that the suspect knew the combination.

Exit. The point of exit in the business burglary is often the same as the point of entry. In many businesses, alarm systems are activated by the opening of doors and windows. Suspects are aware of this fact and will exit through the same entry point that bypassed the alarm. Exceptions occur when the entry point is not sufficiently large to permit the carrying out of large objects or when alarm systems are present.

INVESTIGATIVE PROCEDURES

Investigative procedures relative to burglary encompass three broad areas: the crime scene, official records, and property recovery.

The Crime Scene

The burglary crime scene, in particular, yields much physical evidence. Because force is frequently necessary to effect entry, numerous items are handled, and automobiles are often employed, the burglary crime scene is very likely to reveal important tracing clues. When processing the burglary scene, the investigator must reconstruct the actions of the suspect in as complete a fashion as possible.

Rarely in a forced-entry situation will the point of entry be difficult to locate. The exact method of entry should be determined by a careful examination of damage to the door, window, or other entry point. All marks, striations, fingerprints, and other tracing clues should be recorded by field notes and photography. In a large number of successfully prosecuted burglary cases, the convicting evidence is obtained from the point of entry. During entry attempts, burglars are often very nervous and apprehensive. In their haste to force entry without being seen, they may be careless about leaving such tracing evidence as toolmarks, bloodstains, footprints, and fibers.

The interior of the burglarized dwelling should be investigated with the following questions in mind: What items have been handled by the burglar? Have these items been disturbed by others? What method of search did the burglar employ? Why that particular method? And, of course, what items are missing? Property that might have been touched by the burglar should be processed for fingerprint evidence. The entire scene should be thoroughly searched for hair, fiber, and glass evidence generally associated with burglary.

By analyzing the burglar's prowl, the officer may be able to determine the primary target, such as narcotics. The burglar's prowl is also a strong indicator of the method of operation. The point of exit may not always be apparent since a door forced open during entry can obviously be exited without additional force. The burglar, once in the home or business, may have unlocked a rear door for exit, having gained entry through the front door. It will then be up to the training and experience of the officer to distinguish the exit from the point of entry, if, indeed, they are not the same.

The investigator must always be alert to the possibility of a *staged burglary* (a scene arranged by the "victim" to suggest a burglary). Insurance fraud is the most common motivation for the false burglary report, yet there may be other motives. In one investigation, a man staged a burglary scene for the benefit of his wife, claiming the theft of several hundred dollars. It was discovered that he recently lost his paycheck through gambling. In another case, a jewelry store manager sold a quantity of merchandise to an out-of-town buyer. Staging a burglary of his business and claiming the merchandise had been stolen, the manager attempted to sue the owner of the building from whom he rented for not providing adequate locks on the doors.

A detailed listing of missing property is very important to the success of the investigation. Unfortunately, such a listing is not always simple to secure. Many individuals, particularly victims of apartment and home burglaries, do not have complete descriptions of their property, including serial numbers. In some burglary scenes, it is difficult to determine what items are missing because of extensive damage. Or victims simply may not know. Since the majority of burglary arrests result from tracing recovered stolen property back to the burglar, the lack of missing property identification is a major reason for the low arrest rate.

In far too many burglary investigations, a thorough **neighborhood check** is not attempted. Because of the lack of personnel, or officer carelessness, this essential element of the burglary investigation may be overlooked. All residences or businesses within a reasonable radius should be checked to acquire the following information:

1. Were "strangers" to the neighborhood observed?
2. Were unfamiliar automobiles parked in or cruising the neighborhood?
3. Were unusual sounds heard (e.g., glass breaking)?
4. Are there pertinent personal factors involving the victims—divorces pending, delinquent children, business partner disputes, etc.?

The neighborhood check, in addition to developing leads, will place residents on alert for the return of the burglar or new offenders.

Many business burglaries involve suspects who have visited the business site prior to the commission of the crime. This is particularly true in burglaries of retail businesses or public buildings. Posing as a customer or one who has legitimate business in the establishment, the suspect is actually observing the interior of the building for its risk potential, its vulnerability, and the location of valuables. Accordingly, all burglary victims should be closely questioned regarding recent customers or visitors who aroused their suspicion or were noteworthy in any way. The same method of operation is frequently used in residential burglaries; some suspects "case" potential sites by posing as delivery men or city officials, asking for directions, or using other ruses to gain entry.

Official Records

When the identity of a particular burglar is known or suspected, criminal justice records are invaluable to the investigation. The arrest record of a suspect can be provided by the FBI or state bureaus of investigation, giving the investigator a starting point for the construction of the method of operation. Assuming that the suspect has been arrested for burglary previously, the officer will contact law enforcement agencies that investigated the prior offenses. A comparison of the investigative reports to the method of operation of the current case may be highly significant. Records can additionally supply other helpful information, such as home and business addresses, associates, and fingerprint patterns. The burglary investigation in which the offender's identity is not known truly challenges the skill of the investigator. In this case, methods of operation must be determined solely on the basis of conclusions drawn from the crime scene or interviews. A review of all burglaries having similar characteristics as to entry, prowl, or unique property taken is essential.

Many state bureaus of identification provide statewide matching of methods of operation. Thus, officers can submit MO information from a current case to obtain matching information from past investigations. Police departments that require patrol officers to conduct field inquiries of suspicious subjects are directly aiding burglary divisions. In reviewing field inquiry cards, the burglar's description may be ascertained. There have been many cases in which a burglary suspect was field interviewed before the offense or while leaving the area. When clothing, race, or physical features have been described by a witness, this information can then be matched to similar information on field interview cards.

If the officer is fortunate enough to be working in an agency having an **informant file** (a file containing probable informants listed by type of crime), the task may be greatly simplified. By consulting the file for burglary informants, the officer can contact individuals who have proven their information-gathering ability. Burglary is a crime in which the use of informants is often successful in that the disposal of stolen property is involved. In each instance, the recently acquired property is open to the notice of others, giving the informant an opportunity to obtain descriptions of possible suspects. Burglary informants who have observed stolen property can often give detailed descriptions, providing the basis for a search warrant to be issued.

Property Recovery and Fencing Operations

The crime of burglary is generally perceived by its perpetrators as a relatively low-risk undertaking. Indeed, few suspects are actually apprehended at the scene, and detailed descriptions of perpetrators are uncommon. The disturbingly low national arrest rate for reported burglary of 14 percent reflects the difficulty of on-site apprehension. Accordingly, although the complete burglary investigation always demands a careful analysis of the scene, most arrests result from after-the-fact actions of the suspect. The four greatest points of vulnerability concerning the burglary suspect's actions are

1. actions during the entry,
2. actions during the suspect's search of the property,
3. actions during the exit, and
4. disposal of stolen property.

Of the four suspect behaviors, the disposal of stolen property often has the highest level of probability for enabling investigative success.

The major difficulty of the burglary investigation is in connecting a suspect to the locality that was entered. Few investigations produce witnesses who can place a suspect at the burglary scene, and there are not many instances in which physical evidence is recovered to link a suspect to the premises. There is one constant factor common to the great majority of burglaries, however: physical property is removed by the suspect. When items are stolen from a dwelling, three possibilities exist: (a) property is destroyed, (b) property is sold, or (c) property is kept for personal use. Ultimately, successful property recovery depends on obtaining an initial detailed description of the stolen item. The investigator first attempts to locate the property and then to link the item with the suspect. Once property and perpetrator have been connected, the investigative challenge lies in legally demonstrating that the suspect obtained the property from the burglary scene.

Stolen property occasionally is destroyed. When a burglar becomes aware of a police investigation closing in, an attempt to destroy all linking evidence may be made. Burglars have been known to burn, bury, and even throw weighted stolen property into the ocean to avoid apprehension. Inexperienced burglars, often juveniles having second thoughts about their criminal actions, often destroy property out of guilt or fear.

In a significant number of burglaries, stolen items are kept by the offender for personal use. One of the prime motivations for burglary is a compulsion to acquire material goods that are otherwise unobtainable. Once the burglar possesses a particular type of property that is personally appealing, such as an expensive stereo system, the temptation to keep it for personal use is strong. The property may be given to a second party as a gift or even traded for other items the burglar wants or needs, such as narcotics. The investigator must take considerable care to keep acquired information as secretive as possible, for should the burglar become aware that his or her identity is known, the property may be destroyed or cover stories prepared.

Active burglars frequently use the services of an individual known as a "fence." A **fence** is one who buys stolen items with "no questions asked." In effect, the fence acts as a broker or middleman, selling the property to another buyer. Many professional burglars are contacted by fences before the offense is committed and subsequently steal the type of item needed by the fence. Property is generally sold in this manner for 20 percent or less of the item's real worth. The burglar who has no fence outlet may attempt to sell stolen property to a pawnshop or other type of retail store dealing in used merchandise. Or the items may be sold directly to other individuals via classified ads, flea markets, garage sales, and the like. With increasing regularity, some burglars and fences attempt to sell stolen merchandise through online computer auction Web sites.

Virtually all burglary investigation experts agree that the fence is a major obstacle to reducing the number of burglary crimes. The fence has been highly underrated as a serious criminal problem. To stay in business, professional burglars and thieves of all types depend on the fence. It is the willingness of the fence to buy stolen property that serves as a motivation for many burglars. Fences deal in virtually any type of property, from T-bone steaks to washing machines. All areas of the country have fencing operations; large cities have the highest concentration. It has been estimated by the Los Angeles county district attorney that 95 percent of the stolen items in that area are handled by approximately 400 large-scale fences.[10]

Many antifencing operations have recently been devised by law enforcement agencies. Such programs have four basic goals:

1. to identify and close active fencing operations,
2. to initiate criminal prosecution,
3. to deter burglary and theft, and
4. to develop and maintain fencing intelligence information.

A relatively new method to combat fencing is aimed at burglars attempting to sell stolen property rather than at fences per se. Law enforcement investigators, working undercover, pose as fences. A store is rented and staffed by these investigators, who communicate that they will purchase stolen property. As burglars and thieves bring their stolen items to the business site, efforts are made to identify suspects and link the property to reported cases. After a significant amount of stolen property has been bought, with the transactions typically recorded by hidden videotape, all identified sellers are arrested. Arrests are made only after investigators believe they have identified the maximum number of suspects and gathered the necessary evidence to sustain successful prosecutions. This type of procedure has commonly been known as a **sting operation**. Literally hundreds of government-financed "businesses" have been operated in this fashion by local, state, and federal investigators. An extremely high percentage of those arrested in sting cases have been successfully prosecuted because of the quality of the incriminating evidence.

For sting operations to be successful, investigators must be able to duplicate the most common types of fencing methods. The first variety involves the burglar acting as his own fence. Typically selling stolen property directly on the street, the suspect presents items to passing pedestrians or sells them directly from a vehicle. The second type of fence is the more traditional, an individual who either directly operates a legitimate business or has a business outlet for the sale of stolen property. Burglars and thieves learn of such localities through the criminal subculture and take stolen property to the fence for immediate cash sale. The profits realized by stolen property at minimal rates and selling at retail can exceed 900 percent.[11] A wide variety of businesses can be involved in secondary fencing; such operations have been found in appliance stores, secondhand and antique shops, junk and scrap yards, and various construction businesses, among others.

Antifencing operations must be designed to prove the necessary legal elements common to most state and federal laws pertaining to the receipt of stolen property. Basically, two elements must be demonstrated: (a) that the property item is stolen and (b) the person possessing, selling, or receiving the property has reason to believe the item to be stolen. Sting operations can take either of the aforementioned forms, with officers posing as sellers or buyers of stolen property. The first method poses more of a potential legal problem, as entrapment defenses are common when investigators use proactive methods.

An innovative proactive operation, termed ROPTIDE, was conducted by the Washington, D.C., Metropolitan Police and the FBI. The two agencies effectively formed an antifencing task force, with investigators posing as sellers of stolen property. Intelligence information indicated that three categories of burglary and theft would be targeted: construction site, business and home, and auto vehicle. Posing as burglars or thieves, the investigators approached known fences, offering to sell obviously stolen merchandise. The program was very successful in arresting fences, recovering stolen property already in the possession of fencing targets, and deterring future dealings between burglars and their fences. To date, operation ROPTIDE has produced 276 arrests and the recovery of $8 million in stolen property (see Figure 9.3).

Police strategies such as ROPTIDE are proving to be effective for several reasons. When two or more agencies form a coordinated task force approach to combat a specific crime, the results are typically more impressive than the efforts of a single agency. Additional personnel, enhanced budgets, and a variety of expertise all contribute to this outcome.

Other methods of defeating the fence include checking for stolen goods at places where used property is sold. Many police agencies have investigators who regularly visit pawnshops and secondhand outlets for this purpose. Informants have also been frequently used in fence identification. In addition, the criminal investigator should always question burglary suspects being held in custody as to their fencing contacts. Many investigative leads can be developed in this way, with a suspect occasionally providing information sufficient for a search warrant. Sometimes a suspected or arrested individual may agree to "introduce" an undercover officer to a fence.

FIGURE 9.3   Proactive antifencing operations. Surveillance photos of ROPTIDE task force taken as local and federal investigators gather evidence against known receivers of stolen property. *A.* Undercover detective poses as a burglar to sell stolen property to a fence operating out of a real estate office in downtown Washington, D.C. Fence had been active for more than 40 years. *B.* Investigator, posing as a nurse, sells alleged stolen jewelry to secondhand store that was buying stolen items from more than 30 thieves daily. *C.* To dispose of stolen jewelry, fences transported items to distant antique shows. The undercover detective who previously posed as a nurse (now wearing a wig to disguise her identity) and an FBI special agent locate the sold pieces and repurchase them, completing the evidentiary chain. *(Source: James Trainum, Metropolitan Police Department, Washington, D.C.)*

STUDY FINDINGS

The analysis of burglary research is very important to the successful reduction of this offense. By carefully analyzing findings from the following two studies, the investigator may be able to gain some useful insights.

- A study by John Conklin and Egon Bittner researched nearly 1,000 suburban burglaries for a one-year period. The researchers concluded that although there are more residential burglaries than nonresidential, nonresidential burglaries are proportionally greater as to their overall numbers in the community. Of the buildings burglarized, nearly 6 percent had an alarm system of some type. It is noteworthy that nearly 40 percent of these systems failed to function. The study also revealed that the amount of time between the occurrence and reporting of a burglary to the police related directly to the success of the investigation. The longer the lapse before reporting the case, the less likely it was to be solved.[12]

- A study of burglary sponsored by the California Department of Justice focused on six police jurisdictions, two in northern and four in southern California. A total of 8,137 burglaries were carefully analyzed over a one-year period. The following significant findings resulted from the study:

  Burglary losses were found to be of moderate value and included goods easily converted into cash.

Hard salable items, such as stereo systems, television sets, radios, computers and the like, accounted for more than half of all property reported stolen. Nonresidential structures were more likely to have cash, drugs, and items from inside safes stolen. Residential structures were more likely to have jewelry, furs, and firearms stolen.

  Residential burglaries occurred predominantly during the week and in the daytime.

Nearly 56 percent of all residential burglaries occurred during the day, as compared to only 15 percent of the reported nonresidential burglaries. Nonresidential burglaries occurred more frequently on weekdays, during the hours of darkness. No significant seasonal fluctuation was found to exist for either reporting category.

  Most burglaries involved some degree of forcible entry that was more likely to be associated with nonresidential than with residential structures.

Both categories involved similar means to gain entry, primarily through a door or window. Seventy-three percent of all nonresidential entries involved force of some type, compared with 57 percent of all residential entries. Tools were used more often in nonresidential cases, resulting in higher property damage in this category.

  With the exception of alarm systems, various types of deterrence bore little relationship to the prevention of burglary.

Both residential and nonresidential structures were about equally likely to have streetlights within 100 feet of the premises. A significant finding revealed that an alarm system was not likely to operate about half the time. Eighty percent of the nonresidential and 99 percent of the residential structures did not have alarm systems. Over 90 percent of the burglaries in both categories involved stolen property that bore no identifying serial numbers.[13]

STRATEGIES TO COMBAT BURGLARY

Controlling and reducing burglary crimes poses a particularly difficult problem for the criminal investigator. The large number of burglary investigations strains the resources of the police to a serious degree. With the rapid increase in burglary rates and correspondingly low rates of arrest and property recovery, officers have recognized the need for programs of prevention. In general, burglary reduction programs involve four basic strategies:

1. making structures physically more secure,
2. increasing detective and patrol effectiveness,
3. identifying stolen property and those who sell it, and
4. increasing citizen awareness.

Physical Security

A police agency should first determine the number and locations of structures that are in need of additional security. In making this determination, the **vulnerability analysis** may be used. Reported burglaries are categorized by type of structure involved, location, and method of operation. The data are then analyzed, and the various steps to implement physical security are determined using the findings of the analysis. Many agencies conduct what is termed the *premise security survey*. An investigator provides home owners or business proprietors with recommendations to reduce their probability of becoming burglary victims. The Chula Vista, California, police department determined that 25 percent of its residential burglaries involved a garage. Police officers periodically checked residences looking for unlocked, unattended garages. Upon finding such a garage, an officer would enter it and tag items likely to be stolen with yellow slips of paper. The paper slips stated, "This property could be stolen," and gave the name and telephone number of the police agency.[14] The Arlington, Virginia, police department determined that nearly 50 percent of their residential burglaries involved apartments. A local ordinance was instituted that required secure, deadbolt locks on all apartment doors. A significant decrease in apartment burglaries followed the passage of the ordinance.

A unique physical security program developed by the Milford, Connecticut, police department focused on commercial burglary prevention. Local business structures that were lacking in physical security were photographed at night. An investigator then contacted the business owner during working hours, pointing out various hazards apparent in the photograph (e.g., poor lighting, open windows) and recommended corrective measures.[15]

Burglar alarms have traditionally been used as a means of improving the physical security of a structure. Although the majority of alarms are found in commercial businesses, nearly 9 percent of the nation's 75 million private homes have some form of security system.[16] Commercial buildings use the alarm (either the simple bell type or the more complex electronic type) to a greater degree than the residence. The growing use of burglary alarms is viewed with mixed feelings by many police agencies. In one respect, they increase the probability of burglar apprehension; yet, because of the high number of false alarms, they can be a problem. As mentioned previously, a large number of alarms either fail to operate or are rendered useless by knowledgeable burglars. Ninety-eight percent of the 14 million emergency alarm calls answered by police in the United States are found to be false. It is an international problem: The London Metropolitan Police annually answer more than 130,000 alarms—99 percent of which are false.[17] Many factors account for false alarms, such as high winds, poor maintenance, power failures, and owner carelessness.

Many police departments have urged passage of city ordinances to levy fines on owners of alarms that are habitually activated falsely. As a general practice, fines of $100 or more can be levied after the second or third false alarm. False alarms are generally reduced as a result of such programs. However, alarm systems can be very beneficial in preventing burglaries and apprehending offenders. There is no way of knowing how many burglars are deterred by the presence of an alarm system, although there is reason to believe that many will not even attempt entry once a system is observed.

In some cities, residents and business owners whose security alarms malfunction and cause a police response can escape fines by taking a two-hour class on how to avoid false alarms. Pioneered in Los Angeles, where nearly 130,000 false alarms occur each year, two false alarms are allowed, followed by a choice between an $80 fine or attendance at a False Alarm Reduction Class.

Detective and Patrol Effectiveness

Innovative strategies designed to increase the effectiveness of burglary investigation are constantly being developed. One such program has been used in the Hampton, Virginia, police department. Because of a 31 percent increase in burglary crimes in one year, this agency inaugurated a successful **management by objective** (MBO) concept. MBO involves four basic steps:

1. diagnose the problem,
2. determine the proper action,
3. evaluate the action taken, and
4. make necessary adjustments and repeat the process.

The department first determined the degree of success of existing burglary procedures. It was found that the planning, execution, and assignment responsibility of the burglary unit was in need of revision. New plans of action were instituted, with assignments given to members of the burglary unit commensurate with their duties. All members of the unit were issued a detailed listing of their specific duties, permitting them to conduct investigations confidently within a prescribed framework. In addition, operational procedures were devised to refer detectives with specific investigative problems to the proper person. This prevented investigators from losing time and avoided the bottleneck of duplicated effort. The next MBO phase involved increasing communication among the various divisions of the department. The burglary commander instituted random open-group discussions with investigators, encouraging them to provide suggestions and ideas for improvement. Next, a formal reporting system was designed to evaluate the total performance of the burglary unit. The final step of the MBO concept involved careful analysis of goal achievement. The constant establishment of new goals and redefining of objectives is a continual procedure.

In an effort to reduce a climbing burglary rate, the Albuquerque, New Mexico, police department recently restructured how its burglary detectives would operate. The burglary detective squad is located in the police headquarters and uniquely assigns one detective to investigate all cases in which incidents are believed to involve the same suspect. Rather than having many detectives coordinating their cases, investigations involving a probable single suspect are automatically assigned to one detective who specializes in linking the cases and presenting them to the prosecutor at one time. While this method of investigation allows for better recognition of suspect method of operation, it also generally results in stiffer penalties by demonstrating that a single suspect is responsible for a considerable number of burglaries.

In a program of mutual cooperation, two police agencies often combine investigative personnel to reduce the number of burglaries. A special investigation unit composed of officers from both departments is formed. Separate investigative teams then operate from the unit, each having a specified geographic area of responsibility. The teams are generally required to deal with burglary investigations only and work each case until closed. Such cooperative programs have been very successful, often bringing about a significant reduction of burglary crimes within one year of start of operation.

Special tactics for patrol officers have been put into practice, with varying levels of success. *Bicycle patrols*, in which uniformed and undercover officers patrol high-risk structures, have proved to be very promising. With bicycles, areas that are difficult, if not impossible, to patrol by automobile become accessible. Bicycles also allow officers to reach a burglary crime scene without the noise and light of the patrol vehicle.

The correlation between burglary and school truancy has resulted in the formation of *truancy patrols* in several police agencies. The truancy patrol program is typically publicized in school newspapers just prior to its implementation. A special team of officers then concentrates on a high-risk burglary area, looking for truants. In cities that have tried this type of program, many youthful burglars have been apprehended and numerous burglaries prevented.

Identification of Stolen Property

The identification of stolen property increases the probability of its return to the victim and the successful arrest of the offender. The marking of property serves four basic purposes:

1. theft is discouraged;
2. law enforcement officials can better establish whether an item in possession of a suspect has been stolen;
3. recovered items can be identified, claimed, and returned to the owners more efficiently; and
4. the transfer of stolen property from burglar to fence is deterred.

The majority of the nation's police agencies have some type of program to mark and identify property. Certain basic methods are common to most of these programs. Items that are likely to be stolen are marked with a number that can be traced back to the victim. Driver license numbers or social security numbers are engraved on the item with a special tool. Police officers or community volunteers loan out the equipment from the police agency or travel to the requesting person's home or business.

Some property identification programs use a *property inventory list*. Property liable to be stolen is listed by description and serial number. In the event of a burglary, this detailed listing is given to investigating officers by the victim. Identification of stolen property has been associated with lower burglary rates. In fact, some insurance companies have been prompted to offer lower rates on home-owner insurance to those individuals who have taken advantage of property identification programs.

Citizen Awareness

A major obstacle in combating burglary is citizen apathy. Experienced criminal investigators realize that many burglaries can be prevented, more stolen property recovered, and arrest records improved with greater public awareness.

Community education is one of the oldest services offered by the police, but until relatively recently, such police efforts have failed to have a significant impact in reducing burglaries. Traditional burglary community education consisted of occasional lectures to requesting public groups and distribution of burglary prevention materials. Burglary reduction through community education now involves programs that are considerably more effective.

The ultimate objective of educating the public regarding burglary is to reduce instances of this offense. An additional benefit is that the public becomes aware of the value of the police, thereby reinforcing the police–citizen cooperation necessary to combat burglary. Police departments have found that waiting for the public to come to them for information is simply not effective. Police agencies must take it upon themselves to actively promote burglary awareness, using effective attention-getting methods. A highly promoted Neighborhood Watch Program, originally sponsored by the National Sheriff's Association, is such an example. Neighborhood Watch teaches citizens to make their homes, families, and property less vulnerable to crime. It also promotes a sense of neighborhood responsibility to reduce crime. Police agencies that have successfully reduced burglary through this program have aggressively initiated contact with the community. For example, in San Jose, California, all residents of a particular neighborhood were contacted in person. In addition, a letter was sent to each family explaining the crime prevention program in detail. The letter requested citizens to add their names and phone numbers to an enclosed map of their street and to return the map to the police department. Once the map was completed, copies were returned to all participating residents. The home owners were then encouraged to contact their neighbors and organize a local meeting at which a police crime prevention officer briefed the group regarding burglary prevention. More than 30,000 local watch programs are currently operating in every state.[19]

The Salt Lake City, Utah, police department devised an intense antiburglary campaign that was highly innovative. For a single month, the department implemented what was termed "Burglar Stop Month." With the assistance of private businesspeople, the public was literally bombarded with information on burglary prevention. Following a formidable news media kickoff, Salt Lake City citizens found antiburglary tips printed on their grocery bags, on table napkins in restaurants, on billboards, and even on the milk cartons. Personal property was marked in large volume, and homes and businesses were visited for vulnerability checks. As a result of the total program, an impressive 35 percent decrease in burglary was reported from statistics for the previous month.[20]

The Law Enforcement Assistance Administration was tremendously influential in supporting all types of burglary prevention programs. Although this federal agency is no longer functioning, its funding of nearly 1,000 local crime prevention programs during two decades provided an excellent example for current prevention efforts. Another supporting agency, the National Crime Prevention Institute (NCPI), was founded at the University of Louisville campus in 1971. Following the system of the British police, in which officers are formally trained in prevention tactics, NCPI trains officers throughout the nation to reduce criminal opportunity. More than 30,000 police and security officers have learned various prevention techniques from the institute.

CRIMINALISTIC APPLICATIONS

It is essential to keep in mind that any specific type of physical evidence can, and to varying degrees will, be found at virtually any type of crime scene. Although certain types of evidence are commonly found at burglary scenes and are thus included in this chapter discussion, they can often be encountered in the investigation of other crimes. Not only does this logic apply to the burglary-specific physical evidence presented here, but it is applicable for all physical evidence detailed in other chapters.

The application of criminalistics to the crime of burglary is very significant, for the suspect is rarely seen, much less apprehended, at the crime scene. Therefore, criminal investigators must rely on their ability to locate trace evidence to submit to the crime laboratory in the hope that such evidence will link the burglar to the scene. In the majority of burglary cases, however, evidence is not sent to the crime laboratory. This is due to the following three factors:

1. lack of a thorough crime scene search,
2. unmanageable caseload, and
3. lack of evidence.

The initial crime scene search by either the patrol officer or the detective is, unfortunately, often superficial. The very nature of this offense results in a substantial number of evidence items. Burglars are present inside the structure for a considerable time period; thus, tracing clues are often transferred from burglar to scene and, conversely, from scene to burglar. Consequently, the probability of linking evidence being present at the burglary scene is high, particularly when compared to other felony crimes that are committed more quickly, with little or no contact. For this reason, a thorough crime scene search must be undertaken by a trained officer.

The primary reason so few burglary scenes are properly searched is that the number of cases is so great. With burglary being the most commonly reported felony, most medium-sized to large police agencies simply do not have the necessary investigators to process each scene. Typically, only scenes involving a large loss or scenes in which additional crimes occurred will be thoroughly processed.

Although many types of evidence may be encountered during the burglary investigation, toolmarks, paint, glass, soil, and fingerprints are frequently processed by the investigator. Such evidence is of course not exclusive to burglary and will (as with any type of evidence) be found in other types of crime scenes. In the remainder of this chapter, the first four types will be considered. Latent fingerprints are discussed in detail in Chapter 17.

Toolmarks

The majority of burglaries involve a forceful entry with tools that often leave marks. A **toolmark** is an impression resulting from forceful contact between a tool and surface area of an object (see Figure 9.4A–B). The tools used in burglary are many and varied. Simple screwdrivers (Figure 9.4C) or pry bars may be used, as well as various drills and specially designed burglary tools that are quite complex. The officer often encounters toolmarks at the point of entry. Suspects naturally use a tool when force is required to gain entry (e.g., when a locked door or window is encountered). The marks will then be found on door frames, window ledges, and similar locations in close proximity to the entry point.

When a metal tool comes in contact with a softer material (such as wood) with sufficient force, an impression of the harder object is left. Thus, when a screwdriver is forced into a wooden door frame, an impression of the screwdriver blade results (see Figure 9.4D). In addition, when a tool slides across the surface of an object, the edge of the tool frequently leaves marks.

Toolmark identification is based on the concept of individuality. In theory, all manufactured objects possess small variations, even though they may be mass-produced. The variations, in regard to tools, will occur on the point or edge of the object. The variation may take the form of tiny upthrusts of metal or small depressions across the edge. With such variations at the time of manufacture or resulting from use, the surface of each tool is unique. It is this uniqueness or individuality of toolmarks (or any other type of evidence) that gives the investigator a major tracing clue in connecting a marking from the scene to a particular suspect.

When the officer finds a toolmark, it must be recorded by field notes and photography. It is normally necessary to use magnification and additional lighting while photographing. After the mark has been recorded, the object bearing the toolmark should be removed from the scene and transported to the crime lab. Since many marks will be found on large objects

A

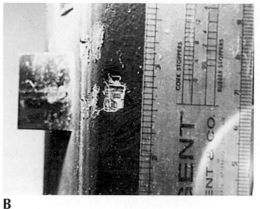

B

C

D

FIGURE 9.4 Toolmark analysis—a case study. *A.* A toolmark is found on a metal door at the scene of a burglary; *B.* A close-up photograph is taken, with a measurement marker included; *C.* A screwdriver is recovered from the burglary suspect; *D.* The evidence screwdriver is forced against lead for testing purposes

E

FIGURE 9.4 *(continued)*   *E.* A cast is taken of the test marks in the lead. This will be compared to a cast made of the marks found on the door. *(Source:* David Townshend, Michigan State Police.)

that are hard to handle, this will not always be possible. When the marked object cannot be transported, a detailed cast should be made. *Casts* are made by applying a soft, pliable substance such as moulage or silicone material to the mark. The various sliding marks and striations are reproduced in this way for further study.

The criminalist can provide valuable information concerning toolmarks (a) when only the mark is present and (b) when a suspected tool is compared to the mark. Photographs and casts of the toolmark will be examined and compared with other similar toolmarks in the attempt to determine the general nature of the tool. Further, the cast may be compared to other, similar casts of recent vintage in the attempt to link a series of burglaries to one offender.

When an arrest is made and a tool recovered or when a tool is found at the scene, a direct comparison may be possible. An experienced criminalist usually can determine whether a specific tool made a particular mark. The suspected tool is used to make a similar mark, termed a *standard*. Standards result from laboratory tests that attempt to duplicate circumstances pertaining to the original evidence. The resulting evidence, or standard, is then compared and contrasted to the original mark. A standard toolmark will usually be made in a material approximating that of the original (see Figure 9.4E).

After comparing the standard to the original toolmark, the criminalist makes one of the following judgments:

1. the tool in question made the specific mark,
2. the tool in question did not make the specific mark, and
3. based on the available data, no determination can be made about whether the tool in question made the specific mark.

The third alternative—that the data are inconclusive—is rarely encountered. Of course, much of the success in making a determination depends on the quality of the data—the original toolmark or the standard to which it is compared. No specific number of matching lines is necessary to conclude a match. The match, or lack of it, will be determined by the training and experience of the criminalist and the manner in which the standard conforms to the original.

Casting and Producing Replicas

Burglary crime scenes and a host of other felony crime scenes routinely produce evidence that must be recorded through the use of the *cast* or *replica*. These procedures are necessary when the object upon which the tracing characteristics are located cannot be physically transported to the laboratory. Tracing clues such as footprints, tire tracks, and toolmarks are often found on nonportable objects. During the search phase of the crime scene process, all officers must use caution not to alter tracing impressions left by the criminal. These are most often of the shoe or tire track category and may be completely obliterated by a single misplaced step.

Shoe and Tire Impressions. When any impression is located by the investigating officer, the evidence should be initially recorded through photography (see Figure 9.5). Shoe impressions occur in both indoor and outdoor scenes. When the impression is located indoors, it must be recorded in a similar fashion to the latent fingerprint. Since the impression is really a dustlike trace, it must be lifted from its original surface by an adhesive material. *Rubber lifters*, which are of contrasting colors to that of the impression, are of value in lifting this type of evidence. In addition to the older adhesive lifters, investigators may employ an electrostatic dust print lifter. The device consists of a high-voltage power supply control unit, a nickel-plated steel ground plane and a metalized lifting medium. As high voltage is applied to the lifting mat, it takes on a negative charge, and

FIGURE 9.5 Portable evidence camera records shoe impression mold for future comparison with suspect's shoe.
(Source: Sirchie Fingerprint Laboratories.)

FIGURE 9.6 The electrostatic dust print lifter allows the investigator to record and collect dust and fine soil at crime scenes. *(Source: Sirchie Fingerprint Laboratories.)*

the ground plane becomes positive. Any dust present under the mat will take on a positive charge and will then be attracted to the negatively charged collection mat. The dust print transferred to the lifting mat then appears as a precise mirror image of the original dust print (see Figure 9.6). When the shoe impression is located in the outdoor scene, the impression will be embedded in the soil. In this case, a plaster of Paris cast is generally employed.

Plaster of Paris or the newer *silicone rubber* compounds provide a detailed impression of the tracing characteristics of the original impression. The value of the shoe or tire mark as evidence lies in its unique or individual qualities. The cast can provide general tracing clues, such as brand or model, or it may clarify a specific impression that could indicate guilt. As each shoe or tire mark undergoes normal wear, imperfections of the sole or tread appear. These imperfections will be unique to the specific shoe or tire that left the impression. The value of the cast will depend upon locating the object that made the crime scene impression. When a suspect is identified and apprehended, the appropriate items should be legally seized for comparison at the laboratory.

Prior to actually taking the cast, the impression should be properly prepared. If twigs have fallen into the impression and are obscuring the details, they should be carefully removed. If the impression is in a granular substance, such as sand or dust, the trace should be sprayed with a chemical fixative. A proper mixture of plaster and water is necessary (see Figure 9.7). The plaster and water must be mixed to result in a creamlike consistency. Before the mixture is poured, a frame should be placed around the impression to contain the liquid. The mixture should then be poured with care and allowed to harden. The plaster should never be poured directly on the impression, for the force of the falling liquid will alter the detailed characteristics. Any suitable hard, clean object can be used to break the force of the falling plaster. When the impression is nearly half full with plaster, reinforcing materials should be added to stabilize the hardened cast. Most casts will be completely hardened within 45 minutes. After approximately 15 minutes—when the cast is hardened yet still impressionable—the officer's identifying marks are applied (see Figure 9.7E). After the cast is carefully removed to avoid splitting, it should be allowed to dry completely. When five hours have passed, the cast can be cleaned of soil debris by running a gentle stream of water over it. Abrasive brushes or scouring pads should never be

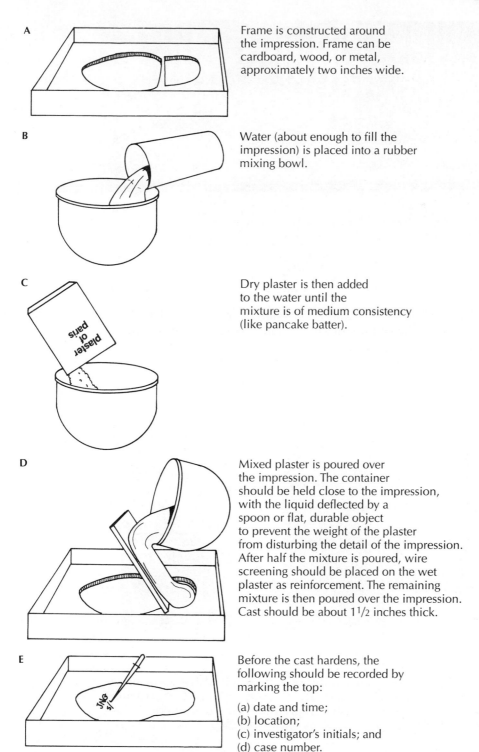

A — Frame is constructed around the impression. Frame can be cardboard, wood, or metal, approximately two inches wide.

B — Water (about enough to fill the impression) is placed into a rubber mixing bowl.

C — Dry plaster is then added to the water until the mixture is of medium consistency (like pancake batter).

D — Mixed plaster is poured over the impression. The container should be held close to the impression, with the liquid deflected by a spoon or flat, durable object to prevent the weight of the plaster from disturbing the detail of the impression. After half the mixture is poured, wire screening should be placed on the wet plaster as reinforcement. The remaining mixture is then poured over the impression. Cast should be about 1½ inches thick.

E — Before the cast hardens, the following should be recorded by marking the top:

(a) date and time;
(b) location;
(c) investigator's initials; and
(d) case number.

FIGURE 9.7 Impression preservation using plaster of Paris.

used to clean the cast. Casts of tire tracks are made in a similar manner to the procedure just described.

When many footprints of the suspect are located in either indoor or outdoor scenes, the pattern of the prints should be recorded and carefully measured. Through analysis of the officer's measurements and photographs, a

FIGURE 9.8   Suspect's shoe and impression of shoe marks left at a crime scene. Note the similarities of the impressions to the actual shoe pattern.

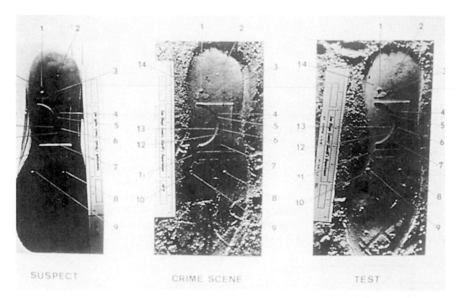

FIGURE 9.9   A suspect's shoe impression was left at the scene of a felony. Following the suspect's arrest, his shoe and a test impression were compared to the crime scene impression. Fourteen unique similarities were found. *(Source: Joseph Orantes, San Diego Police Department.)*

criminalist can often determine estimates of the suspect's height and general pattern of walking (see Figures 9.8 and 9.9).

Paint

Paint is a mixture of a pigment and a vehicle, such as oil or water, that together form a liquid or paste that can be applied to a surface to provide an adherent coating and impart color. Burglars may leave or take away paint evidence during entry or prowl or while exiting the scene. If entry is forced by a metal tool, paint on the tool surface or the surface being forced may chip away. During the prowl of the structure, fresh paint may adhere to the burglar's clothing or shoes. Safe burglaries frequently involve the transfer of paint either from the safe to the tool or from a painted tool surface to the safe.

The investigator must carefully record the location of the paint sample and package it individually in a clean evidence container to submit to the forensic laboratory. The evidence can initially be used as a basic tracing aid. For example, if a freshly painted structure has been burglarized, the officer may have reason to believe the burglar's clothing came in contact with the paint. Assuming an arrest has been made or a search warrant executed, a careful examination of the suspect's clothing for paint smears would be logical. If traces of paint were found on the suspect's clothing, the traces would be compared with paint sampled from the crime scene. Paint evidence may also give officers some indication of a specific tool or automobile used by the suspect. If a criminalist suggests that a toolmark appears to have been made by a crowbar and within the marking paint traces are located, the officer can collect various painted crowbars for a paint comparison. Or, in a case in which older paint chips are encountered, there is the possibility that minute chips have adhered to the burglar's clothing.

Paint evidence (or evidence consisting of other substances, such as plaster or safe insulation) is often encountered on the tips of tools left at the crime scene. The officer should take care to ensure that such evidence is not lost. The end of the tool containing the paint should be wrapped in a plastic envelope and sealed. When paint evidence is located on a stationary object, such as a wall or safe, samples of the paint should be removed for analysis. An excellent method to accomplish this is to place a short strip of tape on one side of the open end of a plastic envelope. Then, attach tape and envelope to the stationary object containing the evidence. With one hand, hold the envelope open, and with the other, scrape the paint into the envelope with a clean knife blade (see Figure 9.10).

Paint evidence is examined and compared in a variety of scientific ways designed to suit a specific investigation. The technique selected by the criminalist will depend on the type of paint, size of the sample, and number of samples obtained. Intact samples may be examined under a microscope to note the appearance of the edges. Since most intact paint samples have edges that are broken and jagged, a matching of two samples (in jigsaw puzzle fashion) may be accomplished (see Figure 9.11). Particularly in hit-and-run automobile cases but in burglary cases as well, samples found at a scene

FIGURE 9.10 Paint sample recovery.

FIGURE 9.11   A fracture match of two paint fragments. One fragment was found at the scene of a hit-and-run; the other was recovered from the suspect's automobile. *(Source: Wisconsin Department of Justice—Crime Laboratory Bureau.)*

have been matched to those carried from the scene, either on the offender's person or automobile.

There are often many layers of paint on a single evidence sample, particularly on those from residential burglaries. The number of layers and the color of each should be carefully noted for comparison with similar samples that may be found on a suspect. If two samples are presented in court—Sample A collected at the scene and Sample B found in the suspect's pants cuff—mathematical probability factors will be cited to prove identical origin. The criminalist can demonstrate mathematically that two paint chips having a number of separate coats of paint of identical color in the same sequence are very likely to have come from the same scene.

Paint evidence may also be examined by infrared spectroscopy or by chemical testing. Infrared spectroscopy is done with a laboratory instrument known as a **spectrophotometer**. This instrument identifies paint, as well as many other types of evidence, by measuring and recording the absorption spectrum. Wavelengths given off by a radiation source in the spectrophotometer produce a graphlike chart that is unique to the evidence being studied. By using the device to measure and record the three types of radiation—ultraviolet, visible, and infrared—various substances can be identified or compared. Paint samples also may be identified and compared by standard chemical laboratory methods. Various chemicals are applied to the sample to identify pigment and other substances intrinsic to the evidence.

Glass

During many burglary investigations, the officer encounters glass evidence, typically in a broken state. *Glass* is a combination of silica and several metal oxides that are mixed, heated together, and cooled into a solid mass. Although quite common at many crime scenes, glass as a valuable tracing and identification clue is often not considered. Although glass is routinely collected in automobile hit-and-run cases, it is more likely to be ignored in the typical burglary investigation. This is perhaps due to a lack of officer training or an underlying assumption that a normal burglary does not justify "bothering the lab."

Different types of information can be obtained by glass analysis. One basic yet highly significant determination can often be made using glass fragments, namely, direction of force. When a suspect breaks a window to enter a structure, force is exerted from one point to another. The criminalist can often determine if the original force came from the outside in or if the force was exerted from inside the structure. This basic information can detect a false burglary; a "victim" may break a window from within and claim a burglar broke it to gain entry from outside the structure.

In determining from which side the striking force was exerted, the forensic scientist carefully studies the manner in which the fragments fractured. Initially, the attempt is made to reconstruct all fragments if possible. If the various glass pieces can be assembled together, analysis of the various fractures is simplified. The three basic fractures are the cone, radial, and circular fracture.

When a striking force pushes through a window pane, the pane will bend toward the origin of the force. The bending effect causes the fracturing and ultimate splitting apart of the fragments. A **cone** (or shell-shaped) **fracture** often indicates the side on which the pane was struck. As the force moves through the pane, pressure directly in front of the striking object creates a conelike opening in the glass. If the glass is still intact or if the pane can be reconstructed at the laboratory, the two sides of the cone opening will be closely examined. The small opening of the fracture will indicate the side from which the force originated; the larger, opposite opening will indicate the exit side.

Radial fracture lines also result from the bending of the pane toward the striking force. As the glass bends, jagged breakage lines run from the cone opening outward. Radial fracture lines often appear on both sides of the glass but in greater number on the side opposite the striking force. **Circular** (or concentric) **fracture lines** appear on the same side as the striking force, although they may be apparent in smaller numbers on the opposite side (see Figure 9.12).

The backward bending of broken glass is a fortunate phenomenon for the criminal investigator, for when the glass is forcefully broken, a large number of small fragments are thrown in the perpetrator's direction. Some of these fragments may adhere to clothing without notice. If the offender is apprehended and the clothes recovered, a search may reveal glass fragments useful for comparison. Glass fragments have distinct chemical and physical properties that can serve as linking factors. Careful analysis, comparing glass from the crime scene and glass that was lodged in the suspect's clothing, can produce a match. Although not possible in all cases, sufficient glass fragments can be linked to the original pane. The criminalist can then again turn to the probability theory to demonstrate the common origin of fragments found on the suspect and fragments recovered at the scene.

Occasionally, large fragments of glass will have been carried from the scene via the clothing or automobile of a suspect. In a manner similar to matching large paint chips, the glass fragments may be pieced together. A match of this type is highly convincing to a jury and frequently results in a conviction. Glass analysis will also aid the officer in determining the order of

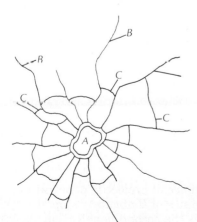

FIGURE 9.12   Primary glass fractures. *A.* Cone fracture; *B.* Radial fracture lines; *C.* Circular or spiral fracture lines.

penetration when more than one object strikes a pane. The sequence of striking objects may be significant to a particular investigation (e.g., a robbery or homicide in which many bullets are fired). To determine the order of penetration, the criminalist studies the radial fracture lines. These lines abruptly stop at preexisting lines of fracture. That is, when the first object strikes the glass, it produces fracture lines at which fractures from subsequent striking objects terminate (see Figure 9.13).

Soil

Soil is commonly found in burglary crime scenes and often plays a part in many other felony investigations. Because of its abundance and the ease with which it is transported, it has become an important evidence item in criminalistics. *Soil* is composed of decayed rock, various minerals, and decomposed plant matter. There is really no such thing as "just plain dirt"; soil is unique, with samples within a few feet of each other frequently differing significantly in composition. The individuality of soil is determined by the degree of humus, minerals, and human-made elements present in a particular sample.

Burglars often deposit soil at the crime scene. This, in itself, is of little significance; but if the burglar retains a similar soil sample (on a shoe, perhaps), a comparison that is highly significant can be made. The object is to show that Evidence Item A, found at the scene, is identical to Evidence Item B, found on the suspect. When officers process a crime scene, the recovery and packaging of soil must be done with care. When soil is discovered on portable objects, the entire object should be packaged and transported to the lab. No effort should be made to remove soil, for contamination and the loss of valuable comparative elements could result. When soil is located on nonportable objects, such as floors or automobiles, the soil should be packaged in a clean individual envelope or glass vial.

Soil may serve as a general tracing clue because of its uniqueness and also as an incriminating indicator. If an investigator has no leads about the identity of the perpetrator of a burglary, soil may provide a general starting point. Because different types of soil are associated with particular geographic areas, the officer may attempt to trace the soil to its original location. After limiting an entire city or county to a specific area, the area would be investigated for likely suspects. Although this method is far from being consistently successful, it has proved helpful in many investigations.

The more frequent use of soil involves tracing like samples to a common origin. If a burglary suspect is arrested and soil recovered from the bottom of his or her shoes, the recovered soil may be compared to similar evidence

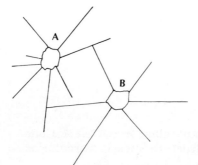

FIGURE 9.13 Sequence of projectile penetration. The radial fracture lines of B abruptly stop at those of A. Thus, B is the second penetration.

found at the burglary scene. If the two samples are found to be similar, the presence of the suspect at the scene is strongly indicated. Even if the suspect has previously denied being at the location, the soil match is a convincing indicator of guilt.

After soil has been discovered at the crime scene, it may be necessary to obtain another sample from a different location. For example, soil recovered in an urban residential burglary may have been transported from a rural cornfield by the burglar. Or, as in one homicide investigation, soil may be recovered from a suspect's shoes at the time of arrest and matched to soil subsequently sampled from a gravesite. Soil selected for sampling purposes need not be in large quantities; amounts approximating the size of a golf ball are normally sufficient. It is extremely important, however, that the localities of the various samples be selected with care. The uniqueness of soil is what gives it value for comparison purposes. If the officer selects a sample only a few feet from the original site, a comparison may not be relevant.

The most commonly used current method of comparing and analyzing soil samples is known as the **soil density gradient test**. Glass tubes of narrow diameter are filled with various liquids of different density value (see Figure 9.14). Sample A, found at the burglary scene, and Sample B, obtained from a suspect's backyard, are deposited into two liquid-filled tubes of the same density. In time, the soil particles filter down into the fluid. Each particle settles at the point in the tube at which the fluid is equal in density to it. When all particles of both soil samples have settled, a similar configuration will be noted in both tubes. The criminalist may use other methods to compare soil samples, such as visually contrasting the color. In addition, chemical testing and analysis by the spectrographic process may be employed.

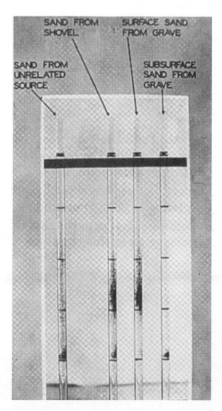

FIGURE 9.14 Results of a soil density gradient test used in a murder case. Sand taken from a shovel recovered from the suspect's home matches sand from the victim's gravesite. *(Source: Joseph Orantes, San Diego Police Department.)*

▲ SUMMARY

As America's most common felony, the crime of burglary requires constant investigative effort. Despite the extremely high rate of occurrence, only 14 percent of all reported burglaries result in arrest. The essence of a successful burglary lies in its not being observed; thus, many normal investigative procedures are frustrated. Because so few offenders are encountered at the scene, the typical burglary investigation centers on the crime scene and the resultant physical evidence.

Burglary crime scenes include residences, businesses, and general dwellings. More residential burglaries occur than any other type, often perpetrated by unskilled offenders. Juveniles have a traditionally high rate of participation, constituting nearly 17 percent of all those arrested. Although burglary is classified as a property-oriented crime, suspects often can be violent, as nearly one in three victims who encounter home burglars are attacked by them in some manner.

The investigation of burglary must be systematic and often concentrates on the suspect's actions at the crime scene. Specifically, the entry, method of search, and exit are processed with particular thoroughness. Although residences are frequently selected for their cash and small valuables, businesses and public sites are perceived to contain considerable amounts of cash in safes. Because burglary of a safe requires prolonged effort and a degree of skill, many investigative clues can be located at the scene of a crime of this nature.

Burglary reduction can be achieved through increased arrests, yet deterrence strategies have proven to be very important. Many of the most effective deterrence programs focus on the ways in which burglary suspects dispose of their stolen goods. Through various undercover and sting operations, investigators are able to arrest burglars as they attempt to sell stolen property. Other types of undercover operations have proactively targeted active fences who knowingly purchase stolen merchandise.

Although any type of physical evidence may be encountered at a burglary crime scene, toolmarks, paint, soil, and glass fragments are commonly located and processed by forensic experts.

■ EXERCISES

1. Prepare a paper listing frequency, rates, offender characteristics, and other data relative to burglary in your community. Contrast your findings with national data found in the FBI's *Uniform Crime Report*.
2. Through local police interviews, discover what strategies have been developed to reduce the number of burglaries in your community.
3. Prepare a forensic science display. Conduct glass experiments to demonstrate the various types of fractures discussed in this chapter.

● RELEVANT WEB SITES

http://www.issinc.ca/index.php?C=Burglary&T=O

British site with links to American burglary Web sites. Detailed discussion on home security, burglary prevention, safe burglaries, burglary statistics, and burglary investigation.

http://www.ojp.usdoj.gov/bjs/glance/burg.htm

Department of Justice site that provides details on the prevalence of burglary in the United States from 1973 to the present. Discusses the degree of burglary as obtained through annual victimization surveys.

http://www.jcsd.org/burglary_prevention.htm

Extensive discussion on how citizens can prevent being a residential or business burglary victim. Includes prevention techniques based on the concepts of light, time and noise.

Robbery

KEY TERMS

atomic absorption spectroscopy

Ballistic Identification System

cargo robbery

carjacking

commercial robbery

crime scene

fiber evidence

home invasion robbery

lands and grooves

modus operandi

neutron activation analysis

paraffin test

pistol

predatory criminal

proactive policing

residential robbery

revolver

robbery

semiautomatic

smart guns

street robbery

truck hijacking

LEARNING OBJECTIVES

1. to know the legal meaning of the term *robbery;*
2. to be aware of the current state of robbery regarding frequency, time, and place of occurrence;
3. to be able to list offender characteristics associated with this crime;
4. to be able to define the four major categories of robbery;
5. to be familiar with the method of operation pertaining to each of the four major categories;
6. to be able to explain the investigative procedures that are followed in the robbery inquiry;
7. to be aware of the two major strategies for reducing the instances of this offense; and
8. to have knowledge of those areas of forensic science that directly pertain to the robbery investigation.

INTRODUCTION

The historical view of robbery is somewhat paradoxical. Early English literature is filled with accounts of the bold and daring highwaymen of the Robin Hood genre. In the United States, literally hundreds of robbers—from Jesse James to John Dillinger—have been portrayed as true folk heroes. Yet, despite the traditional fascination with this offense, robbery has had a tremendous negative impact on the public. The fear of "crime in the streets" is largely a fear of robbery. In many areas, this fear has resulted in self-imposed imprisonment. The dread of becoming a robbery victim has driven the old and young alike, the poor, inner-city resident and the affluent suburbanite, behind their own locked doors.

Robbery is the taking of property of another, from his or her person or immediate presence, by the use of force or intimidation. Actual physical force need not be used to sustain a charge of robbery; when circumstances are such that fear would ordinarily be induced in the mind of a reasonable human being, the fear is sufficient to sustain the charge. Property need not be taken from the victim's person; it is sufficient if it is taken in the person's presence. Furthermore, robbery does not depend on the kind or value of the property taken, so long as the property could be the subject of theft. Many states have two categories of robbery that are generally dependent on the presence of a dangerous weapon. Courts have consistently held that merely being armed with a dangerous weapon, as opposed to actually using one, is sufficient to establish robbery. Also, a dangerous weapon need not be what is commonly thought of as such. Even a toy gun in the hand or pocket can be considered a dangerous weapon if it is used in such a way as to put the victim in fear of bodily injury.

Robbery is commonly misreported to the police. Many victims report what is really a larceny or burglary by stating that they have been "robbed." Although it is unreasonable to assume a general public awareness of the statutory difference, the officer should quickly determine which offense has actually taken place.

CURRENT STATE OF ROBBERY

The crime of robbery is declining from a leveling trend achieved during the 1980s. Currently, nearly 413,000 robbery complaints are annually reported to police. Overall, the national rate is 142 incidents per 100,000 people, a 33 percent decrease in volume from the reported 1994 rate of occurrence.[1] As with most serious crime, government victimization surveys indicate a much larger actual incidence in the population: approximately 1,010,000 victimizations when unreported robberies are included in the total.[2] This offense is closely correlated with population density, for whereas rural areas have 16 victimizations per 100,000 people, cities with a million or more inhabitants average 440 per 100,000. Robbery accounts for a sizable proportion of all reported violent crime—30 percent, or a robbery every 60 seconds. Geographic surveys demonstrate that the southern states have the highest rate of robbery and the midwestern states the lowest. Robbery tends to be a cyclical crime in that the number of offenses tends to rise in the colder months, generally peaking from October to December.

Although robbery can occur anywhere, 43 percent of the offenses are typically committed in the street. Although the object of robbery is money or property, many victims suffer physical injury as a consequence of the attack. The extent of such physical and mental suffering cannot be measured in monetary terms alone; however, in a recent year, the average financial loss for each robbery incident was slightly over $1,244 for a total reported loss of $514 million.[3]

The majority of robberies, 42 percent, are committed with firearms, specifically handguns. The strong-arm technique, or "mugging," which involves violence or fear of violence inflicted by the offender's hands, arms, or feet, accounts for 40 percent of the reported cases. The third highest variety, 9 percent, involves the use of knives or other cutting instruments. All other cases are associated with other types of weapons and intimidation. Law enforcement typically clears 26 percent of the reported robbery incidents through the arrest of a suspect. The statistically average robbery victim is a young, lower-income, unmarried male of a minority group; females generally account for one-fourth of all victims.[4]

OFFENDER CHARACTERISTICS

According to arrest statistics, the average robbery suspect is a black male, 18 years of age or older. The majority of robbery suspects are young adults, with nearly 63 percent being under 25 years of age. Yet juveniles continue to account for a significant proportion of offenders for this crime category—nearly 24 percent. From a racial standpoint, approximately 54 percent of arrested robbery suspects are black, 44 percent white.[5] Robbery is a heavily male-dominated offense: 90 percent of arrested suspects are males.

Generally speaking, there is variation in the motivating factors for the criminal actions of robbers. Research studies have indicated that there is no one stereotype to characterize all offenders or even a sizable proportion of them. However, robbers can generally be classified via one of the following basic categories: (a) the professional intensive offender, (b) the amateur intermittent offender, and (c) the specific-objective offender. *Professional intensive offenders* typically consider crime generally, and robbery specifically, to be their life's work. These offenders will commit numerous robberies throughout their lifetimes and often entertain the notion that they are the most daring and "macho" of criminals. Although such self-images are, of course, grandiose, the professional robber does enjoy relatively high status within the criminal subculture. An LEAA-funded study conducted by the Rand Corporation focused on 49 inmates serving sentences in California for armed robbery. Although all of the offenders had extensive criminal records, one-third were identified as professional intensive criminals. It was additionally found that this type of robbery suspect committed ten times the number of crimes committed by the nonprofessional offenders.[6] An additional study, focused on the most active 10 percent of incarcerated robbery inmates, determined that each subject averaged 85 robberies a year.[7]

Amateur intermittent offenders do not necessarily view themselves as lifetime robbers. This type of offender commits infrequent robbery offenses, often recklessly. Whereas intensive offenders tend to attack victims with known profit potentials, intermittent offenders generally select victims randomly. They are more inclined to attack victims who are obviously more vulnerable, such as women or elderly people. Consequently, they are less likely to be armed, often resorting to the strong-arm technique.

Specific-objective offenders are probably the least numerous of the robbery suspect types. They commit robbery to achieve a specific objective beyond the acquisition of money per se. They may rob to support a narcotics or a gambling habit. A small number commit robbery simply for the psychological gratification derived from the victim's fear. Specific-objective offenders are often first-time offenders and are apt to be apprehended within a short time of the crime. They generally have criminal offenses in their backgrounds but have not adopted robbery as a preferred crime. Specific-objective offenders (with the exception of those deriving gratification from victims' fear) do not enjoy the person-to-person confrontation of the armed robbery. They would prefer to accomplish their objective through a property crime, but they lack either the skill or the means to commit such an offense.

Robbery offenders can be clearly classified as **predatory criminals**, those showing a preference for crimes involving direct confrontation or the stalking of victims. Such offenders are often predisposed to turn to robbery rather than property offenses, inasmuch as robbery offers a match for their predatory personality. The fact that one in three of all robbery victims is injured by the perpetrator underscores the violent nature of this type of suspect.[8] Additional researchers further document the violence associated with robbery in that

1. guns are actually discharged during robberies 20 percent of the time,
2. 11 percent of all murders are linked with robbery as a motive or circumstance, and
3. with the sole exception of homicide suspects, robbery suspects are more likely than any other violent offenders to use a weapon.[9]

ROBBERY TYPES

Street Robbery

Street robberies are those offenses occurring on public streets, thoroughfares, or other outdoor localities that are not obstructed from public view. Forty-three percent of all robberies fall into this category. The typical street attack involves a young suspect and an obviously vulnerable victim. A substantial proportion of strong-arm robberies occurs in the street, as do those purse snatches classified as robberies (see Figure 10.1).

Street muggings often involve more than one offender; typically, a victim is overwhelmed by the presence or force of several muggers. The victim may

FIGURE 10.1   The most common form of robbery, the street robbery is generally a swift and violent occurrence that often results in a poor description of the perpetrator. *(Source: Esbin-Anderson / The Image Works.)*

be attacked from the front or rear and is often pushed or beaten to the ground. During the attack or immediately following, the victim's valuables are taken. Targets of the attack are generally the victim's wallet, purse, watch, or any other jewelry item that is easily seen. Whether a purse snatch is classified as robbery depends on the manner in which the crime is perpetrated. Generally, if the purse is quickly taken off the arm or shoulder, without overcoming the actual resistance of the victim, the offense will be called a theft. However, if some manner of force is used, the offense will be classified as a robbery in many states. Force is typically employed when the theft attempt is thwarted.

Strong-arm street robberies can result in serious victim injury. Victims who physically resist are often attacked in a very violent fashion. Persistent victim resistance may lead to an escalation of the attack, with the introduction of dangerous weapons besides the initial hand/fist.

The typical street robbery occurs so quickly that the victim can provide only a poor description of the offender. Often the victim can offer no description at all. Although the offender is not generally armed, a significant number of victims are injured. One western study revealed that 50 percent of street victims were injured, with 10 percent of them requiring hospital treatment. The high injury rate may be due to the selection of older victims in the street robbery. The same study indicated that nearly 50 percent of the male victims were over 50 years of age, whereas 77 percent of the female victims were over 50.[10] In the majority of street robberies, a relatively small amount of money is taken—usually less than ten dollars. Most street robberies occur at dusk or after dark, with some degree of artificial light.

Although most street robberies normally involve a young amateur offender and a victim selected at random, a small but significant number involve offenders who are more experienced. Occasionally, the officer will encounter the robbery of a bill collector, jewelry salesperson, or some other type of pedestrian known to carry cash or valuables. Older robbers, who tend to plan their attacks more carefully, are often involved in this type of offense, and generally they will be armed with a gun. Street bill collection is declining, however. Rarely is it encountered outside of a large metropolitan area. However, the robbery of jewelry salespersons outside of stores is rapidly increasing.

A rapidly expanding form of street robbery involves victims who are withdrawing money from automated teller machines (ATMs). This form of robbery has grown in proportion to the increase of these banking devices across the nation. In 1985, there were 52,500 ATM machines in the United States, and by 1997, there were an estimated 100,000, with more than $6 million annually passing through each one.[11] The banking industry estimates that there is only one robbery attack in every two million transactions, but the true figure is unknown because most official reports do not separate this form of robbery from others. However, these offenses are growing more common in cities, as more than a half dozen are committed in urban areas such as Los Angeles each day. This form of robbery typically involves an armed suspect who specializes in a particular kind of attack. A suspect may lie in wait and attack the victim before or, more commonly, after an ATM transaction. Others abduct victims and force them to travel to their ATMs and withdraw a maximum amount of cash.

Residential Robbery

Residential robbery takes place whenever an offender forcefully or by deceit enters the domicile of a victim while the victim is present for the purpose of taking that person's possessions and valuables. Fortunately, individuals who enter a residence for the purpose of committing a robbery are relatively rare. Communities that have experienced true residential robberies are understandably alarmed and demand prompt action by their police agencies. Although the majority of residential robberies involve burglars who are surprised by returning residents, the true residential robbery, also known as **home invasion robbery**, involves an offender who is aware that the home is occupied and gains entry by force or false pretense. Unlike the residential burglar who is suddenly confronted by victims, the true home invasion robber purposely targets the resident, rather than the residence. Often carrying items that connote intimidation and confrontation, this type of suspect comes prepared to control victims and frequently engages in violence. Because suspects are unsure of the degree of resistance they may encounter within the residence, the offense almost always is committed by more than one offender.[12] Some residential robbers pose as repair people, city inspectors, or police officers to gain entry initially; others may knock at the door and force their way in after the door is opened.

Although there is some evidence indicating prior offender–victim relationships in many residential robberies, a substantial number do not involve a prior relationship. The victim is generally selected by the location of the house or its appearance (a wealthy neighborhood or expensive home). Or there may be some indicator that the victim possesses specific property. For example, if the offender learns that a certain individual is an active coin collector or that another has substantial jewelry insurance, such knowledge will determine the selection. An increasing number of residential robberies involve narcotics and dangerous drugs as the primary target and cash or property as secondary targets. A victim will generally not tell an investigating officer about a narcotics loss, but the victim's reputation as a drug dealer or possessor of narcotics very likely will have motivated the robbery.

The residential robber often is of the psychopathic type and is almost always armed with a gun or knife. The violent person-to-person nature of residential robbery is ideally suited for this extreme antisocial individual. Other felony offenses may occur during the residential robbery, such as homicide or rape. Because the offender is in close contact with the victim for long periods of time, the victim may be murdered to eliminate subsequent identification.

Vehicle-Related Robbery

In the *business vehicle robbery*, the operator of some commercial type of vehicle is victimized. Generally speaking, taxicab drivers and delivery van operators are particularly prone to this type of offense. It has been found that the geographic area in which a driver works affects the likelihood of victimization. For example, taxicab robberies occur with great frequency in inner-city areas. Most vehicle robberies occur during the evening, with the exception of delivery van robberies, which are common during the afternoon hours.

The taxicab driver is victimized more often than delivery drivers and also runs the risk of serious physical injury. A common method of operation is for the robber to give the driver an address in a quiet, secluded area and, upon reaching the destination, commit the offense. Taxicab drivers are primarily selected as victims because of the cash they carry. Since vehicle robbers tend to be violent, many cab drivers are assaulted, even murdered, following the robbery. The frequency of violence associated with taxi robbery is extremely serious, as taxi drivers have the highest proportional rate of on-the-job homicide of any occupation in the United States.

Another type of vehicle robbery is termed the **truck hijacking**, or **cargo robbery.** This type of offense almost always involves armed offenders who specialize in the seizure and robbery of fully loaded tractor-trailers.

The method of operation is highly specialized and organized, many offenses being linked to organized crime operations. Typically, these robbers select a truck known to carry specific cargo, having planned in advance where the hijacked truck will be unloaded and how the cargo will be disposed of. In a variation of the traditional hijacking, entire trucking terminals were robbed, with offenders locking up terminal employees and driving off with loaded trucks worth a quarter of a million dollars.

The truck robbery often occurs within the limits of a large metropolitan area. The offenders surprise the driver and display firearms to discourage resistance. The driver is held at one locality while the truck is driven to a site at which the cargo is unloaded and transferred to another vehicle. Drivers are seldom injured in this type of robbery, and the stolen truck is generally recovered within a short time. However, the recovery of the stolen property is difficult, for once the merchandise is removed from the original packing cases or separated from the lot with which it was shipped, recovery is unlikely. The type of truck selected for robbery is determined by the cargo; for example, during past gasoline shortages, many fuel trucks were hijacked. Other prime targets include computers, liquor, cigarettes, television sets, and cameras. The financial loss in truck robberies is very high, for one truck's cargo can easily exceed $1 million. It is estimated that hijacking and cargo theft constitute a yearly loss to the trucking industry of more than $1 billion.[13]

The incidence of *non–business-vehicle robbery* has escalated sharply since the early 1990s. This type of robbery involves one or more offenders targeting victims solely because they are drivers or passengers of a vehicle. The typical method of operation is for the suspect to stop a victim's moving vehicle and rob the occupants, typically at gunpoint, of cash and valuables. Victims who appear to be tourists or business travelers are particularly vulnerable, as suspects believe such individuals are more likely to possess cash or items easily sold for cash. Such robberies are often more prevalent in tourist localities by suspects who have developed innovative approaches to halting a victim's vehicle. For example, the Miami, Florida, police department reports many incidents that begin with a suspect bumping the rear of a victim's moving vehicle with his or her own. Upon exiting the auto, believing that he or she has been involved in a legitimate accident, the victim is robbed. Another variation of this form of robbery includes theft of the victim's vehicle following the robbery; sometimes a victim is forcibly stopped for the single purpose of stealing the vehicle.

Commonly termed **carjacking**, or robbery drive-aways, such incidents are rapidly becoming familiar to investigators across the nation. In New Jersey alone, there were 574 carjackings committed in a recent year, of which two resulted in murder. In a single 21-day period, 205 robberies of this type were reported in Detroit, with most other large cities reporting dramatic increases. The Department of Justice estimates that nearly 50,000 completed and attempted carjackings take place annually, with offenders successfully stealing the victim's motor vehicle in 52 percent of the cases. Minority males under age 35 are the most common victims, and although most victims escape injury, 16 percent are seriously hurt resulting in an average of 27 homicides each year. Offenders use weapons in nearly 80 percent of all carjackings, with handguns being the most commonly encountered. Suspects generally commandeer cars stopped at traffic lights, restaurants or mall parking lots, ATMs, pay telephones, or self-service gas stations. A substantial number of reported carjackings are falsely reported to authorities. In the majority of such cases, drugs are at the center of the false report. To secure more narcotics, addicts may willingly loan their vehicles to drug dealers. When the vehicle is not returned, the addict reports a false carjacking. Police estimate that drug-related false reports constitute nearly 30 percent of all carjacking cases. Recent national legislation makes carjacking a federal crime punishable by up to 15 years in prison and by life if death results from the offense.[14]

Commercial Robberies

Robberies perpetrated against any type of profit-oriented operation (e.g., banks, jewelry stores, or grocery stores) are classified as **commercial robberies**. The only common denominator in commercial robberies is that the looted structure normally contains cash or other valuables and is not a residence. The majority of commercial robberies are of small businesses and stores, with the chain store and convenience operation frequently selected for victimization. Commercial robberies often occur in stores that are located in out-of-the-way places and/or are run by lone or elderly clerks. This type of robbery generally involves a limited amount of planning; in most cases, the perpetrator nets less than $700 from the offense. A significant number of victims are seriously injured or killed during commercial robberies, and the extent of injury is normally correlated to the degree of victim resistance. That is, shopkeepers who resist the offender are more likely to be killed or injured.

Gas stations have long been favored targets of commercial robbers. Since their appearance in the 1920s, they have typically been victimized by experienced offenders. Generally speaking, the all-night station on the outskirts of a community is more likely to be robbed than other types of stations. The number of attendants and the amount of business activity will affect a particular station's vulnerability. Invariably, a community has a small number of gas stations that account for a majority of the robberies. Chain stores and gas stations are usually "cased" for a short period of time by the robber to determine when the minimum number of customers will be present. Quite often the robber has been a prior customer of the business.

Jewelry stores and other specialized commercial business houses are not attacked as often as chain commercial establishments, but the individual who favors specialty store robbery tends to be more experienced. Generally, the offender will have been inside the establishment one or more times and will have noted the location of the safe or other valuables. This type of commercial robbery may involve "inside information" given to the robber by a past or present employee. Such information may include the time at which maximum cash will be on hand or the location of certain valuables.

Bank robbery frequently is portrayed in the media as a "glamor" crime, with actual robberies carried out by teams of professional and meticulously trained criminals. This media image, however, is very misleading. Actually, according to an FBI assistant director, the modern bank robber is "young and dumb." Despite the typical bank robber's inexperience and naïveté in criminal methods of operation, there has been a considerable increase in bank robberies in the past five years. More than 8,000 such offenses take place each year, with certain American cities experiencing particularly sharp increases. Los Angeles reports more than 2,000 offenses annually, making this city the bank robbery capital of the nation, with nearly half of all bank robberies taking place in California.[15] The statistically average bank robbery dollar loss is approximately $4,800. However, a small number of high-loss professional robberies are reflected in this figure; the typical loss rarely amounts to more than $2,000. The average loss is less than half of what it was several decades ago. This is because tellers have been keeping

TABLE 10.1   Robbery by Type and Percent Distribution

Type	Percentage
Street/highway	43
Commercial business	15
Gas or service station	3
Convenience store	6
Residence	14
Bank	2
Miscellaneous	17

Source: Federal Bureau of Investigation.

only minimal amounts of cash in compliance with the Bank Protection Act of 1968. Although the monetary loss from bank robbery is large, banks actually lose three times as much money through embezzlement by employees.

Bank robbers rarely injure bank employees or witnesses. In fact, the typical death resulting from this type of robbery is that of the robber. Of the 37 people killed during bank robbery attempts in a recent year, 24 were would-be robbers. A small percentage of the offenders is successful in avoiding arrest; 65 percent are apprehended. The high clearance rate is due to many factors, but high-quality automatic cameras are responsible for the majority of the arrests. Furthermore, since bank robbery of a federally insured institution is a federal offense, highly trained FBI specialists investigate this crime in cooperation with local criminal investigators.

Bank robbery offenders are hard to categorize in terms of specific offender characteristics; however, drug addiction is a significant trait. Nearly 50 percent of the suspects are drug addicts or individuals who use drugs on a regular basis. Although a small number of bank robberies involve professionals who attack vaults and safe deposit boxes, the typical offender leaves the scene after taking money from only one teller. Suspects are often amazingly compulsive and conform closely to specific methods of operation. For example, a robbery suspect held up 29 San Diego banks before being apprehended. His method of operation remained strikingly similar throughout the robbery series, and he continually wore a particular type of sunglasses and an Oakland A's baseball cap. This suspect's use of a disguise is unusual, as research indicates that 76 percent of all bank robbers make no attempt to conceal their identities.[16] The futility of this offense is well documented by an FBI study that calculated the true financial benefit of bank robbery. Findings indicated that the average convicted bank robber's income amounted to about 40 cents per hour for the time spent in prison in relationship to the money gained during the robbery.[17]

See Table 10.1 for a summary of reported robbery incidents as determined by category of victimization.

INVESTIGATIVE PROCEDURES

The investigation of robbery poses many of the problems inherent in person-to-person crime. When victims and witnesses are confronted by an armed suspect, their perceptive abilities are diminished. The presence of a weapon further limits perception, as will any violent action. Since the typical robbery involves a dangerous weapon and an emotionally disturbing atmosphere, the inquiry cannot rely on descriptions as the primary tracing means.

Method of Operation

Because the suspect's identity is almost always unknown to the victim, the investigator's first and foremost goal is to find it out. ***Modus operandi*** has always been considered a strong tracing element in the robbery investigation. Many criminal groups have fixed methods of operation, and robbers tend to develop a methodology early in their careers from which they rarely deviate. Unless a robbery offender becomes aware that a method of operation may provide a tracing clue to uncover identity, the offender will conform to the actions naturally developed during initial robbery attempts. Regardless of the specific category of the robbery, certain method-of-operation traits prevail. The great majority of robberies involve the following elements:

1. selection procedure,
2. entry method,
3. initial actions prior to the display of force,
4. display of force,
5. method of acquiring the object of the robbery,
6. actions prior to escape, and
7. escape method.

The criminal investigator is constantly investigating occurrences after the fact. To develop leads and subsequently learn the offender's identity, the officer should trace the offender's movements from initial to postrobbery actions. If the robbery is other than a typical street mugging, the perpetrator will have utilized some selection process. Such procedures range from sophisticated surveillance of a bank to a two-minute observation of a gas station. The question the investigator must attempt to answer is why and how did the robber select this victim or establishment? Resolution is often difficult, and the question may remain unanswered unless additional information is developed or the offender is arrested. It may be that the victim was selected by his or her appearance or that the particular store was selected for its locality. If it is believed that a prerobbery surveillance was conducted, a careful neighborhood inquiry should follow. Neighbors, shopkeepers, or any person who is usually in the area at the time the robbery took place should be questioned regarding the observation of suspicious persons or automobiles. The success of such neighborhood canvasses will depend on the accuracy of the descriptions given.

Following the selection procedure inquiry, the officer attempts to reconstruct the method of entry. Did the suspect walk into the store without obviously displaying a weapon? Or did the suspect run through the door with a disguise or mask in place? Next, the perpetrator's actions immediately prior to the announcement of the robbery should be determined. Was some stalling type of action involved? Generally, food store robbers pose as customers, waiting for the store to empty out. Bank robbers often walk to a table in the center of the lobby and pretend to write a deposit slip or feign some other activity. Such actions are generally quite fixed and will be repeated in successive robberies.

The display of force is very important to the *modus operandi* of the offense. Fortunately, this event in the robbery sequence is one of the most memorable in the mind of the victim. The investigator needs to know how the offender indicated that a robbery was in progress. Did the suspect shove a weapon at the victim and yell "This is a holdup!" or did the suspect hand a note to the victim, remaining silent? The manner in which money or property was acquired can normally be described to the investigating officer by the victim. In some instances, however, the suspect forces the victim and witnesses to turn away, or to lie face down while the object of the offense is acquired. Generally, the suspect either directs the victim to hand the money over or personally acquires their money or property without assistance. The escape actions of the offender are similarly reconstructed. After receiving the money from the victim or personally acquiring it, did the suspect back toward the door and threaten the victim to stay inside and make no attempt to follow? Finally, a very important method of operation factor and tracing clue must be determined: How did the offender flee the immediate scene and neighborhood? The victim and/or witnesses may be able to provide information in this regard, or information may be gained through the initial neighborhood inquiry.

It is unlikely that the investigator will determine complete answers relative to all seven of the *modus operandi* elements. However, any information can help to connect the offense to past or future robberies. By comparing and contrasting the *modus operandi* information gained in a particular case to similar robbery methods, the names of prior offenders can be checked as possible suspects in the case in question. The use of the computer has fortunately reduced the time required for such checks in many agencies.

The Crime Scene

The **crime scene** is an important starting point in all felony investigations—and the robbery inquiry is no exception. The value of a given robbery crime scene depends on the actions of the perpetrator before, during, and after the offense. Physical traces and clues may be numerous, or they may be virtually nonexistent. If it is determined that the suspect posed as a customer and handled merchandise prior to the display of force, the items handled should be located and processed. If it is determined that the suspect took money from the cash register or was near a showcase, these items must also be protected and processed. It is unusual that items will be touched by a robber during the escape, yet the victim and witnesses should be carefully questioned to determine this. All items having even a remote possibility of contact with the robber's person should be examined and processed to determine the presence of the following types of evidence:

1. fingerprints,
2. hairs and fibers,
3. blood or other bodily fluids if indicated, and
4. soil and footprints.

Certain robbery crime scenes indicate special evidence-processing procedures, such as a scene in which a firearm has been discharged or a victim was bound. A detailed discussion of firearm and fiber evidence is included in the criminalistics section of this chapter.

Continuing Investigation

The *continuing investigation* begins when the investigator leaves the crime scene and terminates when the case is closed or suspended. Information developed during the method-of-operation inquiry and the crime scene processing generally determines the success or failure of the continuing investigation. If the investigator has a complete and well-defined *modus operandi* to work with, a check with other agencies will commence. Teletype messages will be sent to notify other departments of the offense and to distribute tracing information to other robbery investigators. State criminal identification bureaus should be contacted for statewide method-of-operation comparisons.

If the vehicle used during the escape was noted by the victim or witness, it may prove to be an important tracing clue. Although many robbers steal automobiles to avoid tracing, the recovery of the described getaway vehicle is significant. When an auto is recovered that matches the description of a suspect's vehicle, it should be treated and processed as in any important crime scene. Many tracing clues may be found in the auto that cannot be located at the robbery scene. Suspects are generally in the auto longer than they are at the scene; they also tend to relax following the offense, making mistakes that could aid in tracing. If an individual remains in an auto for any length of time, some evidence will generally be left. Hairs, latent fingerprints, fibers, moneybags, disguises, and other items may be located.

Amateur robbers sometimes use personal vehicles to escape from the scene. Some will have afterthoughts concerning the possibility of the car being seen and license noted and will report the car stolen to cover the possibility. They reason that if and when a connection is made, they will be free from suspicion by claiming that the auto was used in a robbery during the time it was not in their possession. Accordingly, all stolen auto reports should be reviewed for comparison of the cars with the perpetrator's vehicle.

The continuing inquiry will focus on the stolen property that was taken from the scene. If cash was the only item taken, this area of inquiry will be short lived. Generally, only in bank or large payroll robberies can currency serial numbers be traced. However, many street robberies and some residential and commercial offenses involve stolen property other than cash. The stolen items should be treated as are items stolen during a burglary in an attempt to locate and trace them to the offender. Investigators often rely upon the informant in attempting to establish the robber's identity. Since many robbers are inexperienced and tend to be boastful, informant information has traditionally been successful in identifying a significant number of robbery offenders.

STRATEGIES TO COMBAT ROBBERY

Robbery is very difficult to prevent through basic uniform patrol. Because of the seriousness and increasing frequency of this offense, many police agencies have developed strategies designed to prevent robbery or to apprehend the robber in a greater percentage of cases. All of the numerous programs that have been implemented to combat robbery can be categorized as either prevention or apprehension programs.

Prevention Programs

Robbery *prevention programs* are often designed to inform probable victims that they are likely to be robbed and to suggest methods to prevent the offense. For example, the Minneapolis Police Department suggests through a letter that shopkeepers carefully note suspicious people and vehicles. The letter explains that when a suspicious person or auto is seen in the store or general area, a description should be recorded in a notebook kept near the cash register for this purpose. Other suggestions include not to keep more than a minimum amount of cash on hand and to use a "bait bill." A *bait bill* is a bill in the cash register that has had the serial number recorded. Thorough analysis and resulting action can also prevent robbery.

Paul C. Marquardt
Senior Special Agent
U.S. Department of Justice
Bureau of Alcohol, Tobacco, Firearms, and Explosives
Kansas City Field Division

Unlike some students majoring in criminal justice, my interest in law enforcement didn't really come into focus until after graduation from college. I majored in business administration, not being certain what profession I wanted to pursue, and it seemed like a solid starting point for various careers. I attended college for a year, then left as money ran short and was soon drafted into the Army. After undergoing challenging training as a combat medic, I was rapidly deployed to Vietnam. My experiences in the Vietnam War not only quickly matured me but also guided me into what would become my life's work as a federal criminal investigator. My tour of combat duty with the First Air Cavalry gave me insight into personal potentials that I hadn't thought myself capable of. I found I liked the challenge of risk to help others, and people observed I operated well under considerable stress. And doing something important and meaningful was extremely significant to me. My tour of duty ended in 1971. I returned to college and graduated from the University of Wisconsin at Oshkosh three years later. At that point I knew I wouldn't really be satisfied with a routine job.

After my military experience and college graduation, my thoughts turned to law enforcement as a career that would fit the insights I had developed about myself. I recalled a term paper I had written in one of my college classes about the U.S. Secret Service. In it I expressed an interest in maybe trying to be a federal agent one day. When the professor returned the paper, he cautioned me not to get too excited over such a career, as such jobs were difficult to get. His words now served as a challenge to me, and I took and passed the Treasury Enforcement Examination. This exam serves to qualify a person for interviewing for a variety of federal investigative positions. The first one I heard from was the Bureau of Alcohol, Tobacco, and Firearms (ATF). I actually knew little about the functions of the ATF at that time but was impressed with the agents conducting the interview in St. Paul, Minnesota. After a lengthy and detailed background investigation, I was offered a position as a special agent. So in the fall of 1975, I began what would become a fascinating and challenging career.

I took my initial training at the then new federal training facility at Glenyco, Georgia, one of the very first classes to be processed. The training consisted of two phases: a general criminal investigative tactics class in which federal agents from various agencies were mixed together and then a specialized ATF training class. After I completed traning, I was assigned to the Kansas City field office, and I've been here ever since. Then, as now, ATF agents work in teams we term "group". These are composed of ten or so investigators working on various assignments, mainly related to our mission of enforcing firearms and explosives laws. Although less frequent, cases dealing with alcohol and tobacco enforcement matters also arise. Although I worked numerous explosive cases, I soon developed as a firearms specialist. In particular, I became skilled in investigating the interstate connection of firearms to criminal activity. I've testified in over a hundred such cases as an expert witness, detailing how a firearm or ammunition has moved or affected interstate commerce, an essential element in proving a federal gun violation.

I've worked a wide variety of criminal investigations during my career, although most have involved firearms or bombings. Many stand out as particularly interesting, including a series of organized crime car bombings that occurred in Kansas City during the early years of my career. Rival La Cosa Nostra members were murdering each other over territory disputes, and because bombs were often used, the cases fell to the ATF. I also worked the Oklahoma City bombing case, in which domestic terrorists destroyed a federal office building, murdering over 160 victims. A large number of ATF personnel participated in various aspects of this investigation, and I was where the suspects assembled the bomb and rented the truck that was exploded at the federal building. Working out of Fort Riley, we gathered evidence detailing their actions prior to the murders. Another notable case involved the investigation and apprehension of the so-called trench coat bank robbers. These were two very active and heavily armed bank robbers who remained at large for

16 years. Stealing over $8 million from 29 banks, they hold the record for the largest single bank robbery loss: $4.6 million from a bank in Tacoma, Washington. The ATF was involved in the case becuase of the illegal weapons and silencers utilized by the suspects. Our investigations also frequently involve undercover operations by agents. My undercover experiences were primarily confined to the first ten years of my career, and I took on many personas posing as a buyer or seller of illegal weapons or explosives.

I've just thoroughly enjoyed my job as a special agent. I've gotten to investigate hundreds of fascinating cases, taught undercover and firearms identification courses to many American officers, and traveled to Budapest, Hungry, to instruct at the International Law Enforcement Academy. But what I've enjoyed the most is the personal satisfaction of helping to convict a serious criminal who has been getting away with major illegal activity for a long period of time. There's no better feeling of accomplishment. This can be done only if you master the whole system and if you think "court" with everything you do. That is, you have to realize that your investigation will be closely examined in court, so field actions must be done properly. The chief negative of the job has been how hard it can be on one's family. Once I was called out on a case on Christmas Eve, right in the middle of opening gifts with my kids. But the positives far outweigh the negatives, and I'd encourage criminal justice students to consider a career with the federal government.

In Gainesville, Florida, robberies of convenience stores fell 80 percent during a six-year period after police established a task force to gather and analyze data on robbery, which had been increasing at a rate of 20 percent a year. Investigators determined that in three years, 96 percent of all convenience stores in Gainesville had been robbed. Accordingly, the police succeeded in having a city ordinance passed that dramatically reduced robbery. The law required that two or more clerks must be on duty during peak robbery times, all clerks must receive robbery deterrence training, all parking lots must be brightly lighted, a visible camera must be in each store, and a very limited amount of cash must be on hand, among other preventive actions.[18]

Other prevention strategies are designed to discourage robbers from committing offenses by instilling fear of consequences. Such prevention programs play on the notion of the omnipresent police officer. This type of program typically involves a well-publicized undercover or *decoy operation* to stress that the police could be anyone, anywhere. A squad of officers often disguise themselves to blend in with the vulnerable victim stereotype. After several arrests are made via undercover officers, the possibility that such officers may be present will deter street robbers.

When law enforcement agencies institute decoy operations, they are practicing a form of **proactive policing**, that is, taking the initiative to deal with crime prior to victimization, rather than waiting to react to the aftermath of victimization. A successful decoy program, termed Operation STAR (Safeguarding Tourists Against Robberies), was used by the Miami police to combat a rising trend in vehicle robbery. The primary victims were visiting tourists robbed while driving rental cars. The victims were selected because of their tendency to carry large amounts of cash and reluctance to return as witnesses for the prosecution. This form of robbery became so frequent and violent that a county ordinance was passed outlawing any sticker or sign that would identify a vehicle as a rental car. Such reactive measures deterred many tourist robberies, and a decoy operation proved to be highly successful in reducing this form of robbery.

Posing as tourists, investigators devised ways to appear vulnerable, often using female officers to increase this impression. A decoy traveling in a car would simulate engine trouble by stopping and raising the hood or stop in a targeted area and appear to make a phone call. As the would-be robber attacked the decoy investigator, surveillance officers assisted in the arrest as others videotaped the incident for prosecution purposes. Operation STAR's effectiveness was immediately apparent, as the city realized a 12 percent reduction in robbery that authorities attributed directly to the decoy program.[19]

Because the connection of handguns to robbery offenses is so strong, many urban police agencies have initiated *gun-suppression* strategies. A test program aimed at reducing gun-related crime in Kansas City, Missouri, demonstrated that vigorous street checks of pedestrians suspected of carrying illegal weapons, plus increased traffic stops, generated a 65 percent increase in gun seizures and a corresponding 50 percent drop in gun-related violence. Officers found that traffic stops were the most productive means of finding illegal guns, yielding an average of one gun discovered for every 28 stops. Areas in which increased proactive searching occurred were computer selected by analysis of past rates of gun-related violence. Even though the frequency of police searching was significantly increased from past levels, all searches of pedestrians and motorists conformed to standard legal guidelines to ensure the protection of civil liberties.[20]

Additional firearm suppression efforts focus upon the relationship of guns used in crimes to where they are originally purchased by suspects. Bureau of Alcohol, Tobacco, Firearms, and Explosives (ATF) research has shown that 1 percent of all gun dealers in the United States were the source of nearly 57 percent of weapons traced to crimes. Yet another study by the Americans for Gun Safety Foundation demonstrated that 15 percent of the guns recovered in crimes during a recent five-year period were traceable to just one-tenth of 1 percent of the nation's gun stores. Such findings have important implications for criminal investigators seeking to prevent common gun crime like robbery. When specific stores are identified as being the source for an unusually high number of crime-related firearms, officers can pay close attention to such localities and their customers to ensure proper procedures and sales. The ATF has compiled a listing of such gun shops that is readily available to police and the general public. The listing names only those shops in which a minimum of 200 guns used in crimes can be traced to a particular store. There are currectly 120 shops on the list, with the greatest number located in the state of Indiana. One shop had 2,370 guns used in various crimes traced back to it, while a close second has sold 2,294 firearms traced to various crime scenes, including seven criminal homicides.[21]

Other prevention programs focus on the reduction of firearm violence through advanced technology. Science is developing various techniques to produce so-called **smart guns**, weapons that can be fired only by their authorized users. Because studies show that up to 40 percent of felons acquire their guns through theft, technologies that prevent the use of stolen weapons could effectively reduce gun violence. Among the various blocking devices being developed are magnetic rings that must be worn to free a firearm's mechanism, fingerprint or palm print recognizers, and voice-activated sensors.[22]

Apprehension Programs

Apprehension programs are designed to reduce the frequency of robbery through the arrest of offenders. Since robbery suspects are often recidivists, a successful arrest program will eventually reduce the robbery rate of a given community for some time. The traditional random stakeout has been replaced in many jurisdictions with tactical holdup alarm systems. In a *stakeout,* plainclothes personnel wait at a site selected for surveillance in anticipation of the robber. Modern *tactical alarms* (Figure 10.2) have greatly expanded the coverage of stakeout squads. Alarm systems can be placed in many localities and monitored by a single officer. The systems are portable and instantly notify officers of the location of a robbery. However, the effectiveness of the alarm depends on the shopkeeper or clerk activating it by depressing a transmitting device by hand or foot. One single monitoring unit is capable of covering 20 localities.

Other electronic aids have helped to apprehend robbery suspects. The Seattle Police Department developed a 35mm camera system that photographs robbers during the offense. The camera is placed in stores having a high incidence of robberies and is activated by the shopkeeper by hand or foot or when a special triggering bill is removed from the cash register. The camera system takes 16 frames in 40 seconds, providing investigators with excellent quality photographs of the perpetrator (see Figure 10.3). Such photos are typically far clearer than videotaped images, often leading to rapid suspect identification. Other businesses and banking institutions utilize a small explosive device hidden in a wad of money that is given to the robbery suspect. The device explodes a cloud of tear gas and red dye; it is triggered by a device hidden in the door. The dye is virtually impossible to remove in a short time so that the escaping robber can be easily recognized.

The police department of Birmingham, Alabama, has increased apprehensions by means of a suspect concentration program. Each investigative robbery team is assigned ten current robbery suspects per month. The investigators become intensely familiar with activities of the assigned suspects, with the intent of making them aware that they are under police surveillance.[23]

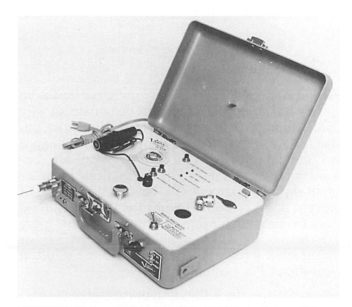

FIGURE 10.2   A silent radio stakeout alarm. When tripped by an offender or victim, the device will broadcast a prerecorded voice message directly to the police while the crime is in progress. *(Source: Varda Silent Alarm Company.)*

FIGURE 10.3   An armed bank robbery suspect is recorded at the scene. Bank robberies are increasing throughout the country and often involve young, unskilled criminals motivated by drug habits. *(Source: Littua Lan/Syracuse Newspaper/The Image Works.)*

CRIMINALISTIC APPLICATIONS

Many types of forensic evidence are encountered at robbery crime scenes, and the possibility of recovering evidence related to firearms is strong. The majority of robbers carry a firearm into the scene; a small number fire the weapon when committing the offense. The robbery scene also is likely to yield evidence from ropes and other binding materials. Fiber evidence comes not only from binding and restraining materials but also from clothing worn by the suspect.

Firearms

The study of firearms and related evidence is a traditional and important area of criminalistics. Annual surveys by the Justice Department demonstrate why familiarization with firearms, particularly handguns, is vital for the investigator. Research analysis reveals that 33 percent of American adults keep a firearm in their home and that 1.3 million people in the United States are confronted each year by criminals carrying handguns. Additionally, firearms were found to be used in 7 percent of all rapes, 40 percent of robberies, 18 percent of aggravated assaults, and 66 percent of all criminal homicides.[24] The criminal investigator normally encounters firearm evidence pertaining to one or more of the following: (a) revolvers, (b) pistols, (c) rifles, (d) shotguns, (e) bullets, or (f) cartridge cases. By examining such evidence, the criminalist can often provide answers to important questions. For example:

1. Did a specific firearm discharge a specific bullet and/or cartridge case?
2. What kind of firearm fired a specific bullet and/or cartridge case?
3. What specific type of ammunition was discharged?

In the recent past, revolvers were the most common type of firearm recovered by investigators. Beginning in the mid-1990s, the pistol began to

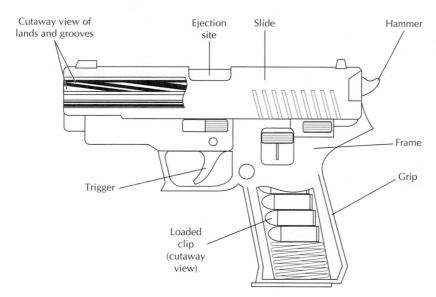

Cutaway view of lands and grooves

Ejection site

Slide

Hammer

Frame

Grip

Trigger

Loaded clip (cutaway view)

FIGURE 10.4   Major parts of the semiautomatic pistol.

equal the revolver in frequency of usage and is currently used in serious crime as much or more than any other type of firearm.

The term **revolver** is based on the revolving multichambered cylinder that is essential to its operation. With each firing, the chambers of the cylinder revolve to align with the barrel prior to discharge. The term **pistol** is normally used to describe a semiautomatic handgun. Although such weapons are commonly called automatics, their true operation is dependent upon separate firings. The **semiautomatic** pistol (Figure 10.4) operates on what is known as a blow-back principle, in which the force of the discharge ejects the fired shell casing, loading and cocking the weapon for the next firing. Consequently, a semiautomatic does not employ the revolving firing chamber. *Rifles* and *shotguns* are long-barreled weapons that, depending on the particular firearm, operate in a similar manner to the handgun. A rifle or shotgun utilizes one of four operational designs: bolt action, semiautomatic, level, or pump action.

In attempting to link a specific firearm to a specific bullet or to identify a general type of gun, the criminalist examines marks on the bullet produced by the barrel of the firearm (see Figure 10.5). When a bullet passes through a firearm's barrel, distinctive markings will be impressed on the projectile. These markings, or *striations,* result from the bullet pressing against the inside of the barrel. The inside surface of all firearms, with the exception of the shotgun, is rifled. The rifling process takes place at time of manufacture and involves a *broach,* or *rifling tool,* being passed and twisted through the barrel. The broach cuts a specific number of *grooves* into the interior of the barrel that are designed to spin the discharged projectile. The spinning effect is necessary to give a fired bullet greater stability and accuracy.

Every firearm manufacturer has adopted a standard number of grooves for its gun barrels. The corresponding number of ridges between the grooves are termed "lands." Accordingly, all rifled firearms have a specific number of **lands and grooves**, normally numbering between four and nine. The general appearance and number of the lands and grooves determine the general type of firearm; the rifling striations are used to judge individuality (see Figure 10.6). At the time of manufacture, the broach imparts a large number of minute marks unique to each particular barrel. The individual marks result through minor accidental movements of the broach and do not affect

FIGURE 10.5 The criminalist test fires a revolver for bullet recovery purposes. Note the bullet in flight. *(Source: Metropolitan Police, New Scotland Yard.)*

accuracy. Thus, the small cuts left by the broach serve to link any bullet fired through the firearm's barrel to that particular firearm.

The criminalist first examines a fired bullet recovered from the crime scene to determine the number and appearance of the lands and grooves. Then, if the suspect's firearm is recovered, a comparison bullet is fired for inspection. After the firing, the comparison bullet and the crime scene projectile are viewed through the *binocular comparison microscope*. This instrument merges the images of the two bullets into a single image, allowing the criminalist to compare the minute striations visually for similarity. If the bullets match, having identical striations, they will be judged to have been fired

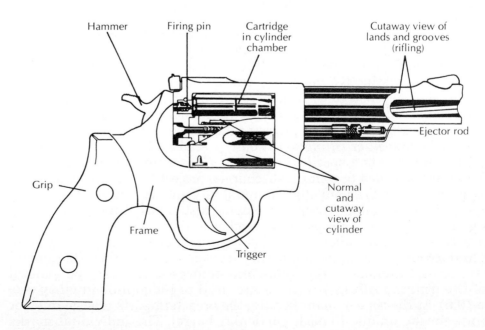

FIGURE 10.6 Major parts of the revolver.

FATAL   TEST

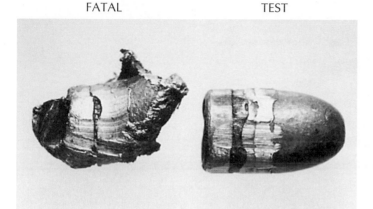

A

FATAL   TEST

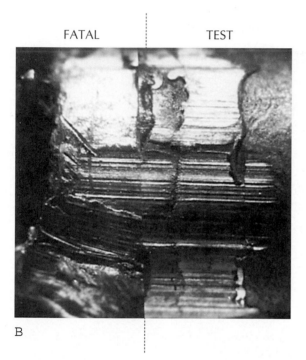

B

FIGURE 10.7   *A.* The left-hand bullet was recovered from the body of a murder victim. The right-hand bullet was test-fired through a handgun recovered from the suspect's home; *B.* When both bullets are compared by means of a comparison microscope, the striations align perfectly—proof that both came from the same gun barrel. *(Source: Wisconsin Department of Justice—Crime Laboratory Bureau.)*

by the same weapon (see Figure 10.7). If they do not match, it can be assumed that different barrels fired each bullet. The results of the comparison will be inconclusive if the crime scene bullet is damaged or if the recovered barrel has been altered in some fashion.

The barrel of a firearm is not the only indicator that can be used to link bullet to weapon. When weapons are loaded, individual marks may be scratched onto the *shell casings.* For example, the semiautomatic handgun generally requires the shooter to place a series of cartridges into a clip (magazine). During this operation, the sides of the magazine scrape the brass casings, leaving distinctive scratch marks. Other identification markings and

A

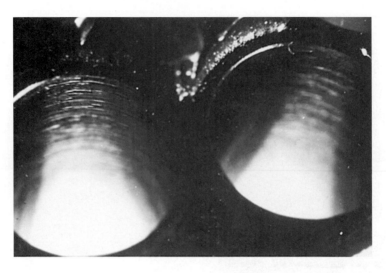

B

FIGURE 10.8   *A.* A cylinder from a revolver. The six openings contain the cartridges and act as firing chambers during discharge; *B.* Close-up of two of the cylinder openings. Note the fine metal striations within each chamber. The unfinished striation markings are transferred to the surface of the shell casings during discharge. Such markings aid in the matching of shell casings to a particular firearm.

impressions occur when the projectile is fired. Upon firing, the primer is struck by the firing pin, resulting in an explosion. The shell casing is forced backward into the breech block, expanding the sides of the casing and producing additional markings (see Figure 10.8). Finally, many valuable identification marks result from the operation of the extractors, ejectors, and firing pin. The *extractor* is a metal rod that places the cartridge in the firing chamber prior to discharge. The *ejector rod* dispels the fired shell casing from the weapon. Both metal parts scratch the brass surface of the shell casing, leaving distinctive and often unique markings for identification. Every cartridge must have its self-contained gunpowder ignited by a spark from the primer explosion. This is accomplished by the *firing pin*—a pointed hammerlike rod that indents either

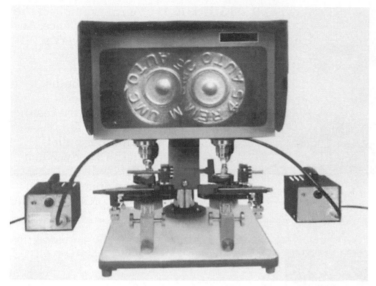

FIGURE 10.9 A bullet comparison microscope comparing the firing pin impressions of two fired shell casings. *(Source: Sirchie Fingerprint Laboratories.)*

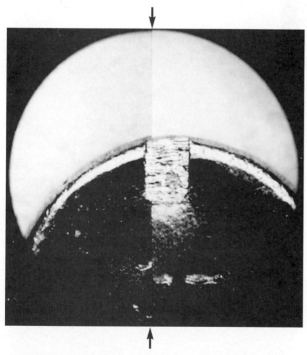

FIGURE 10.10 Close-up of two rimfire firing pin impressions. Note the perfect match of striations made visible under the microscope. *(Source: Wisconsin Department of Justice—Crime Laboratory Bureau.)*

a rim primer or a primer located in the center of the cartridge's base. Since the firing pin is a metal part that has been filed and processed during manufacture, it will often have individualistic marks or imperfections. Such imperfections are impressed on the soft surface of the primer, providing a means of tracing a spent shell casing to a particular firing pin (see Figures 10.9 and 10.10).

FIGURE 10.11   *A*. An example of the importance of firearms evidence. An investigator carefully recovers a murder weapon from a stream; *B*. The criminalist fires the recovered handgun into a bullet recovery unit for comparison purposes; *C*. The expert retrieves the fired bullet from the trap for comparison with another bullet taken from the victim's body. When matched, the bullets will demonstrate a common gun origin. *(Source: Michael Havstad, Los Angeles County Sheriff's Department.)*

Specific ammunition can normally be readily identified by the criminalist. Unless the bullet is badly damaged or fragmented, its appearance and weight will indicate its manufacturer. *Cannelures,* or the indented grooves that hold lubricating grease, are often present on the bullet and generally aid in determining origin. The caliber of the projectile can normally be determined by weighing the projectile and measuring its diameter (see Figure 10.11).

Occasionally, the criminalist encounters a firearm on which identifying serial numbers have been obliterated. In nearly every case of serial number obliteration, restoration can be achieved by means of chemical aids. Firearm serial numbers are stamped in such a way that the impressions of the numbers are still in the metal, even though they may not be visible. By applying various chemical compounds, the number of impressions can be made apparent so that the firearm can be connected to a particular suspect or theft.

Many criminal investigations involve a firearm that has been left at the scene. When such a weapon is recovered, the criminalist attempts to identify the suspect through the weapon. The initial tracing attempt focuses on the latent fingerprint evidence and the possible presence of DNA material. All smooth surfaces that could possibly bear prints are processed. Even if the robber wore gloves during the crime, the possibility of fingerprint evidence should not be discounted. During prior loading or cleaning of the weapon, fingerprints are often inadvertently left on shell casings or other parts of the firearm. If the weapon was concealed in the suspect's pocket, waistband, or jacket, various residues may have attached to it. Consequently, the firearm will be examined for hairs, fibers, and other debris that may be of identification value.

If a suspect is arrested shortly after the discharge of a weapon, an effort may be made to demonstrate that the suspect recently fired a gun. Such a determination cannot identify the individual as the person who fired the specific crime scene weapon, but it can serve to focus the investigation toward that individual. Efforts to determine gunpowder residue on a suspect date to 1953 with the development of the paraffin technique. The traditional **paraffin test**, or *dermal nitrate method,* has been found to be valueless. The test was developed to detect the presence of fired powder residue on a suspect's hands. A paraffin cast of the hand that held the weapon was made, with the inside portion treated with a chemical compound. A specific color reaction was used as an indicator of recent firearm discharge. This test has now been invalidated, as many individuals who had not fired a weapon were shown to react positively to the test because of their occupations.

Neutron activation analysis (NAA) and **atomic absorption** (AA) **spectroscopy** have been far more successful in determining recent firearm discharge. Both methods analyze the noncombustible primer mixture components of barium and antimony rather than gunpowder because gunpowder inside the fired cartridge burns so completely that no laboratory technique can successfully trace unburned powder on the hands or clothing of the shooter. NAA is a modern nuclear method of determining the presence and composition of specific trace elements. By bombarding a substance with neutron particles, many elements can be readily identified and quantitatively determined by measurements made on radioactive end products. In the case of ascertaining a recent firearm discharge, a paraffin cast is made as in the dermal nitrate method; however, the cast is analyzed by NAA to determine the presence of gunpowder residue. Specifically, the NAA process reveals the presence of barium and antimony, metallic elements exploded onto the shooter's hands during discharge. AA has recently become quite popular, for the technique is inexpensive and requires less-sophisticated equipment than NAA methodology.[25] The absorption method requires a specimen to be heated, and the resulting vaporized atoms exposed to radiation emitted from a light source. Sensitive recorders then detect and measure the degree of light absorbed by various trace elements. SEM employs a scanning electron microscopy technique and is believed by many to be the most reliable gunshot residue method.

Firearm evidence recovered at the scene must be handled with care to prevent contamination and damage. When a firearm is recovered, the officer must avoid touching surfaces that may bear fingerprints. The checkered grips or edges of the trigger guard should be used to pick up the weapon. The weapon should never be lifted by placing a pencil or other object in the end of the barrel. If evidence is present on the muzzle of the firearm (blood, for example), a small cellophane bag should be secured around this area. Before shipment to the laboratory, the firearm's serial number, make, and model should be recorded. The gun should be distinctively marked in an inconspicuous area with the officer's initials; occasionally, similar guns have been found with matching serial numbers.

When spent bullets are recovered at the scene, great care must be taken to mark them properly. The officer's mark should appear on the base of the bullet—never on the sides that bear the identifying striations. Each recovered bullet should be individually wrapped in tissue paper and packaged in a container. Cartridge cases should also be marked, with the marking placed inside the open end of the case. Markings should not be placed on the outside surface or base of the cartridge; this may damage breech block, extractor, ejector, and firing pin striations. All fired evidence should be handled as little as possible to prevent alteration of the markings (see Figure 10.12).

In an effort to assist investigators in linking firearms evidence to suspects, the Federal Bureau of Alcohol, Tobacco, and Firearms originated a sophisticated computer database. Termed the **Ballistic Identification System**, the computer electronically compares and catalogs bullets and shell casings located at crime scenes. Commonly termed "ballistic fingerprinting," the computer comparison is far quicker than the former human method, as the system can examine a bullet or casing in 1.7 seconds, whereas a criminalist takes 20 minutes to one hour.[26] The computer searches a federal database for matches between crime scene firearms evidence and test evidence. When criminal investigators find guns at scenes or obtain them through search warrants, test evidence is obtained for comparison and storage in the data bank by test firings. The system has tremendous potential to clear past firearms cases because recovered bullets or shell casings can be compared to present or future test firings.

Beginning in 2003, the Bureau of Alcohol, Tobacco, and Firearms expanded this program to provide sophisticated firearms comparison equipment to local and state agencies in 233 sites across the United States. Termed the National Integrated Ballistic Information Network (NIBIN), nonfederal police agencies are provided with ballistic imaging equipment and linked with regional and federal databases. Firearms evidence can then be instantly entered into the databases from local crime scenes and compared regionally or nationally with bullet, shell casing, or firing pin marks previously entered

FIGURE 10.12 *A.* Fired cartridge cases should be marked on the side of the case, near the mouth. Care must be taken not to deface extractor or ejector marks; *B.* Marks may also be placed inside the mouth of the case, if the case is large enough; *C.* Fired bullets should be marked near the nose or base, avoiding the rifling marks; *D.* For shotgun shells—loaded or fired—marks should be placed on the side. A scriber, needle, or sharp knife should be used to place the marks. Since shotgun cartridges are composed of either paper or plastic, a scriber, ink, or indelible pencil should be used.

into the database. This system eliminates the need to send or physically transport evidence to crime labs for comparison, as a 360-degree photo of the firearms evidence is computer translated into a digital signature for database comparison. Because of the ease in which evidence can be quickly entered and compared, a number of important cases have been solved. In Boston, where the police department requires that all recovered evidence relating to firearms be entered into the system, three handguns carried by several suspects were quickly linked to 15 shootings that had injured ten victims in two states. The program has been so successful that some states now require ballistic fingerprints of firearms. To date, Maryland and New York have enacted legislation requiring that guns sold in those states be test fired and the resulting bullet and cartridge case characteristics entered into their ballistic imaging system's database.[27]

Fibers

Fibers are found in nearly every crime scene and are considered to be the most conspicuous and numerous of all evidence items. Fibers from clothing and binding materials are often located where robberies, homicides, rapes, and other crimes have occurred. The longer an offender remains at the scene and the more active the offender, the greater the probability of fiber evidence. The value of fiber evidence is directly dependent upon its tracing possibilities. Much like human hair, a fiber is used to establish identity or to assist in narrowing the investigation to a specific area. However, fiber evidence is less significant than hair evidence in that fiber comes from a nonhuman source. Criminalists are normally not able to establish, with absolute certainty, the specific origin of a specific fiber. However, through the use of mathematical probability, it can often be demonstrated that it is extremely likely that a specific fiber came from a specific garment.

Most fibers can be classified as either animal, vegetable, mineral, or synthetic (human-made). Textile fibers are perhaps the most commonly encountered, for they are frequently used in the manufacture of clothing. Cotton, wool, and many varieties of synthetic fibers are left at and taken from a large number of crime scenes. Mineral fibers are much less frequently encountered than any other varieties. They may be noted in burglaries, for they are commonly used in the manufacture of safe insulation.

In processing fiber evidence at the crime laboratory, the criminalist first attempts to classify it as animal, vegetable, mineral, or synthetic (see Figure 10.13). Animal fibers are easily identified; they have the characteristics of animal hair. Another method of determining origin involves a burning process. Vegetable fibers burn for longer periods of time than animal fibers do after being withdrawn from a flame; vegetable fibers also emit a unique odor. Synthetic fibers, such as rayon, can normally be identified by low-power microscopic examination. Synthetics generally lack the twisted appearance of vegetable fibers and are hollow or rodlike throughout.

If fibers are recovered at a crime scene and a subsequent arrest is accomplished, the criminalist may attempt to link the fibers to the offender. For this to be achieved, officers must recover the garment from which the recovered fibers originated. Accordingly, an analysis of the recovered fibers generally indicates the color, class, and possibly the type of garment from which they originated.

When a suspect is apprehended, all clothing that resembles the recovered fiber evidence should be confiscated for comparison purposes. However, as mentioned previously, limitations of fiber evidence most often preclude linking it positively to a specific garment. Generally, the tracing value of items

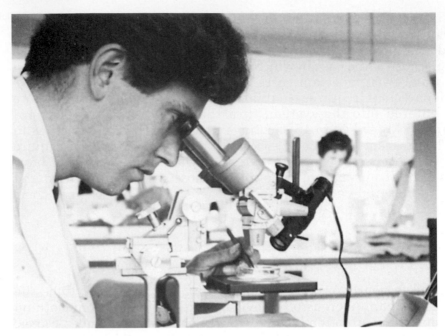

FIGURE 10.13   A criminalist microscopically examines fiber evidence for general and unique characteristics. *(Source: Metropolitan Police, New Scotland Yard.)*

that are not of bodily origin is less than that of such items as blood or hair. The tracing value is even further limited if the nonbodily object lacks striations or serial numbers. Although fiber evidence has no individual markings that can be traced to a specific origin, the fiber may have undergone a limited individualization during manufacture. The criminalist attempts to note features of a particular fiber that impart individuality, for example, the presence of a dye or a "twisting" effect. Generally, the twist effect will resemble a Z; or it could go in the opposite direction, resembling an S. By noting the twist pattern, number of twists, color, presence of other fibers, and other traits, the criminalist can determine the probable value of the evidence.

Many criminals bind victims and witnesses with rope or cords. Such binding materials should be recovered at the scene and submitted to the laboratory for analysis. Rope and other binding materials are constructed mainly from cotton and, to an increasing degree, synthetic fibers. The criminalist determines if the recovered rope can be of any value in tracing; its origin may be so common as to preclude any tracing value. The fact that rope is normally quite bristly is to the advantage of the investigator because the majority of offenders carry the binding material into the scene by putting it in a pocket, and the rope fiber may contain debris from the pocket. The value of the debris will be dependent on its uniqueness. The manner in which the offender has tied the binding material (the use of a particular knot, for example) is also of significant investigative value. Officers should not cut through the binding material so that the knot is destroyed.

In recovering fiber evidence, paper envelopes should be avoided, for they often contain their own manufactured fibers. Fibers should be picked up with tweezers or by hand—never by means of gummed tape. A vacuum sweeping technique should be used in scenes in which fibers and similar types of evidence are common. Only vacuums containing removable filters should be used. After a sweeping of the scene, the filter can be taken from the trap and sent intact to the crime laboratory for analysis.

SUMMARY

Robbery poses an immediate challenge to the investigator of the twenty-first century, as it is increasing both in frequency and in the level of violence against victims. Robbery suspects are predatory offenders in that they purposely stalk and confront victims. Successful robbery investigations tend to detail the offender's method of operation, for robbery is a high-stress crime in which suspects tend to act in a predetermined behavioral pattern. Accordingly, careful attention must be given to victims as they detail the actions of the suspect from the moment of contact to the escape from the scene.

Most robberies are committed in the street by a suspect employing strong-arm tactics. Although residential and vehicle robberies are not as common as street robberies, they too are increasing in frequency. Police are using proactive decoy operations to combat robbery, in addition to traditional apprehension methods. Because the use of weapons plays a prominent role in many robbery cases, investigators must be very familiar with the collection and analysis methods associated with this type of physical evidence.

 ## EXERCISES

1. Prepare a paper listing the frequency rates, offender characteristics, and other data relative to robbery in your community. Contrast your findings with national data found in the FBI's *Uniform Crime Report.*

2. Prepare a forensic science display. Construct a display of projectiles and shell casings illustrating the principles discussed in this chapter.

 ## RELEVANT WEB SITES

http://www.atf.treas.gov/index.htm

Home page of the Bureau of Alcohol, Tobacco, Firearms, and Explosives. A number of links are provided concerning the firearm mission of the ATF, including extensive data on gun-related crime and regulation.

http://www.ojp.usdoj.gov/bjs/glance/rob.htm

Trends and statistics regarding robbery in the United States compiled through Department of Justice victimization studies from the mid-1970s to the present.

http://www.crimedoctor.com/robbery1.htm

Private security consultant discusses robbery facts pertaining to location, rates, suspect method of operation, arrest rates, and suspect weapon usage. Numerous links to other security matters.

Homicide and Aggravated Assault

KEY TERMS

aggravated assault
asphyxia
autopsy
benzidine color reaction
   reaction test
contusions
coroner
defense wounds
deoxyribonucleic acid (DNA)
dying declaration
exhumation
forensic anthropologist
forensic odontology
forensic pathologist
hesitation marks
homicide

lacerations
low copy DNA
manslaughter
medical examiner
murder
postmortem lividity
precipitin test
psychological profiling
putrefaction
rigor mortis
simulated death
victim-precipitated crimes
violent criminal apprehension
   program
workplace homicides

LEARNING OBJECTIVES

1. to be able to define the various types of homicide;
2. to be aware of the current state of criminal homicide as to frequency and victim–offender relationships;
3. to be able to discuss the five basic offender causative patterns;
4. to appreciate the importance and methods of psychological profiling;
5. to know the legal meaning of aggravated assault;
6. to be able to compare aggravated assault regarding frequency and offender characteristics to the crime of murder;
7. to have a working knowledge of the standard investigative methods that apply to the homicide investigation;
8. to be able to define the five major methods that aid the investigator in determining the time of death;
9. to be able to explain the four major causes of death;
10. to understand the legal significance of the dying declaration;
11. to be able to compare and contrast the medical examiner system and the coroner system; and
12. to be familiar with those areas of forensic science that directly apply to the death investigation.

HOMICIDE

The homicide investigation traditionally has been portrayed as the classic test of the criminal investigator. This image originated in the early English detective novel and has been perpetuated through countless U.S. films and television scripts. Although death investigations are relatively common to the police officer, murder inquiries are far less prevalent. **Homicide** is defined as the killing of a human by another human. The common notion that homicide and murder are synonymous is false. The major difference between them lies in the legality of the death, that is, in the presence or absence of criminality. Execution of convicted offenders by the state or the legal taking of life of suspects resisting arrest with deadly force are deaths of a homicidal nature. Such deaths involve human causation and are justifiable or excusable. Thus, homicide is not necessarily a crime.

As nearly 6,000 people die from a variety of causes every day in the United States, criminal investigators are often involved in death inquiries (see Table 11.1).[1] A common reaction following the death of an individual by natural causes is to contact the police, for 80 percent of the population dies outside established care institutions such as hospitals or nursing homes. Similar contacts result when accidental deaths or suicides are encountered. These situations occur with much greater frequency than the crime of murder. The average U.S. police agency does not often encounter a death involving the unlawful killing of a person by another. Such deaths happen more often in large cities and less frequently in rural or smaller suburban areas. As a result of this variation in frequency, specialized homicide investigators are normally found only in agencies serving 100,000 people or more. Because 90 percent of all local police agencies serve populations of fewer than 25,000 people and nearly 50 percent of all police agencies employ fewer than 10 officers, all police officers must be knowledgeable in the techniques of death investigation.[2] It is not practical for small departments to include specialized homicide investigators; therefore, death investigation assignments are generalized among the members of such departments.

TABLE 11.1   Annual Causes of Death in America

Cause of Death	Rank	Number of Deaths (rounded to thousands)
Diseases of the heart	1	700,000
Malignant cancers	2	554,000
Cerebrovascular disease	3	164,000
Lower respiratory disease	4	123,000
Accidents	5	102,000
Diabetes	6	71,000
Influenza	7	62,000
Alzheimer's	8	54,000
Nephritis	9	39,000
Septicemia	10	33,000
Suicide	11	32,000
Liver disease	12	27,000
Hypertension	13	20,000
Homicide	14	16,000

Source: U.S. Department of Health and Human Services, Centers for Disease Control and Prevention.

Murder

All police officers should be trained in murder investigation despite its relatively low frequency, for no other criminal offense has the real and imagined impact of murder. The loss of life by criminal causation is without dispute the most heinous crime in the mind of the average individual. Police agencies must be prepared to respond to such a crime with maximum investigative effort, for an entire community can be upset by an unsolved murder. Although millions of major crimes are committed annually in the United States, only a small fraction are criminal homicides. Nevertheless, criminal homicides are the gravest of offenses because they involve the taking of a human life. Public interest immediately focuses on the police inquiry and demands a successful solution and prosecution. The efforts of the investigator will be additionally intensified by the knowledge that an individual with the proven capacity to kill is at large and may repeat the offense.

With minor variations among the states, **murder** is defined as the unlawful killing of a human being with malice aforethought. The statute description in the Illinois criminal code is typical.

A person who kills an individual without lawful justification commits murder if, in performing the acts that cause the death,

1. he either intends to kill or do great bodily harm to that individual or another or knows that such acts will cause death to that individual or another,
2. he knows that such acts create a strong probability of death or great bodily harm to that individual or another, or
3. he is attempting or committing a forcible felony other than voluntary manslaughter.[3]

A criminal homicide is then murder if the wrongdoer accomplishes the crime with premeditation. The act is frequently referred to as a premeditated design to kill, and the state must prove that the accused consciously intended to kill the victim. It is important to note that premeditation does not always imply the existence of an elaborate plan to commit the offense. The time frame in which the idea to murder was conceived is not as important as the fact that the design to kill was present before the act. A criminal homicide can also constitute murder even when premeditation to kill is lacking altogether. For example, the Florida statutes state that "when perpetrated by any act imminently dangerous to another, and evincing a depraved mind regardless of human life, although without any premeditated design to effect the death of any particular individual, it shall be murder." Finally, murder can be accomplished without premeditation if the killing occurs during the commission of a felony. Many states have assigned varying degrees to the crime of murder for sentencing purposes. Typically, premeditated murder is of the first degree, whereas an act creating a strong probability of harm, which results in death, is of the second degree. Deaths that result during the perpetration (or attempt) of a felony are generally considered murders of the third degree.

Manslaughter

Manslaughter is the unlawful killing of a human being without malice. Thus, manslaughter is not murder, nor is it a homicide through legal means (a legal execution). In most states, manslaughter is classified by means of three specific categories: voluntary, involuntary, and vehicular (often referred to as reckless homicide). *Voluntary manslaughter* is the case if, at the time of the killing, the slayer acted under a sudden and intense passion resulting from serious provocation. The law recognizes that an individual can be violently affected by intense provocation. The serious provocation is judged sufficient if it would incite an intense passion in a reasonable person. The large majority of criminal homicides fall within this category. Deaths resulting from arguments, lovers' quarrels, and family disputes generally make up the bulk of manslaughter offenses.

Involuntary manslaughter can occur during an unlawful act, or it may occur during a lawful act. If a death is without lawful justification and provocation or premeditation is not involved, it may be considered involuntary manslaughter. Deaths that occur during the commission of an unlawful act not amounting to a felony or deaths resulting from actions lacking due caution and involving culpable negligence are also judged to be involuntary.

Investigators encounter involuntary manslaughter offenses that are often erroneously termed "accidental deaths." A case in which a death is caused by carelessness or negligence, such as the crash of an elevator that was known to be in need of repair, is an example. Such offenses are normally far from being purely accidental in that the death occurs as a direct result of some action or omission on the part of a wrongdoer. Deaths in which automobiles are involved and that are the result of gross negligence are often separately defined as a form of involuntary manslaughter. There are types of homicides that are excusable and justifiable and that are not prosecuted. Excusable homicide results from what has been termed "misadventure." A killing in self-defense is an excusable homicide. Deaths that are the unfortunate results of lawful acts, such as the prevention of the commission of a felony, are often considered excusable. Justifiable homicide lacks an illegal or evil design; often it is an action of last resort.

Contrary to widespread belief, an actual body is not necessary to obtain a murder or manslaughter conviction. There have been a number of successful murder convictions in the United States in which the victim's body was never located. Courts have held that *corpus delicti*, the body of the crime, does not mean the actual body of the victim. The *corpus delicti* is proved by showing that the death of a person occurred by the criminal action of another.

Current State of Criminal Homicide

The FBI's annual *Uniform Crime Report* (UCR) is the single most accurate source for determining the status of murder and manslaughter. Authorities are in agreement that murder is the most accurately reported of all offenses. Unlike certain crimes that are often not reported, such as rape and burglary, murder is normally reported when discovered. In a surprising number of cases, it is the perpetrator of the crime who provides the information. Murder is defined in the UCR as the willful killing of another. The statistics gathered in the UCR represent only murder and nonnegligent manslaughter and do not record deaths caused by negligence, suicide, accident, or justifiable homicide.

Although the incidence of criminal homicide reached an all-time high during the early 1990s, the current annual rate of approximately 16,000 criminal homicides indicates a significant decrease of this serious violent crime in the past seven years. Criminal homicide accounts for only approximately 1 percent of the total violent crime. Nevertheless, our present decade rate of criminal homicide is historically very high, surpassing even the murder rates experienced during the violent Prohibition era of the 1920s and 1930s. For example, Chicago's criminal homicide rates are nearly triple the frequency encountered during the city's murderous gangland period during Prohibition.[4]

Although experts have cited many possible causative factors contributing to our current criminal homicide rate, the relationship of drugs to murder is unmistakable. The rapid growth of drug gangs, particularly those dealing in cocaine, is directly linked to significant numbers of murders and bystander deaths. Recently, Washington, D.C., officials reported that 41 percent of all homicides were drug-related, and 56 percent of killings in the city of Savannah, Georgia, were similarly connected.[5] Criminal killings are currently so common in most urban areas that citizens cannot recall a time free from such violence. In Kansas City, Missouri, city officials have unsuccessfully urged citizens to produce a murder-free month; March 1949 was the last month in which no one was killed in that city.

An analysis of murder by month indicates the greatest frequency is in the summer months of July and August. More murders occur on holidays and weekends than on other days. Most occur during the evening and night hours. A geographic breakdown of murder by region indicates that the southern states have traditionally had the highest frequency of murder. Murder rates in large metropolitan areas have always been higher in proportion to population than rates in less heavily populated areas.

Victims.   The victims of murder are male in approximately 77 percent of all instances, and they are most likely to be between 20 and 24 years of age. The residence is the most common murder location.[6] Males account for 78 percent of the victims, with 9 percent being juveniles. Racially, the victims of criminal homicide are nearly evenly split between both blacks and whites. The National Center for Health Statistics has documented that criminal homicide is the leading cause of death among black males 25 to 34 years of age.

Historically, statistics on relationships of victims to offenders show that the majority of murder victims knew their killers, but in the early 1990s, the relationship percentages began to change. The FBI's UCR documents that only 44 percent of all victims knew their killers, compared to a 1970s rate of over 80 percent. Thirteen percent of victims are related to and 31 percent are acquainted with their assailants. Of all female victims, 33 percent are slain by husbands or boyfriends. Nearly 56 percent of all killings are classified as either stranger homicides or cases in which acquaintanceship could not be determined during the investigation. Various studies indicate that the number of victims who know their killers has declined even more rapidly in major U.S. cities. In New York, it was discovered that 33 percent of the victims did not know their killers, giving the city the country's highest rate of slayings classified as "stranger murders."[7] It is apparent that certain other highly "anonymous" cities are also experiencing a rise in stranger-to-stranger murders. The New York City Police Department speculates that the anonymity of the city and the breakdown of closely knit neighborhoods are prime reasons contributing to the high proportion of stranger murders. However, other studies indicate that motives of narcotics and robbery contribute significantly to the increased killing of strangers.[8]

Many homicide investigators fear that the increased murders of strangers may be directly related to the decrease of the murder clearance rate. Nationally, the police clearance rate for murder is the highest of that for all the major crimes—nearly 63 percent. However, major metropolitan areas have shown a significant decline in clearance rates. The arrest rate has dropped from 86 percent in 1970 to the recent decade average rate of 64 percent. New York City reported a clearance rate of 60 percent of all reported cases, Los Angeles 65 percent, and Denver only 46 percent.[9] That such cities are large, impersonal metropolitan areas, ideally suited for such murder, may lend authenticity to the proposed relationship.

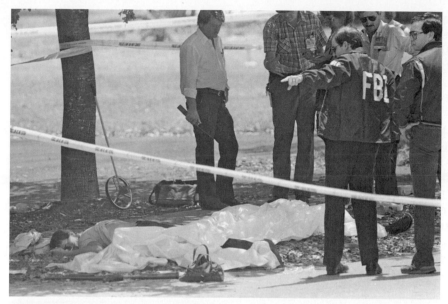

FIGURE 11.1   The homicide investigation tests the full resources of the investigator. Here, FBI agents investigate a multiple murder scene in Florida where two fellow agents were killed in a gun battle with two robbery suspects also shot to death. *(Source: Corbis/Bettmann, © Bettmann/CORBIS.)*

Although the specific percentage is currently unknown, a significant number of murders are **victim-precipitated crimes**. That is, such murders involve a conscious or unconscious action by the victim that is a causative factor in the violent act. Experienced investigators are all too familiar with the typical victim-precipitated murder case. Such investigations either involve victims who dare their slayers to assault or who provoke the assault by some other action. Research studies of several major cities indicate that a substantial number of criminal homicides fall into this category. It is often difficult to establish a clear means of distinguishing the victim-precipitated murder from other types of murders. Do some victims bring about their own deaths by continually insulting individuals known to be armed and violent? Can an unfaithful wife precipitate her death by continuing an affair after her husband has sworn to kill her if the extramarital relationship is not terminated?

It is believed that alcohol and other intoxicating drugs are often associated with the victim-precipitated murder and homicide in general. One New York study revealed that nearly 70 percent of victims were intoxicated at the time they were killed.[10] With regard to racial factors, in victim-precipitated murders, as well as in "normal" criminal homicides, offenders and victims are almost always of the same race, with interracial murders generally accounting for under 10 percent of the cases reported to the police.

It is important to realize that the majority of murders are not victim precipitated, yet the number of such situations should not be overlooked. Officers must be prepared for the possibility of a defense strategy that is built around a victim's precipitating actions.

Offender Characteristics

The majority of arrested murder suspects are from 17 to 34 years of age, as nearly 70 percent are within this age-group. There are currently more than 140,000 inmates serving time for criminal homicide in American prisons.

Criminal homicide is a male-dominated crime; only 10 percent of the arrested suspects are female. Fifty-one percent of the offenders are black; approximately 46 percent are white. The race of the murder suspect varies significantly according to the population area studied. City arrest trends in communities of populations over 50,000 show the majority of offenders to be of minority groups, but in suburban areas, these racial trends are often reversed.

Although no single set of circumstances causes one person to kill another, one common denominator does appear evident in the majority of criminal homicides. Most offenders are in an emotional state of extreme anger when they kill. Of course there are exceptions, such as a coldly calculated murder to eliminate a robbery witness. Yet the typical murder is neither premeditated nor perpetrated in the commission of another crime. Most murders can be categorized as involving either

1. emotional disputes,
2. matters of sex,
3. related crimes,
4. severe mental abnormalities, or
5. benefit factors.

Emotional Disputes.   Criminal homicides involving emotional disputes vary considerably. They may occur within families and between acquaintances outside of the family. All such murders involve sudden emotional explosion, resulting in the death of some individual. Deaths resulting from family fights of long standing or, in a small number of cases, recent family disturbances often fall into this category. A research project sponsored by the Police Foundation demonstrated that individuals who murder their relatives often have a record of domestic quarrels that required police intervention. The study involved the examination of murder records in Kansas City and Detroit and concluded that the police had knowledge of threats or serious domestic conflicts in the majority of murders that eventually took place. Although emotional arguments may originate over a seemingly trivial matter, anger quickly escalates to a violent level. Offenders are often males troubled by feelings of inadequacy. Typically, husbands murder their spouses more frequently than the reverse. Only a very small percentage of marital homicides are planned in advance. In those cases in which such preplanning is a factor, women are more likely to premeditate, for their peril is greater if they attempt the killing and fail.[11] It should be noted that the true source of anger in the emotional dispute is often not the point of the specific argument that precedes the murder but a long-standing problem of a more serious nature.

Some emotional homicides end in the suicide of the perpetrator. Generally, male suspects kill a wife or girlfriend before killing themselves, but some murders may involve entire families or numerous coworkers. Mental health authorities report that the most typical murder-suicide is one in which two partners abuse and depend on each other for affection in a love–hate relationship. The relationship is often marked by many past separations, threats, and accusations of infidelity. The final act symbolically demonstrates that the perpetrator cannot exist separately from the victim but cannot live with him or her either. Studies indicate that more than 70 percent of such homicide-suicides involve murderers who are either husbands or boyfriends of the victims.[12]

Outside the family structure, emotional disputes often occur in bars and similar social gathering places. The consumption of alcoholic beverages is very often a factor in such nonfamily disputes. Friends who murder are often intoxicated—and their victims are likely to have been intoxicated also. An emotional dispute may begin during a card game; it may start as a verbal argument over some triviality. Anger is quickly intensified to the point of mindless rage, and a criminal homicide results. Following the commission of the murder, the anger quickly subsides. These offenders often immediately express disbelief that they could have committed such an offense. Those who murder as a result of emotional disputes are almost always apprehended by the police. The majority make no attempt to avoid arrest and may wait at the crime scene; they may even report the offense. Since such individuals are not generally psychopathic, they feel considerable guilt resulting from their actions. The majority of emotional murders take place between friends or acquaintances.

A significant number of the murders in this category are individuals who have experienced a continual atmosphere of violence. That is, such people have often grown up in environments in which the norm is to settle disputes by physical means. Many inner-city ghettos and certain rural areas breed cultures of violence. Settling emotional disputes through violence may also be conditioned as a result of childhood abuse.

Not all emotional murders are perpetrated by adults. Juvenile murderers may kill victims within their immediate family, but more typically they murder outside of the family. Suspects under 18 years of age account for approximately 8 percent of the willful killings resulting in arrest. Psychological studies of juveniles who have committed murder reveal certain common traits among the offenders, regardless of the type of victim. These juveniles often have experienced parental abuse within the family in which an alcoholic father plays a significant role. In addition, increasing use of firearms by juveniles to settle disputes has significantly escalated the number of homicides by gunshot. Among young black males ages 15 to 19, homicide rates are more than 11 times the rate for their white counterparts.[13]

Sexual Matters.   A substantial number of criminal homicides can be attributed to sexual involvements. Jealousy is the causative factor in the majority of such offenses. Whatever the relationship—husband and wife or unmarried lovers—one partner suspects the other of being sexually unfaithful. The actual murder may be the culmination of numerous assaults, or it may result from a chance discovery of infidelity.

Murders committed as the result of infidelity have been recorded in the earliest criminal records. Until relatively recently, certain countries legally sanctioned or simply ignored such killings, particularly if the husband was the perpetrator. Even in the United States, these murders were often not prosecuted with any regularity until the twentieth century.

Related Crimes.   In this type of murder, offenders kill during the commission of another crime, normally a felony. Such killings have grown alarmingly throughout the United States, with cities evidencing particularly rapid growth. Two decades ago, related-crime killings rarely accounted for more than 10 percent of the total criminal homicides. At the present time, nearly 22 percent of all criminal homicides involve a related crime. The greatest number of related-crime murders are in conjunction with robbery. Narcotics and sex offenses follow in frequency. In some areas, such as inner-city neighborhoods, a significant proportion of related-crime homicides occur during illegal drug transactions. Such murders were once unique to heroin transactions, but now other narcotics and dangerous drugs such as cocaine and methamphetamine are involved. The frequent relationship of drugs to murder is well illustrated by a New York City–based study that examined nearly 4,300 criminal homicides occurring during the course of two years. The research revealed that 31 percent of the victims had cocaine in their systems when slain.[14]

The increase in related-crime murder has been attributed to a variety of factors. The average killer is now considerably younger than the killer of 20 years ago. Some police authorities surmise that the younger armed robber is much more likely to panic during the robbery and kill a victim. Such a theory could be applied to all felony categories involving a young suspect, thus accounting for the increase in related-crime deaths. Some proponents of capital punishment think that the infrequent use of a death penalty for murder causes more offenders to kill victims to eliminate witnesses to the original felony. The offenders would reason that punishment would not be significantly greater if a murder, in addition to a robbery or rape, is committed.

Severe Mental Abnormalities.   Although a large number of murderers have mental problems of varying descriptions, a small number are legally insane or borderline cases. Severely mentally disturbed offenders kill as a result of their illness. They are often totally out of touch with reality—either psychotic or paranoid schizophrenic. They frequently suffer delusions or hallucinations and are often compelled to kill through a sense of persecution. Offenders experiencing such delusions may be mass murderers who continue to kill until apprehended. Mass murderers generally confine their killings to one general area and murder during a relatively short time span. The mass murderer is classified according to three general categories:

1. terrorists,
2. individuals who experience sudden breakdowns, and
3. mentally ill persons who kill to relieve tensions.

Terrorists murder as a means of achieving political recognition or some social outcome not possible by conventional means. Fortunately, this form of homicide is relatively infrequent compared to the overall rate of illegal killings. Although rare, terrorist killings are generally shocking to the public and cause intense media coverage because of the often large numbers of victims killed or injured in a single incident. Cases such as the Oklahoma City bombing of the federal building, the UNABOMBER case, physician murders linked to extremist antiabortion groups, and the terrorist attacks of September 11, 2001, are examples of terroristic killings. Offenders who commit mass murder as a result of a sudden mental breakdown have gradually developed a severe mental illness. The illness may surface as the result of a "sparking" incident or become increasingly apparent with continual mental breakdown. Mass murderers who kill to relieve burdens of persecution or to relieve inner tensions often murder in a bizarre manner. The 1984 murder of 21 people and wounding of 20 additional victims by a single gunman in San Ysidro, California, graphically illustrates this type of mass murder. This type of suspect often kills to gain relief from mental "commands" to kill. The more recent 1999 mass murder of 12 students and a teacher by two fellow students at Columbine High School near Littleton, Colorado, illustrates the terrible results of escalating homicidal mental disturbances.

Workplace homicides, killing at a place of employment, have increased at a disturbing rate during the past decade. Each year more than 1,000 people are victims of occupational homicide (see Table 11.2). For Americans who die at work, criminal homicide is now the third principal cause and is the leading cause of death among women workers. The cause of

TABLE 11.2   Workplace Homicide Victims by Occupation

Top Ten Occupations Most Commonly Victimized by Homicide in 2004

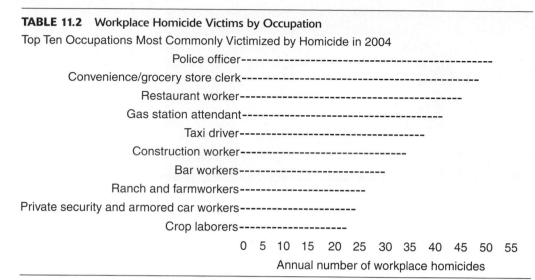

Source: U.S. Department of Labor, Bureau of Labor Statistics.

increased frustration that leads to workplace threats and, for some, homicide is poorly understood. Studies do demonstrate that of all workplace threats, current or former employees account for the majority of hostile actions, not strangers or customers. Workplace homicide suspects are typically of four varieties: the domestic offender, disgruntled employee, obsessive employee, and former employee. The domestic-connected workplace killing involves a perpetrator who kills his wife or girlfriend at her place of occupation. Often as a result of a long-standing history of domestic violence, the typically divorced or separated suspect decides to murder his former intimate at her place of employment. Disgruntled workers who kill are currently employed at the site, but because of various grievances or disciplinary actions against them, they murder one or more coworkers. In many cases, such killers seek out supervisors or others who the offenders believe were responsible for their being passed over for promotion. Obsessive workplace killers have psychologically fixated on another worker who is often stalked or harassed by the suspect over a period of time prior to the murder. Most often such killers are males who develop a sexual obsession with a female coworker. The former employee who commits workplace homicide is a terminated worker who kills for revenge. Often previously psychologically unstable, this suspect transfers the loss of his job into a loss of personal identity.[15]

Serial Murders.   The serial murderer is a type of perpetrator who commits numerous murders but, unlike the mass murderer, kills over long time periods. Additionally, the serial killer often travels widely in the commission of his crimes. Federal authorities estimate that several hundred murders annually may be attributed to this type of killer.[16] Victims are typically women or juveniles, with the suspect almost invariably male. Although many serial murders have occurred in the United States, the two worst examples have occurred overseas. Andrei Chikatilo, a Russian who murdered 53 victims in the former Soviet Union, was arrested in 1990 following a 12-year criminal investigation. Harold Shipman, an English medical doctor, was convicted of serial murder in 2000 and is credited with murdering at least 215 former patients (most of whom had minor ailments) through deadly injections.

Investigative psychologists report two types of serial killers (or "lust murderers" as they may also be referred to): the organized nonsocial and

FIGURE 11.2   A classic sadistic serial murderer, Dennis Rader was convicted in 2005 of committing ten criminal homicides over a seventeen-year period in the Wichita, Kansas, area. A clever and resourceful suspect, the so-called BTK killer left few clues at his crime scenes. After analyzing a mailed diskette meant to taunt the police, criminal investigators traced it back to Rader who had created it on his church's computer. *(Source: Sedgwick County, Kansas, Sheriff's Office/AP Wide World Photos.)*

disorganized asocial personality. The organized nonsocial murderer is totally psychopathic, exhibiting complete indifference and hostility toward society. Methodical and cunning, he is excited by thoughts or media portrayals of cruelty. The disorganized asocial killer has an aversion to others and typically represents the classic loner. This suspect type feels rejected and lacks the nonsocial suspect's motivation to inflict pain and punishment.[17] Although any type of victim may be at risk, serial homicidal offenders frequently target prostitutes or other victims whose occupation or "street life" orientation places them in vulnerable environments.

Most serial killers are sexual sadists who are typically severely psychopathic. Such individuals are marked by antisocial personalities, acting out sexual needs in the ultimate antisocial manner. The sexual psychopathic offender should not be confused with the rapist. Serial sexual murder provides a gratification that the offender is unable to achieve through normal sexual outlets. Sex murderers normally select victims of their own race and are almost always male. A psychological profile of the serial sexually motivated murderer often conforms in many respects to the following:

1. kills three or more victims in separate incidents in varying localities;
2. likely male, in his late twenties or early thirties, more often white than any other racial group;
3. of average or above intelligence;
4. may have poor employment record;
5. tends to be manipulative, emotionally cold, and outwardly passive;
6. predatory offender who fantasizes, plans, stalks, and ultimately kills victims without interpersonal conflict and emotional provocation;
7. generally selects highly vulnerable victims to avoid detection;

8. lacks feelings of guilt or remorse and views victims as mere objects;
9. may have history of childhood sexual or physical abuse and/or violent role models in the home;
10. often has exhibited childhood signs of abnormality involving cruelty to animals or younger children, arson, or extreme vandalism; and
11. generally becomes increasingly confident, violent, and competent in avoiding arrest as crimes increase.[18]

Psychological Profiling

The use of **psychological profiling** has proven quite successful in the investigation of serial murder. Although nothing can replace a logical criminal investigation based on traditional, proven methods, the use of psychology is an additional tool with tremendous potential. Investigative psychology can aid law enforcement officers by providing information that enables them to limit or better direct their efforts. All criminal offenders have unique psychological behavior patterns in addition to their *modus operandi*. Accordingly, the investigator trained in psychological profiling attempts to construct a personality portrait of the offender. By analyzing crime scene photos, physical evidence, and reported conversations of the suspect, investigators can often develop a very accurate portrait of the offender.

The use of psychology to profile an offender's motive and personality is not a totally new concept. The origins of psychological crime solution are

INVESTIGATIVE PROFILE

Gary Plank
Behavioral Profiler
Nebraska State Patrol
Investigative Services Division
Lincoln, Nebraska

I'm a sergeant with the Nebraska State Patrol, and I've worked as a behavioral crime analyst, what many people refer to as a profiler, for 15 years. My position is a very fascinating and challenging one and has been portrayed (often inaccurately) in many television shows and movies. I wanted to get into law enforcement since age four or five. As a child I was very impressed by the way police officers helped people, and my grandfather was a town marshal in Oklahoma. So I knew a criminal justice major was for me, and after starting at a community college, I graduated with a bachelor's degree from Chadron State College. I later earned a master's degree in mental health counseling as well. While I was an undergraduate student, I worked as a dispatcher for a local sheriff's office, and this only confirmed my interest in police work. I entered the Nebraska State Patrol in 1979 and, following academy training, was assigned to road patrol. After about five years, I was promoted to a full-time criminal investigator position. I worked a variety of property and crimes-against-person cases for seven years and attended many in-service training classes, one of which was to completely change my career focus.

I heard an FBI profiler, Roy Hazelwood, who was one of the founders of the bureau's behavioral profiling unit, give a training presentation at Boy's Town in Omaha. I made an immediate connection with everything he was saying and was particularly impressed with the central theme of profiling: how psychology and criminal investigation can merge together to assist the police. At about this same time, the newly appointed superintendent of the State Patrol asked for applicants to become the agency's first behavioral profiler. The superintendent was a retired FBI agent and had observed firsthand the benefits of profiling. I competed for the position and was selected to travel to the FBI unit for training at the

INVESTIGATIVE PROFILE (CONTINUED)

bureau's academy in Quantico, Virginia. So in 1990, my family and I moved to Virginia for the yearlong fellowship training with the FBI's Behavioral Science Unit, which would lead to my profiling accreditation. The training was intense and immensely interesting.

For the first three months, I and other officers attended lectures by experienced FBI experts. The lectures dealt with abnormal psychology, criminal pathology, and research gleaned from numerous interviews with convicted serial criminals. We also reviewed many cases previously profiled by bureau agents to appreciate how crime scene behavior imparts suspect personality, among other factors. We also studied at the Armed Forces Institute of Pathology, audited law classes concerning criminal insanity at the University of Virginia, and observed New York City's homicide crime scene unit for a week. This highly specialized unit processes all homicides throughout New York City. Then we were assigned our own cases on which to apply our new skills. Graduation from the program was granted only when each of us successfully profiled seven cases submitted by police from around the country. My class consisted of only seven criminal investigators, including several from foreign police agencies.

After my fellowship with the FBI, I returned to the Nebraska State Patrol and have worked continuously as a criminal investigative analyst. My work includes cases developed by the state police or, more commonly, submitted by police departments or sheriff's offices from around the state. I specialize in providing insight into homicides, sexual assaults, child molestations, arson, and bombings, among other crimes. Profiling particularly lends itself to crimes in which criminal psychopathology is present. This occurs when something unusual or unnecessary to the commission of the crime is done or said. I'm basically looking for deviant behaviors that identify an unknown suspect, confirm a suspect already identified, locate evidence, or assist in obtaining a confession. Lately, I've also been working a number of threat assessment and stalking cases. I'm often consulted when all other traditional methods of investigation have failed, so my work involves a lot of "out of the box" thinking. In addition to applying principles of abnormal psychology to my cases, I use a lot of imagination to gain insight. I always return to the original crime scenes and try to view the surroundings through the offender's eyes. If the crime happened at night, I visit the scene at night. I ask myself why a particular victim was selected, why a particular weapon was used, and so on. All of this gives me insight into the offender's personality, which is the core of profiling.

There are many things I enjoy about behavioral profiling, but getting to work with a wide variety of law enforcement agencies is at the top of the list. I regularly work with local, state, and federal agencies, and I want to stress that profiling is not a job that involves just one lone person. It's all about interagency cooperation and the sharing of information. Even now, I regularly consult with other profilers around the country regarding cases we are all working. The biggest negative aspect of the job is having to get so close to the human suffering. In order to conduct profiles, you have to mentally re-create aspects of the crime. This means you have to visualize all the details of what the victim went through. This is especially disturbing when the crimes involve child victims. My advice to students who would like to do what I've been fortunate enough to do is threefold. First, get experience as a field law enforcement officer on some level. I'd recommend at least five years of investigative work to develop a basic understanding of criminality. This will serve as the foundation for the advanced psychological information you'll process during your behavioral training. Second, take courses in abnormal psychology and /or mental health counseling in addition to your criminal justice studies. Finally, be realistic about the number of job opportunities in this specialty. Contrary to the media image, there are a limited number of full-time profiling positions with various police agencies throughout the country.

rooted in nineteenth-century fiction, such as that by Edgar Allan Poe and Arthur Conan Doyle.[19] Possibly the first recorded use of psychological profiling in the United States occurred during the 1932 Lindbergh kidnapping case. Using psychological analysis with great accuracy, psychiatrist Dudley Shoenfeld carefully reviewed the circumstances of the case and the contents of ransom notes. Concluding that the victim was dead very soon after the abduction and that the baby had been taken by a lone man, Schoenfeld's predictions were contrary to those held by the authorities. However, when the profile proved to be totally accurate, the value of psychological assessment in criminal investigations was demonstrated.[20] Used frequently in various sensational investigations, psychological profiling remained relatively obscure until its use and promotion by the FBI.

Since 1978, the FBI Academy's Behavioral Science Unit has been assisting local law enforcement agencies in their investigations of violent crime. The unit also trains local and state investigators in the profiling method through on-site internships. The unit's agents are now heavily relied on for their profiling assessments and are credited with solving hundreds of previously unsolved cases. As of 2006, there were only 24 FBI agents and about 15 federally trained local and state law enforcement officers working as full-time profilers. There are relatively few profilers at local police agencies because most departments do not have the resources to free up detectives for the extensive training required—often a yearlong internship based out of the FBI Academy.

The basis of a proper profile is a complete crime scene examination and thorough interviews of the victim and witnesses. Profiling is a form of *retro-classification*, or classification that works backward. Unlike mental health psychologists who may attempt to classify a patient's emotional illness by interviewing the client personally, law enforcement profilers must work backward from behavioral clues left at crime scenes to establish identity through experience, insight, and interpretation. Many types of crime scenes lend themselves to this form of analysis. Such scenes are presumed to reflect the criminal's behavior and personality in much the way furnishings reveal the home owner's character.[21] Obviously, bizarre crimes or those in which the investigator recognizes the presence of psychopathology are particularly well suited for this process. Accordingly, the profile is generally reserved for homicides, rapes, or other serious offenses in which a mental deficiency is exhibited by the suspect. Information essential for the profile is typically drawn from the following:

1. detailed crime scene photos and sketches;
2. results of laboratory tests and autopsy reports, if applicable;
3. a complete report of the offense, including date and time of offense, location, and weapon used; and
4. information concerning the victim, including
   (a) occupation
   (b) general reputation
   (c) detailed physical description
   (d) marital status and number of children
   (e) all known miscellaneous social and personal information, e.g., use of alcohol, financial status, educational level, etc.[22]

Using known psychological concepts, past experience, and instinctive reasoning, profilers review collected information to form the assessment (see Figure 11.3). Although a profile cannot always be expected to yield the following factors, psychological assessments often reveal

1. suspect's race,
2. sex,
3. age range,
4. marital status,
5. general employment,

FIGURE 11.3   FBI behavioral profilers study maps, physical evidence, photographs, and official reports to construct a suspect's identity. *(Source: Spencer Grant / Photo Edit Inc.)*

6. reaction to questioning by police,
7. degree of sexual maturity,
8. whether the individual might strike again,
9. whether the individual has committed a similar offense in the past, and
10. possible police record.

Psychological profiling can be accomplished by trained mental health professionals who are not law enforcement officers. However, experienced investigators who are also skilled psychologists (such as those in the FBI's profile unit) have had the greatest success. Profiling has traditionally focused on murder and rape cases; however, the technique has been used successfully in other types of investigations, including child molestation, arson, and kidnapping.[23]

Closely related to the FBI's psychological profiling program is the **Violent Criminal Apprehension Program** (VICAP). Operated at the FBI's National Center for the Analysis of Violent Crime, the VICAP program is a nationwide data collection effort that receives and analyzes information on specific cases of violence. The late Pierce Brooks, former Los Angeles police captain and chief of police in Lakewood, Colorado, is credited with conceiving the VICAP concept. While investigating a homicide case in the 1950s, Brooks became convinced the killer had probably committed a similar crime at an earlier time. Frustrated by the 14 months he was forced to spend in the Los Angeles public library searching for newspaper articles describing a similar method of operation, Brooks began to imagine the usefulness of a huge computerized national database in which criminal method of operation was cataloged and tracked. His visionary ideas and writings soon motivated FBI interest in establishing the current VICAP program. Any law enforcement agency may submit a solved or unsolved case to the VICAP program if the investigation meets one of the following criteria:

- solved or unsolved criminal homicides that appear to be serial in nature or homicides that are random, motiveless, or sexually oriented;

- missing person cases in which there is a strong possibility of criminality; and
- investigations in which unidentified bodies have been discovered and the cause of death appears to be homicidal.

VICAP analysts study such cases to determine whether there have been prior investigations with similar elements or characteristics. By linking similar cases in various jurisdictions, the program seeks to identify and apprehend offenders who have eluded detection and arrest. Through nationwide data collection, VICAP links and alerts various police agencies in their efforts to solve serious cases. As agencies are often unaware of crimes outside their immediate areas, the program has proven significant in identifying serial offenders and their related crimes (see Figure 11.4).

Benefit Factors.   Possibly the smallest number of criminal homicides are committed to achieve some type of benefit. Some offenders may murder to rid themselves of the attachment of another individual, but the majority of benefit murders are financially motivated. Such homicides may take place between business partners, or they may be committed to profit from life insurance coverage.

Those who murder for benefit generally hire a second party to commit the offense or attempt to deceive the officer by staging a fatal felony crime scene. Occasionally, large police agencies may experience a series of organized crime murders or killings resulting from youth gang conflicts. Such homicides are benefit related in that they are based on either financial gain or the achievement of power.

The benefit murderer is frequently resourceful and coldly calculating in the methods used to achieve the homicide. A San Diego murder case in which

FIGURE 11.4   VICAP Alert notice detailing general identity and forensic findings of a decomposed victim in a suspected criminal homicide. Such notices assist in locating suspects and linking incidents to similar past and future crimes. (*Source: Federal Bureau of Investigation.*)

a wife eventually succeeded in killing her husband involved at least five successive murder attempts of uncommon means. The suspect, motivated by a $20,000 life insurance policy, concealed a sac of tarantula venom in a pie intended for the victim, threw an exposed electrical cord into the victim's shower, attempted to inject an air embolism into the victim's vein while he slept, mixed LSD into the victim's toast, and placed bullets in the carburetor of the victim's truck. The suspect finally succeeded in murdering her spouse by assaulting him with a lead weight of six and one-half pounds.[24]

Another example of murder calculated for benefit was the highly publicized killing of Carol Stuart in Boston. Driving home with her from a hospital birthing class (Mrs. Stuart was seven months pregnant), the victim's husband, Charles Stuart, shot his wife to death to collect nearly $300,000 worth of life insurance. Staging an elaborate hoax, the husband also shot himself to convince the police that a violent robbery suspect had killed his wife and wounded him. The killer convincingly diverted suspicion from himself with a detailed and highly credible description of the alleged robber, inflicted himself with a potentially deadly wound, and wrote the eulogy for his wife's funeral. As the investigation gradually began to focus on him, the murderer committed suicide by jumping from a bridge.

Type of Weapon Used

Firearms again predominate as the weapon most often used in homicide. Nearly 53 percent of murders are committed with the handgun; 8 percent are committed with rifles or shotguns. Of the murders not committed by guns (normally about 30 percent), knives are the most common weapons. The remaining criminal homicides mostly involve blunt objects, poisons, fire, or direct violence applied by hands, fists, or feet. It is significant and pathetic that nearly 5 percent of the victims murdered through direct violence are infants and children from birth to 14 years of age.

Other Causative Factors

Possibly one of the most controversial issues relating to causative factors is the availability of handguns. It cannot be denied that the vast majority of murders are committed with firearms—typically near 70 percent. The debatable factor is whether the murders would take place regardless of the availability of the firearm. The law enforcement community reflects society at large in that opinion is split on the issue of gun control. Many top-ranking police administrators, including many U.S. attorneys general, have strongly supported some method of handgun registration or the outright ban of handguns. One former attorney general favored the banning of handguns in cities of 50,000 or more that have either a 20 percent higher crime rate than the national average or a crime rate 10 percent in excess of the national average with a 5 percent increase in murder over the previous year. Some officials support municipal or state-supervised handgun registration programs. Yet, it is estimated that at least 100,000 firearms are stolen each year from private owners alone. It is doubtful whether registration programs will affect this type of burglary, for stolen firearms are particularly attractive to criminals because of the difficulty in linking the gun to the felon.

There are more than 210 million firearms in the United States, of which 66 million are handguns. Of this number, the Bureau of Alcohol, Tobacco, Firearms, and Explosives estimates that fewer than one million are in the hands of the police. Added to the current number of handguns, more than 2.5 million new handguns will be sold through licensed firearm dealers. Although the majority of victims are killed with handguns, a significant number are also wounded. In light of the fact that handguns are involved in approximately 630,000 crimes each year, the relationship of the firearm to crime is immediately apparent and an issue that continues to be more closely examined.

AGGRAVATED ASSAULT

Aggravated assault is defined as the unlawful attempt or completed attack upon another with the purpose of inflicting severe bodily injury, usually accompanied by the use of a weapon or some other means likely to produce death or serious bodily harm. Aggravated assaults do not result in the murder of the victim. If the victim dies as a result of such an attack, the offender is charged with murder, manslaughter, or another appropriate felony. Aggravated assaults often fall short of death through medical intervention or the lack of a deadly weapon.

Contact is not necessary for the completion of an aggravated assault. A suspect may not be successful in inflicting injury with a weapon, yet if successful completion of the crime would have resulted in serious personal injury to the victim, the elements of the offense are satisfied. There is a wide difference between an assault and aggravated assault. Assault does not require contact between offender and victim, nor does it require that the offender premeditate the probability of a serious attack. An individual commonly commits an assault when he engages in conduct that places another in reasonable apprehension of receiving a battery. Consequently, an assault may be complete when the assailant advances on a victim in a menacing manner. If a reasonable person would conclude that the assailant is about to engage in a battery, the elements of an assault are present. The statutory definitions of aggravated assault differ from one state to another. Despite various state variances, all assaults committed with a deadly weapon will be classified as aggravated for the purpose of this discussion.

Current State of Aggravated Assault

There are more than 860,000 aggravated assaults in the United States each year. This crime accounts for approximately 64 percent of the crimes of violence. Metropolitan areas have the highest rate; rural areas, the lowest. Aggravated assault, like murder, peaks in frequency during the summer months. Frequency is lowest during January and February.

This crime continues to decline, the current rate of aggravated assault being nearly 23 percent lower than the 1994 figure. Police agencies are typically successful in solving approximately 56 percent of the reported cases of aggravated assault by arrest.[25] This relatively high solution rate is consistent with the better-than-average rate of solution associated with crimes against the person. Because of the nature of aggravated assault, arrests are typically made by patrol officers rather than detective personnel. Patrol officers often happen upon the assault in progress or are dispatched to the scene.

Victims. The victims of aggravated assault tend to parallel murder victims in terms of identifiable characteristics. The statistically average victim is a young adult white male. Often he will know his assailant, as aggravated assaults frequently result from arguments between family members. A significant proportion, however, occur between individuals who are not related. Studies indicate that the consumption of alcohol is a prevalent factor in crimes of this nature, on the part of both victims and assailants.

Offender Characteristics

The statistically average aggravated assault offender is a white male, 21 years of age. Those 21 years of age and older account for a majority of the arrests; those under 21 account for approximately 26 percent. Arrests of males outnumber female arrests by seven to one. Studies indicate that aggravated assault offenders tend to be individuals who resolve conflicts by explosive physical means. Although many such individuals have no history of prior arrest or police contact, a large number have backgrounds involving misdemeanor and felony violations. Parental and environmental influences appear to be very important as causative factors in this offense. Studies indicate that a high percentage of such crimes go unreported in many inner-city areas. It is not uncommon for disadvantaged communities to resolve conflicts by unofficial means.

Motives for aggravated assaults vary considerably. The Task Force on Individual Acts of Violence of the National Commission on the Causes and Prevention of Violence reported the most frequent motivation to be an altercation, that is, a dispute or argument between two or more individuals. This type of situation prevailed in over 30 percent of the aggravated assaults, whereas 8 percent were committed during escapes to avoid arrest.[26] All other offenses were committed during the course of other crimes or classified in the "unknown" category. Other studies have indicated that if the offender and victim are related, the assault will generally occur within a residence.

Type of Weapon Used

The majority of aggravated assaults are committed with blunt instruments like a club. Personal weapons such as hands, fists, and feet were used in 28 percent of the crimes, firearms in 18 percent, and knives in the remainder.[27]

Because of the similarity between aggravated assault and criminal homicide, similar investigative procedures are generally used for both offenses.

Homicide Investigation Procedures

Criminal investigation of homicide is a discovery process. The officer seeks to discover and document such facts as type of death, identity of the deceased, cause of death, and motivation and identity of the offender. To resolve these fundamental questions, the investigation focuses on the deceased, the crime scene, and medical expertise.

The Deceased

The *deceased* is often of prime importance as an investigative factor. The victim's body can reveal much through examination of wounds and other types of tracing clues that may be present. The victim's occupation, background, or associates may also indicate areas of inquiry to be pursued by the investigator. Deceased victims are frequently encountered by police officers in every jurisdiction, regardless of the size of the community. As previously mentioned, the majority of deaths are the result of natural causes. A substantial number result from accidents or suicides, with the smallest number classified as homicides.

Establishing Death. The first essential step of the homicide investigation is to establish that the victim is, indeed, dead. It is important to note that police officers do not have the legal authority to pronounce death. Only individuals authorized by law, such as physicians and coroners, can establish the fact of death. For this reason, the officer should never assume death unless the condition of the victim's body demonstrates death in a totally obvious manner. When the vital functions of the body irrevocably cease to perform, a legal state of death is present. The vital functions are generally recognized as respiratory activity, heart function, and activity of the central nervous system.

An initial procedure in establishing death is to rule out the possibility of **simulated death**. Certain conditions such as electric shock, alcoholic poisoning, and barbiturate poisoning can cause physiological reactions that closely resemble death. Prolonged immersion has occasionally been found to simulate death, with the unfortunate result of the victim's actual death because of lack of first-aid attention. In the 8,000 drowning incidents each year, a small but significant number of victims only simulate death; they are likely fatalities unless prolonged immersion is recognized. In New York alone, there have been nine documented cases of prolonged immersion in cold water from up to 38 minutes in which the victim survived.[28] Consequently, so-called obvious signs of death can be misleading. Even if lack of breathing is noted or the absence of a heartbeat, the officer should not assume death. Cardiopulmonary resuscitation should be initiated unless rigor mortis or an equally unequivocal sign is present.

Identifying the Deceased. Identifying the victim may be easily accomplished or very difficult. The majority of criminal homicides are investigated shortly after the death. The body will be intact, and identifying data will often be at hand. Since, in the average homicide, acquaintances, witnesses, or the offender are generally present, they can provide victim identification. Victims who cannot readily be identified are often associated with stranger-to-stranger homicides. Significant numbers of deceased individuals cannot be easily identified by authorities. Such victims lack immediate identifying papers and are often from other unknown geographical locations. Many of them have previously been reported missing to authorities. Nearly 100,000 Americans are the subject of active missing person reports throughout the country, of which 40 percent are adults and 60 percent are juveniles. This problem is more acute in large cities such as New York City, where approximately 3,000 residents die unidentified through accident, suicide, and criminal homicide each year.[29] Decomposition of the body may also preclude immediate identification.

Establishing the identity of the victim is important in that basic tracing clues as to the motive and identity of the perpetrator may be provided. With the identity known, the investigator can focus attention on the victim's background and establish a possible motive through such information. Victims encountered in indoor crime scenes normally have identifying data on the body, or such data will be available throughout the scene. Personal papers, clothing tags and dry cleaner marks that may be traced, and other types of evidence, may be found. In outdoor scenes, such evidence is normally not as readily available since the victim is removed from the personal environment. Also, the outdoor scene may not be discovered for long periods of time; thus, evidence may be destroyed by elements of nature or be carried away by animals.

If there are no identifying papers on the victim's person, as is often the situation in robbery-homicide, fingerprints should be used as a means of identification. A complete set of fingerprints should be taken and immediately forwarded to the FBI identification division. Although a substantial proportion of the population has been fingerprinted, with the prints on file in Washington, D.C., a larger proportion has not. Thus, not all fingerprint searches are successful in identifying the deceased. An additional problem may be encountered when fingertip tissue has decomposed. In this situation, it is advisable that an expert fingerprint technician attempt the printing. If no experts are available at the scene, the fingers or hands can be severed and sent to the laboratory for proper processing. When fingerprints are available and on file in official agencies, they provide the most positive means of victim identification.

If fingerprint identification is unsuccessful, the officer must rely on other methods to establish identity. Dental structures are highly resistant to destruction and are frequently useful when the other portions of the body are totally decomposed. Dental comparisons are successful only if (a) the victim's dental work is present and charted and (b) the dentist who accomplished the work is located. Accordingly, personal identification by dental characteristics **(forensic odontology)** begins with an examination and charting of the teeth. Since the investigator is normally not qualified to perform this task, a dentist should diagram or radiograph the evidence. The investigator then attempts to locate the dentist who performed the work or a portion of the dental repair. Unless other personal tracing information has been located on the body, this task may be quite difficult. There is no national central depository where all dental records are located. California, however, implemented the first statewide dental identification program. State law requires all law enforcement agencies and coroners to supply dental records of missing persons and unidentified deceased persons to the California Department of Justice. The file contains thousands of records and, during a recent year, helped authorities successfully identify 29 deceased persons. Of the identified cases, 25 were victims of criminal homicide.[30] In cases where dental X rays have been taken and identified but no dental repair work has been performed (not uncommon with children), odontologists may be successful in making an identification through examination of the sinus cavity. Unique structural aspects of the sinus cavity, involving bone appearance that is visual in the background of dental X rays, can be successfully matched to after-death X rays taken of the victim's sinus area.

The skeletal remains of the victim may also help to determine identity as well as yield other types of information. If bone fractures are noted, they may be used to identify the deceased, but only if corresponding medical records can be located. The width of the pelvic bones are excellent indicators of the victim's sex; the skull and bones of the nosebridge may indicate race. Determination of the victim's age may be more difficult in that victims past the age of 18 years have generally achieved their maximum skeletal growth. However, general age determinations can be established via dental structure and expert examination of the bone joints.

Forensic pathologists and dental experts have also developed several techniques to establish identity from a skull. Both of the primary methods, three-dimensional clay bust and photographic superimposition, are dependent upon tissue depth research developed by the Federal Aviation Administration. It has been established that different thicknesses of facial tissue occur at known points throughout the human skull. Accordingly, forensic experts using the three-dimensional method systematically add clay to the skull, re-creating a realistic facial image. The facial restoration can then be photographed and publicized for identification. The photographic superimposition method is dependent upon scientifically matching the recovered skull to an identified antemortem photograph of the victim. First, soft-tissue outlines noted on the photograph (Figure 11.5A) are matched to corresponding bone structures of the skull (Figure 11.5B). The identified photograph and skull are superimposed to the respective points of interest, resulting in a positive identification (Figure 11.5C).[31]

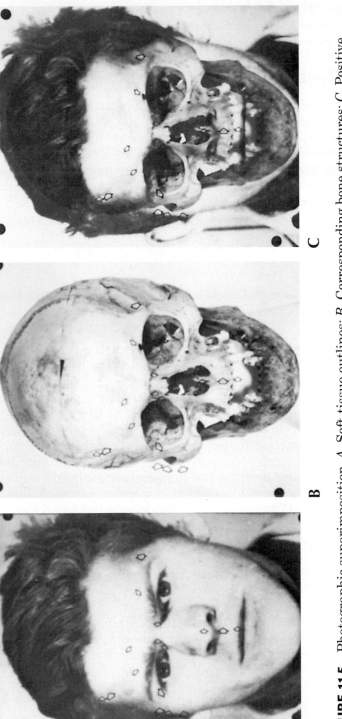

FIGURE 11.5 Photographic superimposition. *A.* Soft-tissue outlines; *B.* Corresponding bone structures; *C.* Positive identification. *(Source: Dr. Robert B.J. Dorion.)*

Finally, DNA samples should always be taken, as all states and the federal government are now maintaining DNA files of those who have been arrested or imprisoned for specific types of offenses.

Time-of-Death Determination

A determination of the time of death should be attempted in all homicide investigations. This fact is significant because of its investigative importance in corroborating or disputing alibis or in establishing the victim's movements prior to death. Determining time of death is not an exact science. No method can precisely establish the time elapsed from the moment of death to the time of examination. However, this period can be approximately calculated, with such estimates occasionally being accurate to within five hours. Five methods of varying accuracy are currently used by physicians to determine time of death:

1. postmortem lividity,
2. rigor mortis,
3. putrefaction,
4. cooling rate, and
5. general body indicators.

Postmortem Lividity.   **Postmortem lividity** is due to the cessation of cardiac activity and the resultant cessation of the body's blood flow. The blood will settle, in response to gravity, to the lowest parts of the body, nearest the ground. Hence, dark blue discolorations appear under the skin in the body's lower surfaces (see Figure 11.6). Lividity typically appears as a deep blue or purplish discoloration but may also have a red appearance, depending on the cause of death. Time estimates based upon lividity are not precise; they can provide the investigator with only a rough approximation. Lividity generally sets in after three hours from the moment of death and will become fixed in ten hours. Many factors can affect the onset and rate of lividity, such as the physical condition of the victim and the amount of blood lost prior to death.

Postmortem lividity determinations are also useful in indicating whether the deceased was moved by another person. For example, if the victim is found lying on his back but lividity is evident on the front part of the body, an unnatural movement of the body has occurred, suggesting a possible act of deception by others.

Rigor Mortis.   Following death, various chemical changes take place in the muscles of the body resulting in **rigor mortis** (also termed rigor). Rigor is a stiffening process, the rate of which is affected by a variety of factors. Generally, rigor will be noticed in the muscles of the face and jaw area within two hours of death. The stiffening process spreads downward through the body to the toes, completing the rigor within 12 hours.

Rigor mortis typically disappears within 36 hours, starting from the head and extending to the lower parts of the body. Determining death from rigor leaves much room for error in that weather and health factors, as well as clothing worn by the victim, all contribute to an acceleration or deceleration of the stiffening process. Hot weather will hasten the onset of rigor; cooler weather has the opposite effect. Rigor should not be confused with the

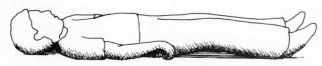

FIGURE 11.6
Postmortem lividity.

physiological reaction of *cadaveric spasm*. The latter is an immediate stiffening of the entire body or of one of the extremities. The exact causes of cadaveric spasm are not fully understood, but it is assumed that severe trauma to the nervous system or intense stress may cause this reaction.

Putrefaction. **Putrefaction** is the decomposition of the body by bacteria, fungi, and oxidation. Following death, tissues, organs, and other bodily elements begin to break down at a general rate. The rate of putrefaction is directly affected by the humidity and the body's access to oxygen. The decomposition process begins soon after death in normal environments and will be apparent within 48 hours of death. The rate of decomposition can be extremely rapid in certain environments. Several cases have been documented in which decomposition to a complete skeleton has taken place within two weeks after death.[32]

Putrefaction is characterized by a general darkening of the skin and accompanying bloating caused by bacterial gases. The onset and rate of putrefaction are not considered to be accurate indicators of time of death.

Cooling Rate. It is known that the normal body temperature is 98.6°F (37°C) and that a deceased body will begin to cool, at a certain rate, to the temperature of its surroundings. Thus, a generalized time of death can be calculated if the temperature of the body when found, the heat-loss rate following death, and the environmental temperature are given. Generally, a body will lose 3°F for the first four hours after death and 1°F each hour thereafter, until the body temperature approximates the environmental temperature of the surroundings.

The rate of cooling is affected by many internal and external variables. Individuals who have considerable body fat or who are heavily clothed retain body heat and cool at a slower rate.

The general appearance of death can be noted in the muscles and eyes of the victim. The muscles will be very relaxed (unless rigor has set in), and there will be a loss of flushing in the fingernails. If the nail is pinched, a change of color because of blood flow will be absent. The eyeball will lack the characteristic tension and will be flaccid to the touch. (The various signs of death are charted in Figure 11.7.)

Causes of Death

All deaths can be classified as to cause: *natural, accidental, suicidal,* or *homicidal*. Although the majority of deaths in the nation are the result of natural causes, a substantial number fall into the other three categories. The criminal investigator can normally classify a death as a homicide without difficulty; homicidal death scenes are generally in a state of disarray, rarely resembling suicidal or accidental death scenes. Furthermore, in only a relatively small number of premeditated murders will the killer attempt a deception as to cause of death. The determination of whether a death is the result of an accident or a suicide may be more difficult, depending on the evidence recovered at the scene.

Determining the precise cause of death is important for many reasons. Knowledge of the means by which death was caused can help the officer to establish the identity of the perpetrator. For example, if it is determined that death was caused by a specific type of strangulation, the investigation can focus on offenders known to have caused past deaths in that manner. Obviously, if the type of weapon that caused death is known, officers search for that specific type during the execution of search warrants. Further, the

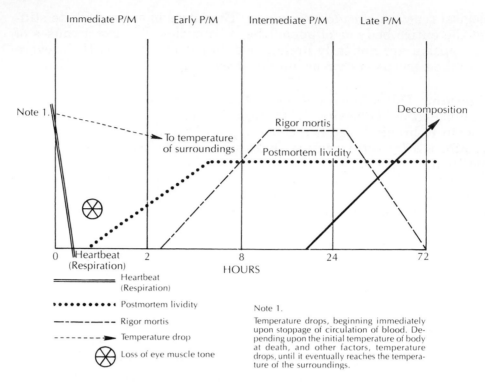

FIGURE 11.7   Positive signs of death—initiation, duration, termination.

cause of death has legal ramifications, affecting payment of insurance or outcome of wills.

Gunshot Wounds.   The majority of criminal homicides within the United States are committed with firearms. Consequently, the investigator will encounter gunshot wounds quite often in death investigation. A substantial number of accidental deaths and suicides also involve guns. Gunshot wounds are carefully examined to answer the following questions:

1. Was the wound inflicted before death?
2. Did the death result from the wound?
3. Can the wound indicate the type of firearm used?
4. How far was the victim from the firearm at time of discharge?

Three general types of firearms are common to death investigations: the *rifle, shotgun*, and *handgun;* each will inflict a characteristic wound. Criminal homicides involving rifles are the least frequent; handguns account for the greatest number of offenses. Rifles and shotguns are more common to accidents and suicides than to criminal homicides.

All gunshot wounds result from the entry of a projectile into the body and the frequent presence of undispersed explosive gases. After entering the body, bullets either shatter and fragment, ricochet off bone, shift to locations away from the entry path, or exit. The relative size and appearance of the wound will be affected by the distance from which the weapon was discharged. Generally, the closer the discharge to the skin, the greater the damage. When a firearm muzzle is flush with the skin surface or very close to the skin surface, the resultant tissue damage will be considerable. This damage is primarily due to explosive gases that precede the projectile at close range. Such wounds are typically larger than the projectile and contain traces of gunpowder (see Figure 11.8). When the muzzle of a firearm is flush

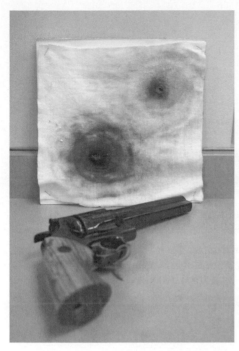

FIGURE 11.8 Gunshot powder residue tests can assist investigators in reconstructing the distance and position of victims to suspects. Additionally, the reliability of self-defense claims can be tested by such examinations. *(Source: Mikael Karlsson/Arresting Images.)*

with the skin surface or within two feet of the skin, the following wound characteristics are noted:

1. A burning or scorching of hairs and skin tissue. Scorching occurs as a result of the discharge flame; it is seldom observed in discharges farther away than four inches.

2. A darkening or blackening of the skin or a grayish ring surrounding the wound. The blackening of the skin is caused by the gunpowder explosion. The gray ring results from fouled materials removed from the sides of the projectile by the skin. Blackening of the skin is seldom observed in discharges farther than seven inches from the skin.

3. A crescent-shaped wound. The so-called *star wound pattern* generally results from contact shots. If the muzzle is flush against the skin, a tearing of the skin will result from the explosive gases. Star wounds are particularly common to the skull or skin directly over bones.

4. A muzzle imprint of the firearm. This imprint will not always be present; however, it will occasionally be noted in contact discharges. The imprint is dependent upon the force with which the muzzle is held against the skin surface at the time of discharge.

5. The presence of numerous small unburnt powder grains. Small particles of powder will be buried into the skin surface, producing what is known as a *tattoo* (see Figure 11.9).

Distant bullet wounds result from discharges that are generally greater than three to four feet from muzzle to skin. The actual distance from which the shot was fired is very difficult to judge from the appearance of "far" bullet wounds since many of the characteristics of near discharge are absent. Only the gray grime ring will be present in typical situations. Distance wounds are smaller than the entering projectile because of the absence of explosive gases.

In some investigations involving firearms, a determination of whether the death was a homicide, suicide, or accident is difficult. In making such

FIGURE 11.9 Powder pattern test on a plaster death mask. This test was conducted in a murder case involving a victim shot in the face at close range to determine, by the pattern of the powder, the distance of the gun from the face at the time of discharge. *(Source: Joseph Orantes, San Diego Police Department.)*

a determination, the distance of the discharge is of great significance. The vast majority of suicidal and accidental gunshot cases involve arm's-length discharges. Accordingly, if the wound indicates discharge beyond the victim's arm length, homicide is indicated. There are, however, a small number of unusual suicides and accidental deaths that involve bizarre circumstances. For example, there have been individuals who committed suicide by shooting themselves with a firearm that was placed across the room in a container designed to hold the weapon. A string, wire, or other triggering device attached to the firearm would allow for discharge of the weapon some 20 to 30 feet from the victim's body. Such unusual suicides are normally made obvious by the devices found in the crime scene.

The location of the wound may also serve to rule out suicide. If the wound is located in an area of the body that is relatively inaccessible to the victim, homicide is indicated. It is also unusual for a suicide wound to be inflicted in an area other than the head or chest; however, there have been a number of suicide cases involving wounds in extremities. Similarly, multiple gun wounds typically suggest homicide. However, such conclusions are far from absolute: several studies indicate that multishot suicides will occur in 1 of 61 gunshot suicides.[33] The presence or absence of a "suicide note" is a poor indicator of suicide or homicide. Since, in a large number of suicide cases, such notes are lacking, their absence in no way rules suicide out. In some cases of criminal homicide, notes have been left to confuse the investigator. The killer may force the victim to write a note prior to death, or a note may have been written in a past suicide attempt.

Recently, homicide investigators have noted certain changes in patterns of illegal killings. Various studies confirm that deaths are occurring more frequently at shooting scenes as a result of higher gun calibers. Victims are currently more likely to be shot by high-caliber handguns than even five years ago, possibly as a result of the increase in gang and drug homicides. Additionally, victims are far more likely to sustain a greater number of gunshot wounds, a factor that may be linked to the increase of semiautomatic weapons, which generally have the capacity to fire a greater number of rounds more rapidly than revolvers.[34]

Edged Weapons.   Deaths resulting from incised wounds are common to the criminal investigator. Although homicides by stabbing are second to deaths by firearms, the frequency of nonlethal stabbings in urban areas typically exceeds gunshot wounds. The U.S. Centers for Disease Control and Prevention documented that victims are twice as likely to have been stabbed as shot and that city residents are five times as likely to require treatment for stabbing as are rural residents.[35] Many aggravated assaults and criminal homicides involve edged wounds, as do a significant number of suicides. Accidental deaths resulting from such weapons are relatively uncommon. The Cuyahoga County, Ohio, Coroner's Office documented the scarcity of the accidental stabbing. Of 15,063 autopsied cases occurring during a ten-year period, only nine were found to be accidental stabbings.[36] Typically, a stabbing or cutting death is caused by the internal bleeding of an artery or the piercing of a vital organ. There will often be considerable blood at the crime scene involving death by an edged weapon; yet, in some scenes, a comparatively small amount of blood is encountered. The quantity of blood is often dependent on the time factor associated with the death. If a vital organ is perforated and death is immediate, there will be very little bleeding. While the term "stab wound" is used to commonly define any type of edged-weapon injury, there are distinct differences between stab and incised wounds. A stab wound occurs when the cut is deeper than its length, while an incised wound's length is greater than its depth.

As with gunshot fatalities, the stabbing fatality may be difficult to classify as to the nature of the death. Although accidental death by stabbing is quite rare, suicide is not uncommon. Males typically commit suicide by cutting the throat area or, to a lesser degree, the chest area. Females generally select the wrists or arteries in the leg. When edged weapons are used in suicide, the presence of **hesitation marks** will often be noted. These are shallow wounds inflicted near the fatal wound to test the weapon before the actual suicide attempt. Sometimes the individual will "back out" after a superficial cut has been inflicted but inflict another superficial cut shortly thereafter. Accordingly, numerous hesitation marks may be encountered near the fatal wound. The presence of hesitation marks is strongly indicative of suicide; however, the total absence of such wounds does not imply that a suicide has not occurred. In many instances, suicide victims succeed in inflicting a fatal wound without weapon testing or the slightest hesitation.

In a further effort to distinguish between a homicide and a suicide, the hands and forearms of the deceased should be particularly scrutinized for small wounds known as **defense wounds**. These are injuries suffered as a victim attempts to ward off an assailant's blows. Wounds of a defensive nature may be located on other parts of the body, such as the back or neck. Such wounds are generally indicators of homicide, but they can be mistaken for hesitation marks. The final judgment as to whether such injuries are hesitation or defense wounds is reached by considering the difficulty of self-infliction and the overall appearance of the scene.

Asphyxia.   Deaths resulting from **asphyxia** are due to a sudden or gradual cessation of oxygen intake. When the oxygen supply is cut off, the respiratory action of the lungs and the blood flow to the brain are impaired or stopped, with the result being death. Asphyxia may occur as the result of conditions caused by an illness, such as pneumonia; it may be self-inflicted; or it may be the result of a criminal homicide. The characteristic appearance of asphyxia victims will be noted in the face. The eyes may show considerable hemorrhaging, the lips will often be bluish, and the neck may show imprints indicating a specific asphyxiation technique.

Asphyxia may be the result of strangulation—either manual or by hanging or ligature. *Hanging strangulation* results from a compression of the air passages or from an interruption of the blood supply to the brain. A common form of suicide, hangings are rarely encountered in accidental deaths or criminal homicides. It is significant to note that the body need not be suspended above the floor to accomplish hanging strangulation. Many hanging suicides involve individuals dying in a sitting or even a prone position. A seldom encountered but significant type of hanging is the accidental autoerotic death. The term *autoerotic* refers to sexual gratification that is obtained without the need or assistance of another person. The investigator may encounter a scene that appears to be a suicidal hanging but is really an accidental hanging resulting from a sexual deviance. Some individuals derive sexual gratification by placing ropes, chains, or other constricting objects around the neck. The sexual gratification is achieved by the constrictive sensation of the rope, which is normally followed by a release of the rope's pressure. However, if the individual slips or falls (from a chair, perhaps) and is rendered unconscious, death will result shortly thereafter. Autoerotic victims often bind themselves or wear clothing of the opposite sex.

Manual strangulation is highly indicative of criminal homicide; imprints from the strangler's fingertips will show on the victim's neck. Death is caused by the pressure of the hands, or the use of the forearm to block the airway and/or compress the arteries in the neck. The popularity of the martial arts has increased the number of accidental deaths by manual strangulation.

Ligature strangulation involves an object, such as a cord, belt, or wire, tightly twisted around the neck. Death is achieved by compression of the airway or blood supply; it is not dependent upon body weight, as in hanging. Ligature marks will be low and transverse and indicate equal pressure; bruises caused by manual strangulation will appear to be spotty and less even than ligature marks.

Asphyxia may also occur as a result of submersion in water. When a victim inhales water into the air passages, a violent choking begins, resulting in the formation of a wall of mucus that blocks the windpipe. Accordingly, the frequent cause of death in drowning is asphyxia. Suicides and homicidal deaths in such situations are rare; the great majority of drownings are accidental.

Smothering, gagging, or the ingestion of certain drugs may also cause death by asphyxia. When the external openings of the body's air passages are blocked by any object, death will result if the blockage is of sufficient duration. Four to five minutes is usually considered the upper limit of time that the brain can function without oxygen. Obstruction of the passages for any greater length of time will initially result in brain damage and eventually death. Smothering in criminal homicides is not common but will be encountered occasionally. This type of murder may follow a rape, for many sex crimes take place in the bedroom where common smothering objects, such as pillows, are located. The incidence of criminal homicide by use of a gag is increasing. Many robbers habitually tie and gag their victims. If the gag is placed directly into the mouth, the tongue may be forced into a blocking position across the airway. Asphyxia resulting from drug ingestion is very common in suicide and will be encountered in accidental deaths to a lesser degree. The drug (usually a barbituate compound) acts on the respiratory center in the central nervous system, so that respiration ceases or becomes so shallow as to cause death.

Blunt Instruments.   Deaths resulting from wounds inflicted by blunt objects are numerous, for such objects may include anything that can be picked up and forcibly brought into contact with the victim. Determining the specific cause of death in such cases is difficult from visual examination alone. Although external injuries may be apparent, the true cause of death may be an internal injury that is not readily visible. The majority of deaths caused by blunt-force injuries involve the head region being struck with considerable force. Typically, a clublike weapon is used, or the victim may be repeatedly kicked in the head region. A blow of sufficient force delivered to the head will cause a fracture of the skull, which, in turn, may injure the brain, causing death. The death may be instantaneous, or it may occur after a period of unconsciousness.

Blunt-force injuries can typically be classified as abrasions, contusions, and lacerations. *Abrasions* are rarely fatal wounds; they are injuries to the outer layer of the skin. Abrasions often result from the victim's body sliding across a surface. Such wounds will be noted frequently in auto hit-and-run cases and in instances in which the victim was delivered a blow and attempted to break the fall by extending the arms and hands.

Contusions are often fatal wounds that result from blows that are forceful enough to rupture blood vessels. Following the blow, an area of bruising forms, which is initially a red/purple discoloration. As time passes, the color will change to green, followed by an off-yellow, and will gradually dissipate. **Lacerations** are ragged tears of the tissue caused by very forceful blunt-instrument blows. The motion of the weapon will be a chopping or shearing, causing considerable tearing of the skin.

Deaths involving blunt instruments are normally homicides or accidents; rarely are they suicides. Accidental deaths that involve machinery or automobiles are often included in this category. The typical blunt-instrument homicide is a "heat of passion" assault. Following an intense argument, the assailant grabs the nearest blunt object available to attack the victim. Accordingly, criminal homicides resulting from blunt-force injuries are rarely premeditated.

The Crime Scene

Although much information can be determined from the body of the deceased, the homicide investigation must also focus intensely on the entire crime scene. A thorough examination of the deceased can usually provide information regarding the nature of the injury, cause of death, and type of weapon used. Yet the crime scene has the potential of revealing other data that may prove very valuable in tracing the perpetrator of the crime. Generally, the most crucial period in death investigation is the initial processing of the scene. Once the scene is processed and police inquiry ceases, the investigative value of the locality is forever lost. Quite naturally, the property owner will make every effort to clean the scene of all traces of violence. Consequently, the investigator must realize that this phase of the homicide investigation is vital. No other felony inquiry is more important, both officially and from an emotional standpoint, than the homicide case. Death is, of course, final and irreversible, demanding the utmost investigative skill from the officer.

Homicide crime scenes are often visually shocking to the inexperienced officer. But even when confronted with the body of the deceased, large quantities of blood, and distasteful wounds, the officer must not forget proper action. Before entering the scene, the officer should stop and survey the area and note the localities of important evidence. Upon entering the scene, the officer must make every effort to avoid contamination of the evidence. Instead of focusing on the deceased and walking toward the body, the investigator should look down and note the path, taking care to avoid stepping through blood or any other evidence. The homicide scene is often in a state of disarray. Tables, chairs, and other furniture may be turned over and otherwise disrupted. The scene should be left exactly as found and recorded, for displaced furniture may facilitate reconstruction of the actions of the criminal and victim.

Since the majority of homicides are not premeditated, the probability of the offender leaving such evidence as latent fingerprints is strong. The investigator's own prints can be avoided by means of gloves or keeping the hands in pockets during the initial inspection. Notations should be made concerning any item in the scene that may shed light on who did what to whom and why. In an effort to determine the time of death, the investigator should observe and record the presence or absence of lights, the condition of ice in drinks, and the relative warmth of radios and televisions. The scene should be thoroughly photographed, with the deceased recorded in detail. Photographs of blood patterns may be significant and should additionally be recorded. The scene should be sketched and the positions of evidence and the deceased carefully measured. An exhaustive search of the scene should be conducted so that evidence can be located and collected. Because of the frequency of firearm-related homicides, care must be taken to locate shell casings that may have rolled out of sight, perhaps under a piece of furniture. It is common for panicked offenders to run from a scene still holding the weapon, which will often be a gun or knife. During the flight, the offender will realize the incriminating value of the weapon and promptly dispose of it. For this reason, investigators should search for evidence outside the immediate scene, for example, in garbage cans, under bushes or parked cars, or on rooftops. These are all likely places to encounter the discarded weapon.

Following a thorough processing of the immediate and external crime scene, officers should begin a neighborhood check. An extensive neighborhood canvass is always justified in a homicide investigation. The type of neighborhood check will depend on the type of death investigation being conducted. If the victim is located in the same room or structure in which the assault took place, the neighborhood canvass will be confined to that immediate area. However, if the victim is located in a place other than the site of the assault, the check will be much wider in range. All individuals within the specified canvass area must be contacted and questioned regarding the habits and associates of the victim.

In the minority of homicide cases, the offender's identity is not immediately known. It may be determined through tracing evidence found at the scene. If this method is not successful, the inquiry will focus on the traditional investigative areas of motive and benefit. Motive and benefit are often determined by a background investigation of the victim.

Thorough processing of homicide crime scenes may often produce evidence indicating the expanding multidimensional aspects of this offense. A significant number of murders are linked to gang-related disputes, drug dealing, and outright robberies. For example, 11 percent of all homicides in Chicago and 34 percent in Los Angeles are directly related to gang disputes.[37] Accordingly, the scene must be searched for evidence linking the killing to these common causative factors if the resulting investigation is to be properly focused. Homicide investigators must also be familiar with the latest intelligence information, current suspects, and other pertinent data available from officers assigned to specialized gang, drug, or robbery details. Cooperation and information sharing among investigators assigned to any unit dealing with violent crime are more important than ever in the twenty-first century, as family and acquaintance homicides decrease and murders related to other felonies continue to increase.

Dying Declarations

There is always the possibility that a seriously injured victim will give a dying declaration that may have a tremendous significance in the investigation. A **dying declaration** is a statement given by a victim who has knowledge of his or her impending death. For the declaration to be valid, the victim must comprehend that death is imminent, and hope of recovery must not be possible. However, death does not have to immediately follow the declaration for it to be valid.

Information gathered through the dying declaration has important judicial significance, for the court considers statements by a dying person to be truthful. The assumption is that individuals will make only truthful statements if those persons are aware that they are about to die. Dying declarations should be taken after a victim is informed of the impending fatal state by a doctor. Typically, the investigator will ask the victim to state the perpetrator's identity. However, a nod of the head by the victim in affirmation of a name posed by the officer has been accepted as a valid declaration.

It is important in establishing the validity of the dying declaration that the investigator can later testify as to the victim's belief that death was imminent. The victim must demonstrate comprehension of such information either by word or by gesture. Thus, after the victim has been informed that death is imminent, the question should be asked, "Do you understand and believe what has just been told to you?" Dying declarations should always be witnessed by the attending doctor or another investigator. Dying declarations are permitted as evidence only in homicide cases. In effect, the court makes an exception to the hearsay rule, which generally prohibits second-hand testimony, that is, information that one person has heard from another. Thus, the investigator is allowed to testify in regard to what the deceased said. Should the victim not die, the investigator would not be permitted to testify, as the victim would be expected to personally provide the court with firsthand knowledge.

Medical Expertise

No other type of investigation depends on the medical sciences more than the death inquiry. Although medical expertise is important in other areas, such as rape cases, the physiological circumstances surrounding death demand knowledge and training unique to the physician. A physician who specializes in this area of medicine is known as a **forensic pathologist**. A pathologist is a licensed doctor who has received additional years of specialized training in the study of abnormal changes in tissues or functions of the body. An expert in autopsy procedures, a pathologist is fully qualified to determine cause of death. There are fewer than 400 full-time forensic pathologists in the United States.[38] Unlike hospital pathologists who perform autopsies to study the effects of disease, forensic pathologists perform medical–legal autopsies to determine cause, manner, and reconstructive aspects of a death.

There are two systems available to the investigator to legally determine the nature and cause of death. The *coroner system* is the most common system; the *medical examiner system* is the more recent. The coroner system originated in England during the twelfth century and is still used extensively in the United States. The **coroner** is normally an elected official who often lacks a medical background. Although the office of the coroner does not infringe upon or limit the police investigation of deaths, coroners have considerable influence that is brought to bear on the eventual determination of the case. Each state, with minor variations, specifies the coroner's duties in a manner similar to the following:

> Every coroner, whenever, as soon as he knows or is informed that the dead body of any person is found, or lying within his county, whose death is suspected of being:
>
> (a) A sudden or violent death, whether apparently suicidal, homicidal or accidental, including but not limited to deaths apparently caused or contributed to by thermal, traumatic, chemical, electrical or radiational injury, or a complication of any of them, or by drowning or suffocation;
>
> (b) A maternal or fetal death due to abortion, or any death due to a sex crime or a crime against nature;
>
> (c) A death where the circumstances are suspicious, obscure or mysterious or where, in the written opinion of the attending physician, the cause of death is not determined;
>
> (d) A death where addiction to alcohol or to any drug may have been a contributory cause; or
>
> (e) A death where the decedent was not attended by a licensed physician;
>
> shall go to the place where the dead body is, and take charge of the same and shall make a preliminary investigation into the circumstances of the death. In the case of death without attendance by a licensed physician the body may be moved with the coroner's consent from the place of death to a mortuary in the same county. . . . In cases of apparent suicide or homicide or of accidental death, the coroner shall, and in other cases in his discretion he may, summon a jury of six persons of lawful age residing in the vicinity where the death occurred, and conduct an inquest into the cause of death.[39]

The coroner generally has considerable discretion regarding the initiation of an autopsy. Further, the coroner must determine through his judgment if a death is an "apparent suicide or homicide."

The medical examiner system was originated in Massachusetts in 1877. This system has replaced the antiquated coroner system in many areas and is generally operative in large metropolitan areas. **Medical examiners** are forensic pathologists who perform the duties traditionally entrusted to the coroner. Because the pathologist is a physician specially trained in death investigation, it is assumed that the death inquiry will be more accurate. The first widely publicized use of medical pathology occurred in 1888, when Scotland Yard detectives requested hospital pathologists to autopsy several murder victims during the infamous Jack the Ripper investigation.

Autopsy. An **autopsy** is a postmortem (after-death) examination of the victim. The use of the autopsy as a discovery process is not a recent occurrence, as history records the Roman physician Antistius examining the body of Julius Caesar shortly after his assassination. Antistius officially reported to the assembled Roman senators that Caesar had received 23 stab wounds, of which one was fatal.[40] Autopsies are mandated by law in certain types of deaths and subject to the coroner's or medical examiner's discretion in other death circumstances. The autopsy should be conducted as soon as the body is discovered. The examination basically involves (a) an exterior visual examination and (b) an interior surgical examination. The pathologist initially notes general observations of the body, such as sex, race, height, and weight. A thorough inspection of the surface of the body follows, with all injuries noted and fully described. Generally, observations are dictated, to be transcribed at a later date. Following the external examination, the pathologist probes the interior areas of the body. During the internal inspection, all vital organs are observed and described. The pathologist of course notes internal injuries. Depending on the pathologist's judgment, samples of tissue, vital organs, bone, and other physiological matter may be obtained for laboratory testing. The investigating officer should be present to note the findings.

The significance of the autopsy can be illustrated by a recent death investigation in upstate New York. Following a mobile home fire, investigators brought the remains of what they believed to be a woman and her infant baby to the community morgue. The examining physician decided not to autopsy the bodies and issued two official death certificates stating that the deaths had resulted from the fire. The inaccuracy of one of the certificates was evident when, several weeks later, the actual body of the infant was discovered within the destroyed mobile home. The unautopsied remains that the doctor had assumed by visual examination to be the infant were determined to be those of the family's pet rabbit.[41]

Exhumation. In a small number of death investigations, a legal **exhumation** may be deemed necessary. Exhumation is the disinterment of a body for examination. The body is then examined to clarify any suspicions surrounding the death. The need for this procedure is rare, for the autopsy normally provides the information necessary to establish the presence or absence of foul play. However, certain deaths may have the appearance of natural causation, but information following burial may justify a legal autopsy.

The decision to exhume the body is not dependent on the judgment of the police or coroner. A judicial official must issue a court order (generally to the sheriff) with the conviction that sufficient cause exists to indicate that the death was the consequence of a criminal action. Because of the insidious nature of homicidal poisonings, a majority of exhumations are performed to establish the presence of toxic materials. The recent exhumation of President Zachary Taylor's body 141 years after his death well illustrates this possibility. A historical writer persuaded the descendants of the former president to allow the exhumation in order to prove that Taylor's death was not natural but a case of assassination by arsenic poisoning. Forensic anthropologists analyzed the remains of the twelfth president for arsenic traces, including hair, bone scrapings, and fingernails. The tests demonstrated that Taylor had not died from arsenic poisoning, thus dispelling the assassination theory.[42]

The results of postinterment autopsies vary according to the time elapsed from interment to exhumation. Although embalming methods do retard the putrefaction process, a body will still undergo decomposition. The adoption of the medical examiner system in all jurisdictions would no doubt reduce the number of exhumations that are deemed necessary.

Forensic Anthropology

Forensic anthropologists are very valuable to certain types of homicide investigations, as they assist medical and police specialists in the identification of human remains. Most have advanced degrees in anthropology and have specialized in assisting criminal cases. A forensic anthropologist's skills are particularly suited to providing information when decomposed human remains are located. Among other determinations, this expert often can

1. distinguish between human and nonhuman remains;
2. determine age, race, sex, and stature at time of death;
3. estimate elapsed time since death;

4. determine the presence and nature of trauma inflicted upon the victim; and,

5. establish positive identification based on skeletal and dental remains.[43]

In an effort to conduct further research in forensic anthropology, the University of Tennessee Medical Center, Forensic Anthropology Center, operates a unique "body farm," as it has come to be known. Located in the Knoxville area, this site allows for the scientific study of decomposition of the human body in various controlled situations and environments. Donated human remains are carefully observed in various stages of decomposition, weather conditions, and differing sites (such as in auto trunks, ponds, shallow graves, etc.) to further forensic skill in determining time of death and other critical investigative factors. The majority of the approximately 60 forensic anthropologists actively assisting the American criminal justice system have trained at this site under the supervision of its founder, Dr. William Bass.

CRIMINALISTIC APPLICATIONS

Criminal homicide initially served as the major inducement for scientists to extend their efforts to criminal investigations. Because of the relative seriousness of the death inquiry, nineteenth-century scientists were prompted to lend their knowledge and talents toward the solution of homicidal crimes. Modern criminalistics has expanded and added to this knowledge considerably, with new methods of forensic homicide testing being developed each year.

DNA

In all humans, as in the majority of other forms of life, **deoxyribonucleic acid (DNA)** contains the entire genetic blueprint of an individual. No two individuals share the same DNA sequence, except identical twins. DNA is an organic substance found in the chromosomes within the nucleus of a cell. Forensic scientists have devised a technique, often referred to as "genetic fingerprinting," that allows them to pick out specific patterns in the arrangement of DNA. Physically, the DNA molecule consists of two strands of randomly stacked chemicals that intertwine to form a double helix resembling a twisted rope. It is the particular appearance of such bands that provide the comparative image for positive identification. Each individual's DNA is contained in various types of cellular material including blood, semen, skin cells, saliva, hair, root tissue, and other physiological substances. When criminal investigators encounter physical evidence that may contain DNA (bloody clothing, semen on undergarments, pulled hair, etc.), the evidence is processed in an effort to associate the suspect with the victim or with the crime scene.

To match recovered DNA samples with a suspect's genetic material, the crime scene material must be probed and associated with a sample from the suspect. The laboratory probing process, as demonstrated in Figure 11.10, seeks to separate the DNA fragments into recognizable band patterns. The banded patterns reveal the highly individual characteristics of the suspect's genetic code and are then matched to a comparative sample (see Figure 11.11). If the genetic fingerprint matches, one can conclude with highly impressive probability that both samples came from the same subject.

With the use of multiple-band patterns, one can identify an individual to a certainty of one in a trillion.[44]

DNA profiling was first used in genetic research and then for determining paternity cases in the 1970s. As research continued to develop the technique, its application expanded into crime investigation. In 1985, British geneticist Dr. Alec Jeffreys published data demonstrating how individuals could be identified on the basis of their individual DNA. England's Bristol Crown Court became the first in the world to convict on DNA evidence when it sentenced a rapist to prison in 1987.[45] Following the highly publicized use of DNA in identifying an English serial murderer in the same year, the DNA technique became an established forensic procedure throughout the world.

1. Stain is identified as bodily fluid, such as blood, semen, or saliva.

2. DNA is extracted from stain and quantified as to amount obtained from sample.

3. DNA is amplified or copied with fluorescent markers.

4. Amplified DNA is then separated in a capillary.

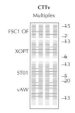

5. Laser is used to strike the fluorescent markers, and emitted light is detected by camera.

6. Image from camera is projected onto a linked computer.

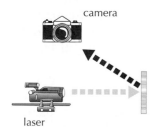

7. A profile is generated demonstrating individualized DNA as diagrammed peaks.

FIGURE 11.10 Laboratory Analysis of DNA. *(Source: Jennifer Johnson, Georgia Bureau of Investigation.)*

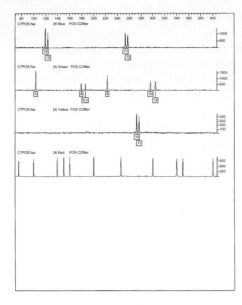

FIGURE 11.11 DNA sample as represented in graph form. Sample is assigned values and will match to common source, such as suspect's blood. *(Source: Jennifer Johnson, Georgia Bureau of Investigation.)*

Forensic DNA profiling has been reviewed extensively by the courts under the varying standards that any newer criminalistic method must pass. Currently all state and federal courts allow properly presented DNA evidence into trial.

Criminal investigators can use the DNA technique in a wide variety of cases, but murder and rape investigations are the most common. Whenever cellular material is left at a crime scene, there is a potential for obtaining DNA samples (see Figure 11.12). Blood is the most commonly tested sample, typically as a liquid or dried stain. Semen is the second most often tested substance, as it is the central evidence in sexual crimes. It is important to note that it is the sperm cell, not seminal fluid, that actually contains DNA. When hair evidence is tested for DNA, only those specimens that have been forcibly removed from a victim will contain the proper amount of cellular material. Hairs that are pulled out generally have the attached root material containing the cells necessary for DNA analysis.[46] The successful extraction of DNA from physical evidence is more dependent on the size and condition of the sample than on its age. Many DNA samples have been obtained from evidence that is more than eight years old; successful testing has been completed on a 2,400-year-old Egyptian mummy.

Evidence that may contain DNA must be collected with great care, as contamination and preservation problems can occur at any time. The investigator and laboratory personnel should always wear disposable gloves, use clean instruments, and avoid touching other objects, including their own body, when handling evidence. Environmental factors, such as heat and humidity, have the potential to accelerate the degradation of DNA. Accordingly, evidence that may contain DNA that is wet or moist should not be packaged in plastic, as a growth environment for bacteria that can destroy DNA often results. To avoid this difficulty, evidence should be thoroughly air dried, packaged in paper, and properly labeled. Handled in this manner, DNA can be stored for years without risk of extensive damage, even at room temperature. Long-term storage often involves keeping the material at a low temperature (4°C) or freezing by expert laboratory personnel.

DNA profiling may well be the most significant breakthrough in forensic science since the development of fingerprinting.[47] The discovery has enabled the resolution of numerous criminal investigations that could never have been successfully concluded otherwise. In addition, DNA has demonstrated

Possible Location of DNA Evidence	*Source of DNA*
Bite marks or area licked	Saliva
Fingernail scrapings	Blood or skin cells
Inside or outside surface of used condom	Semen or skin cells
Blankets, sheets, pillows, or other bed linens	Semen, sweat, hair, or saliva
Clothing, including undergarments worn during *and* after the assault	Hair, semen, blood, or sweat
Hat, bandanna, or mask	Sweat, skin cells, hair, or saliva
Tissue, washcloth, or similar item	Saliva, semen, hair, skin cells, or blood
Cigarette butt; toothpick; or rim of bottle, can, or glass	Saliva
Dental floss	Semen, skin cells, or saliva
Tape or ligature	Skin cells, saliva, or hair
Eyeglasses	Sweat, skin cells

FIGURE 11.12   Identifying DNA Evidence. *(Source: U.S. Department of Justice, National Institute of Justice Commission on the Future of DNA Evidence.)*

the innocence of a significant number of accused suspects. The FBI reports that, overall, 75 percent of the DNA samples it examines can either conclusively link a suspect to a crime or exclude the suspect. Of these successful examinations, nearly one-third of the tests exclude the suspect under suspicion as the source of the evidence collected from the crime scene.[48]

Since 1987, when DNA analysis was used to convict a Florida man of rape, the process has proven to be much more than a prosecutorial aid in U.S. courts. A comprehensive Justice Department report documented 28 cases of men convicted of rape during a recent year who were freed from prison based on DNA testing that proved them innocent. As a result of earlier similar findings, the 1994 Crime Control Act called for the establishment of a nationwide DNA data bank much like the national fingerprint system operated by the FBI. Such a system went online and became a reality in October 1998. The National DNA Index System is currently operational and integrated within most states. The FBI currently holds over 250,000 identified DNA samples from convicted state felons, and DNA evidence from 5,000 unsolved cases is ready to be entered into the computerized system. Eventually, the database will contain millions of samples. All 50 states have laws that make it possible to draw blood, take saliva samples or check swabs, from convicted felons, typically when inmates are processed into the penitentiary. The circumstances in which inmates must give DNA samples vary greatly from state to state. For instance, some currently collect DNA only from inmates convicted of sex offenses, others collect DNA from all newly arrived prison felons, while many collect only from inmates convicted of sex crimes and crimes of violence. Virginia not only was the first state to provide DNA analysis and testing but also enacted the nation's first law requiring convicted sex offenders to provide samples. All states now require convicted sex offenders to submit DNA samples. Virginia's DNA database contains over 220,000 profiles, the largest of any state collection.[49] Although the federal government does not have current legal authority to collect blood from federal prisoners, it is expected that legislation will soon be passed to enable collection. Each state's DNA database is electronically linked by FBI computer software to the nationwide network. By 2005, the FBI DNA collection, now formally known as CODIS (Combined DNA

Indexing System), had successfully matched DNA in more than 11,000 criminal cases. Of this number, 8,000 matches were able to identify the suspect by name, while the remaining 3,000 matches linked current unidentified DNA to identical samples submitted from past crimes.[50]

The practice of collecting and retaining DNA samples from convicted felons for past, present, and future comparison has been legally challenged. However, appellate courts have repeatedly upheld the process, holding that obtaining and comparing DNA from a convicted felon does not constitute additional punishment. Additional court challenges have emerged as a few states, like Virginia, now routinely take and analyze DNA from suspects as part of their booking process following arrest yet prior to conviction or acquittal. DNA samples are required from those arrested for violent felonies and some property crimes, including burglary. Thus far, courts have upheld the practice if state law provides for sample destruction if the case is dismissed or ends in an acquittal.

Low Copy DNA.   As the use and success of DNA evidence has spread throughout the criminal justice system, a new application of the technique, **low copy DNA**, is rapidly being adopted in many investigations. Low copy DNA evidence is being collected and processed in nonviolent property crimes. Formerly, DNA was sought and compared only in major violent crimes because of the necessary large quantity of blood and other properties needed for laboratory testing. New techniques now allow criminalists to compare far fewer cells for a successful match. Accordingly, genetic material from doorknobs, smudged fingerprints, skin cells left inside gloves or a ski mask, and many other sites can now be utilized. As low copy DNA testing becomes more common, already overloaded crime labs will face a major challenge to keep up with testing demands. The U.S. Department of Justice estimates that several hundred thousand DNA samples from violent crimes are currently backlogged and awaiting analysis by the nation's crime labs. The submission of additional hundreds of thousands of low copy samples will demand the hiring of large numbers of new laboratory personnel. Extreme care must be taken with the collection of low copy DNA at crime scenes. Such small samples pose a greater contamination possibility, as extraneous DNA is more easily mixed into and confused with suspect DNA.

Blood

Because of the violent nature of homicide and aggravated assault, blood is a very common type of evidence. The investigator may encounter blood evidence in one or more of four general areas:

1. on the victim,
2. on the offender,
3. within the crime scene, or
4. on a weapon.

Blood is a complex matter containing various substances that are of importance to the criminalist. The fluid part of blood is called *plasma*. Suspended within the plasma are *red* and *white blood cells, platelets*, and *serum*. The serum is significant to the criminalist, for it is the essential liquid necessary for blood typing.

When stains resembling blood are encountered during the course of an investigation, it must first be determined if, indeed, the stains are blood. The **benzidine color reaction test** has traditionally been used to make this judgment both in the field and in the laboratory. However, as benzidine is now recognized as a known carcinogen (cancer-causing agent), its use has been discontinued, and the *phenolphthalein test* is usually substituted. The test utilizes phenolphthalein and other chemicals that react to peroxidase enzyme of the blood. The reaction of the chemicals and enzyme produces a pink color. Unfortunately, there are other substances—certain vegetable matter—that produce the same reaction.

When the laboratory confirms that the blood sample is human, it is normally of investigative value to learn the blood type. Blood group is determined by the presence of individual *antigens*, or factors, of the sample. Human blood either contains A or B antigen, both, or neither. If the sample has A antigen only, the blood type is A. In a similar fashion, B antigen designates only B blood type. If the sample contains both antigens, the type is AB, whereas the lack of both antigens designates type O. The majority of the U.S. population is type O (43 percent); type A accounts for 40 percent. Most of the remainder of the population is type B (14 percent). AB is relatively rare, accounting for only 3 percent. Clearly, then, blood type can be very significant in terms of its relative value in tracing an offender. Individuals may be ruled out as suspects in significant numbers when type AB blood is involved. Type O is of little value, however, because of its relatively common occurrence.

When blood is encountered on humans and inanimate objects, it will be in fresh or dried form. Upon exposure to oxygen, fluid blood will clot quickly. The clotting process begins immediately upon exposure and will be complete within half an hour. Dried blood will be completely clotted, and depending on the time exposed, the sample may be flaking. The temperature of the crime scene and its immediate environment will affect the drying time of the blood sample. High temperatures accelerate the process; cold temperatures retard it.

The Victim.   Bloodstains on the victim can be of investigative value in reconstructing the events of the homicide. The flow of blood from wounds is frequently indicative of the position of the victim when the wound was received. It can also indicate movement after the wound was inflicted. In a similar manner, lividity can indicate to the officer that the body was moved after death. If lividity appears on the back, buttocks, and back of the legs but the victim is found in a sitting position, the investigator can assume postmortem movement of the victim's body. Blood on the victim is not always the victim's own; that is, the bloodstain may belong to the offender. Since many homicides involve violent struggles, the probability that the offender also was wounded should never be ruled out.

The Suspect.   When the identity of the offender is not known, the typing of blood evidence may prove valuable. As already mentioned, the value of this procedure depends upon the relative rarity of the blood type. This is particularly true if the suspect's DNA is not present in various agency files. There is no certain way to differentiate between the victim's and the offender's blood at the scene. For this reason, representative samples should be taken of all separate bloodstains.

Offenders often attempt to wipe their hands clean of blood before fleeing the scene. Consequently, the scene must be carefully searched for this type of evidence. Blood recovered from the scene that is not from the victim will be tested for identifying factors other than type. Recent developments in genetic typing can identify characteristics that were previously not identifiable. Serologists are now capable of identifying not only blood type but also the race and sex of the person it came from through analysis of genetic markers that are unique to individual sex or race.[51] Additionally, tests on a fresh sample can also indicate a syphilitic condition or identify the amount and type of certain drugs in the blood.

The Crime Scene.   The crime scene should be photographed carefully, with all bloodstain patterns recorded in distant and close-up photos. Blood distribution patterns on any type of object are useful in interpreting actions that occurred during the homicide. They may be used to establish the relative positions of the suspect and victim during the attack. A research project by criminalist Herbert Leon MacDonell, a nationally known expert in bloodstain evidence interpretation, concluded the following regarding blood as an aid to criminal investigation:

1. The pattern of spots of blood may be used to determine the direction of the falling drop(s) that produced the pattern.
2. The shape of bloodspots will frequently permit an estimate of their velocity and/or impact angle and/or the distance fallen from the source to the final resting place.
3. The diameter of a bloodspot is of little or no value in estimating the distance it has fallen after the first five or six feet. Beyond this distance, the change is too slight to be reliable.
4. Depending upon the target and impact angle, considerable backspatter may result from a gunshot wound (see Figures 11.13 and Figure 11.14).[52]

Blood droplets, often termed blood splatter, are generally classified into one of three groups depending upon their velocity of flight. High-velocity blood splatter is produced by external force greater than 100 feet per second (fps). The stains resemble a mist and are normally less than 1 millimeter. Blood mist is often the result of gunshots, explosions, or a violent cough or sneeze. Medium velocity drops are created by external forces greater than 5 fps but less than 25 fps and measure 1 to 3 millimeters. These stains are commonly produced by blunt or sharp trauma from cutting instruments, clubs, fists, and arterial spurts. Finally, blood splatters can result from low-velocity force less than 5 fps and will measure 3 millimeters or larger. This form of splatter typically results from a bleeding individual who is walking or running or as blood falls from a weapon.[53]

The analysis of human bloodstains requires considerable training. Although the investigator can make rough crime scene estimates, precise analysis must be accomplished by the criminalist or specifically trained crime scene investigator.

Bloodstains must be treated with care during crime scene recovery and packaging. If the officer is close to the laboratory, the evidence should be personally delivered for analysis immediately. Fresh fluid blood can be recovered through a sterile eyedropper or absorbent filter paper. If the officer cannot immediately hand carry the blood to the laboratory, it should be dried completely before mailing.

Hair

Hair evidence is commonly encountered in a wide variety of crimes, including homicide, rape, aggravated assault, robbery, and burglary. Human hair falls naturally from the head at a fairly constant rate. Accordingly, an offender may leave a hair sample in the course of a nonviolent crime such as burglary. On the other hand, hair may be pulled forcibly from an offender's head during a violent encounter. Sex crimes are likely to yield hair evidence because of the close contact of offender to victim. Finally, in

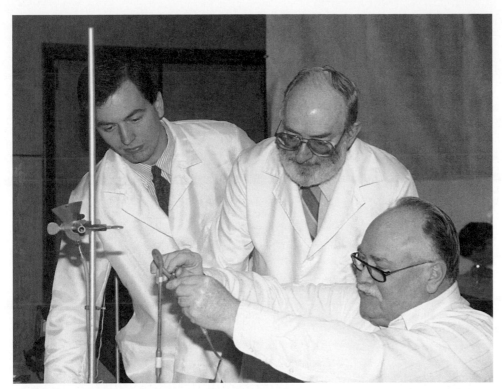

FIGURE 11.13   Criminalist Herbert Leon MacDonell (center) and associates prepare to examine bloodstain evidence. By interpreting the direction and velocity of blood from stain patterns, subject positioning may be deduced. *(Source: Laboratory of Forensic Science, Corning, N.Y.)*

violent crimes in which weapons or blunt objects are used to strike the victim, hairs may adhere to the surface of the object.

The examination of human hairs can help identify both living and dead victims. Hair analysis may also aid in identifying offenders by placing them at the crime scene. The resiliency of human hair is advantageous to the investigator; hairs often remain intact after other parts of the human body decompose. Hairs cannot be positively identified as belonging to a particular individual. However, through various analytical techniques, a hair can be linked to a person with impressive probability.

Hair grows and extends from an organ known as the *hair follicle*. Hair grows naturally in all mammals, with varying degrees of length and thickness in different regions of the body. The hair consists of four major parts, all of which are significant to the criminalist: the cuticle, cortex, medulla, and root (see Figure 11.15). The *cuticle* is the outside covering, or surface of the hair, formed by overlapping scales. The *cortex* consists of elongated cells that surround the center shaft of the hair. The cortex material contains pigment granules that give hair its color. The *medulla* is the core area of the hair; it resembles a central rod running the length of the hair. The *root* is the bulblike, DNA-rich matter on the end of the hair that secures the hair into the follicle.

As with blood, the initial examination of the hairlike material is to determine if, indeed, it is hair. Occasionally, fiber evidence is collected in the belief that it is hair; however, microscopic analysis can quickly reveal the difference between the two. Following the determination that evidence is hair,

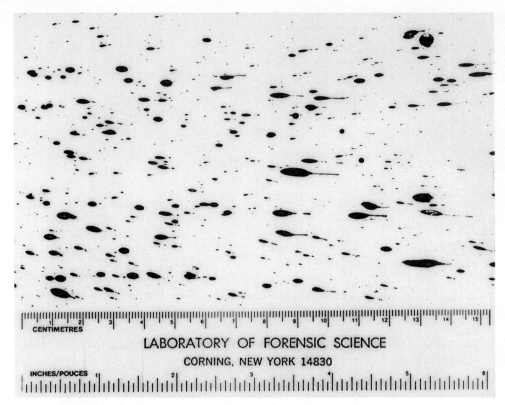

FIGURE 11.14   When blood radiates from a wound origin, the direction of the flow can be deduced by the configuration of individual blood droplets. By interpreting the appearance of the droplets illustrated, criminalists can determine the origin of travel (left to right) and accurately position the victim. *(Source: Laboratory of Forensic Science, Corning, N.Y.)*

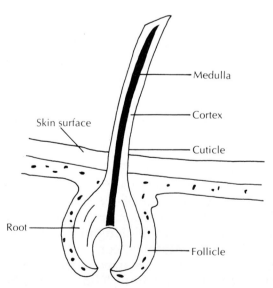

FIGURE 11.15   Major identification components of hair.

the criminalist will attempt to classify it as either animal or human hair. Such a determination will be based on root shape, cuticle shape, pigment distribution, and medulla width. Medulla width is the most distinctive indicator in this regard. Animal hair, in the vast majority of cases, is significantly wider than human hair. Additionally, the matter within the medulla of a human hair is of a fragmented appearance, or, occasionally, there will be no matter within. Conversely, animal medullas are continuous or show breaks in the matter at even intervals.

Offender Identity.   In the majority of investigations, hair evidence can be examined to determine race. It can be resolved that the hair in question came from a member of the Negroid, Mongoloid, or Caucasian race or from a suspect of a mixed racial origin. Hairs from members of the Caucasian race contain pigment that is more evenly distributed than other races. Cross sections of Caucasian hair are also round to oval in shape and straight or wavy. Hair obtained from members of the Negroid race contain heavy, uneven distributions of pigment. A cross section of this type of hair is generally flat to oval in shape and tightly curled. The pigment distribution in hair from members of the Mongoloid race is the most uneven. Mongoloid hair additionally has a heavy black medulla or core. Hair from those of mixed race will show the characteristics of the race that is prominent in other aspects of the individual's physical appearance.

It is very difficult to determine age or sex of an individual accurately from a hair sample. Certain generalized judgments may be offered, based upon the presence of hair dye or other properties unnatural to the hair. Criminalists are able to determine the body area from which the hair sample came with considerable accuracy. Hairs from the scalp typically show less variation in diameter and more constant pigment distribution throughout than do other body hairs. Hairs from the eyebrow, eyelid, nose, and ear are short and stubby and typically have wide medullas. Hairs from the pubic region of the body are very coarse and wiry and generally have continuous broad medullas.

The condition of the hair root is often a telling factor as to how the hair left the body surface. A hair that has fallen out naturally will have a clean, broad root; one that has been pulled forcibly normally has a root that is undeveloped or mutilated on the end that left the follicle. In some investigations, microscopic examination of the hair shaft can indicate the nature of the weapon that struck the region of the body where the hair originated. A sharp cutting weapon will sever the shaft cleanly, whereas a blunt instrument will leave the severed shaft with a jagged appearance.

Recovery and Collection.   If hair evidence is attached to an object or embedded in dried matter, the officer should make no attempt to separate the hair from the object or matter. Hair may be found embedded in blood or caught within glass or metal objects. The object containing the hair should be carefully packaged and sent to the laboratory. Any unattached hairs that are recovered by the officer should be placed in clean vials or plastic containers.

Whenever hair evidence is recovered at a crime scene, sufficient representative samples should be obtained from the victim, family members, and all others who reside there or who have frequented the scene often. This procedure is necessary to rule out hair evidence that does not belong to the offender. When a suspect is apprehended, samples of the suspect's hair should be obtained, through a court order if necessary. A dozen or more representative hairs should be taken from various areas of the suspect's body, packaged separately, and labeled, with care taken not to mix the samples. Combings are generally the preferred method of obtaining such samples, although the hairs may be cut close to the surface.

▲ SUMMARY

The investigation of criminal homicide and aggravated assault cases is increasing in frequency. Although such cases have always been of extreme importance because of their seriousness, the increasing rate of occurrence and decreasing rate of solution have caused considerable alarm. Criminal homicide is not the most frequently encountered death investigation in police agencies. Deaths by natural, suicidal, and accidental causative factors occur with much greater frequency. To knowledgeably exclude the possibility of criminality, investigators must be able to determine professionally the nature of the death. Most criminal killings are the result of sudden violent explosions of anger rather than coldly planned murders. Murder is a legal classification that relates to the degree of preplanning or premeditation involved in the criminal homicide.

Most criminal homicides can be linked to various emotional, sexual, benefit, psychological, or related-crime motivations. Emotional disputes involving long-standing problems often lie behind the killing. Sexual killings generally involve actual or suspected infidelity; murder-suicide is not uncommon in such cases. Mass murders and serial killings are well-documented varieties of killings by mentally abnormal individuals. Mass murder involves a single crime scene and time span, whereas serial killings occur over long periods of time and many geographic areas. Benefit murders are premeditated and typically involve a suspect who will gain financially from the victim's death.

The investigation of criminal homicide is essentially a discovery process focusing on the deceased, time-of-death determination, cause of death, and the crime scene. An additional investigative aid common to the homicide case is the expertise of specialists. Forensic pathologists and forensic anthropologists are particularly valuable. Their participation in investigations as well as their level of expertise are increasing rapidly.

Because of the seriousness of criminal homicide investigations, the application of extensive criminalistics is standard. There is often a wide variety of physical evidence encountered during the course of a homicide investigation, and physiological traces are quite common as a result of the violence that generally precedes a killing. Any linking evidence that can establish a suspect's presence at the crime scene or association with the victim is highly significant. Accordingly, blood traces, hair, semen, and other physical evidence are commonly analyzed by the crime laboratory. The discovery of DNA genetic fingerprinting has greatly expanded the capabilities of forensic experts to identify or exclude suspects in criminal homicide cases.

■ EXERCISES

1. Prepare a research paper detailing the recorded rate of murder in the United States. Using the FBI's *Uniform Crime Report* and other sources, prepare a graph for class display.

2. Prepare a research paper concerning the murder suspect. Compare psychological, sociological, and other causative factors in an effort to explain this crime.

3. Research five of the most recent criminal homicides in your community. Consider the following aspects of each case:
   (a) offender and victim relationship,

    (b) time and location of the offense,
    (c) cause of death,
    (d) criminalistic applications to the crime,
    (e) disposition of the investigation, and
    (f) court action.

4. Research your state's latest court cases in which the DNA genetic fingerprinting technique has been used. Discuss the details of the cases and the results of DNA testing.

 ## RELEVANT WEB SITES

http://www.vcvs.org/facts.htm

Site devoted to victims of violent crime, specifically criminal homicide. Provides homicide facts, information on victims' rights, and numerous detailed essays related to criminal homicide victimization. Essays include reaction to homicide, survivor's trauma, the homicide assailant, and witnessing the homicide event.

http://www.guncite.com/gun_control_gcgvmurd.html

Argues the theory that criminal homicide is the result of criminal offenders misusing guns rather than the need for additional gun legislation. Cites numerous research studies and government data pertaining to murder and manslaughter.

http://www.ncjrs.org/pdffiles/168100.pdf

Department of Justice case study regarding the reduction of homicide in Richmond, California. Describes the nature of the homicide problem and the reduction strategies that were developed in the homicide initiative.

Rape and Sexual Offenses

KEY TERMS

Amber Alert
aspermia
date rape
exhibitionism
fetishism
incest
masochism
pedophile

rape
rape trauma syndrome
sadism
sadomasochism
semen
statutory rape
voyeurism

LEARNING OBJECTIVES

1. to understand the legal requirements for the crime of rape;
2. to appreciate the unique social pressures that affect the reporting of rape offenses;
3. to be able to discuss the current state of rape as to frequency, rate of reporting, and suspect–victim relationship;
4. to be able to describe the various offender methods of operation;
5. to be able to define the four major personality types of rapists;
6. to be familiar with the investigative procedures that are proper for the rape investigation;
7. to be able to discuss the current state of sexual child abuse and the various offender types;
8. to understand the methodology and appreciate the importance of victim questioning;
9. to be able to define and discuss the six sexual crimes covered in the chapter; and
10. to have knowledge of those areas of criminalistics that directly apply to the rape investigation.

RAPE

The crime of rape has become a widely discussed offense in the United States. Although other crimes may be more damaging to a victim (obviously, murder), in recent years, rape has generated more frequent examination in magazines, newspapers, books, and other communication media. The focus on this offense is in part due to a reversal of public attitude. In the past, rape was the "unspeakable" offense because of its sexual character. Until relatively recently, many in this country viewed the rape victim with a mixture of suspicion and embarrassment. In other countries, such as France and Colombia, rape was rarely reported and almost never discussed by the public or by the media. Until the late 1970s, French rape suspects were tried in "correctional courts" that handle only minor offenders. In Colombia, successful prosecution of rape cases is very difficult, with less than 1 percent of all reported cases ever going to court. As society becomes more open generally in its examination of normal sexual conduct, a corresponding openness in the examination of deviant sexual behavior will result.

Rape is generally defined as an act of sexual intercourse against a female by force or against her will. Rape may also occur when sexual intercourse involves a female under a certain age, regardless of that female's willingness to engage in the act. This type of rape is typically referred to as **statutory rape**. In defining rape, all state statutes waive requirements of force and unwillingness when the victim is unconscious or mentally deranged. Any sexual penetration, however slight, is sufficient to complete the crime. The courts have wisely established the legal precedent that "against her will" need not be demonstrated by senseless physical resistance. Resistance is deemed unnecessary when it would be futile or would endanger life.

In the past, it was legally impossible for a husband to rape his wife, although he could be charged in a situation in which he aided another in the rape of his wife. Now the concept of using "marital privilege" as a defense against rape is legally void in all states.[1]

Rape is recognized as a very serious felony that often injures the victim physically as well as emotionally. Many rape victims experience emotional disturbances that may persist for a lifetime. Traditionally, rape was considered to be primarily sexually motivated, but current thought points to aggression as a major causative factor in the crime. Although not all rapes are committed by men who hold all women in contempt, modern research suggests that a significant number of offenses involve hostility, rather than sexual desire, as the prime motivation.[2] Rape poses many difficulties to the criminal investigator. Not only is it difficult to prevent, but its socially sensitive nature often generates information-gathering difficulties. Rape has been the fastest growing of all crimes against the person, yet it also has had the lowest proportion of suspect convictions following arrest.

Current State of Rape

About 90,000 rapes are reported in the United States each year, accounting for approximately 6 percent of all reported crimes of violence. Large cities with populations exceeding 250,000 account for the greatest number of rapes, averaging over 40 percent of all such offenses. Of the total rapes reported to the police, slightly over 44 percent are normally cleared by an arrest. Of all adults arrested, approximately 70 percent are prosecuted, with 40 percent subsequently found guilty of the offense. More rapes occur during the summer months than any other time of the year.

Rape is believed to be the most underreported of all crimes against the person. This is probably due to the victims' fear of their assailants and the sense of embarrassment over the sexual nature of the crime. Although some estimates of unreported rape range from 70 to 90 percent, recent studies do not bear this out. A study by the U.S. Public Health Service does not confirm the widely held belief that most rapes go unreported. The research indicates that at least 57 percent of the victims reported the crime to the police. The data were established by interviewing private physicians, for it is commonly believed that rape victims who do not report the crime seek medical aid through their private physicians.[3]

However, a three-year study released by the psychiatric department of the Medical University of South Carolina is at odds with government victimization findings. The comprehensive study surveyed more than 4,000 women and numerous victim assistance agencies and reported the following:

1. Annually, the number of rapes is actually more than five times the reported figure.
2. One woman in eight is raped at some time in her life.
3. Sixty-one percent of rape victims were 18 or younger at the time of the attack.
4. Only 22 percent of the rapes were committed by strangers to the victim.
5. Thirty-one percent of the victims developed a posttraumatic stress disorder as a result of the attack.[4]

The rape suspect and victim are typically about the same age, with the offender tending to be slightly older. Research studies conflict in regard to victim–offender relationships. The majority of current studies indicate that most offenders and victims are known to each other. It is important for investigators to be aware that acquaintance rapes are far more likely to result in a report to the police than are stranger attacks. One study demonstrated that nearly 30 percent of those raped by acquaintances reported the crime, compared to only 3 percent of stranger rapes.[5] Although the majority of rape reports to the police are legitimate, there are some that are not. In a recent year, 8 percent of all rapes reported to the police were determined by investigation to be unfounded, the highest unfounded rate of all reported serious felonies. Unfounded rape reports are those in which the police establish that no forcible rape offense or attempt to commit rape occurred.[6]

Offender Characteristics

Rape offenders tend to be young, with the greatest concentration from 16 to 20 years of age. Approximately 45 percent of the arrests for rape involve offenders under the age of 25, with 15 percent of the offenses committed by juvenile suspects 17 years of age and younger. Fifty-eight percent of those arrested were white, 41 percent black, and the remainder of other races.

A study by the New York Police Department of 3,000 sexual assault offenders indicates a general profile of the rape suspect. Over 70 percent were under 29 years of age, and 75 percent were not married. Additionally, most were lacking in education and job skills, with a significant number (23 percent) committing robbery or burglary during the same criminal episode.[7]

Rape offenders are highly recidivist, tending to repeat their criminality with far higher frequency than other types of perpetrators. Most offenders who commit crimes with a sexual orientation have disturbing rates of recidivism. A 15-year study by the California Department of Justice examined 1,300 sex offenders and determined that sex offenders were five times more likely than other violent offenders to commit another sex crime. The recidivism rate of violent sex offenders is so alarmingly high that many states have enacted special legislation allowing confinement of selected sex offenders in maximum-security psychiatric treatment centers after they have finished serving their prison terms. Most offenders are committed for indefinite periods of time and can be released only when treatment specialists believe they have a strong likelihood of not reoffending. While some legal authorities believe such statutes are unconstitutional and punish ex-convicts twice for the same crime, the U.S. Supreme Court has upheld the right of states to protect citizens indefinitely from sex criminals who are likely to commit additional sex offenses until they are deemed "cured."

Several detailed rape studies have indicated that men who rape are not psychologically abnormal to an extreme degree. Although many rapists have various forms of mental illness, very few can be characterized as criminally insane. The method of operation used by the rape offender varies significantly. Whereas some offenses involve a relatively quick random selection of the victim, in the majority there is some degree of offender preparation and planning. The type and amount of preparation may range from an initial conversation between offender and victim to a surveillance of the victim for several months prior to the offense. Many rapes, rather than involving a sudden attack, are preceded by an initial conversation in which the offender apparently assesses the victim's vulnerability. Some suspects may habitually roam the streets for many hours, either in a car or on foot, looking for a potential pedestrian or hitchhiker. In the majority of rapes, a single offender is involved; a smaller number involve two or more. Group rapes are rarely impulsive, and victims are less likely to report them than the single rape offense.[8] It is likely that group rapes are perpetrated with greater frequency by adolescents than by older offenders.

The rape offense generally occurs within some type of structure. It is speculated that a sizable proportion, approximately 40 percent, take place in outdoor scenes.[9] Outdoor rapes almost always involve a victim who is a pedestrian. The victim is approached by the offender, who often engages her in a short conversation. Following the conversation, the suspect may communicate his assaultive intentions by word or action. The resulting fear and apprehension displayed by the victim only serve to excite the rapist. Displays of fearful emotion generally reinforce the dominance syndrome, which is often a primary causative factor. In other outdoor rapes, offenders may approach the victim, typically from behind, and force her to a secluded area or inside an automobile. These rape suspects do not typically engage their victims in preliminary conversation. Rapes that occur in indoor scenes commonly take place in the victim's residence. The victim, time, and entry method are generally predetermined from past observance by the offender. Indoor rapes that lack preplanning often take place in office buildings, enclosed parking lots, or structures that allow strangers to enter unobserved, such as college buildings.

Offender Personality Types. No specific personality profile can apply to all rape suspects; however, criminal behavioral experts agree that nearly all rapists can be generally categorized as power-reassurance, power-assertive, anger-retaliatory, sadistic, or opportunistic offenders.[10]

The *power-reassurance* offender psychologically doubts his masculinity and seeks to dispel this doubt by exercising power and control over women. Commonly encountered in stranger-to-stranger rapes, this type of suspect frequently plans his attacks through surveillance of the victim. Using a minimal amount of force, the reassurance rapist generally continues to rape in an ongoing cycle until apprehended. Power-reassurance rapists may show remorse following an attack and seek to apologize or exhibit guilt in some other fashion. Such remorse is only temporary or altogether false, as the suspect will typically continue to seek dominance through additional attacks.

Power-assertive suspects rape to assert their masculinity and dominance over victims. In contrast to the reassurance offender, this type of suspect does not doubt his masculinity but uses rape as a form of symbolic power over women. The assertive rapist is often skilled at social deception and may befriend or know the victim prior to the attack. When the suspect perceives a safe time and place for the attack, he will exhibit his true personality and aggression to overpower the victim. A significant number of acquaintance rapes, commonly referred to as "date rapes," are attributed to this variety of offender.[11] The power-assertive rapist generally uses more severe force than that exhibited by reassurance rapists.

The third type of rapist uses extreme anger to retaliate psychologically for real or imagined past wrongs associated with women. The *anger-retaliatory* suspect's method of operation is characterized by a highly violent attack and his motivating need to punish and degrade the victim. Generally, such suspects do not plan their attacks but impulsively select and attack victims based on similarities in appearance to a past female figure. Victims are typically strangers who are overcome by a sudden, overpowering physical assault, which often causes serious physical injury requiring hospitalization. Whereas extreme anger characterizes the retaliatory rapist, the *sadistic* offender displays the greatest amount of overt hostility toward his victim. Sadistic rapists purposely inflict pain beyond that necessary to subdue their victims, for the visible suffering is found to be sexually arousing.[12] Because of a highly abnormal psychosexual conditioning, the sadistic offender is generally capable of achieving sexual gratification only through extreme violence. After extensive planning, the suspect purposely selects a stranger as his victim, immobilizing and transporting the victim to an isolated environment for a prolonged attack. It is fortunate that sadistic rapists are the least common type of offender, as their attacks have the highest probability of ending in criminal homicide. Most sadistic suspects are highly compulsive and have a strong ritualistic method of operation, which they may record during the rape.

The final type of rapist, the *opportunistic* offender, is generally one who, in association with the commission of an initial felony, commits rape as a secondary offense. For example, a robbery suspect, encountering a lone victim during the course of a commercial robbery, may impulsively rape. This is the only true type of rapist whose motive is directly sexual. The suspect uses only that level of force necessary to commit the rape and often binds the victim prior to exiting the crime scene. Some researchers report a high percentage of opportunist rapists to be intoxicated or under the influence of drugs during their attacks.[13]

INVESTIGATIVE PROCEDURES

The investigation of rape calls for maximum tact and professionalism. In many cases, the officer is confronted by the dilemma of the legitimacy of the victim's report, which adds to the difficulty of the interview. Was it a legitimate rape, or will the facts indicate the report to be unfounded? All crime reports are examined with regard to the possibility that they may be unfounded. Yet because of the trauma connected with rape, this determination is often difficult to make without considerable distress to the victim. If the report is legitimate, the victim must be treated with understanding and sympathy. To determine the offense, the officer must ask specific questions regarding the actions of the offender during the rape. However, such questions may be interpreted by a legitimate victim as indications of the officer's suspicion regarding the validity of her report.

In the past, many people thought that rape victims were doubly victimized, first by the rapist and subsequently by the criminal justice system. It cannot be denied that some victims were treated with a lack of understanding by the police, medical personnel, and prosecution officials. The old stereotype of the rape victim somehow "asking for it" no doubt influenced a number of people in their tactless questions and skeptical actions toward the legitimate victim. Fortunately, a more enlightened attitude is now prevalent. Current rape investigative procedures are professional, not only in the matter of victim questioning but also in all areas of subsequent judicial inquiry.

The investigative method utilized by a given police agency in a rape offense is determined by the size of the department. Medium-sized to large police agencies generally have a specialized sex offense bureau or an investigator who is qualified to handle the rape inquiry.

The Victim Questioning

The initial response to a rape report is typically by the patrol division. Thus, the uniformed officer has a critical role in determining subsequent police actions and instilling a positive attitude in the victim. The police response is usually brought about by the victim rather than a second party. Rapes involving children and adolescents are likely to be reported by parents or other adults. Upon arrival at the scene, the officer must first attend to any first-aid needs that may be necessary. If emergency medical attention is not immediately needed, a description of the offender should be obtained and broadcast. Obviously, the immediate broadcast of an offender description is not indicated if the report is "cold," that is, if it occurs many hours or days after the rape. Although the majority of departments dispatch patrol units to the scene, a small number send specialized investigators to take the initial report. For example, the New York City Police Department has a specialized rape investigation unit that reports directly to many crime scenes. The unit is made up entirely of female investigators who report to any scene in which a victim requests a female officer or to any scene in which the initial patrol officer feels their presence is required. The unit was formed on the assumption that many victims do not feel comfortable being interviewed by a male officer following the rape.

Unless all members of the patrol division have had special training in rape investigation and questioning techniques, the questioning during the preliminary stage should be brief. Questions should establish the criteria for the offense and description of the offender; they should not detail the sexual aspects of the crime. All sensitive aspects of the attack and the offender's method of operation should be determined as soon as possible by an investigator with special sex crime training.

The rape interview is generally a traumatic experience for the victim. Regardless of the tact of the interviewing officer, the victim must recount the details of the offense. The specific details of the rape are necessary to establish the elements of the offense and the method of suspect operation. Since many rape offenders are recidivists, details concerning the specific actions of the rapist are essential for comparison with past and future crimes. The victim's answers should provide information about the following:

1. lack of consent,
2. amount of force,

3. sexual penetration,
4. extent and type of sexually deviant acts,
5. method of suspect operation before the attack,
6. method of suspect operation during the attack,
7. method of suspect operation following the attack,
8. acquaintanceship between suspect and victim, and
9. description of the suspect.

The rape victim should be interviewed in an environment that puts her at ease, preferably in an isolated area free from distractions and other people. Although others may wish to stay with the victim during the interview, their presence is often unnecessary and embarrassing. Victims typically experience shame, guilt, and anger as a result of the offense. The officer should realize that, in addition to the physical attack upon the body, the victim's emotional sensibilities have been injured. The victim may be outwardly hysterical or appear quite calm and unaffected by the offense. Victims who do not cry or otherwise appear emotionally distraught may be internalizing their true feelings. For this reason, a composed victim should not be automatically suspected of giving an unfounded report. Such symptoms are collectively referred to as **rape trauma syndrome**, which, in addition to effecting an unusually calm and relaxed appearance, can cause a victim to delay reporting the rape for days or weeks.[14] During the interview, questions must be asked regarding the type of sexual conduct exhibited by the offender during the attack. This phase of the questioning is often the most difficult for both officer and victim. The officer should not appear embarrassed when asking questions pertaining to sexual conduct. If the victim cannot verbally state what happened, a female officer should be brought to the scene to obtain the information. It has been demonstrated that the sexual conduct of the offender can be learned with greater ease and in more detail by means of female-to-female questioning. Some police agencies have a preprinted checklist of sexual acts that embarrassed victims may complete rather than answering aloud. After victims have completed such lists, they often find it much easier to detail the offenses to the investigator.

Certain types of phrases should be avoided during the phase of the questioning. For example, the officer should ask, "Did the attacker penetrate your vagina?" rather than "Did you and the attacker have sex?" Questions that imply that a victim may have taken the initiative or that suggest possible complicity during the attack should always be avoided. Proper questions should be specific as to the offender's sexual conduct. Questions that are loosely phrased will only encourage the victim to reply with a yes or no answer to avoid embarrassment. If the officer asks, "Did the suspect do anything to you other than have intercourse?" the victim may respond negatively rather than detail an embarrassing deviant act.

As a result of thorough victim questioning, the investigator should be able to determine the offender's experience level. The novice or first-time offender will take minimal or obvious actions to disguise his identity. Actions limited to wearing a mask, changing voice tones, or binding or ordering a victim not to look all indicate a naive suspect unfamiliar with modern medical or police technology. However, the experienced rapist's *modus operandi* will illustrate his past knowledge and encounters with the criminal justice system. This type of suspect often disables the victim's phone, wears surgical gloves, or forces the victim to wash herself or items he has touched.[15]

As in most interviewing situations, the specific questioning technique must be tailored to the behavioral nature of the criminal. With rape and related sexually oriented offenders, two general questioning techniques can be used: the contact suspect method or the aggressive suspect method. The contact rapist tends to know the victim through either a casual or business relationship. Contact rape, also commonly termed **date rape**, occurs with a high frequency although its reporting level is low. Contact rapists believe men should be aggressive in their relationship with women and have sexual stereotypes that blind them to a woman's signal of unwillingness during a dating relationship. Accordingly, this type of offender does not view emotionally coerced sex as a crime and may also engage in using physical force. Although contact offenders do normally feel some degree of remorse, they feel no criminal culpability, believing they have not committed a crime. Successful interview methods for this type of suspect should minimize the moral seriousness of the crime and suggest that others in similar circumstances would probably do the same thing. In order to obtain an admission of guilt or a full confession, the offender's actions should be portrayed as a normal, healthy male response. Although distasteful to the interviewer, "blaming" the victim during questioning often reduces the offender's resistance and associated feelings of guilt.

In contrast to contact offenders, aggressive rapists typically do not know their victims, feel no remorse, and are far more likely to use high levels of force to accomplish the crime. Unlike many contact suspects, this variety of rapist is motivated by power and control rather than sexual pleasure. Often an appeal to the suspect's ego will aid the interview process and will invite bragging, which often leads to an admission of guilt. Since many aggressive rapists view women as insignificant and themselves as highly macho, questions that "condemn" the victim and flatter the suspect often produce positive results.[16] Another interviewing technique that is successful in dealing with rape offenders is the *fantasy-based interview*. Research indicates that most rapists engage in extensive mental rehearsals, or fantasies, which are actually mental exercises for their future crimes. Offenders may fantasize about the details of their attacks for varying periods of time before committing the rape, giving investigators a time period for intervention. When suspects are arrested for other types of crimes, such as warrants or trespassing, but exhibit behavior or have backgrounds that indicate a possible sex offender profile, the fantasy-based interview should be instituted. Acting more as a friendly counselor than stern police officer, the interviewer should motivate the suspect to discuss his fantasies openly. This can be accomplished by making the suspect feel safe, persuading him that everyone has fantasies, and speaking in the language and tone a therapist would use. When the suspect does reveal his rape-oriented fantasies, the detailed method of operation should be matched to unsolved offenses or used as a blueprint for future undeterred crimes.[17]

Medical Procedures

Rape victims should be transported to a medical facility as soon as possible following the rape. The hospital procedure will accomplish two primary objectives: (a) treat the victim for personal injury and (b) collect evidence of investigative significance. So-called rape kits are now commonly used to collect and preserve evidence obtained during sex crime medical examinations. While the kit may be furnished to medical personnel by the police, most hospitals typically have their own. The kit contains various items that are used to examine and package evidence obtained from the victim's person. For evidentiary reasons, the investigator should ensure that all items used are absolutely sterile and free from contamination. Many victims are very apprehensive regarding the medical treatment and often feel more at ease with other women. Citizen groups and domestic abuse personnel are frequently available to lend support to the victim, as are various victim/witness support units. Although many physicians and nurses are now aware of proper evidence-gathering procedures, the investigator should ensure that all necessary steps have been completed before the release of the victim. Although a rape victim cannot be forced to undergo a medical examination, the officer should explain the necessity and importance of the procedure, stressing that it is essential for the prosecution of the perpetrator.

The medical examination of the rape victim includes the following:

1. apparent emotional status of the victim;
2. general appearance of the victim and her clothing;
3. observation of external bodily signs of trauma;
4. internal examination of bodily areas involved during the assault, typically genital, oral, and anal locations;
5. specimens of external and internal semen;
6. cultures for determining possible venereal disease;
7. fingernail scrapings for blood and other traces;
8. general examination and collection of hairs, fibers, and other possible offender-tracing clues; and
9. photographs to illustrate physical trauma.

Interviewing rape victims poses many challenges to the professional criminal investigator. In addition to providing a detailed statement under difficult conditions, many victims are understandably distracted during the interview with health risk concerns. Such concerns are real, as 1 in 30 raped women contracts a sexually transmitted disease as a result of the attack, and 1 in 100 becomes pregnant. Physical health anxieties may block communication during the questioning, but other apprehensions can be even more obstructive to gathering investigative data (see Table 12.1).[18] Rape victims cannot be expected to concentrate fully on complete and accurate answers to police inquiries until such concerns and fears are adequately addressed by the investigator directly or referred to counselors trained to assist victims of violent interpersonal crime.

The Crime Scene

The scene of the rape should be processed without delay, and, in doing so, the investigator should bear in mind the type of offense and the necessary legal elements that must be proven. In an effort to demonstrate the victim's lack

TABLE 12.1 Major Fears of Rape Victims

Fear	Percentage
Family finding out	66
Being blamed by others	66
Becoming pregnant	61
Others finding out	61
Having name made public	60
Getting sexually transmitted disease	43
Getting HIV or AIDS	40

Source: Omaha World Herald; National Victim Center and Crime Victims Research and Treatment Center; U.S. Justice Department; American College of Emergency Physicians.

of consent and the offender's use of force, every type of evidence indicative of these factors should be recorded. Initially, the scene should be recorded through photography. The photographs should indicate the general appearance of the scene, with any indications of a struggle clearly apparent. Following the general photographic survey of the scene, specific items of evidence, such as torn clothing, semen stains, and all other significant items, should be recorded in close-up photographs.

If the rape occurred outdoors, the victim may be asked to return to the locality to indicate the exact area of the attack. Discretion should be used in returning the victim to the scene, for a revisit may be emotionally distressing. Outdoor scenes have a good possibility of yielding soil-tracing evidence and shoe impressions of the offender. To cover the possibility that the offender has deposited soil or taken away soil from the scene, representative samples should be taken. Impressions of the offender's shoes or tire tracks may also be present. Care must be taken not to destroy this fragile type of evidence by inadvertently stepping through an impression. Thus, if the scene is searched at night, portable lights should be used for illumination prior to any searching activity.

Regardless of the rape locality—building, automobile, or outdoor scene—certain types of evidence are likely to be encountered. Clothing from both the victim and the suspect may be scattered about. All undergarments, other clothing, bedding, and other significant articles should be collected. This evidence will be examined to reveal the presence of semen, blood, or hair. Under no condition should the items be packaged together or otherwise contaminated. Many victims will still be wearing the clothing worn during the rape, but others will have destroyed or washed the clothing prior to reporting the offense. The officer should not be unduly suspicious if clothing has been destroyed or washed, for the victim often associates the soiled clothing with the repugnant nature of the offense. If the victim is still wearing the clothing, she should be instructed not to wash or destroy the garments. A change of clothing should be taken to the hospital and the original garments collected for laboratory examination.

The majority of rapes occur indoors, either in the victim's residence or in another type of structure. Rape crime scenes should be processed for latent fingerprints since the sexual nature of the offense often precludes the use of gloves. The victim should be specifically questioned as to the items handled by the offender. Additionally, the victim should be asked to note any missing property. The possibility of forced entry should always be investigated by the officer, although the victim's statement will generally yield information in this regard. Doors and windows may offer tracing clues, such as toolmarks, broken glass, and paint samples. As in all felony investigations, a thorough neighborhood check should be conducted. To facilitate the witness-questioning process, the victim should indicate the identity of all persons who had knowledge of the offense prior to the police report. The witnesses will then be questioned to determine any additional information revealed to them and to document a report that is delayed.

The Suspect

In the event that a suspect is apprehended within a reasonable period of time following the offense, valuable items of evidence may still be present on his body or in his possession. Following a thorough search for stolen property, all appropriate clothing should be confiscated for laboratory examination. The clothing description furnished by the victim will generally indicate whether the offender has changed clothing. If information indicated a clothing change, a search warrant should be obtained to locate the clothing worn at the time of the rape or other items that can be traced to the scene. The close physical contact between offender and victim, including sexual intercourse, often results in the exchange of hair, blood, or fiber evidence. Accordingly, the offender's garments and body may reveal the presence of such evidence.

Occasionally, a rape or sex-related homicide may involve bite marks on the victim. Photographs and casts should be taken of the wound(s) and the offender's teeth in all situations that indicate this procedure. The matching of bite impressions to a specific suspect's teeth has been upheld in several courts as a means of positive identification.[19]

Apprehended rape suspects may agree to be interviewed by the criminal investigator. Although some serial rapists are psychopathic and do not internalize remorse following their crimes, research indicates that approximately 50 percent are not psychopathic and experience guilt.[20] Accordingly, the investigator should emphasize to the suspect that he can relieve his inner feelings of wrongdoing through a confession, while continually stressing, throughout the interview, the unacceptable nature of rape. Because rapists are highly compulsive and tend to commit their crimes in a serial fashion, the investigator should obtain as much detail during the interview as possible. Linking information can then be used to connect past rapes to the suspect. Once the suspect's identity and address are known, a search warrant should be executed as soon as possible. All items that may be connected to the present investigation and to past cases should be secured and removed for analysis. While searching for incriminating evidence, the investigator should be aware of certain characteristics of serial rapists:

1. they often do not wear disguises;
2. they frequently plan their attacks, as evidence may be present to demonstrate this in the form of notes containing addresses, photos of victim, or maps;
3. they may display a weapon (found to be the case in 50 percent of their assaults, commonly a knife);
4. they may bind their victims with materials found at the crime scene;
5. they often take a personal item of the victim (if theft is part of a ritualistic method of operation, it will occur with great probability); and
6. they will often retain instruments used to torture a victim (if the suspect is the sadistic type) and may have photos, videotapes, or audio records of the attack itself or phone calls to the victim, etc., within their residences or vehicles.

Because of the high rate of recidivism connected with sexually oriented criminality, the federal government and the states have instituted various tracking mechanisms to assist investigators and the general public. In 1996, federal legislation was enacted that requires states to track and notify the public regarding the identity and location of dangerous sex offenders. Accordingly, states are required to maintain a sex registry where offenders are mandated to register their identity and residence for ten years after completing a sentence of prison or probation. In addition to registration mandates, offender tracking also includes public accessible online sex offender Web sites operated by the various states. Although the criteria vary from state to state, the Web sites allow citizens to determine if various types of high-threat offenders are residing in their communities. In 2005, the U.S. Department of Justice began its National Sex Offender Public Registry. This

Web site allows the public to search for convicted sex offenders beyond one's state. Using a suspect's name can help one determine if the individual is in the system and where he is currently residing. When the site began, 21 states and the District of Columbia were accessible, and it is epected that all states will soon come online, allowing electronic inquiries from anywhere in the country.

In a related effort to track and deter known sex offenders, most states have passed legislation collectively known as "Megan's Law," named after a seven-year-old sexual homicide victim from New Jersey who was raped and murdered by a twice-convicted child molester who lived across the street. Such legislation requires police to notify the public when a convicted of a certain threat level sex offender is released into their communities.

Public notification practices vary widely. California operates a well-publicized phone number so that residents can call (for five dollars per call) to find out if someone they know is a sex offender. Louisiana requires sex offenders to notify all of their neighbors within three blocks that they are living in the vicinity as well as to pay to publish their name and crime in local publications. Michigan allows police agencies to post sex offender information on the Internet. Many states, such as Nebraska, have different notification programs depending upon the threat level assigned to each offender. The release of high-risk offenders requires that the detention system notify the community in which the offender lives, while the release of moderate-risk offenders mandates notification of day care centers, schools, and religious and youth organizations. Only law enforcement agencies are notified in the case of the low-risk offender.

It is probable that the reported incidence of rape will continue to climb. As the offense loses its traditional social stigma, more women will immediately contact the police following their victimization. Police investigators have made rapid progress in professionalizing the procedures employed in the rape inquiry. The objective of all police officers in their contact with a rape victim should be to leave an impression promoting the victim's confidence. The following letter was written to the editor of a midwestern newspaper:

> To the Editor:
>
> Recently, I was raped, knifed and robbed by [victim names the suspect]. [The suspect] was convicted of the crime of rape, aggravated battery, armed robbery, and theft as a result of that attack after a three-day jury trial during which I took the stand and testified to what had happened that night. I would like to take the opportunity here to commend the high level of competency and professionalism of those who were involved these past three months in the process of arresting and convicting [the suspect]. The detail and precision with which they gathered evidence, presented the case in court, and the skill of those police officers who apprehended [the suspect] that same night is to be highly praised. In particular, I want to express to the community the tremendous sympathy, compassion, and help that has been shown to me by the police, the hospital staff, and the state attorney's office. I had always heard that rape victims are treated poorly by the police, and in spite of that fear, called the police station immediately after I was attacked. From that moment on, I was treated with the utmost respect and understanding by all those police officers and detectives involved in the case.[21]

All rape victims cannot be expected to express their appreciation of the police investigation, but letters such as the preceding indicate the level of professionalism for which all departments should strive.

JUVENILE SEXUAL ASSAULTS

Criminal investigations involving the sexual abuse of children are becoming increasingly standard in most police agencies. The enormity of the problem has been documented by the Department of Health and Human Services, which reports that states received and referred for investigation 1.8 million reports of various forms of child abuse, of which 15 percent, or 405,000 cases, specifically involved sexual abuse.[22] Of the total reported cases of child abuse, approximately one-fourth are substantiated through investigation, resulting in nearly 100,000 criminal prosecutions across the nation. Although the rate of reporting child sex abuse continues to increase, authorities are aware that a significant number of cases are not reported. Many such cases go unreported for two major reasons. First, the crime has a sexual element that, as in cases of adult rape, deters full reporting because of societal embarrassment and suspicion. Second, many perpetrators of child sex crimes are well known to the victim, making reporting by the victim or parents more difficult. The actual rate of abuse is very high, as research even 40 years ago indicated that nearly 25 percent of American women reported a sexual contact with an adult before they were 13 years of age.[23] By all indicators, society is less likely to underreport this offense during the 2000s than in past decades. As in the effort to promote rape awareness in the 1970s, media presentations, citizen group efforts, and the expanded attention of the criminal justice system have combined to bring this crime into a new era of increased reporting, investigation, and prosecution.

Recent studies by the U.S. Department of Justice indicate the extreme seriousness of juvenile sexual assault. Surveys now document that rape is more often a crime against the young, as females under age 18 are victims of 51 percent of all rapes reported to law enforcement agencies. Findings indicate the younger the victim, the less likely the crime will be reported and the more likely a relative or acquaintance will be the perpetrator. Family members or acquaintances accounted for 96 percent of the attacks on girls under 12, with one out of five of such attacks being perpetrated by the victim's father.[24]

Offender Characteristics

Sexual child abusers are commonly referred to as child molesters or the more clinically precise term, pedophiles. **Pedophiles** are individuals who prefer to have sexual contact with children and whose sexual fantasies and erotic imagery focus on children.[25] Perpetrators who engage in the sexual abuse of children are generally, but not always, older than the victims. Their victims, however, are always legally defined as children. The vast majority of cases produce suspects who are significantly older than their victims, as the offender is typically an adult. However, sexual offenses committed by juvenile offenders are becoming more common. Professional counselors, psychologists, social workers, and police officers are reporting a sharp increase in cases of juvenile offenders sexually abusing child victims. A study by the National Center for Juvenile Justice reported that rape arrests of juvenile suspects aged 13 and 14 doubled during a recent ten-year period. For lesser sex-oriented offenses, the arrest increase was 80 percent, and arrest rates for 12-year-olds increased 20 percent.[26]

Sex offenders in general, and child molesters in particular, are highly compulsive and active criminals. A research study funded by the National Institute of Mental Health documented that the typical sexual offender against children is male, begins molesting by age 15, engages in a variety of deviant behaviors, and molests an average of 117 youngsters, most of whom do not report the offense. This study and many others note the rarity of the female sex offender. In California, only 471 of 70,000 registered sex offenders are women, less than 1 percent of the state's total. Child molesters vary as to method of operation and motivation, yet virtually all offenders take advantage of the vulnerability of, easy access to, and communication difficulties of their victims. Most offenders can generally be classified as either situational or preferential.[27] *Situational pedophiles* are not totally focused on children for their sexual gratification. Their attacks tend not to be as continuous or numerous as those of other offenders. Often turning to children as sexual substitutes for a peer sex partner, the situational suspect often has poor social coping skills, low self-esteem, and a generally inadequate personality. His main reason for selecting a child for sexual abuse is often the ready availability of the child, which is why this offender's own children are often molested. Perhaps the most frequent occurrence of situational child molestation involves a parent or relative who molests a child because of stress or while intoxicated.

Preferential offenders have a definite, focused sexual preference for children. They engage in sexual activities with children not because of situational stresses or inadequate social skills but because they are strongly attracted to and prefer children as sex objects. This type of offender is the more stereotypical child molester, who is generally very predatory and responsible for numerous victimizations until apprehended. The preferential suspect can exhibit many methods of operation, the most common being seduction. The seduction method attempts to lower the victim's inhibitions gradually to the point at which sex may be offered for affection or rewards.

It is important to note that either type of suspect can be involved in stranger victimization or the use of force during the criminal act. Either may abduct victims for prolonged abuse, although such cases most typically involve a preferential offender with sadistic tendencies. Various studies have indicated the following traits to be common among child molesters:

1. generally male, significantly older than the victims;
2. preference for female victims, although a significant number of males are abused;
3. often targets victims who are living in a dysfunctional family or living with one parent or whose mother is unavailable owing to employment, disability, or illness;
4. often has interest in child pornography and collects such materials;
5. often seeks out jobs or social activities that provide access to children and exclude adults; and
6. may have unstable employment record and background of frequent moves.

Although all cases of child sexual abuse are serious, the nonfamily abduction is often the most disturbing. A *nonfamily abduction* is a coerced and unauthorized taking of a child, generally for sexual purposes. The victim may be abducted, detained, and released or kept for long periods of time. A minority of cases involve suspects who intend to keep the victim permanently or who murder the child. Of the nearly 3,000 such cases in which victims are abducted for any length of time, approximately 200 cases involve victims who are transported 50 miles or more, ransomed, permanently kept by the perpetrator, or killed. Annually, nearly 100 victims are murdered as a consequence of nonfamily abductions.[28] A three-year study conducted by the Washington Attorney General's Office concluded that stranger child abductions are typically motivated by sexual drives rather than ransom or extortion demands. Additionally, the study revealed that nearly 60 percent of the victims are within a quarter mile of their homes when abducted, and two-thirds of the suspects had a legitimate reason for being in the neighborhood when they committed the abduction, such as living or working there or visiting a friend. Of abducted victims who are murdered, nearly 70 percent are raped or sexually assaulted, and the average age is 11. Finally, the majority (60 percent) were not targeted through stalking but were victims of opportunity for sex criminals predisposed to predatory violence.

Because of increasing public and police concern about child sexual abductions, a notification system known as the **Amber Alert** was instituted in 1997. In a manner similar to the announcement of weather emergencies, the Amber Alert immediately interrupts radio and television broadcasting with details of the abduction. Descriptive data of the suspect, vehicle, and victim are quickly given out to the public during the first critical hours with the belief that offender and victim are still in the immediate area. Many states also flash the information on major highways. When an Amber Alert is instituted in California, the information is instantly flashed on 500 electronic freeway signs. The system is named after a nine-year-old abduction victim, Amber Hagerman, who was murdered in Arlington, Texas, in 1996. To date, there are 44 states using notification programs that are credited with recovering at least 20 children.

The effectiveness of the Amber Alert was well demonstrated in the summer of 2002 when two teenage girls were abducted at gunpoint by a stranger in the Mojave Desert town of Quartz Hill, California. After binding the victim's boyfriends with duct tape, the suspect forced the victims into a vehicle and drove off. Police immediately forwarded the vehicle description to radio and television stations, and the vehicle description was flashed on hundreds of freeway electronic billboards. Because of the public's awareness of the wanted vehicle via the alert, the car was spotted within hours 100 miles from the abduction scene. Although both girls had been sexually assaulted, they were rescued by police who shot the suspect to death when he fired upon the officers. Law enforcement authorities believed the girls were within minutes of being killed and buried by their abductor when they were rescued.

Of the approximately 3,000 child abductions occurring annually, most will involve a suspect who is at least acquainted with the victim. True stranger abductions average about 150 a year. Various studies indicate stranger child abductors share many common traits. Most are men (95 percent) who tend to be unmarried and have few friends. They are often the socially outcast type of individual who harbor continuous sexual fantasies about children, often possessing and using considerable child pornography. Some, however, may actually prefer an adult female sex partner but, because of poor social skills, feel uncomfortable with a person of their own age. Or they may have attempted to restrain an older woman unsuccessfully and feel they can overpower a young child with far more ease. In 40 percent of stranger child sexual abductions, the victim will be killed, with 32 percent of the remaining victims seriously injured. Nearly all stranger abductors are willing to use violence to complete the crime, and 25 percent have been found to be sadistic.

Child molesters typically select female victims, although some molest both sexes. The average rates of child sexual abuse derived from eight random community surveys in the late 1980s indicated that 70 percent of the victims were girls and 30 percent boys.[29] In abduction cases, 75 percent of the victims are female, and half of the victims are 12 or older.

Additional characteristics of the child molester include the probability of abuse in the suspect's own background and, often, a narcissistic personality.

Most victims of child abuse do not become abusers as adults. Adult suspects who do molest, however, show a high incidence of sexual abuse during their childhoods; estimates range from 40 to 80 percent.[30]

Another group of child sexual abuse perpetrators can be termed *familial offenders*. These are suspects who molest children within their immediate or extended families, the victims being daughters, sons, or other close relatives. The American Psychological Association estimates that from 12 million to 15 million people are victims of some form of family-related childhood sexual abuse. The majority of cases involve a father and daughter or stepfather and stepdaughter. The remaining cases involve other related males; in only a fraction of cases is a mother the perpetrator.

Either the number of family-related child molestations is growing rapidly or more cases are being reported to police and social agencies. Offenders may be situational offenders who molest because of anger against their spouses or because of unaccustomed stress that triggers a sexual behavioral change. A smaller percentage are true preferential offenders. In the majority of family molestations, the mother is aware that sexual activity is taking place. When family molestation involves sexual intercourse between individuals of any age too closely related to marry, the abuse is termed incest. Incestuous abuse may be serial or concurrent. In *serial incest*, the offender sexually abuses one child, whereas in *concurrent incest*, the suspect initially abuses one child, then subsequently abuses another child within the family unit.

The presence of incestuous relations may be indicated to the investigator by the following:

1. One child of a large family who is better dressed than her peers (often in provocative clothing), with more money to spend.
2. A child who complains of urogenital or anal injuries or pain.
3. A child reported with venereal disease or semen traces discovered during a routine health examination.
4. A child who is uncharacteristically quiet, fearful, and withdrawn. Such a behavioral change typically occurs suddenly, when the incestuous relationship begins.

Some cases of sexual abuse of children can be classified as sexual exploitation. *Sexual exploitation* of children generally includes child involvement in pornography, child prostitution, and/or child sex rings.[31] This form of child sexual abuse is a growing problem, occurring with greater frequency than is commonly believed. In the Los Angeles area alone, more than 30,000 children a year are estimated to be sexually exploited.[32] Frequently, the victims are runaway adolescents who turn to prostitution to earn money. Although both male and female adolescents are victims, it is often boys from 12 to 17 years of age who are exploited in this manner. Adolescents are commonly involved in two types of cases: runaway and local exploitation. A runaway case generally involves a juvenile who leaves home and travels to an urban area. The youth is often from a dysfunctional home or one in which a suitable father figure may be lacking. Consequently, the youth is attracted to and exploited by older males. He may be forced into sexual activities or take part voluntarily for money or other inducements. The sex acts are often filmed or videotaped and sold for private viewing or Internet posting. Local exploitation cases involve children who remain in their communities. They are coerced into participating or willingly engage in sexual acts with the offender. The acts are often recorded, and the abuse typically continues for long periods of time. Both forms of exploitation involve the abuse of numerous victims by one or more offenders and may include sex acts performed by several victims for the gratification of the suspect. Victims are often induced to bring other peer victims into the relationship.

Online Juvenile Sexual Solicitation

As the number of children regularly using the Internet has grown, so has the risk of sexual solicitation by adult sex offenders via the Internet. Recent studies demonstrate that nearly 20 percent of children who regularly use the Internet report receiving unwanted sexual solicitations online. The 2001 University of New Hampshire study published in the *Journal of the American Medical Association* found that adult offenders generally targeted girls, with nearly 90 percent of the sexual solicitations occurring in chat rooms or via instant messaging. Such research confirms the rapidly increasing number of such cases investigated by law enforcement. In 1998, the FBI officially opened 700 cases dealing with online pedophilia involving either the posting of child pornography or the attempt to lure children under 18 to personal meetings. By 2000, the number of similar new FBI cases had quadrupled to 2,856.

In a way similar to how crack cocaine exploded the world of drugs, the Internet has dangerously expanded the sexual exploitation of children. Because of their immaturity, young girls may actually believe they have fallen in love with the adult they have communicated with during frequent chat room encounters. Rarely informing their parents, the victim may agree to meet the adult offender, with the meeting resulting in sexual assault, pornographic recording, or possible criminal homicide. Of the nearly 100,000 American families who have filed official missing person reports, two-thirds of the reports concern missing juveniles. While most of the missing juveniles have not been lured away through computer solicitation, the numbers are increasing. FBI research indicates that Internet child sex abusers are typically white males, between the ages of 25 and 45, middle to upper class, with professional-type employment. In addition to child sexual solicitation, this type of suspect is generally also active in the sending and receiving of child pornography via the home or office computer.

In 1982, the U.S. Supreme Court first upheld a state law banning child pornography. In 1996, the Child Pornography Prevention Act was passed by Congress banning the possession of any image that appears to portray sexually explicit conduct by a child. Accordingly, suspects who transmit, receive, or print such depictions via the computer are subject to arrest.

Child Sexual Assault Investigation Procedures

Investigations of the sexual abuse of children is often a difficult matter. Initial difficulty is caused by the lack of reporting associated with sex crimes. Underreporting poses an additional obstacle to gauging the extent of the abuse within an investigator's jurisdiction, and linking present offenses to past crimes is thus greatly complicated. In addition, very few cases are reported directly by the victim, which affects the degree of cooperation and number of details provided. The age of the victim and the general lack of witnesses also challenge the investigator. Finally, the criminal investigator must use considerable discretion throughout such a case, as unfounded reports are not unknown and a suspect's reputation may be irreparably harmed.

Most incidents of child sexual abuse are reported by parents or legal guardians. They are generally greatly disturbed and strongly wish to be present during the victim's interview. Because child victims need support, the presence of a nonoffending parent should be allowed during the interview unless the victim indicates an objection by word or action. Prior to the actual questioning, the investigator should obtain general data regarding the victim's developmental status. Being aware of the child's age, siblings, family composition, unusual physical or behavioral problems, and other factors can be helpful to the investigator in questioning the victim. Moreover, the circumstances and details of abuse should be obtained from the reporting party prior to the questioning as well as the circumstances in which the reporting party discovered the molestation.

Interviewing child sexual abuse victims has traditionally been mishandled in a significant number of cases. The major factor for prosecutors not electing to take many cases to court has been faulty interviewing that legally "taints" the victim's answers to the point of inadmissibility during a trial. Until relatively recently, child sexual abuse was viewed as a social rather than criminal problem. Initial interviews were more often than not conducted by social workers or others trained in therapeutic approaches designed to help children discuss what was done to them in order to initiate the emotional healing process. Although psychologically helpful, this form of interviewing legally contaminates the victim's responses. The forensic technique is the preferred interviewing method when interviewing child victims, as it is nonsuggestive, using open-ended questions designed to gain evidence for a search or arrest warrant. Forensic questioning allows victims to provide answers without the probing of therapeutic inquiries. For example, a trained forensic interviewer would ask, "Did anything ever happen to your clothes?" rather than "Did your Uncle Frank ever take off your clothing?"[33]

The child victim should be made to feel as comfortable and stress free as possible. Generally, the older the child, the more difficult this will be. Interviewing male children who have been victimized by male offenders is particularly difficult, as the stigma of homosexuality is generally a barrier to obtaining complete details. The investigator must make a constant effort during the interview to use language appropriate to the victim's level of understanding. As in all sex crime interviews, particular care must be taken not to sound accusatory. After the victim has been made to feel comfortable and a rapport established, the child is directed to tell what happened in his own words.

The child's first telling of the incident of abuse should be a nondirected questioning. When the victim finishes this initial reporting, the investigator carefully uses open-ended questions to determine the legally significant details of the event. Of particular significance are details relating to specific sexual acts and the presence and degree of coercion. Using anatomical dolls or encouraging the child to illustrate abuse through drawing are commonly employed techniques but must be used with great caution, avoiding any form of directed or suggestive input from the interviewer. Accordingly, the interview should be videotaped to document the spontaneous replies of the victim. All child victims of sexual abuse should undergo a complete medical examination by medical personnel specially trained in the examination and collection of cultures and samples pertinent to sexual assaults.

Child molesters often possess incriminating evidence within their residences relevant to an alleged abuse. Just as dealers in narcotics are likely to have narcotics paraphernalia, child molesters are likely to possess and retain various items that connect them to child sexual abuse. Thus, the execution of a search warrant is highly significant to a complete criminal investigation. Physical evidence secured through the warrant can provide proof of abuse or corroborate a victim's statements. Moreover, physical evidence is frequently located that demonstrates past molestations involving other victims. All computers and related items should be named in the warrant and subjected to a thorough search for child pornography and victim images.

Every attempt should be made to interview the sexually abusing offender. Most suspects initially deny the crime or attempt to minimize what they have done, both in quantity and in quality.[34] Others may attempt to rationalize their behavior, most commonly by blaming the victim. Suspects who have committed their crimes within the setting of their occupation (teachers, doctors, counselors, etc.) often fabricate explanations connected with the course of their duties. The investigator should stress the positive aspects of the abuser being discovered, such as the good that can result from proper treatment. The interviewer should also show concern for the offender, regardless of how repugnant the abuse. Suspects are much more likely to cooperate with authority figures who are not judgmental. Additionally, because many child abusers have been molested as children, an empathetic discussion of the suspect's personal abuse is often successful in eliciting a cooperative attitude.

Successful offender interviews generally involve two main phases: the use of minimization and evidence confrontation. Initially, various themes must be developed to provide the suspect with moral excuses that serve to minimize the crime. If this is successfully accomplished, offenders can maintain their self-respect and still provide an admission of guilt or full confession. Minimization can often be achieved by allowing the suspect to use the psychological defense mechanisms of rationalization and projection. The investigator may guide the suspect into rationalization by suggesting he or she was not in a "real" state of mind at the time of the crime as a result of the influence of drugs, alcohol, or some other external force such as stress from personal matters. Projection may be introduced by encouraging the offender to transfer the blame for his or her actions onto others. Common projection targets include blaming a spouse for neglecting sexual needs or some emotionally traumatic event in the suspect's past. In addition to minimizing the crime, offenders should also be confronted with evidence documenting the violation. Any past arrests, medical proof of victim injury, or witness observations should be exhibited and discussed. The suspect should then be informed that given the totality of the evidence, continued denial is useless and would not be believed by a jury.[35]

Some child abuse investigations involve victims who have been abducted or who are otherwise missing from their homes for many years. Computer-generated technology is able to age existing photos and produce an age-progression image, showing how the victim would appear today. In a process that is part science and part art, experts apply known facial aging patterns to a victim's photograph and merge various characteristics of blood relatives, also obtained from photos. The results are often very accurate and aid tremendously in obtaining information from witnesses about the victim's location (see Figure 12.1).

Successful prosecution of offenders in cases of child sexual abuse has traditionally been difficult. The credibility of the child victim is often attacked as well as the child's ability to accurately distinguish fact from fiction. However, the U.S. Supreme Court ruling in *Maryland v. Craig* (1990) has increased the probability of effective prosecution. The *Craig* case ruled that the Sixth Amendment does not invariably require face-to-face confrontation between a defendant and child abuse victim at trial if the victim will suffer emotional trauma by testifying in the presence of the defendant. In such cases, the victim's testimony can be obtained through the use of one-way closed-circuit television.[36]

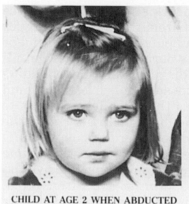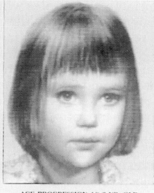

CHILD AT AGE 2 WHEN ABDUCTED   AGE PROGRESSION AS 6 YR. OLD   RECOVERY PHOTOGRAPH AGE 7

FIGURE 12.1 Computer-aided age progression of an abducted child. The center image was created by computer aging the victim's photo taken when she was two years old. *(Source: Horace J. Heafner, National Center for Missing and Exploited Children.)*

SEX OFFENSES AND RELATED BEHAVIORS

Sex crimes involve human behaviors that are defined by legal statute as being unlawful. Although sexual deviations are a matter of social subjectivity (what is offensive in one culture may not be in another), the law of each state has defined those acts that are of significance to the investigator. A large and increasing number of prison inmates are sexual offenders. Nearly 90,000 inmates have been convicted of various sex crimes, comprising 10 percent of the nation's prison population. At least 20 percent of the adult prison population in ten states are sex offenders. Sexual motivations for a particular crime are often not obvious. To certain shoplifters, the act of stealing and concealing an item may involve sexual gratification. On the other hand, the officer will have no difficulty in determining the sexual basis of indecent exposure.

Sensitivity and tact must be practiced in investigations involving sex offenses. Sex crimes are typically shocking and embarrassing to the victim, and often they involve children and adolescents. Although an experienced officer may not be shocked by a common sex crime, it should be realized that the victim is likely to be humiliated. Consequently, the interview and follow-up contacts should indicate that the police view the offense with appropriate seriousness.[37] In all crimes involving juveniles, the parents or legal guardians of the victim should be contacted immediately.

Exhibitionism

Exhibitionism, commonly known as *indecent exposure*, is an exposure of the sex organ for sexual gratification. Depending upon the specific statute, there may be no distinction as to the offender's sex, or the law may apply only to a male exhibitionist. Some states specify that the victim and offender be of the opposite sex; others make no such distinction. The exhibitionist is a compulsive offender who typically follows a fixed method of operation. Frequently, suspects expose themselves from doorways of buildings, parked vehicles, or at windows to passersby. The crime tends to be repeated until the offender is treated or incarcerated.

The majority of exhibitionists are males who lack sexual self-confidence and feel inadequate and inferior to other males. Often, there is no desire for the normal sexual act, of which the suspect may be physiologically and/or psychologically incapable. Sexual gratification is derived from the victim's emotional response—generally shock, fear, and disgust. Very few offenders attempt to touch the viewer. Generally, they expose themselves to women with whom they are not acquainted. Sometimes the offender calls out to gain attention, then exposes his genitalia and masturbates. Since the offender is sexually immature and fears normal sexual relations, a young nonthreatening female may be selected. The investigation of this crime generally results in an arrest. Since the offender is compulsively driven to commit the crime, the locality and *modus operandi* are often fixed. Exhibitionists are individuals who have had an abnormal and incomplete psychological development. Research indicates that a dominating mother and absent father may be common to many of them.[38]

Voyeurism

Voyeurism is the derivation of sexual gratification from surreptitiously observing the unclothed body of another. The voyeur, commonly known as a "peeping and Tom," is typically a young male and may progress to exhibitionism. A disturbed sexual development is typical of voyeurs, who are often unable to achieve sexual stimulation in a normal manner. The sexual gratification is achieved only if their presence is concealed; openly viewing a nude person does not satisfy this kind of deviate.

Like many of the sexual deviates, voyeurs vary in method of operation. Some become sexually aroused only if they view an unclothed heterosexual couple. Others may derive pleasure only by viewing a specific part of a female body. Although the arrest rate for exhibitionism is high, voyeurs are rarely apprehended in the act. When voyeurs are arrested, they are typically charged with trespassing. Few admit to the reason for their presence, leading the police to classify them as probable burglary suspects. An examination of the voyeur's clothing often reveals semen stains resulting from masturbation during the surreptitious viewing. Not all voyeurs progress to contact sex crimes, but a significant percentage of rapists and other violent sex offenders have indicated past histories as voyeurs.

Sadomasochism

Sadomasochism is actually a dual deviation in which sexual satisfaction may be achieved by inflicting pain on another or by submitting to physical ill-treatment at the hands of another. **Sadism**, named for the French writer of torture stories Marquis de Sade, refers to the infliction of pain; **masochism**, named for the Austrian writer Leopold von Sacher-Masoch, refers to the submission to pain. Sex offenses involving sadism may result in minor injuries or in brutal homicides. The sexual gratification of the sadist is achieved by the discomfort and pain exhibited by the victim. The masochist may precipitate his or her victimization by purposely seeking out sadistic offenders.

Although a preference is normally shown for one form of the deviance, a single offender may exhibit tendencies to both abnormalities. Sadomasochism often involves bondage, flagellation, and piquerism as the primary elements of sexual gratification. *Bondage* refers to sexual gratification from tying or restricting movement in some manner. *Flagellation* involves whipping to arouse sexual emotions. *Piquerism* refers to gratification achieved from tearing the victim's flesh by stabbing, piercing, or slashing. Occasionally, a homicide will result from combined deviant actions of sadism and masochism. Sadomasochistic encounters are found in heterosexual relationships, and they are also quite common among homosexuals.

Fetishism

A behavioral deviation involving an inanimate object or a specific body part as the sole stimulator for sexual gratification, **fetishism** typically involves a male subject and inanimate objects, such as female undergarments, shoes, handbags, and the like, as stimulators for sexual arousal. Sexual satisfaction derived through a fetish is not illegal. The fetishist may, however, continually engage in acts of theft to obtain the gratification object. A series of thefts from clotheslines or public washing machines in which female undergarments are stolen is apt to involve a fetishistic suspect. A fetishist, like the majority of other sexual deviates, has undergone an incomplete psychological development. He doubts his masculinity and fears rejection by females.

Certain sexual actions, in all probability, will always be considered illegal by our society. Whereas certain deviations, such as transvestism, were at one time illegal but are now nonarrestable, deviations involving human injury will always be considered dangerous to society. Most people think that society has the right, through its expression in the law, to govern sexual conduct to a varying degree. The high courts of the United States are the final determiners of the extent of control that may be imposed. Investigators should be aware that most sexual deviants are compelled to act in the manner that they do. Their identification and apprehension is an important initial step in treating the psychological motivation for their behavior.

When sexual offenses are encountered, the investigator should use only professionally proper terms to describe the offense rather than words that could be offensive to a jury. Slang terms should not be used in field notes or reports or during courtroom testimony. The following terms are proper descriptors:

Adultery	Voluntary intercourse by a married person with someone other than his or her spouse.
Analingus	Use of the mouth or the tongue on the anus of another.
Anthropophagy	The eating of human flesh to achieve sexual gratification.
Anus	The opening at the lower end of the alimentary canal through which waste is excreted from the body.
Bestiality	A sexual act between a person and an animal.
Buggery	Anal intercourse, often referred to as sodomy.
Coprophagy	The ingestion of fecal excrement to achieve sexual gratification.
Cunnilingus	Use of the mouth or tongue on the external genitalia of the female by a male or female.
Ejaculation	The ejection of seminal fluid during a sexual activity.
Fellatio	Use of the mouth or tongue on the male sex organ by a male or female.

Flagellation	A whipping or flogging that characterizes an abnormal eroticism.
Fornication	Sexual intercourse between unmarried persons.
Frottage	Sexual gratification achieved by pressing or rubbing against a person.
Gerontophilia	The preference for an elderly person as one's sex partner.
Impotence	The inability to perform sexual intercourse.
Incest	Sexual intercourse between persons too closely related to marry legally.
Infibulation	The masochistic self-torture of one's own sex organ.
Necrophilia	Sexual attraction to or intercourse with a dead body.
Pederasty	Anal intercourse with a young male.
Piquerism	Sexual inclination to cut, stab, or pierce the flesh of another person.
Pyromania	Uncontrollable impulse to set destructive fires to secure sexual satisfaction.
Tribad	A female homosexual who assumes the role of the male during sexual acts with a passive partner.
Troilism	An exhibitionistic desire to perform sexual acts with several partners or in the presence of a number of people.

CRIMINALISTIC APPLICATIONS

Any type of evidence may be encountered in sex crimes; however, in many of them, semen will constitute the primary evidential item. The presence of semen may also be noted in scenes other than those of obvious sex crimes. Accordingly, the investigator should be aware of the identification characteristics of semen.

Semen

Semen is the male reproductive fluid that normally contains spermatozoa, the male reproduction germ cells. The presence and appearance of spermatozoa is highly important to the value of semen as a tracing clue. Spermatozoa are long structures with a rounded head, giving the cells the appearance of tadpoles. Sperm cells cannot be seen without microscopic aid and are generally very numerous in a fresh sample. Following their discharge from the male, the cells typically remain in an active state for up to 15 hours. They will become inactive and completely dissolve after 24 hours within a living female. Seminal stains not deposited within the body of the female may remain intact for lengthy periods of time.

Not all seminal samples contain spermatozoa, for certain conditions prohibit their presence. Because of the extremely fragile nature of sperm cells, improper handling may destroy them. Additionally, some suspects may have an **aspermia** condition—a lack of spermatozoa in their semen. Spermatozoa may also be lacking as a result of certain venereal diseases that cause the germ cell to be eliminated. If the sample is to be tested for DNA, the evidence should first be tested to determine whether it contains sperm. It is the sperm cell that actually contains DNA, not the seminal fluid.

Seminal strains are found in three basic localities: on the victim, within the crime scene, and on the suspect. Semen located on the suspect is of the least value to the investigator, for its presence cannot document the criminal offense. Semen located on the victim is of significant value and may be located on an exterior surface of the body or within a body cavity. Semen is often located within the crime scene, normally in the specific area of the sex offense. Any physical evidence from the crime scene that bears suspected semen stains, such as bedsheets, towels, washcloths, paper towels, toilet paper, or tissue paper, should be collected. Stained areas believed to exhibit evidence of the assault should be described or highlighted for later analysis by forensic experts.[39] When semen evidence is submitted to the laboratory, the criminalist employs testing methods to initially determine if the stain is indeed semen (see Figure 12.2). Following the discovery of semen in a specific area of a garment, the sample is converted into a liquid solution for microscopic examination. The most common chemical test is known as the *acid phosphatase test*. This examination tests for the presence of an enzyme that is secreted by the prostate gland into the semen.

The various properties of seminal fluid can be of importance in specific suspect identification. Initially, the appearance of the spermatozoa is analyzed as to dimension and presence of abnormalities. The blood type of the suspect can usually be determined through a chemical analysis of the semen. Approximately 75 percent of human beings secrete evidence of their blood type into their bodily fluids. Accordingly, chemical analysis of a secretor's semen, saliva, gastric juices, and other physiological fluids will reveal blood type.

Collection Procedures

In all sex offenses the victim should always undergo an examination by a physician. The physician should be directed to take smears of the body cavities for seminal fluid. Any garment that may contain semen should be

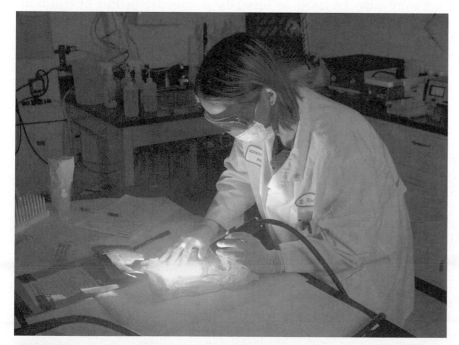

FIGURE 12.2 Criminalist examines evidence under ultraviolet light to determine the presence of semen and other physiological trace evidence. *(Source: Michael Havstad, Los Angles County Sheriff's Department.)*

collected from the victim and scene for laboratory analysis. Because semen will fluoresce under ultraviolet radiation, the use of a portable ultraviolet lamp (black light) will aid the officer in locating semen evidence. When the evidence is located on fabric surfaces, the dried semen will have a stiff, starchy feel. If the semen is still wet or damp, the evidence should be dried completely before packaging. Damp semen evidence may undergo alteration and decomposition if packaged before it has completely dried.

Handling of evidence containing seminal fluid should be kept to a minimum. If clothing is recovered that does not have obvious seminal stains, it should be submitted to the laboratory if there is any indication that it may contain traces. All evidence items should be rolled in paper and placed in separate containers. The evidence containers should be of paper construction rather than plastic, as the latter material may cause contamination.

Condom Trace Evidence

General knowledge of DNA's identification potential is becoming more widespread among the criminal population, and more suspects are taking precautions to avoid leaving bodily fluids at crime scenes. Rape is no exception; offenders are increasingly wearing condoms during their attacks and purposely taking the evidence item with them to avoid any possibility of DNA identification. A study by the Las Vegas Metropolitan Police Department revealed that 34 percent of the rapes during a recent year involved suspects who wore condoms. Although condoms may successfully eliminate the discovery of fluids necessary for DNA profiles, valuable trace evidence may still be present as a result of their use. Manufacturers produce condoms using a variety of materials, both natural and synthetic. As each manufacturer has its own formula, the various lubricants, powders, and spermicides commonly left by condoms can assist the investigator in many ways. After samples of condom residue are obtained by medical personnel, the individualized traces can provide evidence of penetration necessary to establish the *corpus delicti* of rape. Traces may also be used to identify a specific brand of condom, which can assist in linking a suspect to the scene if similar brands are located in his auto or residence. Finally, acts of serial rape may be linked to a single suspect by comparison of condom residues.[40]

▲ Summary

The investigation of sexually oriented crimes poses a unique challenge to the criminal investigator. Crimes that involve a sexual element have traditionally been underreported. When they are reported, victims often suffer from shame and guilt, making complete interviews difficult to obtain. The crime of rape continues to increase in frequency, as reported offenses now exceed 100,000 cases annually. Rape is believed to be the most underreported of all violent crimes in the United States, with nearly half of all victims not reporting the crime to authorities. Although underlying causative factors differ, most rapists commit their crimes as a means of demonstrating power and dominance over their victims. The sadistic rapist displays the greatest amount of overt hostility toward the victim, as the violence involved is a source of gratification.

Rape victims may not always report the crime immediately, for a significant number suffer from rape trauma syndrome and delay the report, often appearing outwardly calm and detached. As rapists are frequently serial offenders, a detailed questioning is very important to establish an offender's specific method of operation. Great care must be taken to avoid an accusatory or judgmental attitude toward the victim, and only open-ended questions should be asked. All rape victims should be examined by trained medical personnel and appropriate physical evidence collected and analyzed by criminalists.

Rape investigations can either involve known suspects named by the victim or focus on a search for a completely unknown perpetrator. Both types of cases demand careful interviewing in which details of force or threat of force will be obtained. Sex crime investigations also traditionally concentrate on the crime scene to demonstrate through physical evidence the various elements necessary to complete the crime.

Juvenile sexual abuse is another criminal offense that has demonstrated significant increases during the 1990s. Previously, relatively few cases of child molestation were reported to law enforcement. When they were encountered, these were generally cases of stranger molestation or abduction. More recent victimization surveys demonstrate that the number of cases reported in the past is inadequate to demonstrate the true extent of this crime. Child molesters, or pedophiles, are individuals who focus their needs for sexual gratification on children. Generally, the suspects are significantly older than their victims, yet an increasing number of offenders are juveniles who abuse other children. Most suspects can be classified as either situational or preferential as to motivation and method of operation. Situational suspects tend to molest children because of an inability to relate to peers, low self-esteem, or a situational stress factor. Preferential offenders have a totally child-centered preference for sexual contact with juveniles. The majority of child molestation cases involve suspects and victims who know each other very well. Sexual intercourse within the family, generally between a father or stepfather and a daughter, is termed incest.

The investigation of reported sexual child abuse is one of the most difficult cases an investigator can encounter. Victims rarely report the crime directly; they are young and impressionable and can easily become confused and intimidated. Accordingly, great care must be taken to document a professionally conducted investigation.

Certain other types of sexually related human behavior may involve the criminal investigator. Some behaviors may be obviously criminal, such as indecent exposure or voyeurism involving trespassing, whereas other sexual behaviors are not crimes but have the potential to increase the probability of an individual's victimization, such as homosexuality or transvestism.

Although many different types of evidence will be encountered in the investigation of sexually oriented criminal offenses, semen and other physical forms of evidence are particularly common. Semen analysis involving DNA profiling may be used to link a suspect to a crime scene or victim.

▌▌ EXERCISES

1. Research the various programs (public and private) in your community that deal with rape prevention and after-the-crime support. Interview the administrators with regard to the purpose and operation of the programs.

2. Prepare a research paper concerning the social aspects of rape. Analyze why this offense has been so underreported and the factors that indicate it is a crime of violent aggression rather than sexual compulsion.

3. Research the extent of sexual child abuse cases in your community. Interview police investigators and child welfare workers. Detail how

your prosecuting attorney presents this type of case in court with regard to the unique age of the victim and sensitivity of the testimony.

RELEVANT WEB SITES

http://www.rainn.org

Home page for the Rape, Abuse and Incest National Network. Extensive information on sexual assult victimization, including statistics, counseling centers, and programs, and on how to access phone and online hotlines.

http://www.vachss.com/help_text/date_rape.html

A comprehensive listing of links detailing acquaintance and date rape. Includes links to many detailed government reports on the topic, including drug-assisted date rape and the National Institute of Justice report on the sexual victimization of college women. Other links access various sites pertaining to juvenile sexual abuse.

http://www.ojp.usdoj.gov/bjs/pub/pdf/saycrle.pdt

Fact-filled report by the U.S. Department of Justice, Bureau of Justice Statistics, pertaining to sexual assault of young children as reported to law enforcement agencies. Includes detailed information regarding victims, nature of incidents, and offender characteristics.

Larceny

KEY TERMS

affinity scams
auto chopping
bank-examiner swindle
booster device
bunco swindle
car clouting
check kiting
confidence swindle
credit card fraud
employee pilferage
forgery
grand theft
identity theft

joyriding
kleptomania
larceny
National Insurance
   Crime Bureau
phishing
pigeon-drop swindle
shoplifting
ultraviolet light
vehicle identification
   number
vehicle stripping
white-collar crime

LEARNING OBJECTIVES

1. to know the legal requirements for the crime of larceny;
2. to be able to explain the current state of larceny as to frequency, objects of theft, and offender characteristics;
3. to understand the current state of vehicle theft;
4. to be able to define and discuss the three major methods of operation unique to auto theft;
5. to be able to explain the investigative procedures that are proper for the stolen vehicle inquiry;
6. to be able to discuss theft from motor vehicles, including suspect method of operation;
7. to be able to discuss shoplifting and the suspect method of operation unique to this offense;
8. to understand the nature of the confidence swindle and those common techniques discussed in the chapter;
9. to be able to explain the concept of white-collar crime and the investigative procedures designed to combat this offense;
10. to be able to explain credit card fraud and the suspect methodology of this crime;
11. to be able to define the three types of check frauds; and
12. to have knowledge of those areas of criminalistics that directly apply to the larceny investigation.

INTRODUCTION

Every four seconds a larceny is committed in the United States. **Larceny** is the formal common-law term for what is popularly known as theft. The frequency of this type of criminal offense is so prevalent that no other measurable crime category can equal it in dollar loss. The yearly reported loss of property and currency to larceny now exceeds $5 billion.[1] This figure does not include losses from worthless checks, stolen automobiles, embezzlement, confidence swindles, shoplifting, employee theft, and many other business-related frauds. If the true loss from criminal theft and fraud could be accurately computed, the total figure would be staggering.

Although the specific statute definition of larceny varies by state, when one unlawfully, without force, obtains or takes an item of value from another, with the intent to permanently deprive, a larceny has occurred. The act of larceny consists of the actions of the offender (exerting unauthorized control of the property); the mental state is demonstrated by the intent to permanently deprive.

Continuing the tradition that originated in early common law, most states have divided theft into two subsections determined by the value of the stolen property. The distinction in value defines a theft as either grand theft or petty theft. **Grand theft** is a felony offense and may involve relatively small amounts, such as a minimum of $500 in Kansas or as much as a $2,000 minimum in Pennsylvania. Petty theft is prosecuted as a misdemeanor. Most states specify that a theft from one person by another, regardless of the value of the object, is a felony. Because of the large number of offenses that are generally thought of as thefts, this chapter will limit discussion to certain larcenies of common frequency.

CURRENT STATE OF LARCENY

Approximately 8.2 million larcenies are reported annually in the United States, including motor vehicle thefts. Larceny and motor vehicle theft thus account for well over 60 percent of the total crime index. Geographically, more thefts are committed in the southern states in proportion to population, followed by the midwestern states. The volume of larceny is highest during the summer months, peaking in July or August. The average value of property stolen in each reported theft is now nearly $740. Through the years, the distribution of larceny as to type of theft has remained relatively constant. As in prior years, a major portion of theft—nearly 40 percent—represents larceny from motor vehicles and accessories. Other types of thefts involve shoplifting and property from buildings, which total about 30 percent.[2] Almost any imaginable item may interest a particular thief. Within one recent month, police reported larcenies of timber, embalming fluid, cattle, grain, 17,000 laptop computers, motion pictures, grease, and 11 million worms.

The frequency of larceny has increased dramatically since the early 1970s, so that it now is the most voluminous of all crimes. Frequency of thefts from motor vehicles has demonstrated the greatest increase; thefts of vehicle accessories, in particular, show the greatest gains. The only specific larceny that has shown a significant decrease in frequency is bicycle theft.

OFFENDER CHARACTERISTICS

Youthful offenders have a heavy involvement in this crime category. Over 28 percent of those arrested are suspects under the age of 18; 57 percent are under the age of 25. Females have a higher involvement in larceny than in any other crime. Nearly 37 percent of all apprehensions for theft are of female suspects. Racially, arrests of white suspects outnumber black arrests by more than two to one, with all other races comprising about 4 percent of the total.

The clearance rate by arrest for this crime has traditionally been one of the lowest, rarely exceeding 18 percent. However, on a national level, more arrested suspects are formally charged for larceny than for any other crime. Of those formally charged, approximately 75 percent are found guilty.

MOTOR VEHICLE THEFT

Current State of Motor Vehicle Theft

Although tabulated within the *Uniform Crime Report* as a separate form of theft distinct from other types of larceny, motor vehicle theft remains a persistent and expensive criminal problem. The rate of auto theft has now surpassed 1.2 million thefts per year—nearly one of every 130 registered motor vehicles is stolen. Automobile larceny is the single most costly crime in the United States, with the average value of a stolen auto being over $6,800 at the time of theft. When the cost of auto theft is computed with the additional expense of police, court, and correctional agency efforts, this offense costs the U.S. public more than $8 billion annually.[3] Of the motor vehicle thefts annually reported, 75 percent are of automobiles; the remainder involve stolen trucks, buses, and other types of vehicles. The western states have traditionally had the highest rate per 100,000 of motor vehicle theft, with the lowest rate occurring in the Northeast. The cities of Miami and New York, where one of every 29 registered vehicles is stolen, are tied for the highest vehicle theft rate in the nation.[4] North Dakota has the statistically lowest rate of vehicle theft of all states, whereas New York State has the highest. Motor vehicle theft is primarily a big-city problem since the highest theft rates generally appear in the most heavily populated sections of the United States.

Vehicle theft has become a worldwide problem, with many foreign countries reporting a dramatic increase in this offense. West Germany had more than 65,000 vehicles stolen during a recent year, which accounted for over 3 percent of all registered vehicles in the country. Italy reported more than 264,000 car thefts, with nearly one-third of the stolen vehicles belonging to visiting tourists.[5]

In all geographic divisions and population groups, the frequent involvement of the youthful offender is indicated by the high proportion of those arrested under 18 years of age. Nearly 30 percent of all persons arrested for auto theft are under 18; those under 25 account for 62 percent. The majority of the arrests are of white male suspects, whereas minorities account for nearly 39 percent. Only a relatively small percentage of vehicle thieves are arrested; law enforcement clears approximately 13 percent of the reported cases.

Various research studies have reported the following data in regard to the current status of vehicle theft:

1. Thefts generally take place at night; most often stolen are vehicles parked near the victim's residence.
2. Stolen vehicles are recovered in approximately 60 percent of all reported cases.
3. Nearly 90 percent of all stolen vehicle incidents are reported to police authorities.
4. In 25 percent of cases, other objects of value are also taken, such as cash, purses, wallets, stereos, and CD players.
5. Victims are present when their vehicle is stolen in approximately 7 percent of all cases. When present, a victim is attacked nearly 20 percent of the time.
6. Young victims experience the highest vehicle theft rate, whereas the elderly have the lowest.
7. If you own a car, chances are one in 42 that the auto will be either broken into or stolen.[6]

Vehicle Identification Methods

Of the many types of stolen property, the vehicle is perhaps the most identifiable—if it remains intact. From the first years of automobile production, some type of identifying system has been used to connect a given auto with the owner and manufacturer. The license number is assigned by a state's department of motor vehicles and will be the primary identifying factor in nonprofessional auto theft investigations. Since the changing of license numbers is a very simple task, a more permanent method of auto identification has been devised. The engine number or motor identification is placed on the engine block during the time of manufacture. Engine block stamping was the first method of permanently identifying a vehicle. What is now referred to as a **vehicle identification number** (VIN) is a means of identification that clarifies the location and nature of the engine block number and other identifying data. Although the VIN system of vehicle identification was initiated in 1954, it was not until 1968 that full compliance was achieved from all U.S. auto companies.[7]

The VIN system requires vehicles to have an identifying plate affixed to the dashboard and to have engine and transmission areas stamped with a corresponding identification code. A VIN plate provides information concerning the automobile's make, model, year of manufacture, plant location, engine type, and sequential production number. The corresponding engine number provides similar information, minus the model type, and transmission numbers generally repeat the engine code.

A standard method of vehicle identification that also deters some thefts is the VIN etching method. VIN etching involves the use of chemicals to place the VIN on all of the car windows. VIN identifications are not noticeable unless one looks closely, but once they are etched on the windows, they cannot be removed. In addition to the VIN, current federal law requires MYLAR stickers to be placed on certain major automobile parts to assist in identification. The stickers contain individual VINs imprinted on bar codes that resemble those found on grocery or clothing items. Since the identifying numbers are disguised, thieves cannot forge false documents or additional codes. The MYLAR codes can be read only with special devices and assist in identifying stolen autos in which the VIN has been removed. Additionally, switched body components can be readily identified and traced back to their original vehicle source. Another means of vehicle antitheft identification is the Stolen

Vehicle Retrieval System. This method of identification is dependent upon a hidden transmitter within the stolen vehicle. When the auto is discovered to be stolen, the police are notified and activate special computers used to track the vehicle through radio signals. Although the cost of homing-device technology is a deterrent for some individuals, the system is highly effective and has a recovery rate of 90 percent within an hour and a half of the theft.[8]

Suspect Method of Operation

Motivations for stealing vehicles are varied, yet such thefts may be categorized in terms of three general intents. Either the vehicle is being stolen for joyriding purposes, for use in other criminal activity, or for profit motives.

Joyriding. **Joyriding** is both a descriptor for a type of offender and a method of operation. Joyriding offenders are generally youngsters, typically under 18 years of age. The vehicle is stolen to provide thrill or pleasure, with the motivation of transportation occasionally a factor. Whereas nearly 75 percent of auto thefts were attributed to this type of offender 15 years ago, a significant reduction has been reported to date. It is now apparent that joyriding has decreased to less than a fiftieth percentile ranking, resulting from an increase in the profit motivation.

Juvenile joyriders are likely to steal an auto because of peer pressure or because they want to experience the "thrill" of driving a desirable model car at high speeds. The crime is typically perpetrated by more than one youth, and the stolen auto is usually abandoned near the residence of one of them or where one of their own cars is parked. Joyriders are apprehended more frequently than are other types of car thieves, and autos stolen for joyriding purposes are recovered in greater numbers than those stolen for other reasons.

Additional Criminal Activity. This motivation for vehicle theft is a factor in the smallest number of actual larcenies. Certain types of suspects habitually steal an auto prior to committing a second criminal offense. Armed robbery suspects are particularly prone to this activity, as are kidnapping offenders. The reason for the theft is to eliminate personal vehicle tracing clues that the victim or witnesses may supply to the investigator. The suspect typically parks a personally owned vehicle near the site of the vehicle targeted to be stolen and proceeds with the theft. The vehicle may be stolen from a residence or from a parking lot or other congested area. Offenders who are more experienced steal autos from residences that they have surveyed previously. In this manner, it can be determined when the owners are asleep or not using the car, avoiding a stolen vehicle report while the auto is being used in a subsequent robbery or other offense. The offender may even attempt to return the car to the residence following the robbery in the hope that the owner will never realize that the car was stolen. If this effort is successful, the auto will be lost as a site of probable evidence.

The majority of vehicles stolen for additional criminal activity are recovered in a relatively short time period. Although some offenders may return the auto to its original site, the majority will not. A small number of suspects attempt to delay the discovery by burning the vehicle, pushing it into a pond or other site of concealment, or parking it in a commercial lot.

Motive in an increasing number of urban auto thefts involves the gang-related drive-by shooting or initiation by theft. Most vehicles used for this purpose are stolen to avoid identification by witnesses and are often taken by three or more juvenile gang members. When recovered, the vehicle should be processed carefully for firearms-related evidence. Another emerging trend is the theft of vehicles for use in the drug trade. This pattern often originates in suburban areas with the theft of an auto. The stolen vehicle is then driven to a nearby urban area and traded for narcotics—usually cocaine.

Profit Motives.   The profit-motivated suspect constitutes what is commonly termed the "professional auto thief." Because this offender's method of operation is very sophisticated, apprehension is difficult. Furthermore, professionals often resell the entire auto, or strip the vehicle, making recovery infrequent. Auto larceny for profit is becoming more prevalent and poses the most serious challenge of all the various types of theft. Whereas 20 years ago nearly 90 percent of all autos stolen for profit were eventually recovered, only 57 percent are currently recovered. The professional thief is attracted to auto theft because the crime is, indeed, lucrative. The FBI estimates that more than $250 million in criminal profit results from this type of auto larceny.

Stripping and Chopping.   Auto theft for *stripping* purposes generally involves the taking of parts and accessories rather than the body of the vehicle. **Vehicle stripping** may be perpetrated by an individual seeking a new or better part for a personal auto or by an organized group of offenders. In the group operation, the parts are often sold to "customers" who have "ordered" a specific part or to unscrupulous auto parts dealers. Stripping, as a method of operation, generally involves one of two techniques. Either the vehicle is stripped at the same location at which it was parked by the victim, or it is towed or driven to another locality. The majority of vehicle strippings occur within concealed locations, such as rented garages. One of the fastest-growing trends of vehicle parts larceny is theft of vehicle air bags, which can be removed from a vehicle in three minutes and have a retail value of more than $1,000. Additionally, headlight bulbs in luxury autos are being stolen due to their high value.

Auto chopping refers to the dismantling of the vehicle's major body components, such as the fenders, doors, hood, and the like. It is estimated that of the nearly one million passenger cars stolen, nearly 40 percent are stolen for chopping purposes. Apparently, this motive is the fastest growing of those pertaining to auto larceny. Chopping is preferred by offenders to engine stripping in that auto body components generally lack identifying numbers. The profit is also an inducement, for it is estimated that the average new car has the potential to clear over three times its normal value when the body components are dismantled and sold. For example, a single door of a new luxury-type vehicle will bring $200 to $300 in the used-parts market. Certain luxury autos, such as Cadillacs or Lincolns, will double their original value.

Chopping occurs principally in major metropolitan areas, and few dismantled vehicles are ever recovered. The general method of operation regarding chopping involves three groups of offenders: the *salvage yard owner*, the *vehicle thief*, and a *chopping crew*. The following hypothetical case is typical. A legitimate salvage part dealer in California orders a front end for a new Cadillac. The order is placed over the auto dismantling industry's "long-line network." The network is composed of leased telephone connections or online Web sites, allowing dealers to communicate instantly with each other regarding parts for sale or parts needed. A dishonest salvage part dealer in Chicago learns of the California dealer's need for the Cadillac component. The dishonest dealer writes what is known as a "pull sheet"—a slang term for a stolen vehicle order. The pull sheet is given to a "car puller"—the thief who will steal the vehicle. Car pullers are highly skilled car thieves who often carry vehicle locator books. These are notebooks compiled by the thief that indicate addresses of desirable cars, including model, year, color, and other data concerning the best time to steal the vehicle.

After the desired Cadillac is located and stolen, it is delivered to the salvage dealer in a specified manner. Instructions for delivery are generally included in the pull sheet. Rather than delivering the vehicle directly to the yard, the thief parks the auto in a prearranged public place. After ascertaining that the police are not watching the car, it is driven away by the chopping crew. The crew normally rents a garage in which to perform the actual work. The chopping method generally employs the use of a circular saw and blowtorch. All flammable materials are initially removed from the vehicle, the doors are removed, and the crew proceeds to cut the car in half across the roof. This procedure leaves the chopping crew with major expensive body components, including the doors and rear- and front-end assemblies. All parts bearing identifying codes are discarded or immediately shredded into scrap. The crew then transports the Cadillac's front end assembly to the Chicago dealer, who sells it to the legitimate dealer in California.

The Chicago dealer pays the thief—generally $200 to $300—and the chopping crew receives up to $500. The front end is sold for several thousand dollars, and the dealer has the remaining valuable parts to sell over the long-line network. The dealer in California has no way of knowing that the purchased part is stolen, for once a body part is removed from a vehicle, there is generally no way it can be identified.

To remedy this type of auto larceny for profit, there is but one solution. Laws must be enacted that will force vehicle manufacturers to put identification numbers, similar to the VIN system, on major body components. This procedure is very expensive, and it is unlikely that vehicle manufacturers will voluntarily comply without statutory enforcement.

Title Switching.   Another illegal operation involving the salvage yard operator concerns *title switching*. Through various unlawful means, a yard dealer obtains the title of an auto that has been destroyed. Generally, this is an auto that has been brought to the yard to be crushed into scrap metal. The dealer destroys the vehicle but retains all identifying data. A second vehicle of the same make, model, and year of the destroyed auto is subsequently stolen. The VINs and license plates of the destroyed auto are then transferred to the stolen auto to "legitimize" the latter vehicle.

Because the title is retained from the destroyed vehicle, no official record exists showing the loss of this auto. Thus, when the identifying data are transferred to the stolen vehicle, a routine file check will reveal no irregularity. The dealer generally sells the stolen vehicle to a consumer or to another dealer.

Resale.   A relatively small number of vehicles, when contrasted to the numbers stolen for joyriding and for stripping and chopping, are stolen for resale. In resale operations, the entire vehicle is sold, either in the United States or in a foreign country. Using various methods, the thief acquires a legal registration certificate or fraudulent title for the stolen auto. The vehicle is sold as quickly as possible to a private party or to a used-car lot. Luxury autos such as those made by BMW, Mercedes Benz, Toyota, Honda, and Mazda and utility vehicles are the most commonly stolen new vehicles in the nation.[9] Yet older cars, especially those manufactured in the 1990s, are stolen more frequently than newer models, as the demand for older model parts far exceeds current vehicle parts.

Many stolen autos find their way into Mexico or South America, where the registration procedures are often lax. Unless the investigator has a lead indicating a specific country, recovery is unlikely.

The transportation of American vehicles to foreign countries is increasing rapidly as a motive for motor vehicle larceny. Whereas stolen vehicles were once transported across state lines and delivered to unsuspecting or cooperating used-car dealerships, shipping stolen vehicles out of the country for sale is emerging as an attractive choice for organized car theft rings. Profits are substantial, as foreign buyers will pay two to three times the value of the stolen car in the United States. The stolen vehicles are shipped overseas with the cooperation of a dishonest exporter or packaged to represent legitimate goods. This form of vehicle theft has become so popular that in some Caribbean countries, 20 percent of all autos in use have been stolen and shipped from the United States.[10] The frequency of this form of larceny is higher in urban cities with large international shipping terminals, such as New York City and port cities in New Jersey, Florida, and Texas. Of the 1.1 million vehicles stolen in the United States in 2003, experts estimate that 200,000 were illegally exported. Additionally, of the 30 metropolitan areas with the highest auto theft rates, 20 have easy geographic access to export markets.

Investigative Procedures

The traditionally low rate of clearance for vehicle theft indicates the investigative difficulties associated with this offense. Several factors unique to vehicle theft are mainly responsible for these difficulties. The first factor is the relative ease with which the crime can be perpetrated. Studies indicate that over 80 percent of stolen cars are left unlocked; 40 percent have keys in the ignition. Even if the vehicle is locked, gaining entry is a simple matter through the use of a "slim-jim" type of device. Any object that is thin and metal-like, such as a coat hanger, can be easily slid along the car window until it hits against the lock and releases it. The knowledgeable thief can then easily bypass any "antithief" device within the steering column.

A second major factor adding to investigative difficulty involves the motive of a substantial number of auto thieves. Many are juveniles seeking a joyride, who will frequently abandon the vehicle in a short period of time. Because the stolen vehicle is not retained, tracing elements helpful in other types of theft are diminished. A third factor involves the nature of the property being stolen. Many vehicles are stolen for parts other than the readily identifiable engine. The parts are difficult, if not outright impossible, to identify. Finally, the professionalism of some car thieves further confounds the vehicle theft investigation. Professional car thieves are typically mechanical experts and are often part of a sophisticated theft ring.

Although many older professional car thieves use more sophisticated methods to enter and start vehicles, most younger thieves break into the steering column to start the car manually through the exposed ignition wiring. An increasing number of car thieves are attempting to steal the keys as well as the vehicle. When vehicles are stolen without their keys, damage invariably results, lowering the resale price. Many luxury auto manufacturers now make keys that cannot be easily duplicated or keys containing computer chips, resulting in an immobilized vehicle without the proper key entry. Such factors have forced car thieves to devise ways of stealing the owner's key prior to the vehicle theft. Stealing from car dealerships or parking garages where keys are stored is common, and some suspects have turned to carjackings.[11] Finally, investigators should be aware that some aspects of motor vehicle theft come under both federal and state laws, with successful enforcement often requiring the cooperation of federal, state, and local police agencies. This is especially true in cases that involve organized crime groups, gang-sponsored theft rings, and carjackings.

National Insurance Crime Bureau.   With each passing year, auto theft becomes more of a specialized investigative area. Although all police officers are acquainted with auto larceny through their training and experience, the complex nature of this offense requires continued in-service training from many sources. The **National Insurance Crime Bureau** (NICB), a civilian organization founded in 1912 and funded by the insurance industry, has been extremely helpful in this regard. Although active in researching and offering assistance in many forms of insurance fraud, the group has traditionally focused heavily upon vehicle larceny. Formerly known as the National Auto Theft Bureau, the NICB offers training seminars and publishes various manuals pertaining to the investigation of auto larceny and other crimes of particular loss to the insurance industry.

The organization recently developed the License Plate Reader Program in collaboration with the Bureau of Customs and Border Protection. This program fights vehicle theft and fraud by utilizing license plate reading devices that digitally record vehicle plate information on 15 million inbound and outbound vehicles at 12 U.S. border crossings each year. In addition to assisting police in individualized fraud cases, the NICB operates the National Insurance Crime Training Academy, in which highly specialized fraud courses and seminars are offered to civilian and police investigators. The NICB spends nearly $30 million a year to combat insurance fraud, of which $6 million is focused exclusively on the investigation of vehicle larceny and recovery.

Gathering Investigative Information.   In order for an auto theft investigation to be successful, the initial report must be accurate. The officer must be certain that the information supplied by the victim is correct in all respects. If an error is made and the wrong identifying data are recorded, the probability of recovering the stolen vehicle diminishes. Data consisting of numbers and letters must be precisely recorded. The investigating officer should not merely take the victim's word as to a VIN or even a license number. The information should be confirmed by an official record check or compared with an official document.

The victim of the theft should be interviewed concerning the time the vehicle was parked prior to the theft. Accurate times are necessary if suspect method of operation is to be determined. The possibility of a friend or relative having borrowed the vehicle must not be overlooked. Also, it may be possible that the auto was repossessed for failure to meet payments due. Although repossession agencies should notify the police before and after each repossession, this may not have been accomplished. Some victims may be aware that a friend or former spouse could have taken the auto but will not tell the officer unless directly asked.

The site where the vehicle was parked should be examined carefully. If the stolen vehicle was parked on a soil surface, there may be tire tracks from the suspect's vehicle. To cover the possibility of a joyride or additional crime theft, license numbers and basic descriptions should be noted for strange autos parked in the vicinity of the theft. As with any felony investigation, a thorough neighborhood check should be made.

Once the identifying data are confirmed, the information will be broadcasted to other units and entered into computers. Local computers will be notified, as will terminals at the FBI's National Crime Information Center.

Field Observation—Patrol.   Uniformed patrol officers on routine patrol have the greatest probability of observing a stolen vehicle. Experienced officers are aware of certain mannerisms that drivers of stolen vehicles may display upon observing a nearby police vehicle. Joyriders are particularly apt to exhibit extreme nervousness when they sight a police officer. A vehicle that suddenly turns off seemingly to avoid the officer should be examined. Since the majority of joyriders are youthful and rarely alone, expensive vehicles with young drivers and passengers being driven in an irresponsible manner bear close observation.

The appearance of the vehicle can also indicate that it may have been forced open and stolen. Common exterior signs are damaged glass or locks, obscured or missing license plates, or damage to the auto's body components. Interior signs are often more reliable, for forced entry may not necessarily result in damage to the exterior. Although some suspects will have a key with which to start the auto, many will not. There may be no key in the ignition, indicating a "hot-wire" technique, or the key in the ignition will appear to be homemade. Occasionally, suspects simply use a screwdriver to defeat the ignition system. Additionally, the occupants, if any, will be unable to document their ownership of the vehicle.

Patrol officers should be observant of the following indicators of possible vehicle theft:

1. Vehicles that conform to local vehicle theft profiles. Generally, such vehicles are easy to steal, as their ignitions are easy to defeat. In many areas, Mazdas, Toyotas, and Nissans are frequently stolen for this reason.
2. Vehicle damage, such as punched-out door locks, damaged windows, and damaged steering columns.
3. License plates do not appear to be proper for the vehicle under observation. For example, new California autos are assigned seven-digit license plates, not the older six-digit plates. Caution must be taken when checking license plates on suspicious stolen vehicles. Some suspects purposely attach plates that are not stolen but match the year and model of the stolen vehicle. Without further investigation a preliminary computer check would not reveal the stolen status of the vehicle. Among car thieves, this practice is known as a "cold plate on a hot car."
4. Vehicles with their lights off at night or showing only parking lights. Such signs, including erratic driving, may indicate that the suspect does not know the location of interior equipment or how to handle the newly stolen auto.

Federal legislation known as the Motor Vehicle Theft Prevention Act has assisted patrol officers in the recognition and apprehension of stolen vehicles. The act has created the Watch Your Car™ program, a national voluntary motor vehicle theft prevention program that encourages citizens to display special decals or state-issued, customized license plates. These decals or license plates serve to alert police that the vehicles are not normally driven between prime vehicle theft hours—typically 1 A.M. and 5 A.M. Motorists may also choose to display another decal or device to signify their vehicles are not normally driven in the proximity of international land borders or ports (see Figure 13.1).

The purpose of the Watch Your Car™ program is to identify vehicles that are not routinely operated during early morning hours or near international land borders so police can investigate an auto theft before a stolen vehicle report is filed.

FIGURE 13.1 Typical Watch Your Car™ decals applied to vehicles to deter theft and assist in car theft apprehension.

Field Observation—Detective. The investigator who is assigned an auto theft case will use an investigative technique that is geared to the specific type of method of operation. If the theft is perpetrated for joyriding or for additional criminal usage, the auto will soon be recovered. In these situations, the automobile itself will become the investigative focal point after the recovery. The investigator must carefully process the vehicle for latent fingerprints and all personal suspect tracing clues. As in the discovery of all stolen objects, a neighborhood inquiry should be made at the recovery site. However, if the vehicle has been stolen for stripping or chopping purposes, the inquiry technique must vary. Obviously, a vehicle stripped for engine and transmission parts will be recovered with these parts missing. The investigator should process the vehicle in the following manner.

1. If possible, a crime scene technician should process the vehicle.
2. The direction in which the vehicle was heading when recovered should be noted. (In the majority of cases, the scene of the stripping is behind the vehicle.)
3. Any residences or garages in the immediate area bearing excessive grease deposits should be noted. (The stripping location is normally close to the recovery point.)

4. It should be noted whether the recovered auto is at the base of a hill or incline. (The auto may have been rolled down from the stripping garage.)

5. A check for latent prints should always be done.

6. The interior of the auto should be thoroughly searched for tracing evidence left by suspects.

7. Checks should be made with appropriate fire departments to determine if local complaints have been made concerning the use of acetylene torches in private garages.

8. A particular suspect method of operation should be noted, if possible. Has oil or gasoline been used to wipe off latent prints? What parts were taken? What valuable items were left behind?

9. When examination of identifying engine numbers indicates that the number has been changed or altered, detailed impressions should be taken. The numbers should first be cleaned with a solvent to remove grease and debris. The numbers should then be photographed in proper light. Following these procedures, an impression of the numbers should be obtained. A surface replica plastic compound should be poured into the impression area, which has been dammed with putty to receive the plastic. Or small squares of lead may be applied to the numbers by a forceful blow.

10. Flea markets, used-auto-parts shops, speed stores, and salvage yards should be checked for missing parts.

11. Investigators should instruct all beat officers to conduct discretionary field interviews of persons traveling in the area where the vehicle was recovered.

12. The license number of the stolen vehicle should be computer checked for summonses regarding parking tickets or other traffic violations. Because thieves rarely bother to pay fines for parking in illegal zones or put money into expired meters, the tickets will show specific locations where the vehicle was parked, possibly at or near the suspect's home or workplace.

Chopping motivations are likely when late-model, generally expensive vehicles are stolen and not recovered. Sometimes the major body components are not recovered, but the engine and transmission are. Chopping operations normally occur around a salvage yard operator. Suspected yards or individual operators should be placed under surveillance. An effort should be made to contact other yard operators to determine if a particular dealer is selling parts at a below-normal wholesale price. (Informants are very important in this type of investigation.) A police agency may also wish to place an undercover officer into a suspected yard as an employee. Autos stolen for complete resale purposes are quite difficult to recover. Generally, an interstate violation is involved, resulting in a federal investigation. Close cooperation between local and federal investigators is necessary with this type of inquiry.

Motorcycle Thefts

Motorcycle theft has also increased rapidly during the past decade. The popularity of the motorcycle and the difficulty with which it is recovered both contribute to the high rate of larceny. Experts report stolen motorcycle recovery to be even lower than auto recovery: Such victims stand only a nine-in-100 chance of ever seeing their motorcycle again.[12] Motorcycles can be easily altered to appear radically different from a victim's description.

Additionally, the VIN system varies greatly with different types and models, making VIN checks difficult for the untrained officer.

To the knowledgeable thief, a motorcycle can be stolen and disassembled with relative ease. Because it is much smaller and lighter than an auto, the motorcycle may be lifted into a van or simply pushed quietly away. To thieves who possess considerable mechanical skill, the locking system can be easily bypassed to start the motorcycle. Motorcycle locking systems are generally not as complex as auto locking systems. Furthermore, duplicate keys for motorcycles are relatively easy to obtain if the lock number from the ignition is known. Some thieves may prefer motorcycles for the reason that they can be disassembled easily for VIN alteration. Identifying numbers are in fewer locations than in automobiles. The VIN can be altered by welding or by overstamping an existing digit; for example, the digit 9 may be altered to resemble an 8.

The investigative methods employed in motorcycle theft are generally similar to those used in automobile theft. Motorcycles are typically stolen for stripping or resale. Some may be stolen for joyrides, but very few are stolen for chopping because of the lack of expensive body components. The investigator should routinely check motorcycle repair shops and localities where parts are swapped or sold. If so-called outlaw motorcycle gangs are known to frequent the immediate area, they should be observed. The history of such organizations indicates a strong probability that they may be involved in motorcycle larceny.

Heavy Equipment Vehicle Theft

Unfortunately, there are no accurate statistics concerning the theft of farm and heavy construction vehicles. However, an analysis of the FBI's National Crime Information Center reveals more than 10,000 such stolen vehicles currently being sought. Rates vary widely from state to state, with Texas reporting nearly 2,000 thefts and Vermont two.

Investigators experience little success in the recovery of stolen heavy equipment, averaging only 6 percent. The low rate is primarily due to the absence of required registration and title and the lack of any standard permanently applied identification number. Each heavy equipment manufacturer has its own individual identification numbering system. Additionally, identification numbers are often mounted in a nonpermanent manner, allowing easy removal. Accordingly, investigators often have difficulty recording thefts and locating victims when vehicles are recovered.

The theft of heavy equipment is one of the fastest-growing forms of rural crime and the most expensive. A single piece of equipment can be worth well over $150,000. Criminal investigators must familiarize themselves with the uniqueness of this type of vehicle theft. Visiting local dealerships, learning individual numbering systems, and eliciting the aid of heavy equipment operators will aid such investigations.[13]

THEFT FROM MOTOR VEHICLES

Larcenies that involve the taking of property from a vehicle, including any item other than an auto accessory or vehicle part, are numerous and costly. Although frequently dismissed as a minor criminal problem, this offense currently accounts for over 34 percent of all reported thefts and averages $712 per incident. Theft from motor vehicles is often referred to as **car clouting** and may be a continual larceny problem in a particular jurisdiction.

Suspect Method of Operation

Offenders who specialize in this crime are of two basic types: organized and unorganized. The organized offender frequently operates in a group and may travel from locality to locality. The unorganized offender is an opportunistic criminal who commits the theft whenever circumstances dictate. Car clouting appeals to both types of suspects; it is a quick and easy crime, often yielding stolen property of considerable value. As in most criminal activities, the offender's method of operation varies. One common element is the continual prowling of an area for likely autos. The thief may operate on foot or drive from scene to scene to vary the pattern of the larceny. In parking lots, the probability of valuable property being left in autos overnight is increased. Motel lots or lots frequented by tourists or salesmen are common targets. Some unorganized suspects will simply walk through residential streets looking for an auto in which valuable property is visible.

Many different types of property are commonly stolen in car clouting. The recent popularity of expensive tape and CD players has boosted the frequency of this crime significantly. Although some departments may classify CB radios as auto accessories, other agencies do not in that the radio is not an original part of the vehicle. Literally any item of value may be stolen—luggage, cameras, sporting goods, briefcases, and so forth. Once the desired object is spotted, the suspect will ascertain that no witnesses are present. The window will then be broken or forced open. Some suspects may gain entry via a coat hanger or more sophisticated car-opening tool. The offender who uses a car-opening tool of a sophisticated nature is generally a recidivist.

In the successful investigation and apprehension of the car clouter, a method of operation must be established. Routine patrol officers will rarely see the offender, who will act only when there are no vehicles in sight. Although some arrests do result from alert citizens who may observe and report the larceny in progress, a planned surveillance is generally the only effective method of apprehension. Past records must be carefully studied that indicate the time of day, locality, and type of property typically stolen. Surveillance teams can then be placed at crucial scenes to observe the offense and arrest the suspect. Many departments film or photograph the offense in progress. The recent development of night-viewing scopes for law enforcement use has greatly aided this and other types of night surveillance activities.

In an effort to increase apprehensions in cases of theft from vehicles, many law enforcement agencies are using various proactive techniques. The Waycross, Georgia, police department has had considerable success with its baited-vehicle detail. This special unit consists of investigators who identify a high-crime area where there is an established pattern of thefts from vehicles. Specific factors, such as the time and type of objects stolen, are determined from an analysis of similar past larcenies. When a bait site is chosen, it must be conducive to surveillance, apprehensions, and making vehicle stops. The baited vehicle is then driven to the site and placed under close surveillance by the unit. The vehicle, often a pickup truck with guns placed in plain view of anyone looking through the rear window, is arranged to appear obviously unoccupied and disabled. The officers then wait for a thief to take the "bait" by attempting to steal the firearms. The act is completely videotaped, and the arrest is made. The baited-vehicle technique has been highly successful, as 63 percent of theft attempts of the baited vehicle have resulted in arrest.[14]

Shoplifting

Shoplifting refers to a theft committed in a retail business during the hours of commercial operation. The larceny may be committed by a customer or by an employee of the store. When employees steal from their employers, the larceny is often termed **employee pilferage.** Shoplifting may well be the most frequent and expensive of all types of theft and involve the greatest financial loss. The true frequency is difficult to determine, for only those cases resulting in an arrest or loss report by a business are officially recorded. There are well over 600,000 arrests for this offense—nearly three times as great as the rate in 1970. Shoplifting constitutes nearly 15 percent of all reported larcenies, and the average value of property stolen during a single offense is $181. A U.S. Department of Commerce study estimates collective merchants' losses at $24 billion annually. A recent national survey of 200 leading retail chains across the country documented that suspects of the ages 30 to 50 account for nearly 60 percent of all shoplifting apprehensions, with juveniles composing 22 percent of all arrested suspects. Of all shoplifters apprehended, 48 percent were female, with more arrests taking place on Saturday than any other day.[15]

Suspect Method of Operation

Shoplifters operate either from outside the organization or from within. External offenders are those who are not part of the victimized organization; employees victimize the business through internal theft. Expert opinion differs as to which general group accounts for the larger loss. It has been demonstrated that nearly 40 percent of the nation's workforce has engaged in "on-the-job" stealing. However, it is estimated that only 10 percent of all employees are recidivists who systematically steal.[16]

External suspects run the gamut of criminal types from the totally amateur to the skilled and prepared professional. Amateurs typically shoplift for secondary motivations. Adolescent peer pressure, thrill, or the desire to simply acquire an item free of charge are common reasons. Whereas the professional shoplifter derives a livelihood from this larceny, the amateur does not generally steal for profit or resale. Males and females are nearly equally distributed among both types, with all racial backgrounds represented. The professional offender does tend to be older and often works with one or more accomplices. **Kleptomania,** the well-known mental illness that compels one to steal, has been overly portrayed as a common shoplifting motivation. This illness occurs infrequently, although the investigator may encounter many suspects who rationalize their criminal actions by claiming falsely that they are kleptomaniacs. All shoplifters utilize the same basic methods, with variations, in specific details.

Booster Devices. A **booster device** (Figure 13.2) is any object other than the suspect's clothing that is used to accomplish the theft. The traditional device is a package, generally wrapped and tied with ribbon, with a hollowed-out section. The hollowed section may be operated with a springlike trapdoor, allowing the shoplifter to quickly place stolen merchandise within the box. To the untrained eye, the box appears completely sealed.

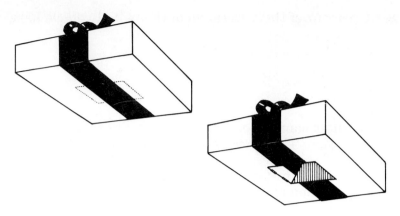

FIGURE 13.2   Booster device.

This device can be very effective. Some do not require the use of the suspect's hands to operate the trapdoor—a wire or cord performs the operation. The bogus package can be placed over a counter item, the item being "flipped" into the box by the action of a spring opening.

Clothing or Body Concealment.   This method is the most common technique used by the shoplifter. Personal clothing or some part of the body is used to conceal the stolen item. Oversized coats, maternity dresses, or a series of hooklike devices inside the clothing are often used. Generally, the amateur offender places the item inside a jacket or pants pocket; the professional is more inclined to utilize the hooks or special clothing to acquire a large number of items and to provide greater concealment.

Other concealment tactics may involve taking several garments into a dressing room with the intention of wearing those to be stolen under personal clothing. A small number of shoplifters are proficient at using the body to conceal stolen merchandise. Cases have been reported in which shoplifters have hidden small items in their mouths or between their upper legs. The leg technique is practiced by a female offender wearing a skirt. The stolen object is quickly placed under the skirt and held in place by the leg muscles. Suspects have been known to steal sizable items—as large as portable televisions—through this technique.

Switching Techniques.   The most common switching method involves taking a price tag or sticker from an inexpensive item and placing the tag on an expensive one. The offender then purchases the valuable item at a greatly reduced price. More sophisticated switching techniques, involving distraction and speed, are often practiced in jewelry stores. For example, the thief asks the jewelry store clerk to display a diamond ring or expensive watch. When the item is picked up for examination by the thief, an accomplice distracts the clerk's attention. In those few seconds, the thief conceals the original item, substituting an imitation. The unsuspecting clerk is handed the bogus piece of jewelry, and the two shoplifters depart.

Professional shoplifting teams, using a method of operation similar to that of pickpocket teams, frequently pass the stolen item from one member of the team to another immediately after the theft. Suspect A initially steals the item from the counter. The item is quickly passed to Suspect B, who may pass it to yet another accomplice. The switching is done to confuse security personnel who may have observed the first suspect stealing the merchandise. If the first suspect is stopped and searched for the item, the search will not reveal it. The other suspects, upon observing the search, quickly dispose of the item.

Investigative Procedures

The sheer volume of business larceny has forced commercial industry to adopt numerous private security deterrents. Although all local police agencies will aid in apprehending shoplifters, police officers cannot be stationed in stores at all times. Private security forces that combat business larceny may utilize uniformed or plainclothes personnel; however, undercover operations prove to be a more successful deterrent. If the presence of security personnel posing as customers is well publicized, both internal and external offenders are hesitant to shoplift. The security squads are typically augmented by electronic theft prevention systems, two-way mirrors, and hidden observation posts.

The criminal investigator generally works shoplifting cases involving professional suspects. Police agencies should be contacted when such teams are observed or when losses indicate that a criminal group has victimized the store. Professional shoplifting teams account for sizable losses of merchandise. Many South American nationals operating as shoplifters throughout the nation have been reported. Suspects from Chile, Colombia, and Peru were reported to operate mainly in stores and suburban shopping centers in Miami, Chicago, and Los Angeles. The teams generally ranged from five to ten members, with as many as 100 teams in operation simultaneously.[17]

Shoplifters can often be detected by their mannerisms. Pickpockets and shoplifters use similar tactics; both types of criminal depend upon quick movement, concealment, distraction, and occasional switching from one thief to another. Persons carrying objects to screen hand movements should be suspected, as should individuals who move from place to place in the store with no real interest in shopping. Persons who meet in a conference, disperse, and regroup should be kept under surveillance. Persons who appear to be more interested in observing the locations of clerks or who nervously glance about should also be observed. A principle with wide application in many areas of police work applies particularly well to shoplifting: *Watch the suspect's hands—the hands, in one way or another, will do the stealing.*

Legal Procedures

When a person is observed stealing merchandise, care must be taken to observe the offender from the moment the item is taken until the person is physically stopped. Although the suspect may be apprehended inside the store, prosecution is normally very difficult in such situations. To confirm the intent of the suspect to permanently deprive, an out-of-the-store arrest is always preferable.

CONFIDENCE SWINDLING

Confidence swindles or **bunco swindles** involve deceit and trickery to accomplish the swindler's aim—to induce the victim to part with something of value. Although this type of fraud has captured the public's imagination through countless books, stories, and movies, the reported frequency is not in proportion to that which the media would suggest. It is impossible to determine the true number of bunco victims accurately. The humiliation of being swindled or the reluctance to admit one's greed prohibits many victims from reporting the fraud. Swindling is an age-old crime that preys upon human character traits and specific character weaknesses. Bunco swindles invariably appeal to one or more of the following traits or weaknesses:

1. greed,
2. superstition,
3. frugality,
4. cooperation, and
5. ignorance.

Confidence swindles vary considerably as to the method of operation and skill of the offender. The old-time professional flimflam man has in many cases been replaced by a younger, less skilled offender with computer skills. There is no limit to the number and variety of swindles that occur in a community. Some involve false products or services; others revolve around "get-rich-quick" schemes. Although some bunco suspects operate alone (particularly those specializing in computer fraud), the majority of confidence games involve two or more operators. The following confidence swindles are common frauds grouped by the motivating factor, or "bait," that entices the victim.

Although all age groups are victimized by bunco criminals, the elderly are frequent preferred targets. The elderly are often selected because of their diminished physical strength, making them less of a physical threat. Also, elderly people may have retirement savings readily available. Fraud against this group of victims is often underreported, as victims are reluctant to admit their victimization. Many elderly fear that if people think they can't control their finances, they will be institutionalized. Thus the combination of embarrassment and the fear of losing one's independence persuades many elderly victims to remain silent. With this in mind, investigators should make every effort to educate the elderly regarding the prevalence of bunco fraud among all age groups and encourage full crime reporting.

Greed

The **pigeon-drop swindle** typifies the requirements for a successful bunco operation. A perfect mixture of greed, fast talk, confusion, and frequent sleight of hand, it results in a considerable money loss to the victim. There are several varieties of the pigeon drop, all of which are successful to a surprising degree. One common technique requires two swindlers, say Tom and Dick. Tom engages a likely victim, or "pigeon," in normal polite conversation. Dick suddenly appears, pretending not to know his accomplice. Dick claims to have just found a large sum of money in a wallet and attracts the attention of the victim to his lucky find. Fictitious documentation inside the wallet indicates that the money came from an illegal source. Or Dick may explain that he saw the wallet drop from a "known" criminal's pocket. Dick asks Tom and the victim for their help in deciding what to do with the money, whereupon Tom explains that he happens to work for an attorney. All three eventually agree that Tom should contact his employer to determine the proper course of action. Tom leaves the victim and Dick alone while he pretends to contact his attorney.

When Tom returns, he says that the attorney showed him a law or explained that they may keep the "illegal" money and that it is his feeling that all three should split the money, all being parties to the discovery of the wallet. Tom states that the attorney pointed out that the law requires each party to produce "good-faith" money. This money must be a substantial amount, to demonstrate each individual's ability to handle money and show trust. According to Tom, the attorney has offered his office safe as a secure place to keep the money for a specified number of days. After the set number of days have passed, the good-faith money will be returned, and the contents of the wallet will be equally divided.

The victim then accompanies both Tom and Dick to banks, where he observes them withdrawing good-faith money. Each swindler makes an obvious display of placing the money into an envelope. The victim then withdraws his money, as Tom and Dick have apparently done. All three then walk to the attorney's office. When they are outside the building, Tom, who supposedly works for the attorney, offers to take the good-faith money and wallet inside to be placed in the safe. The victim and Dick hand over all their money and wait outside. When Tom returns, the victim is told that the attorney wants to see him. The victim goes inside the building and soon realizes that no one knows what he is talking about. Quickly returning outside, the victim discovers that Tom and Dick have both disappeared with his good-faith money.

The pigeon drop is perpetrated thousands of times a year. Swindlers who commit the pigeon drop may dress to gain the victim's confidence, appearing as nurses, priests, or security guards. The Los Angeles Police Department Bunco Squad estimates the victims of this swindle lose in excess of $500,000 annually in the Los Angeles area alone.

Another type of swindle that depends on the greed motivation also uses a group affinity appeal. Generally termed **affinity scams,** this variety of fraud targets a specific ethnic or racial group. Suspects use media advertisements or personal contacts to entice victims to invest in various illegal investment schemes. Victims are guaranteed unusually high interest rate returns. The typical victim is a recent immigrant from a less developed country who has a small lifetime savings to invest. Suspects capitalize on the victim's distrust of outsiders and promote the natural affinity with members of their own ethnic group. To date, various real estate, securities, and commodity swindles have targeted Hispanic, Haitian, Iranian, Vietnamese, and Korean groups, among others. After obtaining the victim's money for alleged high-interest investments guaranteeing a return from 25 to 500 percent, the suspect vanishes with the investment capital.[18]

Superstition

Superstition swindles are successful with victims who irrationally fear that harmful consequences will result from their failure to act or comply with some type of action. The swindle invariably revolves around an "evil omen" or "curse" that will certainly befall the victim if he or she fails to act. The well-known chain letter or more sophisticated operations of this nature are often successful with poorly educated victims.

Frugality

The desire to be thrifty in matters regarding money is common to most people. Confidence operators are aware of this and often design a swindle to appeal to the person who is not greedy or superstitious but who wants to "save a buck or two." Numerous home- and work-repair schemes exemplify this type of swindle. For example, a truck that outwardly appears to belong to an established house painting company drives to the victim's home. The "work crew" offers to paint the home for a cut-rate fee, explaining that their company is on strike or that they need extra money that the boss will not know about. The victim agrees and is told that a 50 percent down payment is required before the job can commence, with the remaining 50 percent to be paid upon satisfactory completion. The victim pays the first installment and work begins. After a short time, the crew informs the victim that union rules require a coffee break. The crew drives off and is never seen again. Either bogus paint has been used, or the victim is left with a house partially painted.

Cooperation

Swindles that exploit the cooperative nature of the victim are often the most pathetic of all reports. The victim is duped into action through a desire to cooperate with the government or other type of proper authority. The **bank-examiner swindle** is the most common type. In this operation, the victim, normally at home, receives a telephone call from a fictitious bank examiner. After deceiving the victim into revealing the name and location of his or her bank, the "examiner" explains that the bank suspects one of its employees of stealing money. The victim is asked to help the bank in apprehending the dishonest employee by withdrawing a specific amount of money, usually several thousand dollars, in order to catch the thieving employee. The victim is instructed to go to the bank, withdraw the money from a certain teller, and go back home to await the arrival of the examiner. The examiner arrives at the victim's home, acquires the money as "evidence," and gives the victim an official-looking receipt. The examiner explains that the teller will now be arrested and that the victim's money will be redeposited. The victim is thanked profusely and often expects to receive a reward for cooperating. When the victim does not hear from the examiner again or when he or she attempts to withdraw additional money, the swindle is discovered.

Ignorance

Ignorance swindles are frequently combinations of the other standard confidence schemes, often involving an incredible lack of knowledge or gullibility on the part of the victim. Victims are selected for their apparent lack of intelligence or ignorance of criminal operations. Two common swindles that exploit the ignorance of victims are the bill-machine and medical-quackery swindles.

The *bill-machine swindle* requires a device fashioned to look impressive by means of blinking lights, wires, and other bogus "scientific" gadgetry. The machine is purported to make exact copies of money or to make larger bills from smaller denominations. After several slight-of-hand demonstrations that seem to produce $100 bills out of $1 bills, the machine is sold to the victim for a considerable amount of money.

The *medical-quackery swindle* is often the most ruthless in that victims who are seriously ill and unfortunately ignorant frequently suffer in terms of health as well as money. The swindler may pose as a physician or "healer" or claim to possess a secret formula or special treatment.

In one medical-quackery case, a swindler set up an office in a western state advertising a fortune-telling health advice business. Complaints were soon received that this individual was offering to cure serious illnesses, such as cancer, with a "sex cure." An undercover female police officer approached the suspect complaining of cancerlike symptoms. The suspect diagnosed her condition as resulting from a "hex," which only he could cure by sexually cleansing her body cavities.

WHITE-COLLAR CRIME

Some of the fraudulent practices previously described and many other types of illegal acts are known as **white-collar crime.** This term refers to offenses that include elements of deceit or concealment in their methods of operation but do not involve the application of physical force. Although many white-collar frauds are of a criminal nature, many will be resolved via civil proceedings. The National Chamber of Commerce and other authorities have estimated that common white-collar crimes cost the U.S. public $40 billion to $70 billion each year.

Investigative Procedures

White-collar crimes are generally very difficult to prevent—and when detected or reported, they pose many investigative difficulties. The prevention and detection of crimes of this nature are best accomplished by the industries in which they occur. It is to the advantage of business organizations to screen employees and reduce opportunities to commit fraud. Within the business, various preventive measures should be taken, including spot checks and unannounced audits. Finally, when a dishonest employee is detected, he or she should be prosecuted. All too frequently, a firm will "cover up" an employee's actions for fear of negative publicity. Or the business will allow the employee to make restitution rather than contact the police.

Law enforcement officials now fully realize the widespread problem of white-collar crime. Many agencies on the local, state, and federal levels have organized special units to detect and apprehend the white-collar criminal. For example, the San Diego City Attorney's Office operates a consumer protection unit that has recovered more than $1 million in restitution for fraud victims and $800,000 in civil and criminal fines. The 11-member unit investigates more than 1,000 cases annually.[19] Local units have been effective, but state and federal units have the jurisdictional authority and budget to make a significant impact on this crime with the aid of private industry. Investigations on the state level generally originate from the attorney general's office, in which special consumer affairs divisions are frequently located. The following federal agencies are also equipped and trained to investigate white-collar crime:

- Department of Justice, Antitrust Division;
- Department of Justice, Criminal Division;
- Federal Bureau of Investigation (the larger offices have specialized fraud units);
- Federal Trade Commission (investigates unfair, monopolistic, or deceptive fraud practices);
- Internal Revenue Service, Intelligence Division;
- Department of Housing and Urban Development, Office of Interstate Land Sales Registration;
- Postal Service (postal inspectors are frequently involved in combating white-collar crime that depends on the U.S. mail as a means to operate);
- Securities and Exchange Commission;
- Secret Service (investigates frauds involving U.S. coins, currency, and securities of the United States);
- Department of Agriculture (this agency and its Commodity Exchange Authority conduct investigations to prevent fraud to both the farmer and consumer);

- Department of Health and Human Services (enforces many federal acts that protect the public); and
- U.S. Attorney's Office.

While the true number of fraud crimes in the United States is difficult to estimate, complaints filed with the federal government are an accurate method of measurement. The Federal Trade Commission tracks the annual volume of citizen fraud complaints, which totaled 635,000 in 2004 (see Table 13.1).

CREDIT CARD AND CHECK FRAUD

Throughout history, society has encountered law enforcement problems directly related to the purchasing of goods. In the early years of the United States, most goods transactions were accomplished through barter or direct cash exchange. The law enforcement problem encountered in those times concerned counterfeiting of the currency. As the use of the check in lieu of cash became more prevalent, the check forgery problem increased. Following World War II, the concept of purchasing goods by means of credit cards gained popularity. Now the United States is well on its way to becoming a cashless, checkless society. If business experts are to be believed, the twenty-first century will find virtually all business being transacted by credit or debit card.

Credit Card Frauds

There are at least 800 million credit cards currently used in the United States.[20] The daily usage of credit and debit cards is nearly beyond imagination, as one company alone, VISA, reports that its cards are used to purchase merchandise 6,000 times a second. Consumers charge an estimated $1.7 trillion each year on their general-purpose credit cards during in-person and online shopping. Although the majority of credit card holders use them in a lawful manner, a small but significant number use the cards to commit theft. **Credit card fraud** is also the most commonly reported form of identity theft. Thirty percent of all methods of identity theft involve the misuse of credit card accounts. As in many crime-related situations, the lawful are

TABLE 13.1 Top Ten Categories of Consumer Fraud Complaints for 2004

Type of Fraud	Percent of Total Complaints
Identity theft	39
Internet auctions	16
Shop-at-home/catalog sales	8
Internet services/computers	6
Foreign money offers	6
Prizes/sweepstakes/lotteries	5
Advance-fee loans/credit protection	3
Business opportunities/work at home	2
Telephone services	2
Other	12

Source: Federal Trade Commission.

penalized financially by the criminally inclined. Credit card–issuing companies and subscribers to companies that require a fee must absorb the $790 million annual loss attributed to this type of fraud.

Suspect Method of Operation.   To perpetrate credit card fraud, the suspect must first obtain the card. A small number of offenders obtain their cards through lawful standard methods of application. An individual with the required financial background and no criminal history simply applies for and obtains the card. A considerable number of offenders (approximately 20 percent) obtain cards by means of false applications. For example, a person's name and credit card number may be obtained from a past card transaction. With this information, offenders can apply to another card company with information supplied from the victim's background but have the card mailed to themselves. An equal number of offenders obtain cards issued to but never received by legitimate applicants. Generally, the cards are stolen at the time of manufacture or from the mail. Yet the most common means of obtaining a credit card for fraud is through the commission of another crime. Purse snatches, pickpocket thefts, burglaries, thefts from autos, and many other crimes result in stolen credit cards. Many credit card frauds are committed by dishonest employees who commit the crime with a victim's legitimate card. A growing form of credit card fraud involves the use of counterfeit cards. Suspects either obtain blank plastic cards and design them to appear authentic, alter genuine cards by embossing new numbers, or steal unnumbered cards from a manufacturer.[21]

Credit card frauds occur in all jurisdictions, without regard for age, sex, or race. Amateur first-time offenders may be involved as the result of a burglary in which a card was stolen, or professionals may saturate a given community with hundreds of purchases using counterfeit cards. Most often, one of the following profit-making techniques is involved:

1. An item is purchased and sold to a fence or other party.
2. The stolen card is presented to a bank for a cash advance.
3. A dishonest clerk imprints two sets of charge slips: one is used for the current transaction; the other is filled in and the cardholder's signature is forged.
4. A dishonest clerk or waitress presents a bill for $25, receives cash as payment, and pockets the cash. Using a lost or stolen card, the clerk or waitress prepares a charge slip for $25 and forges the cardholder's signature.
5. A dishonest clerk or merchant operates a card fraud scheme with a holder of a lost or stolen card. Using the card the thief has stolen, the merchant simulates a normal expensive purchase. The merchant pays the thief a "user's fee" for the card, then pretends to have suffered a loss. The merchant then collects a sum of money equal to the value of the item from the company that issued the card. (Card issuers generally reimburse stores that are victimized by card fraud.)

Investigative Procedures.   Credit card investigations are dependent on accurate witness information and physical evidence for their success. Clerks and merchants must be trained to observe suspects accurately and provide accurate physical descriptions. The suspect's method of operation—the type of items purchased and shopping mannerisms exhibited—should also be noted. For example, some offenders always purchase items that are below the store's floor limit. The *floor limit* refers to a given cash value requiring an automatic check on the validity of the card number. Or the suspect may attempt to rush or distract the clerk to avoid a floor-limit check.

Fortunately, credit card transactions generally require a personal signature. Although the suspect typically forges this signature, a handwriting sample has been left. Some businesses require a fingerprint sample in addition to the signature. The enormous loss through credit card fraud has necessitated many systems of prevention. Many of the large credit card companies have instant phone-check systems in which a computer searches reports for a lost or stolen card matching the reported number. The clerk calls in the number before the purchase or may visually search a computer printout of stolen cards. When a suspect is apprehended via such a system, the investigation works backward from the last purchase attempt to the original theft. Since many employees or business owners are involved in this type of fraud, any patterns regarding method of operation that may occur in a particular business should be noted. Most major card companies now have specialized investigators to aid local police agencies in credit card fraud investigations.

In addition to traditional credit card investigative methods, officers will also generally search various Web sites for stolen credit card numbers. Such sites, like the one operated by CardCops, collects information from Internet chat rooms where credit card thieves have been checking to see if stolen card numbers are still valid or have been deactivated. The relatively new site already contains over 100,000 stolen credit card numbers that can be verified by police and citizens. Cardholders and investigators can check credit card numbers against the database to see if suspects are currently using credit card numbers without the knowledge of the owner. If a number is in the database, it indicates that someone has inquired whether the number has been reported stolen, and someone will likely use the number for illegal purposes if it has not been discontinued. Many of the stolen card numbers are obtained by computer hackers who break into databases of Web commerce sites. Other suspects trick unsuspecting computer users into providing card numbers. The goal of such sites is to reduce the time factor between the theft of one's card number and the victim's discovery of fraudulent charges.

Check Frauds

Fraud perpetrated through the use of the check has been a constant problem to both private industry and law enforcement. Although traditionally portrayed as a nonviolent, sophisticated criminal, there has been a growing trend toward the amateur bad check perpetrator. Commonly known as a "paperhanger," the check fraud suspect accounts for nearly $10 billion in loss of cash and property annually. In California alone, bad check cases account for an annual $400 million loss. Check investigations are generally of three types: *forgery, alteration*, and *insufficient funds*.

Forgery.   The **forgery** of a check involves the signing of another's name to a check without authority with the intent to defraud. The name signed on the check may be totally fictitious or may be the true name of the party to whom the check is issued. Obviously, the suspect must first obtain the check before the fraud is committed. The check can be stolen in a variety of ways— burglary, theft from auto, mail theft, pickpocket operations, and so forth. Or the suspect may have access to a check-printing machine by which a totally fictitious check is issued. Unfortunately, many thefts in which checkbooks are stolen also involve a matching set of personal identification.

In most situations, the suspect is prepared to authenticate the forged signature with some type of identification. False drivers' licenses and other identity documents are readily available in the criminal subculture; often they are made to order for a particular fraud.

Computer-Aided Forgery.   The proliferation of personal computers and printers has brought about a rapidly rising rate of computer-generated check counterfeiting. Using software graphics to copy corporate logos and check designs, suspects are capable of duplicating authentic checks with relative ease, printing the counterfeit check on laser printers loaded with check paper. Such paper is readily available at many stationery stores. Other offenders feed their computers images of good checks drawn on good accounts, change the date and the name of the payee, and make dozens of fake copies. Far easier to counterfeit than money, desktop-publishing counterfeit checks are the most serious crime problem facing banks, according to the American Bankers Association.

Altered Checks.   The altered check operation involves a rearrangement of preexisting information or erasures or additions. Many altered checks are written to the suspect who commits the alteration, precluding the need for a forged signature. The amount of the check is the primary object of alteration; that is, the existing amount is increased by some method of forgery. The suspect will alter the numerical and written amount of the check through physical or chemical alteration. Professionals prefer to alter commercially printed rather than personal checks, as the latter normally require more identification. In one common alteration technique, a bill is deliberately overpaid in order to receive a refund check from the company. This check is then altered so that a $10 refund becomes a $100 refund.

A growing form of check alteration commonly known as "check washing" has been recently noted in numerous states. Suspects generally obtain checks through mail theft, stealing people's outgoing mail bills that look as though they might contain a personal check. A chemical is then used to wipe away the pen ink from the payee and dollar portions of the check, leaving the victim's signature and check face intact. The check is then made out to match false identification and cashed. Check washing first surfaced in Arizona and California in the mid-1990s and has now spread across the country.

Insufficient Funds.   Banking officials estimate that 1 percent of the 50 billion checks written in the United States each year are returned because of insufficient funds. This translates into nearly 500 million such checks annually, or 15 every second.[22] In situations involving insufficient funds, checks are drawn on accounts that do not contain enough money to cover the amount of the check. An overdrawn checking account is frequently the result of unwitting error. By contrast, the criminally inclined and premeditated act utilizes two common techniques: kiting and less-cash operations.

Check kiting is a relatively sophisticated technique that involves manipulating accounts and capitalizing on bank error. A stolen check is generally used to open a new checking account in a bank. The suspect indicates that part of the check is to be credited to his or her account, with the balance to be returned in cash. A second account is then promptly opened with another worthless check, drawn on the first check before it has had time to "bounce." The suspect again withholds part of the intended deposit in cash. This procedure may continue until the suspect feels the risk is too great. By manipulating a series of accounts in many banks, the offender often builds up a sizable bankroll before discovery. Other forms of check kiting involve personal insufficient funds rather than stolen checks. Suspects write checks on one bank when there are insufficient funds in the account to cover them. To conceal the fraud, they then deposit checks drawn on a second bank at which an account with no funds was maintained. It is the pattern of depositing insufficient funds (checks) among two or more banks that characterizes check kiting. Put simply, this fraud is accomplished by taking advantage of the time required for a check deposited in one bank to be physically presented for payment at the bank on which it was drawn.[23]

Investigative Procedures.   The criminal investigator who handles check frauds must be a specialized officer. Experience, training, and a capacity to absorb detail are needed to be effective in this area of investigation. The officer must be familiar with the many varieties of check fraud and the identities of known suspects within the jurisdiction. Cooperation from state bureaus of identification and federal enforcement agencies is often needed. Since forgery of government checks is commonplace—particularly welfare, pension, and unemployment payments—various state and federal agencies are authorized to handle certain cases. As in all criminal investigations, the necessary elements that constitute the offense must be established. Thus, in check forgery, the intent to defraud must be demonstrated, as must the suspect's knowledge of the false nature of the check.

The investigation may begin with a complaint by an individual victim who has received a forged check showing a withdrawal from his or her account. Or a banking institution or business may contact the police. Any person in a position to identify the suspect must be interviewed without delay. As undue time passes, memory of physical description may begin to fade. The clerk or bank teller should be carefully questioned regarding the suspect's method of operation and physical characteristics. The type of identification used to cash the check should also be ascertained. Further, the investigator should note any type of property, other than cash, that may have been obtained for the check; certain types of property may be traceable. When a check has been altered or forged on an individual's bank account, the victim may be able to provide tracing clues. The officer should determine whether the victim has any knowledge of the check or how the forger may have obtained it. Additionally, the victim should be given the opportunity to possibly identify the handwriting. Check fraud commonly involves female suspects in much higher proportion than found in other index crimes. Since 80 percent of the 60 billion legitimate checks written in the United States are written by women, it is logical that female criminality would predominate in this form of fraud.

Prevention Methods.   The nature of check fraud demands effective methods of prevention if this offense is to be significantly reduced. Merchants, clerks, and bank tellers should be trained to recognize common features indicative of forged or altered checks, such as the following:

1. improperly set type of printed checks, misspellings, or "crowding" of handwriting or numbers;
2. areas of the paper that are off color, because of erasure or chemical alteration;
3. ink that does not match preexisting ink colors or that indicates a second writing instrument;
4. the payee's name endorsed differently from the way it appears on the name of the check;
5. an individual attempting to cash a check who is "wrong" for the type of check presented (e.g., a juvenile who presents a pension check);

6. a person who has "forgotten to bring identification" or who uses methods of distraction; and

7. a person who uses a check of a large amount to pay for a purchased item of very low worth.

Banks and other institutions have adopted devices to reduce check fraud during the cashing transaction. Many institutions stamp the back of a check with special chemical compounds. The customer is then instructed to touch the area, leaving an indelible fingerprint. Other businesses use the *regiscope*, a photo-identity camera that records the customer's image before the check is cashed. The use of computers has additionally achieved a marked effect in reducing check frauds. Lost or stolen check numbers are fed into a citywide computer system into which merchants phone prior to the cashing of any questioned check.

Police agencies are increasingly using computers to record and file information gathered in each check investigation. Systems known as Automated Worthless Document Indexes (AWDI) are being used throughout the country. In addition to storing selected data on each reported incident, the computer identifies trends and methods of operation. AWDI has saved investigators countless hours of time in connecting one or more suspects to a given series of frauds.

IDENTITY THEFT

Identity theft is one of the fastest-growing crimes of the new century. Law enforcement authorities estimate that there have been 27 million victims of this crime in the past five years. Highly profitable, this crime accounts for losses amounting to $1 billion annually. The criminal profit is so great that federal authorities report many organized crime groups are actively engaged in it, particularly Russian and Nigerian groups within the United States. Identity theft is the criminal act of assuming someone else's identity for some type of gain, normally financial. Identity theft is now the most common type of consumer fraud complaint and in 2004 comprised 40 percent of all complaints to the Federal Trade Commission (FTC). In the year 2000, identity theft complaints to the FTC comprised only 23 percent of all reports.

The crime is commonly committed by a suspect assuming another person's identity by obtaining the victim's Social Security number, date of birth, bank account, or credit card account numbers. Such data can be obtained through mailbox theft of billing statements, checks, or obtaining credit card numbers during store or restaurant purchases. Some suspects specialize in phone deception, posing as authority or financial figures, and obtain the victim's personal data through "verification" schemes. Others rummage through trash, steal records from their employer, or hack into an organization's computers.

Another common method of operation is termed "prctcxt calling," in which suspects misrepresent themselves to obtain the private data of a victim directly from banks and other financial institutions. Posing as social workers, police officers, potential employers and other figures of authority, suspects persuade employees to reveal the victim's personal identifying data. Other commonly encountered methods include quickly photocopying a victim's driver's license during a business transaction or searching through the victim's trash for credit card statements or other documents with personal data.

Some offenders employ a device commonly termed a "skimmer." This small object electronically reads or skims the information contained within a credit card magnetic strip: the black strip on the back of the card. This information gives the thief access to full account information, identification numbers, and other personal data. This device is commonly sold at business supply stores or over the Internet. After obtaining personal data, suspects either make immediate purchases or attempt to obtain various forms of credit or loans assuming the victim's identity as their own. Using what is termed as an "account takeover" methodology, criminals use the stolen identity data to request duplicate checks from a mail-order or Internet company or apply for multiple credit cards in the victim's name.

One of the latest methods of identity theft is termed **phishing** and first became prominent in 2003 and early 2004. Phishing involves suspects who create and use e-mails and Web sites designed to look like those of actual, well-known legitimate businesses, financial institutions, or government agencies. The intention is to deceive Internet users into disclosing their personal information such as bank account or password user names. The phishers then use such information for criminal purposes, committing frauds commonly associated with other forms of identity theft.

Indicators that one has been the victim of this form of theft include unauthorized withdrawals made from bank accounts, charges the holder did not make on a monthly credit card statement, and frequent creditors calling wanting payments for bills the victim has no knowledge of making. Efforts to reduce the frequency of this crime have included warnings to the public not to reveal personal information to strangers over the phone; not carrying their Social Security card, birth certificate, or passport; and never printing their Social Security number on bank checks. Large numbers of Americans are now routinely using home shredders to eliminate personal data being accessible in their trash in addition to requesting a review of one's credit history at least annually.

Most states have passed laws specifically aimed at identity theft. Nebraska's 2002 Identity Theft statute is typical of most in that offenders can be charged with identity theft rather than a more vague offense of theft or business fraud. The Nebraska statute (and those of many other states) specifies that if the loss is over $500, the suspect will be charged with a felony, and if more than $1,500, he or she can face up to 20 years in prison. The new laws also generally allow victims to seek restitution, attorney's fees, and other costs resulting from the identity fraud. Investigators can alert potential victims through publication of the facts listed in Figure 13.3.

Criminalistic Applications

Document Examination

All crime laboratories conduct extensive examination and analysis of questioned or disputed documents. A document can be literally anything upon which a mark is made for the purpose of conveying a message. A seemingly insignificant document involved in an investigation may offer many tracing clues:

1. Handwriting can exonerate an innocent suspect.
2. A specific suspect may be traced to a specific document through handwriting, a writing instrument, latent fingerprints, or DNA.
3. A specific computer printer, photocopy machine, or typewriter may be traced to a specific document.
4. Alterations, forgeries, erasures, or obliterations may be noted, and, depending on the evidence, original marks may be restored.

- Never give credit card number, Social Security number, or other personal information over the phone unless you initiate the call.
- Avoid giving similar information to online businesses, and shop only at secure computer sites. Such sites use encryption to protect personal information. Generally identified with an icon of a closed padlock or unbroken key. Secure websites begin with "https" instead of "http."
- Never put credit card numbers, Social Security number, or other personal information in e-mails.
- Minimize the number of credit cards carried; carry only the one needed.
- Avoid carrying Social Security card, passport, or birth certificate in wallet or purse.
- Since a Social Security card number is especially sought after by identity thieves, only give when absolutely necessary. Find out how the information will be used and whether it will be shared with others. Ask to use other forms of identification, and never have it printed on personal checks.
- Always take ATM and credit card receipts with you, and shred papers with personal information such as bills and pre-approved credit card offers.
- Pay attention to billing cycles. Contact creditors immediately if bill doesn't arrive on time.
- Deposit outgoing mail containing personal identifying data in post office, or collection box, to avoid mailbox theft.
- Check credit card statements as soon as you receive them for unknown charges.
- Order a copy of your credit report annually, making sure it's accurate and includes only authorized transactions. Many times people are unaware their identity has been stolen until they apply for a credit card or loan for an auto or home.

FIGURE 13.3 Minimizing Identity Theft Victimization. *(Source: The Better Business Bureau of the Heartland, Omaha World Herald, Consumer Protection Divisions of the Attorneys General of Nebraska and Iowa.)*

5. Indented writing or torn edges of a document may link one document to another or reveal tracing information.

Care and Handling of Documents. All documents should be handled so that their condition will not be changed from collection to examination. Documents submitted for examination should be placed in protective transparent folders and handled as little as possible. The document must never be folded or creased in any way. No attempt should ever be made to repair a damaged document with adhesives, staples, or other materials. Charred paper should be packed in cotton or similar material and preferably transported personally to the laboratory.

Types of Examinations. Handwriting analysis and comparison are common laboratory procedures. Handwriting gradually becomes as individualistic as speech and other personal mannerisms. In the vast majority of cases, it is possible to identify a particular sample of writing as the product of a certain suspect, given the following conditions:

1. A sufficient quantity of questioned writing must be available (the evidence item in question—forged check etc.).
2. A sufficient quantity of known standards (comparison writings) must be available for analysis.

Although many factors are considered in comparison examinations, the criminalist is primarily concerned with matching individualistic writing characteristics peculiar to the suspect present in both documents. It should be noted that the scientific examination of handwriting has no connection with the pseudoscience of graphology, or "character reading," from handwriting.

Before a positive identification of the writer can be made by the criminalist, both questioned and known writings must display a sufficient number of individualistic writing characteristics that, when considered in combination, are sufficient to establish beyond doubt that both writings are the product of the same individual. If one of the documents lacks the required number of matching individualistic characteristics, the criminalist will be unable to reach an absolute conclusion.

The ease with which documents can be matched to one another varies considerably. Some individuals write in a highly distinctive manner; the writing style of others offers little variation. When the writing is determined to have been achieved through tracing or some type of direct copying method, identification may be impossible. In such cases, the suspect is not writing but drawing. It is usually possible to determine that the questioned document is a forgery, but identification of the writer may be difficult. The surface on which the writing is done, the writing instrument and paper, the mental and physical condition of the writer, and the purpose for which the writing is prepared (signature, letter, and so forth) all influence handwriting variation. One of the most common causes of handwriting variation in questioned and standard writings is intentional disguise.

Standards of Comparison.   Standards are handwriting, printing, typewriting, and so on from a known source that are used as comparative samples in conjunction with a questioned document. Standards of comparison are vital for positive identification of questionable handwriting. The investigator should obtain handwriting standards in all questioned document investigations. Handwriting standards fall into two basic groupings: *collected writings* and *requested writings*.

Collected Writings.   Collected writings are products of the ordinary writing activities of the suspect. At the time they are prepared, the suspect has no knowledge that they will eventually serve as standards. Collected writings should include words and letters that are also included in the questioned document. Additionally, the collected standard should be in the same style as the questioned writings. If the writing in question involves a hastily written signature or a printed note, comparable standards should be obtained.

Requested Writings.   These are standards executed at the request of the investigator. It is wise to obtain specimen writing from all suspects, whether or not a confession has been obtained. The type of paper, writing implement, content, and so on should duplicate the questioned writing as closely as possible. The suspect should be put at ease and then write from dictation rather than copy a sample. The suspect should never be allowed to see the questioned writing until the standard has been obtained. Each standard should be removed from the suspect's view as soon as it is written, with the speed of the dictation varying from slow to fast. There is no specific number of standards that should be obtained in all cases; however, as a general procedure, the suggestions outlined in Table 13.2 may be followed.

Typewriting

While the computer has replaced the need for typewriting in many tasks, the typewriter continues to be encountered during various criminal investigations. The typewriter has proven to be an extremely useful tool—both in

TABLE 13.2   Example of Standards for Requested Writings

Questioned Document	Standards for Comparison
Writing on the face of the check	Ten to fifteen blank checks of the same size as the check in question completed by the suspect, using the same text (words, numbers, etc.).
Endorsement on the check	Same signature as that in question written on the back of ten to fifteen blank checks or separate slips of paper comparable in width to the questioned document.
Extended writing, such as obscene letter, extortion or holdup note	Same text as that in question written two to five times on separate sheets of paper of approximately the same size. If disclosure of the contents of the note is undesirable, another text should be dictated containing similar words, misspelled words, numbers, and so forth.
Miscellaneous signatures or notations	Same signatures or notations as those in question written ten to fifteen times on separate slips of paper.

Source: Information Concerning the Document Section of the Crime Laboratory (Tallahassee: Florida Department of Criminal Law Enforcement), p. 5.

business and in personal use. At the same time, it has aided and abetted criminal activities. The first patent for a typewriting machine was granted in England in 1714. Although the first U.S. typewriter was patented in 1829, it was not until Christopher Sholes invented the first commercially practical machine in 1868 that typewritten communication became widespread.

Types of Examinations.   There are three general examinations required in typical typewriter investigations:

1. to determine the make of a typewriter used to produce a specimen of typewriting,
2. to determine whether a document was typed at one sitting or if certain portions of the typing were added later, and
3. to determine whether a certain typewriter was used to execute a certain typewritten specimen.

Standards of Comparison.   When a typewriting specimen is questioned, it is preferable to submit the suspected machine or removable character cartridge to the laboratory if at all possible. Otherwise, the standard should be duplicated and typed three times. Several imprints of each character, separated by single spaces, should also be obtained with capital and lowercase impressions. The make, model, and serial number of the machine should be noted and shown on the specimens.[24]

Miscellaneous Document Examinations

It is often possible to determine the source of a particular paper by examining the watermark and other features. It may also be possible to determine whether two or more papers are from the same source. Further, it may be possible to determine whether a certain piece of paper was once attached to another by examining torn edges and other features. Documents that have been charred but not completely reduced to ash can often be rendered decipherable through chemical treatment. Erasures, obliterations, and alterations also can normally be determined.

Indented writings (impressions transferred through one sheet of paper to another by physical pressure) may be made visible through chemical or electrostatic detection, depending on the proximity of the submitted paper to the original at the time the impressions were made. The age of a particular document may be of investigative importance in a certain case. The exact age is generally very difficult to determine; however, it is sometimes possible to establish the age within broad limits. Inks also may yield various types of forensic information or investigative leads. Ink analysis typically entails the removal of a small sample from the suspect document through chemical means. The ink is then separated into component dyes for analysis and comparison. Additionally, the rate of the ink's physical decay may be significant. For comparison, the U.S. Treasury Department contains the world's largest collection of ink samples—more than 4,000 varieties.[25] It is sometimes possible to show that different inks were used to complete different portions of a document. Yet it is rarely possible to determine that ink from a certain pen or bottle was used on a specific document.

In submitting documents to the crime laboratory, originals should be used, if possible. The criminalist requires an original, and evidence rulings of the courts require that the original rather than a copy be submitted. The *best evidence rule* requires that the best evidence available be used to minimize the possibility of error during a judicial proceeding. Furthermore, the criminalist requires the original document to properly analyze the uniqueness of the handwriting or other factors.

Ultraviolet Tracing and Photography

Ultraviolet light (UV light) is radiation that lies beyond the violet, visible end of the spectrum. Sometimes referred to as *black light* because it cannot be seen, UV light is currently finding widespread use in criminalistics and many field investigations, in addition to document examinations. When a larceny suspect has established a method of operation, the use of UV light and fluorescent materials may help to identify and trace the offender. Ultraviolet light is also used to examine objects and to produce photographs that may yield information that would not be visible using normal light sources.

Ultraviolet Tracing.   Ultraviolet tracing is dependent upon the fluorescent effect achieved when UV light strikes an object. Some types of evidence will fluoresce naturally; other types will fluoresce only when a synthetic material is present. Fluorescence is achieved when the UV light is exposed and absorbed by certain substances, which then appear to glow, or luminesce, in a darkened area.

Fluorescent materials are available to the criminal investigator in many forms. Powders are frequently used, as are crayons and inks. For these materials to serve their intended purpose, the officer must know what type of object the suspect is likely to touch and have some notion of the suspect's identity. Larceny lends itself well to this tracing method, particularly employee theft. For example, a merchant may contact a police agency stating that one of ten employees is continually stealing boxes of shotgun shells from his sporting goods store. The merchant does not know which employee is the thief, only that the shells are being stolen from a storeroom accessible to his employees. The officer could apply a fluorescent powder to a shell box and subsequently examine the hands of all ten employees following a theft.

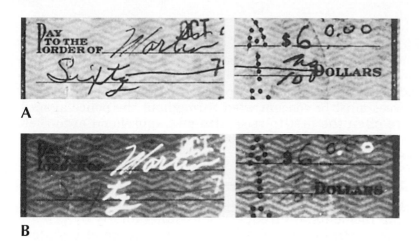

A

B

FIGURE 13.4   A check was cashed for $60 by a forgery suspect. The writer of the check insisted that it was made out for only $6, not the $60 claimed by the suspect. *A.* This photograph was taken using normal lighting and photographic techniques; *B.* The same areas were photographed using techniques to detect and record infrared luminescence. Obviously, the check had been altered as to the amount and name. *(Source: Wisconsin Department of Justice—Crime Laboratory Bureau.)*

The powder selected should be similar in color to the object being dusted; that is, a yellow powder should be applied to a yellow box of shotgun shells. The hands of the employees would then be examined with UV light to observe any fluorescent effects. This could eliminate some of the employees as possible suspects and may even link a particular employee to the thefts. This type of ultraviolet tracing is applicable to any situation in which continuous and systematic offenses occur. Thus, false fire alarms, pickpocketing, and a wide range of thefts may be traced to a particular individual.

Ultraviolet Examination and Photography.   Ultraviolet light can be used to examine certain types of evidence that may produce natural fluorescence. Blood, semen, and urine, for example, can all be located through natural fluorescence. Ultraviolet light is additionally helpful in locating hairs and fibers on clothing or within a crime scene. However, the most frequent use of UV light is in the examination of questioned documents.

When UV light is used on a questioned document, evidence of tampering or alteration may become visible. When a suspect erases or obliterates a word or number on a check, for example, the alteration may not be visible to the eye. But when UV light strikes the paper surface, the "smudginess" present within the paper fibers will generally be apparent (see Figure 13.4). For court purposes, it is frequently desirable to photograph the fluorescent effect upon a given object. Ultraviolet photography does not generally require special emulsion compounds within the film; any film sensitive to all colors of the visible spectrum (panchromatic film) can be used. No particular type of camera is required. Various filters or UV light can be placed over the camera lens to screen out nonultraviolet radiation light rays.

▲ SUMMARY

Larceny is the most common serious crime in the United States. Theft may be legally classified as a misdemeanor or felony, depending on each state's financial-loss determination. Approximately eight million thefts are reported annually, involving every conceivable type of property. Youthful offenders and women show a heavy involvement in this crime category, as 30 percent of all arrests are of juveniles, and one in three overall arrests is of a female suspect.

Motor vehicle larceny is a growing and costly form of theft. Most stolen vehicles are automobiles, although a significant percentage of cases involve motorcycles. Motor vehicles are stolen for a variety of purposes, which commonly include additional criminal activity profit and thrill motivations. Investigative resources must be concentrated throughout the police agency, as patrol officers are often the first to recognize and apprehend auto theft suspects. Following an initial arrest, investigators can often determine whether a larger car theft ring is operating.

Common larcenies are also encountered within retail business operations. Although substantial losses are incurred through internal employee theft, local police investigators are more likely to be summoned in shoplifting cases. Shoplifting incidents are frequently handled totally by private security personnel, but police may assist in the investigation of high-loss cases. Confidence swindles involve various forms of deceit and trickery to accomplish acts of larceny. Most swindles involve some type of appeal to greed, superstition, frugality, cooperation, or ignorance.

White-collar crime is a term applied to illegal acts of deceit or concealment found within professional or business operations. Often ignored or given scant attention in the past, investigations of white-collar crime are currently quite common. Many such cases involve credit card or check fraud, as well as other more specific fraudulent acts. Criminalistic assistance in many larceny investigations commonly focuses on check and document examination.

EXERCISES

1. Prepare a research paper on the topic of white-collar crime. Explain why this area of criminality has not been heavily prosecuted in the past and why current investigations are difficult.

2. Research the auto theft situation in your community, making available data regarding type of vehicles being stolen, time and place of theft, and offender characteristics.

3. Using role-playing methods, act out various confidence swindles with other students. Demonstrate the swindles to the class.

RELEVANT WEB SITES

http://www.auto-theft.info

An online auto theft information clearinghouse site containing numerous essays relating to the prevention of motor vehicle theft, stolen vehicle reporting, and vehicle identification. Many links to other national sites concerned with motor vehicle larceny.

http://www.nicb.org

Web site of The National Insurance Crime Bureau, a not-for-profit organization funded by nearly 1,000 insurance companies. Contains extensive material relating to vehicle theft and other forms of actual and fraudulent claims typically handled by the insurance industry.

http://www.ncjrs.org/spotlight/identity_theft/facts.html

National Criminal Justice Reference Service site pertaining to the facts and figures of identity theft. Details recent identity theft reports by the Federal Trade Commission and contains links to other related government sites and publications.

http://www.ftc.gov/bcp/conline/pubs/credit/cards.htm

Operated by the Federal Trade Commission, site details numerous tips on avoiding credit and charge card fraud. Also discusses the proper method of reporting credit card losses.

Narcotics and Drug Investigations

KEY TERMS

amphetamines
anabolic steroids
barbiturates
civil forfeiture
cocaine
crack cocaine
depressants
drug abuse
drug addiction
freebasing
Global Positioning System
hallucinogens
heroin

inhalants
injection kit
marijuana
methamphetamine
morphine
narcotic
narcotic tolerance
opium
physical dependence
sinsemilla
surveillance
undercover operations
withdrawal symptoms

LEARNING OBJECTIVES

1. to be aware of the historical use and abuse of narcotics and dangerous drugs;
2. to understand the relationship of opium to the production and sale of heroin and other narcotics;
3. to be able to define the opium derivatives and state their effects on the user;
4. to be able to discuss the origin, method of use, and current status of cocaine;
5. to be able to define the four major classifications of dangerous drugs;
6. to be familiar with the physical and mental effects of dangerous drugs;
7. to understand the three basic traditional investigative procedures of the drug inquiry;
8. to be able to recognize the various indicators of narcotic and dangerous drug misuse;
9. to understand the principles of the undercover operation; and
10. to be able to explain the various methods of surveillance and their application to the drug investigation.

INTRODUCTION

Human beings have used drugs since ancient times; unfortunately, drug abuse also dates back that far and has persisted to the present day. Drugs fulfill essential medical purposes. They relieve pain and aid in the cure of countless physical and mental afflictions. The abuse of drugs, however, defeats their originally intended purposes and often results in the loss of mental and physical well-being. In a legal and medical sense, **drug abuse** refers to the consumption of a controlled substance without medical authorization. Abuse also exists when illegal drugs not used by medical science are consumed. Since not all drugs are controlled and restricted by statute, drug abuse may also include the misuse of any natural or chemical compound that produces a negative effect. Organized societies have continually sought to identify and prevent the spread of drug abuse. Early customs and codes resulted in the many federal and state laws that now govern the use of drugs.

In the United States, a disturbing trend of growing drug dependency has taken place. Until the mid-1800s, a relatively small percentage of people in this country abused drugs. From the close of the Civil War to the present time, an increasingly greater proportion of the nation's population has become involved in drug abuse. The growth in population is not the sole factor responsible for this phenomenon. Apparently, a wide variety of factors are to blame, most of which have emotional, economic, or social implications. Regardless of the specific causes of drug abuse, the criminal investigator faces a difficult area of inquiry. In the late 1960s and early 1970s, a virtual "explosion" of drug abuse and experimentation took place. Much of the drug abuse centered on marijuana and various hallucinogenic compounds rather than highly addictive narcotics. Beginning in the early 1980s, however, cocaine use produced a major epidemic within five years, as crack cocaine became the narcotic of choice for millions of Americans. In the late 1990s to the present, methamphetamine reemerged and grew into a highly serious problem. Although there are indications of a leveling trend with some narcotics like cocaine, the drug problem is still extremely serious and costly to all Americans. The monetary cost of drug abuse is very high, but the emotional and physical suffering is beyond calculation.

CURRENT STATE OF NARCOTIC AND DRUG ABUSE

Illegal drug usage is highly prevalent among American career criminals. Nearly 45 percent of state prison inmates report that they used a major drug before committing the crime for which they were convicted. Nearly half of those sentenced for robbery, burglary, larceny, or a drug offense report having been under the influence of an illegal drug when they committed their crimes.[1] Programs forecasting drug use in major American cities have documented that arrested suspects will more likely than not test positive for drugs when arrested. For example, males testing positive for drugs ranged from a low of 48 percent in Houston to a high of 82 percent in New York City.[2] The national average of arrested Americans of either sex who test positive for drugs is 64 percent. Drug-testing rates are only slightly lower for arrested females. Nationally, of all persons charged with a felony in the 75 most populous counties, 35 percent are charged with drug offenses. In addition, in the federal prison system, 61 percent of all inmates are convicted drug offenders versus more than 22 percent of all state inmates.[3]

The widespread American drug problem, however, is not confined to criminal populations. Approximately 16 million Americans admit to currently using some type of illegal drug or narcotic during the past month, representing 7 percent of the population age 12 or older.[4] Moreover, 53 percent of all high school seniors acknowledge that they have used an illegal drug. Yet despite the national severity of the problem, drug use among the general population has dropped. In the late 1970s, 23 million Americans were using illegal drugs of all types, and in 1981, 66 percent of all high school seniors acknowledged drug usage. But a 12-year decline in drug use halted abruptly in 1992. Since then, drug usage has gradually increased to the point that one in four school-age children has used illegal drugs before reaching high school, and marijuana usage among teens increased 300 percent since 1992.[5]

The federal government estimates that Americans spend $49 billion annually to purchase illegal drugs. Of this total amount, $31 billion is spent for cocaine, $7 billion for heroin, $9 billion for marijuana, and $2 billion to purchase various other drugs.[6] It is ironic that this amount of money approximates the amount spent to combat the national drug problem. Federal, state, and local law enforcement share responsibility for investigating drug crimes. Most of the 1.3 million annual drug arrests are made by state and local authorities, whereas the Drug Enforcement Administration and FBI arrest approximately 25,000 suspects each year.

NARCOTICS

The term **narcotic** historically refers to drugs that produce a depressant effect on the central nervous system. There are many synthetic forms of narcotics, but the term most often describes derivatives obtained from the opium poppy such as morphine and heroin. Additionally, the federal government, through the Controlled Substances Act of 1970, classified cocaine and other nondepressants as narcotics. Cocaine differs from the traditional family of narcotics: first, it is not derived from the opium poppy, and, second, it acts as a stimulant rather than as a depressant.

The Opium Poppy

The opium poppy (Figure 14.1) is a deceptively beautiful flowering plant that has paradoxically relieved and caused much suffering throughout the world. From the poppy comes a saplike substance called **opium**. Morphine, codeine, and heroin are all alkaloid derivatives of opium. The opium poppy is planted and harvested for both legal and illegal uses. The legitimate uses for opium are directly connected to the medical field. Physicians typically use opium and morphine to relieve pain; codeine is used to suppress coughs and to control diarrhea. The poppy plant is grown in many countries for legitimate use. Poppies are grown for illegal purposes in four areas of the world: Mexico, South America, Southeast Asia, and Southwest Asia.

Opium poppy plants are harvested in the late summer or early fall through a painstaking process. The first step involves the cutting or "scoring" of the plant's seedpod with a specially curved knife. Opium then seeps forth from the incisions, drying into a brown mass overnight. The dried substance is then collected. If it is destined for legitimate use, it is graded by morphine content and further refined. If, however, it is destined to be used illegally, it is boiled with glycerine and water until it takes on a tarlike appearance and consistency. It is then pressed into cakes and sold in kilo (2.25-pound) lots.

Opium Abuse. Opium is commonly abused in many Eastern countries, but in the United States, opium abuse is now relatively rare. Opium usage in the United States was at its highest point during the late 1800s and early 1900s.

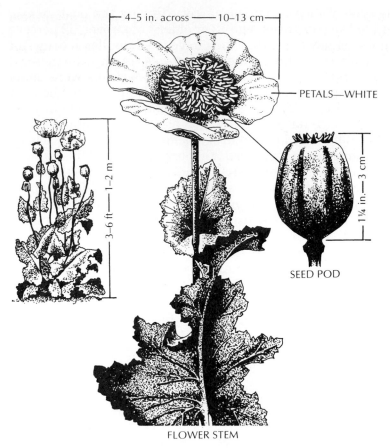

FIGURE 14.1   The opium poppy (*Papaver somniferum*).
(Source: Smith Kline and French Laboratories, Philadelphia, Pennsylvania.)

The majority of illegally produced opium and its derivatives (morphine and heroin) used in the United States currently comes from the Middle East, Southeast Asia, and Mexico.

The most frequent method of opium abuse is through the smoking process. The opium smoker needs three essential ingredients: a small amount of opium, a pipe, and a heat source. A long, metal, needlelike instrument is dipped into the opium to form a small pellet or ball, which is heated until it begins to give off fumes. The small ball is placed into the pipe, whereupon the smoker inhales the fumes of the heated opium for a period of time. Opium is a powerful narcotic that gives the smoker a sense of general euphoria and gradually induces a relaxed sleep, accompanied by hallucinations and pleasant dreams. As with all the opiates, continued use results in tolerance, physical dependence, and finally addiction.

Narcotic tolerance refers to the ever-increasing drug quantities needed to achieve the same effect obtained initially. Larger doses or greater purity are required to produce the euphoric condition that resulted, at first, with a small quantity of the narcotic or a dosage of low purity. **Physical dependence** is involuntarily achieved through continual use of a narcotic. This condition is evidenced by withdrawal symptoms when use of the drug is ceased. **Withdrawal symptoms** are serious and normally very painful, the extent of pain depending on the degree of tolerance acquired by the user.

An individual who regularly uses an opiate several times a day physically experiences symptoms of withdrawal within approximately ten hours after the last dose. Symptoms generally include feelings of extreme anxiety, sweating, muscle cramping, vomiting, and hot and cold flashes. The symptoms peak after three days, gradually diminishing over the succeeding week.

Drug addiction is a state of chronic dependence produced by repeated consumption of a substance. True addiction is a two-edged sword: the individual is affected both physically and mentally. The physical effect is characterized by tolerance and withdrawal symptoms, whereas the mental consequence takes the form of a psychological dependence on the drug.

Morphine.   **Morphine**, the principal alkaloid of opium, is converted from raw opium through a relatively simple boiling and filtering process. Opium is placed in a hot container of water and broken down into a liquid state. Chemicals are added to filter the impurities from the opium, resulting in a chemical separation of the morphine base from the original substance. The conversion process takes ten pounds of opium to achieve one pound of morphine. Morphine generally is found in tablet or a white crystalline powder form. Approximately three times stronger than opium, it is typically injected under the skin or into the muscles for medical purposes; however, the addict most often injects morphine directly into the bloodstream via a hypodermic needle or an improvised equivalent.

Although addiction to morphine is uncommon today, a substantial percentage of the male population was addicted to the drug following the Civil War. Morphine was freely used to treat the wounded, causing thousands of veterans to become dependent upon continued consumption of the opiate. Commonly referred to as the "soldier's disease," the addiction rate did not decrease until the early 1900s through natural mortality of the veterans. Unfortunately, morphine addiction still tends to show an increase following every war.

Heroin.   **Heroin** is chemically synthesized from morphine via a complicated laboratory procedure. The conversion is equal in that one pound of morphine results in one pound of heroin if the chemical process is completed correctly. Discovered in England in 1874, the drug was widely promoted as the latest cure for morphine addiction. Before scientists and the public realized that the new drug was at least five times more powerful than morphine in its pharmacological effects, thousands had become addicted.

The use of heroin is a highly serious narcotic problem in the United States, second in frequency of addiction only to the use of cocaine. Although estimates vary as to the number of addicts, a recent congressional study indicates that 500,000 to 750,000 people may be addicted to heroin.[7] An even larger number of individuals are users but not addicts. Law enforcement officials have noted an alarming return of heroin popularity in the 1990s, even though many addicts had switched to cocaine during the past decade. However, as cocaine usage stabilizes and declines, many hard-core addicts are returning to heroin abuse. Moreover, an increasing number of cocaine users are using heroin in combination with cocaine, creating dual addiction problems. Cocaine and crack abuse has proven to be highly debilitating in that the "crash" effect after ingestion is particularly difficult for users to deal with. Accordingly, many cocaine addicts now blend heroin into their drugs to modify the destructive effects of continual usage. Heroin can be injected, snorted, or smoked in conjunction with cocaine. The returning popularity of heroin has doubled the worldwide production of opium in the past several years, and the number of American seizures of this drug has risen 100 percent. As crack cocaine usage continues to decrease, heroin abuse continues to rise. Heroin is more available and purer than ever, causing both a growing acceptance of its use and the emergence of new groups of users and traffickers. Heroin prices are at a 30-year low, costing about as much as crack when purchased by street addicts.

Most of the heroin currently abused in the United States originates in South America, primarily in Colombia, with significant percentages also coming from Asia and Mexico. In the early 1990s, almost all the heroin seized on U.S. streets came from Asia. In the 1960s, the vast majority of opium was produced in Turkey, processed in France, and smuggled into the United States. Following the collapse of the so-called French Connection, producers and distributors moved their operations to Mexico, growing the opium poppy primarily along the western slopes of the Sierra Madre. Intense pressure by law enforcement authorities drove much of the heroin production from Mexico. Resurfacing in Pakistan, Afghanistan, and other Asian regions, heroin production shifted to its current primary site as Colombian organized crime groups began to invest heavily in its production and distribution. Heroin from Asia and the Middle East is generally white, whereas heroin from Mexico and South America is often brown or black.

Heroin abuse is still most prevalent in inner cities of large metropolitan areas, yet new middle-class young adult and late adolescent users in the suburbs are heavily contributing to the growth rate of this narcotic.[8] The National Institute of Drug Abuse estimates that New York City currently has the largest number of addicts—nearly 200,000. While New York may have the largest total number of heroin addicts, Baltimore may have the highest proportional heroin problem of any large American city. A study by the University of Maryland found that 40 percent of those arrested in Baltimore tested positive for heroin, twice the rate in New York City and four times that of Washington, D.C. An estimated 60,000 people—nearly 1 in 11 Baltimore residents—are addicted to heroin. This unusually high rate of addiction significantly contributes to the city's criminal homicide rate and other forms of street crime.[9]

Heroin Distribution Cycle   Heroin is bought and sold by individuals who may be typed according to four basic categories: principal distributors, wholesalers, ounce distributors, and street dealers. *Principal distributors* reap the greatest profits from illegal opiate sale and conversion. Heroin is the most common product of opiate conversion and the greatest moneymaker. Principal distributors are usually organized crime figures or freelance operators who have the funds and connections to establish a production source. Frequently, one organized crime group works with another to establish a mutually profitable operation. For example, the U.S. Cosa Nostra (Mafia) conducted regular heroin transactions with the so-called Mexican Mafia. The latter group controlled most of the poppy production in Mexico and was composed of Mexican and Mexican American individuals. Other organized crime groups have included the Chinese and Nigerians. Chinese ethnic groups remain the dominant overseas importers and wholesale distributors of heroin. Nigerian involvement is the newest link in the heroin distribution cycle; officials estimate that as much as 40 percent of the American heroin supply is controlled by Nigerian suppliers and dealers.[10] However, the principal heroin threat to the United States continues to come from poppy cultivation in Colombia and Mexico.

Principal distributors will pay from $18,000 to $25,000 for a kilo of pure, unadulterated heroin. The distributors finance the growth of the poppies, perform the chemical conversions, and finally smuggle the heroin into the United States. Nearly all opium-to-heroin chemical conversions are performed in foreign countries; however, one U.S. laboratory (in California) has been located to date. Following its conversion, heroin is transported by "mules" (persons who illegally transport drugs) into the United States. Many methods are used, such as body concealment, concealment in luggage or other goods, or shipment by mail. From the beginning of heroin production in Mexico, there have been sharp increases in heroin smuggling by the same suspects who routinely smuggle illegal Mexican immigrants into California. Although the federal government uses a variety of methods to seize the incoming narcotic, it is estimated that only 6 percent is actually intercepted.

When heroin reaches the United States, the principal distributors sell the narcotic to wholesalers for nearly $175,000 per kilo. *Wholesalers* are individuals who have considerable funds for narcotic purchases but lack the connections to produce opium poppies. At this stage of the distribution process, the heroin is "cut" or diluted into lower levels of purity. Wholesalers typically dilute 100 percent pure heroin to kilos that are 80 percent pure. In the cutting process, milk sugar or quinine is usually added to the heroin to reduce its potency. By cutting the heroin, the wholesaler quickly turns one kilo into two kilos of an adulterated nature. The wholesaler then sells the cut kilos to an ounce distributor, who will again dilute the heroin.

An *ounce distributor* generally buys heroin in pound quantities and cuts the pound many times until the purity is reduced to 60 or 50 percent. This distributor then sells the heroin in ounces (five grains to an ounce) or in smaller quantities to street dealers. The *street dealer* is almost always an addict whose addiction is financed by the sale of small amounts of heroin to other addicts. By the time the heroin reaches the veins of the addict, its purity has been reduced—although purity levels are currently rising. The purity of heroin abused by street addicts now averages approximately 36 percent, compared to 7 percent a decade ago. The profit inherent in the distribution process is enormous. When all profits are computed at the various levels, the $18,000 kilo of heroin has profited many persons for a total of approximately $1.5 million.

Methadone

Methadone is a totally synthetic narcotic, the effects of which are similar to those of the natural opiates. Originally developed to serve as a pain reducer, the drug is widely used in medically supervised heroin detoxification programs. Methadone eliminates the physical withdrawal symptoms that normally occur when an addict ceases to use heroin. However, the use of one drug to replace another has resulted in controversy. Although methadone does not produce the euphoric "high" experienced with heroin, a similar tolerance and dependency can develop in the user. When methadone usage ceases, the resulting withdrawal symptoms are not as severe as symptoms exhibited with heroin withdrawal, but they may be more prolonged.

Methadone treatment maintains an addict's physical and mental dependency on a drug but seeks to keep the individual free from the criminal lifestyle necessary to purchase heroin. Unfortunately, many addicts in methadone maintenance programs revert to heroin usage. The strong psychological need for the "uplifting" effect of heroin may account for this. Although the methadone does satisfy physical needs, the need for a euphoric experience is very strong.

Methods of Opiate Abuse

Opium, morphine, heroin, and codeine are abused in a variety of ways. The substance may be smoked, ingested through the mouth or nostrils, or injected into the system. Intravenous injection has always been the method of preference for the addict. When a drug is injected directly into the bloodstream by means of a hypodermic needle, the effect of the drug is maximized. When other techniques are used, such as smoking, sniffing, or swallowing, the drug is broken down and reduced in potency before it enters the bloodstream. The addict wishes to achieve the fastest and most powerful effect possible from a narcotic that is generally low in potency. Thus, nearly all addicts use the injection technique.

The narcotics addict possesses an **injection kit** or "outfit," consisting of a syringe, cooker, filter, tourniquet, and heat source (see Figure 14.2). The heroin is initially reduced from a powder to a liquid since only a liquid substance may be injected. The heroin powder is placed in a spoon (cooker) and heated from beneath until the solution reaches the boiling point. A small piece of cotton or cloth material is then used to filter impurities while the solution is drawn into the syringe. The tourniquet is applied to "raise a vein," and the heroin is subsequently injected into the bloodstream.

Low purity levels of heroin in the past led abusers to inject heroin directly into the bloodstream to produce the greatest possible "high," but purity levels of heroin are currently much higher, in some cities as high as 50 percent, so that approximately one in three addicts now smokes or snorts the narcotic. The threat of AIDS transmission through shared needles has also caused many addicts to change their method from traditional injection.

Cocaine

Cocaine is a narcotic that is extracted from the leaf of the coca bush (Figure 14.3). The coca bush is entirely unrelated to the opium poppy; hence, cocaine bears no generic relation to opium. The leaves of the bush are harvested and soaked with solutions to yield coca paste. This paste, or unrefined

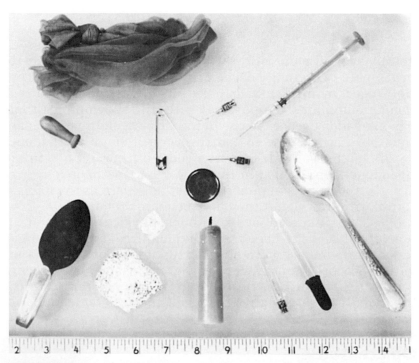

FIGURE 14.2   The heroin user's injection kit, common to many types of illegal drug use. Tourniquet, spoons, needles, and other items are for dissolving, heating, and injecting narcotics. *(Source: Wisconsin Department of Justice—Crime Laboratory Bureau.)*

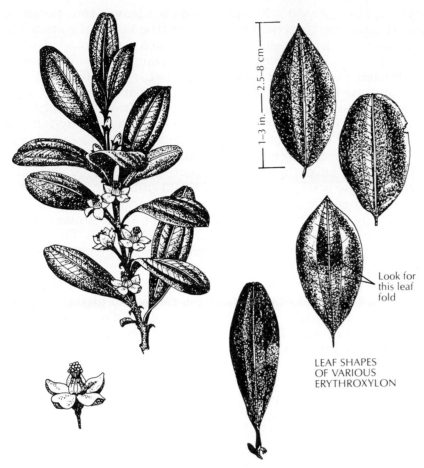

1–3 in. — 2.5–8 cm

Look for
this leaf
fold

LEAF SHAPES
OF VARIOUS
ERYTHROXYLON

FIGURE 14.3   The coca bush (*Erythroxylon coca*). *(Source: Smith Kline
and French Laboratories, Philadelphia, Pennsylvania.)*

cocaine, is then shipped to a processing laboratory for refinement. When
cocaine reaches the street for sale, it is in the form of a white crystal-like
granule that is often processed into rock form.

As with the opium poppy, several countries legally produce coca leaves for
medical and commercial use. Regarding illegal production and shipment to the
United States, many South American countries contributed in the past.
Currently, however, Peru and Bolivia grow most of the leaves on more than
200,000 acres. After the leaves are rendered into paste, the bulk is transported
to Colombia for refinement and distribution. Accordingly, Colombia is directly
responsible for most of the white crystalline cocaine reaching the United
States. It seems that Colombia's northeastern Caribbean region of Guajira is
economically dependent upon the production and trafficking of cocaine and
high-grade marijuana. It is estimated that 90 percent of all inhabitants of the
province are directly engaged in the illegal drug trade. Further, Colombian law
enforcement officials indicate that the profits realized from illegal cocaine now
rival those from coffee as the country's biggest moneymaker. The vast majority
of South American cocaine, at least 70 percent as reported by the Drug
Enforcement Administration, reaches the United States through Mexico.

Methods of Cocaine Abuse.   The abuse of cocaine in the United States is
not a recent phenomenon, as is popularly believed. Cocaine was widely used
in hundreds of "tonics" and patented medicines during the late nineteenth

century and early in the twentieth. So safe were coca leaves considered in 1885 that a concoction of coca leaves and kola nuts (the latter, the source of caffeine) was introduced as a quick-energy drink named Coca-Cola.[11] But as the dangers of coca leaves were recognized, the formula of the drink was changed to the present nonnarcotic beverage. In 1910, President William Taft reported to Congress that use of cocaine was the most threatening drug habit to have ever appeared in the United States. It was not until the passage of the federal Harrison Act in 1914 that cocaine was declared illegal to possess and sell. During the 1960s, cocaine again gained widespread popularity. By the mid-1980s, more than four million people here regularly used the narcotic at least once a month, with more than 500,000 seriously dependent upon it.[12] One study estimates that 20 million people in this country have now tried cocaine at least once. Among those ages 18 to 25, cocaine use is especially high. The National Institute on Drug Abuse reports that 19 percent of people in this age-group have tried cocaine. The House Select Committee on Narcotic Abuse and Control estimates that 45 tons of cocaine illegally reach the United States each year.

Although cocaine is classified as a narcotic drug, along with the highly addictive opiates, some authorities state that tolerance and physical addiction do not result from continued usage. However, other drug researchers feel that the narcotic can be addictive in a physical sense. Further research is needed to determine positively the extent of physical addiction related to cocaine. It is clear, though, in the minds of most experts, that the narcotic is highly addictive from a psychological standpoint. Cocaine is a very powerful stimulant to the central nervous system. It is commonly inhaled, although some users inject the drug intravenously. Users typically "snort" the drug by reducing the crystal granules to a light powder. A small spoon containing the cocaine is inserted in one nostril while the other nostril is squeezed shut. The drug is then drawn into the mucous membranes of the nose by inhaling.

Freebase Cocaine.   Cocaine abuse throughout the 1970s and early 1980s was almost exclusively centered on the narcotic's hydrochloride powder. The white crystalline powder was expensive and primarily abused through nasal inhalation. In 1974, California abusers began to popularize a new method of cocaine use termed *freebasing*. **Freebasing** is a chemical process that "frees" base cocaine from its hydrochloride powder. The powder is first dissolved, then chemical catalysts are added to obtain nearly pure cocaine. Freebase cocaine is created through an unstable chemical process involving ether and elaborate paraphernalia, such as acetylene or butane torches. By 1980, authorities estimated that between 10 and 20 percent of all addicts were using freebase exclusively.[13]

Crack cocaine is another form of freebase cocaine. However, unlike the older original freebase method, crack freebase is produced through a process that is cheaper, simpler, and safer. Crack cocaine is obtained by combining the narcotic with baking soda and cooking the mixture. The former heating method was highly explosive because of the ether-heating process, but the crack method uses simple heating sources such as stoves, microwaves, or coffee machines, among others. Crack is nearly pure cocaine, stripped of the hydrochloride granules that make it a powder. After heating, the crack is quickly cooked and compressed into a dense chunk about one-fourth the volume of the powder from which it was converted. Abusers melt the crack, or "rock," onto layers of screens within a pipe bowl, invert the bowl, and smoke the resulting fumes. Crack is extremely powerful—at least five times as powerful as powdered cocaine. The Drug Enforcement Administration (DEA) estimates that 75 percent of those who abuse crack cocaine will become addicted after three uses and that as many as 50 percent may become addicted after the first use.[14] The reality of the government estimates can be appreciated when one realizes that 400,000 Americans regularly use crack, whereas as recently as 1980, there were no crack abusers.

Beginning in 1999, drug investigators noted a gradual decline in crack usage in many urban American cities. For the first time in nearly a decade of rising crack arrests, apprehension rates are now dropping. The crack epidemic is declining for a variety of reasons, including zero tolerance by the police for anyone using or selling drugs in the open. Since crack is highly dependent upon open "drug bazaars," police pressure has dramatically affected the ability of crack dealers to sell their products. Additionally, there has been a general revulsion against the drug that is not associated with other drugs. As a result, crack is often shunned by potential younger users and is becoming a drug used primarily by older, previously addicted abusers.

Cocaine Distribution Cycle. Unlike the traditional three-tiered distribution cycle for other narcotics, cocaine distribution is essentially a two-step cycle. Principal distributors reap the greatest profits, as they coordinate purchase and transportation of coca paste from its origin in Central American countries. Organized crime groups dominated by Colombians are primarily involved at this highest level. Principal distributors first process leaves from plants grown in Peru and Bolivia into coca paste. The paste is then refined into powdered cocaine at various sites overseas and within the United States. At this point, most principal distributors sell the refined cocaine to secondary dealers, whereas others handle the secondary distribution themselves. Secondary dealers typically take the refinement process a step further, transforming the cocaine powder into crack cocaine (see Figure 14.4).[15] Many large secondary dealers then sell the cocaine directly to the street addict population, avoiding the traditional wholesale level of distribution common to heroin dealing. Because of the simplicity involved in converting cocaine to freebase crack, a wide variety of secondary dealers is common. However, much of the total volume is controlled by either Jamaican or black street-gang organizations.

Initially, most of the imported cocaine came from Colombia into the United States through south Florida. However, intensified law enforcement efforts successfully forced many principal dealers to move their operations to Mexico. Accordingly, the first signs of crack cocaine originated in California during the early 1980s, as refined cocaine moved from Mexico into Los Angeles. California-based black street gangs, primarily the Crips and the Bloods, were quick to realize the profits of secondary crack cocaine dealing and marketed the narcotic eastward across the country. Jamaican organized crime groups known as "posses" originally dominated East Coast

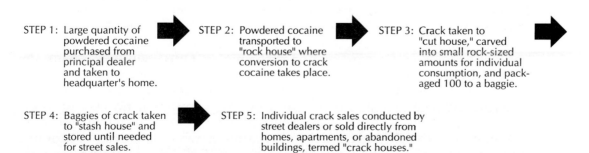

FIGURE 14.4 Crack cocaine distribution process.

operations but have expanded into the Midwest. As a result of aggressive sales by both groups, crack first appeared in New York City in 1985 and soon dominated addicts throughout the city.[16] Authorities estimate Crip and Blood gang membership at nearly 40,000; Los Angeles–based gangs control up to 30 percent of the crack trade. Approximately 40 Jamaican posses with a total membership of 22,000 have also been involved.[17] Many other groups and individuals are also active in large-scale secondary cocaine dealing, including white motorcycle gangs and Dominican and Haitian organized crime groups.

Physical and Mental Effects of Narcotics

Opiates. Natural and certain synthetic opiates have a depressant effect in a mental and physiological sense. When the narcotic first enters the body, the so-called rush is experienced. A rush is the most intense euphoric sensation resulting from use of the drug. The rush generally lasts only several minutes, after which the user "goes on the nod," or exhibits drowsy, stupor-like behavior. The user may appear to be asleep at this time or to be drifting back and forth from sleep. Speech is often slurred and rambling, and the pupils of the eyes are very constricted. Psychologically, the user experiences a "mellow" state of well-being in which all worldly problems and cares are insignificant.

The duration of the effects resulting from an opiate varies according to its purity and the tolerance of the user. An addict who has regularly used heroin for a year generally experiences the euphoric effects for only two to three hours; a first-time user experiences the effects for a much longer time. After approximately five hours, the experienced addict feels physical and mental discomfort. If ten hours pass without another injection (fix), mild withdrawal symptoms begin. Intense withdrawal suffering will be evident within 12 to 24 hours.

Cocaine. Cocaine produces an immediate psychological and physical rush sensation. Since individuals react to cocaine in much the same way as they react to amphetamines, it is often difficult to determine whether cocaine was ingested or a strong amphetamine. Increased heartbeat, elevated blood pressure, and dilation of the pupils typically result from cocaine ingestion.

The physical dangers of cocaine usage have now been well documented. Ailments range from minor nasal membrane damage to fatal heart and lung failure. Medical problems related to cocaine abuse constitute the most common drug-related reason for visits to hospital emergency rooms. Thirty-six percent of all drug-related visits are connected with cocaine, resulting in 2,500 deaths yearly.[18]

The psychological delusions resulting from cocaine use are highly desirable to the addict. A sense of increased vigor and physical strength is typically experienced. The user may also become excitable, verbose, and anxious. Some exhibit antisocial behavior—becoming loud, overly aggressive, and sometimes physically abusive. The euphoric sensations from cocaine do not last as long as those associated with opiates. Often, within an hour, the effects of the narcotic will have worn off, leaving the user with a depressed, "washed-out" feeling. The "high" from crack lasts a very short time, generally no longer than 5 to 15 minutes. In a significant number of cases, hallucinations and feelings of persecution may be experienced. Such behaviors may occur with a large dose of cocaine or when the drug is of much greater purity than what is customarily ingested. Crack cocaine smokers are more likely than other cocaine users to be violent or psychotic.

DANGEROUS DRUGS

Synthetic and natural substances, other than narcotics, that have the potential to injure through abuse are commonly referred to as *dangerous drugs*. The many drugs that fit this general description can be classified as depressants, amphetamines, hallucinogens, and inhalants.

Depressants

Depressants are drug compounds, commonly referred to as **barbiturates** and *tranquilizers*, which have a sedative effect on the nervous system. Drugs such as Seconal, Valium, Nembutal, and scores of others are unfortunately often abused in our society. Depressants are commonly prescribed by physicians to relieve apprehensive and anxious mental conditions, muscle spasms, and high blood pressure. Additionally, an individual suffering from insomnia may resort to depressants to induce sleep.

The abuse of barbiturates may lead to tolerance and physical dependency. Further, if the user suddenly stops taking a depressant that has been habitually abused over a long period of time, serious withdrawal symptoms can develop. A person under the influence of a depressant may appear to be intoxicated. That is, coordination, speech, and thinking patterns may be slowed or altered. Depressants are abused by many different types of people, ranging from the inner-city youth to the affluent suburban housewife. More adults than juveniles are habitual users, and, for the most part, they obtain the barbiturates from legitimate sources. The abuse of all prescription drugs has become widespread, of which depressants are the most commonly encountered. Federal studies indicate that 15 million Americans are currently abusing prescription drugs, which includes two million teenagers. One in five teens has abused a prescription painkiller, more than have experimented with Ecstasy, cocaine, crack, or LSD. A major factor in juvenile prescription abuse is the easy home access to drugs prescribed to parents.[19]

As the user increases the drug dosage to accommodate tolerance, the daily dosage can grow to dangerously high levels. Depressants are generally taken orally, in pill form. However, chronic users who are addicted may inject the substance intravenously by dissolving the tablets or capsules. Barbiturate users may accidentally or intentionally mix other substances with the drug. Depressants mixed with opiates are not uncommon. Mixtures with alcohol can result in death. In fact, a substantial number of accidental and suicidal deaths are the result of depressant abuse.

A powerful sedative, *Rohypnol*, became a serious drug of abuse in the late 1990s. Although illegal in the United States and Canada, the drug is commonly prescribed in other countries, including Mexico and Colombia, as a sedative. It is ten times as powerful as a standard sleeping pill. Also known as "roofies," the small white pills are generally smuggled into the United States from Mexico and sold for less than five dollars per unit. Although some abusers use Rohypnol to enhance the effects of alcohol or marijuana, most attention regarding this drug centers on its ability to erase memory through its amnesiac effects. Suspects commonly place the pill into the drinks of unsuspecting victims and proceed to rape and otherwise abuse the victim. In about ten minutes, Rohypnol creates an intense blackout, a drunklike effect that can last up to eight hours. In Florida alone, more than 100 reports of sexual assaults on victims incapacitated by Rohypnol were reported in a recent year.[20]

Another depressant drug compound that is increasing in popularity is *GHB*, or gamma hydroxy butyrate. Commonly abused by juveniles and young adults, GHB is a "designer drug" or synthetic drug easily mixed if one has the formula and knowledge of where to purchase the necessary chemicals. The chemicals needed to produce GHB are easily obtained, with the main ingredient being paint thinner. As with most such drugs, formulas and preparation instructions abound on the Internet.

Originally developed as a surgical anesthetic, bodybuilders first abused GHB in the early 1990s, then it became well known as a date-rape drug in a similar fashion to Rohypnol. Currently, the drug is used as a "party drug" and is often abused by those who would not use other illegal narcotics such as cocaine. GHB produces a relaxed, uninhibited feeling similar to the drunken state of alcohol intoxication. However, such effects are often followed by severe headaches, nausea, vomiting, fever, muscle rigidity, and slowing of respiration. When GHB is combined with alcohol or used in high enough quantities to result in an overdose, seizures, cardiac arrest, coma, and even death may occur. Hospitals have reported a rash of recent deaths from GHB—at least 72 people have died—and 5,000 people have been treated for overdoses since it became popular ten years ago.

The powerful synthetic painkiller OxyContin has recently become a drug of widespread abuse. OxyContin acts upon the brain and body in a similar fashion to morphine and is highly effective in reducing chronic pain among the seriously ill. However, drug abusers have increasingly sought the prescription drug because of the intense "high" achieved by ingesting the pills orally, snorting, or crushing the pills and injecting the substance directly into the bloodstream. Abuse patterns began in the late 1990s in rural Appalachian areas of the country and by 2003 had spread widely across the nation. Overdoses of the drug during the past three years killed nearly 40 people in rural Virginia alone and is attributed to 120 deaths nationwide. In addition to buying the tablets through drug dealers, addicts may fake intense pain symptoms to obtain a doctor's prescription. The popularity of the drug has lead to a rash of pharmacy burglaries and armed robberies in which OxyContin is the specific target.

Stimulants

Commonly known as "uppers," stimulants have a stimulating effect on the central nervous system. The most commonly abused stimulant of dangerous drugs are the various **amphetamines.** Physicians do not prescribe amphetamines as often as they do barbiturates, but prescriptions for such stimulants as benzedrine and dexedrine are still quite common. Tolerance can develop through abuse, although most authorities feel that physical dependence does not. As in the case with many dangerous drugs, an unnecessary medical prescription often accounts for the user's initial experience. Complaints focusing on obesity, depression, and fatigue are commonly heard in countless physicians' offices in efforts to obtain prescriptions for stimulants.

Certain physiological reactions result from using amphetamines, and the behavior of the user will be affected. When the drug is first ingested, the heart and respiratory rates increase. An increased sense of general excitement and alertness is experienced. Fatigue diminishes, giving way to renewed mental and physical energy. Individuals under the influence of stimulants may appear to be hyperactive—constantly moving about, with quick and restless actions. If the dosage is high, aggressive behavior may be displayed. The user may be irritable or easily provoked to violence. The majority of stimulants are taken orally, but those who chronically use amphetamines on a daily basis typically inject the substance.

Methamphetamine.   The abuse of **methamphetamine**, a powerful stimulant, is currently a serious and rapidly increasing drug problem in most parts of the United States. First encountered during the late 1960s, this powerful amphetamine, commonly known as "meth" or "crank," can be abused through snorting, injecting, or smoking. Currently, the most common method of abuse is inhalation, although addicts often advance rapidly to injection, which is the most effective delivery system for most drugs. Smokable methamphetamine, known as "ice," has the same chemical properties as common methamphetamine but is converted into a rocklike form for smoking. Smokable rock methamphetamine is more potent than other forms of amphetamine and is highly addictive. Contrary to widespread predictions, smokable methamphetamine has not materialized as a leading drug problem in the United States. Only one state, Hawaii, has reported an unusually high number of abusers of smokable methamphetamine.[21]

Rapidly increasing in popularity during the latter part of the 1990s, methamphetamine has even surpassed cocaine as the drug of choice among a substantial number of users. By 2005, the head of the DEA reported that methamphetamine enforcement had become a national priority and was the largest drug problem facing rural America. Deaths attributed to this dangerous drug in Phoenix were up sixfold in a single year, and the Midwest states tracked a 510 percent increase in methamphetamine arrests in a recent three-year period. In Des Moines, Iowa, authorities make more arrests for methamphetamine abuse or sale than for drunk driving. The "high" of this drug lasts up to ten times longer than that created by a similar amount of cocaine. Substantially more potent than methamphetamine abused two decades ago, today's methamphetamine is often six times more powerful. While a substantial amount of this drug finds its way into the country from Mexico, methamphetamine is a popular homemade commodity.

Using a relatively easy mixing process, methamphetamine can be created through the combination of common over-the-counter products, such as cold and asthma medicines, anhydrous ammonia fertilizer, drain cleaner, antifreeze, lye, and starting fluids. Using formulas spread by word of mouth or by the Internet, suspects utilize various types of plastic tubing, glassware, and propane tanks to mix the chemicals to produce methamphetamine. Since the chemical process produces telltale odors and other suspicious indicators, the makeshift labs are typically located in garages, empty barns, vans, rental storage units, and even bathtubs (See Figure 14.5). The number of methamphetamine labs continues to grow, posing an explosive and environmental danger to those living nearby. From 1973 to 1999, the DEA seized 9,469 secret meth laboratories across America. The rapid growth of the meth problem is evidenced by the discovery of 8,500 labs in 2005 alone. As police crack down on methamphetamine in cities and rural towns, makers of the drug have set up operations with increased frequency in state and national forests. In 2000, the U.S. Forest Service alone located 488 meth labs, a 356 percent increase from the previous year. Another newer, rapidly growing phenomena involves "roving labs." Such operations utilize vehicles in which the mixing and purifying of meth is done. Cars, rental trucks, and tractor trailers are converted into rolling laboratories to avoid detection. The distinctive rotten-egg smell is dispersed along the highway, and the by-product waste is kept out of suspect's homes.

Each year, the DEA reports nearly 1,500 methamphetamine labs found in vehicles, with the true number no doubt being much higher, as local and state police are not required to report lab seizures to the federal government. Yearly vehicle lab seizures ranged from only one in Alaska to 172 in the state of Washington. The volatile nature of the various chemicals used to make meth causes a dangerous environment regardless of where the lab is located. Of the 2,000 chemicals commonly available to make the drug, at least 50 percent are explosive. While most meth labs are discovered through traditional police work such as undercover investigations, one in five is discovered

FIGURE 14.5 The cleanup and removal of methamphetamine labs can be very hazardous. Here a narcotics agent who is specially trained in such procedures begins to dismantle a meth laboratory. *(Source: Russell Schanlaub, Bi-state Drug Task Force, Northwestern Indiana.)*

because of an explosion. The environmental cleanup costs of removing a hazardous meth laboratory can range from $50,000 to $100,000 for a large operation. The general public can be educated to assist law enforcement by recognizing the presence of meth labs. Indicators often include the following:

1. The presence of strange ether odors, a sweet-smelling substance. Other foul odors are often present because of the common usage of ammonia in the "cooking" process.
2. Suspicious activity in neighboring homes, hotel rooms, or other localities, which includes unusual items being discarded into the trash, such as numerous propane tanks, glass containers, red-stained coffee filters, and empty lantern fuel cans.
3. Continual traffic into the house, individuals smoking outside the locality (done to avoid explosions of the highly flammable chemicals inside) and houses or apartments with reinforced doors and windows.
4. In rural areas, the theft of fertilizers such as anhydrous ammonia from sales sites or from individual farm or ranch tanks.

While a considerable amount of methamphetamine is produced in home labs, much of the drug comes into the United States from production sites in Mexico.

Law enforcement has been far more successful in tracing and eliminating small meth labs within the United States than international processing facilities. Foreign labs are often protected by corrupted officials and political obstacles. Small domestic "stove-top" operations are typically run by one or a few suspects known as "cooks" or "cookers." After easily obtaining various legal products that combine to create meth, the suspects directly sell the product to lower-level dealers or addicts in their community. A federally funded study of California meth labs raided in Riverside and San Bernadino counties yielded information that can be applied to investigations throughout the nation. Annual lab seizures in the two counties totaled 373, constituting 35 percent of all meth labs discovered in California. Findings from the study indicated the following regarding small-time meth lab operators:

- 33 percent admitted they were long-time meth users who were in treatment programs when their labs were raided.
- 20 percent had been arrested previously for manufacturing meth.
- 88 percent preferred to cook meth on Tuesdays and Wednesdays, usually between the hours of midnight and six in the morning.
- The majority of cookers had fires in their labs within a 36-month period, with 33 percent experiencing multiple fires.
- Friends were present during the cooking process 35 percent of the time, spouses or significant others 20 percent, and neighbors 5 percent.
- 25 percent stated their immediate neighbors knew of their meth labs.
- 60 percent learned how to cook meth under the supervision of a close friend or relative.
- Cookers teach four other people to make meth each year and on average had used the drug for nearly six years before trying to manufacture it.[22]

As with all stimulant users, a wide variety of individuals from varying socioeconomic groups abuse methamphetamine. Although traditionally associated with "biker types" and disadvantaged Hispanic populations, the addiction problem has rapidly spread to the middle class. A substantial number are not chronic but "situational" users who take the drug only when a given situation arises. Business executives or students who wish to continue mental work-study activities often take stimulants to relieve their fatigue. Truck drivers, cab drivers, construction workers, and individuals in many other occupations take the drug to continue physical activities. But most people take amphetamines for the "thrill" these drugs provide.

Methamphetamine gives an immediate and intense rush or a delayed euphoria, depending on how it is taken. The drug decreases the appetite, increases alertness, causes paranoia, and decreases the need for sleep. As the potency of methamphetamine has increased, situational users run the continual risk of addiction. Chronic users ("speed freaks") often alternate between states of exhilaration and total mental and physical exhaustion. Continued high dosages of stimulants act to delude both the body and mind. While the user is "high," sleep is impossible, eating is ignored, and the body is in a general state of stress. The drug literally changes the brain so that the user feels a need for more drugs to return to a "normal" state. Some users will display schizophrenic or psychotic behavior. Often the user's body is already exhausted when another dosage of methamphetamine is ingested, reducing physical reserves and defenses against illness even further.

As with all forms of drug abuse, any type of person can be a potential addict. However, the typical meth abuser is a white male in his mid-20s to early 30s. Research indicates that most users try the drug at age 20 and have extensively used alcohol and marijuana starting at age 14. While most meth users are male, a rapidly increasing number are female. Experts believe that 40 percent of users are now women and fear the number may rise during the next five years. The drug appeals to women because it is relatively inexpensive and easy to obtain and gives them energy to take care of children, among other tasks. Nationally, of all women in drug treatment programs, 47 percent identified meth as their primary drug. In Iowa, 43 percent of women entering prison in 2002 said meth was their drug of choice, compared to 25 percent in the year 2000.

A leafy substance known as *Khat* is appearing with greater regularity across the nation. When ingested, the Khat plant produces an amphetamine effect, enhancing alertness and mood, and suppressing appetite. Regular use can lead to insomnia, anxiousness, irritability, hallucinations, and violence. The active ingredient is cathinone, which generally loses its potency after 48 hours. Police link a recent influx of immigrants from Somalia and other African and Middle Eastern countries with the increased prevalence of the drug.

Khat has been illegal in the United States since 1993 but is legal and widely used within other cultures, particularly within the countries of Somalia, Ethiopia, Kenya, and Yemen. While still mostly confined to immigrant groups from such countries, the abuse of Khat has spread to nonimmigrants. The shiny, bright-green or reddish-green Khat leaves are often sold attached to rhubarb-appearing sticks. A bundle of 15 to 30 sticks sells for about $40 and is either chewed or brewed in a tea-like fashion. Most of the Khat being used in the United States is not grown domestically but is shipped by air express or courier from African or Middle Eastern countries. Because the potency of Khat drops dramatically 48 hours after the leaves are harvested, it is quickly used by suspects before the amphetamine effect diminishes.

Hallucinogens

Although many of the hallucinogenic drugs became household words during the past three decades, the use of so-called consciousness-expanding substances can be traced to primitive human beings. **Hallucinogens** can be found in nature, made within a laboratory, or combined through a semisynthetic process. Drugs that dramatically alter perception, behavior, and thought processes have a strong potential for abuse by certain types of individuals. Those looking for an "answer to life" or simply a mind-altering "trip" are quick to experiment with any hallucinogenic compound. As with any other dangerous drug, hallucinogenic abuse may result in mental or physical injury to the abuser.

Lysergic Acid Diethylamide (LSD). LSD was first synthesized in Switzerland by biochemist Albert Hofmann from the lysergic acid present in a certain fungus that forms on rye and wheat. Although its hallucinogenic effects were not discovered until 1943, the drug is without doubt the most widely known psychedelic compound. LSD is typically produced in illegal drug laboratories throughout the country, where it is converted into liquid, pill, or powder form. Generally, liquid-impregnated substances, such as sugar cubes, brownies, tomato juice, whole tablets, or crushed tablets packed into gelatin capsules, are encountered by the investigator. Although liquid or tablet LSD is still encountered, the drug is commonly found on sheets of perforated paper squares onto which LSD has been absorbed. The sheets of paper are often termed "blotters" and illustrated with cartoon characters or other designs. The drug is odorless, tasteless, and clear of color, unless another substance has been mixed with it.

True lysergic acid is not produced or abused in the quantities that many people believe. Frequently users think they are buying LSD when the substance actually purchased is another drug such as PCP or some other hallucinogenic. A common reaction to LSD ingestion is altered perception, resulting in hallucinations of varying degrees. The effects of the drug are felt only 30 minutes to an hour after ingestion. As with all drugs, the intensity of the effects is dependent on the purity of the dosage. Although the potency of a single tablet can vary from 100 to 1,000 micrograms of LSD, as little as 25 micrograms can cause hallucinations in an adult. The dangers of LSD are now widely known, largely as a result of repeated reports by the media of "bad trips," ending sometimes in disaster. Users may lapse into severe forms of mental illness, exhibiting symptoms of schizophrenia, psychosis, and paranoia. In addition, some users have been seriously injured or killed through accidents brought on by LSD.

Physical dependency on LSD does not occur, but the user may develop a tolerance to the drug. LSD is highly profitable to those who illegally produce it in that one pound can provide 3,600,000 individual doses. Since one tablet or sugar cube of LSD sells for three to five dollars, the laboratory-produced pound has the capability of profiting the producer in excess of $15 million. Many synthetic drugs have effects similar to those of LSD. As mentioned previously, these are often sold as lysergic acid to users. Drugs such as Ecstasy, GHB, MDMA, and other "alphabet" variations produce hallucinations and perception distortion.

Drug authorities report that LSD made a comeback in popularity during the 1990s and early 2000s. Users are centered in the middle class, and there is growing involvement among high school and college students. The DEA reports that LSD constitutes the third-largest category of dangerous drugs removed by its agents, nearly 500,000 doses annually. Although the current number of LSD abusers is high and growing, the height of the drug's popularity was reached in 1970, when nearly two million Americans tried the drug.[23]

Phencyclidine (PCP).   PCP, commonly referred to as "angel dust," is a preferred hallucinogenic. PCP is a very powerful nonaddictive anesthetic drug with hallucinogenic properties. Drug authorities and drug abusers are in agreement that PCP produces more violent behavior changes than any other illegal substance yet encountered. PCP has been the causative factor in hundreds of deaths, having been linked to at least 214 murders, suicides, and accidental fatalities in Detroit during a one-year period.[24]

Developed in the early 1950s as an anesthetic, PCP was first tested on humans in 1957 as a surgical anesthetic agent. However, use was quickly discontinued when patients reported such erratic side effects as hallucinations, feelings of hostility, and disorientation. Often erroneously described as a general animal tranquilizer, the drug is used only as an anesthetic on monkeys and apes. Despite the known negative effects of PCP, its use is increasing, particularly among juveniles. The age of an average user decreased from 19 to 14 years in only two years. A corresponding increase in hallucinogen injuries caused by the drug has also been noted, resulting in more than 4,000 emergency room visits in one year. Furthermore, a government study reports that PCP has been used at least once by 14 percent of the population between the ages of 18 and 25, with more than seven million Americans of all ages having used the drug.

PCP can be ingested in pill form, or it can be inhaled or smoked. Users typically dust or spray the drug on mint leaves, parsley, or marijuana and smoke the substance. Small dosages may cause behavior resembling drunkenness, but irrational or violent behavior may also be exhibited by some individuals. Common reactions include convulsions, uncontrollable rage, stupor, or prolonged coma. In many cases, extended comas have resulted, lasting for five days or more, followed by a psychosis that persists for several weeks. The behavioral psychosis resembles the serious mental illness of paranoid schizophrenia.

The frequency of phencyclidine usage can be directly traced to its availability on the street. The equipment and chemicals needed to produce the drug are readily available, and no extended chemistry background is required. For $100, a suspect can assemble an amateur laboratory and manufacture PCP worth $100,000 in illegal sales. In the first six months of one year, 22 separate "underground" laboratories were discovered by law enforcement authorities. The labs ranged from larger mass-quantity operations in basements or warehouses to small production units located in kitchens or bathrooms.[25] On the street level, PCP is generally sold in small packets that contain one to two grams costing ten dollars. A single two-gram purchase can often produce eight or more "highs."

Beginning in the early 2000s, narcotics investigators noted a rapid rise in the number of PCP users, evidenced by a 48 percent increase in emergency room visits from 1999 to 2000. Many of today's users are too young to remember the negative reputation the drug acquired during the 1970s and 1980s. A recent National Household Survey on Drug Abuse documented that 264,000 Americans are now trying the drug for the first time each year. Currently, PCP is most commonly encountered as a liquid soaked into marijuana, a practice known as "wet" or, less frequently, "water." Often such PCP-soaked marijuana may also contain embalming fluid or the drug Ecstasy.[26]

Mescaline and Psilocybin.   Both psilocybin and mescaline are natural hallucinogens that may cause tolerance but do not produce physical dependence. Mescaline is obtained from the peyote cactus that grows naturally in Mexico and the U.S. Southwest. In the past, certain American Indian groups were by tradition allowed to use mescaline during religious ceremonies. The U.S. Supreme Court ruled in 1990, however, that state drug laws may prohibit the use of mescaline without violating constitutional religious rights. Fifteen states and the federal government have statutory exemptions allowing religious usage of mescaline by specified Indian groups. Mescaline ingestion produces effects similar to those produced by LSD. The drug is found on the street in powder, tablet, or other forms, or pieces of the actual cactus may be consumed. The hallucinogenic effects and disorientation derived from peyote are generally weaker than the effects of LSD.

Psilocybin is obtained from a mushroom species that grows predominantly in Mexico, but it is also found in the United States. A derivative of psilocybin, *psilocin*, also produces hallucinogenic reactions and varying behavior changes. Both drugs are encountered as liquids, tablets, and powders and occasionally in natural form. Although the effects of psilocybin and psilocin are very similar to those of mescaline, a much smaller dosage of the first two drugs will produce hallucinations.

Methylenedioxy amphetamine (MDMA).   Commonly known as *Ecstasy* or the "love drug," this synthetic drug's chemical properties are similar to the hallucinogen mescaline but with additional amphetamine effects. It increases energy and feelings of sensuality and empathy toward others, but it also raises blood pressure and heart rate, impairs memory, and can cause seizures. The drug often completely masks fatigue and has been known to cause death through heart failure, convulsions, dehydration and exhaustion. Generally brought into the United States from Mexico and Europe in capsule form, the drug is also seen as tablets, pressed pills ingrained with symbols, or a loose powder. Ecstasy users primarily are middle-class teenagers who frequent all-night dance parties popularly called raves. It is a mild hallucinogenic that creates a sense of euphoria, with one tablet affecting the brain for up to six hours.

Ecstasy has continued to show increased usage well into the 2000s. Once relatively confined to large dance gatherings, the drug is now commonly encountered in a variety of settings. Widespread and usually inaccurate information on the Internet has encouraged many young users. Often thought of as a designer or "party" drug, Ecstasy is actually a cross between a hallucinogenic and an amphetamine. Some speculate that Ecstasy is becoming the current generation's LSD. A recent survey of teenagers indicates that 20 percent have a friend or classmate who has used the drug, and 17 percent said they knew more than one user. Items associated with Ecstasy use may include colored contact lenses or sunglasses. Pupils often become extremely dilated, sometimes to the point of not being able to see the iris, and then constricted as the drug wears off. Glow sticks are often used at social gatherings and dances, as light trails become visually distorted, enhancing the visual effect while under the drug's influence. Some users may possess or use pacifiers since intense grinding of the teeth is common. Some users will engage in "stacking," or taking more than one tablet in an effort to enhance the drug's euphoric effect. Rapid, sometimes deadly, overheating of the body can result, causing users to continuously drink large quantities of water to stay hydrated. This behavior is particularly common at raves where abusers dance vigorously for long periods of time, further causing dehydration problems.

Ecstasy pills can originate from many countries, but the Netherlands is the manufacturing origin for an estimated 80 percent of all Ecstasy. Other countries in which the drug is now produced include Belgium and Greece. The standard Ecstasy lab is generally more complex than labs producing methamphetamine in the United States. Two chemical precursors are necessary and are imported from Eastern Europe and, in smaller amounts, from Southeast Asia. Profits are substantial, as the one dollar or less production cost converts to a $20 per pill street price.

Marijuana. Although there is a large body of literature on the subject of **marijuana** (also spelled marihuana) and its derivatives, considerable disagreement still exists over the effects and abuse potentials of the drug. A federal survey indicates that marijuana has been smoked by at least one-fifth of all people in this country. It has also been estimated one-third of the U.S. population has used the drug at least once and that 12 million are currently daily users. National self-reporting studies indicate that 2.5 million Americans try marijuana for the first time each year. However, marijuana usage among youth appears to have peaked during the late 1970s. A recent poll of reported marijuana use by high school seniors within the previous year indicates a 36 percent usage level. Unfortunately, this rate indicates a gradual climb in the number of young people using marijuana following a decade of steady decline. It is clear, then, that the U.S. public has had more experience with marijuana than with any other illicit psychoactive drug.

Marijuana is a drug derived from the flowering tops and leaves of the Indian hemp plant *Cannabis sativa* (Figure 14.6). The plant grows naturally in mild climates throughout the world, especially in Mexico, South America, Jamaica, and the United States. Approximately 60 percent of the marijuana used in the United States comes from Mexico; the remaining amounts are grown locally or imported from other countries. In the past few years, Canada has become the source for significant amounts of indoor-grown, high-potency marijuana. Marijuana has an ancient history of use, with Chinese pharmacological accounts citing the drug in 2737 B.C. This drug has been used as a medical aid in China and India and throughout the Arab world for thousands of years with unproven claims of benefit.

In Europe and the United States, the drug was viewed primarily as a commercial product until the late 1920s, when large numbers of individuals began to smoke it for euphoric effects. It is reported that in 1611, the Jamestown colony in Virginia planted marijuana with the intent of using it

FIGURE 14.6   The marijuana plant (*Cannabis sativa*), showing typical leaf formation. *(Source: Joseph Orantes, San Diego Police Department.)*

for hemp, the durable fiber found in the plant, particularly throughout the stem. There was a continual need for hemp in the economy for clothing, sail, and rope products from colonial times to the end of World War II.

The marijuana plant may grow to heights of 15 feet in a natural state; plants grown by users are typically two to five feet in height before they are processed. Plants are of the male and female variety, containing an odd number of leaflets in each section. The leaf is generally as long as a pencil, dark green on the upper side and a lighter shade of green on the underside. The plant's leaves are always of an odd number, generally from 5 to 11 per grouping.

Only the female marijuana plant contains any appreciable amount of *tetrahydrocannabinol* (THC), the substance that produces the euphoric "high." Depending on the specific plant and region of growth, the THC content varies from relatively weak levels to high potency, near 20 percent. The leaves and flowers of the plant are dried and crushed into small pieces for use as a drug. A mature marijuana plant typically yields about three-fourths to one pound of marijuana for sale. Although marijuana is eaten and chewed in some cultures, U.S. users almost always smoke the substance. The dried mixture is generally rolled into cigarette form or inserted into a pipe for smoking (see Figure 14.7). The fumes are inhaled, held in the lungs for three to five seconds, and slowly exhaled. When marijuana enters the bloodstream, various physiological effects result. These are dependent upon the individual user, the strength of the drug, and the duration of ingestion. Continued abuse of marijuana can lead to tolerance; however, it does not appear that physical dependence develops (see Figure 14.8).

Although some marijuana users experience mild hallucinations, most do not, unless the potency of the drug is very high. A more common effect is an altered sense of perception, particularly with regard to color, sound, and taste. Some users may become loud, aggressive, or generally talkative; others may become quiet, drowsy, and introverted following ingestion.

FIGURE 14.7 An assortment of drug paraphernalia often encountered in narcotics investigations, including smoking pipes, syringes, pills and other illegal substances. *(Source: Tom Croke/Getty Images, Inc.–Liaison.)*

Generally, the ability to react quickly and to make decisions that require clear judgment is negatively affected. It follows that marijuana abuse clearly has the potential to cause serious traffic accidents. A study conducted by the California Highway Patrol to determine the incidence of marijuana use by drivers suspected of being intoxicated revealed a startling finding. Of the thousands of people involved in traffic accidents in California, the patrol found a greater percentage of drivers (38 percent) to be intoxicated from marijuana than from alcohol.

Smoking marijuana cigarettes is frequently compared with consuming alcoholic beverages. Although there are some similarities, there is one major difference. Alcohol has only one chemical ingredient that is dissolved in the blood within an hour. However, marijuana has up to 50 different chemical

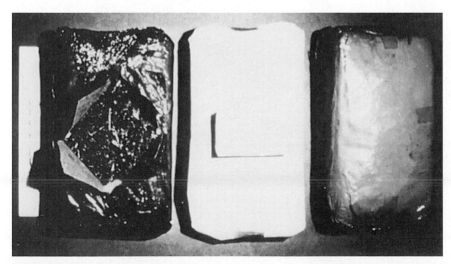

FIGURE 14.8 Typical kilo packages of marijuana. When sold in quantity, it is generally packaged as illustrated. *(Source: Joseph Orantes, San Diego Police Department.)*

ingredients, with the most health-threatening (THC) being accumulated in the bloodstream for up to 30 days.

Sinsemilla. As a result of the recent high-intensity efforts to stop narcotics importation on the East Coast and across the U.S.–Mexican border, foreign marijuana smuggling operations have been significantly curtailed. Consequently, numerous domestic marijuana growers have begun to cultivate and sell the plants in the United States. U.S. growers produce more than 5,000 tons of marijuana each year, at least 35 percent of the nation's demand.[27] An unusually potent form of marijuana, **sinsemilla,** is currently being cultivated. Domestic marijuana is believed by many to be the largest cash crop in California and the fourth largest throughout the nation (see Figure 14.9).[28]

American-grown sinsemilla is most commonly grown in outdoor plots, but an increasing number of growers are using the new indoor *hydroponic method*. Through this technique, plants are grown under high-intensity lights, with water and nutrients pumped through the plants' submerged root systems. Growers cultivate the marijuana in basements, large greenhouses, rural buildings, underground bunkers, and other isolated indoor locations. Specialty supply houses based in northern California, Oregon, Washington, and Canada sell the often-sophisticated equipment needed for indoor cultivation. The hydroponic method typically takes 10 to 12 weeks to bring a marijuana plant to maturity, allowing suspects to produce four crops a year. Indoor operations are increasing in number each year and becoming more sophisticated; crop quantities often equal outdoor production. In Lancaster, California, investigators recently discovered a concrete-walled greenhouse containing 6,000 marijuana seedlings. The 7,000-square-foot hydroponic operation was larger than a basketball court and would have produced an annual crop with a street value of more than $75 million.[29]

Although hydroponic marijuana production is an expanding problem, traditional outdoor plots still predominate. Sinsemilla can be cultivated in backyard gardens or produced in massive farm-grown quantities. A recent

FIGURE 14.9 A portion of the nation's fourth-largest cash crop being destroyed. Here, Mississippi narcotics agents burn part of the state's $80 million worth of marijuana seized during one year. *(Source: James Wallace, Mississippi Bureau of Narcotics.)*

seizure in Minnesota yielded more than 80 tons of marijuana from a 275-acre growing site, and a similar raid on a farm in Mercer County, Kentucky, produced more than 100,000 marijuana plants being cultivated on 200 acres. Marijuana is often planted among corn or sunflower crops to screen the illegal crop as it matures. After harvesting, suspects dry the plants, clip the potent parts, and package the marijuana in heat-sealed plastic trash bags. Some large-scale growers have moved their sinsemilla operations into national forests to evade attention. Because of the violence commonly associated with drug operations, nearly 400,000 acres of forest-land have been declared by the government as unsafe for visitors.

The continued high demand of American marijuana users has caused a rapid increase in the amount of potent Canadian marijuana grown and smuggled into the country. Because of increasing seizures of the drug along the border, the U.S. Customs Service began a doubling of its enforcement efforts along our northern border, with particular focus on Washington State. Marijuana harvesting now ranks as British Columbia's most lucrative agricultural product, with illegal revenue estimated at $2 billion a year. Considered by drug users to be far more potent, Canadian marijuana, commonly termed "BC bud," can bring as much as $6,000 a pound in parts of California—ten times the typical price for marijuana from Mexico.

Hashish. "Hash" is a derivative of marijuana that is typically much stronger than the marijuana commonly smoked. It was discovered thousands of years ago that the resin of the top leaves produce the most powerful euphoric effects. Hashish is obtained by a scraping and beating process that forces the resin, very high in THC content, from the leaf. The resulting substance is generally ten times as powerful as marijuana.

Hashish may be found in liquid form as an oil base. To obtain hashish oil, a quantity of high-quality marijuana, generally from Mexico or Jamaica, is heated with a solvent. The heating, or percolationlike process, extracts an oil with concentrated amounts of THC.

Anabolic Steroids

The generic term **anabolic steroid** pertains to any drug related to testosterone that promotes muscle growth. Steroids include a synthetic version of the male hormone testosterone. Anabolic refers to a substance that promotes growth. Testosterone is a primary male sex hormone that produces physiological changes in the body, stimulating muscle growth and the development of male sex characteristics. Until relatively recently, abuse of steroids was not considered a significant national problem; few states had specific legislation prohibiting unauthorized possession and sale. However, the current high level of abuse has prompted the federal government and all 50 states to prohibit the drugs without a prescription.[30]

Anabolic steroid abuse is associated with suspects who use the drugs to increase sports-related abilities or for enhanced muscular appearance.[31] National surveys indicate that 7 percent of all young men aged 15 and older have used steroids. Abuse in urban areas is higher than in other areas, as reported by the Illinois State Pediatrics Society. Its studies found that 12 percent of all male high school students in the Chicago area had used steroids.[32] Until a few years ago, only males were commonly associated with this drug problem, but a recent trend of steroid abuse involves girls. The National Institute of Drug Abuse reports that 175,000 girls annually use anabolic steroids. The increased usage among girls, which some researchers attribute in part to a kind of reverse anorexia, produces a "fashionable" lean-but-muscular look. As with male usage, the abuse of steroids can cause females severe medical problems, including infertility. Steroids are commonly abused through intramuscular injection, but investigators have encountered orally ingestible steroids in tablet, capsule, and liquid forms.

Anabolic steroids have the potential for serious adverse reactions that can result from unsupervised use. Many abusers have reported heightened aggression commonly known as "roid rage." Physical problems can include increased risk of heart disease, liver tumors, and growth reduction, among other emotional and physical disturbances. Indicators of steroid use may include the following physical changes:

1. rapid muscle growth or weight gain;
2. aggressive, combative behavior;
3. slight yellow tint to the skin;
4. purple or red spots on the body;
5. trembling, unpleasant breath, and sudden outbreak of facial acne.

Inhalants

Inhalants are generally noncontrolled chemicals that emit fumes when dispensed from an air-sealed container. Volatile chemicals such as glue, nail polish, and furniture polish may be inhaled, as well as many household sprays packaged in aerosol cans. A relatively small number of individuals inhale ether, nitrous oxide, and other types of anesthetics. Hydrocarbon substances, such as gasoline, may also be abused. Some teens may even begin to inhale fumes from air-conditioning units. Youth have been found unconscious beside outdoor air-conditioning units from inhaling Freon fumes given off by the cooling unit. Subjects seek out air conditioners which have exposed adjustable valves and release Freon fumes on rags for inhalation. The abuse of inhalants is mainly among juveniles and is a very difficult problem for law enforcement to control. The possession of gasoline, spray paint, butane, or computer duster is legal, as is possession of most other inhalants, with the exception of certain anesthetics.

Classic inhalation abuse is exemplified by the "huffer," typically a juvenile who habitually inhales fumes to produce a short alcohol-like intoxicated sensation. The offender empties a bottle, tube, or contents from a spray can into a bag or surgical glove or onto a handkerchief, places the bag or cloth tightly over the mouth and nose, and inhales the fumes. Some subjects will place the entire bag over their head to heighten the fume effect. The general effects take place within five minutes: "drunken" speech and muscle control, possible hallucinations, and deterioration of concentration and memory. Inhaling glue, gasoline, and other inhalants is highly dangerous in that the user may suffocate or damage body organs. Inhalants enter the bloodstream quickly and seek out fatty organs, such as the brain, liver, and kidneys. Besides causing irreversible brain damage, chronic abuse can cause the heart to beat irregularly or to stop beating. Inhalants, a growing form of substance abuse that is often overshadowed by campaigns against more commonly feared dangerous drugs, are tried by one in five teenagers. The drug of choice for American eighth graders, inhalants rank fourth in popularity among all schoolchildren, behind alcohol, tobacco, and marijuana but ahead of LSD and cocaine. The National Institute on Drug Abuse estimates that 1,000 teens die every year from breathing fumes from the inexpensive, legal, and easily obtained products favored by offenders.

One inhalation abuse trend involves so-called room deodorizers containing butyl nitrite. Butyl nitrite is a chemical substance that produces an instant euphoric state in most individuals upon inhalation. The "high" is the result of blood rushing to the head and other parts of the body through expanded blood vessels. The physical effect is similar to that of *amyl nitrite*, a controlled drug used to treat heart ailments. Amyl nitrite is in the same general chemical family as is butyl nitrite, but the former drug was given a controlled status in 1969. Amyl nitrite abusers simply switched to butyl nitrite, which is still decontrolled, to achieve the same "rush."

Butyl nitrite typically has an instantaneous effect that lasts for a short period of time. As with most of the inhalants, tolerance may be built up, whereas physical dependence is not reported. The abuse of butyl and amyl nitrite can be dangerous to certain people. If an abuser has a weak spot in the blood vessels of the head, the expansion of the vessels that occurs during the rush may cause a cerebral hemorrhage. Furthermore, such negative side effects as severe headaches, vomiting, fainting, dizziness, and incontinence have been reported.

In an effort to categorize degrees of drug abuse potential, the federal government created five levels, or "schedules," of controlled substances classification. Originally created by Congress in 1970, the Controlled Substances Act is regularly amended with newly emerging dangerous drugs and narcotics as needed. The act has served as a model for similar state legislation and assists prosecutors and judges in charging and sentencing determination in drug cases (see Table 14.1).

TABLE 14.1 Controlled Substances Act—Schedules of Controlled Substances

---

Schedule 1

1. The drug has a high potential for abuse.
2. Drug has no currently accepted medical use in treatment within the United States.
3. There is a lack of accepted safety for use of the drug under medical supervision.
Examples: heroin, codeine, peyote, Ecstasy, marijuana, psilocybin

Schedule II

1. Drug has a high potential for abuse.
2. Drug has current medical use in treatment.
3. Abuse of the drug may lead to severe psychological or physical dependence.
Examples: cocaine, fentanyl, methadone, PCP, OxyContin, methamphetamine, LSD

Schedule III

1. Drug has potential for abuse but less than schedule I or II drugs.
2. Drug has currently accepted medical treatment use in United States.
3. Abuse may lead to moderate or low physical dependence or high psychological dependence.
Examples: anabolic steroids, barbiturates

Schedule IV

1. Drug has low potential for abuse when compared to drugs in other schedules.
2. Drug has currently accepted medical treatment use in United States.
3. Abuse may lead to limited physical or psychological dependence relative to drugs contained in schedule III.
Examples: chloral hydrate, GHB, various stimulants, depressants, and tranquilizers

Schedule V

1. Drug has low potential for abuse relative to drugs in schedule IV.
2. Drug has current accepted medical treatment use in United States.
3. Abuse may lead to limited physical or psychological dependence relative to drugs contained in schedule IV.
Examples: drugs that contain very limited extracts of codeine, morphine, or opium.

Source: Drug Enforcement Administration, U.S. Department of Justice.

INVESTIGATIVE PROCEDURES

The investigation of narcotics and dangerous drugs is often a long and difficult procedure but one in which success can be very gratifying. The difficulty of the drug investigation can be attributed to many factors. The world of the drug dealer and user is a true world of its own; those who are not part of the drug scene are often "foreigners" to its culture. An extensive and constantly changing drug terminology exists, along with certain patterns of speech and behavior, all of which must be mastered by the criminal investigator. Obviously, drug culture behavior and terminology must be totally familiar to the officer working in an undercover capacity, but other investigators must also be knowledgeable. Patrol officers and detectives frequently field-interview addicts and general drug abusers. These individuals may be interviewed as suspects or in a victim or informant capacity. They can be interviewed more effectively and with greater rapport if the officer can relate to them in their own terms.

Another difficulty of the drug investigation stems from the international nature of this crime category. Whereas other types of offenses are confined to a specific jurisdiction, the drug inquiry often involves production, sales, and distribution in many different areas. Consequently, it may be difficult for the officer to see "the whole picture" relative to the pattern occurring in a single jurisdiction.

A third difficulty relative to drug abuse and dealing is a low suspect visibility risk compared to other types of crime. Burglary and larceny suspects, for example, run the hazard of being seen during commission of their offenses. Narcotic transactions, however, occur in clandestine locations and often among very few individuals. Although this offense is often termed "victimless," in a realistic sense, the crime is far from without victims. Few other crimes have the potential to so totally disrupt lives—the lives of the users and those close to them. However, the term does correctly imply the absence of the traditional victim report to the police.

Directions of the Inquiry: Production, Distribution, and Abuse

The investigation of drugs must take three distinct directions if the total objective of eradicating drug abuse is to be achieved. All police investigations must be directed toward (a) sources of production, (b) sources of distribution, and (c) sources of abuse.

Sources of Production.   The locations at which illicit narcotics are produced are generally known to law enforcement officials. The difficulty is that nearly all such locations are outside of the United States. When a crime situation originates in another country but comes to involve the United States, resolution of the situation is complicated by politics and lack of coordination. There can be no doubt that if the opium poppy and coca bush grew only in the United States, near total eradication would be more readily achieved. But these plants originate throughout the world—South America, Mexico, and Asia. Only federal investigative agencies, such as the DEA, have the information and resources to affect the sources of narcotic production. The DEA has made significant progress in aiding foreign governments in narcotic investigations. For example, under the direction of the agency, the Mexican government has operated an opium poppy eradication program for many years. Additional source eradication programs are operating in Colombia and other South American countries, as DEA agents assist local investigators in search-and-destroy operations against cocaine growing and processing sites.

The sources of production for the majority of controlled depressant and stimulant drugs are legitimate pharmaceutical companies. Although dangerous drugs are produced in "underground" laboratories, a substantial proportion of the legitimately produced drugs also reach abusers without being prescribed. Each year, U.S. drug manufacturers produce more than 20 billion doses of controlled drugs. Of these, an estimated 200 million to 250 million dosage units are diverted into the hands of abusers.[33] The drugs are diverted from their intended medical use through theft and falsification. They may be stolen during the actual manufacture, during shipment, or after their arrival at the point of distribution. Physicians' offices, pharmacies, veterinary offices, hospitals, and other medical facilities are often burglarized for drugs. In the past, many suspects forged documents identifying them as physicians or pharmacists, placing sizable orders to drug manufacturers. However, federal regulations and closer supervision have now made such practices quite rare. Although the forgery of drug orders has diminished, clandestine drug laboratory operations have increased. "Underground" labs secretly produce various types of drugs and are often found in private residences, motel rooms, house trailers, and commercial establishments. Most laboratories that investigators encountered produce stimulant drugs, with most of the labs raided by the police engaged in methamphetamine production.[34]

For more than 30 years, the U.S. government has combated major drug operators from its El Paso Intelligence Center (EPIC). Created in 1974 to stop a major influx of Mexican heroin, EPIC has grown into the world's leading drug intelligence and training network. More than 300 staff employees from ten participating federal agencies, plus the Department of Defense and the Central Intelligence Agency, respond to thousands of requests per week. The center's mission is to provide complete and accurate intelligence on worldwide drug movement by land, sea, and air. EPIC's investigative and interdiction resources provide rapid computer-based data on drug suspects and couriers as well as anticipate and counteract the movements of drug traffickers. In its role as the nation's electronic eyes and ears of both law enforcement and the intelligence community, the center also tracks the smuggling of arms and aliens across the U.S. border, as these activities are typically linked to drug production and importation. In a recent year, EPIC responded to more than half a million inquiries and provided information that contributed to the seizure of 44 tons of cocaine, 88 tons of marijuana, and the arrest of nearly 1,200 suspects.[35]

Sources of Distribution. These are the individuals who illegally profit by selling drugs—the dealers. All levels of law enforcement work to combat drug dealers; that is, violations can be either federal, state, or local. The investigative task is to identify and apprehend the dealer. If interstate operations are involved or if dealings are widespread, federal and state investigators are generally the first to become aware of the activity. If the dealer is a local dealer or one who operates intercounty, municipal and county police agencies are typically alerted to these operations.

In an effort to more effectively identify and arrest high-level sources of drug distribution, the FBI and the DEA merged investigative drug operations in 1982. The combined effort has resulted in joint investigations of thousands of cases since the merger. Similarly, the Internal Revenue Service has directed 600 of its agents (nearly one-fourth of the agency's total investigation staff) to focus upon drug distributors. Since all profits are taxable, including those gained from illegal drug transactions, narcotics traffickers are regularly prosecuted for tax evasion.[36]

Civil forfeiture of real property used during felony drug violations has become an effective investigative option. **Civil forfeiture**, also known as assets seizure, is a legal punishment in which property used for illegal purposes is transferred to government ownership. In illegal drug dealings, civil forfeiture has become a common means of reducing the profits and incentive of drug dealers. To seize valuable assets such as homes, apartments, business facilities, and vehicles, the criminal investigator must document that the property was used or was intended to be used to commit or to facilitate a felony drug violation. Typically, the conviction of the owner of the property serves as the necessary probable cause to initiate civil forfeiture against a specific type of property.[37] To seize property successfully, drug investigators must demonstrate the property actually facilitated or aided the drug trafficking. Drug cases in which suspects use their homes or vehicles to sell drugs from or have drugs delivered to often qualify for forfeiture. Once the government establishes probable cause that a particular property facilitated drug trafficking, the burden shifts to the owners of the property to prove they did not know of or consent to the drug dealing. Should a convicted offender be unsuccessful in establishing the "innocent owner" defense, forfeiture proceedings can be instituted.

Forfeiture sanctions are currently being used by all states and the federal government. As a criminal investigation strategy, forfeiture can be used to eliminate continuing criminal enterprises. Although most commonly associated with drug cases, forfeiture has also been used in other types of cases, such as gambling and hazardous waste violations.[38] Through the seizure of cash, cars, homes, and luxury items, the "working capital" of criminal organizations is disrupted. Moreover, forfeiture is an effective crime deterrent.

The distribution of illegal drugs is accomplished by various means, often limited only by the imagination and resourcefulness of the suspect. The most common method of moving drugs throughout the United States is by vehicle, with private cars being used the most. Drug seizures from private autos are accomplished either by alert patrol officers during routine traffic stops or by investigators responding to informant information. During traffic stops, the suspicious behavior of the vehicle's occupants alerts the officer to conduct a more detailed drug-related search. When an officer suspects a vehicle may be carrying drugs, the occupant should be made to feel at ease initially, then asked if the auto contains anything of an illegal nature. Drug couriers who are first placed at ease often react with exaggerated nervousness when suddenly asked a question designed to elicit a strong psychological and physiological response if answered deceptively.

Other methods of distributing narcotics involve swallowing large amounts of drugs, typically wrapped in condoms or balloons. Drug couriers who swallow drugs for later retrieval are often termed "body packers" or "internals" and are increasingly being discovered by drug investigators. About 50 percent of all Colombian heroin seized at Miami International Airport came into the United States concealed in couriers' stomachs. Suspects run the continual risk of being poisoned by leaking packages, leading to the use of other live means of drug concealment. An English sheepdog that had just arrived on a flight from Colombia was inspected by U.S. Customs investigators. The unusually lethargic dog was discovered to have more than five pounds of cocaine crudely implanted in her abdomen. The drugs were recovered by a veterinarian, and a suspect was arrested when he arrived to claim his dog. The sheepdog is now being used as a trained drug dog for Customs investigators.

Drug distributors may occasionally be identified by patrol observation, but the majority come to the attention of the police through informants.

Additionally, the sudden presence of a drug that has not been prevalent in the community may indicate a new source of distribution. Regardless of the information source indicating the presence of a dealer, the information must be confirmed. The confirmation process may involve the surveillance of a suspect on the street or the surveillance of a suspect's home. The following occurrences are indicators of drug dealing:

1. known addicts or drug users coming and going from certain premises;
2. unusual security precautions by an individual, suggesting a "lookout" for the police at a residence;
3. individuals who leave their residence to use a telephone booth when that residence is equipped with a phone;
4. an individual who is approached by many people on the street and who, after conversing very briefly, quickly walks away;
5. individuals who pass money, envelopes, plastic bags, balloons, or tinfoil to others;
6. individuals who regularly purchase drug paraphernalia and substances commonly used in "cutting" narcotics;
7. individuals who have no apparent employment or means of support but who continually give evidence of having large sums of money; and
8. individuals who regularly visit or communicate with known narcotics dealers.

Not all drugs are sold by "typical" dealers with criminal backgrounds. A relatively small but highly significant percentage of the nation's physicians and pharmacists illegally dispense drugs. The California Department of Consumer Affairs estimated several years ago that 200 to 1,000 California physicians supplied significant amounts of the dangerous drugs abused in that state.[39] These doctors write "script" (street jargon for prescriptions) for anyone willing and able to pay a certain price. Typically, the physician charges the user a $10 to $30 fee for the prescription, which is often filled by a pharmacy that is paid by the doctor to cooperate.

This trend of abuse began during the early 1970s, when new federal laws cut off supplies of pharmaceuticals from Mexico. Physicians have more recently been arrested for having written incredible numbers of prescriptions. In one case, a doctor wrote 5,017 prescriptions for 130,442 pills in a single 90-day period. Another doctor was cited as having more than 200,000 pills in his office at the time of arrest, and still another was arrested driving a truck containing nearly two million amphetamines destined for unlawful sales.[40] It is important to note that physicians who dispense drugs unethically account for only 2 percent of all doctors. However, a small number of physicians can provide enough drugs of potential abuse for an entire city of addicts. Stimulants, such as Ritalin and Desoxyn, and depressants, such as OxyContin, Dilaudid, and methaqualone, are commonly unlawfully prescribed.

Some drug dealers and users are very adept at deceiving legitimate physicians, using physical symptoms to acquire drugs. They will feign a particular illness with the hope of securing a prescription containing a dangerous drug commonly prescribed to combat the illness. They may prepare for the encounter with the physician by consulting a medical book or the *Physicians' Desk Reference* to match fictitious symptoms with a particular controlled drug.

Source of Abuse. Narcotics investigations frequently begin with a suspect who habitually or intermittently abuses drugs (see Figure 14.10). Without the user or source of abuse on the street, dealers and producers

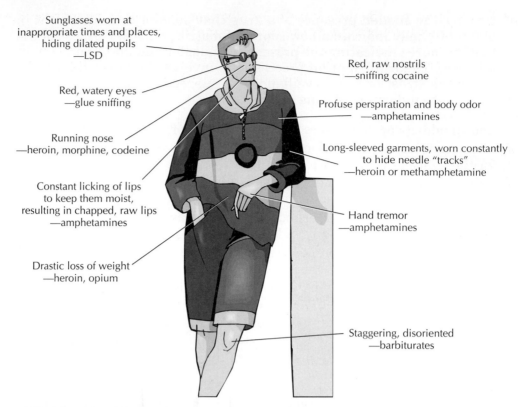

Sunglasses worn at inappropriate times and places, hiding dilated pupils —LSD

Red, raw nostrils —sniffing cocaine

Red, watery eyes —glue sniffing

Profuse perspiration and body odor —amphetamines

Running nose —heroin, morphine, codeine

Long-sleeved garments, worn constantly to hide needle "tracks" —heroin or methamphetamine

Constant licking of lips to keep them moist, resulting in chapped, raw lips —amphetamines

Hand tremor —amphetamines

Drastic loss of weight —heroin, opium

Staggering, disoriented —barbiturates

FIGURE 14.10 Physical appearance of the drug abuser.

would have no ready market for their criminal operations. Because of such substantial numbers of drug users (see Table 14.2), the demand now involves 7 percent of the American population aged 12 or older. The criminal investigator may attempt to work backward from the street addict in an attempt to identify and apprehend higher-level suspects. This investigative procedure is very difficult since dealers are very suspicious to sell to anyone not known as a drug user. Before the tracing process can begin, the street addict must be identified. There are many physiological and behavioral indicators that may facilitate identification (see Table 14.3).

In an effort to further identify those who habitually use dangerous drugs and narcotics, various studies of abusers (arrested, unarrested, and in treatment programs) indicate the following:

- The single most common factor among both heroin and cocaine users is their repeated use of marijuana.
- Contrary to the media stereotype of the inner-city user, cocaine abuse in all forms is greatest among white single men.

TABLE 14.2 Illegal Drug Use among American Population Aged 12 or Older

Age	Percent within Total Population of Similar Age
12 to 17	11 percent
18 to 25	19 percent
25 and older	5 percent
Total of Americans 12 and older using illegal drugs	7 percent

Source: U.S. Department of Justice, National Household Survey on Drug Abuse.

- Street-level drug dealers stand a 1-in-70 probability of being murdered (100 times higher than those in the general work force), a 1-in-14 chance of severe injury, and a 2-in-9 probability of imprisonment. Approximately 16,000 drug addicts die each year from various medical problems directly associated with their addiction.

TABLE 14.3   Indicators of Drug Misuse

Opiates

- Scars ("tracks") on the arms or on the back of hands, caused by injecting drugs.
- Constricted and fixed pupils; possibly dilated during withdrawal.
- Frequent scratching.
- Loss of appetite; possible consumption of candy and other sweets with great frequency.
- Sniffles; red, watery eyes; and coughing, indicating the need for an injection. Flushed skin, frequent yawning, twitching, and nausea, indicating the onset of withdrawal.
- Alternate periods of dozing and awakening ("going on the nod").
- Sudden weight loss and unkempt appearance, for no apparent reason.
- Need for isolation at fixed intervals, in order to inject the opiate.
- Possession of the paraphernalia of an injection kit (bent spoon, needles, etc.).

Cocaine

- Irritation at the base of the nostrils or permanent damage to the cartilage in chronic abusers.
- Dilated pupils while under the influence of the narcotic.
- Excessive talkativeness and excitability.
- Depressive, withdrawn behavior possibly following the "high."
- Possession of the common paraphernalia of cocaine abuse (tiny spoon, crack pipe, plastic vials used to carry crack; or cocaine-smeared dollar bills, matchbooks, etc., which are rolled to form a tube for inhalation).

Barbiturates

- Behavior such as that associated with alcohol intoxication, but without the odor of alcohol on the breath.
- Staggering, stumbling, or poor muscle coordination.
- Falling asleep at unnatural times.
- Slurred speech.
- Constricted pupils.
- Difficulty in concentrating and problem solving.
- Sudden manifestation of quick temper or quarrelsome disposition.

Amphetamines

- Excessive activity, irritability, belligerence, or nervousness.
- Sudden excited movements or talking.
- Dilated pupils.
- Curtailed eating or sleeping for long periods.
- Tremors of the hands.
- Rise in blood pressure or a rapid pulse, accompanied by heavy perspiration.
- Possible needle scars in chronic users.

Hallucinogens

- Wide variance in mood and behavior. The user may sit or recline quietly, or may appear fearful or terrified.
- Dilated pupils, in some cases.
- Increased blood pressure and heart rate.
- Possible nausea, chills, flushes, and trembling of the hands.
- Difficulty in time and space perception.
- Altered perceptions of colors and sounds.
- Gross behavioral changes, which may resemble mental illness.
- Difficulty in communicating with others; thought patterns that are fragmented and inconsistent.

(Continued)

TABLE 14.3   (Continued)

Inhalants

- Odor of common inhalants (glue, solvents, gasoline, etc.) on the breath or clothing.
- Excessive nasal secretion and watering of the eyes.
- Poor muscle control (staggering) within five minutes of exposure.
- Slurred speech.
- Dilated pupils.
- Possession of plastic bags or paper bags containing dried glue, or the odor of some inhalant.

- Cocaine and crack usage increases with age, education, and employment status.
- Sixty-five percent of all persons arrested on drug charges are under age 30.
- Women are far less likely than men to use drugs; however, women who commit other types of crime are just as likely to use drugs as males.

Another study demonstrated that over an 11-year period, some 243 addicts committed nearly a half million crimes to support their habits. That averages 2,000 crimes for each offender, or a serious crime every other day. The study further indicated the following:

- Half of all jail and prison inmates regularly used drugs before committing their offenses.
- Addicts committed nine times as many property crimes each year as did nonaddicted offenders.[41]

Stages in the Development of Drug Use Patterns

Researchers and criminal investigators have long noted certain recurring elements or stages that are common to the development of new drug groups in American society. When police are able to identify the following stages of drug use, the emerging drug abuse pattern may be effectively forestalled or stopped altogether.

Stage 1. Use begins with small, isolated groups.   This is the lowest level of use during which a drug can be contained by law enforcement. Drug abuse always starts with some relatively small group of individuals or within an isolated subculture. In this stage, investigators should identify and attempt to infiltrate the group in an effort to eliminate the drug threat before it progresses.

Stage 2. Users experiment with other forms of drug abuse.   Users often tire of their drug of preference and begin to experiment with other forms of abuse, or, if the police have been successful in eliminating one type of drug from a given community, another may arise. This stage demands continuous surveillance and field searches of suspects, with a sustained effort to identify the new "replacement" substances.

Stage 3. Users focus on a specific drug, and dealing accelerates. Frequent drug abusers select a particular drug for their attention, often justifying the drug by its ease of usage or degree of availability. As a particular drug becomes more popular, local drug dealerships begin to emerge.

Suspects involved are generally those who reject legitimate methods of success but seek to prosper economically. Marginally employed residents of the drug-using community are those most likely to begin relatively small-time dealing. If investigators are to prevent large-scale drug organizations from forming and the resulting violence endemic to such gangs, lower-level dealers must be arrested in "buy and bust" stings using informants or undercover personnel.

Stage 4. Drug use increases, as does the level of dealing. Sharp increases in the use of a drug are propelled by ready availability, low cost, and a widespread belief among drug users that the substance is desirable. As word of mouth spreads stories about the drug's potency or desirable effects, demand increases and more suppliers are drawn into the market. By this stage, local investigators are often unable to suppress the level of the problem and often must request help from state or task force drug squads. The drug problem has now spread to a degree that a quick police response alone will not eliminate the problem.

Stage 5. Drug use reaches epidemic proportions and overloads police and other public agency resources. The number of new users is now being constantly added to by numerous and aggressive drug dealing organizations. Existing and new drug abusers add to an accelerating demand. Specific areas of town or abandoned houses are used to deal the drug, and emergency room admissions reflect the problem. Rising crime levels in burglary, larceny, and robbery to support drug habits strain police resources. This final stage is the most difficult to control by any level of criminal investigation. Often a local, state, and federal police effort is demanded.[42]

This pattern of drug emergence has been noted many times in the history of drug abuse. Crack cocaine, LSD, and methamphetamine have all progressed from being nonexistent to emerging as major drug abuse problems. With quick and legally aggressive action, investigators can work to contain emerging drug trends before they spread beyond the first level.

Undercover Operations

Undercover operations require a law enforcement officer to assume a fictitious role to accomplish a particular task. Although undercover operations are common to many investigative areas, they are used perhaps most frequently in narcotics cases. Although repeatedly glamorized in the media, the undercover operation is often a tedious and demanding assignment for the investigator in which mental and physical stamina is challenged and strained. Undercover work requires constant alertness since the false identity assumed is one that is unnatural to the officer. The hours are almost always long, and the assignment generally requires work during the peak hours of criminality—late into the night and on weekends.

Not all officers are suited to work undercover. Relative to both behavior and physical appearance, undercover officers must "become" the very criminal types they have been trained and conditioned to regard with aversion. It is natural for the majority of officers to find it hard to mingle with or befriend criminal types, for whatever purpose. Generally speaking, the undercover officer must be quick thinking. There is no way to prepare completely for the many unpredictable situations that invariably occur during this type of assignment. For example, the officer may be asked to participate in a crime or be offered an injection of heroin. The officer's cover may be

Noel E. Griffin III
Special Agent Supervisor
Florida Department of Law Enforcement
St. Augustine Field Office

I'm the supervisor of one of 20 field offices of the Florida Department of Law Enforcement (FDLE). This is a state organization that investigates a wide variety of crimes occurring within the boundaries of Florida, in addition to assisting local law enforcement agencies and operating forensic labs. About half the states have similar investigative bureaus separate from their highway patrols, and the FDLE is the largest in the United States. Law enforcement has always been in my blood, as my dad was the sheriff of Lake County, Florida. I enrolled at Florida State University right after high school and thought about becoming a dentist. However, I soon discovered that majoring in criminology was really a match for my interests and obtained a bachelor's degree in this area.

After college I became a police officer with the Mt. Dora Police Department, which is located in central Florida. As a third-generation Floridian, I didn't want to work in any other state, so I was really pleased to obtain this position. I worked there for nine years and rose to the rank of captain, leaving to become an investigator for a Florida prosecutor's office. I worked for the fifth Judicial Circuit State Attorney's Office for five years and among other duties supervised several drug task force operations. In 1995, I became a special agent with the FDLE and was assigned to the St. Augustine Field Office. This office has six field agents assigned to it and covers three counties. Although our field office operates as a full-service unit of the FDLE, we formally are part of the Jacksonville Regional Operations Center. The FDLE was created back in 1967, when it was known as the Bureau of Law Enforcement. Prior to that, the State of Florida had a small investigative unit known as the Florida Sheriff's Bureau, which assisted the various sheriff's offices with difficult cases. The importance and responsibilities of the FDLE have rapidly expanded since its founding and is headquartered in the state's capital, Tallahassee. We now have close to 500 special agents assigned around the state. From the beginning, the organization has actively recruited college graduates from across the nation, and all initially undergo specialized training, even though most have previous criminal justice field experience.

Of course, when I first came on with FDLE, I wasn't a supervisor, so I worked a lot of different criminal investigations. However, the majority of my cases involved some type of narcotics violation. I'd worked in an undercover capacity prior to joining the FDLE and quickly put those skills to use yet again. But after a year or two, the amount of undercover work decreased, as I was being recognized from prior investigations. This can be a problem unless you work in a very large urban area. One of my important early drug cases involved over 200 pounds of cocaine being brought into St. Augustine. The cocaine was coming from Jamaica to Miami and then on to St. Augustine, where it was converted to crack cocaine. I worked this case for over a year and a half, and it led to the indictment of 20 suspects. We primarily work mid- to upper-level drug cases, quite often with agents from the federal Drug Enforcement Administration. While we could prosecute suspects in state court, the majority of the major drug cases end up in federal court because of the complicated legal conspiracy violations and enhanced penalties. With narcotics cases our investigative goal is to work backward to the source of supply, tracking the flow of narcotics and money through the various levels of dealing as far as we can. Unlike on TV, these types of cases don't always involve undercover work with police or civilian informants. Many of them are what we call "historical investigations," in which past actions document a criminal conspiracy. We make such cases by tracking and connecting phone calls, records of criminal contracts between people, money exchanges, pager transmissions, and so on. A major interagency drug task force is also run out of our field office, and we were the first office in the state to have one. The task force is composed of the FDLE (I serve as the initiative commander), three federal agencies, the Florida Highway Patrol, and a number of local and country departments. It has an annual $200,000 federal budget that supports the operations of the group.

I've been the office supervisor since 2002 and direct, manage, and supervise the work of six special agents, one crime analyst, and a staff assistant. I'm particularly honored to have been selected in 1999 as the Special Agent of the Year for FDLE. I like the diversity of the work and greatly enjoy the camaraderie that comes with helping each other during investigations. We are like a family, and it has led to lifelong friendships with many whom I've worked with. However, the job has a lot of stress connected to it, and it's very difficult to leave the work at the office and not take it home. For criminal justice students who would like to join state investigative bureaus, they'll need a four-year degree and generally five or more years of investigative experience. I'd stress to students that to succeed in law enforcement, they should be guided by a work ethic that includes three principles: proper attitude, always giving your best performance, and being accountable for your work. Finally, a career in law enforcement means making a sincere commitment to your agency, to your law enforcement partners, and to the citizens you serve. It truly is a way of life.

challenged or other difficult situations arise, demanding quick and decisive thinking.

Case Preparation.   An undercover assignment should never be initiated until the officer has been thoroughly prepared. As much information as possible should be gathered on the suspect who will be the target of the operation, and this information should be scrutinized by the officer to better adapt to the undercover role. The role itself must also be carefully researched and prepared. The fictitious identity should fit the environment to be infiltrated and be compatible with the officer's background and personality. If false documents are required, they must be prepared before the officer begins the fieldwork.

Information gathering will necessitate many hours of surveillance of the suspect's comings and goings and general behavior. The undercover officer should not participate in such surveillance, to avoid the risk of being recognized later. Associates of the suspect should also be researched and studied.

Field Operations.   Generally, an undercover officer will not be able to penetrate an organization or gain the confidence of a suspect without a credible introduction. All criminals, and particularly narcotics dealers, are suspicious of strangers to the point of paranoia. To avoid this difficulty, most undercover officers work with the aid of an informant. The informant is typically known to the suspect, often as a friend or "customer." The informant will introduce the officer to the suspect, thus establishing the officer's credibility. All the principles of informant handling discussed in Chapter 7 should be applied in this situation.

The investigator should attempt to work the informant out of the active investigation as quickly as possible following the introduction. To protect the informant as the source of introduction in making direct buys of drugs, the informant should cease to accompany the officer as soon as is practical. Although the danger of undercover operations has been overly stressed, it is always present. Narcotics undercover operations pose a very dangerous paradox: If the investigator is successful in convincing the dealer that the assumed identity is real, the investigator runs the risk of the "drug rip-off." A narcotics rip-off occurs when one party in a drug transaction robs the other of either money or drugs. Consequently, a drug dealer who truly believes that the officer is just another buyer may decide to rob and assault when the "buy" occurs.

A narcotics dealer should not be arrested after the first undercover sale to the officer. Several buys of increasing quantities should be completed until the dealer has been worked to "sales capacity." A major purpose of the investigation is to trace the dealer's source of supply, although this is frequently difficult. A final "buy and bust" should be arranged by the officer in which the suspect will be placed in the best physical environment for arrest.

The secret to success for the undercover officer is to "live" the role that is assumed. The officer must convincingly act as though buying or selling narcotics is a part of the daily routine. The investigator should be under surveillance by other officers whenever meetings with suspects occur. In many situations, the various buys of drugs will be recorded by means of hidden transmitters worn on the officer's body and photographs taken by the surveillants.

Some drug buys do not require long-term undercover operations by investigators, such as street sales of small amounts of cocaine and heroin. Because dealers in these instances routinely sell to strangers, undercover investigators generally employ short-term buy-bust or reverse sting arrests. The *buy-bust* arrest uses undercover officers to make street drug buys either on foot or in vehicles. After the drug purchase, surveillance officers quickly move in and arrest the dealer. The *reverse sting* operation uses undercover officers posing as drug dealers rather than buyers. Officers locate themselves in areas known to attract buyers and wait to be approached by those ready to buy drugs. When suspects offer to purchase drugs, an exchange of drugs for money is made, and the suspect is arrested by the surveillance team. As reverse operations frequently lead to accusations of illegal entrapment, investigators must be thoroughly knowledgeable about their state's laws concerning entrapment. In particular, the details of who must initiate the transaction and what the undercover officer may and may not say must be fully understood.[43]

Drug Purchases.   For a suspect to be charged with sale and possession of a narcotic, the actual sale must be legally demonstrated. Drug buys are generally accomplished in one of two ways: the *controlled informant buy* or the *undercover officer buy*. Drug purchases through informants are very common since not all agencies have an officer available for the buy. Furthermore, some suspects will never sell drugs to anyone but known drug users. The controlled informant drug buy should be conducted in the following manner:

1. Before meeting the suspect, the informant should be thoroughly searched for contraband. This is to avoid defense claims of entrapment, insinuating that the informant possessed drugs before the meeting with the suspect. All personal monies and medications should be relinquished by the informant. Money furnished for the buy should be recorded by serial number.

2. The informant should be transported to the buy location or followed so that the investigator can testify that the informant was always in sight until the arrival at the buy location. If the informant drives a personal vehicle, that vehicle should be thoroughly searched.

3. The building in which the buy is to take place should be put under surveillance. The times at which the informant enters and exits should be carefully noted.

4. Upon exiting, the informant should be followed to a prearranged meeting place and always kept in view of the officer. The officer must be able to later testify that the informant had no opportunity to meet someone else to secure drugs.

5. At the meeting location, all items purchased should be taken from the informant and marked for evidence. Money not used during the buy

should also be recovered. A search of the suspect's person and vehicle should again be conducted. The evidence should promptly be entered into the evidence room of the agency.

6. The informant should be carefully interviewed as to what transpired during the buy (conversations, actions, presence of other people and drugs, and so forth).

If an undercover officer makes the buy, which is always preferable, close surveillance of the operation is mandatory for the officer's protection. Research by the DEA demonstrates that the probability for violence is highest when buys are being conducted. Although there is danger of violence during any phase of the undercover operation, the investigator is at greatest risk when money is being shown to persuade suspects to deliver narcotics. Other factors that make undercover operations in the 2000s more dangerous than in recent years include the increased paranoia produced by cocaine-based drugs, methamphetamine and PCP, longer mandatory prison terms, and larger amounts of money involved.[44]

Once inside the suspect's premises, the officer should note the physical layout of the building for future raid purposes. Drug purchases should always be planned to facilitate the subsequent securement of a search warrant. The buy should take place inside the suspect's home, if at all possible. A search warrant can then be easily secured and the search conducted at this locality.

The Search. The execution of a search warrant or the execution of an arrest warrant requires planning and coordination. Whenever a suspect is arrested in a raid or premises are searched where drugs are present, there is the possibility of officer injury. Narcotics dealers, in particular, often possess firearms, and they may violently resist arrest, fearing the consequences of the sudden cessation of their narcotics habit. The warrant should be executed at a time that is optimal for the suspect's apprehension and the securement of a maximum quantity of drugs. A sufficient number of officers must be on hand to control unexpected suspects and to cover all avenues of escape. Since female suspects are frequently encountered in drug raids, a female officer must be present to perform searches. The major difficulty in the narcotics raid is that drugs can be quickly and easily disposed of as soon as the police announce their presence and authority. Consequently, the officers should attempt to gain rapid entry.

Once inside the residence, officers should move quickly into rooms that have been predesignated before the raid. All occupants of the premises should be controlled and searched. In addition to a normal, thorough search for weapons and evidence, officers must exercise extra care to avoid accidental needle sticks. As a significant number of drug addicts carry exposed needles that may be AIDS infected, caution must be exercised while searching suspects and their possessions.

The warrant should be read to the owner (suspect), who will be furnished with a copy of the document. A thorough search of the premises, in the owner's presence, can then be conducted. As evidence is located, it should be processed as it would be in any given crime scene. Following the search, the owner should be given an inventory list of the items seized. Many agencies routinely take before and after videos of the homes and businesses where they have executed a search warrant. This practice will disprove a claim that officers ransacked a residence or otherwise conducted an improper search. Prior to searching the interior of the premises, a videotape is taken to document its condition. A second recording is subsequently made when the search is completed.

Narcotics users and dealers seem to have a genius for concealing drugs within homes or automobiles. There is literally no limit to the hiding places that may serve this function. Evidence has been found under dog collars, in doorknobs, and behind television picture screens. The investigator must be guided by instinct, training, and information acquired through informants or undercover activities. When suspected drugs are located, under no condition should they ever be tasted. Although it has been commonly portrayed as "standard operating procedure" on television, the tasting of any drug, even in minute quantities, can be very dangerous.

Surveillance Techniques

Narcotics investigations and many other types of cases involve the use of surveillance. **Surveillance** is a secretive, close watch kept over persons, objects, or locations. A vital tool of the criminal investigator, covert observations are used with greater frequency than commonly realized. The FBI reports that after informant information, surveillance is the most frequently employed investigative technique in obtaining arrests, indictments, and convictions. The technique is employed to learn information that could prove useful to the investigation. It is used to develop both intelligence and evidence by identifying subjects, their activities, associates, residences and places of business, hangouts, and other related locations. There is no fixed point common to all inquiries at which the officer will decide to place a suspect under surveillance. Each case is unique and requires different information-gathering techniques. Surveillances are commonly used when information has been developed on the identity of a suspect who cannot yet be charged and arrested. The information implies that the suspect is either currently committing criminal acts or will be committing an offense in the near future. In addition, a surveillance may be employed to obtain probable cause for the issuance of a search or arrest warrant, to check the reliability of an informant, or to protect an undercover investigator.

Surveillances may be continuous or sporadic, depending on the nature of the investigation. In a *continuous surveillance,* the subject is constantly observed; the *sporadic surveillance* is situational in nature. For example, the surveillance of an undercover officer would be sporadic in that the officer would be watched only during his field contacts with the suspects.

Presurveillance Activities. Before a surveillance of either type is begun, planning, coordination, and research must be undertaken by all members of the surveillance team. The object of such presurveillance activities is to eliminate errors that could expose or confuse the operation. Each member of the surveillance team should be fully briefed as to the identities of the suspects, geographic locality of the surveillance, and communication procedures to be used.

There can never be too much planning before a surveillance. This type of activity is one of the most difficult investigative procedures to properly manage since unexpected occurrences are always a possibility. Investigators cannot control the behavior of those they observe and follow; consequently, they must react to the unexpected actions of the suspect without jeopardizing the surveillance operation. Officers who have not seen the suspect should be shown photographs and briefed as to the suspect's mannerisms. Each officer should totally understand his or her individual role and the overall purpose of the exercise.

As with undercover operations, not every officer is ideally suited to function as a surveillant. Officers must be able to blend into surroundings and have the ability to think quickly. In addition, the ability to observe and remember accurately and to be patient for long periods of time is essential.

Surveillance Methods

Moving Surveillances.   Surveillances are often of the moving variety in that the suspect is followed while in motion. The *moving surveillance* is generally accomplished in a vehicle, on foot, or from the air (helicopter or airplane). The automobile is most commonly employed, followed by the foot method, or a combination of the two. If only one police vehicle is to be used, it obviously must stay behind the suspect's auto. Care must be taken not to follow too closely, yet the suspect's auto must be in view at all times. Because of the difficulty of the single-auto surveillance, it is rarely used in significant cases.

Multivehicle surveillances are standard procedure for investigations deemed important. When there are many police vehicles secretively observing a suspect's auto, their chances of being discovered are considerably reduced. This is because the positions of the vehicles may be interchanged. Surveillance vehicles can use parallel routes to keep pace with the suspect, or the autos can be stationed at intervals along the suspect's route of travel. If the number of vehicles is sufficient not to arouse suspicion, they may alternately pass the suspect and take up positions waiting for the suspect to pass.

When many police vehicles are employed, communication should be constant and accurate. The position of the suspect should be constantly communicated to officers who do not have the suspect's vehicle in sight. Only investigators with a sound knowledge of the streets of the surveillance area should participate in the exercise. The suspect may attempt to "test" for police surveillance by ignoring traffic safety devices or by doubling back. Consequently, officers must use discretion and constant communication to combat such evasive techniques.

The foot surveillance is somewhat simple to conduct, as the suspect is moving at a slow rate of speed. However, it is easier to lose sight of an individual than an automobile. Foot surveillances are rarely practical unless suspects are in heavy pedestrian traffic or are totally unaware that they are being followed. If there are many officers engaging in the foot surveillance, tactics should be similar to those used in the multivehicle exercise. A combination of foot and vehicle surveillance is often used for greater flexibility.

Suspects may test for a foot surveillance, particularly when about to engage in an illegal activity. One common testing method is for the suspect to abruptly enter a building or vehicle to see if the investigator will follow. The suspect may also confront the officer, demanding to see identification. In this case, the suspect may not really know the person confronted to be a police officer. Many suspects routinely confront individuals they see more than once on the street. If surveillance officers think that they are drawing a suspect's attention, they should inform other members of the surveillance team and leave the area. Some suspects may use an associate to follow an officer's movements. Consequently, surveillance officers should be alert for individuals whose movements are consistent with the suspect's. Regardless of the moving surveillance technique, a good memory is essential. This is particularly true in foot surveillances, in which the investigators may not have an opportunity to record descriptions of suspicious persons, vehicles, or localities.

Fixed Surveillances.   *Fixed surveillances* are also termed *stakeouts* and *stationary surveillances*. This surveillance involves no movement initially, although it may become a moving type of surveillance at any time. In the stakeout, generally one or more investigators observe a premises or parked vehicle. Fixed surveillances are generally conducted for one or more of the following purposes:

1. to gather evidence by observing the activities within a premises (for example, activities associated with militant groups, vice operations, or organized crime);
2. to obtain information that can be used to secure a search warrant (for example, activities associated with fencing operations, narcotics dealing, stolen property, and/or known criminals coming and going from a premises);
3. to identify, locate, and/or apprehend suspects or wanted persons;
4. to observe, protect, and control an informant's activities, or to protect material witnesses;
5. to analyze the physical structure of a dwelling for a subsequent raid or apprehension activity; or
6. to protect and document the movements of an undercover officer.

Investigators who participate in the fixed surveillance must blend into the environment, attracting no undue attention. They are generally concealed in a vehicle that will not arouse suspicion or engaged in an activity that is commonplace to the neighborhood. A fixed surveillance normally allows the officer to make precise notes, as writing materials and observation equipment can be carried within the vehicle. Movements of the suspect should be noted in a chronological log and recorded through the use of surveillance photography.

Since many fixed surveillances are conducted at night, *night-vision devices* are often used to aid the investigator (see Figure 14.11). Night-vision

A   B

FIGURE 14.11   *A.* A night-viewing device, which greatly intensifies a small amount of light, allowing the viewer to see the subject in near total darkness; *B.* A photograph taken with a night-viewing device, in near total darkness, showing the apprehension of a suspect. *(Source: Kelly Showalter, Night Vision, ITT Industries.)*

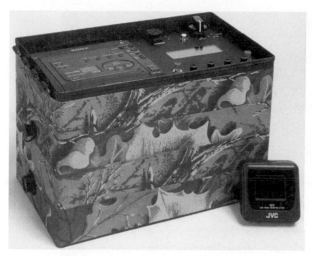

FIGURE 14.12 The Covert Unattended Surveillance System visually records criminal operations without the risk of detection, as the police need not be present to activate the device. The system is ideal for a variety of cases, including narcotics, organized crime and terrorist surveillances *(Source: Paul Feldman, Law Enforcement Associates.)*

viewing instruments greatly intensify small quantities of light via an electron-amplification process. This process allows the officer to view or photograph the object of the surveillance in near total darkness. Other surveillance devices include the covert unattended video system. This form of suspect observation needs no human attendance, and is generally concealed in the ground, woods, or other forms of cover. A totally wireless device, the system is ideal for video recording suspect activities involving outdoor marijuana operations, drug laboratories, extremist group surveillance, and a host of other applications. The system includes a pinhole camera in a camouflaged weatherproof housing. Images from the camera are recorded within the system's 8mm VCR, with a passive, infrared detector switching the recording process from standby to active when triggered by suspect motion or footsteps (see Figure 14.12).

The most recent surveillance methods involve the use of space-age technology. Investigators now have the ability to track the movement of suspects by utilizing satellite technology, which makes suspect awareness of the surveillance an impossibility. Remote tracking technology using **Global Positioning Systems** (GPS) has actually been available to police for decades. However, until recently, receivers could not transmit further than a fraction of a mile. Because of advanced tracking methods utilizing satellites and cell phones, police can now follow the movements of an individual virtually anywhere in the world. GPS techniques can also be used by protective surveillance teams to provide effective yet unobserved tracking of undercover officers or informants.

A recent State College, Pennsylvania, arson case illustrates how GPS was successfully used to connect a suspect to an arson scene. The suspect caught the attention of the police after several witnesses observed him at various arsons. Obtaining a warrant from the court, investigators secretly installed a GPS receiver on the suspect's vehicle. Then, using satellites and cell-phone technology, they tracked his movements on a laptop computer at police headquarters, never having to expose their presence to the suspect. Through the computer, they tracked the man from town to town and even street to street. Officers would occasionally verify the technology, visually confirming that the suspect was still the driver of the car on which the tracking device was placed and the car was actually where the computer detailed. Eventually, the GPS system proved the suspect was at the scene of an arson and provided the probable cause for his arrest. He was charged with setting 25 fires, including a car fire and an apartment building blaze that caused $500,000 in damage (see Figure 14.13).

FIGURE 14.13   Using GPS technology, investigators can track criminal suspects without fear of detection. Here officers determine a suspect's movements through the use of a hidden modem unit within his vehicle. Mapping software then enables officers to position his daily whereabouts. Such information is then retrieved and run as demonstrative evidence during court proceedings. *(Source: David M. White, State College, Pennsylvania, Police Department.)*

GPS surveillance methods have three major advantages over traditional foot and auto tracking: they are extremely accurate, reduce manpower for surveillance, and pose no hazard of being discovered by the suspect.

CRIMINALISTIC APPLICATIONS

Criminalistics is vitally important to narcotics enforcement for two reasons: identification and prosecution. In all criminal trials involving sales and/or possession of drugs, the state must establish the fact that the drug in question is, indeed, a drug. Only the qualified criminalist can serve as an expert witness in this regard. The criminalist may also link one drug to another to establish a pattern or to locate a clandestine laboratory in a specific geographical area. Although the majority of states have their own state laboratories to perform drug analysis, the DEA operates the largest drug forensic laboratory system in the world. DEA laboratories are staffed by more than 120 professional chemists in six regional labs, averaging more than 45,000 examinations each year.[45] Any authorized law enforcement agency in the world may use the services of this laboratory system.

Source Identification

It is often desirable to identify the source of the drugs that are involved in the investigation. The so-called *ballistics examination* of drug tablets is a common method of source identification. It is a combination of chemical analysis and toolmark examination of tablets and capsules that attempts to identify the manufacturer of the drug. The technique involves accurate measurements of size, scoring (indented impressions on the tablet's surface), imprints, bevels, and sealing devices. Additionally, microscopic imperfections are noted, and the components of the drug are identified via microchemical tests. The data obtained from these examinations are then compared with known samples obtained from drug firms, and samples are identified as having been produced in a clandestine laboratory.

Through this method of examination, it can be determined whether the drug has been diverted from legal channels of production. The source of manufacture may be traced to illegal laboratories by comparing the markings imprinted on the tablets to corresponding pill machines or to tools that were appropriated upon the discovery of the laboratory.

Substance Identification and Analysis

The forensic chemist must first determine whether the suspected substance is a narcotic or dangerous drug compound. Following this determination, qualitative and quantitative analyses are generally performed. Qualitative examinations determine the elements of which the substance is composed; quantitative tests determine the purity level of the substance.

Many different laboratory procedures are used to confirm that a suspected substance is a controlled drug. The chemist may subject the substance to tests that are physical in nature, such as determining the boiling point. *Crystalline precipitation tests* are commonly used to identify opiate derivatives and cocaine. Such analyses utilize chemicals that form crystals within the questioned substance. The formations of the crystals are unique to specific drugs. In addition to the preceding methods, the color spectrum of the substance may be examined through *spectrographic analysis*. Certain substances, such as barbiturates, can be identified and compared by means of *X-ray diffraction*. Researchers have recently developed a test for determining the presence and amount of marijuana in an individual's blood. The test, known as the *Soares-Gross technique*, involves a radioimmune assay for the THC present in the bloodstream. It is effective when performed within two hours of the ingestion of the marijuana. A blood sample, obtained from the subject, is mixed with animal blood antibodies and radioactive THC molecules. A constant percentage of antibodies chemically bonds with the nonradioactive THC in the sample, allowing criminalists to measure exactly the amount of marijuana in the blood.

Quantitative tests are important to the investigation since the nature of the charge and sentencing of the suspect may be dependent on the amount and purity of the drug. This type of examination is generally performed through chemical analysis.

Substance Detection in the Body

Forensic chemists are often called on to examine physiological evidence for the presence of dangerous drugs or narcotics. Such analysis may be requested for investigative leads or as a legal element for prosecution purposes. Whereas testing blood and urine for drug traces is commonly performed by medical personnel and associated labs, crime labs often test hair samples for drugs of abuse. Drug traces remain sequestered in the hair shaft indefinitely, thus providing detection for a much longer period than blood or urine. Each inch of hair represents approximately 60 days of substance usage. Drug levels in urine decrease rapidly through excretion, and in many cases, evidence of drug abuse can be eliminated in three days. Ingested drugs circulate in an individual's bloodstream, which nourishes the developing hair follicles. Trace amounts of abused drug entrapped in the hair core shaft are proportional to those ingested. Such traces cannot be washed or bleached out. It is always advisable for investigators to obtain court orders to collect physiological evidence and to get and preserve hairs, using the same level of care exhibited during crime scene processing.[46]

DESCRIPTIONS OF COMMONLY ENCOUNTERED DRUGS

Amphetamines   As with many other drugs, amphetamine slang terms are derived from the shapes and colors of the various capsules and tablets, their effects, or uses:

Amphetamine Sulfate: Rose-colored, heart-shaped tablets, known as peaches, roses, hearts, or bennies. In the form of round, white, double-scored tablets, they are known as cartwheels, whites, or bennies. In capsule form, they are of many colors and are known as black beauties, L.A. turnabouts, browns, or copilots. In oval-shaped tablets of different colors, they are often known as footballs, bullets, or greenies.

Injectable Amphetamine: Generally pharmaceutically packaged for medical injection. Known as jugs, bottles, or bombido.

Dextroamphetamine Sulfate: Orange-colored, heart-shaped tablets, known as hearts, oranges, or dexies. All types of amphetamines are generally referred to as uppers or pep pills.

Barbiturates   Generally known as goofballs, downers, barbs, candy, or sleeping pills. Specific types are nicknamed for their colors or shapes:

Pentobarbital Sodium: May be encountered in tablet form—either white, pink, or green. May also be encountered in capsule form and known as yellow-jackets or nimbies.

Secobarbital Sodium: May be encountered in tablet or capsule form. Often known as reds, pinks, red birds, red devils, or seggy.

Amobarbital Sodium: Typically encountered in solid blue capsule form and known as blues, blue birds, or blue devils.

Amobarbital Sodium/Secobarbital Sodium Combination: Typically packaged in red and blue capsule form and known as rainbows, red and blues, or double trouble.

Cocaine   Snow, "C," crack, rock, boulder, coke, cecil, dynamite, flake, speedball (when mixed with heroin), dust, paradise, chalk. Generally encountered as a white, crystal-like powder packaged like heroin, in flat folded papers or tinfoil. Crack cocaine is often rock-sized, white chunks, sold in plastic vials.

Codeine   Schoolboy. Generally encountered as a liquid in controlled cough medicines, or in pill or powder form.

Ecstasy   May be encountered in the form of capsules, tablets, pressed pills, or loose powder. Tablets are most commonly encountered, ranging in color and often with stamped designs. Common street names include the love drug, hug drug, X, XTC, Adam, or E.

GHB   Typically encountered as a colorless and odorless liquid, GHB may also be sold in powdered form. Known as Liquid Ecstasy, Liquid X, Invigorate, Longevity, and Blue Nitro.

Hashish   Hash, kif, quarter moon, soles. Generally sold to high-level drug dealers in dried, thin block form as a brown or black substance. Also encountered loosely ground, in ounce quantities.

Heroin   Snow, stuff, "H," junk, smack, skag, hard stuff, boy, diesel, dynamite, horse, white stuff, shit, joy powder. Typically wrapped in tinfoil or encountered in balloons as a fluffy brown (Mexican) or white (Middle Eastern) powder.

Lysergic Acid Diethylamide (LSD)   Cubes, blotter, royal blue, acid, sugar, blue acid, LSD 25, zen, sugar lump, sunshine. Generally encountered in or on other substances, such as in sugar cubes, on the backs of postage stamps, on small slips of paper, in blue pills, or occasionally in pharmaceutically prepared vials. LSD is colorless and odorless.

Marijuana   Grass, smoke, skunk, boom, straw, Texas tea, Acapulco gold, bhang, boo, pot, weed, "J," mary jane, reefer, roach, B. C. bud (from British Columbia, Canada). Generally encountered in a rolled cigarette form (joint), packaged loosely in ounce quantities (lid), or packed in kilo squares (K's or bricks).

Mescaline (peyote)   Mescal button, cactus, button tops, moons, "P," the bad seed, big chief. May be encountered in natural form as a cactus portion or a section of the cactus known as a button. Generally sold in ground form within a capsule, giving a brown appearance.

Methamphetamine   May be encountered in tablet form—light green, orange, pink, or white. More commonly encountered as a fluffy white powder packaged like heroin or in pharmaceutically packaged injection vials. Generally known as speed, crank, meth, chalk, cristy, crystal, or splash. Smokable type termed "ice" and found in hardened rock form.

Morphine   "M," dreamer, white stuff, hard stuff, morpho, unkie, Miss Emma, monkey, cube, morf, tab, hocus.

Generally encountered in powder, pill, or pharma-ceutically packaged liquid form.

Opium   Black stuff, gum, hop, skee, tar, "O," mud. Typically found as a hardened, black, tarlike substance, or in pill form.

Phencyclidine (PCP)   Angel dust, peace pill, animal dust. Generally encountered as a white powder or a pill.

Psilocybin   Silly, sacred mushrooms, magic mushrooms. Generally encountered in natural form—a brownish mushroom with or without stem. May also be sold in ground powder form, tablet, or liquid form.

▲ SUMMARY

The investigation of illegal drug possession and sale is a top law enforcement priority for the new millennium. It is currently estimated that more than 13 million Americans are illegal drug users. The generic term *drug* actually includes substances that are legally classified as narcotics or dangerous drugs. *Narcotics* refers to substances that have a high potential for addiction and generally produce a depressant effect on the central nervous system. Some classified narcotics are an exception to those producing this physical reaction, as cocaine and its various derivatives stimulate rather than depress the nervous system. The most serious depressant narcotic drug of abuse is heroin, a chemically converted narcotic from the opium poppy. Heroin is again gaining in popularity, as thousands of addicts switch back to it from crack cocaine. Heroin is abused by approximately one-half million addicts throughout the country, who are most commonly encountered in urban areas. Whereas nearly all heroin addicts formerly injected the narcotic, growing numbers are inhaling it because of the current higher levels of purity and the fear of AIDS transmission through contaminated needles.

Cocaine, as well as its freebase form, crack, is a second type of narcotic highly prevalent today. Like heroin, cocaine originates outside the United States and, through a chemical conversion process, is transformed into a crystal-like powder. American users then convert the powder into the more powerful crack form by a simple heating process. Cocaine is highly addictive psychologically, particularly when smoked as crack.

Synthetic and natural substances, other than narcotics, that have the potential to injure through abuse are commonly referred to as dangerous drugs. Most dangerous drugs can generally be classified as depressants, stimulants, or hallucinogens. Barbiturates are the most commonly abused depressant drugs; users are found among all classes of people. Stimulant abuse centers on amphetamines and the more powerful methamphetamine. Most barbiturates and stimulants are ingested by tablet or capsule, but methamphetamine abusers often inject or smoke this powerful derivative. Hallucinogens include any substance that is legally classified as possibly harmful because of the drug's ability to alter perception and thinking. The most well-known hallucinogen, LSD (lysergic acid diethylamide), is returning to popularity among high school and college students. LSD may be encountered in a variety of forms, but strips of paper soaked with the drug are most common. Marijuana is a mild hallucinogenic, and more Americans have direct experience with this drug than with any other illegal substance. Increasing amounts of marijuana are grown within the United States by hydroponic or outdoor farming methods. Anabolic steroids are unique dangerous drugs that promote muscle growth. Use of these drugs is growing rapidly, generally among those who wish to improve sports performance and personal appearance.

Criminal investigations targeting drug operations focus on various levels of suspect involvement. Principal distributors are difficult to investigate on all but the federal level of enforcement. Secondary and street-level dealers and users are frequently investigated by local police, as they are visible and generally known through surveillance or informants. Upper-level drug dealers are often targets of asset forfeiture. Forfeiture is a legal punishment in which valuable property used to facilitate illegal acts is surrendered to government ownership. Drug investigations often require undercover operations. Undercover assignments may involve the investigator working directly to purchase drugs or informants working under the investigator's care. When informants are employed in an undercover capacity, their actions must be tightly controlled and regulated.

Although the abuse of narcotics and dangerous drugs is showing signs of stabilizing and even decreasing, the level of use is still very high. It is probable that investigators will continue to devote considerable time and resources to this serious national problem.

▪ EXERCISES

1. Prepare a research paper on the historical uses of narcotics. Specify the country of origin, how the drug came to be abused, and early methods of ingestion for each of the major narcotics.

2. Locate a drug rehabilitation agency in your community. Interview several former narcotics users, attempting to find out their motivations for using drugs and the manner in which the substances were used. Report your findings to the class.

3. Interview a local narcotics investigator. Determine the estimated extent of drug abuse in your community. Record the arrest data for the past five years. Compare this information with national trends.

● RELEVANT WEB SITES

http://www.dea.gov/pubs/state_factsheets.html

Operated by the federal Drug Enforcement Administration (DEA), this comprehensive site provides detailed drug summaries specific for each state. Links to sites detailing drug policy, DEA resources, law enforcement drug operations, and drug trafficking patterns.

http://www.nida.nih.gov/infofacts/methamphetamine.html

National Institute of Drug Abuse (NIDA) site devoted to methamphetamine data. Includes associated health hazards and extent of usage. Links to NIDA home page in which data regarding all major drugs of abuse are detailed.

http://www.inhalants.org/

National Inhalant Prevention Coalition, a nonprofit referral and information clearinghouse concerned with inhalants, operates this site. Extensive inhalant information, including characteristics of users and details of many of the nearly 1,000 products commonly abused.

http://www.usdoj.gov/ag/readingroom/undercover.htm

Complete text of the U.S. Attorney General's Office report on the use of FBI undercover agents and informants in sensitive criminal investigations.

Youth Gang Investigations

KEY TERMS

Crips and Bloods gangs
drive-by shootings
expressive violence
female gang
founding member
gang unit

graffiti
hard-core member
MS-13 (Mara Salvatrucha 13)
street gang
tagging

LEARNING OBJECTIVES

1. to understand how and why gangs are a growing crime problem;
2. to know the four elements that define a street youth gang;
3. to be aware of the connection of drugs and firearms to street gangs;
4. to comprehend motivations for joining a youth gang;
5. to be able to define the four major types of gang members; and
6. to understand the various investigative methods commonly employed against violent youth gangs.

INTRODUCTION

Criminal conduct associated with youth gangs has become a serious investigative problem throughout the United States. Once considered primarily a dated urban crime problem, organized street gangs have spread alarmingly throughout the nation. Hundreds of thousands of young individuals are affiliated with gangs or are "wannabes." Gang violence among adults and youth is not a new phenomenon in the United States, as such activity had its origins in the eighteenth century. What is new is the high level of membership and associated criminal activity that faces today's criminal investigator.

The youth gang problem has risen and fallen in various historical cycles. Street gangs were not seriously studied until the 1920s, as prior to this date such groups were small in membership and typically involved minor delinquent acts. Many Americans first became concerned with youth gangs during the focus on juvenile delinquency in the 1950s. As recently as the mid-1970s, many criminal justice researchers documented the near extinction of gangs in America. Yet by the mid-1980s, a combination of factors created a dramatic acceleration in gang growth that continues to today. Youth gangs are also linked to the steady rise of general violent juvenile crime in the past decade and are specifically associated with startling increases in juvenile homicide, drug arrests, and gun violence. Because of the prevalence and intensity of this growing law enforcement problem, investigators in large and small communities must be able to recognize and successfully confront this dilemma.

Current State of Youth Gangs

Youth gangs are often known as street gangs or more commonly given the generic term *gang*. Although many law enforcement agencies and researchers have attempted to clarify what constitutes a youth gang, the Chicago Police Department definition is complete and has been widely adopted: A **street gang** is an association of youthful individuals, generally ranging in age from 13 to the early 20s, who exhibit the following characteristics in varying degrees:

1. a gang name and recognizable symbols;
2. a defined geographic territory;
3. regular meeting patterns; and
4. an organized, continuous course of criminality.[1]

The exact degree of gang involvement is not known, but a National Institute of Justice survey documented that gangs are a formidable problem in the overwhelming majority of large and small cities surveyed. The study revealed that nearly 846,000 gang members belong to more than 31,000 gangs in nearly 5,000 jurisdictions throughout the United States.[2] With such large numbers of young individuals belonging to groups that are inherently geared toward criminal behavior, it is highly likely that the growth of youth crime is also linked to gang growth. By any measurement, youth crime increased dramatically in the past two decades. Nationally, 2.3 million juveniles were arrested in 1995, an increase of 175 percent from 1975. From 1990 to 1995, violent crimes by youth under 18 rose nearly 70 percent, with more than 110,000 children under the age of 13 arrested annually for felonious acts. By 2005, the Department of Justice documented that juveniles commit 20 percent of all violent crime, a rate far out of proportion to their numbers in the population. Such increases in violent youth crime are predicted to continue and even worsen, as the nation's juvenile population is expected to grow through the beginning of the new century.

The recent surge in juvenile crime does not parallel adult increases in reported criminality. In most crime categories, adult offenses decreased significantly in the past two decades, whereas youth crime increased rapidly even though the population of teenagers declined. The discrepancy is poorly understood by justice researchers but is partially attributed to various negative social conditions and expanding gang affiliation. Our present juvenile criminal situation is extremely serious, but the near future holds even more cause for concern. There are now 39 million children in the United States under the age of ten, more of this age group than the country has had for decades. Should current trends of youth crime and gang growth continue, experts predict a wave of violent juvenile "superpredators" as the youngsters come into their teen years.[3]

Gang-related crime may occur in any size jurisdiction—urban, suburban, or rural (see Figure 15.1). Even on isolated Native American reservations, once noted for their lack of organized criminality, youth gangs are now considered the leading form of criminal behavior. The Arizona Department of Public Safety cites Native American youth as one of the state's fastest-growing ethnic groups involved in gang activity. In the Salt River Reservation, more than 25 gangs with 300 members are operating, membership that comprises 17 percent of the entire reservation population. Accordingly, the image of gangs operating solely in urban cities is a false stereotype, as gang growth in the United States has been noted in every imaginable jurisdiction.

Offender Characteristics

Although the majority of youth gang members are black or Hispanic males, the proportion of white and female involvement is increasing. As in many patterns of American criminality, the racial and ethnic makeup of gang participants has changed. In the early part of the last century, gang involvement in crime was mainly associated with second-generation white immigrants from eastern and southern Europe. As greater numbers of African Americans and Hispanic immigrants migrated into northern inner cities,

FIGURE 15.1   Percentage of jurisdictions reporting gangs by region.

TABLE 15.1   Types of Youth Gangs by Jurisdictional Size as Determined by State Prosecutors

Types of Gangs	Percentage Operating in Large Cities (population of 250,000 or more)	Percentage Operating in Small Cities (population of 50,000 to 250,000)
Locally based, African American	83%	60%
Hispanic	64	43
White hate gang (e.g., skinhead)	53	23
Asian	52	14
Crips and Bloods (e.g., gangs originating in Los Angeles)	50	41
Caribbean (e.g., gangs with origins in Jamaica, Dominican Republic)	43	16

Source: U.S. Department of Justice, National Institute of Justice.

the composition of youth gangs changed to reflect these populations. More recently, gangs have begun to reflect Central and South American, Asian, and Jamaican populations, among others. A national study surveyed prosecutors to indicate the type of gang offenders operating in their jurisdictions. As detailed in Table 15.1, survey respondents in large and small localities reported the presence of locally based African American gangs as being most prevalent, with Caribbean youth gangs the least frequently encountered.[4] A National Youth Gang survey sponsored by the Justice Department sampled over 3,000 police agencies regarding age, race, and gender data of gang members within their jurisdictions. The results indicate the vast majority of gang members are males (90 percent) from 15 to 24 years of age (71 percent) (see Figure 15.2). Police also report that Hispanic gang members comprise 44 percent of total gang membership; African Americans, 35 percent; caucasians, 14 percent; and Asians, 5 percent.

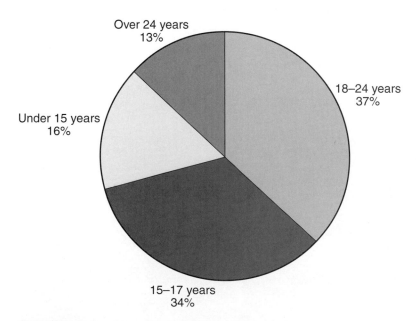

FIGURE 15.2   Age of gang members.

A study of 40 youth gangs in Chicago, a city with nearly 60,000 members, revealed only four gangs constituting half of all street gang memberships. The dominant gangs were composed predominantly of African American and Hispanic males, reflecting the city's population dynamics. Although media accounts often portray new gangs emerging as mere satellite operations of long-standing big-city street gangs, this is rarely the case. The majority of newly formed gangs are actually homegrown, creating unique local problems that can be effectively addressed only by local law enforcement efforts. Most new gang members do emulate more well-known urban gangs such as the Crips and Bloods, but true alliances between distant geographically based groups is uncommon. Most gang offenders are youths who willingly join an emerging or established street gang. Generally, membership satisfies some unfulfilled need in their often dysfunctional or disadvantaged lives. Yet the growth of gangs in middle-class, affluent suburbs indicates that excitement, rather than poverty alone, may be a motivating foundation element.

The urge for excitement is closely linked with youthful feelings of being powerless. Gang membership has traditionally attracted the most vulnerable youths, those who are failing or dropping out of school, have low opinions of their future prospects, or have early criminal arrest histories. A study of African American gangs in Milwaukee, Wisconsin, noted that every gang leader had left school prematurely, most having been expelled for assaultive behavior.[5] In many of the nation's larger cities, gang membership is a multigenerational family tradition. Interviews with members demonstrate that joining gangs is simply following the behavior of brothers, cousins, or even fathers. Informal social or family recruitment is also reinforced through incarceration in local jails or state prisons. Crime-prone youths know that prison life will be less dangerous and threatening with gang protection. Although intimidation does play a role in about 20 percent of gang recruitment, most members adopt gang affiliation through family, friends, or drug-dealing activities (Figure 15.3).

FIGURE 15.3 Typical gang graffiti associated with urban black gangs such as the Crips or Bloods. Writing identifies members and establishes territory. *(Source: Dennis Porter, Los Angeles County Sheriff's Department.)*

Female offenders constitute a growing segment of American gang membership. Females may be found as auxiliary branch members of exclusive male gangs, or they form fully autonomous organizations. Surveys indicate that at least 100 female gangs are operating in the nation, with females comprising an estimated 10 percent of gang membership, or approximately 84,000 girls. Female gangs are typically structured to resemble male groups, having similar initiation rites, meetings, and associated criminality. Female gang members appear to have three behavioral constants in their backgrounds: early sexual activity, delinquency, and strong susceptibility to peer pressure.[6]

Although large street gangs lack the more precise hierarchy of adult organized crime groups, the general elements of a social hierarchy can often be identified:

1. **Founding members.** Often referred to as "original gangsters," **founding members.** are the oldest members of the gang and may have helped found the group. They are held in high esteem because of their street skills, prison experiences, and material possessions acquired through years of drug dealing.

2. **Hard-core members.** Generally 16 to 24 years of age and totally dedicated to gang enterprises and activities, these individuals are likely to wear gang colors and similar clothing styles; they direct most street-level sales of cocaine.

3. **New members.** Often referred to as "baby gangsters," they range in age from 12 to 16 years old. These juveniles are typically used as drug couriers for older gang members and often sell small amounts of crack cocaine. Some individuals in this group are gang "wannabes" and are awaiting or seeking initiation into the gang.

4. **Street lookouts.** Sometimes known as "tiny gangsters," they represent the youngest level and usually serve as outlooks and messengers for older gang members.

Gang Crime Patterns

Street gangs engage in a wide variety of criminal behavior. Yet gang-related crime is above all a violent crime problem for criminal investigation. Homicides and other violent crimes account for nearly 50 percent of all recorded gang-related crime incidents. American youth gangs have been associated with crime for decades, but the frequency and degree of violence in the past ten years has risen considerably. Individual gang members, gang cliques, or entire gang organizations now traffic extensively in narcotics; commit shootings, assaults, robbery, and extortion; and terrorize entire neighborhoods. Whereas the gangs of past generations mainly engaged in relatively minor crimes or fought among themselves for territory, today's gangs are far more aggressive and externally focused in their criminality. An ever-increasing number are supported by drug dealing, extensively using firearms to intimidate and kill rivals. The extreme violence now associated with gangs has become an integral function of the group. According to prosecutors in large cities, more than 70 percent of gangs located in their communities are routinely involved in violent crime. It is estimated that more than 46,000 serious felonies are committed by gang members annually.[7] Gang-related felonies typically center on drug dealing, homicides, and associated violence.

Drug Dealing

Federal researchers have established that 10 percent of the nation's gang-related crime is associated with drugs. It is important to note that this percentage is based solely on police arrest statistics and is assumed not to reflect the much higher actual degree of drug participation among most street gangs. The surge in overall violent juvenile crime coincided with increases in drug arrests, increases that were particularly evident in the nonwhite urban environment in which gangs have thrived. One of the most distinguishing characteristics of today's gangs is the drug connection—specifically the using and selling of crack cocaine and methamphetamine. A significant percentage of all crack cocaine sold in the United States—at least one-half—is distributed by street gangs. Although youth gangs routinely sell other illegal drugs, such as marijuana, PCP, and heroin, their involvement in crack cocaine and meth is far more extensive.[8]

The Los Angeles–based **Crips and Bloods gangs** personify the drug-gang connection. Both gangs formed in southern California during the late 1960s, associating themselves with colors that identify membership and allegiance: blue for Crips and red for the Bloods. Initially, the two gangs patterned themselves after the traditional 1950s gang model of territorial violence and minor crime. Realizing the huge profit potential of the drug demand that had continued to build from the late 1960s to the mid-1980s, the two gangs began to supply marijuana and PCP. When powdered cocaine became popular among white users in the late 1970s, the organizations began to act as midlevel distributors. By the late 1980s, the old drug routes through Florida had been eliminated by law enforcement, and drug smuggling shifted into Mexico and California. The enormous popularity of crack cocaine among inner-city residents soon dominated Crips' and Bloods' crime activities, swelling membership to an estimated 30,000 in the 1990s. Both gangs have been engaged in establishing drug operations outside of California and regularly transport crack cocaine to various midwestern and eastern cities.

Naturally, Bloods and Crips are not the only street gangs engaged in drug dealing. Many of the Asian and Caribbean gangs also sell drugs as their chief source of income, as do most local inner-city gangs. For example, 56 percent of all arrests involving Chicago's oldest African American street gang, the Vice Lords, are for drug dealing or possession of narcotics. Although most local gangs stick to their area, gangs trafficking large quantities of illegal narcotics are more likely to expand their dealing outside traditional territories. As gangs increase their involvement in dealing drugs, they tend to become more organized. When a group's narcotic dealing reaches interstate or international involvement, the street gang might more properly be termed an organized crime group.

A rapidly growing gang with Central American roots is believed to be even more violent and organized than most other Los Angeles–based youth gangs. The **MS-13 Mara Salvatrucha** gang has a particularly vicious reputation and is heavily involved in violent crime. The group is named for a street in San Salvador and for guerilla fighters who battled in El Salvador's civil war. Founded by the children of refugees who fled Central American civil war in El Salvador to southern California in the 1980s, the gang is estimated to have 50,000 members in North and Central America. Deported American gang members have organized large MS-13 gangs in El Salvador, Honduras, Guatemala, and other countries in the region. These units communicate closely with American branches and, in addition to drug dealing, participate in smuggling, immigrant extortion, robbery, and many unusually violent crimes.

The gang has spread rapidly from the Washington, D.C., area to North Carolina and is especially prevalent in northern Virginia. Unlike many other gangs that specialize only in drug dealing, MS-13 is criminally flexible. Members may wear blue and white, colors symbolizing the national flag of El Salvdor, and often tattoo their bodies and faces with MS-13 slang and symbols.[9]

Criminal Homicide

The Department of Justice estimates that nearly 1,100 gang-related killings occur each year; that is, nearly one of every 21 homicide victimizations is gang related. Whereas juvenile homicides declined nearly 20 percent between 1980 and 1984, by 1993 the number had increased 94 percent, the largest rise in juvenile homicide ever recorded.[10] The mid-1980s also marked a nationwide expansion of gang activity, and many believe gang violence has directly contributed to the accelerating juvenile murder rate.

Mirroring most large gangs, juvenile homicide victims are disproportionately male and African American. Whereas between 1980 and 1994 the number of white juveniles killed rose 15 percent, the number of African American juvenile victims increased 97 percent.

The new street gang is far more focused on deadly violence than were past generations of gangs. In 2005 Chicago, police estimated that 50 percent of all murders were gang related. Homicides are often committed using the **drive-by** shootings, in which two or more gang members fire weapons at rivals from a moving vehicle. Such shootings, which have spread across the country as a standard method of gang retaliation, have resulted in hundreds of innocent people being killed or wounded. In Los Angeles County, which has become the focal point of gangs in contemporary America, gang-related homicides increased more than 250 percent in a recent ten-year period. By contrast, during the same period, the number of non–gang-related killings declined significantly. Authorities attribute the higher instance of gang killings to drug dealing, more lethal weaponry, and frequent drive-by homicides.

Associated Violence

Street gangs are also responsible for other forms of violence, particularly **expressive violence**, which is destructive behavior that has no practical purpose. Gang violence for the sake of violence takes the form of random beatings, arson, auto theft, and frequent use of firearms. Real or imagined insults or demonstrations of "disrespect" trigger frequent assaults among gang members. Violence may erupt over the flashing of hand signs, mode of dress, or challenging graffiti.

Although any of the social trappings associated with gang behavior can lead to aggression, the use of graffiti is particularly common. **Graffiti** is a general term for wall writing or **tagging**, that is applied to buildings or public property. Generally the work of young offenders using cans of spray paint, the wall messages are commonly associated with gang activity. Although those who make graffiti ("taggers") are often affiliated gang members, some are outsiders who hope using graffiti will help them to gain acceptance into a particular street gang. Tagging messages usually resemble handwriting but may be difficult for law enforcement officers to read because suspects often invent their own letters or symbols. Gang taggers typically use graffiti to threaten or show disrespect to rival gangs. Another purpose of the message may be to announce the presence of a gang or immortalize murdered gang members.[11]

Graffiti has been a form of gang communication for nearly 20 years, primarily used to mark a gang's territory. Defining specific neighborhood blocks as belonging to the group is an important part of the gang territorial mind-set (Figure 15.4). Creators of graffiti often operate in groups, known as "tagging crews," which are capable of spraying a staggering amount of graffiti throughout a community. In a recent year, more than $36 million was spent just in Los Angeles County cleaning wall markings.[12]

A new form of high-tech graffiti is now spreading rapidly online. Commonly referred to as high-tech tagging, gang members known as *cyberbangers* routinely invade Web sites with written graffiti-like challenges and threats. Either through their own Web sites or by posting messages on non gang sites, cybertaggers use the anonymity of the Internet to glorify the gang lifestyle, claim territory, or threaten rival gangs.[13]

Firearm violence is also closely associated with the national gang problem. As street gangs began to turn to drug dealing, possession and use of guns increased dramatically among them. While the number of juvenile murderers has tripled in the past ten years, the number of guns used in these killings has quadrupled. In 1994, eight out of ten juvenile killers used a gun, compared with five out of ten in 1983. The previously mentioned Chicago street gang study confirmed that a gun was the lethal weapon used in almost all gang-motivated homicides, and the use of high-caliber, automatic, or semiautomatic weapons dramatically increased. Gang members have a fascination with firearms beyond the normal attachment of most other criminal types. Guns have replaced fistfights or the carrying of knives in many gangs, and increased homicide has been the result. During a recent three-year period in Chicago, 32 percent of all nonlethal cases of gang violence involved a gun, as did 94 percent of killings perpetrated by or against members of the city's 40 youth gangs.

FIGURE 15.4   Grafitti writing style of Californian Cambodian gangs. Note that "Crazy Brothers Clan" has been crossed out by "Tiny Rascal Gang," symbolizing a direct challenge that often results in violence.   *(Source: Dennis Porter, Los Angeles County Sheriff's Department.)*

The increasing use of guns by violent juvenile offenders is potentially far more dangerous to society than increased adult firearm violence for several reasons. Many juveniles are more willing to fire guns at others, as their immaturity often prevents any consideration of the consequences. Since most gang members come from poor, powerless lower-class environments, the gun has become an important symbol in their self-image. The use of firearms, particularly large-caliber semiautomatic weapons, becomes the fastest route to empowerment. Peer support and pressure by fellow gang members to carry and use guns only serve to increase the likelihood of firearm violence. The spread of guns through the nation's youthful population, combined with the cumulative, desensitizing effects of media-glamorized violence, has led to an alarming increase in shootings by gang members and nongang youths alike.

Investigative Procedures

The criminal investigation of gang offenses can be particularly challenging, as an unusually wide variety of criminal behaviors may be involved. Police responses to gang crime take two basic forms: reactive and proactive. Since most larger gangs are involved in the drug trade, investigations often focus on drug possession or sale; that is, police react to a crime that has been committed. Similarly, since many violent street gang members carry firearms, gun arrests can be expected. Proactive investigations, however, seek to eliminate or contain illegal gang crime before the behavior becomes widespread. For example, eliminating independent drug sources before they become established with a local gang would be a proactive step, as would the surveillance and identification of visiting gang recruiters from larger, out-of-town street gangs. Unless a jurisdiction has no gangs, the proactive method must be used in conjunction with after-the-crime investigations.

Crimes stemming from gang activity should be identified and separated from other criminal offenses occurring in a community. This is necessary for effective investigative response and proper record keeping. To determine if an incident is gang related, police investigators must analyze each case to see if it meets any of the following criteria:

1. *Identification*—Crimes that stem from the significance a gang places on certain symbols of its identity or alliance (such as hand signs, language, graffiti, or clothing). Such symbols may provoke others to violence.
2. *Recruitment*—Offenses related to recruiting gang members, such as intimidation by word or action.
3. *Extortion*—Efforts to exact payments as tribute or "protection" from individuals or businesses.
4. *Territory violations*—Crimes committed to guard a gang's "turf" or to show disrespect to another gang's territory.
5. *Prestige*—Crimes committed either to glorify the gang or to gain rank or peer status within the group.
6. *Internal conflict*—Offenses that result from internal conflicts or power struggles within the leadership or rank and file of the gang.
7. *Vice*—Offenses typically involving the distribution of drugs, generally cocaine, crack meth, marijuana, PCP, or heroin; occasionally may involve gambling or prostitution.
8. *Retaliation*—Criminal acts of revenge for real or imagined insults against the gang by rival street gang members.[14]

INVESTIGATIVE PROFILE

April L. Tardy
Detective-Gang Investigator
Operations Safe Streets Bureau
Los Angeles County Sheriff's Department
Compton Station

I've been a law enforcement officer with the Los Angeles County Sheriff's Department (LASD) since 1994. Although I have a degree in business administration from California State University at San Bernardino, I didn't apply for any business jobs after graduation, preferring a career with the Sheriff's Department. I took an Introduction to Criminal Justice course in college, as it sounded interesting, and then two other justice courses in criminal investigation and gang investigations. After that, I knew I'd found the career I wanted to pursue. My agency has a policy that, after academy training, all new deputy sheriffs are assigned to work as correctional officers in our county detention facilities. We are the largest sheriff's department in the United States, and our county jail system holds the largest number of inmates of any jail or prison in the country as well. So I went from the academy directly into Sybil Brand Institute, L.A. County's female county jail. I worked as a correctional deputy for five years, and although I wouldn't want to do institutional corrections for my whole career, I found the experience to be invaluable. When one works in corrections, you learn so much about criminal behavior: how they think, their culture, and the attraction of the gang lifestyle.

I was then assigned to the patrol division at the LASD's Temple Station. This part of Los Angeles County has significant gang membership, and I had frequent contact with them while a uniformed patrol deputy. They were so numerous that on average I'd FI (field interview) up to ten gang members a day. I found this type of offender quite interesting and also discovered I had the ability to communicate effectively with them. After two years on patrol, I successfully competed for a detective position in the gang unit. Most of our stations have gang units, formally termed the Operation Safe Streets Bureau. This unit is in addition to the general crime detectives and narcotics investigators also assigned to the station.

The gang unit is composed of two separate groups of detectives: gang investigators and gang suppression deputies. I'm one of nine gang investigators in our station, and my primary duties are both proactive and reactive. We respond to crimes in which gang suspects are involved, and we often target specific gangs or members for our attention. A lot of our work is focused on gathering information that can be used as probable cause to obtain search warrants. We gather information from informants and the suppression unit to obtain our warrants, often resulting in drug and weapon arrests at the residences we search. I'd say about half my time is spent dealing with preparing and executing search warrants. There are eight Compton Station gang suppression deputies. The suppression investigators are mainly responsible for gathering intelligence, conducting surveillance, and other tactics used to prevent or deter gang crimes. The major gangs I deal with are various set or subgroups of Crips and Bloods, although we also have quite a few Hispanic youth gangs. The majority of the gang-related crime is linked to narcotics, mainly dealing in crack cocaine, but methamphetamine is also a problem. Hispanic gang violence tends to be more territorial in nature, while much of the trouble from the other gangs is linked to drug dealing and personal challenges.

Although my station has law enforcement responsibility for several communities outside the city of Compton, the majority of my work is centered within this community. Unfortunately, Compton has an exceedingly high rate of violent crime and associated gang activity. With an overall population of 97,000 people, nearly 1,600 violent crimes are reported annually. A great deal of our crime is directly related to the 10,000 gang members who belong to 60 various Compton gangs. Since the beginning of this year, we've already investigated 45 gang-related murders in the city—and the year has over four months to go. This level of violence has a terrible effect on the law-abiding people of Compton, and this is what motivates me to work as hard as I can. I grew up in a city where this type of problem didn't exist, but I work in a place where children are held hostage by crime and spend their lives looking over their shoulders. So when I took that gang investigations course back in college, I knew I wanted to eventually do this type of work.

There are a number of great things I enjoy about my position. I particularly like helping families who have been trapped by gang wars or who just need help. I assist them in

(Continued)

obtaining aid, and sometimes we have to totally relocate them because of death threats. I also participate in a mentoring program for sixth- to eighth-grade girls. We try to provide a positive role model for inner-city girls and show them there is another world out there beyond the gang life. We have frequent field trips, for although they live in southern California, many of the girls have never even been to the beach or a zoo. Two negatives quickly come to mind: time away from my family and seeing the continuous damage that gangs do to so many people.

If a criminal justice student wants to do this type of work, I'd recommend they first get some type of job within the community where they plan to be an officer. It could be a part-time job while they are still in college, but they'll learn how to build rapport and the culture of the community. Also, you can't really do an investigative job like mine unless you've first worked in uniformed patrol. It's as a patrol officer that you'll find your niche, what really interests you, and what you may want to specialize in as an investigator. Finally, if you're going to work gang investigations, you have to be ready to deal with a lot of terrible, senseless violence. A few years ago we worked a case in which a young gang member was shot to death in the middle of the morning. We found him dead in the street with a spray can in one hand and a handgun in the other. It was the day before Thanksgiving, and a rival gang caught him trying to spray paint over their gang graffiti. For that, they chased him down and murdered him.

When specific gang crimes are separated from similar non–gang-affiliated offenses, law enforcement officers can concentrate on identifying specific gang suspects and design effective investigative strategies.

Research has identified three types of gang-infested high-crime neighborhoods: turf hot spots, drug hot spots, and combination neighborhoods. Areas classified as turf hot spots are neighborhoods in which fights frequently occur over territorial boundaries. Gang crime in such areas generally focuses on intergang rivalries in which one group attempts to gain another's territory. Territory-focused gangs are often not engaged in extensive drug operations and operate to promote the material and psychological well-being of the membership. Drug hot spots are areas in which gang-motivated drug crimes predominate. Assaults and homicides related to narcotic deals are common, and there is heavy traffic from outside the neighborhood to purchase drugs. In combination neighborhoods, gang-motivated crime often includes both turf and drug criminality.

Once investigators classify a gang neighborhood, patrol and investigative strategies can be initiated to curb or prevent crimes. Gang violence associated with territorial disputes can be discouraged if patrols conduct frequent field interviews to uncover gang members' possession of weapons. Frequent stop-and-frisk tactics serve to disperse large groups of gang members gathering for retaliatory fights. Investigators assigned to gang units can easily identify rival gang members coming into another group's neighborhood. Follow-up field inquiries help to discourage further interaction between the two groups. Neighborhoods that are predominantly drug gang oriented require standard antidrug investigation tactics associated with most narcotic inquiries. The constant use of gang informants and undercover police officers as well as other methods of gathering intelligence are essential in such cases. Since most gangs "import" their drugs from others prior to sale and distribution, every effort must be made to track the supply chain to its highest source. If the supply source cannot be pinpointed, law enforcement can attempt to suppress the drug activity by vigilant search-and-arrest operations against the lower-level members engaged in street sales. Standard buy-and-bust operations, in which undercover officers cruise neighborhood drug sale areas simulating typical outside buyers, should be mounted frequently. In combination neighborhoods, both types of enforcement pressure must be brought to bear against gang members. In all three types, specialized officers are often needed to supervise the operations.

In medium to large police agencies, **gang units** are composed of volunteer officers who receive special training in antigang policing. Gang unit officers receive intensive in-service training to help them recognize gang members through their *modus operandi*, graffiti, hand signs, clothing, and other means of communication. Specialized police gang units often team up with similarly trained attorneys from the prosecutor's office. Such specialization allows one prosecuting attorney to handle a gang case from its inception rather than having many different prosecutors handle a single felony.

Recent technological advances have also helped gang investigators. Most large police agencies rely on unique computer programs designed to track gang members and gang-related criminal activities. Programs specifically designed to search for and identify gang members and gang crimes expedite rapid searches using any number of partial identifiers, including nicknames, gang tattoos, aliases, dates of birth, residences, scars, probation status, and other details. Although some civil liberty groups object to databases that list and categorize suspects based on neighborhood or clothing styles, strict criteria determine inclusion. To be listed, a suspect must have admitted previous gang affiliation or have been included in a gang roster. Such databases are dependent on the degree of detailed information that patrol and detective officers can provide through field interviews or arrests of suspected gang members.[15]

Because of the frequent connection of gangs to drugs and firearms, successful investigations require close coordination with robbery, narcotics, and homicide detectives. In addition, various federal agencies have a cross-jurisdictional interest in such offenses. The ATF, DEA, FBI, and Immigration and Customs often can provide additional gang intelligence to local authorities or assist in enhanced federal prosecutions. In areas in which gangs have become an extremely serious threat to the community, local, state, and federal agencies may form an antigang task force, pooling their resources for drug buys, gang member surveillance, and other suppression tactics.

Investigators and prosecutors should be aware of the unique difficulties concerning victims and witnesses of gang crime. Often extraordinary measures are necessary to protect witnesses in gang cases before, during, and after trial. Although reluctant victims and witnesses are not uncommon in many felony investigations, fear of threats or retaliation is a particular concern in gang-related cases. In a major survey, nearly 90 percent of prosecutors in large cities and 74 percent in small jurisdictions agreed that obtaining the cooperation of victims and witnesses is one of their most significant problems.[16] Accordingly, a major task of gang investigators is to provide protection to cooperating citizens. Unfortunately, the problem of cooperation is further complicated by the fact that many victims and witnesses are similarly involved in gang-related activities.

The identification and arrest of violent gang members have been enhanced by some targeted legal prosecutions. Even though the dynamics and motivation of youth gangs are unique, violators in many states have usually been charged only with offenses proscribed by existing criminal laws. Some states, however, such as Oklahoma, have developed statutes specifically targeting gangs in an effort to increase penalties and deter gang violence. Other states beef up penalties by applying special statutes aimed at organized crime groups engaged in "ongoing criminal enterprises" and criminal conspiracies. Even in jurisdictions that rely totally on existing laws to prosecute gang members, those laws may be prosecuted to their maximum capacity.

▲ SUMMARY

Gang crime will only be eliminated by a combined effort of justice professionals and the general public. Because the motivation for gang membership is rooted in social and psychological dysfunction, police alone can never eradicate the problem. Criminally oriented youth are increasing in number in the United States and are closely linked to the country's widespread drug and firearm problem. Although criminal investigators must work vigorously to identify and contain gang crime, this form of criminality will only be fully controlled when the root causes of organized youth violence are identified and eliminated.

■ EXERCISES

1. Interview the head of a local law enforcement agency to determine if youth gangs are present in your community. If so, establish the locations and membership characteristics of each gang. Finally, determine if the gangs are drug dealing or primarily territorial in nature.

2. Interview a probation officer or similar correctional official who has worked with gang clients. Find out the official's opinions regarding why some youth are so strongly attracted to gang membership. Compare this person's opinion with a police investigator's opinion as to causation factors.

3. Prepare a research paper detailing gang communication. Describe how and why gang members use hand signs and graffiti to communicate.

4. Explore your community for examples of graffiti. Photograph several sites for classroom presentation. Describe the communication as to whether it is gang related or nongang tagging and so on. Ask local criminal investigators to help interpret the wall paintings.

5. Prepare a classroom report on the history of youth gangs in America. Attempt to explain the social and historical forces that may have contributed to gang growth during a particular decade. Detail how youth street gangs in the 1920s and 1950s differ from gangs of today.

● RELEVANT WEB SITES

http://www.gangsorus.com

Highly informative site operated by a former Customs special agent providing details on over 900 American street and prison-based gangs. Particular areas include gang identifiers and the historical background of each group among numerous other gang links.

http://www.msnbc.msn.com/id/7244879/site/newsweek

Detailed article on the origins and current status of the gang Mara Salvatrucha, a recently emerging violent gang causing considerable concern to law enforcement within the United States.

Special Investigations

KEY TERMS

accelerants

arson

child abuse

domestic abuse

elder abuse

hate crime

high-velocity explosives

incendiary fire

intelligence

La Cosa Nostra

loan-sharking

organized crime

point of ignition

pornography

protection orders

pyromaniac

spouse abuse

stalking

strategic intelligence

tactical intelligence

LEARNING OBJECTIVES

1. to be able to define the major types of domestic abuse;
2. to be able to explain the four types of child abuse that may be brought to the attention of the criminal investigator;
3. to be able to list characteristics that are common to the child abuse offender;
4. to be familiar with the origin, method of operation, and current status of La Cosa Nostra;
5. to be able to discuss how organized crime converts illegal funds into legitimate operations;
6. to be able to discuss the investigative methodology that can be used to combat organized crime;
7. to understand the definition and significance of hate crime;
8. to comprehend the seriousness of the current status of arson regarding financial loss and human injury;
9. to be able to define the five classifications of a fire;
10. to understand the four common motivations behind the incendiary fire; and
11. to be able to discuss the investigative methodology used in arson cases, with reference to the crime scene, victim and witness interview, and suspect inquiry.

INTRODUCTION

Special investigations are cases that are unique and often require special training to fully understand their broad significance. Domestic abuse, organized crime, hate crimes, arson, and explosions are examples of offenses that call for special investigations. Despite their relatively low frequency when compared with "standard" crimes, offenses involving special investigations are increasing, and their impact on society is being felt more strongly.

DOMESTIC ABUSE

Short of the battlefield, the U.S. home is the most common site of violent interpersonal conflict. **Domestic abuse** may take the form of a conflict between married persons, or (frequently) the abuse may be directed toward children. Domestic abuse, or family violence, implies crimes committed against members of the perpetrator's family. Family violence accounts for 8 percent of all reported violent crime in the United States. When family members engage in violent crime against relatives, 90 percent commit either simple or aggravated assault. Victimization surveys indicate that approximately 2.3 million cases of violence occur annually between relatives. Significantly, 60 percent of such cases involve the spouse or ex-spouse of the victim. Of the remainder, 12 percent involve violence between parents and children of 12 years or older, and 30 percent involve violence caused by other relatives.[1] Police arrest nearly 86,000 individuals each year for offenses against adult or child family members. The average arrested suspect is a white male 25 to 29 years of age. Although females arrested for family violence constitute only 16 percent of all family violence arrests, their rate of apprehension has increased dramatically. In the course of the past nine years, female arrests have increased 130 percent.[2]

Criminal investigators have been aware of the end result of domestic violence for many years. The many homicides and aggravated assaults that occur within the family have traditionally come to the attention of the police. Furthermore, the frequent domestic-quarrel call for patrol service has statistically ranked high as a situation resulting in police injury and death. According to recent studies, however, the vast majority of batteries against wives, husbands, and children go unreported.

Spouse Abuse

The term **spouse abuse** refers to a battery committed by one married partner on the other. *Battery* occurs when one individual inflicts bodily harm on another individual. The bodily harm may be inflicted by any means—from touching to throwing an object. Although there have been cases involving battered husbands, in the typical spouse battery the wife is the victim. The Centers for Disease Control and Prevention estimated that at least 1.5 million U.S. women are battered each year by their spouses, whereas nearly 835,000 men are beaten by wives. Additionally, 2,000 to 4,000 women annually are beaten to death by husbands, former husbands, or live-in boyfriends.[3] According to FBI statistics, 15 percent of all murders in the United States are domestic homicides, and the odds are nearly 2.5 times more likely that a husband will kill his wife than that she will kill him. Research also documents that women are more prone than men to kill their offspring and significantly more inclined to kill sons than daughters.[4]

There are many widespread myths concerning wife beating that are misleading as to the background and attitudes of both offender and victim.

Husbands who commit spouse abuse are generally not mentally ill, although numerous studies indicate that they are exceptionally insecure and emotionally stunted individuals, often unable to cope with the traditional masculine role. Although many abusers drink frequently, they typically use alcohol or drugs as a release mechanism. Offenders are from all socioeconomic classes; they are as likely to be lawyers as bricklayers. Battered wives also represent the full spectrum of U.S. society. The notions that most batteries occur as a result of financial arguments and that most involve masochistic victims are false. The battery may be precipitated by a wide variety of incidents, including what appear to be trivialities. Many battered wives do appear to have similar psychological traits and personalities. Abused women tend to be more submissive, trusting, and reserved than the general adult female population. Additionally, they tend to assume the guilt for the battery—often seeing themselves as the causative factor.[5] Continual batteries and verbal abuse often result in a demoralization of the victim and a general loss of self-esteem.

Numerous studies document that domestic abuse typically follows an established pattern. The batterer's primary motivation is to control the life of the victim. Generally beginning with emotional abuse, abusers repeatedly undermine victims' self-confidence with degrading remarks. This stage is often followed by efforts to isolate victims by controlling where they go, what they do, or whom they associate with. Threats then follow, generally directed against the spouse or children. Eventually, the abuse progresses to destroying belongings and then reaches the physical stage. In an effort to assert ultimate control, the suspect initially engages in shaking or pushing, with many cases escalating to episodes of extreme physical assault. In spite of occasional periods of contrition by the suspect, the violence typically gets more severe if nothing is done, especially if only the victim seeks help. When domestic battery between partners escalates, it can ultimately result in criminal homicide. In an attempt to identify which cases of domestic abuse are more likely to end in death, Johns Hopkins University researchers surveyed 30 women who had survived murder attempts by intimate partners. The number one risk factor was found to be a history of prior incidents of domestic violence. Other risk factors included the combination of a gun owned by the perpetrator prior to the attempted homicide and estrangement where the woman had left the relationship. Additional risk factors included forced sex and the in-home presence of a child belonging to the woman from a previous relationship.[6]

The police can play a significant part both in identifying battered spouses and in reducing their number. Continual domestic violence generally comes to the attention of the police agency. Victims, children of the spouses, neighbors, relatives, and others eventually contact the police. The patrol division responds to the call and attempts to resolve the conflict. Officers used to be concerned only with stopping the immediate violence and restoring the peace. Recent training in the field of domestic violence has greatly improved the quality and long-range effectiveness of police crisis intervention, however. The increasing seriousness and growth of family violence has resulted in the development of specialized domestic violence units within many large police agencies.[7]

The criminal investigator generally becomes involved with domestic abuse as the result of a serious battery or aggravated assault. Additionally, reports of **stalking** against domestic partners or acquaintances may initiate a police inquiry. All states and the federal government have enacted laws to combat this form of abuse, as it is a common problem among mere acquaintances, strangers, or husbands and wives who seek out their former mates to terrorize. Most laws are similar to those of Kentucky, which defines stalking as an intentional course of conduct directed at a specific person, serving no legitimate purpose, that seriously alarms, annoys, intimidates, or harasses the targeted individual. Stalking may take various forms, including phone calls, letters, e-mails, or violent personal confrontations.[8] Public awareness of stalking as a dangerous criminal offense can be traced to the 1989 murder of actress Rebecca Schaeffer. Her death by a persistent stalker was highly publicized and precipitated the enactment of many of the original antistalking laws. Recent data from the National Violence Against Women Survey demonstrate that stalking is far more widespread than previously thought. The survey found that 8 percent of women and 2 percent of all men—an estimated 1,100,000 women and 371,000 men—have been stalked at some time in their lives. The average duration of a stalking episode is one year and eight months, but increases to two years and two months if a current or former intimate partner is involved.[9]

Although the legal definition of the crime of stalking is gender neutral, 78 percent of stalking victims are women, while 87 percent of the stalking perpetrators are male. While most stalking cases involve perpetrators and victims who know each other, 23 percent of all female victims and 36 percent of all male victims are stalked by strangers. About half of all stalking victims report their victimization to the police, with only 25 percent of such reported incidents leading to an arrest. Finally, the seriousness of stalking can be realized when one considers that 25 percent of all victims will obtain protection orders and that one in five victims will eventually move to a new location to escape their stalker.

Protection orders are a special type of court mandate issued by a judge that orders someone who has been harming another not to attempt to harm that person again. Most states have two types of protection orders: the domestic abuse protection order and the harassment protection order. If the victim's stalker is a spouse, former spouse, or a person currently (or in the past) living with the victim, a domestic-type protection order may be obtained. Generally, the court requires the victim to show that the stalker was physically violent or threatened physical violence, with the threat placing the victim in great fear. The harassment protection order may be issued against anyone who is harassing, regardless of their relationship or lack of such. The victim must prove to the court that the harassing behaviors had a threatening element causing fright.

While there are many different types of stalker profiles, some common traits exist in all investigations. Perpetrators are desperate for any type of attention from their victims, whether it be positive or negative. All suspects are seeking to control the behavior of their targets in some fashion. This may range from threatening harm against the victim or her family pets, property destruction, or threatening suicide. Overall, 87 percent are male; however, in cases involving female targets, 94 percent of the offenders are male. In cases involving male victims, 60 percent of the stalkers are male. In nearly 80 percent of stalking episodes, there will be a precipitating event. Typically, these involve a relationship ending, illness or death of a family member, or some emotionally upsetting incident. The anger and helplessness resulting from such events are then often projected onto the victim.

Various studies now categorize stalking offenders into three distinct groups: simple obsessive, love obsessional, and erotomanic. Simple obsessive suspects make up approximately 48 percent of offenders and are the most commonly encountered by the investigator. Most are males who were in prior relationships with their targets. Because of their social immaturity, they are unable to let the relationship end. A history of substance abuse is common, and they rarely can maintain a lasting relationship. Simple obsessive stalkers are the most likely to make threats and actually harm victims.

Ninety-seven percent make various threats against former partners, of which 30 percent are actually carried out. Love obsessional stalkers make up 43 percent of offenders and are male 97 percent of the time. They have had no prior relationships with victims and are generally between 30 and 40 years of age. Offenders become obsessed with their targets through media presentations and begin to fixate upon establishing a relationship with the celebrity target. Nearly 25 percent of offenders make threats against their victims, with only 3 percent actually being carried out. The final suspect category, the erotomania stalker, is the rarest of the three types at 10 percent. They develop a strong delusional belief that they are loved by the victim. Offenders are generally females who rarely have met their victims and represent the least dangerous form of stalker.[10]

The investigation of stalking is often a challenge, as offenders can be unpredictable and the potential for violence an ever-present possibility. Initially, a threat assessment must be made that evaluates the suspect's potential for violence. Overall behavior is examined with particular attention placed upon the nature of his or her threats. Other areas of concern include access to weapons, violations of protection orders, substance abuse or mental illness, and prior physical violence. In addition to detailed victim and witness interviews, these risk factors can be revealed through examining presentence reports, protection order applications, and past arrest records. After assessing the facts, investigators can gauge the reliability of the victim's report and determine the stalker category best representing the suspect. These actions will determine if an immediate arrest is justified or the degree of surveillance or warning to be used by authorities.

Abuse of the Elderly

Another growing form of domestic abuse concerns the mistreatment of senior citizens. The elderly are the fastest-growing and, in many ways, the most vulnerable segment of the nation's population. Since 1981, there has been an increase of 100,000 cases of physical abuse of older people reported each year, with actual physical harm occurring in 50 percent of the cases. A thorough study conducted in 2002 by the U.S. Administration on Aging reported that **elder abuse** had reached one million victimizations a year, with only one in five of the abuse incidents actually coming to the attention of a social, medical, or police authority. The American Medical Association estimates that 10 percent of all individuals over 65 suffer some form of elder abuse. Additional research reveals that elderly victims are three times more likely to be abused if they live with someone, and females often suffer greater physical harm than males. Investigators have noted that this form of abuse also continues over a period of years, with mistreatment found among all ethnic and economic groups. Nearly half of all abusers are the children or younger relatives of the victim, with spousal abuse accounting for 40 percent of all cases. Finally, the suspect often is suffering from some form of psychological, emotional, or mental disability or other form of external stress in addition to his or her role as the victim's caregiver. It is not uncommon for the offender to have drug or alcohol problems and be financially dependent on the victim.[11]

Successful investigation of this form of domestic abuse is particularly difficult, as many seniors have disabilities that keep them isolated and hidden from public view. Additionally, they may hesitate to cooperate with the police for fear of losing their primary caretaker. Accordingly, when officers interact with the elderly for any reason, care must be taken to observe signs of abuse. Obvious signs of injury or an appearance demonstrating poor hygiene and physical care may indicate an abusive environment. When interviewing, the investigator should show patience and understand that elderly victims are often fearful not only of their abuser but also of losing control of their independent living through an official inquiry.[12] Many larger police agencies have specially trained elder abuse investigators, and similar prosecutory specialization is becoming more common. The San Diego County Prosecutor's Office developed one of the first highly specialized elder abuse units nearly 15 years ago. Iowa has assigned two state investigators to assist agencies in reviewing cases of elder financial exploitation, and Illinois has opened 100 caregiver resource centers to educate and assist elder caregivers, an effort that should reduce abuse incidents.

Domestic Child Abuse

Nearly three million cases of **child abuse**, neglect, and abandonment are annually recorded by various state child welfare agencies, resulting in one million specific investigations of abuse.[13] In addition, recent Gallup polls indicate that 10 percent of all females and 5 percent of all surveyed males report that they were past victims of some form of child abuse.[14] Prior to 1973, when federal funding became available through the Mondale Act to detect, prosecute, and prevent child abuse, this form of criminality was rarely reported to authorities. Following the creation of new tracking agencies and methods of reporting, the annual rates of abuse began to increase rapidly. Although increased reporting has undoubtedly saved thousands of children from substantial harm, the number of unsubstantiated cases reported has also increased dramatically. In 1975, 35 percent of all child abuse reports were unsubstantiated; by 1996, 66 percent of reports were found by investigation to be unsubstantiated.[15] Nebraska's child abuse figures are typical of most states. In the year 2000, authorities received reports of 8,254 suspected cases of child abuse, of which only 1,932 were substantiated by subsequent investigation. Many individuals see this offense in terms of its physical implications only. Actually, in a legal sense, child abuse is any act or omission that endangers or impairs a child's physical or emotional health and development. Thus, child abuse may take the form of physical assault, emotional assault, neglect, or sexual exploitation (see Figure 16.1). For a detailed discussion of child sexual abuse, see Chapter 12, "Rape and Sexual Offenses." Child abuse is clearly illegal in all states, as defined in the criminal or child welfare codes. Additionally, all states have now enacted

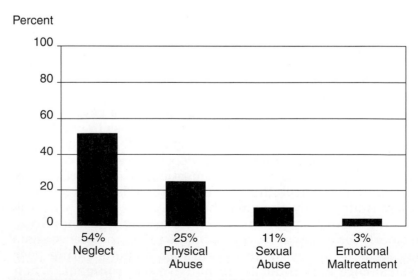

FIGURE 16.1   Types of reported child abuse.

laws requiring certain professionals, such as health practitioners, social workers, teachers, and police officers, to report cases of child abuse. For example, the state of California requires that the following cases be reported:

1. children who have sustained injuries that appear to have been inflicted by other than accidental means,
2. children who have been sexually molested,
3. children who have sustained unjustifiable physical pain or mental suffering,
4. children who have been injured or permitted to be injured by those legally responsible for their care, and
5. children who have been placed or permitted to be placed by those legally responsible for their care in a situation injurious to their health or welfare.[16]

Child abuse is the infliction of physical or mental injury, the degree of the injury notwithstanding. It is essential that the police and other service workers attempt to identify and apprehend child abusers at the earliest opportunity. A parent or caretaker may begin by inflicting minor injuries and go on to cause more serious harm over time. Therefore, detecting child abuse at the outset and intervening with preventive action may subsequently save a child from permanent injury or death. The investigator will generally be able to detect instances of inflicted physical injuries, physical neglect, or malnutrition—such cases are obvious. Damage to the psyche or emotional deprivation is often difficult to perceive, however. Adults who know the child's behavior patterns, such as teachers, are in an excellent position to determine this type of abuse.

Child Abuse Investigations.   The investigation of child abuse may be initiated through the patrol or detective division or by an agency outside the police department. In most states, child abuse investigations are handled jointly by law enforcement officials and local child protective services workers. Most large police departments have special child abuse investigative units. Of all police agencies serving 250,000 or more populations, 83 percent have such units in operation.[17] Typically, an abusive situation becomes known as the result of an injury or a domestic disturbance. A physician notes injuries that the parent cannot explain, or a dentist may note similar unexplained injuries. In many cases, child abuse is noted when patrol officers are dispatched to scenes in which spouses are quarreling. In the course of investigating the family fight, the officer may encounter an abused or neglected child. Some police agencies have separate detective units to handle all cases involving juveniles. In large departments, only investigators in the juvenile division handle cases of child abuse. Regardless of the size of the agency, all police officers must be trained to recognize the victims of child abuse and the offenders.

Physical Assault and Corporal Punishment.   Each year in the United States, at least 1,000 children die from injuries inflicted by their parents. During the past ten years, more than three children died each day as a result of parental maltreatment. Additionally, hundreds of thousands are physically abused by parents or others who are "caring" for them. It is important to note that these figures are reported statistics; they do not reflect the large number of unreported cases. The most common cause of inflicted physical injury results from unreasonably severe corporal punishment of the child (see Figure 16.2). Generally, the injury occurs when an enraged parent strikes or throws a child with undue force. Although many experts are of

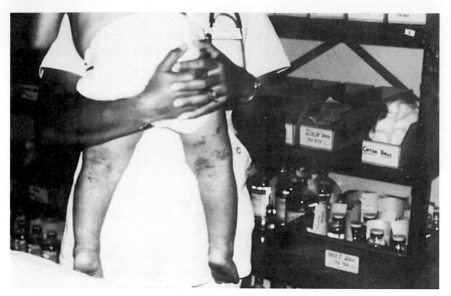

FIGURE 16.2   In this typical example of physical child abuse, the victim was struck repeatedly across the back of the legs with a belt. *(Source: San Diego Police Department.)*

the opinion that corporal punishment in any form is counterproductive as a disciplinary technique, the law has traditionally held that parents have the right to punish their children corporally. However, when the corporal punishment inflicts injury and/or constitutes an emotional assault that endangers or impairs the child's health and development, child abuse is indicated.

Physical child abuse should be suspected and investigated by officers who encounter the following:

1. Children with injuries on several surface areas of the body.
2. Children who show evidence of previous injuries (scarring or abrasions and bruises in varying stages of development).
3. Children with wraparound injuries (generally caused by flexible objects— electrical cords, belts, or straps).
4. Children with bruises of odd size or who show the imprint of the striking object (e.g., belt buckle imprints).
5. Children with injuries under the clothing. Some offenders take care to inflict injuries in nonvisible locations.
6. Children with burn injuries. A typical method of operation for some abusive parents is to burn the child. The burn will often appear on the lower portion of the child's body, for example, the legs or buttocks.
7. Children who are extremely fearful of adults or who refuse to speak in front of parents.
8. Parents who cannot explain a child's injury or who offer explanations that are unlikely.
9. Parents who continually blame injuries on siblings or friends or who claim the child is "accident prone."

Emotional Assault.   The results of emotional assaults obviously are not as apparent as physical injuries. Yet this form of child abuse can be just as incapacitating to the victim. Emotional cruelty can handicap a child behaviorally and intellectually. And if the emotional abuse is severe and prolonged, serious psychological disorders may develop.

The emotional assault can consist of constantly blaming or belittling the child, unpredictable or inconsistent responses to the child's actions, continual negative moods, or constant family discord. Impossible demands on the child or use of the child as a weapon during marital disputes also constitute emotional assaults.

If the officer notes the following, emotional assault should be suspected and investigated:

1. Children who are withdrawn, depressed, or apathetic.
2. Children who are discipline problems in school because of "acting out." They may also exhibit antisocial behavior outside of the school environment.
3. Children who show signs of emotional turmoil. Inordinate attention to details, a lack of verbal or physical communication with others, or a display of pathological rhythmic movements (e.g., head banging) may indicate emotional disturbance.

Emotional Deprivation. Children need the emotional involvement of their parents if they are to develop properly. When parents do not provide their children with love, support, and security, the children will be thwarted in their emotional growth. Further, parents who fail to show any interest in a child's activities or who fail to show any affection, generally, are emotionally depriving their children. Children past infancy will suffer emotionally (which may lead to physical problems as well); infants can die from the emotional deprivation of parents. So-called emotional starvation is one of the most difficult types of abuse to detect. Unfortunately, this type of child abuse has the greatest potential to produce delinquent behavior in adolescents and criminal behavior in adults.

Investigators should suspect emotional deprivation upon noting the following:

1. Children who refuse to eat or who eat very little. They may be very frail in appearance and generally not thriving.
2. Children who engage in aggressive or delinquent behavior.
3. Children who continually seek out adults (teachers, neighbors) for attention and affection.

Physical Neglect. When a parent or caretaker of a child fails to provide adequate food, shelter, clothing, protection, supervision, or health care, physical neglect is indicated. Neglect is the most common type of child abuse, for nearly 55 percent of all reported cases are of this variety.[18] Physical neglect is generally not difficult to determine by law enforcement officers and others. It should be suspected in the following circumstances:

1. When unsanitary conditions exist in the home (garbage, animal or human excretion).
2. When potential health or safety problems are a factor (e.g., lack of heating, fire hazards, insect or rodent infestations).
3. When meals are of poor nutritional quality or are not prepared at all. Food may be spoiled.
4. When the general appearance of the child indicates neglect. Obvious medical and dental problems have not received attention.
5. When the child's clothing indicates neglect. It may be dirty or torn.
6. When certain factors are present, indicating a lack of parental protection and/or supervision. Clothing may be inadequate for weather conditions, or the child may be walking the streets at late hours.

Child Abuser Characteristics. Child abusers are from a wide variety of backgrounds and are of various psychological types. Parents and relatives comprise the majority of those responsible for abuse and neglect. The federal Department of Health and Human Services reports that parents account for 75 percent of those responsible for maltreatment, relatives 10 percent, and nonrelated individuals 6 percent. Frequently, abusing parents were abused themselves or experienced difficult childhoods. Such parents tend to use the same destructive techniques on their own children, perpetuating the syndrome of the "battered child." Abusing parents often reverse roles with their children; they expect and demand the children's love but have considerable difficulty providing a warm, caring environment in which the children can express such emotions. Abusive parents and caretakers are often experiencing marital or emotional conflicts. They may be immature, anxious, unreliable, and untrusting. Abusing appears to be more prevalent in young marriages and among parents who have a poor self-image.

The following characteristics are common in the majority of abusive families:

1. The parents are isolated individuals who feel they cannot trust themselves or others.
2. The children are "different" in some way. The child may be mentally or physically retarded or unusually intelligent.
3. The parents have unrealistic expectations of the child's abilities or accomplishments. Or they may be intolerant of immature behavior, which is normal in young children.
4. The family experiences one or more crises, large or small, setting the stage for the act of child abuse.
5. The parents have explosive tempers; they may be alcoholics or drug abusers.
6. The parents are raising an unwanted, premature, or illegitimate child.
7. The parents or caretakers are not the natural parents.

When a parent is predisposed to abuse a child, for whatever reason, a precipitating factor will generally "spark" the actual abuse. One child abuse authority cited three common precipitating factors:

1. One or both parents have moved away from close friends and family within the past year.
2. There is an acute flare-up of a chronic marital problem, which may cause one of the partners to "walk out" of the relationship.
3. The parents cannot control the child's behavior; for example,
   (a) the child will not stop crying,
   (b) the child will not go to sleep,
   (c) the child will not eat,
   (d) the child resists toilet training, or
   (e) the child shows evidence of illness.[19]

The majority of abusive parents (80 percent or more) do not consciously intend to injure the child. They abuse the child through impulsive angry actions during which they are out of control. Consequently, they feel great guilt after inflicting the injury and will often take the child to an emergency room for medical treatment. It is estimated that nearly 20 percent of the children seen in hospital emergency rooms are treated for the results of child abuse. There is, however, a small but significant percentage of child abusers (10 to 20 percent) who suffer from mental illnesses.[20]

Gathering Evidence. When the investigator gathers evidence to support a charge of child abuse and/or neglect, that evidence must be carefully documented. Photography is a very important tool in documenting physical injuries. Also, home environments that are unhealthy for the child should be exhaustively documented through color photographs. Each room of the residence should be photographed (including the use of close-ups) to convince the court of the environment of neglect forced upon the victim (see Figure 16.3). Typical conditions include the following:

1. **The Kitchen:** Dirty glasses and dishes, insects, filthy standing water in the sink, spoiled food, dirty refrigerator.
2. **The Sleeping Areas:** General dirty and unkempt appearance, unmade beds, dirty bed linens, lack of linens, clothes thrown on the floor.
3. **The Bathroom:** General unsanitary appearance, waste in the toilet, contents of medicine cabinet accessible to children, waste material on the floor, grime in the tub.
4. **General Signs of Neglect:** Exposed wiring, trash accumulations, oven or burners left on, lack of heat, pets abused or neglected, young children left unattended.

Victims of child abuse should be interviewed with care. Such children are often hesitant to name a parent or caretaker as the abuser. The child may be frightened of the parent or ashamed of the abuse. Loyalty to the parent or fear of losing whatever little security they have is also normally very

A

B

C

D

FIGURE 16.3 A photographic survey documenting physical neglect.
A. Close-up of the unsanitary kitchen sink; *B.* Bathroom area;
C. Living room; *D.* Bedroom. *(Source: San Diego Police Department.)*

strong. Parents are usually very defensive during the interview and often persist in denying the abuse, despite evidence to the contrary. The investigator should gather supportive evidence by interviewing those in a position to testify to past abusive actions of the parent. Teachers, relatives, other children in the family, or neighbors can often be helpful in this regard.

Child abuse often motivates the victim to escape the abusive environment. The U.S. Department of Justice reports that nearly 450,000 children run away from their homes each year. This figure does not include the nearly 130,000 "thrownaways," children who are expelled from their homes and refused reentry.[21] National concern regarding missing children led to the passage of the Missing Children Act in 1982. The act authorizes the entry of related identification data in the FBI's National Crime Information Center and allows parents to verify such information. In addition to governmental efforts to prevent and investigate child abuse, the National Center for Missing and Exploited Children serves as a national clearinghouse of information on abused, exploited, and missing children. The center provides considerable assistance to citizens and criminal investigators and routinely distributes photos and descriptions of missing children. A toll-free telephone line is continuously open for those who have information that could lead to the location and recovery of missing children: 1-800-843-5678.

ORGANIZED CRIME

There is considerable confusion in the United States regarding the definition of organized crime, the composition of its membership, and the illegal activities it controls. In a basic sense, **organized crime** pertains to any group of suspects who have formed a highly organized, disciplined association engaged in criminal activities. Such groups may be small, but they typically involve a sizable number of individuals in the planning and execution of illegal acts. A true organized crime group requires a continuous commitment by its members, although there may be some nonmembers participating for short periods of time. A major factor that distinguishes organized crime members from other, more numerous criminals is their elaborate planning and lack of impulsiveness in committing crimes.

Organized crime groups have as their fundamental goal economic gain. Economic gain may be achieved through many means—both legitimate and illegitimate. Organized crime groups generally operate so that illegal activities support legitimate enterprises. Group members use a wide variety of tactics to accomplish the criminal enterprises—violence and intimidation, inspired by corruption and greed, are common working tools.

Another characteristic of an organized crime group is the close-knit nature of its membership, which serves to make the group extremely difficult to penetrate from outside. Loyalty to the group is ensured by tight control; there is swift discipline for those who reveal information concerning the group. These factors contribute to the recidivism and incorrigibility common to organized crime members who have been incarcerated.

Organized Crime Groups

La Cosa Nostra.   The average U.S. citizen immediately connects organized crime with the Mafia or the newer derivative of this group, **La Cosa Nostra** (LCN). There are, in fact, many organized crime groups that vary greatly in size and ethnic composition. Yet the Mafia or, more correctly, the Americanized LCN, continues to be judged the most sizable and powerful organized crime group in this country. The LCN can be historically traced to the Sicilian Mafia, an ancient criminal organization that originated in Palermo, Italy, in 1282 as a radical political organization. The purpose of the original Mafia was to free Italy from foreign domination. One theory is that Mafia is the acronym of the motto, "*Morte alla Francia Italia anela*" (death to the French is Italy's cry).[22] During the early 1800s, the character of the organization shifted from a political group to a violent criminal unit. It is probable that numerous criminal types were drawn into the organization by the violent tactics used during the political phase. Attracted by the power and fear the organization could generate, criminals began to realize the possibilities of using the group for criminal gain. When Italy and Sicily united under an Italian king, the Italian government endeavored to rid Sicily of the Mafia. But the organization had grown so strong that many members would not give up their positions of power. In fact, the Mafia came to exert a political and criminal force that rivaled the island's legitimate government. The Sicilian Mafia, to this day, continues to exercise considerable control on the island of Sicily.

The Mafia's influence spread to the United States during the late 1800s, with the thousands of European immigrants who settled primarily in the major East Coast cities. The newly formed Italian ghettos were immediately victimized; transplanted Mafia members merely continued established criminal operations in the new locality. The growth of the U.S. branch of the Mafia was constant but slow until the enactment of what has been considered the greatest boost to organized crime in the history of the United States. On January 16, 1920, Prohibition was enacted, making the sale and possession of alcoholic substances illegal. The Mafia and many other organized crime groups used the enactment of Prohibition to their advantage by providing alcohol to a more-than-willing public. The profit realized during this era catapulted the Mafia into positions of influence and power that had not been obtainable before.

During the late 1930s and early 1940s, a shift in power began to occur in the organization. Younger members contested for positions of power with older Sicilian members. After considerable infighting and scores of murders, the LCN emerged. The term can be loosely translated to mean "our thing"; it completely replaced the older designation, Mafia, within the organization. Thus, the traditional U.S. branch of the Sicilian Mafia was transformed into a younger organization composed of Italian American criminals. It is estimated by federal investigators that the LCN comprises 24 subgroups, or "families," operating in various geographic areas. The members of each LCN family range from 20 to 700 males who identify with other members as being of the same organization. Approximately 5,000 men are known members of the LCN.[23] Large numbers of criminals who are not members of the organization also support the criminal activities. Such nonmembers may take gambling bets, sell narcotics, drive stolen vehicles, and engage in loansharking and other illegal activities. Accordingly, a totally realistic LCN organizational chart would reveal that organized crime is actually responsible for much of the crime with which it is normally not connected. For example, many high-loss burglaries are motivated by the knowledge that valuable goods can be fenced through a local LCN family member (see Figure 16.4).

Illegal Operations. The LCN's moneymaking operations are basically twofold: illegal methods and legal operations, the latter supported by the profit from the former. It is impossible to estimate accurately the LCN's gross income from both illegal and legal activities. However, experts speculate that profits from illegal activities alone are nearly $50 billion annually. The single largest revenue source of an illegal nature is gambling. An estimated $38 billion a year is generated through illegal bets on horse races, dog races, lotteries, sporting events, and other activities. In the judgment of most

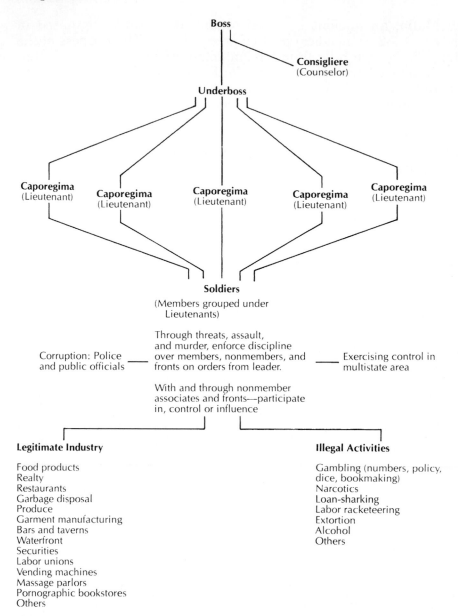

FIGURE 16.4   The organizational structure of a Cosa Nostra family.
(Source: President's Task Force on Organized Crime.)

law enforcement officials, *usury*, or **loan-sharking**, is the second-largest source of revenue for the LCN. This is the lending of money at higher interest rates than the legally prescribed limit. Loan-sharking has provided many organized crime groups with an ideal medium for the investment of funds initially obtained through gambling operations. Interest rates vary greatly, depending on the lender and borrower, and can range from 12 to 200 percent.

The LCN has been involved in the criminal sale of narcotics and dangerous drugs for at least 40 years. The structure of this operation is the opposite of the gambling structure: In narcotics, the product originates at the highest level, with profits moving down the chain of command (Figure 16.5). The LCN has developed extensive international connections, concerned mainly with the production and sale of large quantities of opiates and cocaine. Many experts, however, believe that Asian organized crime groups have begun to replace the LCN as principal suppliers of heroin and will dominate American heroin importation.

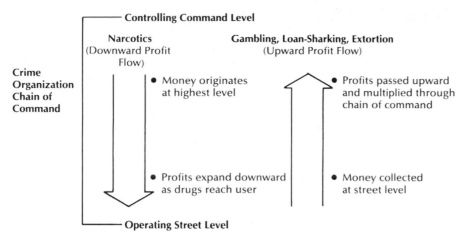

FIGURE 16.5 Organized crime profit flow.

Prostitution, alcohol and cigarette bootlegging, and counterfeiting appear to be playing smaller and smaller roles in the operations of the LCN. Members of the LCN have been wary of investing too heavily in prostitution since the conviction of important members during the 1940s and 1950s in connection with this offense. The illegal production and distribution of alcoholic beverages has been declining since the 1950s and never was considered a major activity after the repeal of Prohibition.

Legitimate Operations.   During the past three decades, the LCN has increasingly realized profits by infiltrating legitimate business enterprises. The method of operation is normally quite consistent. Businesses that are easy to exploit are selected, particularly those that require a low capital investment and limited investigations for license requirements. Certain types of bars, restaurants, massage parlors, parking lots, and pornographic bookstores are often selected by organized crime for investment purposes.

The LCN typically uses one of three methods to infiltrate a legitimate business enterprise other than legal investment. The group may systematically invest concealed profits from illegal activities into a legitimate firm. Continual investment gradually gives the organized crime group a controlling interest in the business. Or an organized crime family will accept usury payments in the form of controlling interests in a business. This occasionally happens when businessmen become indebted to loan sharks through gambling losses. Finally, the crime group may revert to traditional violent methods to gain control of a business. Extortion, outright physical violence, or intimidation are used to gain control of a firm or to force a business to use LCN products or services.

Businesses acquired through legal or illegal means are disposed of for quick profit in many cases. A common method of disposal is through bankruptcy fraud. One version of this technique is to conceal the transfer of ownership from the firm's creditors and operate on the credit rating of the original owner(s). The crime group then orders quantities of merchandise that are quickly sold at a loss and subsequently declares bankruptcy. Another method is known in street terms as the "bust out." After acquiring a business, the organized crime group invests some of its own funds in bank deposits to establish a favorable credit rating. Then, over a period of many months, merchandise is ordered from suppliers in ever-increasing quantities. Generally, just prior to a major holiday, huge merchandise orders are placed on credit. The goods are sold for cash, sometimes for less than the wholesale price. Before the suppliers can collect for their large shipments, the business is declared bankrupt.

Control of labor and the infiltration of various labor unions by the LCN have become growing problems to the criminal investigator. When a business is owned by the LCN, the affiliation of the employees with an LCN-controlled labor union is likely to be mandatory. An organized crime member may obtain a charter from a legitimate union and organize a number of local chapters. The locals are then used as instruments to extort local businesses, or false labor contracts are sold to dishonest businessmen who are eager to keep employee wages as low as possible. Additionally, organized crime frequently embezzles or subverts sizable funds from union treasuries. It appears that the LCN will continue to invest in legitimate business with increasing frequency. The Internal Revenue Service estimates that at least 85 percent of high-level LCN members are currently engaged in legitimate business activities covering a broad spectrum of operations.

Miscellaneous Organized Crime Groups. Although the LCN in particular is linked to organized crime in the minds of the U.S. public, there are many other ethnic crime organizations currently operating in the United States. Groups other than the LCN have not received the extensive media coverage given the LCN since the Kefauver hearings of the early 1950s. However, from a historical standpoint, Italian Americans were not the first but one of the last groups to engage in the "ethnic succession" of organized crime.[24] Irish American crime groups were the first truly organized criminals, succeeded by Jewish organized crime groups in the early 1900s. As these ethnic groups gradually transferred their illegal profits into legitimate enterprises, their illegal activities diminished. The Italian American syndicates then dominated illegal organized activities and were stereotyped by the media as the only organized crime group in the country.

Federal law enforcement analysts report the emergence of African American, Hispanic, Russian, and Chinese organized crime groups as the possible major groups of the future. In certain geographic areas of the United States, these groups are already rivaling the LCN for control of illegal operations. For example, New York City, in addition to having five LCN family operations, currently has many sizable African American, Jamaican, and Puerto Rican groups engaged in gambling and narcotics activities. Rapidly expanding Russian organized crime groups in New York City are of particular concern. New York's FBI office recently formed a special Russian Organized Crime Squad to combat this new threat, which emerged in the United States following the collapse of the Soviet Union. Southern Florida (traditionally an "open" LCN state) has several Cuban organized crime groups that are instrumental in narcotics and vice crime, and certain vice activities in southern California are being conducted by various Mexican American and Central American organized crime units. In the past decade, several other emerging organized crime groups have begun to exert considerable influence. More than 43 Colombian organized crime families dominate the U.S. and international cocaine trade. Their impact on southern Florida's crime rate has been particularly severe. This region's recorded crime increased by 132 percent, with nearly 25 percent of all homicides during a single year resulting from the use of machine guns.[25] Various Asian gangs are also increasing their involvement in organized crime. In a manner similar to early Mafia operations, Vietnamese and Chinese criminals are preying on their own ethnic communities. The Asian gangs are most active in large East and West Coast cities.

Other nontraditional organized criminal groups include prison-based crime families and various outlaw motorcycle gangs. Groups operating primarily within the California prison system, such as the La Nuestra

Familia, Mexican Mafia, Aryan Brotherhood, and Black Guerilla Family, are heavily involved with drug dealing and violence. Although founded within the correctional system, such gangs are branching out their criminal activities from prison to the community. Authorities report that some 800 outlaw motorcycle gangs have developed around the country and in foreign countries. Top officials of the Bureau of Alcohol, Tobacco, Firearms, and Explosives cite outlaw motorcycle gangs as the largest and best-armed criminal organizations in the United States. Four large motorcycle gangs—the Hell's Angels, Outlaws, Pagans, and Bandidos—are identified as the principal U.S. organizations. Outlaw motorcycle gangs began forming shortly after World War II, when a small number of former military personnel established groups based on antisocial attitudes and a mutual interest in motorcycles. The Hell's Angels organization is recognized as the largest, currently fielding 63 chapters in 13 countries.[26] Such groups have accumulated substantial wealth through a wide range of organized criminal activities, but their primary source of revenue is drug trafficking, particularly in methamphetamine production and sale.

In the mid-1990s, various criminal groups with extreme political views emerged, sharing many of the characteristics of true organized offenders. Violent militia groups and racist skinhead factions are typical of this second category of organized offenders, but they are not truly organized crime groups, as their motives are political and social upheaval rather than purely financial gain. In many other respects, however, such groups share most of the necessary qualifications, such as continuous commitment, elaborate crime planning, and extreme group loyalty.

Investigative Methods

The organized crime investigation often taxes the abilities of the criminal investigator to the limit. The difficulties of this inquiry result from the complex methods of operation utilized by organized criminals and from the secrecy that surrounds their activities. Organized crime is often the result of intricate conspiracies carried on over many years. The operations of the group are conducted under extreme secrecy, with swift and violent reprisal to members who violate the code of silence. These factors make for an uncommonly difficult investigation in which months and even years of skillful effort may be needed for a single conviction.

The investigative method employed in organized crime cases may take various directions. However, the key to the successful prosecution of this type of crime is the combined cooperation and sharing of information. Since organized crime is normally multicounty and interstate in nature, federal, state, county, and municipal agencies must interact, sharing information and combining investigative effort. Investigators have traditionally relied upon the criminal informant to provide leads in organized crime cases. However, effective organized crime informants tend to be actual group members, and their fear of violent reprisals from the groups to which they belong is justified. Thus, although such informants may provide much valuable information, they tend to be extremely recalcitrant witnesses during a criminal trial. For this reason, legislation providing effective contempt sanctions against witnesses who refuse to testify before criminal courts, grand juries, or investigating commissions should be enacted in each state. Such legal statutes already exist in many states, but enforcement is often lax or noneffective because of the comparatively light punishment for violations.

When organized crime members do agree to testify, it is imperative that protection suited to this type of investigation be provided. In many organized crime cases, witnesses have been geographically relocated by the U.S.

Marshal's Office and provided with completely new identities. However, until organized crime informants are ensured that such methods do, indeed, afford them complete protection, their testimony will continue to be relatively rare in the courtroom.

The federal government has intensified its efforts to contain organized crime. Many new organized crime strike forces have been formed combining the investigative expertise of federal law enforcement agencies with state and local investigators. Finally, the FBI has committed nearly a quarter of its workforce to specific organized crime investigations.[27]

While the LCN remains America's largest organized crime group, its power and influence is significantly diminishing. Beginning in the mid-1990s, the coordinated efforts of several federal agencies, directed by the FBI, achieved numerous arrests and convictions of upper-level LCN members. By 2002, the director of the FBI estimated the LCN had lost at least 40 percent of its power and influence across the nation. A number of factors have diminished the strength of this organized crime group, including improved surveillance technology and frequent use of the federal RICO (Racketeer Influenced and Corrupt Organizations) statute for enhanced prosecutions. Previously, LCN members strictly adhered to "omerta," the code of silence prohibiting informing to the police. However, many arrested mob members now routinely testify against their LCN families and are placed in the federal Witness Protection Program, which presently contains approximately 5,000 people. Although the LCN will remain a serious crime threat, police authorities believe it will continue to decline as newer organized crime groups emerge and gain nationwide power.

Gambling.   Because gambling is the largest source of revenue for some types of organized crime, there must be continuous and effective investigative effort waged against it. The enactment of legalized lotteries and offtrack betting has not significantly reduced illegal gambling. Legalized gambling lacks one essential element that is always available to the illegal gambler: credit. Gambling cases are often initially developed at the municipal level; however, an arrest at this level alone will seldom eliminate the problem. Most gambling operations are dependent on or controlled by organized crime interests, which provide the funding and sanctions for local operators.

Cooperation among various police agencies may result in tracing and identifying the "chain of operation" from the local bet taker to the organized crime connection. Frequently, the materials used in gambling operations are transported over many different state lines, enabling federal officers to enter the investigation. Since gambling operations are dependent upon communications for payoff information, court-authorized electronic surveillance is invaluable in this type of investigation.

Narcotics and Dangerous Drugs.   Organized crime's involvement in the area of illegal drugs is concentrated mainly on heroin and cocaine. Because of the international aspects of this problem, agency cooperation must extend to foreign police departments to stop the operation at its source. The task force approach has also been found to be highly successful in identifying and apprehending high-level drug distributors. Although the Drug Enforcement Administration and the FBI are the lead federal agencies empowered to investigate narcotics, they depend on considerable intelligence information developed by other agencies for continued success.

As with gambling, the investigator attempts to trace the local drug dealer through many levels to the organized crime source of distribution. Although drug cases are often initially developed by local police agencies, state and federal investigators should be contacted in the early stages of the inquiry. Early contact is generally essential since many local agencies have neither sufficient funds nor experience to trace the drug source.

Electronic surveillance has been used effectively in many narcotics investigations. Yet the undercover operation has traditionally been the key to successful drug inquiries. Identifying the organized crime distributor is difficult, however. The undercover officer will meet greater resistance in penetrating this type of group than others.

Prostitution and Pornography-Related Areas.　Organized crime groups are still involved in the business of prostitution, although their involvement has declined through the years. The focus of operations is generally on call girls (prostitutes who are typically contacted by customers over the telephone) and, to a lesser degree, the brothel (the dwelling from which one or more prostitutes operate). Organized crime is generally not involved in the more visible street-walking type of prostitution. Investigations of businesses that are fronts for prostitution operations are difficult since the organized crime figure is typically insulated and protected by others named on ownership documents. Consequently, the investigator must be familiar with how to research licenses and other official documents. Much investigative time and effort will be spent at the local courthouse. Many experts have concluded that the recent growth of such legal businesses as massage parlors, certain types of therapy centers, and dating services has sparked renewed interest in prostitution profits by organized crime.

Since the late 1960s, there have been few clear legal guidelines for investigators to follow in adult **pornography** cases. The 1967 *Redrup v. New York* Supreme Court decision cast much doubt not only on what constitutes pornography but what is legal or illegal material for legitimate business distribution. Organized crime is known to have invested in all areas of the pornography industry: literature and films, sexual devices, and the production, wholesaling, retailing, and distribution of such products. For example, federal investigators estimate that one LCN family in the New York City area has obtained over 60 percent control of the pornographic film and video industry in its geographic area. The centers of control for organized crime's pornography activities currently are Los Angeles and New York City.

Since there is still no judicial clarification of what constitutes an illegal pornographic product, investigators should concentrate their efforts on licensing and business code violations. If it is ascertained that an organized crime figure is behind a pornography operation, every effort must be made to uncover the true ownership of the business, thus exposing licensing violations resulting from concealment of the owner's identity.

Intelligence Gathering.　Intelligence gathering aimed at organized crime groups must take place during many types of seemingly unrelated investigations. **Intelligence** is the synthesis of data, systematically gathered and evaluated, concerning individuals or activities suspected of being connected to organized crime. The information obtained from fellow officers, citizens, criminal informants, electronic surveillance, and other means constitutes the raw data from which intelligence is produced.

Two types of intelligence are used to meet the needs of organized crime investigators: tactical and strategic. **Tactical intelligence** is used to meet short-term needs; **strategic intelligence** indicates patterns of activity useful in planning and decision making for future operations. For example, strategic intelligence provided by federal agencies may provide local investigators with the means to understand the structure and movement of organized crime elements within their jurisdictions. An organization composed of numerous police agencies, the Law Enforcement Intelligence Unit (LEIU), evaluates and disseminates such information to member agencies throughout the United States. This type of information, if properly compiled and understood, enables the police to predict organized crime activity so that it may be prevented. Every agency concerned with organized crime operations must systematically gather and disseminate intelligence to other agencies, using either the task force or the LEIU approach.

HATE CRIMES

A **hate crime,** also known as a *bias crime,* is a criminal offense committed against a person, property, or society that is motivated, in whole or in part, by the offender's bias against a race, religion, disability, sexual orientation, or ethnicity/national origin. In response to a growing concern about hate crimes, Congress enacted the Hate Crime Statistics Act of 1990 on April 23, 1990. The U.S. Attorney General designated the FBI's Uniform Crime Reporting Program to include data related to offenses in which victim selection was motivated by hate toward one's race, religion, sexual orientation, or ethnicity. In September 1994, the Violent Crime Control and Law Enforcement Act amended the Hate Crime Statistics Act to add disabilities, both physical and mental, as factors that could be considered a basis for hate crime prosecution. Following the federal example, most states have also enacted hate crime laws.

Hate crimes are not separate, distinct crimes but traditional offenses motivated by the perpetrator's bias. Accordingly, crimes such as criminal homicide, rape, assault, robbery, vandalism, and others can be classified as hate crimes only if an investigation demonstrates a motive linked to the above hate-related factors. In a recent year, there were nearly 7,490 hate crime incidents reported to the FBI involving 9,100 victims. Of the total reported incidents, the majority were motivated by racial bias, followed by religious hatred, sexual orientation bias, ethnicity/national origin prejudice, and disability bias (see Figure 16.6).

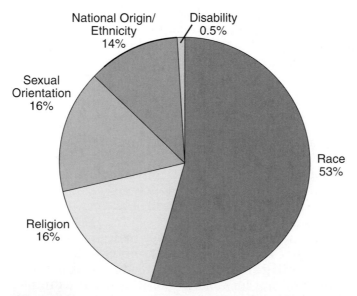

FIGURE 16.6 Hate crimes by the motivation of the perpetrator. *(Source: Federal Bureau of Investigation,* Uniform Crime Report.*)*

Crimes that are based upon an underlying bias and hate can be committed by lone offenders who are not affiliated with specific hate groups or by one or more suspects who belong to a hate group. Hate groups are organizations that seek members with similar views, have an organizational structure, and often either advocate or participate in discrimination or violence against victims who are the object of their prejudice. The Southern Poverty Law Center, a highly respected civilian research group that identifies, tracks, and compiles intelligence information on hate groups, reports 751 active hate groups currently operating throughout the United States (see Figure 16.7). Hate groups can be classified into six general categories; Klan, neo-Nazi, Skinhead, Christian Identity, black separatist, and Neo-Confederate. Klan groups follow the traditional ideology of the Ku Klux Klan, which emphasizes white separatism and superiority and anti-Catholic and anti-Jewish hatred (anti-Semitism). Neo-Nazi groups strongly identify with Adolf Hitler and the Nazi racist and anti-Semitic beliefs, while Skinheads hold similar beliefs but limit their membership to teens and young adults. Christian Identity members identify whites as the Bible's chosen people and Jews as Satanic. Black separatist organizations have strong bias against whites, advocate separation of the races, and are often anti-Semitic as well. Neo-confederate groups seek to revive the racist principles of the antebellum South. Members from each of the groups have been involved in various recently reported hate crimes.

Unaffiliated groups or lone suspects are also responsible for a considerable number of hate-motivated criminal acts. While any of the defined victim groups can be the victim of such attacks, homosexual victimizations are particularly frequent. Male or female homosexuals may be sought out for violent assault (commonly referred to as "gay bashing") solely because of the sexual preference of the victim.

The number of hate groups operating in this country has risen significantly in the past ten years. Many groups are increasingly turning to the Internet and racist rock music to increase their influence in mainstream society. In the past ten years, the number of hate group Web sites has virtually exploded in quantity. Beginning in 1995 with the first hate Web site (a neo-Nazi group), similar Web sites now number close to 500. Almost half of the Internet sites represent actual organized associations that can be contacted or joined or from whom racist materials can be ordered. Others are generally operated by lone racist or anti-Semitic individuals.

Hate crimes are actually enhanced prosecutions in which sentencing punishments are more severe if the suspect's motive is proven to be based upon hatred of one or more of the legally defined protected classes. While a suspect may still be charged with aggravated assault, the punishment can be increased if the assault originated due to hate. The term *hate crime* can be used to describe suspect motive or, within jurisdictions that have enacted hate crime legislation, can pertain to additional charges that can, if proven, lead to enhanced punishment.

The largest portion of hate crimes were actual physical attacks against another person, accounting for 60 percent of all reported hate offenses. The remaining crimes were mainly offenses against property. The most common person-to-person hate crime was intimidation, followed by simple assault and aggravated assault. Fourteen people were victims of hate crime murder. The most common hate-motivated property offense was vandalism or property destruction, followed by burglary and theft. Of the crimes motivated by race hatred, most were anti-black, followed by significantly less offenses against whites and Asians. Religious-oriented crimes were mainly against Jewish Americans, followed by attacks against Islamic citizens. The vast majority of sexual orientation hate crimes were perpetrated against male

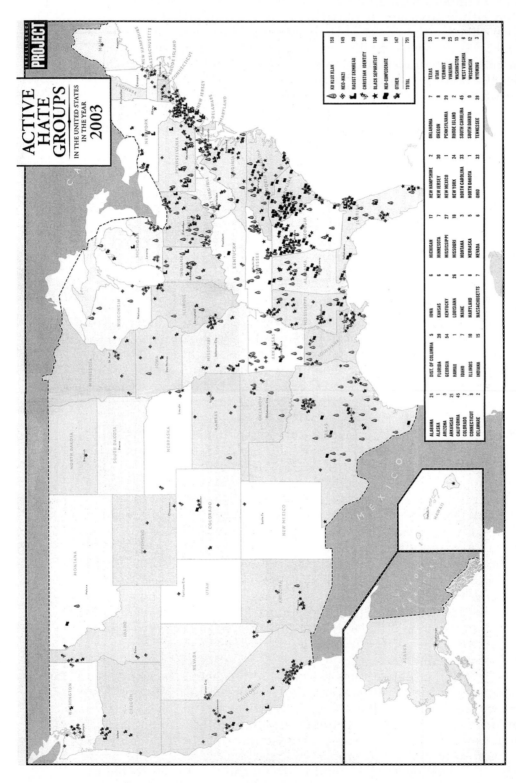

FIGURE 16.7 Location of active hate groups in the United States. (*Source: Intelligence Project of the Southern Poverty Law Center.*)

homosexuals, with most national-origin attacks against Hispanics. Disability bias crimes were directed mainly against the physically impaired, with a far smaller number of incidents involving those with mental disabilities.

The focus of hate crime investigations is documentation of motive. Since the motive of the suspect is essential to demonstrate that his or her actions were motivated by hate of a protected class of victim, the burden of proving this element of the crime lies with the state. Hate crime detectives are specialists in screening crimes to determine if they should be classified as hate offenses. They typically have advanced interviewing skills and understand the psychological makeup of suspects who victimize individuals based upon race, religion, sexual orientation, and other protected factors. Finally, hate crime investigators often have the responsibility of educating fellow officers about this emerging area of law and serve as agency representatives in promoting community awareness. Many police departments have formed special units whose sole responsibility is the determination and investigation of hate/bias crime. The New York City Police Department's Bias Incident Investigation Unit has 22 detectives, while the Los Angeles Police Department has 19 sworn officers assigned to its Hate Crime Investigation Unit.

When an alleged hate crime is reported, the investigator must screen all known information to determine if the case should be classified as a hate offense. The following questions can be posed to help identify hate/bias crimes and initiate a formal investigation:

1. Was the victim a member of a targeted class?
2. Does it appear that the victim and the suspect belong to different groups?
3. Would the criminal act have taken place if the victim and the suspect were of the same group?
4. Is there evidence that the suspect used biased oral comments, gestures, or written statements?
5. Did the suspect leave bias-related objects or symbols at the crime scene?

If it is established that a hate crime has occurred, the investigation will focus upon locating and arresting the offender. Once the perpetrator has been located or if he or she was apprehended at the scene, officers will concentrate upon interviewing, linking present *modus operandi* to past cases, and investigating the offender's background investigation. Hate criminals can be classified into five types: thrill seeking, organized, missionary, reactive, and identity conflicted. A proper classification is significant to a successful interview and illuminates offender motivation. Thrill seekers are usually young and offend in groups. They commit hate crimes for psychological or social excitement. They rarely know their victims and often engage in verbal or physical assault in addition to hate graffiti. Organized suspects may act alone or in groups and are motivated by the need to express deep resentment against minority group victims. To enable their criminal acts, they look for a role model or leader to organize and encourage their offenses. Missionary offenders identify with or believe a higher power has authorized their hate crimes. They seek to remove targeted groups by extreme means. Such offenders are pathological in their hate and are capable of committing very violent crimes, including criminal homicide. Reactive hate crime occurs when offenders believe they are protecting and defending what is theirs from protected-status individuals. These crimes are generally linked to economic, psychological, or territorial threat, such as an attack upon a racially minority immigrant who the suspect believes is willing to work for less than him- or herself. Finally, some hate crimes may be identity conflicted. Some suspects have intense self-hatred to the extent that they will harm others with whom they share common traits.[28]

ARSON

When property is burned for some improper and illegal motive in a willful and malicious manner, **arson** has been committed. This offense has become alarmingly serious in terms of financial loss and human injury. The estimated annual loss from arson is $2 billion, or nearly $12,000 per reported incident—a loss figure second only to that from motor vehicle theft. In addition to the staggering property loss, it is estimated that more than 1,000 deaths and 10,000 injuries annually can be attributed directly to arson.[29]

One would assume that such a serious offense would have gained official and public attention long before now. It continued to receive but scant notice for at least two reasons. First, arson was not listed in the FBI's *Uniform Crime Report* until 1979 following a congressional mandate. Second, the historic attitude of the police has been that arson is a "fire problem"; hence, the responsibility for prevention and investigation lies with the fire department. Fortunately, most police officials now realize that the only way to combat the growing incidence of arson successfully is to recognize it for what it is: a felony.

Nearly 71,300 arsons were reported during a recent year, part of a tenfold increase since the 1950s. The national clearance rate was 17 percent. Fifty-one percent of the arrests involved suspects under 18 years of age—the highest percentage of juvenile involvement for any major crime. Males comprise 85 percent of all arsonists, and nearly 77 percent of all arrested suspects are white.[30] The majority of burned property is structural, and vehicles, crops, timber, and other targets account for 46 percent of all reported losses (Figure 16.8).

Arson Types

Fire departments and police agencies generally classify the cause of a fire into one of five broad categories:

1. natural,
2. accidental,
3. suspicious,
4. incendiary, or
5. of unknown cause.

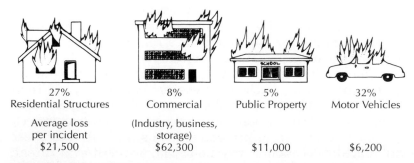

27% Residential Structures	8% Commercial	5% Public Property	32% Motor Vehicles
Average loss per incident $21,500	(Industry, business, storage) $62,300	$11,000	$6,200

FIGURE 16.8 Major arson targets. (*Source: Federal Bureau of Investigation, Uniform Crime Report.*)

The *natural fire* results from the workings of the forces of nature. For example, if a structure is struck by lightning during an electrical storm, the fire is of a natural causation. *Accidental fires* typically are caused by faulty equipment within the structure, such as electrical wiring. Other accidental fires are caused unintentionally by human beings. Smoking in bed or carelessly storing oily rags in poorly ventilated places may result in fires in this category. Fires may be classified as being of *unknown cause* if the investigation is improper or if the scene is so thoroughly burned that a definite conclusion about cause cannot be reached. *Suspicious fires* (suspected of being intentionally set) or obvious **incendiary fires** are classified as arson.

Incendiary Fires.   The incendiary fire is intentionally set, the method of operation varying according to the motivation and skill of the arsonist. The means of ignition (the manner in which the fire is started) may be simple, such as setting a match to dry vegetation, or it may be very complex. Basically, the means of ignition will be of two general types:

1. **Handheld Flame:** A match, cigarette lighter, candle, flare, or some other handheld heat source applied directly to a combustible material.
2. **Delayed Devices:** Fuses, electrical devices or wiring, timers, chemicals, or other materials that will not cause ignition immediately but some time after they are set up. The time of delay may range from seconds to hours after the device has been set to ignite.

The motivations for setting a fire run the entire gamut of criminal reasoning. They include but are not limited to *financial profit, revenge, vandalism*, and *crime concealment*.

Financial Profit.   Arson for financial profit nearly always involves an insurance fraud. When an owner of a particular structure determines that a greater profit can be achieved through insurance payments than from legitimate sales, arson may result. This reasoning may apply to both residential and business structures. The standard insurance fraud by arson involves a business executive who has acquired a property that is not making an acceptable profit. The business may be a retail store with considerable stock or a vacant apartment building in an economically depressed area of a city. Regardless of the type of business, one factor is always consistent: The insurance is worth more than the actual operation would warrant.

In certain depressed areas of cities, such as the South Bronx in New York, the buying of vacant buildings for eventual arson has become commonplace. The building is acquired for a very low price and insured for several times its worth. The structure is burned (generally by a professional arsonist hired by the owner), resulting in a considerable profit for the holder of the insurance policy. One property owner apparently specialized in such practices: within a two-year period, he received nearly $500,000 in insurance payments for 54 different structure fires.[31]

Revenge.   The revenge motive is common to all types of crime. Typically, it involves an offender whose hatred, spite, or jealousy is directed toward a specific second party or parties. To achieve the revenge, the offender burns the property of a targeted victim(s). Many revenge fires involve a vehicle in addition to a dwelling. Revenge is considered by most arson authorities to be the primary motivation of adult arsonists.

Vandalism.   The arson attributed to vandalism generally occurs for "the thrill" of setting the fire or simply as a general protest against the establishment. A very high percentage of school fires and fires in noninsured autos and structures are set for these reasons. Vandalism is primarily the work of juvenile offenders.

Crime Concealment.   The investigator may occasionally encounter the arson that has been committed to conceal a crime. The fire is set to obliterate the evidence of another criminal act, such as burglary or murder. The arsonist hopes that the fire will destroy all incriminating evidence of his or her identity or evidence that the initial crime was even committed. The white-collar criminal may set a fire to destroy evidence of embezzlement or some other type of fund diversion. In such cases, records and documents of the illegal transactions are the target of the offender.

Although the preceding four motives are the most frequently encountered in arson investigations, there are other reasons for incendiary fires. Arson may be used as a means of intimidation (a common tactic of organized crime), or it may be the work of a mentally ill individual. The **pyromaniac** is someone who derives gratification (often of a sexual nature) from the viewing of a fire. Other mentally ill offenders may start fires for reasons unique to their illness. For example, schizophrenics may burn buildings because "voices" instruct them to do so; psychotic individuals may commit arson in the belief that those inside the targeted structure are plotting against them. Regardless of the pyromaniac's specific mental illness, he or she generally exhibits considerable repressed rage and hatred toward society and authority figures.[32]

Arson Investigation

The arson investigation is often difficult for all but the most highly trained criminal investigator. This felony is a stealth-related crime that, by its nature, leaves very little direct evidence as to the identity of the arsonist.[33] The utter destruction and disorder unique to a burned-out structure make that crime scene one of the hardest to process. For this reason, in many jurisdictions, the fire department investigates the arson scene, and police investigators assume responsibility for the case after the arson has been detected. The reasoning behind this approach is that fire investigators are more accustomed to dealing with the physical aspects of a burned structure, whereas police investigators are more efficient in questioning witnesses, tracing suspects, making arrests, and the like. However, given the extent of insurance premium increases, job loss, and injury potential, the offense is generally considered a police problem. Some communities utilize a police/fire task force approach. With this method, police, sheriff's, and fire department personnel in a multijurisdictional region jointly investigate suspected arsons. Because 85 percent of the 28,700 fire departments in the United States are staffed by volunteers, such a technique ensures investigative thoroughness.[34]

Crime Scene.   The initial focus of the arson crime scene investigation is to determine the **point of ignition** of the fire and then, by careful examination, to determine the method of operation. Typically, the point of ignition can be determined visually. Parts of the structure that are charred to a deeper color than the surrounding areas generally indicate the area in which the fire originated. Such areas are further examined for a unique pattern of charring known as "alligatoring," which refers to a pattern of crevices resembling the skin of a reptile. When the segments of alligatoring become smaller and a deep charring is noted, the point of ignition is strongly indicated.

The arson investigator must thoroughly process all areas of the scene for evidence to confirm or deny an assumption of arson. This task is often frustrated in that the very evidence needed to determine a finding of arson may be destroyed by the fire. In addition, the firefighting operations and postfire procedures of the fire department may also destroy evidence. When the firefighters respond to an active fire, their first concern is to save lives and put out the fire. In so doing, walls and other structural elements of the building may be torn down or otherwise altered. The postfire operations include removing objects that might ignite at a later date and opening up the structure for ventilation. Such procedures are necessary to combat the fire and prevent rekindling, but they may also destroy evidence of arson.

After the fire has been extinguished, the true arson crime scene search begins. Yet even when the fire is still active, valuable clues of arson may be gained by noting the color of the flame and the color of the smoke. Some fire departments routinely photograph suspicious fires with motion picture cameras using color film since a detailed study of the flame and smoke pattern can indicate the type of combustible material used to set the fire.

The investigator will carefully examine the entire fire scene for the presence or absence of burn indicators, ignition materials, and fire accelerants. *Burn indicators* are the effects of heating or partial burning on specific materials, used to determine the point of ignition and direction of heat flow. *Ignition materials* start the fire, whereas fire **accelerants** are flammable materials used by arsonists to accelerate the burning or to increase the amount of destruction. If more than one point of origin is found or ignition materials or fire accelerants are present, then arson is strongly indicated.

As previously mentioned, the actual ignition procedure may be simple in some cases and complex in others. Fires set for revenge and those that are set by vandals generally involve the more obvious ignition methods. One of the most common methods of operation is to pour gasoline against the side of the structure and ignite it with a match. Yet, in cases motivated by financial profit, great care may be taken to conceal the method of ignition and the presence of fire accelerants.

The professional arsonist, commonly known as a *torch*, generally selects a delayed ignition process (see Figure 16.9). This is done to establish an alibi for whereabouts at the time of the actual ignition and to eliminate the personal danger of being inside the structure when the fire starts. Delayed ignition can be accomplished by improvising a fuse consisting of a smoldering cigarette and a book of matches. Or a burning candle may be placed on top of highly flammable materials. When the candle burns to its base, the flammable materials are ignited. More complex delayed ignitions often involve chemicals, that, when mixed together, burst into flame after a specified time period.

After the ignition has been achieved, accelerants may be used to spread and intensify the fire. Skilled arsonists rarely use crumpled newspapers and strongly prefer accelerants. As ignition temperatures are typically in the 500° to 700° Fahrenheit range, only chemicals can burn hot enough to ignite yet still be easy to set. Common accelerants include gasoline, kerosene, charcoal lighter fluid, paint thinner, and lacquer solvents. Gasoline is the most frequently encountered fire accelerant at the arson crime scene. Accelerants are often poured over flammable materials on the floor of the structure, but they may be found also on walls and ceilings. Traces of accelerants can frequently be found inside the burned structure. Since liquids are commonly used, they will flow to the lowest level, seeping into porous or cracked floors. Accordingly, the floors should be carefully inspected, as should the earth beneath the flooring materials.

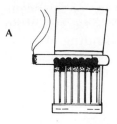

A smouldering cigarette placed within a book of matches. Delayed ignition occurs when the cigarette burns to the match heads. The device is typically placed on clothing or other material that has been soaked with accelerant.

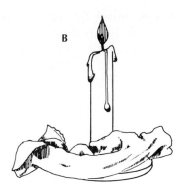

Candle burns until the flame reaches the paper or cloth placed near base.

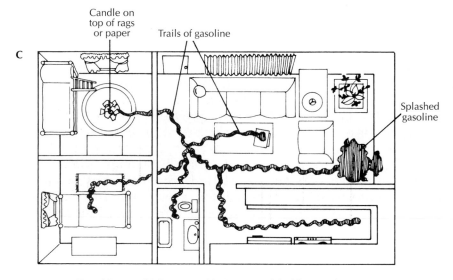

Candle on top of rags or paper

Trails of gasoline

Splashed gasoline

To achieve multiple points of ignition, "trails" of fire accelerants may lead from the initial point of ignition to other rooms. Trails often terminate against walls splashed with accelerants.

FIGURE 16.9   Common methods of delayed ignition.

Accelerant Detection Devices.   Several types of equipment can help the criminal investigator detect the presence of fire accelerants in a crime scene. Although the sense of smell has been heavily relied upon in detecting accelerants, other more scientific means are far superior. Investigators have successfully used *chemical dyes* to detect hydrocarbon residues and vapors. (Hydrocarbon is a mixture of hydrogen and carbon commonly found in accelerants.) The portable *catalytic combustion detector* is the most frequently used device to detect accelerants. This device operates according to a heated-vapor principle by which vapors at the scene are tested for oxidization. When combustible gases are heated, they are oxidized and can be analyzed electronically to indicate their accelerant origin. The *gas chromatograph* is also widely used to test for the presence of accelerants at arson scenes. Residues are gathered at the scene and transported to the crime laboratory for chromatographic testing. At the laboratory, the criminalist places small amounts of the debris into a sealed glass tube and subjects it to intense heat, forcing volatile residue to the upper air space of the tube. The criminalist then removes the vapor with a syringe and injects it into the gas chromatograph. The device separates the various components of the vapor, producing a graph, known as a chromatogram. This graph is contrasted to other graphs of previously tested known accelerants in the identification process (see Figure 16.10).

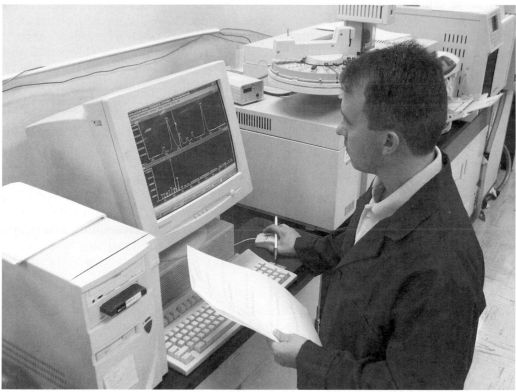

A

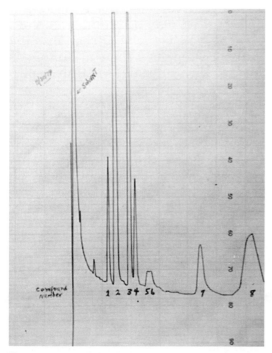

B

FIGURE 16.10 The gas chromatograph process. *A.* Vapor is injected into the gas chromatograph for analysis; *B.* The resulting chromatogram identifies the vapor.
(Sources: Michael Havstad, Los Angeles County Sheriff's Department; Sirchie Fingerprint Laboratories.)

A number of investigative agencies have recently begun to use dogs trained in arson detection. Conditioned dogs have been found to respond to accelerant odors with potentially greater accuracy than accelerant detection devices commonly used in the field. Experiments by the Connecticut State Police established that only 40 percent of arson evidence recovered through traditional means resulted in positive laboratory confirmation of accelerants, whereas dog-located evidence produced a 95 percent success rate.[35] Although instruments and dogs both differentiate among accelerants and similar chemical gases at suspected arson scenes, dogs produce far fewer false-positive findings. Many breeds can be trained to detect fire accelerants, but Labrador retrievers are particularly well suited to the task. Trained accelerant-detection dogs are being used in most states.

Although scientific instruments are used to detect the presence of accelerants, the investigator must still visually search and record the scene carefully. The smallest bit of evidence, such as the formation of irregular cracks in glass, can indicate the rapid, intense heat produced by an accelerant. Burnt matches near the scene should always be recovered and carefully packaged. Many arson cases have been solved by matching the torn end of a match to the stub in a matchbook still in the arsonist's possession. The scene should be thoroughly photographed in color, using the traditional general-to-specific method. Photographs can help to determine arson when studied by criminalists skilled in this area.[36]

When evidence is located at an arson scene, the collection and packaging method often depends on the material's volatility. Arson evidence is typically quite fragile and highly susceptible to contamination. Items that are suspected of containing the volatile elements that give accelerants unique identifiable qualities should not be packaged in plastic containers. Because such containers are produced from a petroleum base, an imprecise laboratory analysis may result when the container elements mix with petroleum evidence from the scene. Some crime laboratories routinely use standard gallon metal paint cans that are new and have never been filled with paint to package volatile scene materials. The metal lid may be hammered shut, sealing the gases of the evidence item. A small hole is then punched into the can and immediately sealed with a rubber stopper. When a sample is needed, the criminalist can penetrate the seal with a needle to obtain a specimen without fear of contamination.[37]

Victim and Witness Interviews.   One of the primary reasons that arson cases frequently remain unsolved is that there are generally no eyewitnesses to the offense. Nevertheless, all arson cases should be thoroughly explored for the possibility of witness information. A thorough neighborhood check should be conducted, as should an interior check if the structure is an apartment building or office building. In cases involving occupied homes and apartments, victims should be closely questioned as to the possibility of revenge or jealousy motives. In cases that involve commercial businesses or abandoned insured buildings, the following should be researched:

1. **Identity of the True Property Owner:** Because many businesses and apartment buildings have "front or straw ownership" (i.e., ownership designed to conceal the true owner's identity), thorough research is often necessary.
2. **Insurance Data on the Building:** When was the property last appraised by an insurance agent? What is the age of the structure? The true value of the building? The amount of the insurance in excess of the true value?

3. **Business History of the Structure:** Has the business been operating at a loss? What is the type and amount of stock in the building? Was stock removed or orders canceled before the fire?

4. **Background Information on All Parties Involved in the Insurance Coverage:** This would include information on the owner, insurance agent, appraiser, insurance company, policy adjuster, and fire marshal in an effort to determine possible collusion to commit arson for profit.

The Suspect.   Professional arsonists tend to be specialists—they rarely commit other types of crimes. Thus, their methods of operation also tend to be fixed. *Modus operandi* files should be established for suspects as to ignition methods, accelerant usage, alibi patterns, and other identifying factors. This type of information should be readily shared with other departments since the arsonist often travels widely.

Although most arsons are committed by hired professionals or amateur suspects, serial arsonists are occasionally encountered. Serial suspects set repeated fires and lack the traditional motive of profit or crime concealment. *Serial arsonists* are highly compulsive fire setters who may be classified as either mass, spree, or recurring. Mass arson involves a single offender who sets various fires at the same location during a very limited time period. A spree offender sets fires at separate locations within a limited time period, and recurring arsonists set numerous fires between time periods of days, weeks, or even years.[38] Serial arson is motivated by various factors, including mental illness or revenge. Such fires are generally indicated when traditional motives are lacking and similar arsons with matching methods of operation are reported between various time intervals.

When a suspect is apprehended shortly after the arson, the suspect's clothing should be secured for purposes of analysis. The criminalist will examine the clothing for the presence of residues similar to those recovered at the scene. The contents of the suspect's pockets (particularly the belongings of a juvenile or nonprofessional adult arsonist) may reveal the ignition means in the form of a matchbook or lighter. The suspect's skin and clothing should also be examined for the presence of burns since many inexperienced arsonists are burned when they ignite flammable materials. Hospital emergency personnel and local doctors should be questioned as to individuals seeking treatment for burns suffered during the ignition. The suspect should be extensively interviewed regarding past fires that appear to have involved a similar method of operation since arson tends to be a recidivistic offense.

Bombing Investigation

The investigation of bombing includes completed as well as attempted incidents that involve explosive devices. Public interest in bombing inquiries intensified following the massive 1995 bombing of the federal building in Oklahoma City, which killed 168 and wounded 600. The UNABOMBER and World Trade Center bombings and the bombing during the 1996 Olympics are additional examples of high-profile criminal explosions. Yet such cases are far from typical, as most bombings in America are neither serial nor terroristic. The typical bombing reflects the more everyday criminal motives of revenge and profit.

According to the Bureau of Alcohol, Tobacco, and Firearms, the number of Americans who illegally use explosive devices has nearly doubled from 1991 to the present. Nearly 3,200 completed or attempted bombings are reported annually in the nation, of which only about ten can be classified as terrorist planned.[39] Rather than being international terrorists, bombing suspects tend to represent a wide spectrum of ordinary criminality. The majority of suspects are motivated by personal revenge or hatred and often target spouses, acquaintances, or neighbors. Others use explosives for pure financial gain, typically expecting to collect insurance. A much smaller number are antigovernment or tax protestors who use explosive devices to vent their anger or paranoia. Regardless of motive, bombs are cheap and easy to construct and often result in a prolonged investigation dependent on trace evidence.

The oldest known explosive propellant is black powder. Mentioned by Marco Polo in the 1400s, many ancient civilizations take credit for its discovery. Most authorities, however, cite the Englishman Roger Bacon as the inventor of black powder in the thirteenth century. Black powder bombs are *low-velocity explosives*, so named because of their rate of detonation, which is generally less than 3,000 feet per second. Black powder bombs remain the most commonly encountered American explosive device. Black powder is very hazardous, as it is easily ignited and susceptible to heat, friction, and electricity. Such bombs often explode while the suspect is assembling them, accounting in large measure for the fact that 35 percent of all bomb injuries are sustained by the bomber. Black powder explosives are often encountered as pipe bombs, made by densely packing powder into a pipe and capping its ends. Unlike higher-speed explosives, black powder is a propellant that has a pushing rather than shattering effect.

A disturbing trend concerning black powder pipe bombs is the increasing number of juveniles involved in such offenses. The Bureau of Alcohol, Tobacco, and Firearms reports that 34 percent of all pipe bombings in the United States are perpetrated by juvenile suspects. High juvenile involvement can often be traced to the simplicity of pipe bomb construction and the easy availability of instructions for bomb assembly on the Internet, in bookstores and libraries, and at gun shows.

High-velocity explosives have a rate of detonation that easily exceeds 3,000 feet per second and have a violent shattering effect. Dynamite, nitroglycerine, and the military explosives of TNT (trinitrotoluene) and plastique are examples. Most high-velocity explosives contain nitric acid and other mixtures and are capable of destroying large areas. Other common, often easily and legally obtainable items, such as sugar, flour, and ammonium-nitrate fertilizers, can be mixed with various substances to become lethal bombs.[40]

A new variation of bombing threat centers upon the use of chemical agents either within other explosive devices or self-contained without an external propellant. While a number of chemical agents have been reported, the threat of anthrax-laden bombs has posed a particular challenge to law enforcement. In 1998 alone, there were over 100 anthrax bomb threats reported by police across the country. *Anthrax* is a virulent livestock bacillus and has become a favorite threat device used against abortion clinics, women's health centers, and government agencies. Although the vast majority of such devices are found to be hoaxes and contain no anthrax, police and health authorities are forced to take all threats and suspected devices seriously. In one five-month period, Los Angeles authorities investigated 40 anthrax threats, with 17 cases recorded in Indianapolis during a similar period.

Anthrax spores, like many other potentially deadly chemical agents, must be transformed into a usable weapon, a process that requires in-depth knowledge and experience. Experts predict this form of chemical bombing, often termed "bioterrorism," to continue, if not dominate, bombing threats through the new century.

The investigation of suspected bomb incidents initially entails standard crime scene and interviewing techniques. Because the investigation is often dependent on physical trace evidence, the scene must be sealed from the possibility of contamination quickly and completely. Additionally, every effort must be made to interview anyone who may have seen the suspect entering or fleeing the scene before or immediately after the explosion. A thorough neighborhood check should be done to ascertain if any out-of-the-ordinary person or vehicles were observed near the scene several days prior to the bombing. Because the location, collection, and packaging of bomb evidence is a highly specialized form of crime scene processing, local authorities frequently enlist the assistance of federal agents or nearby military experts. As the motive of most bombings remains interpersonal conflict or greed, investigators use the standard examination of motive, opportunity, and means to guide their inquiry. Once suspects are developed, the investigation will focus on offender interviews and forensic examinations at crime laboratories. Although many suspects do confess through the use of standard interviewing methods, many will be convicted only through forensic linkage of bomb scene evidence to their residence or person.

▲ SUMMARY

Various forms of criminal investigation are unique, requiring training and insight to comprehend their significance. Crimes of domestic abuse occur in a home environment and may involve married couples or unmarried partners or may be directed toward children. Such conflicts have the potential to eventually lead to serious acts of violence, including criminal homicide. Domestic child abuse is a major American problem; millions of cases are reported annually to law enforcement or social welfare authorities. Proper and timely intervention in the abuse cycle is very important, for child abuse can have lifelong effects upon the victim. Abuse of children takes many forms, including physical abuse, emotional abuse, and neglect.

Organized crime is a historical problem dating back to the origins of this country. Many groups have succeeded each other as identifiable criminal organizations engaged in continuing illegal enterprises. The Americanized Mafia, La Cosa Nostra, is a highly organized crime syndicate operating throughout the United States. Other more recent organized crime groups include outlaw motorcycle gangs, prison-based crime families, minority street gangs, and various ethnic groups closely linked to cocaine and heroin distribution. Many such groups use profits from illegal operations to support legal investments. Organized crime groups are further characterized by exclusive racial or ethnic membership, continuous crime involvement, and the frequent use of corruption and violence to accomplish their objectives.

Arson investigations became increasingly important in the 1990s, as more police agencies joined with traditional fire personnel to determine the origin of suspicious fires. When property is burned for an improper and illegal motive in a willful and malicious manner, arson is indicated. Arsonists set fires for many reasons, including profit, revenge, vandalism, crime concealment, or serial motivations. Suspects are generally adult, yet this felony has the highest proportionate involvement of juvenile participation of all serious felonies. The use of sophisticated instrumentation is essential for complete arson investigation.

Bombing incidents are increasing across the United States. Although some are terroristic, the great majority of such cases are motivated by ordinary criminal reasons: revenge and profit. Most criminal explosions use detonated black powder and are termed low-velocity bombings. Other explosives are termed high velocity, as their rate of detonation is far greater in feet per second. The investigation of this type of crime is generally complex, as physical evidence is often of a trace nature and must be subjected to laboratory analysis.

EXERCISES

1. Visit the department of social welfare or department of family services in your community. Determine the extent to which domestic abuse exists and how such cases are handled and referred to law enforcement agencies.

2. Prepare a research paper on the history and development of La Cosa Nostra. Discuss in detail the current methods of operation used by this organized crime group.

3. Determine the extent of arson in your community. Interview a fire investigator or police investigator specializing in arson inquiries. Research local growth rates, suspect characteristics, and typical methods of operation.

RELEVANT WEB SITES

http://alcoholism.about.com/od/abuse/

Comprehensive domestic abuse site that provides a potential abuse screening quiz, various personalized stories of abuse by victims, and information on the association of drinking and spousal abuse and the effect on children and adults of witnessing repeated domestic abuse.

http://www.elderabusecenter.org/

National Center on Elder Abuse site that is a gateway for information on elder abuse, neglect, and exploitation. Provides links to state legislation pertaining to elder abuse, among other related links.

http://www.americanmafia.com/

Wide-ranging site containing numerous articles and data pertaining to organized crime with particular emphasis upon the American Mafia.

http://www.sp/center.org/center/about.jsp

Site of Southern Poverty Law Center, which tracks hate groups and reports upon hate crimes. Many links providing details on specific extremist hate organizations.

Suspect Identification

KEY TERMS

arch fingerprint
Automated Fingerprint
  Identification Systems
computer-aided identification
cyanoacrylate fuming
dactyloscopy
external perception factors
face recognition technology
fingerprint classification
fingerprint ridges

internal perception factors
iodine fuming
latent fingerprints
lineup
linguistics
loop fingerprint
voiceprint
Wade decision
whorl fingerprint

LEARNING OBJECTIVES

1. to be aware of the importance of suspect identification to the overall task of criminal investigation;
2. to be able to define the three basic patterns of all fingerprints;
3. to be able to discuss the three types of latent fingerprints that may be encountered at a crime scene;
4. to understand the mechanics of processing, developing, and lifting latent fingerprints;
5. to understand the computerized fingerprint identification technique;
6. to be able to explain the technique and function of voice identification; and
7. to be able to discuss the major categories and significance of eyewitness identification.

INTRODUCTION

A primary task of criminal investigation is to identify the perpetrator. Many of the cases referred to the investigator are of the unknown-suspect category—the suspect's actions are known, but personal identification has not been made. Even when the suspect's identity is known, identification procedures may be required to confirm information furnished by victims or witnesses. There are two basic types of suspect identification: positive and tracing. *Positive identification* refers to information that identifies an individual beyond question and is legally acceptable as pertaining to and originating with that particular individual. *Tracing information* refers to all other information that may be indicative of the personal identity of an individual. There are relatively few positive indicators of personal identity that are encountered at crime scenes or otherwise obtained. Fingerprints have traditionally been considered the single most positive indicator of personal identity.

FINGERPRINTS

The study of fingerprints for identification purposes, **dactyloscopy**, is based upon distinctive ridge outlines that appear on the bulbs on the inside of the end joints of the fingers and thumbs. **Fingerprint ridges** are actually raised layers of skin along which are scattered the ends of tiny ducts, or pores, from the sweat glands in the dermal layer underneath. The skin between the ridges contains the nerve endings, through which touch, temperature, and pain are perceived. The ridges of each fingertip have definite contours and appear in several distinctive pattern types.

There are three basic fingerprint groups, each having a unique general and specific appearance. For purposes of classification (the process by which fingerprints are assigned a formula for filing and future identification), each of the general groups may be further divided into subgroups. Subgroups are determined by the smaller distinctive differences that exist among the patterns in the same general group.

It is important for all police officers to have a basic understanding of fingerprint patterns and the technique for recording them. This knowledge is needed in fingerprinting suspects and in processing crime scenes for latent prints left by suspects. Arrested suspects are routinely fingerprinted following their apprehension, and fingerprint cards are submitted to various state and federal agencies. If the fingerprints are improperly rolled onto the card, the receiving agency will not be able to classify the suspect's prints. A properly rolled fingerprint will clearly include the essential ridges necessary for classification. Obviously, without knowledge of the essential characteristics of the three basic patterns, the officer will not be able to determine their presence or absence on the card. Furthermore, when processing a crime scene for latent prints, the officer must be able to distinguish between useful prints and a useless smudge.

Fingerprint Patterns

All fingerprints are of the loop, whorl, or arch configuration. A loop is the most commonly encountered; approximately 60 percent of all patterns will be loops. Whorls account for 35 percent, and arches are the scarcest configuration, occurring in only 5 percent of the patterns.[1] To define the three pattern types, the following fingerprint terms must first be introduced (see Figure 17.1):

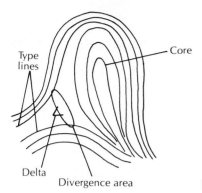

FIGURE 17.1   Common fingerprint terms.

1. **Pattern Area.** The pattern area is the only relevant part of the finger-print in terms of interpretation and classification. This area contains the important ridges of the print, such as the delta and core. The pattern area is enclosed by type lines.
2. **Type Lines.** These lines are the two innermost ridges that start as parallel lines, diverge, and surround the pattern area.
3. **Divergence.** The spreading apart of the two lines (ridges) that have been running parallel or nearly parallel.
4. **Delta.** That point on a ridge at or in front of and nearest the center of the divergence of the type lines. Deltas are present only in loops or whorls.
5. **Core.** The approximate center of the fingerprint. Cores are located for classification purposes only in loops.

Loop.   A **loop fingerprint** is formed by ridges entering one side of the pattern, recurving (turning back to the direction of entry), and exiting the pattern. In all loop fingerprints, type lines, a delta, and core can be located. If the ridges of the pattern area slant toward the thumb of the hand on which they are found, the pattern is termed a *radial loop*. If the ridges of the pattern area slant toward the little finger, the pattern is termed an *ulnar loop* (see Figure 17.2A). For purposes of pattern recognition during suspect printing and crime scene processing, an investigator need only be concerned with the characteristics thus far discussed. For purposes of individual suspect identification and classification, the print must be further individualized by ridge counting. The number of intervening ridges between an imaginary line drawn from delta to core is termed an individual's *ridge count*.

Whorl.   **Whorl fingerprints** can occur in four distinctive configurations. Generally speaking, the pattern appears as ridges that encircle a central circular pattern. All whorls have at least two deltas, typically located on the lower edges of the patterns' sides (see Figure 17.2B). The two most common whorls, *plain* and *central pocket loop*, conform to this basic description. The two other whorl patterns, *double loop* and *accidental*, have different appearances. The double loop is composed of two looplike patterns that generally surround each other. The accidental whorl is often difficult to recognize since it contains unusual ridges, making it impossible to classify as one of the traditional patterns.

Arch.   The **arch fingerprint** is the simplest fingerprint configuration to recognize. Ridges enter from one side of the pattern, rise in the center (in an

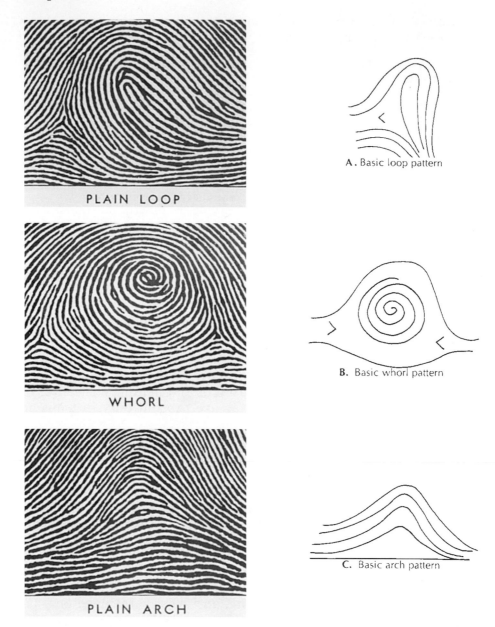

FIGURE 17.2   Basic fingerprint patterns.

archlike fashion), and flow out the other side of the pattern (see Figure 17.2C). A *plain arch* conforms to this description; a *tented arch* generally conforms, with one exception. The tented arch contains a ridge or many ridges, forming a tentlike rise in the center of the pattern.

Fingerprint Classification

Fingerprint classification, as computed by experts, involves the use of various numerals and letters assigned to the ten prints in a multistep process. The classification system developed by Sir Francis Galton and Edward Richard Henry is still in use by present-day fingerprint identification experts. Many suspects purposely give a false name in the expectation that past criminal history will not be revealed. Fingerprint classification defeats this purpose. A comparison of the suspect's fingerprint classification formula with similar formulas previously filed will bring to light the offender's past. Many fugitives and escapees are apprehended in this manner.

Latent Fingerprints

Latent fingerprints are ridge impressions that are found at a crime scene rather than obtained through an inking rolling procedure. They are often of great importance in an investigation. No other crime scene evidence is accepted so readily in the courtroom or is judged to have more credibility than the latent fingerprint. As the confession comes to be relied upon less as a sole indicator of guilt, physical evidence becomes more important to a successful prosecution. If a suspect denies any knowledge of a crime scene but one or more latent fingerprints from that suspect are recovered at the scene, the prints will serve as indisputable proof to place the offender within the scene, despite protestations to the contrary (see Figure 17.3). A latent print is the direct result of contact of the sweat pores located on the ridge surface. When a fingertip comes in contact with a surface, an oily deposit or residue of perspiration is transferred to that surface. An exact impression of the ridge configuration may result, according to the pressure and movement of the fingertip. Not all transfers of perspiration will be of value because the individual may slide or press the fingertip to smear the resulting impression beyond recognition. Latent fingerprints are invisible until some material renders them visible.

Visible fingerprints, as the name implies, can be perceived without the use of a developing material because of the transfer of existing materials from the fingertip to the surface of the object. If the suspect's fingers are soiled or stained (e.g., with dirt or blood), impressions may be left when the fingertips are pressed against a surface. A third type of print, the *plastic impression*, may result when the fingertip comes in contact with a soft, impressionable material. For example, the suspect may leave prints on wax, soap, or grease.

Latent prints are not encountered at crime scenes as often as one might expect. Some suspects purposely wear gloves to avoid latents; others leave

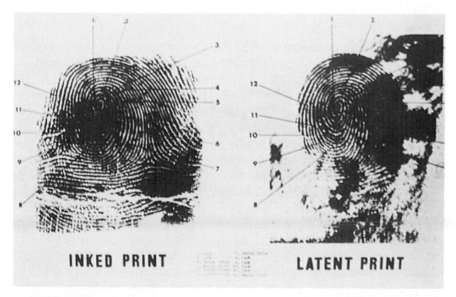

FIGURE 17.3 Latent fingerprint recovered at a crime scene positively matched with the suspect's inked print. *(Source: Joseph Orantes, San Diego Police Department.)*

latent impressions that are of no value for identification. The majority of the impressions developed at a crime scene are sliding smudges, in which detailed ridge impressions are blurred. Furthermore, not all surfaces are suited to record a latent fingerprint. Generally, a hard, smooth surface of a nonporous nature is ideally suited for latent impressions.

Locating Latent Impressions.   To maximize chances of locating latent impressions, the crime scene must be protected from those who could alter the latents. All unauthorized persons should be prevented from entering the scene, and anyone who does enter should ideally wear gloves. The investigator's search for latent impressions will be guided by the suspected nature of the crime. In the case of a burglary, points of entry (windows, doorknobs, locks) should be processed. Areas of the suspect's prowl should be processed, with special attention given to smooth, polished objects (glass or china, for example) and metal surfaces. Finally, the suspect's point of exit should be determined and processed. Paper items should not be ignored. Although paper impressions do not always last as long as impressions made on other surfaces, they can reveal detailed fingerprints. Locating latent prints also depends upon victim or witness testimony. Such individuals must be questioned carefully as to the actions of the suspect. For example, a clerk may indicate that during an armed robbery, the suspect posed as a customer, opening the glass door of a cooler before confronting the clerk. The glass door would then be processed for possible latents.

Because many crimes involve automobiles, this potentially valuable source of latent fingerprints should always be processed. The search for latents is similar to the room search in that the auto is systematically processed. The exterior surfaces should be processed first, one side at a time. Front and rear sections should follow, with the roof being processed as the last exterior step. The interior of the vehicle then should be examined, with particular attention given to all hard, smooth surfaces. Regardless of the type of scene being processed, the investigator will attempt to reconstruct the actions of the suspect. How would a typical burglar open a locked window? How would an auto thief generally gain entry without the key to the vehicle? If the general movement of the suspect can be determined, the search for latents can be more precisely directed.

Developing Latent Impressions.   When the investigator encounters visible or plastic impressions, the object bearing the print should be photographed and transported to the criminalist. Latent prints that are hidden or concealed need to be developed or made visible. Fingerprint powders are used for this purpose through a process known as *dusting*. Fingerprint powders are available in many different colors. The color of the powder used should always provide good contrast with the color of the surface to be dusted. Obviously, black powder on a black surface will not show up clearly. Powder renders the latent visible by adhering to the oil or perspiration deposits. Depending on the manner in which the latent was deposited on the surface, the powder will reveal a classification pattern or a partial impression. In a small number of cases, the latent will be complete and readily identifiable as a loop, whorl, or arch. The investigator may even be able to see the details of the pattern area, such as the delta and core. However, most latent prints will only be partial in that only a portion of the fingertip contacted the surface. Consequently, it is not unusual for the investigator to be unable to identify the pattern's general configuration. Partial prints should also be recovered, since their identification value may still be significant.

Latent fingerprints may also be developed by means of a spraying technique. If an entire wall of a scene is to be processed, a portable spraying device can distribute a light coating of powder over the entire wall to indicate any latents. Additional powder is then applied by hand to determine the value of the impression.

A final nonchemical method of latent fingerprint detection involves the use of *alternate light sources* and *fluorescent powders*. The basic principle of this method is that some trace evidence either glows brightly when exposed to ultraviolet light in the proper wavelength or glows when treated with fluorescent powder. Because a large variety of evidence items are invisible to the naked eye, ultraviolet light, lasers, and other forensic light sources are increasingly being used to render such objects visible. Visible light is only a small portion of the spectrum of electromagnetic energy. If a special light source reflects energy at the proper wavelength, objects not typically seen can become visible. Accordingly, investigators commonly use special hand-held lights to convert white light from a flashlight to the exact wavelength necessary to uncover fluorescent powdered prints and other forms of trace evidence.[2]

Lifting Latent Impressions.   After the impression has been developed and photographed, it is normally desirable to physically remove the impression from the surface. This stage of the process is often the most difficult. In some cases, the print may be destroyed; hence, the photographic procedure is essential before lifting is attempted. Fingerprint lifting involves the placement of a clear adhesive tape or an adhesive rubber lifter against the powdered latent impression. The impression is then transferred intact onto the tape or rubber surface. The lifting tape is adhered to a clean paper card for preservation. The adhesive rubber surface is covered with a transparent celluloid cover. During any lifting process, air bubbles may be trapped under the adhesive material, causing obliteration of some of the ridges. To avoid this problem, the officer must exercise care in placing the adhesive over the developed impression. As a final step, the card or rubber lifter containing the impression should be marked for identification, as is the case with all valuable evidence items.

Chemical Means of Development.   The oldest and most common of the chemical methods of latent development is the **iodine fuming** technique. This method is generally used when paper objects are suspected of bearing latent impressions. Crystals of iodine are exposed to a heat source, so that they sublime (pass from the solid to the vapor state). The fumes are absorbed by the perspiration and oils in the latent print, resulting in the sudden appearance of the ridges. Portable iodine fumers can be used; however, the most satisfactory results are obtained with an enclosed chamber. The document is suspended within the chamber by clips, and an iodine crystal is placed on a heat source in the bottom of the chamber. As the vapors rise to envelop the document, the latent prints are made visible (see Figure 17.4).

A second method of chemical development involves the use of *ninhydrin*. This chemical is typically sprayed on a latent impression whereupon it reacts with amino acids. Amino acids are the chief components of proteins, and proteins are present in perspiration—the primary components of the print. The ninhydrin method is particularly valuable in developing old latents on paper. Under dry conditions, the amino acids adhere to the cellulose fibers of paper. Unless they are disturbed in some manner, the acids will persist for an indefinite period of time.[3] Ninhydrin spraying has developed paper latents that were more than 30 years old. The only drawback to this

FIGURE 17.4   *A.* Latent fingerprints made visible through the use of an iodine fuming cabinet. *B.* Cyanoacrylate (superglue) fuming chamber. *(Source: Sirchie Fingerprint Laboratories.)*

technique is that the amount of amino acids in perspiration varies with temperature. Dry "winter hands" may leave hardly any amino acids or none at all, whereas summer temperatures result in a high level of amino acid secretions.

The latest technology in the chemical methods of latent development is the **cyanoacrylate fuming** technique, commonly referred to as the *superglue method.* Certain types of glues discharge cyanoacrylate ester during evaporation. When properly directed, the fumes can develop a hard, highly resistant latent fingerprint on a wide variety of surfaces, including weapons, plastic bags, and glass. The superglue fuming technique has proven very effective in developing latent fingerprints on nonporous surfaces but not on various porous items of evidence.

When superglue is exposed to air at room temperature, the fumes make visible previously invisible latent fingerprints. The size of the area to which the fumes are confined determines the quantity of superglue required. Several grams of superglue generally develop latent prints on objects in a confined space approximately the size of a ten-gallon fish tank.[4] Specific objects to be processed by the superglue method must be isolated. The evidence item can be placed in a tightly sealed container, such as a large plastic trash bag supported by a cardboard box. The evidence is placed upright, not flat, as airborne superglue fumes circulate, for maximum exposure. As the latent prints develop, they generally materialize as a white color and should be immediately photographed. Using laser light on such latents often darkens and defines the image.[5]

Latent Flesh Fingerprints.   For decades, investigators and criminalists have sought to develop a method of obtaining latent prints from human skin. Until relatively recently, there had been no method of obtaining prints from the skin of a victim touched by a suspect. In nearly all sex crimes and a substantial number of cases involving criminal homicide or assault, latent fingerprints are left by the offender on the victim's skin. An initial method developed in the early 1970s involved covering the victim's skin with a fine lead powder. The powder would be brushed away to reveal the presence of latent prints that were covered with a piece of fine-grained emulsion photographic film. An inflatable balloonlike device similar to a physician's blood pressure cuff was then placed against the impression, inserted with filters, and X-rayed to expose the film. Such a transfer method enjoyed only limited success when measured by today's standards, but it provided the foundation for more effective and simple procedures, such as applying magnetic powder directly to flesh.

The first American criminal conviction based on fingerprints recovered from skin involved a triple homicide in North Miami Beach, Florida. The 1978 investigation focused on three victims found brutally executed in a health spa. Latent prints from a victim's flesh were successfully obtained, even in the humid spa crime scene, by using the magnetic powder method. Using the technique, the investigator first brushes magnetic powder onto the skin where fingerprints are suspected. When latent prints are developed, photographs should be taken prior to any attempt at lifting the impression. Finally, latent print tape is used to remove the impression and place the evidence on a fingerprint card.[6] Although the magnetic powder method is popular, the FBI recommends combining this method with glue fuming. Fumes produced from heated superglue are directed onto the skin, after which magnetic or fluorescent powder is applied to reveal latent prints. Research indicates that successful latent print recovery from skin is enhanced with younger victims, as aging and element exposure can cause the skin to be rough. Additionally, a woman's skin is better suited to latent print recovery because it is smoother and has less body hair than does the skin of a male.[7]

Success with powder and glue methods has led to extensive experimentation with other methods. Latent skin impressions have been obtained using the iodine-silver plate method, dusting with magnetic powders, and the laser. The *laser technique* has particularly great potential for field use. The laser method is dependent on the fluorescent effect of human perspiration. As perspiration contains various components that glow when exposed to laser light, the latents are first treated with fluorescent powder or evaporating fluorescent dye. When viewed through special camera filters or a treated lens worn by the investigator, the latents are clearly visible. Of all current methods, the laser technique has been found to be the most effective in locating otherwise undetectable latents, old prints, or those on unusual surfaces. In addition, the method is nondestructive, allowing evidence to remain intact.

Computerized Fingerprint Processing and Identification

Even when a latent fingerprint is located at a crime scene, the investigator still faces a major obstacle in identifying the suspect. Contrary to popular belief, police departments cannot generally identify an individual through a latent fingerprint alone; other personal information is most often required. The investigator must have an indication of the suspect's name before a comparison of the latent print and previously taken fingerprints may be contrasted for identification. Fingerprints are classified and filed according to a formula derived from a full ten-finger set of prints. Since it is highly unlikely that the officer will recover a complete set of the suspect's prints at the scene, there has been no workable method available to compare a latent print with prints from a file containing thousands.

Fortunately, the computer has been applied to this identification problem with enormous success. The FBI and other agencies have developed a *FINDER* (FINgerprint reaDER) *system* capable of performing latent searching automatically. The computer system locates minutiae data, consisting of the location and orientation of fingerprint ridges at points of termination (ridge endings) or at points of bifurcation (where they branch into two ridges). The minutiae for a given fingerprint are converted to digital data and are then stored in this form in the fingerprint file. When a latent print is obtained from a crime scene, the computer locates all identifying minutiae. This digital information is fed into a matcher that compares the latent data to any number of other known fingerprint patterns. The computer then scores a match on the basis of probability, printing out the identifying data for human configuration of similar origin.

The development of the FINDER system has resulted in the widespread adoption of **Automated Fingerprint Identification Systems** (AFIS) by most of the states and hundreds of city or county law enforcement agencies.[8] Using the technology of the original federal system, AFIS computers are faster and more affordable. The new systems can effectively compare a latent print with a 300,000-file database in less than 15 minutes. The system can produce up to 25 prints in its database that have a strong probability of being similar to the compared latent fingerprint. Then fingerprint examiners compare the group of database samples to the crime scene latent. Recent AFIS databases have the expanded capacity to hold nearly five million fingerprint samples.

Automated fingerprint computer matching has produced immediate results for criminal investigators in many states. In the first year of New Jersey's use of AFIS, 631 criminal suspects were identified from nearly 900,000 prints in the computer's database.[9] In the first six months of New York State's AFIS operation, the system provided nearly 200 identifications, including suspect matches in 30 criminal homicides. As more large police agencies obtain their own AFIS computers, clearance rate increases can be expected. For example, the San Francisco Police Department has reported a 25 percent reduction in burglaries, directly attributed to fingerprint matches not possible before the installation of the automated system.[10] While various local and state AFIS computers are effective, no automated fingerprint comparison system in the nation is superior to the main system within the FBI's data center just outside of Clarksburg, West Virginia. On an average day, 40,000 fingerprints are fed into the computers, which are capable of processing 3,000 searches a second. As a result of processing prints of recently arrested suspects from thousands of local and state agencies, the FBI system identifies approximately 8,000 wanted fugitives a month.

The now common use of AFIS computers has positively affected how arrested suspects' fingerprints are obtained and processed. Traditionally, arrested individuals were fingerprinted at police agencies or county jails using the standard method of inking the fingers and rolling the impressions onto cards. The fingerprint card was then carried or sent by mail or fax to various records and identification divisions. Too often, wanted suspects with concealed identities were released on bond before fingerprints revealed their fugitive status. Fortunately, much of the same technology that developed the AFIS concept has also created the *live-scan fingerprinting process* (see Figure 17.5). Live-scanning allows police to place a suspect's fingers on a glass plate that is then "read" by a special device to produce a digital image of the prints. The image can then be transmitted over phone

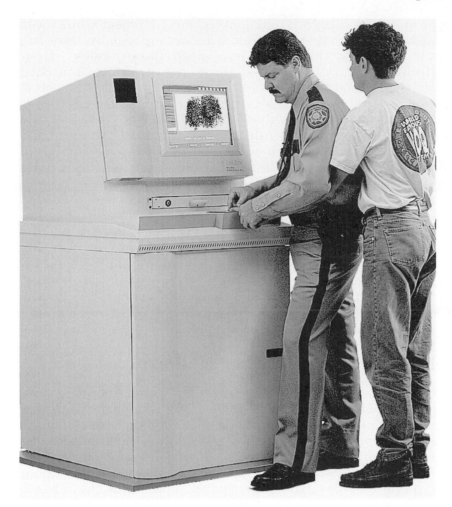

FIGURE 17.5   Live-scan technology now enables law enforcement to print and compare a subject's fingerprints rapidly without linking the fingertips. *(Source: Printrak International, Anaheim, California.)*

lines to a main AFIS computer center for immediate comparison for outstanding warrants or arrest history. The largest live-scan system in the world is operated by Los Angeles County authorities and includes 97 live-scan fingerprinting stations serving 48 different police agencies. As investigators estimate that more than 15 percent of all arrested suspects give false identities, the live-scan system has proven extremely valuable in identifying individuals prior to their release and possible escape. Additionally, the technology has virtually eliminated the taking of poor-quality inked fingerprints.[11]

The use of computers to file, classify, and identify fingerprints automatically is a major advance in criminal identification. In the past, a latent print had to be visually matched with other prints on the basis of a "hunch." This process involved countless hours of tedious and often unsuccessful work. Computerized fingerprint search systems have succeeded in turning what seemed like science fiction into practical reality. For example, the murder of a Miami police officer was solved through an

AFIS computer match. A single latent located on a suspect's auto was matched successfully by the computer from a collection of more than one million prints.[12] Similarly, the highly publicized Los Angeles "Night Stalker" serial murderer was identified through a computer-matched latent recovered from a stolen vehicle. The apprehended suspect is believed to have murdered as many as 17 victims. Automated fingerprinting systems have also proven their value in solving previously unsolvable felony investigations. In 1990, Los Angeles investigators matched the prints of a murderer to latent crime scene prints recovered during an unsolved 1963 criminal homicide. The 27-year-old strangulation case is believed to be the oldest case ever solved by any automated fingerprint identification system. Since 1990, many other police agencies have used AFIS searches to solve past felonies. So-called *cold-case squads*, or investigative units that reopen and expose old unsolved cases to new forensic techniques, commonly make use of new technology related to blood, bodily fluids, and fingerprints. The Dallas Police Department's squad is reinvestigating more than 70 unsolved homicides and reports significant success because of automated fingerprint matching of latent crime scene prints from the 1960s to the present.

Legal Requirements for Fingerprint Identification

Latent fingerprints recovered from a crime scene are compared by experts with impressions from the suspect (see Figure 17.6). The suspect's prints might have been obtained in past arrests or following the arrest for the current offense. If latent prints were of the same quality as those obtained during routine fingerprinting at the police agency, there would never be a problem of determining an absolute match. However, the majority of latent prints are partial impressions of the fingertips or impressions that are too light or too dark. Consequently, the comparison process may be difficult. The same difficulties may be encountered in comparing partial palm prints with full palm prints obtained after an apprehension (see Figure 17.7).

The fingerprint expert attempts to conclude whether the latent is from the same origin as another impression through a careful comparison of the ridge impressions of both prints. Ridge characteristics that are identifiable from common ridge patterns are noted with regard to appearance and location in the pattern. Ridge endings, bifurcations, ridge islands, and ridge crossings are generally located. A ridge-by-ridge comparison is then made between the two points. United States courts have not specified a certain number of points that must be identical for positive identification. However, most courts require 10 to 15 ridges that are identical in both appearance and relative location to justify a conclusion of common origin.

Fingerprint identification in the United States has always been linked with the FBI. As the nation's central collection point for print identification, the FBI's identification division has traditionally been located in Washington, D.C. In 1998, the bureau moved its massive collection of 35 million fingerprint cards dating from 1925 to a new complex in Clarksburg, West Virginia. The print collection will be converted to digital images that will be stored in the agency's automated fingerprint system. The new facility will be able to computer check fingerprints submitted by local agencies against its national collection in less than two hours. The system will utilize special software to check the typical daily load of 50,000 requests, helping police identify and arrest many of the 390,000 fugitives wanted throughout the nation.

FIGURE 17.6 The fingerprint expert seeks to locate similar points of identification on latent and inked prints through observation of unique ridge patterns. *(Source: Michael Havstad, Los Angeles County Sheriff's Department.)*

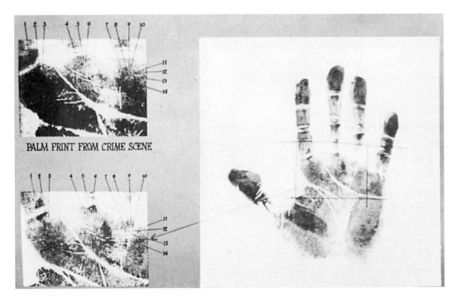

FIGURE 17.7 Many important points of identification can be located on the palm of the hand as well as on the fingertips. *(Source: Joseph Orantes, San Diego Police Department.)*

VOICE IDENTIFICATION

The identification of a suspect based on the hearing of voice sound has been of legal significance for centuries; however, this means of identification is subject to many errors. Accordingly, such identifications are likely to be challenged as to their reliability. Unless the sense of hearing is constantly relied upon to a greater than average extent (as, for example, with the blind), information gathered by this means alone generally requires further substantiation.

The only voice identification method that is legally acceptable in some courts as proof of identity is known as the **voiceprint** or *spectrograph*. The voiceprint method of speaker identification consists of the identification and/or elimination of suspects by both aural and visual comparison of voices with a known voice. The aural evaluation involves testing both voices to determine similarities and/or differences. The pitch, rate of speech, and articulation are evaluated, as are anatomical traits of the speaker(s). The visual phase of the examination compares acoustical patterns for visual similarities and/or differences. For this to be accomplished, a graphlike pattern of the suspect's voice must be compared to a pattern of the known individual's voice. A device known as the *sound spectrograph* is used to convert the sound of the voice recorded on magnetic tape to the visual form. A criminalist trained in interpretation and comparison of sound spectrograph visual displays then examines both patterns for common origin.

Serious development of a system of criminal identification through voice analysis began during the 1920s. As the *New York Times* reported in 1926:

VOICES IDENTIFY CROOKS
Berlin Police Test Machine for Recording Individual Rhythm

BERLIN, Aug. 26—Beside every picture and set of fingerprints and hand writing in the Rogues' Gallery will be a chart with a series of curves characteristic of the rhythm of the voice if a scheme worked out by Dr. Eduard Sievers of Leipzig proves to be all he claims for it. Police authorities are now testing his apparatus for recording the harmonious measures of the human voice and it is already asserted that identification of individuals by it is almost infallible. At least it is better than the handwriting test.

Dr. Sievers even goes so far as to say the characteristic rhythm of voice is transmitted to writing and that writers of anonymous letters can be detected by reading their compositions into a machine and noting the curve produced. He is able in every instance to distinguish between the curves produced by the voices of poets and musicians from laborers who are not appreciative of the finer arts. The method of classifying voice curves is worked out on lines similar to the Bertillon system of indexing fingerprints.[13]

Such early efforts, however, were apparently unsuccessful, for it was not until shortly after World War II that the voice spectrograph was developed by Bell Laboratories. Research at that time was not conclusive and was discontinued after the war. A high frequency of telephoned bomb threats prompted Bell Laboratories to resume testing under the direction of Lawrence Kersta during the early 1960s. Throughout that decade, many law enforcement agencies used the voiceprint technique. The Michigan State Police evaluated and tested the device with particular thoroughness. It has now been refined by Kersta and others to the point that a speaker's voice can be identified with a very low probability of error. Although some courts have yet to be convinced of its positive identification value, many courts have accepted the voiceprints as a positive means of personal identification.

The underlying theory on which voiceprint is based is that each person's speech is unique. This is due to the uniqueness of those parts of the anatomy that play a part in articulation. Assuming that no two individuals have identical vocal cords, nasal cavities, and other body parts involved in particularizing speech, a unique sound will be produced by each individual. Further, according to Kersta, the "articulators" (lips, teeth, tongue, soft palate, and jaw muscles) work together in a unique manner for each speaker.[14]

The voiceprint has developed into an important suspect identification tool. Only when the suspect's voice has not been recorded, or when a comparison recording has not been obtained, is its use precluded.

LINGUISTICS IDENTIFICATION

The use of forensic experts skilled in linguistics is becoming more frequent during investigations and in the courtroom. **Linguistics** is the scientific study of language. Individuals skilled in linguistic interpretations can assist the criminal investigation in three forms of analysis: author/speaker comparison, author/speaker assessment, and discourse analysis. All three areas focus on language usage and rely on comparison methodology. In the first type of comparison, linguistic examiners analyze and compare elements of one communication with a second communication believed to have been made by the same individual. A threatening letter sent to the victim may be compared to letters recovered from the suspect's residence during the execution of a search warrant, or a recorded bomb threat may be compared to previously recorded statements by the suspect. Various communication elements are analyzed and compared, such as vocabulary selection, syntax, phraseology, spelling, and rate of speech. Author/speaker assessment seeks to profile the suspect through an evaluation of characteristics linked to one's demographic or psychological characteristics. Commonly termed *forensic psycholinguistics*, the technique merges the projective methodologies of general profiling with the study of written and/or spoken words. By again examining the suspect's usage of vocabulary, syntax, and phraseology, a linguistics expert can provide a qualified determination of the speaker or author's age, sex, education, occupation, ethnic background, and possibly regional origin. Because of continued research and development by the FBI, psycholinguistics currently has the potential to determine a suspect's level of threat or the actual risk of the crime being carried out. Additionally, false allegations can often be determined through analysis of written threats. Occasionally, rape or stalking victims make false allegations of victimizations, that, upon examination by experts, prove to be written by the reporting party. Finally, psycholinguistics can be of great value in determining the probability of action in potential workplace violence communications. As disgruntled or terminated employees often provide clues of future violence through verbal statements, e-mails, or notes, their actions may be predicted and prevented through careful language assessment.[15]

The final linguistic method of comparison, discourse analysis, is the examination of conversations recorded on audio- or videotape that are used as evidence in court. Testimony is offered to help the triers of fact facilitate accurate listening or accurate understanding of what was said in the recording. Often working from a transcript, the linguist identifies the topics raised in the conversation, who raised them, and the responses to them. Often used to correct or highlight differences between what is stated in a written transcript of a recording and the actual content of the recording, discourse analysis seeks to provide a corrected, more accurate rendition of what was stated. Linguistics experts have been allowed to testify in many cases but have been prohibited in others. A judge's decision to allow linguistic analysis as expert testimony often depends on whether the judge believes the testimony would aid the trier of fact. A second determination centers on whether the judge reasons that the benefit to the trier of fact outweighs the influence that scientific testimony may have on a jury.[16]

Eyewitness Identification

In the majority of cases in which the suspect is unknown, such positive identification methods as fingerprint and voiceprint analysis cannot be employed. In an effort to identify the suspect, the investigator must depend upon tracing clues discovered at the scene and eyewitness descriptions, should they be available. Eyewitness descriptions furnished by victims and witnesses, however, are of notoriously questionable accuracy. The perception of an event is affected by both internal and external factors. Thus, no two individuals will perceive a given event in exactly the same way.

Internal perception factors that can affect perception include personal drives and interests, emotions, prejudices, and past experiences and conditioning. **External perception factors**, by contrast, are not intrinsic to the individual but also affect perception. Weather conditions, distance of the witness from the event, and obstacles between the witness and event are examples. A witness may notice a poorly dressed person in a wealthy neighborhood since such a person, by contrast, would seem out of place (external factor), but a detailed description of the event may be distorted by class prejudice of the witness (internal factor).

Most people have the use of all of their five senses: sight, hearing, smell, taste, and touch. When an event is perceived by a victim or witness, one or more of the senses is involved. The information is processed by the individual in a complex "filtering" process, with varying accuracy. From a legal standpoint, the sense of sight is generally given more credibility than any of the other four senses. However, many individuals with excellent eyesight may witness a crime and yet give a totally distorted description upon questioning.

When interviewing victims and eyewitnesses, the officer must take care not to add to possible inaccuracy of the statement by suggesting mental images. Many interviewing techniques may be used to help victims and witnesses describe a suspect, but regardless of the technique, caution must be exercised not to suggest a suspect's identity or to violate legal identification procedures.

Verbal Identification

When victims or eyewitnesses state that they have seen the suspect, they should be asked to provide a physical description without delay. Witnesses should be separated from one another before the questioning to avoid distortion of their testimony. If witnesses are allowed to discuss the events among themselves, some may be tempted to change their accounts to conform with others. The following items pertaining to identification should be systematically covered during the questioning:

1. **Name.** The officer should never assume that the witness will furnish the suspect's name automatically. Many witnesses will not provide this information unless they are specifically asked to do so. Any name mentioned by a witness could be significant—including first names or nicknames.

2. **Race.** Racial determinations may be obvious, but some witnesses may provide inaccurate information because of their personal prejudices. The officer should ask for detailed descriptions with regard to skin color, hair, eye color, and facial features.

3. **Sex.** Generally an obvious descriptive feature. If the witness has some doubt, this should be noted as possibly significant for future identification.

4. **Age.** Often difficult for the average witness to describe. The officer should suggest different age groupings in increments of five years. For example, "Was he 30 to 35? Thirty-five to 40?"

5. **Height and Weight.** Most individuals are poor judges of height and weight. It is generally easier for a witness to provide accurate information with regard to this item if they are allowed to view different-sized individuals for comparison. Because of internal factors, such as fear, witnesses generally perceive suspects to be taller and heavier than they actually are.

6. **Color of Hair and Eyes.** Typically, witnesses cannot state the color of eyes and/or hair with precision. However, general impressions are easy to obtain. Further, the suspect may have a distinctive hair color or style that may be noted.

7. **Complexion.** Description should include skin tone (pale, ruddy, fair, flushed, dark, etc.) and apparent skin marks, such as scars, acne, birthmarks, and burns.

8. **Miscellaneous Data.** These data include facial hair, style and length of hair and sideburns, limps, condition and absence of teeth, tattoos, speech mannerisms, or any factor tending to personalize the suspect.

9. **Clothing.** Many witnesses perceive clothing details more accurately than the suspect's features. The officer should not ask the general question, "Can you describe the suspect's clothing?" Rather, each basic clothing item from head to foot should be systematically covered.

10. **Objects Worn or Carried.** It should be ascertained whether the subject wore jewelry, such as a ring. If the suspect wore eyeglasses, the frame style, color, and shape of the lens should be noted. Any item that the suspect carried, such as a weapon or bag, should be fully described. Weapon descriptions will vary in accuracy, depending on the familiarity of the witness with weapons. Photographs or drawings illustrating the difference between a revolver and pistol and a rifle and shotgun should be shown to the witness.

In-the-Field Identification

Courts have held that allowing a witness to view a single suspect shortly after a crime is permissible. This type of identification has been allowed in the belief that a witness can best identify an offender while the memory of the person is still fresh, shortly after the crime. This form of suspect identification must be conducted in a proper manner to avoid possible constitutional violations. A suspect may be returned to the crime scene or viewed in the police agency by victims or witnesses if

1. the suspect is apprehended shortly after the offense;
2. a formal complaint, warrant, or indictment has not been issued;
3. counsel has not been appointed to represent the suspect; and
4. police officers make no suggestions, by speech or action, that the individual is suspected of any wrongdoing.

The *field identification* generally involves a victim or witness seeing the suspect at the crime scene. An arrest takes place shortly after the description is obtained from the witness, and the suspect is taken back to the scene to be viewed by the witness. In this circumstance, there is no formal lineup, in which many individuals are viewed in an effort to identify the suspect. Here, a single suspect is viewed for possible identification. Courts have not limited the required time period in regard to a viewing "shortly" after the apprehension. Generally speaking, the viewing should take place within five hours of the offense. Officers must not suggest to witnesses that the suspect may be the actual offender viewed at the scene. It is recommended that in any questionable circumstance, the field identification be substituted for the formal lineup.

Lineup Identification

The **lineup,** as a means of identifying the perpetrator of a crime, has been used for centuries. The lineup was devised to increase the accuracy of identification by circumventing the errors of suggestibility that could result in a single-suspect viewing. In a lineup, a number of persons, including the suspect, are viewed by a crime victim or witness. The witness attempts to identify one of the individuals positively as the perpetrator. If an identification by this procedure is to be admissible in court, certain legal requirements determined by the U.S. Supreme Court in the ***Wade* decision** must be met:

1. All lineups should include a reasonable number of participants, in addition to the suspect. Generally, five to nine persons including the suspect can be used in this procedure.
2. Individuals placed in the lineup must be of the same sex, race, and approximate age as the suspect. They should also be of similar body build. Any outstanding item reported to have been worn during the crime that is still being worn by the suspect (a head bandage, for example) should be worn by all participants.
3. The suspect should be randomly placed in the lineup so that position will not indicate guilt.
4. The witness should never be told which individual is suspected. Each witness should view the lineup separately.
5. The witness should identify the suspect by number. Number positions should be assigned by the police during the procedure rather than addressing the participants by name.
6. A photograph of each of the participants in the lineup should be taken to demonstrate the fairness of the procedure.
7. The investigator should prepare a lineup report indicating who was present at the lineup and who the participants were. Time and place should be stated, and a detailed description of all participants, including lineup position, should be given.[17]

A suspect has no legal right to refuse to appear in a lineup. As a result of a 1972 Supreme Court decision reversing the automatic suspect right to legal representation during a lineup if requested, only suspects who have been legally indicted are entitled to counsel at lineups. If the indicted suspect waives the right to legal representation during the lineup, a written waiver should be obtained. If, during the course of the offense, the suspect is reported to have spoken a specific word or phrase, each member of the lineup can be required to repeat that word or phrase during the viewing.

Photograph Identification

The investigator often has occasion to show a victim or witness a series of photographs in an attempt to identify the perpetrator. This procedure is typically carried out when a specific offender is suspected but is not in custody. Although the Supreme Court held in *United States v. Ash* (1973) that a suspect has no right to have an attorney present during a photographic viewing, it is essential that the same regard for fairness demonstrated during a lineup be present during a photographic viewing. Photographic displays can be conducted at the police agency or at the home of the victim or witness. A photograph of the suspect is displayed along with photographs of other individuals. All photographs must be similar in shape, color, and subject matter. There should be at least ten photographs, including the suspect's photo (Figure 17.8). Witnesses should be shown the photos when they are not in the presence of other witnesses.

When a witness makes an identification, he or she should mark the photo in some identifying manner. All photographs should then be retained for possible court examination. At no time during the photo viewing should the officer make any suggestion, through speech or action, that a picture of the suspect will be seen. After the arrest of the suspect, a formal lineup should be held to confirm the photo identification.

Photo/Voice Identification.   The Nassau County (New York) Police Department has developed a unique and innovative method of suspect identification. If an individual suspected of having committed one of 30 designated major crimes is apprehended, identification data in the form of photographs and speech are added to the department's "Talking Rogues' Gallery." The arrested suspect is photographed full length in color and requested to state name, address, place of birth, age, date of birth, and height. Signs are posted to help the suspect remember the information to be given. The suspect's voice is recorded directly onto a sound/slide frame that will enclose the full-length photograph.

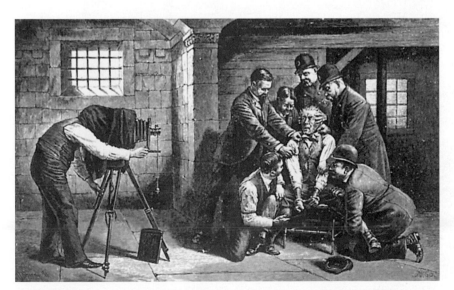

FIGURE 17.8   An early attempt at capturing a suspect's likeness through photography. Criminals tried to distort their facial features to avoid a realistic photograph. Here six police officers "assist" the suspect in sitting still. *(Source: New York Public Library.)*

A victim or witness who has reported having seen or heard the suspect is requested to participate in the sight/sound identification process. A specific room in the agency is set aside for this purpose. The identification room is equipped with a floor-to-ceiling projection screen, projection equipment, loudspeakers, and slide storage containers. The witness actually controls the viewing by operating a remote control unit of the slide projector. Each suspect's slide is projected full length in front of the witness and "speaks" the standard phrases recorded previously.

The Rogues' Gallery is now fully computerized (Figure 17.9). Arresting officers fill out coded physical description cards at the time of apprehension, filing the information in a computer. Consequently, when a witness provides a physical description of a suspect, the computer can provide a listing of sound/slide frames that correlate with the description according to a prescribed formula. There are more than 80,000 slides in the Nassau County Rogues' Gallery. Officers have found this method of identification to be far superior to the traditional photograph display method. Since the witness controls the rate of speed of the viewing, interest and attention are maintained for longer periods. The number of positive identifications has increased dramatically through use of the system. The realism of the color, full-length photo, combined with the suspect's actual speech, is more likely to result in a reliable identification by the witness than other less realistic techniques.[18]

Police Artist

Verbal descriptions are generally very difficult to visualize mentally unless the witness is a skilled observer who can relate information effectively and without distortion. For this reason, the police artist has long been relied upon to convert verbal descriptions to realistic images. Furthermore, the

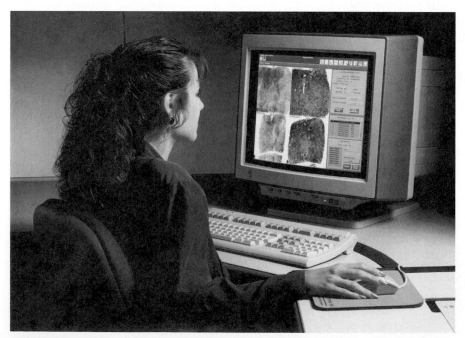

FIGURE 17.9   Computer programs allow law enforcement personnel to view multiple evidence items at one time in addition to assisting victims and witnesses in viewing of multiple suspect photos. *(Source: Printrak International, Anaheim, California.)*

perpetrator of a particular crime may never have been arrested before. Thus, efforts to identify that suspect through photographic displays will be futile.

More than 100 police artists are currently working in the United States.[19] To produce a realistic drawing of the offender, both artistic skill and good interviewing ability are necessary. The artist must be able to ask the right questions in such a way as to elicit the information required to produce a recognizable likeness. A four-step process is usually followed. Initially, the artist engages the witness in light conversation, putting the witness at ease to recall events without undue stress. Second, the artist creates a basic sketch, indicating general shapes—skull, hair, ears, and configuration of the cheeks. Then, guided by the witness, features and shading are added. Finally, finishing refinements are made, giving the face a lifelike appearance and expression. The entire process is a slow one, often taking many hours, as the work is detailed and necessarily precise. Many of the most realistic sketches have been guided by child witnesses. Children often have a keen eye for detail and are less prejudiced than adult witnesses in the way in which they view an object. The police-artist process is generally regarded as the most accurate method of likeness reconstruction.

Mechanical and Computerized Identification Aids

Various devices are currently being used in police agencies to mechanically produce a likeness of a suspect through witness descriptions. For example, the *Identi-Kit*, developed by a retired police official more than 20 years ago, is widely used by hundreds of agencies. The kit consists of more than 500 acetate overlays of hairlines, eyes, noses, chins, eyebrows, scars, beards, and many other identifying features. These are superimposed, one at a time, to create a composite drawing that resembles the suspect (see Figure 17.10). Each overlay has an individual number, allowing one investigator to telegraph or phone the entire code for an image to another investigator. The likeness of the suspect can then be assembled by the recipient of the code without waiting for the composite to arrive by mail.

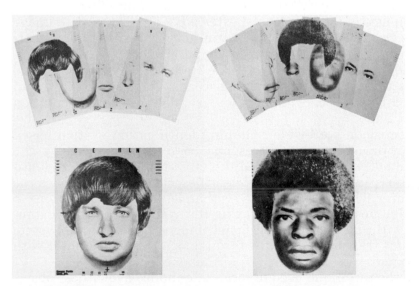

FIGURE 17.10 By superimposing various overlays, realistic images of two suspects are created. *(Source: Identi-Kit Company.)*

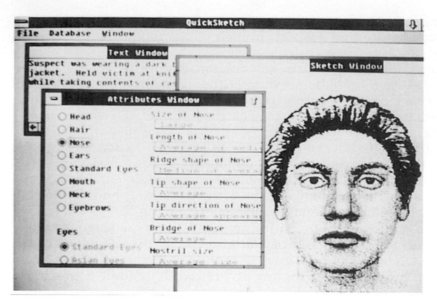

FIGURE 17.11 A computer-generated suspect likeness produced by software containing thousands of facial features. *(Source: Visatex Corporation, Campbell, California.)*

Another mechanical identification aid is the Mimic Image Compositor. This is a special projector, with the characteristic parts of the human face stored on 35mm filmstrips. There are six films in all, one for each major component of the face. The filmstrips are superimposed and projected on a life-sized screen contained at the front of the unit. When the desired composite image has been constructed through witness or victim questioning, photographic prints can be made via an internal camera system (see Figure 17.11). As with the Identi-Kit, the Mimic Image is coded by feature for communication among agencies having similar equipment.

Many larger police agencies are switching their victim/witness identification systems to computer programs utilizing special software. **Computer-aided identification** uses software that stores more than 100,000 different predesigned images of facial features. After a generally accurate image of the suspect has been produced by the victim or witness, further details are added by key commands or by use of a computer mouse. When the finished image is ready for reproduction, it can be electronically composed and printed by dot-matrix printers in a matter of seconds. The printed image can then be reproduced by photocopying or photographed for wide-circulation distribution.[20]

A rapid-transmission statewide criminal identification system based upon computerization of facial features has been implemented by the Wisconsin Department of Justice. Termed the OIC System (Optical Identification of Characteristics), the computer identifies, classifies, and codes the various facial features. The system uses more than 350 facial illustrations to portray a suspect likeness. Each agency using the system has its own standardized manual with uniformly coded facial images. This unique system allows instantaneous transmission of the facial image to any computer with the proper hookup.[21]

Regardless of the technique used to recall or enhance eyewitness observations, great caution must continually be employed by the investigator. There is ample evidence that eyewitness identification is highly fallible and that eyewitness confidence is a poor indicator of observational accuracy. Mistaken eyewitness identification is the leading cause of wrongful conviction. One study demonstrated that in 90 percent of such cases, mistaken witness or victim identification played the primary role in the miscarriage of justice. Faulty eyewitness identification is linked to three problem areas: poor encoding, faulty memory, and officer-generated procedural errors. Poor encoding occurs when external factors such as weather, poor lighting, distance, or other external conditions interfere with the perception process. Research continues to demonstrate the inherent faultiness of human memory. There appears to be a natural tendency for remembered events to be incomplete, with blanks filled in from other sources not present or perceived during the criminal event. Newspaper accounts, statements from other witnesses, and past memories all can be used to create a false memory. While poor encoding and faulty memory are serious obstacles to accurate eyewitness observation, improper information-gathering techniques used by the police are the most serious and are easily preventable.

When investigators conduct lineups and use photo displays, they must use continuous care not to suggest identification to the witness or victim. Witnesses will often observe the officer's body language during such procedures, searching for nonverbal clues as to which subject in the lineup or photo display is indeed the perpetrator. Or they may assume that the suspect is in a photo array or lineup and then feel a sense of obligation to pick a likely individual although they are far from being certain. Many studies show that such false identifications can be reduced if investigators make a point of explaining to witnesses that the suspect may not even be in the lineup or photo array. To further reduce the possibility of transmitting nonverbal clues to victims and witnesses, the office conducting the identification session should not know the suspect.

Face Recognition Technology

Rapid suspect identification linked to computer databases through closed-circuit television is now a reality through **face recognition technology**. The ability to scan a crowd of faces while computers continuously compare facial characteristics to known or wanted criminals was truly science fiction only a few years ago. Such technology was originally developed to secure access and document control in government facilities but is now being rapidly adopted by police agencies throughout the United States. As closed-circuit television captures an image of a person's face, computer software then analyzes contours and various bone structures, converting the image into a code. The digitized code is then compared to a database of suspects, with automatic notification given when a match is made (see Figure 17.12).

This form of criminal identification was first tested in 1997 in several English cities. After noting over 30 percent reductions in serious felony crime within the test communities, the technology grew in popularity and practice throughout England. In 2001, Tampa, Florida, became the first American city to use the system for routine surveillance purposes, digitally dissecting facial features of people in a popular nightlife district and comparing their faces to over 1,000 photos of known felons and fugitives. To some, this form of criminal identification can be alarming as a possible violation of one's right to privacy. Yet no specific court challenge to date has declared the practice unconstitutional. While the Supreme Court did recently rule that police must obtain a search warrant before scanning a home with an infrared camera, there is no expectation of privacy when an individual knowingly exposes himself to public view.[22]

FACIAL SURVEILLANCE
FaceIt Face Recognition Technology

FIGURE 17.12   Facial recognition technology has great potential to deter serious crimes and bring about fugitive apprehensions. *(Source: Identix Corporation.)*

Criminal identification technology of this kind also has wider application than just facial recognition. License plate numbers can be scanned and compared through databases, and, given the nation's terrorism concerns, the system could be utilized at border crossings, airports, and other points of entry. The system can also be designed to notify police when a specific type of wanted automobile make or model is observed by unmanned cameras. The same could be accomplished for boats, trucks, bikes, or any type of vehicle. Facial scanning can also be used in the field by detectives and patrol officers as they interact with individual suspects. Digital cameras installed in police vehicles allow officers to photograph offenders on the street. The cameras are then placed in a docking station within the car, and the facial image is transmitted through a wireless communication to a subject image database. The photo is then compared to previous arrest photos using the agency's face cognition system to determine true name, previous arrest history, current warrants, and other important information. However, the present technology is not without its limitations. Suspects may be able to deceive the computer comparison through various disguises or by wearing large or very dark sunglasses that obscure the eyes. Since the characteristics of the eyes are very important for a successful match, an identification could be prevented. Also, camera angles that are less than a straight viewing or poor illumination could produce disappointing results or false identifications. Despite such potential problems, facial recognition technology has resulted in numerous arrests and will no doubt be used with increasing frequency by the investigator.

Facial recognition technology—or any other new means of criminal identification that produces information destined to be used in court—must meet the necessary standards set forth in the Daubert Rule. Replacing the outdated "general acceptance" standard originally defined in *Fry v. United States* (1923), the Supreme Court in *Daubert v. Merrell Dow Pharmaceuticals* (1993) set forth criteria under which new forms of scientific discovery could be admitted as evidence in criminal trials. The Daubert Rule criteria include five factors that are reviewed by the judge to determine the admissibility of expert testimony pertaining to a new or emerging area of science: (1) Has the scientific theory been tested? (2) Has it been subject to peer review and publication? (3) Does it have a known error rate? (4) Does the theory have widespread acceptance? (5) Does the scientific theory have operating standards?

▲ SUMMARY

The identification of criminal suspects is highly pertinent to successful case solution. Efforts in identification are made in cases of both known and unknown perpetrators. When a suspect is unknown, identification efforts focus on trace evidence and/or eyewitness. In investigations of cases in which identity is known, efforts are focused on placing the suspect at the scene or confirming the claimed identity.

The most reliable and common means of identification through physiological trace evidence is by fingerprint. The locating of latent fingerprints belonging to suspects is highly significant, for such prints can be matched to previously obtained prints for positive identification. Latent prints can be located through various methods. The traditional and oldest locating method involves the use of powders to make perspiration traces visible. The latent prints are then photographed and transferred by tape for permanent storage. Chemical means of print location have generally proven superior to the traditional powder method. Chemical methods include the use of iodine fuming, ninhydrin, and the newer techniques of cyanoacrylate fuming and laser light resolution. The widespread use of automated fingerprint identification has greatly increased the probability of matching crime scene latents with prints of known identity. Voiceprint technology for identification purposes is not as commonly used as fingerprinting. Unlike fingerprint evidence, voice spectrographs have not been successfully introduced as evidence in all courts.

Identification by eyewitness includes in-the-field and lineup procedures. In-the-field identifications are generally conducted prior to the filing of formal charges, whereas lineups are typically held after indictment. Suspect identification may also be accomplished by displaying a photographic series to a witness. As with all forms of suspect identification, the investigator must make every effort to ensure fairness in regard to similarity of the suspect when presenting photos to be viewed by a witness.

In investigations in which the identity of the suspect is completely unknown, victims and witnesses can often provide sufficient verbal description to create an accurate likeness of the perpetrator. Although many believe the police-artist method to be superior, mechanical and computer-aided technologies are also commonly used in discovering a suspect's identity.

■ EXERCISES

1. Obtain the fingerprints of several class members. Using the pattern information given in this chapter, classify each fingerprint as either a loop, a whorl, or an arch.
2. Prepare a research paper on the history of personal identification. Determine how various early civilizations attempted to identify criminals.

RELEVANT WEB SITES

http://members.cox.net/bnminalpine/history.htm

Comprehensive history and time line of fingerprinting around the world and in the United States. Link explains the Henry fingerprint classification system.

http://www.biometrics-101.com/face-recognition.htm

Industry site that explains the principles of biometric face recognition technology. Contains links to biometric recognition sites dealing with the face, iris and retina, hand, and fingerprint recognition methodologies, among others.

The Investigator in Court

KEY TERMS

accusatorial procedure
appeal
cross-examination
direct examination
first arraignment
grand jury

indictment
nolo contendere
preliminary hearing
pretrial conference
pretrial preparation
testimony

LEARNING OBJECTIVES

1. to understand the purposes and procedures of criminal trials;
2. to appreciate the importance of police testimony during a criminal trial;
3. to appreciate the importance of pretrial preparation;
4. to be aware of those aspects of police testimony that are likely to receive special scrutiny by defense and prosecuting attorneys during cross-examination; and
5. to be familiar with the manner in which investigators should conduct themselves while testifying.

INTRODUCTION

Police investigators are absolutely essential to the U.S. judicial criminal proceeding. Our system of determining truth is known as the **accusatorial procedure**, in which innocence is assumed until properly proven otherwise. Police investigators assist the court by providing information that can help a judge or jury to make a just determination of innocence or guilt. The police provide courtroom testimony in all criminal cases in which the suspect pleads not guilty. Even when the suspect pleads guilty and avoids the trial, police testimony is generally given in the pretrial hearings. Furthermore, the officer may give testimony in civil trials that often result from initial criminal contacts.

U.S. jurisprudence places great importance on the perceptions of the police officer: Police testimony is often the determining factor in reaching a verdict. Although the importance of police testimony during a trial cannot be overstated, the investigator also testifies in pretrial proceedings. All investigators must be familiar with the judicial process, as their testimony may be required at any point from the arrest to the formal trial.

The role of the prosecutor is very important throughout all phases of the trial process. The prosecutor and criminal investigator work as a team to ensure the most professional effort possible in presenting the state's case to the judge or jury. Because investigators and prosecutors work closely during a trial, they should meet frequently before actual cases are presented to the court. The prosecutor's office should be accessible to police at all times and a specific contact person appointed to whom police can direct any inquiries.[1]

NATURE OF CRIMINAL PROCEEDINGS

Criminal law and procedure may be thought of as a body of practices or rules designed to protect the accused and the interests of society. The formal judicial process is set into motion following the apprehension of the suspect. Actually, before the first formal judicial hearing, a decision to proceed with prosecution must be reached by the prosecuting attorney. In reaching this decision, the prosecutor informally confers with the investigator and discusses the details of the case. The prosecutor may also review official police documents that have been completed at that time. Upon the arrest of a criminal suspect, a **first arraignment** and **preliminary hearing** before a judicial officer follow as soon as it is practical. All states have various statutory requirements as to the time of the initial judicial appearance.

The first arraignment is typically a short hearing in which the essential facts are presented to the court and generally read to the defendant. The judge informs the accused of his or her legal rights, fixes bail, and sets a date for the preliminary hearing. Depending upon the specific state system, a police officer may briefly testify or offer no testimony at this time. Following the initial appearance of the defendant, a formal accusation of the offense is presented in the form of an *information* or an **indictment**. The information document form of accusation is more common than the grand jury indictment. Both formalize the criminal procedure by determining that the case merits continued judicial review.

The historical grand jury indictment involves presentation of the facts of the case, statute violation, and witness testimony by the prosecutor to the grand jury. A **grand jury** is composed of citizens who vote to either indict the suspect or to dismiss the case. Informations have streamlined the time-consuming grand jury process by allowing the prosecutor to file a formal paper in which the suspect is indicted without the intervention of the grand jury. Following the accusatorial stage, a second arraignment is conducted to hear the defendant's plea. The defendant may enter any one of the following before the court: *guilty, not guilty*, or **nolo contendere**. Or the defendant may choose to *stand mute*. Only the plea of guilty will bypass the trial procedure. However, the court has the option of refusing this plea and entering an automatic not guilty plea. A plea of nolo contendere carries the implication of guilt from a legal standpoint but is not a formal admission of guilt. Many defendants use this plea to avoid admissions of guilt being used against them in subsequent civil proceedings. Not all states, however, allow a plea of nolo contendere in a criminal case. Indiana, for example, allows the defendant to plead only guilty or not guilty. If the defendant stands mute by entering no plea, the court will automatically enter a plea of not guilty to determine justice. Finally, a not guilty plea can be entered based upon various defenses, such as insanity, which will be ruled upon by the judge. A not guilty plea based upon innocence sets in motion the formal trial procedure.

Trial Procedures

Although criminal investigators may testify during the various pretrial hearings, their primary testimony will be heard during the formal trial. The defendant has the right to either a court or jury trial. In a *court trial*, the judge renders a verdict of guilt or innocence besides performing other duties. In a *jury trial*, which is commonly requested in criminal pleas of not guilty, a group of people (normally 12) hears the facts and determines guilt or innocence. Following the selection of a jury, agreeable to both the defense and the prosecution, *opening statements* are normally given—first by the prosecuting attorney and then by the defense attorney. Many defense attorneys waive the right of making an opening statement to avoid alerting the prosecution to the anticipated defense strategy. Police testimony is not offered during opening statements. Witnesses for the prosecution are then called and questioned by the prosecuting attorney in **direct examination**. Police officers are typically essential to this phase of the prosecution's case since they frequently provide eyewitness information or information supportive to the testimony of other witnesses.

Following the direct examination of the witnesses by the prosecuting attorney, the defense attorney generally elects to engage in cross-examination of the prosecution witnesses. **Cross-examination** reexamines information revealed during the direct questioning, enabling the defense attorney to challenge a witness's veracity and accuracy. Following the cross-examination, the prosecution and defense may elect to reexamine a witness again.

After the prosecution has presented its side of the case, the defense may elect to formally enter a *motion for acquittal*. The motion is generally based on the grounds of insufficient evidence to demonstrate guilt. If the judge agrees, the trial will be immediately concluded, with the case being dismissed and the defendant released. If motions to dismiss the trial are denied, as they are in the majority of cases, the defense may then allow the case to go to the jury at that time with the hope that they will doubt the defendant's guilt, or the attorney may present evidence on behalf of the defendant to create such a doubt. If the attorney elects to present evidence, witnesses will be called for direct and cross-examination, as were the prosecution witnesses.

After the defense rests, both the prosecution and the defense may engage in the *rebuttal phase* of the trial. During rebuttal arguments, the attorneys present new evidence and/or additional witnesses. Both sides finally summarize their efforts in the form of *closing arguments* to the jury. Each presents the most persuasive argument possible and reviews points of the trial that are favorable for their respective positions. After closing arguments, the focus of the trial shifts to the jury.

The judge now performs a crucial phase of the trial process by *instructing the jury*. Legal principles, statute definitions, and definitions of judicial terms are typically explained to the jury.[2] The jury then attempts to reach a verdict through careful deliberation of the facts and testimony they have heard during the course of the trial. A verdict of guilty or not guilty must be reached on an offense. If the jury cannot agree on a verdict, it is known as a *hung jury*. In this case, a mistrial must be declared by the judge and the trial restarted with a new jury. If the jury turns in a verdict of not guilty, the defendant is released with the charges officially dismissed by the court. A guilty verdict requires a judgment and subsequent sentencing by the judge. Throughout the entire trial procedure, the defense has the option to enter various motions, which generally seek to dismiss the charges or institute a new trial. Furthermore, if a defendant is found guilty and sentenced, an **appeal** may be filed and presented before an appellate court.

Police testimony is very important throughout the trial process in that a jury will generally give an officer's testimony more credence than that of a lay or ordinary witness. In addition, the manner in which an investigator testifies may influence the prosecution and defense strategies to a considerable degree at many points throughout the trial. Proper courtroom testimony results from a combination of common sense, training and education, and respect for the U.S. accusatorial system.

Pretrial Preparation

Preparation for the trial should begin from the moment of the crime's discovery and continue right up until actual courtroom testimony begins. Actually, the entire police investigation of an offense can be thought of as preparation for trial. If officers viewed the trial rather than the arrest as the natural conclusion of their efforts, there would be a greater number of successful prosecutions. **Pretrial preparations** lay the foundation for sound courtroom testimony.

Investigators are notified by the prosecutor's office that a specific time and date have been set for the trial of an arrested person. In some cases, the officer may have a fresh recall of the particular circumstances surrounding the case; in others, only the most general of facts are recalled. Accordingly, upon receipt of the prosecutor's notification, most officers initiate a review of the case in question. If field notes are still available, they will be reviewed, as will all formal reports of the investigation. This review of pertinent materials is preparatory to the next pretrial step—the pretrial conference.

Pretrial Conference.   A **pretrial conference** is an informal meeting between one or more investigators and the attorney who will represent the state in the trial. The purpose of the conference is to exchange information, answer questions, help the prosecuting attorney decide whether to proceed with the case, and prepare the officers for their trial testimony. Most prosecuting attorneys have copies of the investigator's formal reports, yet the officer should bring all pertinent reports to the conference. The prosecutor will question the investigator closely concerning all matters in need of clarification.

Frequently, the prosecutor knows from past experience that some aspect of the officer's report is "sketchy"; most likely the defense will focus on that aspect during cross-examination to undermine the officer's testimony. Some common important aspects that are often reported in insufficient detail are the following:

1. **Initial Probable Cause:** Why did the officer suspect this particular individual of committing a crime? Was there sufficient probable cause to search the suspect and/or suspect's vehicle? Was there sufficient probable cause to detain or arrest the suspect?
2. **Constitutional Protections:** Was the suspect afforded constitutional rights in a complete and legal manner? At what point during the investigation did officers advise the suspect of the Miranda warnings? Did the suspect request that the interview cease, or request to see an attorney?
3. **Evidence Gathering:** Was evidence of investigative importance gathered in a proper manner? Was a proper chain of custody observed from the discovery of the evidence to its placement in the evidence room? Was evidence marked in a proper manner? Was it tested by experts when applicable?

If the prosecutor notes that any of the above points in the officer's report are unclear, the officer will be questioned to clarify them. If the prosecutor does not question the officer in this manner, the defense attorney will do so in open court, with the officer unprepared. Thus, complete and truthful answers must be given during the pretrial conference. Pretrial conferences are often attended by many officers at the same time. Each investigator should pay attention to the others to understand the complete police investigation. Obviously, however, an officer should never attempt to alter testimony to corroborate the perceptions of another.

The prosecutor will interview and confer with witnesses other than the police during the pretrial conference. All individuals who will be presented as witnesses for the state will be questioned by the prosecutor. Some witnesses may resent prosecution questioning since they have previously been questioned by the police. However, it is the responsibility of the prosecutor to judge witnesses in terms of their credibility and general ability to testify.

Testifying in Court

Before assuming the witness stand to offer **testimony** into the record, the investigator must have a knowledge of the rules governing testimony. Only testimony that is *relevant, material*, and *competent* will be allowed into evidence. Either the defense counsel or the judge may object to testimony that fails to conform to any one of the three categories. Furthermore, a witness generally must restrict conversation to answering questions from the prosecution or the defense.

Depending on the wishes of the defense attorney, the police witness may be allowed to sit in the courtroom during the entire proceeding or be present only to testify. Defense attorneys often request that investigators not listen to other witnesses (particularly fellow police officers) in an effort to reveal contradictions in testimony concerning a common event.

The law allows a witness to review documents (notes, reports, and other materials) during testimony if the materials were written during the time to which they pertain. However, if an investigator produces and refers to such writing during the proceeding, the defense counsel may examine the witness concerning the writing. Additionally, the defense has the legal right to introduce into evidence any portion of the notes that may be pertinent to the testimony of the witness.

Prior to actually testifying, the officer must be prepared, both psychologically and physically, for the witness stand. All witnesses, police officers included, are nervous to some degree at the prospect of courtroom testimony. The nervousness, at least in part, stems from knowing that the case may hinge on the testimony offered. Further, the often overly dramatic media presentations of the "grueling cross-examination" instill unjustified nervousness and fear in many witnesses.

Creating a Favorable Impression. Personal appearance is a very important factor regarding how the officer will be perceived in terms of credibility and reliability. The investigator's appearance should be properly professional and as inoffensive as possible. Extreme clothing styles, hairstyles, or other details of personal grooming may offend a biased member of the jury. The witness chair is not the place to make a personal social statement.

Upon entering the courtroom, the officer should not converse with others (with the exception of the prosecutor) in reference to the testimony about to be given. In particular, conversation with the defense attorney or any witnesses testifying for the defense should be avoided. Jury members typically observe and study police witnesses even before they actually testify. Consequently, officers in view of the jury should present a professional image by being attentive to the proceedings. Carrying on a conversation with other officers while court is in session or while other witnesses are testifying is offensive to the jury.

There is disagreement among prosecutors as to the proper attire of the officer. A police uniform may be advantageous in that some members of the jury may be favorably impressed by the authority associated with it. Other jurors, however, may be automatically hostile to the uniform or feel that the officer has worn his uniform in order to "show off" the professional position. Accordingly, each prosecutor must determine the proper dress of the officer, which may vary from case to case. Whether in uniform or not, the apparel should be neat and clean.

First impressions are important in many situations, and the courtroom is no exception. Upon approaching the stand and taking the oath, the officer will have all the attention of the jury for the first time. Therefore, the officer should strive to appear calm and professional in taking the oath and initially occupying the witness chair.

On the Witness Stand. If the officer has reviewed the case, conferred with the prosecutor, and otherwise made thorough preparations, testifying should be a satisfying experience. Thorough preparation inspires a confident attitude—there are few surprises that can "shake" the prepared investigator. Police testimony in an open courtroom is a necessary and proper test of our system of criminal justice. The prescribed manner in which attorneys question witnesses is designed to ensure fairness. Thus, cross-examination by the defense attorney should not be viewed as a personal attack on the testifying officer.

The investigator will initially be questioned by the prosecution. As a result of the pretrial conference and the officer's experience, the prosecutor's questions should come as no surprise. In short, the officer will be questioned as to personal knowledge about the facts of the case. During direct examination, a serious, interested attitude should be maintained. Even if the investigator recognizes a question before the prosecutor has finished stating it, the officer should not answer so quickly as to create the impression of a staged arrangement between prosecutor and witness. Questions should be answered in a manner that is respectful to the attorneys yet firm and direct. During direct examination, defense counsel may object during a question from the prosecution or during an answer by the officer. When an objection is raised, the officer should cease to speak and wait for the judge to rule on the objection. Answers should be stated in a clear, firm voice. Slang expressions, humor, or nonverbal affirmations or denials, such as by head movements, should always be avoided. In addition, investigators should provide as much relevant detail during their testimony as possible. Various research studies have demonstrated that when eyewitness testimony conflicts, the testimony that provides the most detail is perceived to be the most credible by jury members.[3]

When the prosecuting attorney finishes direct examination, the defense will have an opportunity to cross-examine the officer. The television image of the abrasive, browbeating defense attorney is generally very overstated. Although some defense attorneys may engage in theatrics to increase the officer's nervousness, most defense attorneys are aware that a jury will be offended by attempts to browbeat a witness and that jurors will sympathize with witnesses subjected to this type of questioning. It is perfectly proper and understandable strategy, however, for defense attorneys to attempt to discredit witnesses who are effective in demonstrating a defendant's guilt. Since investigators are often important witnesses for the prosecution, they can expect vigorous defense cross-examination.

The defense attorney systematically attempts to discredit either the overall credibility of the witness or specific information revealed during direct examination. Some attorneys focus on the officer personally, some on statements made by the officer. Personal attacks on the officer are rarely successful; in fact, they are counterproductive. By insulting or verbally abusing the officer, the defense attorney damages his or her credibility rather than the officer's. Further, when the cross-examination takes this form, the prosecution will object, reinforcing the improper activities of the defense counsel in the minds of the jurors. The tactic of striving to discredit previous statements of the officer is much more common. Previous statements may be twisted around or taken out of context in an attempt to cast doubt on their authenticity. Or other information that conflicts with the officer's may be introduced. Questions may be fired very rapidly to cause the officer to falter in answering. Again, if the investigator is thoroughly prepared for the trial, informational attacks usually will be unsuccessful. However, an officer who is ill-prepared or lacking in self-confidence can often be discredited by a skillful defense attorney.

It must be remembered that the defense attorney has carefully noted the exact answers given by the officer during direct testimony. If, during direct examination, the officer is unsure as to the accuracy of certain information and attempts to "bluff" with a seemingly precise response, the officer is very vulnerable to being discredited. Officers sometimes lose sight of the fact that the defense has reviewed all police reports pertinent to the case. Additionally, some defense attorneys conduct their own detailed investigations into the circumstances of the event in question. Accordingly, they often know all the official facts and are in the advantageous position of having questioned other police officers as to the same event. For these reasons, when the answer to a given question is not known, the officer should state so. Also, questions should be answered with a yes or no response; answers should not give more information than is being called for. Keeping in mind that the jury is closely observing the investigator during cross-examination, a polite, professional demeanor must be maintained at all times. Even if it seems that a questioning technique is abusive or that a particular question is improper, the investigator should never refuse to answer or ask the judge to censure the defense. These are the responsibilities of the prosecuting attorney, who is a much better judge of legally improper questions. If the investigator is called as a witness, the following can be considered a basic summary of considerations in testifying before a judge or jury:

1. Research the nature of the hearing. Not all subpoenas specify the type of judicial hearing. It could be a trial, a deposition, a grand jury appearance, or a preliminary hearing, among others. Also, there may be no indication as to whether the hearing is a civil or a criminal case. Knowing the type of hearing is very significant, as differing rules of evidence and varying standards of proof can apply.

2. Thoroughly review all case reports and notes and meet with the prosecutor prior to giving testimony. Reviewing reports will refresh memory and give confidence to testimony. The prosecutor can provide insight as to the expected questioning style of defense counsel, review evidence exhibits, and review the officer's testimony.

3. Dress appropriately. Juror research demonstrates that for males, the most credible witnesses dress in a dark conservative suit and tie, with a white shirt. Females should choose business suits with a conservative length and style, avoiding loud colors and high-heeled or open-toed shoes. Refrain from testifying in uniform when possible, as juror perceptions are generally more receptive and free from stereotyping and prejudice when officers are in business suits.

4. Speak clearly and loudly. It is important that every juror and the judge can hear the testimony.

5. Assume proper body positioning. Sit straight but comfortably. Avoid displaying distracting personal habits and maintain eye contact with the questioner. When answering questions, turn and deliver responses directly to the jury and/or judge.

6. Be calm. Although testifying can test one's nerves, opposing attorneys often try to discredit or confuse nervous witnesses.

7. Testify from memory if possible. This does not mean memorizing, but it is usually better not to use notes unless necessary. Research indicates that law enforcement officers are perceived to be more credible if appearing to know facts without referring to notes.

8. Listen to the question before answering. Do not anticipate the question. Rather, the officer should wait for the entire question before answering and answer only the question asked.

9. Do not guess or speculate. If you do not know the answer, say so.

10. Be yourself. A witness's credibility is enhanced when one does not attempt to act.

11. Don't argue. Arguing may portray the witness as arrogant or antagonistic, damaging the state's case and reducing the overall credibility of the testifier.[4]

In answering questions, the attention of the officer should alternate between the defense and the jury in an effort to gain the jurors' attention and respect. Ideally, following the cross-examination, the jury should have the impression that a responsible, composed police investigator has just testified. By maintaining composure under the pressure of vigorous cross-examination, the officer will have successfully completed the final responsibility in the investigative process from crime scene to courtroom.

▲ SUMMARY

Criminal investigators must be as proficient in the courtroom as they are at the crime scene. Should a defendant elect to plead not guilty and exercise the right to trial, the participation and necessary testimony of the investigator will generally be required. Judicial criminal proceedings place the burden of proof on the government to demonstrate a defendant's guilt beyond a reasonable doubt. The detailed testimony of the investigator will often be the determining factor in establishing guilt or innocence. To testify competently during a criminal trial, law enforcement officers must be fully prepared to take the witness stand.

Trial preparation actually begins when the police first become aware of a criminal offense and does not end until the conclusion of the trial. Because virtually any observation or communication may become the source of later courtroom testimony, all significant communications should be documented and retained. Prior to any preliminary hearings or the trial, the investigator and prosecutor should confer to prepare the state's case. The pretrial conference is very important because it is at this time that the prosecuting attorney and police develop an overall trial strategy. In addition, information is exchanged, questions are answered, and individual investigators are prepared for their testimony during the conference.

Courtroom testimony must be given in a professional manner, as most jury members give close attention and attach considerable credibility to the statements of law enforcement witnesses. Investigative testimony must be given precisely and courteously, with full details revealed when properly called forth by either prosecutor or defense counsel. As it is the professional duty of the defense attorney to discredit the state's case, the investigator should expect rigorous questioning during cross-examination.

Regardless of how professionally evidence has been located and analyzed or how thoroughly suspects have been interviewed, contested criminal cases will not be successfully terminated unless the investigator's courtroom responsibilities are met.

■ EXERCISES

1. Prepare a research paper tracing the historical origins of U.S. criminal judicial procedure.
2. Observe several criminal trials in your community. Note the judicial procedures followed by both the defense and the prosecution. Observe the manner in which police officers testify during a trial. Evaluate such testimony in accordance with the principles presented in this chapter.

● RELEVANT WEB SITES

http://www.lasvegasnevada.gov/

A list of suggestions of value detailing the proper manner of testifying in criminal and civil trials. Of use to both law enforcement officers and citizen witnesses.

http://www.childtrauma.org/ctamaterials/testifying.asp

Comprehensive site maintained by the Child Trauma Academy to educate victims, witnesses, officers, and experts on the unique testimonial challenges often required for cases involving children.

http://www.usdoj.gov/usao/

Developed by the U.S. Department of Justice, this site details 21 essential tips for testifying in federal trials that are also directly applicable to state proceedings.

The Future of Criminal Investigation

KEY TERMS

biometrics
career criminal
cold-case squad
crime scene investigator
digital evidence
explosive tagging
futures research

geographic information system
geographic profiling
investigative research
iris recognition technology
major offense bureau
multiagency unit
virtual reality

LEARNING OBJECTIVES

1. to be aware of past and present influences on today's criminal investigator;
2. to be able to cite recent research findings that may have a bearing on the future status of the investigator;
3. to understand the workings and significance of the multiagency investigation unit;
4. to be able to explain the operations and potential of the major offense bureau;
5. to appreciate the importance of the increase in specialized evidence processing;
6. to understand the significance of investigative flexibility and increased patrol/detective communication;
7. to understand the necessity for the humanistic approach to the successful future of criminal investigation; and
8. to be able to define those areas of forensic science research that have the potential to facilitate the investigative process.

INTRODUCTION

Criminal investigation today is a nearly equal blend of old concepts and relatively new ones. Concepts such as the independent function of the plainclothes officer and heavy reliance upon informants have changed little for more than 100 years. Yet the investigator of the past would be truly baffled by today's emphasis on the crime scene, criminalistics, psychology, and automated data processing systems. Today's investigative officer is both guided and restrained by tradition—and, at the same time, compelled by modern trends in the field and technology toward change.

In projecting trends for the future, one must consider past occurrences and present developments. The past seems to indicate that change in policing does not come easily, or at least it does not come without considerable cautious experimentation. The present reveals crime trends that strain the resources and ability of the investigator, while the public demands greater accountability and results from the criminal justice system.

Policing in general has undergone significant change in projecting its status as a true profession. The police have upgraded their operations, technology, management techniques, and other developmental areas. However, specific areas of policing, such as the investigative area, have been criticized by some for conserving traditional methods that are ill-suited for today's crime environment.

Investigative Efficiency

While room for improvement continues to exist, the efficiency of American criminal investigation has significantly improved from the past three decades. A study of detective efficiency contracted by the Department of Justice in the mid-1970s found that the majority of reported offenses received no more than superficial attention from investigators. Additionally, the research found that if information that uniquely identifies the suspect were not presented to the responding officer when the crime was reported, the suspect would generally not be identified. Finally, it was found that most unknown suspects who were eventually identified and arrested were apprehended by routine police procedures and that nearly half of an agency's investigative efforts could be eliminated.

The twenty-first century has seen much improvement regarding such negative findings. While large detective caseloads still demand selective time allotment, software programs now commonly review most reported crimes and advise officers regarding prioritization. Low copy DNA and other forensic techniques not available or commonly used in the 1970s are now used to greatly increase the probability of suspect identification. And as crime continues to become more specialized and high tech (as with computer crime), its solution is more resistant to routine police procedures. Accordingly, today's specialized investigative function has become more rather than less necessary today. However, one finding in the original study is timeless: the desire of victims to be officially informed as to the status of their cases.

INVESTIGATIVE CONCEPTS OF THE FUTURE

Because of the reactive nature of police work in general, law enforcement officials also tend not to be overly concerned about the future. The volume of reported crime and the natural resistance to change inherent in any government agency often slow police willingness to change. But the pace of change in the twenty-first century is so rapid that law enforcement has become increasingly innovative in attempting to develop more effective investigative techniques. Change is now so complete that many Americans cannot remember a world without cell phones, computers, faxes, and automated teller machines. As a result of expanding demands for service, far greater numbers of college-educated officers, technology, and future-oriented management, various projects have been designed to further the capabilities of the criminal investigator. The following concepts, currently in use in some agencies, show significant promise for widespread future adoption.

The Cold-Case Squad

The **cold-case squad** concept began to appear in the mid-1990s and is a direct result of the utilization of DNA processing. Investigators now realize that many unsolved cases of the past have the potential of being solved through the application of modern technology and newly developed investigative practices. Some specific types of crimes are particularly well suited for the cold-case concept. For example, one-third of all homicides in the United States are not cleared within the year they are committed. The most obvious example of the concept is applying DNA identity testing to evidence from old, unsolved crimes. A significant number of felony cases in past decades resulted in the collection of evidence bearing human trace stains. We now know such evidence can produce DNA even though it may be 40 or 50 years old. In a similar fashion, latent fingerprint evidence, which could not be matched to any particular suspect at the time, now has the potential of yielding an identification through automated fingerprint scanning of national databases. Utilizing similar rapid scanning technology, old firearm-related evidence can now be matched via the computer to guns linked to specific subjects.

While scientific, technological advances have the greatest potential for clearing former unsolved criminal investigations, newly emerging investigative techniques can also produce similar results. The application of psychological profiling techniques and linguistic analysis to previously unsolved cases are two examples of relatively new procedural techniques that can be highly successful in producing new investigative leads, if not outright identification of the perpetrator.

Before dated cases are reinvestigated, a cold-case squad must first be implemented within the agency's existing detective division. The squad will typically be staffed with volunteers who generally are experienced homicide investigators and officers who possess in-depth knowledge in forensics and psychological profiling. Prior to actually investigating cases, the cold-case unit must develop a realistic set of criteria to select cases that will receive their attention. Since not all unsolved dated felonies can be reinvestigated, criteria that are fair and realistic will result in effective case selection. Standard criteria typically focus on whether physical evidence still exists that is conducive to modern forensic technology. Also, highly important will be the current availability of witnesses and the possibility of an identifiable and living suspect. Finally, the squad will evaluate cases to determine if there is an opportunity for clearing other crimes by solving the cold investigation and if the original case was presented to a grand jury or prosecutor's office for judicial action.[1]

After various cases have been subjected to review criteria, the entire squad or a supervisor will classify the case as to its solution potential.

Cold-case squads that have heavy workloads may accept only cases judged to have "excellent" arrest potential, while those with lighter caseloads may accept only those rated as "good."

Many local, state, and federal law enforcement agencies now realize the potential of reexamining major unsolved cases of the past by assigning investigators to cold-case units. To maximize the effectiveness of such units, investigators should be assigned on a full-time basis and should methodically review past cases for their potential for successful solution.

Multiagency Investigative Units

The **multiagency unit** (MA) has proven very effective in many police jurisdictions throughout the United States. This type of investigative effort allows local city and county, state, and federal police agencies to apply their combined resources more effectively to a specific investigative problem. By consolidating their efforts, two or more agencies can establish uniform enforcement priorities, participate in undercover operations with greater success, and conduct transjurisdictional investigations. The problems connected with jurisdictional independence and desire for autonomy of some local police departments (e.g., duplication of effort, ineffective coordination, and lack of cooperation) are minimized in the MA approach.

The MA concept works well in areas with a history of cooperation among local police agencies. For example, if departments have helped each other in the past, as in the case of emergency riot control, there is typically less difficulty in creating an MA investigative unit. Multiagency units currently exist in several areas, the Kansas City Major Crime Unit and the St. Louis area Major Case Squad being two of the oldest. These units make use of the investigative skills of numerous police agencies in the greater Kansas City area upon the commission of certain key crimes. The MA investigative approach proved effective in the sniper homicides of October 2002. Numerous local, county, state, and federal agencies pooled their resources and investigative skills in reaction to ten murders and two woundings occurring in the jurisdictions of Washington, D.C., Maryland, and Virginia. Following the arrest of the two suspects, the "Sniper Task Force" eventually coordinated case management with authorities in the states of Washington, Alabama, Georgia, and Louisiana, where the suspects are accused of committing three additional murders (see Figure 19.1). Yet the largest number of MA units are directed toward narcotics enforcement. There are several hundred **multiagency narcotics units** operating in the United States.

The initial impetus for creating an MA unit typically comes from several local police chiefs and sheriffs who see its advantages in investigating specific crimes more effectively. The chiefs delegate several command officers who have administrative and planning experience to design the new unit. The second major step is to verify that such a unit is truly needed. By demonstrating that a specific or general crime problem is of sufficient magnitude to warrant the MA unit, local government officials and the general public can most often be convinced that the unit is justified.

After it has been demonstrated that an MA unit is justified for a given region, the planners must determine goals and objectives. These should be truly based on local needs. In determining specific goals and objectives, the factors that currently impede effective investigation must first be identified. Then the planners must decide which actions are needed to resolve them. Generally, the following basic objectives are considered the backbone of any MA investigative unit:

FIGURE 19.1 The successful arrest of the Washington, D.C., sniper suspects John Lee Malvo and John Allen Muhammad illustrated the importance of interagency cooperation and careful attention to ballistics evidence. The pair were accused of shooting 20 victims throughout the United States. *(Sources: Reuters/Brenden McDermid, Corbis/Bettmann, and Reuters/Jahi Chikwendiu, Corbis/Bettmann.)*

1. to allow and encourage officers assigned to the unit to pursue their investigations throughout the designated region regardless of individual city and county jurisdictions,

2. to coordinate the investigative effort of those officers not specifically assigned to the MA unit with regard to crimes that are the primary focus of the unit,

3. to solicit and obtain funds necessary to operate the unit and purchase equipment,

4. to use undercover officers in jurisdictions in which they have not been used before,

5. to focus unit officers' investigative efforts toward the apprehension of "high-level" suspects and to administrate the apprehension of other suspects by nonunit officers,

6. to establish an areawide intelligence system to actively gather information and intelligence on the unit's crime focus,

7. to provide training (formal and informal) in the crime focus area to local officers,

8. to review input from all cooperating local agencies through regular meetings of department command officers, and

9. to ensure the equal representation of all participating police agencies.

The success of the Violent Traffickers Project in Philadelphia well illustrates the effectiveness of the MA approach. Originally formed to combat widespread street-level drug dealing, the project brought together investigative personnel from the city's police department; the Pennsylvania State Police; the Philadelphia District Attorney's and U.S. Attorney's Offices; the FBI; the Drug Enforcement Administration; the Bureau of Alcohol, Tobacco and Firearms; and the Immigration and Naturalization Service. The Violent Traffickers Project has produced 441 arrests, with a conviction rate of 100 percent and seized more than $2 million in assets. Defendants are tried in federal courts, which typically give longer sentences than state courts.[2]

The MA unit is a logical means of combating the modern crime problem. Certainly, the majority of career criminals have no regard for jurisdictional boundary lines. Unfortunately, jurisdictional boundaries have often been barriers to effective criminal investigation. Although police officers have statewide authority, their true effectiveness often depends upon the willingness of other agencies to cooperate. By having representatives of many police departments working together as an investigative team, the age-old problem of obtaining free access to records, intelligence information, and informal "street knowledge" is eliminated.

The Major Offense Bureau

The **major offense bureau** (MOB) developed as a result of several significant federal research studies. The studies concluded that a relatively small number of offenders are responsible for a disproportionate number of serious crimes. For example, surveys of thousands of felony cases in cities throughout the country reveal that 10 percent of the active offenders are responsible for 55 percent of the crimes.[3] This finding and similar statistical evidence confirmed what many investigators had always believed and was instrumental in the formation of the MOB concept.

The MOB unit is a special organizational structure located in a prosecutor's office, in a detective division, or in both. The unit is designed to identify, apprehend, and successfully prosecute the **career criminal.** The MOB unit focuses attention on crimes that are particularly heinous or on criminals who are serious recidivists. The swift prosecution of these offenders is the primary goal.

Investigators in some major police agencies are primarily responsible for assisting the MOB unit of the local prosecutor's office. Although police identification of a suspect as a career criminal is essential to the MOB process, the eventual success of the concept lies with the prosecutor. There are currently more than 20 MOB units operating out of prosecutor's offices throughout the country. The Bronx County, New York, district attorney's MOB unit is an excellent example of a cooperative police/prosecutor concept that is reducing felony crime.

The major objective of the unit is to prosecute offenders who are career criminals. Further, the unit serves to reduce delay in processing serious cases, to increase the certainty and severity of punishment, and to restore public confidence in the criminal investigation and prosecution process. The MOB unit uses an objective case-screening and evaluation system to determine whether a particular case warrants the unit's efforts toward prosecution. Three primary factors are evaluated:

1. the seriousness of the offense,
2. the criminal record of the suspect, and
3. the evidentiary strength of the case.

The first step in the successful prosecution of a career criminal is to accurately identify a particular suspect as such. Prior to the actual arrest, investigators may have already identified the suspect as fitting into the career criminal category. Special investigative effort may have been focused on the suspect through surveillance, undercover operations, use of informants, and so forth. Or a career criminal may be identified only following the arrest through an evaluation of criminal history and/or the recent criminal offense.

Traditional plea bargaining is very restricted in MOB cases; in fact, many units disallow any plea bargaining. The cases handled by the special unit are either heard in separate trial sessions, in which only MOB cases are heard, or given a priority scheduling status within the traditional court system.

Using techniques unique to the special unit, the Bronx MOB has a median time of 97 days from arrest to case disposition. When contrasted with the median time of 400 days for other cases in the prosecutor's office, the MOB unit has achieved a remarkably swift prosecution period. Further, the unit has a conviction rate of 92 percent, compared to the 52 percent conviction rate of non-MOB prosecutions.[4] The MOB exemplifies the impressive results that can be achieved through cooperative effort. When criminal investigators and prosecutors pool their expertise to identify, apprehend, and prosecute career criminals, a major reduction of serious crime is inevitable.

Other programs aimed at career criminals are not centered in the prosecutor's office but managed and directed by police investigators. San Jose's Habitual Offender Tracking Team (HOT) was created to focus on identified predatory sex offenders. The California State Department of Justice identified more than 400 subjects in San Jose who had committed multiple sex crimes and were highly likely to offend again. Although convicted sex offenders in California are required to register their addresses, the HOT team discovered that 80 percent of the offenders provided incorrect or nonexistent addresses. Investigators then conducted surveillances on selected suspects, as sex offenders are known to have one of the highest recidivism rates of all felons. Close monitoring for four months resulted in 115 arrests for parole violations and other crimes, demonstrating the effectiveness of investigative tracking teams.[5]

Specialized Evidence Processing

There is no question that many more criminal cases would be resolved successfully if evidence processing were more complete. Studies estimate that a considerable amount of the significant evidence present at a crime scene is not located and processed by law enforcement personnel.[6] Consequently, a sizable number of cases are lost for lack of specialized crime scene processing.

If there is to be a reduction in crime, police agencies must develop strategies that place more importance on the crime scene. Although many large departments have mobile crime scene units or criminalists who routinely report to crime scenes, the majority of U.S. police agencies do not. Fortunately, the concept of the **crime scene investigator** (CSI) shows considerable promise in alleviating this problem. The CSI concept is basically a simple one. Within each police department and on each working shift, there should be one or more specially trained officers designated as CSIs. The CSI officer would be trained to process a wide variety of crime scenes on the professional level of a criminalist. In felony cases in which a crime scene is located, the CSI would be dispatched to assist the assigned officer in a thorough processing of the scene.

The CSI concept enables a police agency to more completely serve its citizens by ensuring that only the most competent and motivated officers will gather evidence in serious crimes. CSI officers are generally patrol officers, with normal patrol duties, and they are administratively assigned to a crime scene for whatever period of time is necessary to process the scene professionally. Vehicles of CSI officers will be equipped with a complete collection of crime scene equipment so that response time will be rapid. The value of the CSI concept lies not only in having highly trained officers process scenes but also in the cumulative effect of specified officers gaining expertise through experience. When a small number of officers continually process crime scenes, their thoroughness and competence increase with each scene assignment.

Other futuristic crime scene–based procedures will focus on *on-site crime scene analysis*. For nearly a century, investigators have mainly searched and collected tracing evidence for off-site processing at a crime laboratory. New technology is rapidly emerging that will allow highly trained investigators or lab personnel to test evidence at a crime scene, eliminating the risk of contamination that is always possible in the transportation phase of maintaining the chain of evidence. For example, investigators will soon be able to test crime scenes for DNA evidence with a computer-linked microchip device no larger than a credit card. The device will perform examinations in seconds that now take weeks or months. Physiological evidence such as blood or saliva will be placed directly on the chip, which then produces a unique genetic code contained within the cells of the fluid. A small computer probably mounted in the officer's car will then electronically transmit the information, seeking an identity match against a national DNA database of previously identified suspects.

Similar on-site analysis and identity matching can be performed with fingerprint or firearms evidence. Other devices will be able to analyze crime scene vapors. If police suspect that fumes coming from a suspected location could be the by-product of drug production, common in making methamphetamine, for example, on-site technology could collect and identify the fumes, providing immediate probable cause for a search warrant.

On-site crime scene technology is close to becoming a standard crime scene technique and is significant because of its speed of analysis, the high probability of successful identifications, and its economic cost relative to the results produced.

Defense Technology Assistance

The Government Technology Transfer Program holds great potential for the future improvement of criminal investigation. This government initiative enables the Department of Defense and commercial organizations to work together to assist law enforcement through the application of technology originally developed for national defense. Five regional offices of the National Institute of Justice are currently coordinating the program and provide specialty support and training in the utilization of the new technologies.

The assistance program operates upon the philosophy that law enforcement and defense missions share similar concerns and strategies. The program reviews existing technology previously developed for national defense and recommends specific strategies or devices for civilian law enforcement utilization. For example, traditional military needs have prompted the development of technology aimed at monitoring conversations, speaker identification, or instant conversation translation from a foreign language to English. Other defense technology originally reserved for military use includes long-range surveillance, concealed weapons detection, gunshot location tracking, and advanced night-vision devices. All of these technologies have immediate and apparent application to the investigation and suppression of crime. The defense technology assistance program will identify military devices that have a proper usage potential by civilian law enforcement and make such information known to respective police agencies.

Geographic Information System

Police agencies have consistently sought to find ways to use their considerable amounts of data to show past, present, and future crime trends. Until recently, most agencies were limited to using large wall maps on which variously colored pushpins were physically placed to designate types of crime by geographic location. However, a far more advanced method of mapping, known as the **geographic information system** (GIS), is now becoming a reality for some departments and should become a standard investigative tool in the near future. The GIS translates and displays data into various computerized maps. The maps display images in the form of patterns and clusters that make possible interpretation and effective police response. This form of information display is faster, more accurate, and far more comprehensible than simply reading data or using the older pin maps.

The GIS method also is superior in manipulating and displaying large quantities of data. Information is displayed in visual form that makes clear various relationships between time, place, trends, or specific events that would be lost or less evident if analyzed by reading data. The GIS method is excellent for illustrating specific quantities, densities, or changes. While a street map may specify the location of an apartment complex or hospital, it won't indicate the number of apartments or rooms in the hospital or how many people are actually in the buildings. This type of information could be very significant for police tactical planning, such as a major raid or surveillance operation. Or, by analyzing increased traffic count flow patterns, an investigator may conclude that a particular residence or street corner is being used to sell drugs.

Some jurisdictions have enhanced sentencing penalties for certain crimes committed within specific geographic boundaries. In many states, the possession of a firearm or possession and/or sale of narcotics within a defined distance from a school mandates a far more serious sentence. Although street layouts often make it difficult to determine if such offenses fall into a protected zone, GIS software can easily place a computerized circle around a school to illustrate if the offense qualifies for more serious punishment.[7]

A less precise outgrowth of general GIS methods is the use of **geographic profiling.** Geographic profiling is based on the theory of patterned living, or the fact that everyone has a pattern to their lives, especially when the geographical areas they frequent are examined. As people typically travel a limited distance in their daily lives, insight can be gained by linking crime to living quarters. Traditionally, crime prevention theory focused upon where crimes were most likely to occur in the future based on where criminals lived. Geographic profiling reverses the concept by seeking to discover where an offender might live based on the locations of the crimes committed.[8] This form of computer-assisted geographic data interpretation seeks to predict where future crimes may occur or the residence or workplace of a suspect based on past offenses. Profiling software based on a number of known assumptions regarding criminal behavior, such as rapists or burglars generally preferring to commit crimes in close proximity to their residences, reviews past offenses seeking a common geographic link. When a series of crimes are linked by type, method of operation, location, or other factors, a prediction as to the suspect's residence or future criminality can be made.

Enhanced Investigative Training

The quantity and quality of training provided for criminal investigation will be greatly expanded in the future. As criminals become more knowledgeable and crime scenes more complex, the investigative process will become more demanding. Only innovative training techniques, along with better-educated personnel, can successfully meet this challenge. A foundation of police training has always mandated that techniques be clear, concise, and relevant.

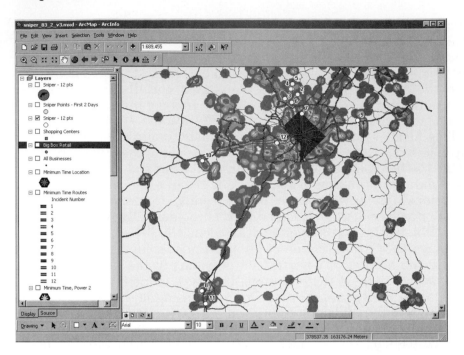

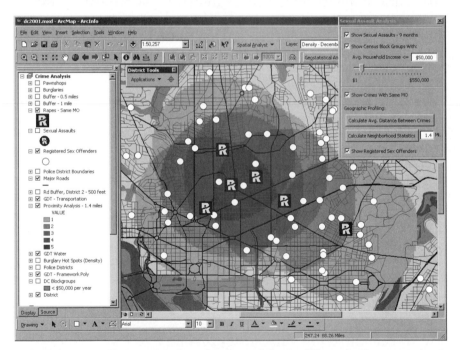

FIGURE 19.2   Two examples of geographic profiling. *A.* Computerized crime mapping attempts to link sniper shooting incidents to possible areas of suspect residence. *B.* A series of sexual assaults are linked to the known residences of registered sex offenders. *(Source: Lisa Horn, Environmental Systems Research Institute.)*

Whereas in the past much of the training for criminal investigation relied on the lecture and demonstration method, future law enforcement training may use another method—virtual reality. **Virtual reality** is a computer-generated, three-dimensional environment that engulfs the senses of sight, sound, and touch. Once the user enters the training environment, it becomes a sensory reality. Virtual reality allows the user to interact with objects and situations that are wholly the products of computers. By completely immersing one's senses, the artificial scene becomes reality, greatly enhancing the training experience and comprehension.

Following the designs of police training specialists, computer programmers create three-dimensional images to educate and inform the user. Head-mounted devices restrict the user's vision to video monitors as the trainee views and interacts with the created environment. Originally developed by the Department of Defense in the early 1980s, the technique was successfully used in combat training. Subsequently, police training used virtual reality to simulate shooting scenarios, then expanded the technique to investigative instruction.

Virtual reality has many training uses of value to the investigator, including incident re-creation, surveillance training, high-risk management, and crime scene processing. Police agencies routinely collect data from officers, victims, witnesses, and suspects following a major incident. Using the data, officers can re-create the various elements leading to the arrest or incident in virtual reality, learning valuable lessons for similar future cases. Surveillance simulations also lend themselves well to the use of virtual reality, as suspect pursuits and evading tactics can be created and experienced. High-risk simulations involving critical incidents common to the detective function, such as drug raids, hazardous arrest and search warrant operations, and firearm confrontations, are also possible. In addition, various crime scenes may be created to challenge the trainee's searching, recording, and collection skills.[9]

Increased Patrol and Detective Communication

In any discussion of strategies for improved criminal investigation, more effective communication and cooperation between patrol and detective units must be stressed. Although many departments have made significant progress in this traditional area of concern, a number of agencies still regard lack of communication as a major internal problem.

Techniques that facilitate a team effort and voluntary sharing attitudes must be developed by all agencies in which there are separate patrol and detective divisions. Personnel must be constantly reminded through in-service training that the preliminary and follow-up phases of the investigation are interdependent. Investigators should periodically advise patrol officers of the status of cases the officers initially handled. When both divisions are aware that a combined effort is being made in a crime investigation, the outcome is more likely to be favorable. Enhanced communication between the patrol and detective units has been significantly improved in police agencies that utilize frequent internal computerized e-mails. Software can be created that automatically forwards case status updates to patrol officers who have worked the preliminary investigation of a case that is now the responsibility of the detective division.

Investigative Research

Investigative methods have largely been based on tradition and the experience and expertise of senior officers.[10] As criminal investigation proceeds through the twenty-first century, such standards will no longer be sufficient. To utilize fully the limited resources of a police agency and respond effectively to more complex and varied investigations, continuous and meaningful research will be necessary. Actually, investigative research is not a totally new concept. Police pioneers such as August Vollmer and O. W. Wilson conducted considerable research pertaining to the investigative function during the early years of the twentieth century. The 2000s, however, demand widespread investigative-oriented research on all levels of enforcement. The term "research" often conjures up an image of mind-numbing formulas and incomprehensible statistical findings. Actually, research is only the careful, systematic study of a particular subject or event.[11]

Investigative research seeks to test or discover various areas of inquiry important to criminal investigators. Often investigators or agency heads wish to discover whether a traditional or current field practice actually works. Although it is common within law enforcement to assume that traditional methods are indeed effective, relatively few standards of operation have actually been tested through proper research methodology. In addition, investigative research can be used to discover new data. Successful research designs can provide answers on how an agency can best react to a newly emerging crime problem or gather previously unknown data on current criminality.

There are two basic types of research of value to the investigative process: analytical and experimental. *Analytical research* is dependent on extensive data collection, followed by analysis and the drawing of conclusions. For example, a detective unit commander may wish to know whether the hours spent processing burglary crime scenes are cost effective. Accordingly, data will be gathered concerning the specific amounts of time spent in crime scene processing relative to the number of cases successfully concluded. Conclusions will then be rendered that will affect the continuation, modification, elimination, or future expansion of burglary crime scene processing. *Experimental research* is focused on demonstrating the cause-and-effect relationship between various conditions. Investigators may suspect that certain burglary crime scene processing methods are superior to others in producing evidence. For example, it may be believed that scenes processed by criminalists produce more suspect-linking evidence than those processed by other individuals. To demonstrate the premise, investigators can control the ways in which similar burglary crime scenes are processed. Some scenes will be processed by patrol officers, a second group by investigators, and a third group only by criminalists. Results are then analyzed to determine any changes in the existing conditions that can be attributed to a specific cause and effect created by the experiment.[12]

Futures Research

Traditionally, the police have given little serious thought to the nature of criminal investigation in the twenty-first century and beyond. The use of **futures research** seeks to accurately predict trends, incidents, and organizational policy in anticipation of future realities. As research becomes standard police practice and college-educated personnel the norm, the use of futures research will become commonplace in law enforcement. The need for continuous future-oriented research is linked to the complex and technologically oriented society of the new century and beyond. Those who will formulate future investigative policy must be able to predict the conditions that will necessitate specific police responses. Accordingly, those who will shape the future of law enforcement need reliable and valid future-oriented data.[13]

There are several methods of accurately looking ahead toward the future, often referred to as forecasting. Four of the most effective for the investigative effort are the use of scenarios, the delphi technique, and qualitative and quantitative methodologies.[14] The scenario method involves the creation of a hypothetical but factually based story. After considerable thought and research, future outcomes concerning an investigative matter are predicted and generally depicted as three possible outcomes: the best, worst, and most likely cases. The agency then analyzes its reaction to each scenario and prepares suitable reactions and policy to meet it. Forecasting through the delphi technique involves a group effort. A panel or group of experts on a particular subject are brought together to give their responses or predictions anonymously. Answers are often written out and then tabulated by an independent member, and results are subsequently displayed and discussed. The delphi method has many variations, but all depend on experts giving anonymous opinions to avoid the negative consequences often found in group dynamics. Predictions or policy formulation result from a consensus of the panel or by averaging answers to a medium response.

The more traditional methods of qualitative and quantitative analysis are often of use for futures research. Qualitative methods generally specify a particular future need and work backward in determining the means necessary to satisfy it. The utility of qualitative thinking is apparent in the technique of brainstorming or similar dynamic group thinking among knowledgeable individuals. Such techniques encourage spontaneous answers and creativity. Ideas are exchanged without prejudgment, and individuals are encouraged to use considerable imagination in their responses or predictions in an open give-and-take atmosphere. Quantitative forecasting often involves mathematical models of varying complexity. This method lends itself well to investigative matters that occur with regularity and in a fixed pattern. Often aided by computerization, quantitative forecasting examines past and present data, introducing future variables into the analysis. On the basis of the known and projected data, a prediction typically based on statistical probability can be established.

As our society undergoes change throughout the twenty-first century and into the next, futures research will become a vital police responsibility. Leading futurists have predicted the decades ahead to be some of the most turbulent ever experienced in the history of the nation. Several factors have been cited as contributors to this troubling forecast, including the breakdown of government service systems, an increase in societal singles and loners, a decrease in the number of blue-collar jobs, and the rapidly changing racial composition of the country.[15] Because of rapid social change and the consequent destabilization experienced by many thousands of individuals, crime patterns will undergo corresponding changes. For the criminal investigator to challenge effectively the new criminality of the future, efforts to predict trends and problems must be undertaken.

While a number of future-oriented groups have projected coming changes that will impact the investigative process, few have been more focused than the Society of Police Futurists International. This group has detailed a number of societal chances that will demand repose by law enforcement if agencies are to keep pace in the future. One area of rapid change is the aging of the American population. By 2030, those aged 65 and older will be 20 percent of the population. An increasingly aging population will cause change in both victimization patterns and those who perpetrate crime. This factor will also cause a shortfall in the police workforce due to a smaller percentage of younger applicants. Accordingly, more general policing and some specific investigative duties will be increasingly delegated to the private sector. These could include private involvement in taking investigative reports, scene interviewing, evidence processing, and surveillance monitoring, among others.[16]

The rapid growth of technology will affect future investigative competency in a dramatic fashion. Detectives will have to be continually trained to keep pace, and a background knowledge or degree in various technological majors may even become required to become an investigator. Computer crime will expand to the point where it may dominate investigative effort in a similar fashion to the current status of drug crimes. Experts predict that by 2030, computers will demonstrate the ability to develop human-level intelligence. Although not realized yet, the future of criminal investigation may include heavy reliance upon computers with super-reasoning ability. Such devices will be extremely valuable in predicting crime trends, linking method of operation, rank ordering probable suspects, analyzing physical evidence, and tracking complex interstate or international crimes. Yet the greatest positive aspect of the future-oriented computer may be its ability to creatively suggest investigative leads.

The continued rapid growth of the crime of identity theft will no doubt make it a significant future investigative problem. Not only will a far greater number of detectives specialize in investigating such cases, but it is likely the crime will grow to such a magnitude that it will be classified as an index crime in the annual FBI *Uniform Crime Report*. In a similar fashion to the recent inclusion of arson as an index crime, the future toll of identity theft will justify far more attention and reaction from all segments of the criminal justice system. A suspect's method of operation will continue to expand as technological advances occur that facilitate the stealing of one's identifying data. Additionally, as more identity theft perpetrators operate from outside the boundaries of the United States, a greater cooperative international investigative effort will be demanded in the future.

The various strategies presented here are but a sampling of concepts that hold considerable promise. Criminal investigation has always adopted the necessary methodology to cope with a current crime situation. Certainly, the opening years of the twenty-first century will witness new and difficult challenges to our criminal justice system. There is little reason to doubt, however, that criminal investigation will not rise to those challenges with new and successful strategies.

CRIMINALISTIC CONCEPTS OF THE FUTURE

In the view of the general public, the field of criminalistics has made the greatest advances in crime detection and investigation. In fact, local, state, and federal crime laboratories have made impressive advances from earlier studies that criticized some aspects of evidence testing accuracy. The inherent difficulties that crime laboratories encounter generally are due to three factors: (a) the large and ever-increasing amounts of evidence submitted for analysis, (b) the time and budget expenses associated with drug analyses, and (c) the media image of the criminalist who "always has the answer" and solves virtually all crimes within a 30- or 60-minute television program. Despite such problems, crime labs continue to fascinate the public and play an essential role in modern crime investigation.

It is logical that the judiciary will continue to emphasize the importance of physical evidence and place less weight on confession during the criminal proceeding. As more officers are trained in the specialty of crime scene investigation, a larger volume of evidence will be submitted to the nation's forensic laboratories. Thus, there will be a need for more criminalists, greater accuracy in testing, and the development of new tests to positively link a specific suspect to a specific offense. Criminal investigation simply cannot keep pace with growing crime and judicial requirements unless the field of criminalists experiences similar growth.

There are approximately 2,500 criminalists in the United States, assisted by nearly 2,000 technicians and support personnel. Most states have a central crime laboratory typically located in the capital city, while the more populated states also have a network of smaller satellite labs serving various regions. Larger police jurisdictions may also have their own independent laboratories, such as the Los Angeles County Sheriff's Department. Serving the forensic science needs of all police agencies within the county except the Los Angeles Police Department, the lab employs 80 criminalists and 120 technicians and clerical support personnel. The heavy workload of this urban crime lab is typical, as nearly 70,000 cases are annually submitted for forensic analysis, including 800 homicides.[17] Fortunately, forensic science is attracting experienced individuals with extensive scientific background, for example, graduates of criminal justice programs holding masters or doctorate degrees in criminalistics. To continue to attract qualified criminalists, crime laboratory budgets must be expanded so that the laboratory will no longer be regarded as the "stepchild" of the police function. With significant staff and equipment increases, the testing accuracy of most laboratories will surely improve. Since many testing errors can be traced to unmanageable caseloads caused by a scarcity of staff, this conclusion is obvious.

Possibly one of the greatest criminalistic advances that will be made will concern the facility with which a given item of evidence can be linked to the suspect positively. Although forensic laboratories can make such determinations at this time, they can do so with near absolute certainty only when fingerprints or DNA samples are involved. To develop and perfect other positive tests to link a suspect to an offense, criminalistic research must be encouraged and funded to a greater degree. Because of the heavy workloads of nearly all laboratories, few criminalists have enough time to engage in experimentation. Although many universities have departments of criminalistics, their number is still inadequate to meet research needs.

It is likely that much of the future forensic science research will involve some aspect of **biometrics.** Biometrics pertains to any form of identification or technological development linked to the use of unique biological material. Earlier forms of such identification methods included individualized fingerprints, identity through the iris of the eye, or voice recognition. The modern era of biometrics will always be connected to the development of DNA analysis. While now relatively commonplace as an investigative tool, new research is expanding the accuracy and application of DNA. Recent discoveries have expanded traditional DNA testing in that crime laboratories are now processing evidence for what is termed mitochondrial DNA (mtDNA). This form of genetic material is found outside the nucleus of the cell and allows criminalists to extract a greater quantity of mtDNA than traditional samples. Additionally, more mtDNA can be extracted from smaller crime scene objects than regular DNA as well as from older or less well preserved evidence. Criminalists are now even able to obtain mtDNA from latent fingerprints. This is particularly important in cases where the latent lacks the number of ridges to make an identification. Continued future advances in the sequencing of the human genome will yield greater amounts of information of value to the criminal investigator. Characteristics such as eye and hair color, race, gender, and even age may become standard tracing information obtained from DNA evidence.

One area of biometric identification that will likely expand in the near future is identity through the iris of the eye. **Iris recognition technology** was pioneered by University of Cambridge professor John Daugman (see Figure 19.3). The eye's iris is an elastic, pigmented, connective tissue that controls the pupil. Fortunately, it has a complex textured appearance that, much like the randomness of fingerprint ridges, produces a highly individualized pattern area. The uniqueness of the iris pattern can be recorded

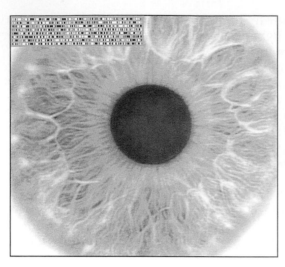

FIGURE 19.3 Iris recognition technology is a rapidly advancing area of biometric identification. Much like the randomness of fingerprint ridges, the complex and unique pattern of the eye's iris can be analyzed for individual identification. *(Source: Dr. John Daugman, University of Cambridge.)*

through a photographic coding technique developed by Daugman. The individual iris code can then be stored in databases and compared to identify individual subjects. Controlled studies demonstrate the reliability of the biometric technique in that a false match can be expected in only one out of a billion eye comparisons. Iris recognition technology is currently in use at many airports and border-crossing points in the Middle East and Europe and may well become a standard part of future American arrest-booking procedures.

Considerable research is being undertaken to improve how law enforcement determines deception. Given the limitations of the traditional polygraph in accuracy and courtroom acceptance, new methods that focus upon electrical brain waves, blood flow patterns, and facial expressions are generating considerable forensic interest. Rather than just measuring the body for signs of stress during deceit, new methods attempt to examine brain responses to deceit. Researchers believe they have isolated a specific electrical brain wave that activates only when one sees a familiar object. Thus, suspects may be shown a photo series that includes a picture of a murder victim or missing person. If the suspect had no interaction with the victim, the brain wave would not register recognition, whereas if they had, the brain wave would activate. Other methods involve the use of brain scanning technology to monitor what brain areas suddenly receive increased blood flow during police questioning. Such research seems to demonstrate that different brain regions fill with blood when people lie or tell the truth. Forensic research also indicates that most individuals give off clues of deceit or honesty through fleeting facial expressions that can be "read" by highly trained interviewers.

Other emerging technology that must be further developed forensically, involves **digital evidence.** Any evidence that can be obtained in digital form is generically termed digital evidence. This includes but is not limited to computer systems, videos, cellular telephones, pagers, digital photos, or fax machines. Investigators and criminalists are increasingly challenged to keep up with such digital advances and to develop methods to access information within the devices without compromising the evidence. Many experts, such as Barry Fisher, director of the Los Angeles County Sheriff's Office Scientific Services Bureau, predict that digital evidence will have the same impact on the criminal justice system as DNA has had.

Several research teams are close to determining certain physiological characteristics that could serve to identify a suspect with a high degree of probability. Some forensic microbiologists are investigating individual microorganisms for possible application to suspect identification. It has been hypothesized that each person has unique microscopic bacteria that remain for specific periods of time wherever they are deposited. If such microorganisms could be recovered and identified, they could conceivably be matched back to a particular suspect. While this theory and other similar ones may seem unlikely, we must remember the skepticism that surrounded the concept of linking the sound of a voice or perspiration from a fingertip to a specific individual.

Work is also under way to improve accuracy in tracing inanimate objects to crime scenes and suspects. Techniques have been developed to "tag" explosives to help the investigator trace them to a source. In **explosive tagging**, minute noncombustible coded particles are added to the explosives in the manufacturing process. The chemical tags (coded particles) are recovered after the explosion by using a magnet, decoded and microscopically examined. The type of chemical additive reveals who made the explosive, when and where it was produced, and its commercial destination following production.

Other innovative research has focused on identifying glove prints left at crime scenes, similar to latent fingerprints. Leather (animal skin dressed for use) has distinctive "prints" that may be left and linked to a suspect's glove. It may also be possible to transfer fingerprints through the thin material of rubber gloves or to leave identifiable latents on the interior surface of the gloves. If a rubber glove is recovered during the crime scene search, the interior surfaces could be valuable in tracing the suspect if various recovery and identification techniques are perfected.

New methods for detecting drug use through hair analysis are being researched and may prove to be more accurate than any current method. Finally, forensic advances in fingerprint technology will also occur. Despite the achievement of DNA profiling, the fingerprint remains the most frequently used tool for identifying criminal suspects.[18] Discoveries and improvements in fingerprint laser technology and other latent methods will continue. In addition, considerable effort will be made to enhance automated fingerprint identification systems on the state and federal levels, with cross-searching between systems becoming a reality in the near future.

In 1981, the American Society of Crime Laboratory Directors established a national forensic laboratory. Modeled after England's research laboratory at Aldermaston, the Forensic Science Research and Training Center (FSRTC) is managed by the FBI. The FSRTC houses a permanent staff that engages in continuous research in addition to providing expert instruction to visiting criminalists. The long-awaited research facility is expected to further advance various breakthroughs in the forensic field.[19]

▲ SUMMARY

The investigative concepts of the future will depend on the expansion of existing proven techniques and the creation of new methods suited for changing criminal trends. The multiagency approach and the major offense bureau are concepts particularly well suited to deal with the growth of serial crimes and the continuing problem of the career criminal. The use of investigative research will become essential for future investigators as criminal investigation moves from the traditional toward methods that can be proven effective scientifically. Investigative research seeks to discover various areas of inquiry that are significant to the investigative function or at least to test existing methods for their efficiency. Analytical and experimental research are the two major forms of such research.

Other research will attempt to forecast proper investigative policy and response. Although the police have traditionally given little thought to the future in formulating policy, a rapidly changing world will challenge the criminal investigative response as never before. Many methods can be employed in futures research; the scenario, delphi technique, and qualitative and quantitative methods are well suited for investigative predictions. All such forecasting methodologies attempt to predict trends or incidents in anticipation of new investigative policy.

Changes and new challenges in the area of criminalistics will also be evident in the coming decades. Improvements in laboratory processing, DNA databases, and automated fingerprinting systems are only some of the advances being researched.

The future of criminal investigation and criminalistics promises to be exciting and rewarding. The student of criminal justice will be entering the law enforcement profession during a phase of unparalleled competence and professionalism. Criminal investigation offers a career opportunity with few equals in terms of challenge and diversity. The investigator of the future will continue to acquire the high status the position merits by skillfully merging scientific technology with the investigative theory and practice of criminal investigation.

EXERCISES

1. Prepare an imaginative research paper on the criminal investigator of the future. Using current crime trends and data, speculate regarding crime trends of the next decade. Suggest some investigative techniques that could be developed to combat these trends.

2. Researching criminal justice publications, list and explain several scientific techniques that have been developed during the past five years in the field of criminalistics.

RELEVANT WEB SITES

http://www.kcpd.org/kcpd2004/coldcase.htm

Web site of the Kansas City Police Department's Cold Case Squad, one of the oldest such units in the United States. Contains a statement of its mission and links to the unit's cold-case tip form designed for online utilization by the general public.

http://www.ojp.usdoj.gov/nij/maps/

National Institute of Justice site details the concept of crime mapping. Extensive links to associated research areas of spatial data analysis, geographic profiling, and various available crime mapping publications.

http://www.policefuturists.org/

Official home page of Police Futurists International. Links to numerous essays regarding future investigative and forensic possibilities, developments, and challenges. Site also maintains a Web log regarding futuristic concepts and events.

Notes

Chapter One

1. A. C. Germann, Frank D. Day, and Robert R. J. Gallati, *Introduction to Law Enforcement and Criminal Justice* (Springfield, Ill.: Charles C Thomas, 1974), p. 43.
2. Germann et al., *Introduction to Law Enforcement*, p. 47.
3. Arthur Griffiths, *Mysteries of Police and Crime*, Vol. 1 (New York: G. P. Putnam's Sons, 1899), p. 65.
4. Arthur L. Hayward, ed., *Lives of the Most Remarkable Criminals*, 2nd ed. (1735; reprint ed., New York: Dodd, Mead & Company, 1927), p. 322.
5. Hayward, *Most Remarkable Criminals*, p. 270.
6. Griffiths, *Mysteries of Police*, p. 120.
7. Hayward, *Most Remarkable Criminals*, p. 31.
8. Griffiths, *Mysteries of Police*, p. 83.
9. Griffiths, *Mysteries of Police*, p. 85.
10. George W. Walling, *Recollections of a New York Chief of Police* (New York: Caxton Book Concern, 1887), p. 29.
11. Walling, *Recollections*, p. 31.
12. James D. Horan, *The Pinkertons* (New York: Crown Publishers, 1967), p. 23.
13. Howard O. Sprogle, *The Philadelphia Police* (1887; reprint ed., New York: AMS Press, 1974), p. 118.
14. Sprogle, *Philadelphia Police*, p. 120.
15. Thomas J. Fleming, "The Policeman's Lot," *American Heritage*, **21**, no. 2 (February 1970), p. 7.
16. Joseph Miller, ed., *The Arizona Rangers* (New York: Hastings House, 1972), pp. 257–258.
17. "100th Anniversary of the Royal Canadian Mounted Police," *Police Chief*, **40**, no. 9 (September 1973), p. 31.
18. Horan, *The Pinkertons*, p. 25.
19. *Education and Training in Forensic Science: A Guide for Forensic Science Laboratories* (Washington, D.C.: National Institute of Justice, 2004), p. 2.
20. Joseph L. Peterson, *Use of Forensic Evidence by the Police and Courts* (Washington, D.C.: U.S. Department of Justice, National Institute of Justice, 1987), p. 5.
21. Henry T. F. Rhodes, *Alphonse Bertillon* (1956; reprint ed., New York: Greenwood Press, 1968), p. 24.
22. Rhodes, *Alphonse Bertillon*, p. 82.
23. *Fingerprint Identification* (Washington, D.C.: Federal Bureau of Investigation, 1975), p. 7.
24. Raymond B. Fosdick, *American Police Systems* (New York: Century, 1920), pp. 348–353.
25. Sir Arthur Conan Doyle, *The Adventures and Memoirs of Sherlock Holmes* (New York: The Modern Library, n.d.), p. 75.
26. Fosdick, *American Police*, p. 332.
27. Joseph Wambaugh, *The Blooding* (New York: William Morrow, 1989), pp. 275–282.
28. Geoffrey R. Stone, *Search and Seizure* (Washington, D.C.: U.S. Department of Justice, National Institute of Justice, 1991), p. 1.

29. Rolando V. del Camen and Jeffery T. Walker, *Briefs of 100 Leading Cases in Law Enforcement* (Cincinnati: Anderson, 1991), pp. 13–14.
30. Richard A. Myren and Carol H. Garcia, *Investigation of Determination of Fact* (Belmont, Calif.: Brooks/Cole, 1989), pp. 32–33.

Chapter Two

1. Callie Rennison, *Criminal Victimization 2002* (Washington, D.C.: U.S. Department of Justice), p. 1.
2. Ted Miller, Mark Cohen, and Brian Wiersema, *Victim Costs and Consequences: A New Look* (Washington, D.C.: National Institute of Justice, February 1996), p. 2.
3. Crime in the United States, 1994, *Uniform Crime Reports* (Washington, D.C.: U.S. Government Printing Office, 1995), p. 6.
4. Carole Wade and Carol Tavris, *Learning to Think Critically* (New York: Harper & Row, 1990), pp. 1–18.
5. *Instructor's Resource Guide: Annual Editions in Criminal Justice* 1996–1997 (Guilford, Conn.: Dushkin, 1996), pp. 3–4.
6. Gene Blair and Sam Slick, "Survival Spanish: Needed Training for Police," *Police Chief*, **57**, no. 1 (January 1990), pp. 42–47.
7. Bernard Cohen and Jan Chaiken, "Investigators Who Perform Well," *National Institute of Justice—SNI*, no. 207 (January/February 1988), p. 14.
8. James N. Gilbert, "Investigative Ethics," in Michael Palmiotto, ed., *Critical Issues in Criminal Investigation* (Cincinnati: Anderson, 1988), pp. 7–14.
9. Kathleen Maguire and Ann L. Pastore, eds., *Sourcebook of Criminal Justice Statistics—1994* (Washington, D.C.: U.S. Department of Justice, 1995), p. 151.
10. Joycelyn M. Pollock-Byrne, *Ethics in Crime and Justice* (Pacific Grove, Calif.: Brooks/Cole, 1989), p. 156.
11. O. W. Wilson and Roy C. McLaren, *Police Administration* (New York: McGraw-Hill, 1972), p. 374.
12. Charles A. Sennewald, *The Process of Investigation* (Boston: Butterworth Publishers, 1981), p. 3.
13. *San Francisco Chronicle*, 19 July 1999, p. B1.

Chapter Three

1. William B. Anderson, *Notable Crime Investigations* (Springfield, Ill.: Charles C Thomas, 1987), p. 328.
2. Larry Holtz, *Criminal Evidence for Law Enforcement Officers* (Longwood, Fla.: Gould Publishers, 1994), p. 21.
3. Charles D. Hale, *Fundamentals of Police Administration* (Boston: Holbrook Press, 1977), p. 157.
4. *National Advisory Commission on Criminal Justice Standards and Goals* (Washington, D.C.: U.S. Government Printing Office, 1973), p. 233.
5. Scott C. Hill, "Technology Making IDs Quicker, Easier, and More Accurate," *Police Chief*, **57**, no. 4 (April 1991), p. 52.
6. *Criminal Investigation* (Gaithersburg, Md.: International Association of Chiefs of Police, 1975), p. 10.
7. Marianne W. Zawitz, ed., *Report to the Nation on Crime and Justice* (Washington, D.C.: Bureau of Justice Statistics, 1988), p. 68.
8. Barbara Boland et al., *The Prosecution of Felony Arrests* (Washington, D.C.: Bureau of Justice Statistics, 1989), pp. 32–43.

Chapter Four

1. George T. Payton, *Patrol Procedure* (Los Angeles: Legal Book Corporation, 1971), p. 170.
2. Donald G. Hanna and John R. Kleberg, *A Police Records System for the Small Department* (Springfield, Ill.: Charles C Thomas, 1973), p. 4.
3. *Public Access to Criminal History Record Information* (Washington, D.C.: Bureau of Justice Statistics, 1988), pp. 2–3.

4. "Report Writing and Documentation," *Nebraska Jail Bulletin*, no. 117 (March/April 1995), pp. 5–7.
5. *Manual of Police Records* (Washington, D.C.: Federal Bureau of Investigation, 1966), p. 12.
6. *Los Angeles Times*, 18 December 1977, sec. 8, p. 8.
7. Paul Szczesny, "Effective Incident Reports," *Law and Order*, **44**, no. 8 (August 1996), pp. 82–85.

Chapter Five

1. D. H. Garrison Jr., "Protecting the Crime Scene," *FBI Law Enforcement Bulletin*, **63**, no. 9 (September 1994), pp. 18–20.
2. Paul L. Kirk, *Crime Investigation*, ed. John I. Thornton (New York: Wiley, 1974), p. 19.
3. George Cuomo, *A Couple of Cops* (New York: Random House, 1995), p. 17.
4. Bill Clede, "3D Eyewitness Draws the Scene, *Law and Order*, **42**, no. 12 (December 1994), p. 12.
5. Robert H. Lloyd, "Crime Scene Documentation and Reconstruction," *Law and Order*, **42**, no. 12 (December 1994), p. 12.
6. Bill Siuru, "Laser Technology Helps Preserve Crime Scenes," *Law and Order*, **52**, no. 5 (May 2004), pp. 52–55.
7. Vernon Geberth, "An Equivocal Death and Staged Crime Scene," *Law and Order*, **52**, no. 11 (November 2004), pp. 117–119.
8. John E. Douglas, *Crime Classification Manual* (New York: Lexington Books, 1992), pp. 249–258.
9. *Harris v. U.S.*, 331 U.S. 145 (1947).

Chapter Six

1. Arthur S. Aubry Jr. and Rudolph R. Caputo, *Criminal Interrogation* (Springfield, Ill.: Charles C Thomas, 1974), p. 21.
2. Robert J. Wicks, *Applied Psychology for Law Enforcement and Corrections Officers* (New York: McGraw-Hill, 1974), p. 42.
3. Richard D. Knudten et al., *Victims and Witnesses: Their Experiences with Crime and the Criminal Justice System* (Washington, D.C.: U.S. Department of Justice, National Institute of Law Enforcement and Criminal Justice, 1977), p. 6.
4. Ted Miller, Mark Cohen, and Brian Wiersema, *Victim Costs and Consequences: A New Look* (Washington, D.C.: National Institute of Justice, 1996), p. 1.
5. Brian C. Della, "Non Traditional Training Systems," *FBI Law Enforcement Bulletin*, **73**, no. 6 (June 2004), p. 7.
6. "Cognitive Approach Aids Interviewers," *Law Enforcement News*, 14 February 1990, pp. 1, 6.
7. Laura Olsen, "Cognitive Interviewing and the Victim/Witness in Crisis," *Police Chief*, **58**, no. 2 (February 1991), pp. 28–32.
8. R. Edward Geiselman and Ronald P. Fisher, *Interviewing Victims and Witnesses of Crime* (Washington, D.C.: National Institute of Justice, 1985), p. 1.
9. "Cognitive Approach Aids Interviewers," *Law Enforcement News*, 14 February 1990, p. 1.
10. *Omaha World Herald*, 24 April 2005, p. 6-B.
11. Frank J. Cannavale Jr., *Improving Witness Cooperation*, ed. William D. Falcon (Washington, D.C.: U.S. Department of Justice, National Institute of Law Enforcement and Criminal Justice, 1976), p. 28.
12. *Escobedo v. Illinois*, 378 U.S. 478 (1964).
13. *Miranda v. Arizona*, 384 U.S. 436 (1966).
14. Kimberly A. Crawford, "Custodial Interrogation: Impact of Minnick v. Mississippi," *FBI Law Enforcement Bulletin*, **60**, no. 9 (September 1991), pp. 28–32.
15. *Omaha World Herald*, 24 September 1995, p. 18-A.
16. *Fraizer v. Cupp*, 394 U.S. 731, 739 (1969).
17. A. Louis DiPietro, "Lies, Promises, or Threats: The Voluntariness of Confessions," *FBI Law Enforcement Bulletin*, **62**, no. 7 (July 1993), pp. 27–32.

18. Joe Navarro, "A Four-Domain Model for Detecting Deception," *FBI Law Enforcement Bulletin*, **72**, no. 6 (June 2003), p. 19.
19. James Janik, "Dealing with Mentally Ill Offenders," *FBI Law Enforcement Bulletin*, **61**, no. 7 (July 1992), p. 23.
20. Arthur S. Aubry Jr. and Rudolph R. Caputo, *Criminal Investigation* (Springfield, Ill.: Charles C Thomas, 1974), p. 21.
21. James T. Reese, "Obsessive Compulsive Behavior," *FBI Law Enforcement Bulletin* (August 1979), pp. 6–12.
22. Vincent Sandoval, "Strategies to Avoid Interview Contamination," *FBI Law Enforcement Bulletin*, **72**, no. 10 (October 2003), pp. 1–10.
23. Stephanie Slahor, "It's What They Say and How They Say It," *Law and Order*, **43**, no. 6 (June 1995), pp. 94–95.
24. Howard N. Snyder and Melisa Sickmund, *Juvenile Offenders: A National Report* (Washington, D.C.: National Center for Juvenile Justice, August 1995), p. 101.
25. In re Gault, 387 U.S. 1 (1967).
26. Susan Adams and John Jarvis, "Are You Telling Me the Truth: Indicators of Veracity in Written Statements," *FBI Law Enforcement Bulletin*, **73**, no. 10 (October 2004), pp. 7–12.
27. William A. Geller, *Videotaping Interrogations and Confessions* (Washington, D.C.: National Institute of Justice, March 1993), pp. 1–3.
28. Diane Ingalls, "Video Confessions," *The National Centurion*, **1**, no. 8 (November 1983), pp. 47–49.
29. "Lights, Camera, Interrogation," *Law Enforcement News*, 15 January 2003, p. 9.
30. Ronald M. Furgerson, "Evaluating Investigative Polygraph Results," *The Detective*, Fall 1990, pp. 20–23.
31. *Manual of Investigative Operations and Guidelines* (Washington, D.C.: Federal Bureau of Investigation, n.d.), p. 1198.05.
32. Anne Cohen, "Hypnosis under Attack," *Police Magazine*, **6**, no. 4 (July 1983), p. 38.
33. Martin T. Orne et al., "The Forensic Use of Hypnosis," *National Institute of Justice Reports* (December 1984), p. 1.
34. Martin Reiser, "Hypnosis as an Aid in a Homicide Investigation," *American Journal of Clinical Hypnosis*, **17**, no. 2 (October 1974), pp. 84–87.

Chapter Seven

1. James H. Morton, "'Robby' the Informer," *Police Chief*, **40**, no. 8 (August 1973), pp. 42–43.
2. *Kearney Hub* (Nebraska), 1 June 1996, p. 7A.
3. "The Big Prize," *U.S. News & World Report*, 7 May 1990, p. 21.
4. "Informers under Fire," *Time*, 17 April 1972, pp. 77–88.
5. Gary S. Katzmann, *Inside the Criminal Process* (New York: W. W. Norton, 1991), pp. 40–41.
6. William Webster, "Sophisticated Surveillance—Intolerable Intrusion or Prudent Protection?" *Washington Law Review*, **63**, 1985, p. 351.
7. "How You Can Join the War against Crime and Drug Pushers" (Pleasantville, N.Y.: The Reader's Digest Association, 1973), p. 5.
8. "Selected Supreme Court Cases," *FBI Law Enforcement Bulletin*, **59**, no. 11 (November 1990), p. 29.
9. "Models for Management," *Police Chief*, **57**, no. 1 (January 1990), pp. 56–57.
10. Publicity Release Office of the United States Attorney General, December 28, 1977.
11. Kimberly A. Crawford, "A Constitutional Guide to the Use of Cellmate Informants, *FBI Law Enforcement Bulletin*, **64**, no. 12 (December 1995), pp. 18–23.
12. *Omaha World Herald*, 8 July 1996, p. 5.
13. David F. Nemecek, "NCIC 2000 Technology Adds a New Weapon to Law Enforcement Arsenal," *Police Chief*, **57**, no. 4 (April 1990), pp. 30–33.
14. William Y. Doran, "The FBI Laboratory: Fifty Years," *Journal of Forensic Sciences*, **27**, no. 4 (October 1982), p. 743.
15. "The Brave World of Data Surveillance," *Unesco Courier*, July 1973, p. 17.

16. *Baltimore Sunday Sun*, 13 July 1975, p. 1.
17. *Champaign-Urbana* (Illinois) *News Gazette*, 24 December 1976, p. 24C.
18. *Illinois Revised Statutes*, Chap. 38, pp. 206–207.
19. "Freedom of Information," *U.S. News & World Report*, 9 August 1976, p. 55.
20. Howard Swiggett, *The Rebel Raider: The Life of John Hunt Morgan* (Indianapolis: Bobbs-Merrill, 1934), p. 61.
21. "Keeping the Cybercops Out of Cyberspace," *Newsweek*, 14 March 1994, p. 38.

Chapter Eight

1. Bill Clede, "Laptop Computer Expo," *Law and Order*, **42**, no. 7 (July 1994), p. 10.
2. Bill Clede, "The Advantages of Electronic Mail," *Law and Order*, **43**, no. 6 (June 1995), p. 12.
3. "Using Microcomputers to Enhance Police Productivity," *Police Chief*, **57**, no. 3 (March 1990), p. 10.
4. "Screams of Warning in Cyberspace," *Law Enforcement News*, **21**, no. 429, p. 12.
5. "Expert Systems," *Law Enforcement News*, 30 April 1991, pp. 1, 17.
6. Bill Clede, "The Advantages of Electronic Mail, *Law and Order*, **43**, no. 6 (June 1995), p. 12.
7. Vernon Geberth, "State-Wide and Regional Information Systems," *Law and Order*, **42**, no. 4 (April 1994), pp. 65–66.
8. Bill Clede, "The Internet: Link to the World," *Law and Order*, **43**, no. 6 (June 1995), p. 34.
9. Greg Evans, "Internet: Learning to Surf," *On Patrol*, **1**, no. 1 (Spring 1996), pp. 56–58.
10. "Taming the Internet," *U.S. News & World Report*, 29 April, 1996, pp. 60–64.
11. "Internet Produces FBI Web Page Arrests," *Omaha World Herald*, 21 June 1996, p. 4.
12. Bill Siuru, "Spotting a Face in a Crowd," *Law Enforcement Technology*, **23**, no. 6 (June 1996), p. 84.
13. Catherine H. Conly and J. Thomas McEwen, *Computer Crime* (Washington, D.C.: National Institute of Justice Reports, January 1990), p. 2.
14. "Florida's Computer Crime," *FBI Law Enforcement Bulletin*, **59**, 2 (February 1990), p. 30.
15. "Computer Fraud: An Analysis for Law Enforcement," *Police Chief*, **43**, no. 9 (September 1976), pp. 54–55.
16. David L. Carter, "Computer Crime Categories," *FBI Law Enforcement Bulletin*, **64**, no. 7 (July 1995), pp. 23–24.
17. Robert D'Ovidio and James Doyle, "A Study on Cyberstalking," *FBI Law Enforcement Bulletin*, **72**, no. 3 (March 2003), pp. 10–18.
18. Judith Martin, "Electronic Crimefighting," *Law and Order*, **51**, no. 12 (December 2003), pp. 52–55.
19. Loren Mercer, "Computer Forensics Characteristics and Preservation of Digital Evidence," *FBI Law Enforcement Bulletin*, **73**, no. 3 (March 2004), p. 29.
20. Michael R. Anderson, "Retrieving Information from Seized Computers," *Police Chief*, **57**, no. 4 (April 1991), pp. 152–155.
21. Hugh Nugent, *State Computer Crime Statutes* (Washington, D.C.: National Institute of Justice, November 1991), pp. 1–10.

Chapter Nine

1. *Crime in the United States 2003, Uniform Crime Reports* (Washington, D.C.: U.S. Government Printing Office, 2004), p. 45.
2. Craig Perkins and Patsy Klaus, *Criminal Victimization* (Washington, D.C.: Bureau of Justice Statistics, 1996), p. 1.
3. Warren R. Nicholes, "Putting Our Best Foot Forward: Burglary Victims Answer the Questions," *Police Chief*, **57**, no. 5 (May 1991), pp. 31–34.
4. *The Seasonality of Crime Victimization* (Washington, D.C.: Bureau of Justice Statistics, 1988), pp. 5–10.

5. *Household Burglary* (Washington, D.C.: Bureau of Justice Statistics, 1985), pp. 1–5.
6. Marianne W. Zawitz, ed., *Report of the Nation on Crime and Justice* (Washington, D.C.: Bureau of Justice Statistics, 1988), p. 51; Drugs and Crime Facts, 1990 (Washington, D.C.: Bureau of Justice Statistics, 1991), p. 5.
7. "For Your Information," *Law Enforcement News*, 30 April 1991, p. 9.
8. "Seattle Citizens Launch Burglary Counterattack," *Target*, **6**, no. 7 July/August 1977), pp. 5–6.
9. *Criminal Victimization in the United States, 1989* (Washington, D.C.: Bureau of Justice Statistics, 1991), p. 14.
10. *Los Angeles Times*, 11 November 1977, part 1, p. 3.
11. James Trainum, "ROP-ing in Fences," *FBI Law Enforcement Bulletin*, **60**, no. 6 (June 1991), p. 7.
12. John E. Conklin and Egon Bittner, "Burglary in a Suburb," *Criminology* (August 1973), pp. 206–232.
13. Pope, *Crime-Specific Analysis*, p. 43.
14. White et al., *Police Burglary Prevention*, p. 23.
15. "Sustained Police-Citizen Cooperation in Milford," *Target*, **6**, no. 9 (October 1977), p. 1.
16. Irving B. Zeichner, "Insight Criminal Justice," *Law and Order*, **31**, no. 12 (December 1983), p. 8.
17. John J. Moslow, "False Alarms: Cause for Alarm," *FBI Law Enforcement Bulletin*, **63**, no. 11 (November 1994), p. 1.
18. Arthur G. Brighton, "Reducing Burglary through Management by Objectives," *Law and Order*, **24**, no. 6 (June 1976), pp. 42–55.
19. Michael Strope, "The Springfield Experience," *Law and Order*, **31**, no. 12 (December 1983), pp. 22–24.
20. "Police Department Sponsors 30-Day Antiburglary Campaign," *Police Chief*, **41**, no. 5 (May 1974), pp. 57–58.

Chapter Ten

1. *Crime in the United States 2003, Uniform Crime Reports* (Washington, D.C.: U.S. Government Printing Office, 2004), p. 31.
2. Joan M. Johnson and Marshall M. DeBerry Jr., *Criminal Victimization 1989* (Washington, D.C.: Bureau of Justice Statistics, 1990), p. 14.
3. *Uniform Crime Reports* 2003, p. 30.
4. Johnson and DeBerry, *Criminal Victimization*, pp. 16–25.
5. *Uniform Crime Reports* 2003, p. 31.
6. Richard H. Ward, Thomas J. Ward, and Jayne Feeley, *Police Robbery Control Manual* (Washington, D.C.: National Institute of Law Enforcement and Criminal Justice, 1975), p. 5.
7. Marianne W. Zawitz, ed., *Report to the Nation on Crime and Justice* (Washington, D.C.: Bureau of Justice Statistics, 1988), p. 44.
8. Caroline W. Harlow, *Injuries from Crime* (Washington, D.C.: Bureau of Justice Statistics, 1989), p. 4.
9. Zawitz, *Report to the Nation*, p. 5.
10. Ward et al., *Robbery Control Manual*, p. 5.
11. *Omaha World Herald*, 8 December 1991, p. 38A.
12. James Hurley, "Violent Crime Hits Home," *FBI Law Enforcement Bulletin*, **64**, no. 6 (June 1995), pp. 9–13.
13. "Combined Effort by Law Enforcement Agencies to Combat Increases in Hijacking and Cargo Theft," *Police Chief*, **50**, no. 11 (November 1983), p. 17.
14. Michael R. Rand, "Carjacking," *Crime Data Brief: Bureau of Justice Statistics* (Washington, D.C.: Bureau of Justice Statistics, March 1994), p. 1.
15. "Bank Heists Surge in DC," *Law Enforcement News*, 15 June 1995, p. 5.
16. "DC Area Bank Heists Rising," *Law Enforcement News*, 31 March 1996, p. 6.
17. *Los Angeles Times*, 11 May 1975, p. 12.
18. "Florida Robberies Dip," *Law and Order*, **42**, no. 9 (September 1994), p. 4.
19. "Operation STAR," *FBI Law Enforcement Bulletin*, **60**, no. 7 (July 1991), pp. 16–17.

20. "The Kansas City Gun Experiment," *FBI Law Enforcement Bulletin*, **64**, no. 5 (May 1995), pp. 4–5.
21. "ATF Data Traces Retail Origins of Crime Guns," *Law Enforcement News*, May 2004, p. 5.
22. "The Search for Smart Guns," *U.S. News & World Report*, 28 November 1994, p. 59.
23. Ward et al., *Robbery Control Manual*, p. 42.
24. "Guns and Crime," *FBI Law Enforcement Bulletin*, **65**, no. 6 (June 1996), p. 21.
25. Roger W. Aaron, "Gunshot Primer Residue: The Invisible Clue," *FBI Law Enforcement Bulletin*, **60**, no. 6 (June 1991), pp. 19–22.
26. "ATF Office to Install Bullet Analyzing Computer," *Omaha World Herald*, 25 May 1996, p. 53.
27. Jennifer Budden, "ATFs NIBIN Program," *Law and Order*, **60**, no. 11 (November 2001), pp. 101–106.

Chapter Eleven

1. Andrew H. Malcolm, "The Ultimate Decision," *New York Times Magazine*, 3 December 1989, p. 50.
2. *Data Report—1989* (Washington, D.C.: Bureau of Justice Statistics, 1990), p. 50.
3. Donald G. Hanna, *Criminal Law for Illinois Police* (Champaign, Ill.: Stipes, 1972), p. 30.
4. *Omaha World Herald*, 1 September 1991, p. 18A.
5. "Homicide Surges in 1990," *Law Enforcement News*, 31 December 1990, p. 1.
6. Donald T. Lunde, "Our Murder Boom," *Psychology Today* (July 1975), pp. 35–42.
7. *New York Times*, 23 March 1975, p. 1.
8. James N. Gilbert, "A Study of the Increased Rate of Unsolved Criminal Homicide in San Diego, California, and Its Relationship to Police Investigative Effectiveness," *American Journal of Police*, **2**, no. 2 (Spring 1983), pp. 149–163.
9. James N. Gilbert, "The Stranger Homicide: Investigative Challenge," *Law and Order*, **31**, no. 11 (November 1983), p. 73. New York City figure from "What's Driving New York's Crime Rate Down," *Law Enforcement News*, 30 November 1996, p. 8.
10. Bruce J. Cohen, ed., *Crime in America: Perspectives on Criminal and Delinquent Behavior* (Itasca, Ill.: F. E. Peacock, 1977), p. 98.
11. John Sedgwick, "A Case of Wife Murder," *Esquire* (June 1990), p. 200.
12. George Esper, "Study of Murder-Suicide," *Omaha World Herald*, 6 December 1989, p. 19.
13. "Kids Who Kill," *U.S. News & World Report*, 8 April 1991, pp. 26–27.
14. "Three Out of Ten Victims Had Taken Cocaine," *Omaha World Herald*, 11 July 1994, p. 2.
15. T. Stanley Duncan, "Death in the Office," *FBI Law Enforcement Bulletin*, **64**, no. 1 (April 1995), pp. 20–25.
16. "Catching a New Breed of Killer," *Time*, 14 November 1983, p. 47.
17. Robert R. Hazelwood and John E. Douglas, "The Lust Murderer," *FBI Law Enforcement Bulletin*, **49**, no. 4 (April 1980), pp. 18–20.
18. *Los Angeles Times*, 17 December 1977, part 1, p. 1.
19. Bruce Porter, "Mind Hunters," *Psychology Today*, **17**, no. 4 (April 1983), p. 46.
20. Emanuel Tanay, "The Lindbergh Kidnapping—A Psychiatric View," *Journal of Forensic Sciences*, **28**, no. 4 (October 1983), pp. 1076–1082.
21. John E. Douglas, *Crime Classification Manual* (New York: Lexington Books, 1992), p. 21.
22. Richard Ault and James Reese, "A Psychological Assessment of Crime," *FBI Law Enforcement Bulletin*, **49**, no. 3 (March 1980), p. 24.
23. Ronald Holmes, *Profiling Violent Crimes* (Newbury Park, Calif.: Sage, 1989), pp. 122–123.
24. *Los Angeles Times*, 8 December 1977, part 1, p. 24.
25. *Crime in the United States 2003, Uniform Crime Reports* (Washington, D.C.: U.S. Government Printing Office, 2004), p. 38.
26. Christopher S. Dunn, *The Patterns and Distribution of Assault Incident Characteristics among Social Areas* (Washington, D.C.: National Institute of Law Enforcement and Criminal Justice, 1976), p. 10.

27. *Uniform Crime Reports*, 2003, p. 37.

28. *Champaign-Urbana* (Illinois) *News Gazette*, 7 August 1977, p. 11.

29. Edward Conlon, "To the Potter's Field," *The New Yorker*, 19 July 1993, p. 42.

30. Paul Pane, "Dental Identification Program: An Overview," *FBI Law Enforcement Bulletin* (August 1982), p. 12.

31. Robert B. J. Dorion, "Photographic Superimposition," *Journal of Forensic Sciences*, **27**, no. 3 (July 1983), pp. 724–734.

32. R. A. Driscoll, "Summary of Skeletal Identification in Tennessee," *Journal of Forensic Sciences*, **28**, no. 1 (January 1983), p. 162.

33. Page Hudson, "Suicide with Two Guns Fired Simultaneously," *Journal of Forensic Sciences*, **27**, no. 1 (January 1982), p. 6.

34. "Trauma Team's Rush to Trim Death Rate for Gunshot Wounds," *Omaha World Herald*, 12 November 1994, p. 4.

35. "News in Review," *Law Enforcement News*, 15 April 1995, p. 2.

36. Marilee Frazer and Sharon Rosenberg, "Russian Roulette with a Knife," *Journal of Forensic Sciences*, **28**, no. 1 (January 1983), p. 268.

37. Irving A. Spergel and Ronald L. Chance, "National Youth Gang Suppression and Intervention Program," *National Institute of Justice Reports*, no. 224 (June 1991), p. 21.

38. Michael M. Baden, *Unnatural Death* (New York: Random House, 1989), p. xii.

39. Illinois Revised Statutes, chapter 31, sec. 10.

40. Baden, *Unnatural Death*, p. 23.

41. "Mistaken Identity," *Time*, **135**, no. 18 (30 April 1990), p. 43.

42. "A Tale of Arsenic and Old Zach," *Newsweek*, **118**, no. 1 (1 July 1991), p. 64.

43. Robert W. Mann and Douglas H. Ubelaker, "The Forensic Anthropologist," *FBI Law Enforcement Bulletin*, **59**, no. 7 (July 1990), pp. 20–23.

44. *DNA Profiling for Positive Identification* (Washington, D.C.: Bureau of Justice Statistics, 1990), p. 2.

45. *Forensic DNA Analysis: Issues* (Washington, D.C.: Bureau of Justice Statistics, 1991), p. 4.

46. *Forensic Testing Facts* (Germantown, Md.: Cellmark Diagnostics, 1989), p. 3.

47. Jay V. Miller, "The FBI's Forensic DNA Analysis Program," *FBI Law Enforcement Bulletin*, **60**, no. 7 (July 1991), p. 15.

48. Miller, "Forensic DNA Analysis," pp. 11–12.

49. "DNA Database Marks Its 1,000th Cold Hit," *Law Enforcement News*, 30 November 2002, p. 6.

50. "DNA Samples the Crime-Fighting Equal of Fingerprints," *Omaha World Herald*, 25 March 2004, p. 5A.

51. Mary Gibbons Graham and Joseph Kochanski, "Individualizing Bloodstains," *Research in Action: National Institute of Justice*, November 1983, p. 6.

52. Herbert Leon MacDonell, *Flight Characteristics and Stain Patterns of Human Blood* (Washington, D.C.: National Institute of Law Enforcement and Criminal Justice, 1971), pp. 1–77.

53. Louis L. Akin, "Blood Spatter Interpretation at Crime and Accident Scenes," *FBI Law Enforcement Bulletin*, **74**, no. 2 (February 2005), pp. 21–24.

Chapter Twelve

1. Nancy Gibbs, "When Is It Rape?" *Time*, 3 June 1991, p. 52; *Omaha World Herald*, 2 August 1992, 16A.

2. "Rape: The Sexual Weapon," *Time*, 5 September 1983, pp. 27–29.

3. Kathleen Maguire and Timothy J. Flanagan, *Sourcebook of Criminal Justice Statistics—1990* (Washington, D.C.: Bureau of Justice Statistics, 1991), p. 271.

4. *Omaha World Herald*, 24 April 1992, p. 1.

5. *Omaha World Herald*, 19 December 1993, p. 10A.

6. M. Joan McDermott, *Rape Victimization in 26 American Cities* (Washington, D.C.: U.S. Department of Justice, 1979), p. xi.

7. H. H. Bonheur, "Psychodiagnostic Testing of Sex Offenders: A Comparative Study," *Journal of Forensic Sciences*, **28**, no. 1 (January 1983), pp. 49–60.

8. Bruce J. Cohen, ed., *Crime in America: Perspectives on Criminal and Delinquent Behavior* (Itasca, Ill.: F. E. Peacock, 1977), p. 356.

9. Harold J. Vetter and Ira J. Silverman, *The Nature of Crime* (Philadelphia: W. B. Saunders, 1978), p. 102.

10. Robert R. Hazelwood and Ann W. Burgess, *Practical Aspects of Rape Investigation* (New York: Elsevier, 1987), pp. 175–182.

11. Nancy Gibbs, "The Clamor on Campus," *Time*, 3 June 1991, pp. 54–55.

12. Thomas E. Baker, "The Sadistic Rapist," *The Detective*, Spring/Summer 1991, pp. 22–26.

13. Hazelwood and Burgess, *Practical Aspects of Rape Investigation*, pp. 181–182.

14. *Omaha World Herald*, 15 February 1990, p. 9.

15. Robert R. Hazelwood, "The Behavior-Oriented Interview of Rape Victims: The Key to Profiling," *FBI Law Enforcement Bulletin*, **52**, no. 9 (September 1983), pp. 8–15.

16. William F. Merrill, "The Art of Interrogating Rapists," *FBI Law Enforcement Bulletin*, **64**, no. 1 (January 1995), pp. 8–12.

17. Mark Mann, "Fantasy-Based Interviewing: An Investigative Approach for Predatory Sex Offenders," *Law and Order*, **44**, no. 5 (May 1996), pp. 117–119.

18. *Omaha World Herald*, 20 December 1993, p. 6.

19. *Los Angeles Times*, 23 July 1976, part 4, p. 1.

20. Robert R. Hazelwood and Janet Warren, "The Criminal Behavior of the Serial Rapist," *FBI Law Enforcement Bulletin*, **59**, no. 2 (February 1990), p. 15.

21. *Champaign-Urbana* (Illinois) *News Gazette*, 19 January 1978, p. 4A.

22. W. C. Overton, "Child Sexual Abuse Investigation," *Law and Order*, **42**, no. 7 (July 1994), p. 97.

23. Sheila Crowell and Ellen Kolba, *Men Who Molest/Children Who Survive* (New York: Film Makers Library, 1985), p. 3.

24. Patrick Langan and Caroline Wolf Harlow, *Child Rape Victims—1992* (Washington D.C.: Bureau of Justice Statistics, June 1994), pp. 1–2.

25. Kenneth V. Lanning, *Child Molesters: A Behavioral Analysis* (Washington, D.C.: National Center for Missing and Exploited Children, 1987), p. 2.

26. *Omaha World Herald*, 11 June 1989, p. E1.

27. Ana Alicea-Diaz, "Child Abuse: Problems in Investigating," *The Detective*, (Winter 1989), pp. 14–15.

28. David Finkelhorn et al., *Missing, Abducted, Runaway, and Thrownaway Children in America* (Washington, D.C.: U.S. Department of Justice, 1990), pp. 8–10.

29. Ann W. Burgess, *Children Traumatized in Sex Rings* (Washington, D.C.: National Center for Missing and Exploited Children, 1988), p. 4.

30. Donald K. Wright, "Too Late for Tears," *The Detective*, Summer/Fall 1989, p. 18.

31. Kenneth V. Lanning, *Child Sex Rings: A Behavioral Analysis* (Washington, D.C.: National Center for Missing and Exploited Children, 1989), p. 7.

32. *Los Angeles Times*, 19 November 1976, part 1, p. 1.

33. Overton, "Child Sexual Abuse," p. 97.

34. Lanning, *Child Molesters*, p. 27.

35. Blaine D. McIlwaine, "Interrogating Child Molesters," *FBI Law Enforcement Bulletin*, **63**, no. 6 (June 1994), pp. 1–4.

36. William McCormack, "Selected Supreme Court Cases: 1989–1990," *FBI Law Enforcement Bulletin*, **59**, no. 11 (November 1990), p. 32.

37. "Interviewing the Rape Victim—Training Key #210" (Gaithersburg, Md.: International Association of Chiefs of Police, 1974), p. 2.

38. James L. Mathis, *Clear Thinking about Sexual Deviations* (Chicago: Nelson-Hall, 1972), p. 33.

39. Robert Grispino, "Serological Evidence in Sexual Assault Investigations," *FBI Law Enforcement Bulletin*, **59**, no. 10 (October 1990), p. 18.

40. Robert D. Blackledge, "Condom Trace Evidence," *FBI Law Enforcement Bulletin*, **65**, no. 7 (May 1996), pp. 12–16.

Chapter Thirteen

1. *Crime in the United States 2000, Uniform Crime Reports* (Washington, D.C.: U.S. Government Printing Office, 2001), p. 47.

2. *Uniform Crime Reports*, 2000, p. 53.

3. *Uniform Crime Reports*, 2000, p. 53.

4. "Stolen Cars Out of the United States," *Law and Order*, **44**, no. 4 (April 1996), p. 43.
5. *Los Angeles Times*, 20 February 1977, part 1, p. 18.
6. Caroline W. Harlow, *Motor Vehicle Theft* (Washington, D.C.: Bureau of Justice Statistics, 1988), pp. 1–3.
7. David Brickell and Lee S. Cole, *Vehicle Theft Investigation* (Santa Cruz, Calif.: Davis, 1975), pp. 5–9.
8. *Omaha World Herald*, 23 September 1991, p. 13.
9. "The Autos Thieves Love," *Parade*, 6 September 1995.
10. Mary E. Beckman and Michael R. Daly, "Motor Vehicle Theft Investigations: Emerging International Trends," *FBI Law Enforcement Bulletin*, **59**, no. 9 (September 1990), p. 16.
11. Mary Ellen Beckman, "Auto Theft: Countering Violent Trends," *FBI Law Enforcement Bulletin*, **62**, no. 10 (October 1993), p. 18.
12. Sheila Goldman and Edward Illam, "Facts of Motorcycle Theft," *Law and Order*, **31**, no. 9 (September 1983), p. 92.
13. George J. Lyford, "Heavy Equipment Theft," *FBI Law Enforcement Bulletin*, **50**, no. 3 (March 1981), p. 2.
14. Jimmy W. Mercer, "Baited Vehicle Detail," *FBI Law Enforcement Bulletin*, **60**, no. 5 (May 1991), pp. 24–25.
15. "Baby Boomers Lead in Shoplifting," *Law and Order*, **42**, no. 7 (July 1994), p. 4.
16. "'Tis the Season to Be Wary," *Time*, 12 December 1977, p. 11.
17. *Los Angeles Times*, 28 November 1977, part 1, p. 11.
18. *Omaha World Herald*, 12 August 1990, p. 17-A.
19. *White-Collar Crime* (Washington, D.C.: U.S. Chamber of Commerce, 1974), p. 33.
20. "In the Spotlight Identity Theft," NCJRS Web site, Office of Justice Programs, http://ncjrs.org/spotlightidentity_theft/summary, 11 May 2005.
21. Vinse J. Gilliam, "Taking the Bounce Out of Bad Checks," *FBI Law Enforcement Journal*, **60**, no. 10 (October 1991), p. 15.
22. Johnny Turner and W. Steve Albrecht, "Check Kiting," *FBI Law Enforcement Bulletin*, **62**, no. 11 (November 1993), pp. 12–16.
23. *Information concerning the Document Section of the Crime Laboratory* (Tallahassee: Florida Department of Law Enforcement), pp. 6–7.
24. *Los Angeles Times*, 12 November 1983, part 1A, p. 4.
25. Ibid.

Chapter Fourteen

1. *Drug Data Summary* (Washington, D.C.: Office of National Drug Control Policy, 2003), pp. 1–6.
2. *Drug Use Forecasting* (Washington, D.C.: National Institute of Justice, November 1995), pp. 19, 22.
3. *Drug Use Forecasting*, p. 21.
4. "The Widening Drug War," *Newsweek*, 1 July 1991, p. 32.
5. "Teen Pot Use Turns Upward," *Law Enforcement News*, 15 November 1996, p. 5.
6. *Omaha World Herald*, 20 June 1991, p. 1.
7. "Heroin Comes Back," *Time*, 19 February 1990, p. 63.
8. "Heroin Makes an Ominous Comeback," *Newsweek*, 1 November 1993, p. 53.
9. "Heroin Addiction," *Parade*, 31 July 1977, p. 5.
10. "The Nigerian Connection," *Newsweek*, 19 February 1990, p. 63.
11. *Questions and Answers about Drug Abuse* (Washington, D.C.: Special Action Office for Drug Abuse Prevention, Executive Office of the President, 1975), p. 30.
12. "Crashing on Cocaine," *Time*, 11 April 1983, pp. 23–31.
13. "The Men Who Created Crack," *U.S. News & World Report*, 19 August 1991, p. 44.
14. Thomas A. Constantine, "Drug Wars," *Police Chief*, **57**, no. 5 (May 1990), p. 37.
15. William M. Adler, "From Rocks to Riches," *Esquire*, **113**, no. 1 (January 1990), pp. 105–112.
16. Mike McAlary, *Cop Shot* (New York: G. P. Putnam's Sons, 1990), pp. 41–42.
17. "The Men Who Created Crack," p. 51.
18. "Database," *U.S. News & World Report*, 24 December 1990, p. 12.

19. "Pill-Popping Teens Become Generation Rx, Study Finds," *Omaha World Herald*, 22 April 2005, p. 10-A.
20. "The Date Rape Drug," *The Chronicle of Higher Education*, 28 June 1996, p. A29.
21. Susan Pennell, "Ice," *National Institute of Justice Reports*, no. 221 (Summer 1990), p. 12.
22. "What's Cooking? Study Finds Surprises in Its Picture of Small-Time Meth Cookers," *Law Enforcement News*, 15 June, 2003, p. 10-A.
23. "LSD Makes a Comeback with Middle Class," *Law Enforcement News*, 15 September 1991, p. 7.
24. "PCP: A Terror of a Drug," *Time*, 19 December 1977, p. 53.
25. "The Perils of PCP," *Drug Enforcement*, **1**, no. 3 (Spring 1974), pp. 8–9.
26. "I Felt Like I Wanted to Hurt People," *Newsweek*, 22 July 2002, pp. 32–33.
27. "DEA's Good News: Pot Prices Soar as Availability Plummets," *Law Enforcement News*, 15 September 1990, p. 4.
28. Ken Liska, *Drugs and the Human Body* (Upper Saddle River, N.J.: Prentice Hall, 1997), pp. 284–285.
29. *Omaha World Herald*, 18 November 1990, p. 19A.
30. Thomas Bower, "Anabolic Steroids," *The Detective*, Spring/Summer 1991, p. 27.
31. Charles Swanson et al., "Abuse of Anabolic Steroids," *FBI Law Enforcement Bulletin*, **60**, no. 8 (August 1991), p. 20.
32. John Taylor, "Anabolic Steroid Use among Teenagers," *Omaha World Herald*, 26 August 1991, p. 25.
33. Stephen E. Stone, "The Investigation and Prosecution of Professional Practice Cases under the Controlled Substances Act," *Drug Enforcement*, **10**, no. 1 (Spring 1983), p. 21.
34. Stephen L. Hermann, "Clandestine Drug Laboratory Hazards," *Law and Order*, **42**, no. 4 (May 1994), p. 93.
35. "Drug Intelligence Center Enters Third Decade," *DEA World*, Winter 1995, p. 19.
36. Margaret Gentry, "Five Years Later, It's Judge Webster's FBI," *Police*, **6**, no. 2 (March 1983), p. 32.
37. Ronald J. Getz, "Civil Forfeiture Benefits Police," *Law and Order*, **43**, no. 10, p. 65.
38. Lindsey D. Stellwagen, *Use of Forfeiture Sanctions in Drug Cases* (Washington, D.C.: Bureau of Justice Statistics, 1985), pp. 1–5.
39. *Los Angeles Times*, 2 March 1978, part 1, p. 1.
40. *Los Angeles Times*, 2 March 1978, part 1, p. 15.
41. William F. Smith, "Organized Crime Today," *Drug Enforcement*, **10**, no. 1 (Spring 1983), pp. 7–8.
42. Marcia R. Chaiken, "The Rise of Crack and Ice," *National Institute of Justice Reports*, March 1993, pp. 2–3.
43. Edward F. Connors and Hugh Nugent, *Street-Level Narcotics Enforcement* (Washington, D.C.: Bureau of Justice Assistance, 1990), pp. 13–14.
44. Gary E. Wade, "Undercover Violence," *FBI Law Enforcement Bulletin*, **59**, no. 4 (April 1990), pp. 15–18.
45. *Guidelines for Narcotics and Dangerous Drug Evidence: Handling and Security Procedures* (Washington, D.C.: Drug Enforcement Administration, n.d.), app. 4.
46. Tom Mieczkowski, "Hair Analysis as a Drug Detector," *National Institute of Justice*, October 1995, pp. 1–4.

Chapter Fifteen

1. Carolyn Block and Richard Block, *Street Gang Crime in Chicago* (Washington, D.C.: National Institute of Justice, December 1993), p. 3.
2. G. David Curry, *Gang Crime and Law Enforcement Record Keeping* (Washington, D.C.: National Institute of Justice, August 1994), p. 1.
3. "Superpredators Arrive," *Newsweek*, 22 January 1996, p. 57.
4. Claire Johnson, *Prosecuting Gangs: A National Assessment* (Washington, D.C.: National Institute of Justice, February 1995), p. 4.
5. Alan Brantley and Andrew DiRosa, "Gangs: A National Perspective," *FBI Law Enforcement Bulletin*, **63**, no. 5 (May 1994), p. 4.
6. Melanie Laflin, "Girl Gangs," *Law and Order*, **44**, no. 3 (March 1996), p. 87.

7. Curry, Gang Crime, p. 1.
8. Cheryle L. Maxson, *Street Gangs and Drug Sales in Two Suburban Cities* (Washington, D.C.: National Institute of Justice, September 1995), pp. 1–13.
9. "Locals Look to ICE to Chill Street Gangs," *Law Enforcement News*, May 2005, pp. 8–9.
10. James A. Fox, *Trends in Juvenile Violence* (Washington, D.C.: Bureau of Justice Statistics, March 1996), pp. 1–3.
11. Christopher M. Grant, "Graffiti: Taking a Close Look," *FBI Law Enforcement Bulletin*, **65**, no. 8 (August 1996), pp. 11–15.
12. John Maxwell and Dennis Porter, "Taggers: Graffiti Vandals or Violent Criminals," *Police Marksman*, **21**, no. 2 (March/April 1996), pp. 34–35.
13. "Gang Members Are Moving Online to Trade Threats, Recruit Members," *Omaha World Herald*, 6 March 2005, p. 12-A.
14. Block and Block, *Street Gangs Crime in Chicago*, p. 3.
15. Laura E. Quarantiello, "Tracking the Homeboys," *Law and Order*, **44**, no. 6 (June 1996), pp. 80–82.
16. Johnson, *Prosecuting Gangs*, pp. 5–6.

Chapter Sixteen

1. *Criminal Victimization in the United States, 1989* (Washington, D.C.: Bureau of Justice Statistics, 1990), p. 135; *Omaha World Herald*, 29 November 2002, p. 5A.
2. *Crime in the United States 1990, Uniform Crime Reports* (Washington, D.C.: U.S. Government Printing Office, 1991), p. 179.
3. "Wife Beating: The Silent Crime," *Time*, 5 September 1983, p. 23; *Omaha World Herald*, 29 November 2002, p. 5A.
4. "Homes Not Havens for Everyone," *Omaha World Herald*, 2 January 1995, p. 24.
5. *Los Angeles Times*, 20 February 1978, part 4, p. 1.
6. "Domestic Homicide Tipoffs May Be Missed," *Law Enforcement News*, February 2004, p. 9.
7. Kathleen Maguire and Timothy J. Flanagan, *Sourcebook of Criminal Justice Statistics—1990* (Washington, D.C.: Bureau of Justice Statistics, 1991), p. 35.
8. Ronald M. Holmes, "Stalking in America," *Law and Order*, **42**, no. 5 (May 1994), pp. 88–92.
9. "Stalking Fact Sheet," Victim's Voices in Corrections, Office on Violence Against Women, U.S. Department of Justice, Fall 2003, p. 9.
10. Robert A. Wood and Nona L. Wood, "Stalking the Stalker: A Profile of Offenders," *FBI Law Enforcement Bulletin*, **71**, no. 12 (December 2002), pp. 1–9; George E. Wattendorf, "Stalking Investigation Strategies," *FBI Law Enforcement Bulletin*, **69**, no. 3 (March 2000), pp. 10–14.
11. "Elderly Vulnerable to Mistreatment," *Kearney Hub*, 12 December 1994, p. 11A.
12. Christopher Fox, "Shattering the Silence of Senior Abuse," *Law and Order*, **43**, no. 3, pp. 95–99.
13. "Child Abuse on the Rise," *Law Enforcement News*, 15 April 1990, p. 13.
14. Maguire and Flanagan, *Sourcebook of Criminal Justice Statistics*, p. 244.
15. Armin A. Brott, "Child Abuse Industry Perpetuates Itself," *Omaha World Herald*, 20 August 1995, p. 11B.
16. *California Penal Code*, sec. 11161.5.
17. Maguire and Flanagan, *Sourcebook of Criminal Justice Statistics*, p. 35.
18. Katie Leishman, "The Extent of the Harm," *The New Republic*, **52**, no. 5 (November 1983), p. 24.
19. Kent Jordan, "Child Abuse" (Speech given before the San Diego Community Child Abuse Coordinating Council, 16 October 1973).
20. Lawrence A. Greenfield, *Child Victimizers: Violent Offenders and Their Victims* (Washington, D.C.: Bureau of Justice Statistics, March 1996), pp. 1–3.
21. David Finkelhor et al., *Missing, Abducted, Runaway, and Thrownaway Children in America* (Washington, D.C.: U.S. Department of Justice, Office of Juvenile Justice and Delinquency Prevention, 1990), pp. 11, 14.
22. John Drzazga, *Wheels of Fortune* (Springfield, Ill.: Charles C Thomas, 1963), p. 16.

23. *Task Force Report: Organized Crime*. Report to the President's Commission on Law Enforcement and Administration of Justice. (Washington, D.C.: U.S. Government Printing Office, 1967), p. 7.

24. Francis A. J. Ianni, *Ethnic Succession in Organized Crime* (Washington, D.C.: National Institute of Law Enforcement and Criminal Justice, 1973), pp. 1–2.

25. William French Smith, "Organized Crime Today," *Drug Enforcement*, **10**, no. 1 (Spring 1983), p. 8.

26. Alan Brantley and Andrew DiRosa, "Gangs: A National Perspective," *FBI Law Enforcement Bulletin*, **63**, no. 5, p. 2.

27. *San Diego Union*, 7 November 1983, p. A4.

28. Walter Bouman, "Best Practices of a Hate/Bias Crime Investigation," *FBI Law Enforcement Bulletin*, **72**, no. 3 (March 2003), pp. 21–31.

29. John F. Boudreau et al., *Arson and Arson Investigation* (Washington, D.C.: National Institute of Law Enforcement and Criminal Justice, 1977), p. 17.

30. *Crime in the United States 2000, Uniform Crime Reports* (Washington, D.C.: U.S. Government Printing Office, 2001), pp. 56–58.

31. *St. Louis Post-Dispatch*, 10 February 1972.

32. Nolan Lewis and Helen Yarnell, "A Profile of the Typical Pyromaniac," *FBI Law Enforcement Bulletin*, **49**, no. 6 (July 1980), p. 14.

33. Frank Hart, "The Arson Equation," *Police Chief*, **57**, no. 12 (December 1990), p. 34.

34. Kenneth Braun and Robert Ford, "Organizing an Arson Task Force," *FBI Law Enforcement Bulletin*, **50**, no. 3 (March 1981), pp. 22–26.

35. Andrea A. Moenssens, *Scientific Evidence in Civil and Criminal Cases* (Westbury, N.Y.: Foundation Press, 1995), pp. 403–426.

36. Adam F. Berluti, "Arson Investigation: Connecticut's Canines," *Police Chief*, **57**, no. 12 (December 1990), p. 44.

37. George Cuomo, *A Couple of Cops* (New York: Random House, 1995), p. 195.

38. David J. Icove, "Serial Arsonists," *Police Chief*, **57**, no. 12 (December 1990), pp. 46–47.

39. "Bank Attacks in U.S. Are More Frequent in 1990s," *Omaha World Herald*, 31 July 1996, p. 10.

40. William A. May and David Dunn, "Terrorists and Bombs," *Law and Order*, **44**, no. 3 (March 1996), pp. 108–114.

Chapter Seventeen

1. Andrea A. Moenssens, *Fingerprint Techniques* (Philadelphia: Chilton, 1971), p. 64.

2. Scott Hoober, "Detecting Fingerprints Easier," *Law and Order*, **42**, no. 5 (May 1994), p. 103.

3. *Iodine Fuming and the Use of Ninhydrin Spray* (Raleigh, N.C.: Sirchie Fingerprint Laboratories, n.d.).

4. William O. Jungbluth and Gary Griffiths, "Investigative Equipment: Superglue Techniques," *The Detective*, Summer/Fall 1989, p. 4.

5. E. Roland Menzel et al., "Laser Detection of Latent Fingerprints: Treatment with Glue Containing Cyanoacrylate Ester," *Journal of Forensic Sciences*, **28**, no. 2 (April 1983), pp. 307–317.

6. Eric W. Fricker, "Lifting Latents from Skin," *Law Enforcement Technology*, **19**, no. 5 (May 1992), pp. 44–47.

7. Ivan R. Futrell, "Hidden Evidence: Latent Prints on Human Skin," *FBI Law Enforcement Bulletin* (April 1996), pp. 21–24.

8. "AFIS Technology for Rural States," *FBI Law Enforcement Bulletin*, **59**, no. 11 (November 1990), p. 24.

9. "Around the Nation: New Jersey," *Law Enforcement News*, 15 November 1991, p. 2.

10. Dunstan Prial, "Computerized Fingerprint Plan," *Omaha World Herald*, 5 March 1990, p. 9.

11. Bonnie Clay, "Los Angeles County's Live-Scan Fingerprinting Network Is World's Largest," *Law and Order*, **42**, no. 11 (November 1994), pp. 24–27.

12. Raymond Lang, "Automated Fingerprint System Works in Miami," *Law and Order*, **31**, no. 9 (September 1983), pp. 26–28.

13. *New York Times*, 27 August 1926, p. 6.
14. Harrison C. Allison, *Personal Identification* (Boston: Holbrook, 1973), pp. 59–63.
15. Sharon S. Smith and Roger W. Shuy, "Forensic Psycholinguistics," *FBI Law Enforcement Bulletin*, **71**, no. 4 (April 2002), pp. 16–21.
16. Penelope Pickett, "Linguistics in the Courtroom," *FBI Law Enforcement Bulletin*, **62**, no. 10 (October 1993), pp. 6–9.
17. *U.S. v. Wade*, 388 U.S. 218 (1967).
18. "Talking Rogues Gallery," *Law and Order*, **25**, no. 5 (May 1976), pp. 20–21.
19. *Los Angeles Times*, 29 August 1979, part 1, p. 1.
20. "Police Sketches Meet Computers," *Law Enforcement News*, 30 April 1989, pp. 1, 7.
21. "Computerized Faceprints," *Police Chief*, **50**, no. 6 (June 1983), p. 15.
22. Matthew Grinnell and Tod Burke, "Face Recognition Technology," *Law and Order*, **49**, no. 11 (November 2001), pp. 36–40.

Chapter Eighteen

1. John Buchanan, "Police-Prosecutor Teams," *National Institute of Justice Reports*, no. 214 (May/June 1989), pp. 2–8.
2. Blair J. Kolasa and Bernadine Meyer, *The American Legal System* (Englewood Cliffs, N.J.: Prentice Hall, 1987), pp. 58–60, 234–278.
3. "Detailed Testimony Given Most Weight by Jurors," *Chronicle of Higher Education*, **35**, no. 39 (7 June 1989), pp. A5–A6.
4. Joe Navarro, "Testifying in the Theater of the Courtroom," *FBI Law Enforcement Bulletin*, **73**, no. 9 (September 2004) pp. 26–30; M. P. Gunderson, "Five Tips for Testifying in Court," *Law and Order*, **51**, no. 7 (July 2003), pp. 110–113; "Elements of Litigation and Proper Courtroom Demeanor," *Nebraska Jail Bulletin* (February 1995), p. 3.

Chapter Nineteen

1. Vivian B. Lord, "Implementing a Cold Case Homicide Unit," *FBI Law Enforcement Bulletin*, **74**, no. 2 (February 2005), pp. 1–6.
2. Ordway P. Burden, "Crime Fight for the Long Haul," *Law Enforcement News*, 15 May 1991, p. 2.
3. William A. Gehler, *Local Government Police Management* (Washington, D.C.: International City Management Association, 1991), p. 79.
4. Daniel McGillis, *Major Offense Bureau* (Washington, D.C.: National Institute of Law Enforcement and Criminal Justice, 1977), p. 5.
5. Stephen D'Arcy, "Tracking Habitual Offenders," *Law and Order*, **43**, no. 3 (March 1995), p. 111.
6. Kenneth W. Goddard, *Crime Scene Investigation* (Reston, Va.: Reston, 1977), p. xii.
7. Tim Dees, "Understanding GIS," *Law and Order*, **50**, no. 8 (August 2002), pp. 42–46.
8. Jim Weiss and Mickey Davis, "Geographic Profiling Finds Serial Criminals," *Law and Order*, **52**, no. 12 (December 2004), pp. 33–38.
9. Jeffrey Hormann, "Virtual Reality: The Future of Law Enforcement," *FBI Law Enforcement Bulletin*, **64**, no. 7 (July 1995), pp. 7–11.
10. George L. Kelling, "What Works—Research and the Police," *National Institute of Justice Research—Crime File*, 1988, p. 1.
11. Gehler, *Local Government Police Management*, p. 333.
12. Kelling, "What Works," pp. 3–4.
13. John H. Campbell, "Futures Research: Here and Abroad," *Police Chief*, **57**, no. 1 (January 1990), p. 30.
14. William L. Tafoya, "Futures Research: Implications for Criminal Investigations," in James N. Gilbert, *Criminal Investigation: Essays and Cases* (Columbus, Ohio: Charles E. Merrill, 1990), pp. 203–212.
15. Alvin Toffler and Heidi Toffler, "The Future of Law Enforcement: Dangerous and Different," *FBI Law Enforcement Bulletin*, **59**, no. 1 (January 1990), pp. 2–5.

16. Alan Youngs, "Law Enforcement in 2003 and Beyond," *Law and Order*, **51**, no. 4 (April 2003), pp. 96–99.
17. Diane Jay Bouchard and Judith Martin, "Improving the Quality of Justice," *Law and Order*, **49**, no. 11 (November 2001), pp. 31–34.
18. Richard M. Rau, "Forensic Science and Criminal Justice Technology: High-Tech Tools for the 90's," *National Institute of Justice—Research in Action*, no. 224 (June 1991), p. 9.
19. William Y. Doran, "The FBI Laboratory: Fifty Years," *Journal of Forensic Sciences*, **24**, no. 4 (October 1982), p. 743.

Glossary

Accelerants Flammable materials used by arsonists to accelerate the burning of property or to increase the amount of destruction.

Accessory A person who aids or contributes before, during, or after an unlawful act in a subordinate or secondary capacity.

Acquittal A setting free or deliverance from a charge by verdict.

Adjudication A formal judicial decision that ends a proceeding by a judgment of conviction, acquittal, or dismissal.

Admissible evidence Evidence deemed material and relevant so as to be allowed in a judicial proceeding.

Affidavit A written statement made under oath or an attachment to a warrant wherein the police detail probable cause.

Affinity scams Bunco frauds that target a specific ethnic or racial group to entice victims to invest in illegal investment schemes.

Aggravated assault An attack by one person on another with the purpose of inflicting severe bodily injury; usually involving a weapon or some other means likely to cause death or serious bodily harm.

Alias A false name used to conceal true identity.

Alibi A statement or defense attempting to prove that a subject suspected of a crime could not have committed the offense.

Alligatoring A pattern of deep cracking on the surface of a material that has been burned, indicative of the point of ignition of the fire.

Amber Alert A notification system that uses the media, highway signs, and other means to inform the public of details pertaining to the abduction of a juvenile by a stranger suspect.

Amphetamines Drug compounds that have a stimulating effect on the central nervous system.

Anabolic steroids Drug compounds related to the hormone testosterone that stimulate muscle growth and the development of male sex characteristics.

Anoacrylate fuming A method of developing latent fingerprints in which the fumes of cyanoacrylate ester are discharged from certain types of glues.

Anthropometry A system of criminal identification developed by Alphonse Bertillon based on 11 measurements of the human frame.

Appeal A request that a case be removed from a lower court to a higher court for the purpose of judicial review.

Arch fingerprint A fingerprint pattern in which ridges enter from one side, rise in the center, and flow out the other side.

Arrest To take a person into custody, by authority of law, for the purpose of answering legal charges.

Arson The willful and malicious intentional act of setting fire to property for some improper and illegal motive.

Artificial intelligence A computer program that manipulates data and infers conclusions.

Aspermia A lack of spermatozoa in semen.

Asphyxia Death caused by a sudden or gradual cessation of oxygen intake.

Assignment by caseload Assigning investigative duties without consideration of the nature of a crime; a method that assumes all officers to be generalists equally competent to investigate any offense.

Assignment by priority A case assignment method in which investigations are assigned by their perceived importance.

Atomic absorption spectroscopy A laboratory technique used to detect elements based on the absorption of light by vaporized atoms.

Auto chopping The dismantling of the major body components of a vehicle for profit.

Automated Fingerprint Identification Systems Computerized systems that compare fingerprints to a local, state, or federal fingerprint database to produce identification.

Autopsy A postmortem surgical examination to determine cause of death.

Bailiff An officer of the court who aids in the judicial proceeding.

Ballistic Identification System Computerized program that compares and catalogs bullets and shell casings.

Ballistics The science dealing with the flight behavior of various types of projectiles.

Bank-examiner swindle A type of fraud in which a victim is deceived into withdrawing money under the pretense of aiding a bank investigation.

Barbiturates Drug compounds that have a depressing or sedative effect on the central nervous system.

Benzidine color reaction test A test that indicates the presence of blood.

Bill of Rights First ten amendments of the U.S. Constitution, which through judicial interpretation guide the actions of criminal investigators.

Biometrics Any form of identification or technological development linked to the use of unique biological material.

Blackmail Some form of payment obtained from a person to prevent disclosure of information that would bring disgrace or ruin if made public; also referred to as extortion.

Bookmaker An individual who takes and records bets on various events, typically sports activities or horse racing. Often called a "bookie."

Booster devices Any object used to assist in a theft, other than the clothing of the thief; typically encountered in shoplifting cases.

Bow Street Runners An early group of English criminal investigators who operated from a court located on Bow Street in London.

Bribery The giving, offering, or taking of anything, especially money, as an inducement to do something illegal or wrong.

Bunco swindles Frauds that involve deceit and trickery as the main method of operation.

Burden of proof The requirement of a continuous demonstration of guilt or a proving of each element of a crime against the accused by the prosecution.

Burglary The unlawful entering of a legally defined structure with the intent to commit a felony or theft.

Car clouting A suspect method of operation involving the theft of property from a vehicle.

Career criminal A criminal perpetrator who has made criminal activity his or her life's work.

Cargo robbery The seizure and robbery of loaded tractor trailer trucks by armed offenders; also known as truck hijacking.

Carjacking A form of robbery in which occupied vehicles are targeted for auto theft.

Chain of custody Pertaining to the process by which evidence is handled, transferred, and accounted for between the time of discovery and the disposition of the case.

Check kiting A method of suspect operation in which several checking accounts based upon nonexistent funds are opened in the attempt to withdraw funds.

Child abuse Any action or failure to act that endangers or impairs a child's physical or emotional health and development.

Circular fracture lines Rounded fractures resulting from an object striking glass that appear on the same side of the striking force.

Circumstantial evidence Evidence that does not directly prove the truth of a fact in issue, but that may establish a strong inference as to the truth of that fact; also known as indirect evidence.

Civil forfeiture Government seizure of assets used during a criminal enterprise.

Closing report The concluding investigative report that causes further investigative action to cease due to the lack of leads, arrest of suspect, or expiration of statute of limitations.

Cocaine A narcotic extracted from the leaf of the coca bush that produces an intense stimulant effect.

Coercion The use of forceful or physically compelling means to obtain information.

Cognitive interview An interviewing technique based on questions designed to improve or focus memory recall.

Cold-case squad Investigative unit that reopens and investigates formerly unsolved cases.

Common law Early English judge law that was common to the English people. It formed the basis for subsequent English and American criminal law.

Computer-aided identification Using computer software to assist victims and witnesses in the identification or facial reconstruction of criminal suspects.

Computer crime Frauds that are perpetrated through the misuse of electronic data processing devices.

Concluding investigation The final phase of the investigation—terminating an unsuccessful case or preparing a successful case for prosecution.

Cone fracture Cone-shaped opening produced from an object passing through a glass surface. The smaller fracture opening indicates the side from which the force originated.

Confession A direct acknowledgment of guilt for the commission of a criminal act.

Confidence swindles Frauds or other crimes that are based on deceit or a misrepresentation of facts.

Consensual crimes Offenses that are committed by mutual consent of all parties involved, hence said to be "victimless." Vice offenses are typical.

Conspiracy An agreement between two or more persons to commit a crime in concert.

Contusions Injuries in which the skin is not broken but blood vessels are ruptured.

Coordinated photo series A series of crime scene photographs taken in a sequential manner from general to specific subject matter.

Coroner An official, generally elected, who is legally responsible for investigating deaths within a jurisdiction as determined by law.

Corpus delicti The facts constituting or proving the body of a crime, or the necessary elements of a crime that together demonstrate its commission.

Crack cocaine Nearly pure cocaine that through a heating process is stripped of its hydrochloride granules. After heating, the cocaine is cooled and compressed into dense chunks and typically smoked.

Credit card fraud Illegal transactions to defraud individuals or businesses utilizing a personal, altered, or stolen credit card number.

Crime scene A location at which a suspected criminal offense has occurred.

Crime scene equipment kits Portable forensic science kits that contain commonly needed crime scene processing items used to protect, record, search, and collect physical evidence from indoor and outdoor scenes.

Crime scene investigator An officer specially trained in the processing of physical evidence commonly found at crime scenes.

Crime scene sketch A measured drawing of a scene, showing the relative location of all important items, particularly physical evidence.

Criminal insanity A mental state that precludes understanding of the criminal nature of the act committed and/or the inability to determine right from wrong during the commission of the crime.

Criminal investigation An inquiry involving possible criminal activity based on logic, objectivity, and legal guidelines.

Criminalistics The application of many fields of natural science to the detection of crime.

Crips and Bloods gangs Black street gangs based in Los Angeles, heavily involved in the sale and distribution of narcotics in many states.

Critical thinking A reasoning process characterized by fair-mindedness, intellectual caution, and an openness to question common or assumed beliefs.

Cross-examination The courtroom questioning of a witness by an attorney.

Cross-projection A method of crime scene sketching allowing for a three-dimensional view of the scene.

CSI effect Unrealistic jury expectation that convincing forensic evidence will be located at all crime scenes and dramatically be presented as evidence during a trial. The lack of such evidence may induce jurors to believe that reasonable doubt exists, and a verdict of not guilty may result.

Cyanoactylate fuming Latent fingerprint development method that uses the ester released from cyanoactyle during evaporation. Commonly termed the "superglue method."

Cyberstalking A computer crime in which victims are harassed, stalked, or threatened by e-mails or some other form of computer-generated communication.

Cyclical crimes Offenses that occur or recur in certain patterns of regularity involving persons, time, or place.

Dactyloscopy The study of fingerprints as a means of personal identification.

Date rape Rape directed at an acquaintance victim through a casual social or business relationship.

Deductive reasoning Forming a general conclusion prior to having a complete examination based on facts.

Defense counsel An attorney who represents the defendant in a legal proceeding.

Defense wounds Injuries suffered as a victim attempts to ward off an assailant's blows; typically located on the hands or arms.

Density gradient technique A laboratory method used to compare and analyze soil evidence through observation of liquid density samples.

Deoxyribonucleic acid (DNA) An organic substance found in the chromosomes within the nucleus of a cell containing unique genetic materials.

Depressants Drug compounds, commonly referred to as barbiturates and tranquilizers, that have a sedative effect on the nervous system.

Digital evidence Any evidence that can be obtained in electronic digital form, such as computer data, videos, cellular transmissions, pages, fax transmissions, or digital photos.

Digital photography Photos that are recorded and transmitted by computer in electronic digital form rather than in film form.

Direct evidence Evidence that directly establishes the main fact of issue without an inference or presumption; gathered directly from sensory perception.

Direct examination The courtroom questioning of a witness by the attorney who called the witness to testify.

Doctrine of informer privilege A legal principle recognizing that an informant's identity should not be disclosed during a trial if such disclosure would result in retaliation to the informant.

Document examiner An expert in the examination of documents, handwriting, typewriting, and associated areas of communication.

Documentary information Information of a printed nature or data otherwise recorded and stored in official agency files.

Domestic abuse Physical or emotional forms of abuse that take place in a domestic environment.

Drive-by shootings Method of operation common to violent street gangs in which occupants within a vehicle fire weapons at selected victims.

Drug abuse When narcotics or dangerous drugs are used improperly and/or illegally.

Drug addiction A physical or mental state of chronic dependence on a drug substance often characterized by tolerance and withdrawal symptoms.

Duress The use of mental compulsion to obtain information, usually involving the imposition of restrictions or restraints on physical behavior.

Dying declaration A statement given by a victim who has proper knowledge of his or her imminent death; such statements are exceptions to the hearsay prohibition and are generally allowed into evidence.

Elder abuse A form of domestic abuse in which an elderly victim is neglected or injured through physical or emotional actions of another.

Electronic mail A means of communicating through electronic messages transmitted by computer.

Electronic surveillance A method of listening to and recording spoken interactions by using devices that gather, amplify, and record communications.

Emotionally affected victims Victims who have experienced direct contact with a criminal suspect and require special considerations during the questioning process.

Employee pilferage Theft committed by employees against their place of employment.

Entrapment Police action that induces an individual to commit a crime he or she was not predisposed to commit.

Equivocal scenes Death crime scenes that are open to interpretation because of natural conditions or circumstances.

***Escobedo* decision** A criminal case resulting in a U.S. Supreme Court decision affirming the right of the accused to be provided with assistance of counsel when requested.

Evidence Any type of proof that, when legally presented during a trial, is admitted into the official record for the review of judge and jury.

Exclusionary rule Legal principle excluding evidence from trial that has been obtained illegally by the authorities.

Exculpatory evidence Evidence that exonerates or clears a person of blame or legal guilt.

Exhibitionism The exposure of the sex organ, under other than conventionally lawful circumstances, for sexual gratification; commonly known as indecent exposure.

Exhumation Disinterment of a body from a tomb or grave.

Expert testimony Testimony given during a judicial proceeding by an individual who by virtue of education, training, and experience has knowledge or skill in a particular field beyond the knowledge of the average person.

Explosive tagging A technique in which minute coded particles are added to explosives during their manufacture for future identification purposes.

Expressive violence A form of violence associated with street gangs in which destructive behavior is expressed without apparent reason.

External perception factors Conditions that are not intrinsic to an individual but that affect his or her ability to acquire and relate information.

Extradition A legal procedure by which a person who commits a crime in one jurisdiction and flees to another can be arrested in the second jurisdiction and returned to the original jurisdiction to be tried for the charge.

Face recognition technology The use of computer-guided cameras to scan a number of faces while comparing facial characteristics to a database of wanted suspects.

Felony A crime more serious than a misdemeanor, generally punishable by incarceration in a state or federal prison for at least one year.

Female gang Street gang composed exclusively of female membership that commonly acts in support of male gangs.

Fence A buyer and seller of stolen property.

Fetishism A sexual perversion involving an inanimate object or a specific body part as the sole stimulator for sexual gratification.

Field notes Notes typically made in the field during the preliminary phase of the investigation and used to form the foundation of the formal report.

Fingerprint classification A file-and-retrieval system in which various numbers and letters are assigned to fingerprints in a multistep process.

Fingerprint ridges Raised layers of fingertip skin that form unique patterns of use in criminal identification.

Forensic anthropologist Specialists, generally anthropologists, skilled at providing investigative clues from decomposed human remains.

Forensic odontology The matching of bite impressions to a specific suspect's teeth.

Forensic pathologist A physician who specializes in the study of changes in body tissues as a result of disease or death and the impact of such evidence on legal cases, typically homicides. This person may work with the coroner in determining the cause of death.

Forgery The making or alteration of a document without authority and with the intention to defraud.

Founding member Street gang member who was instrumental in creating the gang.

Fourteenth Amendment An 1868 Amendment to the U.S. Constitution that, in time, applied due process requirements to state criminal cases.

Freebasing A chemical or heating process that frees base cocaine from its hydrochloride powder.

Freedom of Information Act A federal law providing a formal request procedure for public access to government records.

Futures research Research activities that seek to accurately predict investigative trends, incidents, and organizational policy in anticipation of future realities.

Gang unit An investigative unit specializing in the identification, tracking, and apprehension of street gang members.

***Gault* decision** U.S. Supreme Court decision that extended various constitutional rights to juvenile suspects previously reserved for adult offenders.

Geographic information system A computerized mapping system that translates and displays data into patterns useful for investigative insight or interpretation.

Geographic profiling Computer-assisted geographic data interpretation useful in predicting where future crimes may occur or where a serial suspect lives or works.

Graffiti Wall painting with cans of spray paint commonly associated with gang members.

Grand jury A jury of inquiry that receives complaints and accusations in criminal cases, hears the state's evidence, and issues bills of indictment if applicable.

Grand theft A form of theft classified as a felony on the basis of amount of property loss or circumstances of the act.

Grid search method A crime scene search method in which searchers process the area in a crisscross fashion; often used for large outdoor scenes.

Habeas corpus See *Writ of habeas corpus*.

Hallucinogens Drug substances, both natural and synthetic, that distort the perception of objective reality.

Hard-core member Older street gang members who are committed to criminal activity often including drug sales.

Hashish A derivative of the cannabis (marijuana) plant obtained from leaves that produce a resin having the most powerful euphoric properties.

Hate crimes Crimes that are motivated by a particular victim's race, religion, sexual orientation, or ethnicity.

Heroin An opiate derivative chemically converted from morphine.

Hesitation marks Wounds that indicate the testing of an edged weapon prior to an attempted or completed suicidal cutting.

High-velocity explosives Explosives with a high rate of detonation that typically produce a shattering effect.

Home invasion robbery Residential robbery in which the offender knows a home is occupied and gains entry by force or false pretense.

Homicide The killing of a human by another human; may be criminal or authorized by law.

Homosexuality An erotic attraction to or sexual preference for a member of the same sex.

Hypnosis A state of complete physical relaxation and intense mental concentration in which the subject's suggestibility is maximized.

Hypothesis An assumption or explanation for an occurrence that is then tested for its validity.

Identity theft The criminal act of assuming another's identity for some type of gain, normally financial.

Immunity Exemption from prosecution, generally for information or testimony of value to the state.

Incendiary fire An intentionally set fire in which the means of ignition varies accordingly to the skill and motive of the arsonist.

Incest Sexual intercourse between individuals of any age who are too closely related to marry.

Inculpatory evidence Evidence that is incriminating, as it tends to establish guilt.

In-depth investigation A phase of the investigative process that follows up initial leads developed during the preliminary investigation and attempts to open new areas of inquiry.

Indictment A written document charging one or more persons with a criminal offense.

Inductive reasoning A thinking process in which a conclusion is reached only after all particular facts are gathered and considered.

Industrial Revolution An economic phase characterized by intense industrial development in urban areas and related population shifts to the cities.

Informant file A repository for information pertaining to informants—names, addresses, photographs, fingerprints, and so forth.

Informants with ulterior motives Individuals who provide information to the police for self-seeking motivations other than financial gain.

Information A document prepared by the prosecuting attorney setting forth the charge against the defendant.

Inhalants Controlled or noncontrolled chemicals that emit fumes taken into the body to achieve an altered mental state.

Injection kit Materials typically carried by an intravenous drug addict necessary to inject narcotics into the bloodstream.

Intelligence A law enforcement function concerned with gathering, evaluating, and disseminating data related to criminal activity.

Internal perception factors Factors intrinsic to witnesses that influence perception and observation.

Internet An interconnected electronically linked network of data transmitted and accessed through computers.

Interrogation A law enforcement questioning procedure involving an individual suspected as a law violator.

Interview A communication involving two or more people for the purpose of obtaining information.

Investigative ethics The study of rightful and wrongful human conduct as it applies to the actions of criminal investigators.

Investigative research The application of scholarly methods of data acquisition as it applies to the investigative process.

Iodine fuming A technique in which crystals of iodine are exposed to a heat source for the purpose of revealing latent fingerprints.

Iris recognition technology Unique random patterns of the eye used to identify an individual through comparison of an unknown sample to a previously identified iris pattern.

Joyriding The stealing of a motor vehicle for pleasure rather than profit motives.

Jurisdiction A geographical area of legal authority within which an individual, agency, or court operates.

Jury A body of individuals, legally selected and sworn to consider matters of fact during a trial, that renders a verdict of guilty or not guilty.

Kleptomania A persistent neurotic impulse to steal, frequently without economic motive.

La Cosa Nostra An American organized crime group with origins in the Sicilian Mafia.

Lacerations Ragged wounds of body tissue, as from blows inflicted with a blunt instrument.

Lands and grooves Raised and indented portions of a firearm barrel, generally known as rifling, that serve to impart a spin to the bullet. The cutting tools used in the rifling process often produce characteristic marks that may assist in individualized identification.

Larceny The unlawful obtaining, taking, or withholding without force of an item of value from another with the intent to deprive permanently; commonly known as theft.

Latent fingerprints Ridge impressions located at a crime scene that are generally not visible before processing.

Lineup An assembly of persons, including the suspect, viewed for identification purposes by a crime victim or witness.

Linguistics The scientific study of language—used to assist investigators when spoken or written words are present.

Loan-sharking The lending of money at exorbitant interest rates.

Loop fingerprint A fingerprint pattern characterized by ridges entering one side, recurring, and exiting the pattern and also by the presence of type lines, delta, and core.

Low copy DNA DNA evidence obtained from previously untestable low source amounts at either standard violent scenes or theft or property scenes.

Lysergic acid diethylamide (LSD) A hallucinogenic originally derived from a rye fungus, first synthesized in 1938. Depending upon its chemical potency, the drug produces mild to psychotic-like hallucinations.

Major offense bureau A special investigative unit located in a prosecutor's office or detective bureau, designed to identify, apprehend, and successfully prosecute career criminals.

Management by objective A management technique involving diagnosis of a problem, determination of proper action, evaluation of the action taken, and provision for necessary adjustments.

Manslaughter The unlawful killing of a human without malice, generally specified as voluntary, involuntary, or reckless.

Marijuana A dangerous drug produced by drying the leaves and flowering tops of the cannabis plant.

Masochism Submission to physical ill treatment at the hands of a sadist or another in order to achieve gratification, often of a sexual nature. Compare with *Sadism*.

Material witness A witness who possesses important information in regard to a criminal trial.

Measurement marker An easily recognizable object placed next to an item of evidence during crime scene photography.

Medical examiner A physician, generally a forensic pathologist, who performs the duties traditionally entrusted to a coroner.

Mescaline A hallucinogenic obtained from the peyote cactus that grows naturally in Mexico and the southwestern parts of the United States.

Methamphetamine A dangerous drug that produces a stimulating effect on the central nervous system that is more intense than simple amphetamine reactions.

Metropolitan Police Act English legislation that led to the development of the London Metropolitan Police.

Microcomputer A small computer system consisting of a keyboard and video screen.

Miranda **decision** A criminal case that resulted in a U.S. Supreme Court decision specifying mandatory preinterrogation warnings concerning self-incrimination and the right to legal counsel.

Miranda **warning** Notification by police to suspects they intend to question that they have the right to remain silent, what they say can be used against them, they have the right to have an attorney present during questioning, and an attorney will be provided if they cannot afford one.

Misdemeanor An offense not as serious as a felony, generally punishable by incarceration in a correctional facility for up to but not more than a year.

Modus operandi The specific method of operation, employed by a criminal during the commission of an offense, that is likely to be repeated to form an identifiable pattern.

Morphine The principal alkaloid of opium converted through a boiling and filtering process.

MS-13 (Mara Salvatrucha 13) A rapidly growing violent street gang with Central American roots in E1 Salvador. Found in many American communities but particularly evident in Los Angeles and the Washington, D.C., area.

Multiagency unit Two or more law enforcement agencies working jointly to apply combined resources to one or more criminal investigations.

Murder The unlawful killing of a human with malice aforethought.

Narcoanalysis A medical interviewing technique in which drug compounds are used.

Narcotic In a medical sense, it refers to opium and opium derivatives or synthetic substitutes; in a legal sense, other nonopium substances are included.

Narcotic tolerance Physical need for increasing narcotic quantities to achieve the initial effect of the substance.

Narcotics paraphernalia Items used in connection with injecting, ingesting, or smoking various narcotics and dangerous drugs.

National Insurance Crime Bureau A national investigative bureau founded and funded by the insurance industry to assist law enforcement officers in the investigation of crimes involving stolen motor vehicles.

National Crime Information Center A computerized center operated by the FBI to assist law enforcement agencies in the apprehension of suspects and recovery of stolen property.

Neighborhood check A systematic checking of residences near a crime scene for investigative leads.

Neutron activation analysis A nuclear method of determining the presence and composition of trace elements by bombarding a substance with neutron particles.

Nolo contendere A judicial plea declaring that the defendant will not contest the charge(s) but will not admit formal guilt.

Obsessive-compulsive Mental disorder characterized by fixation, or constant focusing, on a thought, idea, or person.

Opium A narcotic substance extruded from a type of poppy plant. Frequently used illegally but also used legally in medicine.

Ordinance A law of a state subdivision, such as a county, city, or village.

Organized crime Pertaining to the criminal activities of any group of individuals who have formed a highly organized, disciplined association engaged primarily in illegal operations.

Outfit Narcotics paraphernalia used to inject a substance into the bloodstream; also known as an injection kit.

Outline note-taking Crime scene or field notes that are arranged in traditional outline form, generally by time sequence or some other orderly fashion.

Paid informant An individual who receives monetary compensation for providing information to a law enforcement agency.

Paraffin test A method of determining whether a suspect has fired a firearm within a given time period by coating the hands with melted paraffin to note the presence of or absence of nitrates. This method of testing is often replaced by the more reliable neutron activation analysis method.

Paranoia A mental disorder characterized by fixed delusions, typically of a suspicious nature.

Parliamentary reward system An early English practice in which officials were paid for the apprehension and prosecution of criminals, thus encouraging a high arrest and conviction rate.

Parole A conditional and revocable early release from a correctional institution.

Partial fingerprint A latent fingerprint in which only a portion of the pattern area is visible or able to be recovered.

Pedophile An adult who has a sexual desire to fondle or sexually violate a child.

Perjury The intentional making of a false statement while under oath to tell the truth during a judicial proceeding.

Personation Imparting unique personality traits at a crime scene by actions or evidence.

Petty theft A legal distinction of larceny in which the value of the stolen object results in a misdemeanor prosecution.

Phencyclidine (PCP) A powerful synthetic hallucinogenic compound originally developed as an anesthetic.

Phishing Computer fraud technique in which suspects create e-mail or Web sites to look like those of actual, well-known legitimate business, government agencies, or financial institutions for the purpose of fraudulently obtaining money or goods.

Photographic distortion An inaccurate photographic result in which true relationships between objects are not achieved.

Physical dependence A physical dependence on narcotics characterized by withdrawal symptoms when drug usage ceases.

Physical evidence Evidence of a tangible nature that may be of importance during an investigation or a subsequent judicial proceeding.

Pigeon-drop swindle A common bunco method of operation in which a victim is persuaded to produce money in order to share in the division of "found" money. By sleight of hand or some other technique, the victim's "good faith" money is stolen.

Pistol A handgun that operates on a blow-back principle: the force of the discharge ejects the fired casing, loading and cocking the weapon for the next firing.

Plea bargaining A legal practice involving an agreement between the prosecutor and the defense counsel in which a plea of guilty is accepted in exchange for a reduction of charges.

Point of ignition The specific location within an arson crime scene where the fire was started.

Police report The official police document ideally stating the who, what, when, why, where, and how of a suspected criminal occurrence along with victim and witness statements.

Polygraph An instrument that measures certain physiological changes of the body, triggered by emotional responses to specific verbal questions; generally used to determine deception.

Pornography Subject matter that is judged to be morally offensive to the degree of being obscene. There is considerable latitude over what constitutes pornographic material since there is no national legal definition of obscenity.

Portrait parlé An early method of criminal identification in which the human head and facial features were described in a detailed manner.

Postmortem lividity A dark blue discoloration of parts of the body nearest the ground; an after-death process caused by the force of gravity. Color may also be cherry red or pink depending upon the cause of death.

Precipitin test A laboratory test to determine whether a blood sample is of animal or human origin.

Predatory criminal A criminal type characterized by crimes that involve confrontation and the selection or stalking of vulnerable victims.

Preliminary hearing A judicial examination of the arrest and charges brought against the accused.

Preliminary investigation The first exposure of a criminal offense to the investigative process.

Preliminary report The first formal reporting of a criminal offense, used as the foundation report for all subsequent reports.

Premeditation A degree of planning and forethought sufficient to indicate the intention to commit a crime.

Privacy Act A federal law designed to protect an individual's right to privacy by prohibiting the review or release of information unless certain conditions are met.

Private investigator Nonsworn investigators who are paid by private citizens and organizations to gather information in private matters, generally of a civil rather than criminal nature. A small percentage of private agency cases may be concerned with criminal defense.

Privileged communications Information obtained in certain confidential relationships that would not ordinarily be received in evidence.

Proactive policing Law enforcement efforts that respond to a crime threat before the commission of the offense rather than reacting to a victimization.

Probable cause Reasonable grounds to connect a suspect to a crime and justifying various searches and/or an arrest.

Probation A conditional sentence that avoids imprisonment if the offender agrees to and abides by the requirements of the court.

Progress report An investigative report regarding a specific criminal investigation that formally documents the progress or lack of investigative leads.

Projection Crime scene sketching technique in which walls and ceiling are pictured as if on the same plane as the floor.

Prosecution report Document that contains information of judicial significance only. Intended to assist government attorneys in locating victims and witnesses for interviewing, evaluating evidence, and testing the strength of a case.

Prosecutor A lawyer who acts on behalf of the government during a criminal proceeding.

Psilocybin A natural hallucinogenic compound obtained from mushrooms.

Psychological profiling An attempt to identify crime perpetrators through the application of psychological theory, crime scene review, and victim/witness statement analysis.

Psychopath A mentally ill or unstable individual who is typically incapable of normal feelings of guilt. Also known as sociopaths, such people are also characterized by their need for immediate gratification and their ability to manipulate others.

Psychotic An individual suffering from a severe mental illness characterized by the inability to determine reality.

Public investigators Sworn or nonsworn investigators employed by a public agency who perform specific information-gathering tasks.

Punch attack A method of safe burglary in which the dial is removed by force, leaving the spindle and locking mechanism open to attack.

Putrefaction Postmortem darkening of the skin accompanied by bloating caused by bacterial gases.

Pyromaniac An individual who sets fire because of a compulsive mental illness.

Radial fracture lines Glass fractures that result from the bending of the pane toward a striking force causing jagged lines from the point of impact outward. The lines are more common on the side of the glass opposite the striking force.

Rape The act of sexual intercourse by force or against the victim's will.

Rape trauma syndrome A common rape victimization reaction characterized by emotional distress, denial, delay of reporting, anger, guilt, or unusual calm after the attack.

Recidivist A repeat offender who commits additional crimes after having been arrested or imprisoned for criminal activity in the past.

Rectangular coordinate method A crime scene sketching method in which two right angles are drawn from the evidence item to the nearest permanent object.

Res gestae declarations Spontaneous words or phrases spoken during the commission of an offense; generally admissible evidence during a judicial proceeding.

Residential robbery Robbery offense in which occupied homes are targeted.

Response time The time required for law enforcement officers to arrive at a crime scene after receiving a complaint or call for service.

Revolver A handgun in which a revolving multichambered cylinder aligns with the barrel prior to discharge.

Reward program Programs operated by law enforcement or citizen groups that encourage the reporting of criminal activities or investigative information.

Rigor mortis A postmortem stiffening of the muscles in the jaw and neck area and spreading downward through the body.

Rip attack A method of safe burglary in which the exterior metal sheets of the safe are peeled from a weakened corner location.

Robbery The taking of property from a person, or immediate presence of that person, by the use of force or by threat of the imminent use of force.

Rule of discovery The pretrial right of the adversary to examine documents, reports, and other types of information in the possession of the opposition that are anticipated to be introduced as evidence during the trial; created primarily for the benefit of the defendant.

Sadism The infliction of pain on a living thing as a means of obtaining pleasure, typically of a sexual nature. Compare with *Masochism.*

Sadomasochism Dual sexual deviation in which sexual satisfaction is achieved by the inflection and reception of pain.

Sanity hearing A judicial procedure or examination ordered by the court to determine whether a defendant is legally sane.

Search warrant A written court order authorizing the police to search a specific premise for stolen property or illegal substances and to seize and produce the property before the court.

Sector search method A crime scene searching technique in which the area to be searched is divided into equal areas of searching responsibility.

Semen The male reproductive fluid that normally contains spermatozoa, the male reproduction germ cell.

Semiautomatic A type of firearm firing operation commonly found at criminal events. Operating on the blow-back principle, the trigger must be pulled for each discharge rather than once for a continuous firing as found in fully automatic weapons.

Serial crimes Serious crimes characterized by numerous offenses committed by the same suspect or suspects over long periods of time.

Simulated death A physiological state in which the victim may appear to be deceased; can be induced by drug overdoses, electrical shock, and many other factors.

Sinsemilla From the Spanish, meaning "without seed." Commonly refers to high-potency marijuana grown in the United States.

Smart guns Weapons that, through technological intervention, can be fired only by their authorized owners.

Soil density gradient test Analysis and identification technique in which soil is distributed within a liquid to determine density value.

Solvability factors A method of determining if a specific investigation warrants further investigative effort by examining the presence or absence of common indicators of successful case solution.

Spectrophotometer An instrument that identifies physical evidence by measuring and recording the absorption spectrum.

Spiral search method A crime scene searching method in which the searchers move through the scene in an ever expanding fashion from the center to the outer perimeter.

Spouse abuse Pertaining to battery committed by one married partner on the other.

Staging Attempts to redirect an investigation away from logical truths.

Stalking Intentional course of conduct directed at a specific person, serving no legitimate purpose, that seriously annoys, intimidates, or harasses the targeted individual.

Statute A law enacted by the legislative branch of a government.

Statutory rape Illegal sexual intercourse with a female under a specified age, the female's willingness to engage in the act notwithstanding.

Sting operation A police arrest tactic in which officers simulate criminal operations causing suspects to complete a criminal act. Often used to arrest burglars, fences, and narcotics suspects.

Stipulation An agreement between the prosecuting attorney and the defense counsel to allow a questionable item of evidence to be entered without objection.

Stolen Vehicle Retrieval System A method of locating stolen motor vehicles through the placement of hidden transmitters within the vehicle.

Strategic intelligence Pertaining to information gathering that provides for long-range planning and decision making.

Street gang Association of youthful individuals who inhabit and defend a defined geographic territory and engage in an organized and continuous pattern of criminality.

Strip search method A crime scene searching method in which the searcher starts at one end of the scene and walks directly across until the opposite end is reached. The searcher then turns and walks back toward the original end searching to the right or left of the original path.

Subpoena A writ commanding the person designated to attend a judicial proceeding.

Summons A warning or citation to appear in court.

Surveillance The secretive watching of persons, places, or objects.

Suspended case A case that receives no current investigative effort but remains open should new leads develop.

Tactical intelligence Pertaining to information gathering that is designed to meet short-term planning needs or deal with immediate problems.

Tagging The act of spray painting communications on buildings or vehicles that identify gang members or specific gangs.

Terry v. Ohio A criminal case resulting in a U.S. Supreme Court decision affirming the right of police to search suspects for deadly weapons when circumstances indicate a need for self-protection.

Testimony A solemn declaration or affirmation usually made orally by a witness under oath in response to interrogation by an authorized public official.

Tests of suitability Three evidence admissibility standards used to determine if an item of evidence will be allowed to have a bearing on a case; evidence must be competent, relevant, and material.

Theory of transfer When two objects come in contact with each other, evidence will be exchanged from one surface to another, with traces left at the scene and taken from the scene.

Thief-taking An early method of criminal investigation and apprehension that was based on the premise that only a criminal could successfully apprehend another criminal.

Toolmark An impression resulting from forceful contact between a tool and the surface area of an object.

Trajectory The flight path of a projectile, such as a bullet discharged from a firearm.

Triangulation A crime scene measuring method in which measurements are taken from two fixed points to the evidence object, thus forming a triangle as a frame of reference.

Truck hijacking A form of vehicle robbery in which trucks are seized for the valuable cargo contained within.

Ultraviolet light Radiation situated beyond the violet, visible end of the light spectrum.

Undercover operations Pertaining to the fictitious identities assumed by police officers and the roles they play to accomplish an investigative objective.

Uniform Crime Report Annual statistical reports, published by the FBI, that analyze and record crime rates in the United States.

Vehicle identification number The metal plate now referred to as the permanent identification number. Data on the plate include vehicle make, model, year of manufacture, plant location, engine type, and sequential production number.

Vehicle stripping The theft of vehicle parts and accessories.

Verbatim notes Notes or a formal statement taken in the same words actually used; word for word.

Verdict The formal decision of a jury in a criminal or civil trial.

Victim compensation Financial or other forms of assistance given to crime victims by the state, especially those victimized in person-to-person crimes.

Victim-precipitated crime Criminal offenses involving a conscious or unconscious action by the victim that is a causative factor in their victimization.

Videotaping A visual and aural method of recording suspect confessions, admissions, or statements given by victims or witnesses. Also used to record crime scenes, undercover operations, and other investigative operations.

Violent Criminal Apprehension Program A data collection program in which specific violent crimes are reported to the FBI and studied for similarities in method of operation. The crimes of murder, rape, arson, and child sexual abuse are particularly well suited for serial analyses.

Virtual reality Computer-generated, three-dimensional environment that engulfs the senses of sight, sound, and touch.

Voiceprint A method of speaker identification in which the pitch, rate of speech, and articulation are evaluated as well as certain anatomical factors not under the speaker's conscious control; also known as sound spectrograph.

Voice stress evaluator A device that monitors the vocal quality of an individual producing a graphlike reading indicating the possibility of deception.

Voluntary informant Any individual who provides information to the police without ulterior motive or payment.

Voyeurism Surreptitious observation of another for sexual gratification.

Vulnerability analysis A security evaluation of a structure by trained crime prevention officers to determine points of risk regarding crime victimization.

***Wade* decision** U.S. Supreme Court decision affirming the right of police to hold a lineup without the presence of defense counsel if the identification was not part of a critical stage of the proceedings. Subsequent cases determined that any pretrial identification prior to the filing of a formal charge was not part of the critical stage, and therefore no counsel is required.

***Will West* case** A case in which two inmates so closely resembled each other in physical characteristics that the traditional Bertillon method of identification was discredited.

White-collar crime Pertaining to business, professional, and consumer frauds or to various other criminal offenses that occur to customers or clients.

Whorl fingerprint Fingerprint patterns that encircle a central pattern classified as plain, central pocket loop, double loop, or accidental whorls.

Withdrawal symptoms Physical and/or mental effects produced by sudden or gradual withdrawal of drug usage. Symptoms may include anxiety, muscle cramping, vomiting, and general nausea.

Witness An observer who sees or knows by personal presence and perception and/or a person who is requested to testify in a case or before a judicial proceeding.

Witness protection unit Police units designed to provide security to victims and/or witnesses who have been threatened of feel intimidated by suspects or their associates before, during, and after a trial.

Workplace homicides Criminal homicides that occur within one's place of employment.

World Wide Web An electronic locality that contains text, graphics, sound, and interactive potential.

Writ of habeas corpus A legal document calling for immediate judicial review of the circumstances pertaining to the continued confinement of an accused individual; designed to obtain the prompt release of a person who is unlawfully detained.

Bibliography

Allison, Harrison C. *Personal Identification*. Boston: Holbrook Press, 1973.

Alpert, Geoffrey, and Dunham, Roger. *Policing Urban America*. Prospect Heights, Ill.: Waveland Press, 1992.

Anderson, William B. *Notable Crime Investigations*. Springfield, Ill.: Charles C Thomas, 1987.

Arson: The Complete Investigator's Manual. Boulder, Colo.: Paladin Press, 1990.

Basic Elements of Intelligence: A Manual of Theory, Structure and Procedures for Use by Law Enforcement Agencies against Organized Crime. Washington, D.C.: U.S. Government Printing Office, 1971.

Block, Peter, and Weidman, Donald. *Managing Criminal Investigations*. Washington, D.C.: National Institute of Law Enforcement and Criminal Justice, 1975.

Blumstein, Alfred, et al. *Criminal Careers and Career Criminals*. Washington, D.C.: National Academy Press, 1986.

Bourque, Linda B. *Defining Rape*. Durham, N.C.: Duke University Press, 1990.

Brenner, John C. *Forensic Science Glossary*. Boca Raton, Fla.: CRC Press, 1999.

Brodyaga, Lisa, et al. *Rape and Its Victims*. Washington, D.C.: National Institute of Law Enforcement and Criminal Justice, 1975.

Byrnes, Thomas. *1886 Professional Criminals of America*. New York: Chelsea House Publishers, 1969.

Child Abuse. Sacramento: California Department of Justice, 1976.

Coleman, James W. *The Criminal Elite*. New York: St. Martin's Press, 1985.

Criminal Investigation Process: A Dialogue on Research Findings. Washington, D.C.: National Institute of Law Enforcement and Criminal Justice, 1977.

Criminal Victimization in the United States. Washington, D.C.: Department of Justice, 1992.

Critchley, T. A. *A History of Police in England and Wales*. Montclair, N.J.: Patterson Smith Publishers, 1972.

Cromwell, Paul. *Breaking and Entering*. Newbury Park, Calif.: Sage, 1991.

Cuomo, George. *A Couple of Cops*. New York: Random House, 1995.

De Francis, Vincent. *Protecting the Child Victim of Sex Crimes Committed by Adults*. Denver: The American Humane Association, 1969.

Del Carmen, Rolando, and Walker, Jerry T. *Briefs of 100 Leading Cases in Law Enforcement*. Cincinnati: Anderson, 1991.

Di Maio, Vincent. *Gunshot Wounds: Practical Aspects of Firearms, Ballistics, and Forensic Techniques*. Boca Raton, Fla.: CRC Press, 1999.

Douglas, John E. *Crime Classification Manual*. New York: Lexington Books, 1992.

———. *Mindhunter: Inside the FBI's Elite Serial Crime Unit*. New York: Charles Scribner, 1995.

Dudycha, George J. *Psychology for Law Enforcement Officers*. Springfield, Ill.: Charles C Thomas, 1976.

Dunn, Christopher S. *Patterns of Robbery Characteristics and Their Occurrence among Social Areas*. Washington, D.C.: National Institute of Law Enforcement and Criminal Justice, 1976.

Eckert, William G. *Introduction to Forensic Sciences*. Boca Raton, Fla.: CRC Press, 1997.

Farr, Robert. *The Electronic Criminals*. New York: McGraw-Hill, 1975.

Finkelhor, David, et al. *Missing, Abducted, Runaway, and Thrownaway Children in America*. Washington, D.C.: U.S. Department of Justice, 1990.

Fisher, Barry. *Techniques of Crime Scene Investigation*. Boca Raton, Fla.: CRC Press, 2004.

Fosdick, Raymond B. *American Police Systems*. New York: The Century Company, 1920.

Fuqua, Paul. *Drug Abuse: Investigation and Control*. New York: McGraw-Hill, 1978.

Gabor, Thomas, et al. *Armed Robbery*. Springfield, Ill.: Charles C Thomas, 1987.

Gaines, Larry, and Kraska, Peter. *Drugs, Crime and Justice: Contemporary Perspectives*. Prospect Heights, Ill: Waveland Press, 2003.

Gardner, Ross. *Practical Crime Scene Processing and Investigation*. Boca Raton, Fla.: CRC Press, 2004.

Garza, Manuel R. *Multi-Agency Narcotics Unit Manual*. Washington, D.C.: National Institute of Law Enforcement and Criminal Justice, 1976.

Geberth, Vernon. *Practical Homicide Investigation: Tactics, Procedures, and Forensic Techniques*. Boca Raton, Fla.: CRC Press, 1996.

Geller, William, ed. *Local Government Police Management*. Washington, D.C.: International City Management Association, 1991.

Gerber, Samuel R., and Schroeder, Oliver, Jr. *Criminal Investigation and Interrogation*. Cincinnati: Anderson, 1972.

Gilbert, James N. *Criminal Investigation: Essays and Cases*. Columbus: Charles E. Merrill, 1990.

Goddard, Kenneth W. *Crime Scene Investigation*. Reston, Va.: Reston, 1977.

Goldstein, Arnold P. *Delinquent Gangs: A Psychological Perspective*. Chicago: Research Press, 1991.

Goldstein, Seth L. *The Sexual Exploitation of Children*. Boca Raton, Fla.: CRC Press, 1998.

Grau, Joseph J., ed. *Criminal and Civil Investigation Handbook*. New York: McGraw-Hill, 1981.

Green, Gary S. *Occupational Crime*. Chicago: Nelson-Hall, 1990.

Griffiths, Arthur. *Mysteries of Police and Crime*. New York: G. P. Putnam's Sons, 1899.

Harries, Keith. *Serious Violence: Patterns of Homicide and Assault in America*. Springfield, Ill.: Charles C Thomas, 1990.

Hayward, Arthur L. *Lives of the Most Remarkable Criminals*. New York: Dodd, Mead & Company, 1927.

Hazelwood, Roy, and Burgess, Ann W. *Practical Aspects of Rape Investigation*. New York: Elsevier, 1987.

Hazelwood, Roy, and Steph, Michael. *Dark Dreams: Sexual Violence, Homicide and the Criminal Mind*. New York: St. Martin's Press, 2001.

———. *The Evil That Men Do: FBI Profiler Roy Hazelwood's Journey into the Mind of Sexual Predators*. New York: St. Martin's Press, 2000.

Hoffman, Lance J., ed. *Security and Privacy in Computer Systems*. Los Angeles: Melville, 1973.

Holmes, Ronald M. *Profiling Violent Crimes*. Newbury Park, Calif.: Sage, 1989.

———. *Sex Crimes: Patterns and Behaviors*. Thousand Oaks, Calif.: Sage, 2002.

Holtz, Larry E. *Criminal Evidence*. Longwood, Fla.: Gould Publishing, 1994.

Horan, James D. *The Pinkertons: The Detective Dynasty That Made History*. New York: Crown Publishers, 1967.

Ianni, Francis A. *Ethnic Succession in Organized Crime*. Washington, D.C.: National Institute of Law Enforcement and Criminal Justice, 1973.

Inciardi, James, et al. *Street Kids, Street Drugs, Street Crime*. Belmont, Calif.: Wadsworth, 1993.

Inman, Keith, and Rudin, Norah. *An Introduction to Forensic DNA Analysis*. Boca Raton, Fla.: CRC Press, 1997.

Jaffe, Natalie. *Assaults on Women: Rape and Wife Beating*. New York: Public Affairs Committee, 1980.

James, Stuart. *Forensic Science*. Boca Raton, Fla.: CRC Press, 2005.

Jewkes, Yvonne. *Dot.cons: Crime, Deviance and Identity on the Internet*. Cullompton, England: Willan Publishing, 2002.

Katzman, Gary S. *Inside the Criminal Process*. New York: W. W. Norton, 1991.

Keppel, Robert D. *Serial Murder*. Cincinnati: Anderson, 1989.

King, Joseph F. *The Development of Modern Police History in the United Kingdom and the United States*. Lewiston, N.Y.: Mellen Press, 2004.

Klein, Malcolm, and Maxson, Cheryl. *The Modern Gang Reader*. Los Angeles: Roxbury, 1995.

Klockars, Carl, and Mastrofski, Stephen. *Thinking about Police*. New York: McGraw-Hill, 1991.

Knox, George W. *An Introduction to Gangs*. Bristol, Ind.: Wyndham Hall, 1994.

Kubic, Thomas. *Forensic Science Laboratory Manual and Workbook*. Boca Raton, Fla.: CRC Press, 2005.

Laurie, Peter. *Scotland Yard*. New York: Holt, Rinehart and Winston, 1970.

Lester, David. *Questions and Answers about Murder*. Philadelphia: Charles Press, 1991.

MacDonald, John W. *Burglary and Theft*. Springfield, Ill.: Charles C Thomas, 1980.

MacDonell, Herbert L. *Flight Characteristics and Stain Patterns of Human Blood*. Washington, D.C.: National Institute of Law Enforcement and Criminal Justice, 1971.

Maguire, Kathleen, and Flanagan, Timothy. *Sourcebook of Criminal Justice Statistics—1990*. Washington, D.C.: U.S. Department of Justice, 1991.

Matson, Jack. *Effective Expert Witnessing*. Boca Raton, Fla.: CRC Press, 2005.

Memon, Amina, Vriji, Alden, and Bull, Ray. *Psychology and Law: Truthfulness, Accuracy and Credibility*. Holboken, N.J.: John Wiley, 2004.

Mosse, George L. *Police Forces in History*. London: Sage, 1975.

Motto, Carmine, and June, Dale. *Undercover*. Boca Raton, Fla.: CRC Press, 1999.

Musto, David F. *One Hundred Years of Heroin*. Westport, Conn.: Auburn House, 2002.

Myren, Richard, and Garcia, Carol H. *Investigation for Determination of Fact*. Belmont, Calif.: Brooks/Cole, 1989.

Nash, Stephen G. *A History of Scientific Computing*. New York: ACM Press, 1990.

O'Connor, Thomas R., and Gotthoffer, Doug. *Quick Guide to the Internet for Criminal Justice*. Boston: Allyn and Bacon, 2000.

Pace, Denny F., and Styles, James C. *Organized Crime*. Englewood Cliffs, N.J.: Prentice Hall, 1971.

Palmiotto, Michael J., ed. *Perspectives on Criminal Investigation*. Cincinnati: Anderson, 1984.

Pinkerton, Allan. *Criminal Reminiscences and Detective Sketches*. Freeport, N.Y.: Books for Libraries Press, 1970.

Pocket Guide to Arson Investigation. Norwood, Mass.: Factory Mutual Engineering Corporation, 1979.

Pollock-Byrne, Joycelyn. *Ethics in Crime and Justice*. Pacific Grove, Calif.: Brooks/Cole, 1989.

Privacy and Security of Criminal History Information: A Guide to Dissemination. Washington, D.C.: National Criminal Justice Information and Statistics Service, 1977.

Rachlin, Harvey. *The Making of a Detective*. New York: W. W. Norton, 1995.

Ratledge, Edward, and Jacoby, Joan. *Handbook on Artificial Intelligence and Expert Systems*. New York: Greenwood Press, 1989.

Report to the Nation on Crime and Justice. Washington, D.C.: Bureau of Justice Statistics, 1988.

Ressler, Robert K., et al. *Sexual Homicide.* New York: Lexington Books, 1988.

Rhodes, Henry. *Alphonse Bertillon: Father of Scientific Detection.* New York: Greenwood Press, 1968.

Robin, Gerald. *Violent Crime and Gun Control.* Cincinnati: Anderson, 1991.

Ronczkowski, Michael R. *Terrorism and Organized Hate Crime.* Boca Raton, Fla.: CRC Press, 2004.

Saferstein, Richard. *Criminalistics: An Introduction to Forensic Science.* Englewood Cliffs, N.J.: Prentice Hall, 2004.

Sanders, William B. *Gangbangs and Drive-Bys.* New York: Aldine de Gruyter, 1994.

Schell, Bernadette, Dodge, John, and Moutsatsos, Steve. *The Hacking of America: Who's Doing It, Why, and How.* Westport, Conn.: Quorum Books, 2002.

Schlegel, Kip. *Just Desserts for Corporate Criminals.* Boston: Northeastern University Press, 1990.

Segal, Bernard. *Drug-Taking Behavior among School-Aged Youth.* New York: Haworth Press, 1990.

Sennewald, Charles A. *The Process of Investigation.* Boston: Butterworth Publishers, 2001.

Shipley, Bernard, and Ruder, Linda. *Attorney General's Program for Improving the Nation's Criminal History Records.* Washington, D.C.: U.S. Department of Justice, 1992.

Simon, David. *Homicide.* New York: Houghton-Mifflin, 1991.

Sims, Victor. *Small Town and Rural Police.* Springfield, Ill.: Charles C Thomas, 1988.

Stojkovic, Stan, et al. *The Administration and Management of Criminal Justice Organizations.* Prospect Heights, Ill.: Waveland Press, 1990.

Tobias, J. J. *Crime and Industrial Society in the 19th Century.* New York: Schocken Books, 1967.

Turvey, Brent. *Criminal Profiling.* Orlando: Academic Press, 1999.

Violent Crime in the United States. Washington, D.C.: U.S. Department of Justice, 1991.

Wadman, Robert, and Allison, William. *To Protect and to Serve: A History of Police in America.* Upper Saddle River, N.J.: Pearson Prentice Hall, 2003.

Waller, Irwin. *Crime Victims: Doing Justice to Their Support and Protection.* Monsey, N.Y.: Criminal Justice Press, 2003.

Walters, Glenn. *The Criminal Lifestyle: Patterns of Serious Criminal Conduct.* Newbury Park, Calif.: Sage, 1990.

Waltz, Jon R. *Introduction to Criminal Evidence.* Chicago: Nelson-Hall, 1994.

Wicks, Robert J. *Applied Psychology for Law Enforcement and Correction Officers.* New York: McGraw-Hill, 1974.

Yarmey, A. Daniel. *Understanding Police and Police Work.* New York: New York University Press, 1990.

Zulawski, David E. *Practical Aspects of Interview and Interrogation.* Boca Raton, Fla.: CRC Press, 2005.

Index